Music in Ohio

Music in Ohio

WILLIAM OSBORNE

THE KENT STATE UNIVERSITY PRESS

KENT & LONDON

© 2004 by The Kent State University Press, Kent, Ohio 44242

ALL RIGHTS RESERVED

Library of Congress Catalog Card Number 2004012544

ISBN 0-87338-775-9

Manufactured in the United States of America

08 07 06 05 04   5 4 3 2 1

Library of Congress Cataloging-in-Publication Data

Osborne, William, 1937–

Music in Ohio / William Osborne.

p.   cm.

Includes bibliographical references and index.

ISBN 0-87338-775-9 (hardcover : alk. paper) ∞

1. Music—Ohio—History and criticism. I. Title.

ML200.7.O4O83 2004

780'.9771—dc22   2004012544

British Library Cataloging-in-Publication data are available.

Contents

Preface and Acknowledgments

Long fascinated with musical Americana, my interest in Ohio music dates to the summer of 1991, when I was recruited to lead a seminar on the subject at the Ohio State University, substituting for an ailing Susan Porter, a member of the faculty of the Lima branch campus, who had offered a similar course the preceding summer. During the summer of 1992 I was involved with the planning of eight public programs on "Ohio's Music" sponsored jointly by Ohio State and the Ohio Historical Society, and also created the session that dealt with a variety of solo songs and the white gospel song movement. Dr. Porter, still very much present, moved to Colorado soon thereafter and died on October 3, 1993, but not before informally challenging me to write this book in her stead.

A recent survey via the WorldCat system suggests that this study will prove unique. Of course, there exists a wondrous myriad of local, regional, and topical studies, plus a fair number of attempts to deal with music making within a state in a comprehensive, albeit non-encyclopedic manner. However, many of these are circumscribed by the dates of their provenance (for example, studies of music in Kentucky issued in 1894, of Maine in 1928, and of Minnesota in 1956). Other more recent studies are by intent limited so that, again by example, one can learn of the music made in New Hampshire prior to 1800 or in Rhode Island before 1820. I am aware of only two relatively current comparable ventures: George S. Kanahele's *Hawaiian Music and Musicians: An Illustrated History* (1979), which deals with the subject via an extended series of brief articles presented alphabetically, and Rick Koster's *Texas Music* (1998). The latter, however, employs a casual, chatty style (for example, there are many sidebars profiling "Criminally Overlooked Artist[s]"), and it can hardly be considered encompassing, since its part 7, section 1, "Opera (Not Soap or Oat), Classical, and Musical Theater," extends to only six pages. Lota M. Spell's *Music in Texas: A Survey of One Aspect of Cultural Progress* (1936) is much more inclusive but by now is only a period piece.

Ohio can be considered the quintessence of everything American. Contemplate its juxtapositions: rural and urban, agricultural and industrial, a state considered politically conservative, which sent to Washington for years a most liberal senator, a state that houses both cosmopolitan urbanites and Appalachian dirt farmers, a state straddling the boundary between the Appalachian plateau and the Great Plains, whose citizens converse with diverse accents.

For a period, that portion of the Northwest Territory that became Ohio was little more than a cultural colony of New England astride some of the principal westward migration routes. During the twentieth century another major migratory path surfaced as many fled poverty in the South for factory jobs in Ohio's industrial centers. Thus Ohioans are all immigrants, even including, sad to say, those American Indians who are present residents of the state. This study will attempt to reflect and illuminate that history.

Consider, for example, Cleveland, where Severance Hall houses one of the world's most renowned and recorded symphony orchestras only a few miles from the Rock and Roll Hall of Fame and Museum in its flamboyant I. M. Pei–designed quarters, or where one can visit the National Cleveland-Style Polka Hall of Fame in the northeastern suburb of Euclid, as well as the noted collections of the Riemenschneider Bach Institute in the southwestern suburb of Berea.

I hope to demonstrate that a study of music made by or for Ohioans over more than two centuries can offer considerable delight and more insight than has been allowed by general historians. For example, George W. Knepper in his *Ohio and Its People* (Kent: Kent State Univ. Press, 2004) devoted only a part of the chapter, "Arts and Leisure-Time Activities" to a cursory overview.

At times I have felt overwhelmed by the amount of information I have encountered. Mine has been to some degree an act of synthesis—assembling, sifting, and collating the work of many predecessors. I have often been forced to deal with secondary sources, many of them contradictory, even self-contradictory. Early writers felt no need to acknowledge their sources, so I sometimes have swallowed hard and accepted their authority when they referred to otherwise irretrievable information. I spent much time deciding what to exclude and realize that some will probably take offense at obvious omissions. I felt it unnecessary to linger over universal musical idioms and practices, concentrating instead on those events, organizations, and individuals that have something a bit unique about them.

I trust that my decision to present the material in a topical rather than chronological manner will prove efficacious. I thought that taking historical cross-sections—the

"This-is-your-musical-life-from-1860-to-1870" approach—could be become infinitely confusing and preclude any clear understanding of crucial continuities.

I owe enormous thanks to the staffs of those institutions that have provided the bulk of the raw material: the Public Library of Cincinnati and Hamilton County, the Cincinnati Historical Society, the University of Cincinnati, the Ross County Historical Society, the Ohio Historical Center, the Ohioana Library, the Ohio State University, the Cleveland Public Library, the Western Reserve Historical Society, and the Library of Congress. Fearing sins of omission, I will not attempt a catalog of the individual staff members whose diligence and patience have proved invaluable. However, let me express gratitude to three scholars whose advice and counsel I have sought: Dr. J. Heywood Alexander, a retired member of the Cleveland State University faculty, who has plumbed the depths of Cleveland's early music history; Lloyd Savage, a retired public school music teacher, who knows everything about music making in Ross County and among the Welsh; and Dr. Richard D. Wetzel of Ohio University, another pioneer in the study of music here in Ohio. And mostly to the late Dr. Susan Porter, the real pioneer, who put me up to all of this. I can only hope that the outcome would have met with her approval.

I would also like to acknowledge financial support for this venture from the Denison University Research Foundation.

Part One

The Pre–Civil War Beginnings

CHAPTER 1

The Pre-Urban Wilderness

Lack of evidence precludes anything but a surmise that the trappers, traders, soldiers, and adventurers who during the latter half of the eighteenth century infiltrated what was to become the Northwest Territory in 1787 and the State of Ohio in 1803 surely employed music as a means of self-entertainment. Fragmentary evidence suggests that the American Indian tribes that were gradually dispersed elsewhere as their lands were appropriated by war and treaty practiced their own musical dialects, although hardly with enough specificity to allow a sense of how these might have sounded. Since theirs was a purely oral tradition, it would be presumptuous to suggest that the music of the American Indians who have resettled in the state bears a resemblance to that practiced two centuries ago.[1]

The earliest observation is found in a journal of English-born Christopher Gist, who during 1750 and 1751 was sent by the Ohio Company to observe and report on the quality of the land and rivers in what was to become Ohio. He was also to "observe what Nations of Indians inhabit there, their Strength & Numbers, who they trade with, & in what Comodities [sic] they deal." During late January 1751 Gist and his party arrived at a Shawnee town at the mouth of the Scioto River where it meets the Ohio near present-day Portsmouth. He lingered there from January 31 until February 11, observing a sort of mate-swapping dance described as "a very extraordinary kind of Festival."[2] He promised a description at the end of the journal in language considered sufficiently racy to suffer expurgation in early editions of the volume. The ceremony encompassed several days. On the evening of the second day, the men and women were dancing separately, the women

> in their manner in the form of a figure 8, about 60 or 70 of them at a time. The women, the whole time they danced, sung a song in their language, the chorus of which was,

ī am not afraid of my husband;
I will choose what man I please.

Singing those lines alternately.

The third day, in the evening, the men, being about 100 in number, danced in a long string, following one another, sometimes at length, at other times in a figure of 8 quite around the fort, and in and out of the long house, where they held their councils, the women standing together as the men danced by them; and as any of the women liked a man passing by, she stepped in, and joined in the dance, taking hold of the man's shroud, whom she chose, and then continued in the dance, till the rest of the women stepped in, and made their choice in the same manner; after which the dance ended, and they all retired to consummate.[3]

The next account appeared in a memoir originally published in 1799 by Pennsylvania-born James Smith (1737–1812). Smith was one of a party of cutters employed to create a wagon road through the wilderness for the doomed troops of British Gen. Edward Braddock, marching against the French at Fort Dusquene. Smith was captured and spent 1755 to 1759 in the company of Delaware, Caughnewaga, and Mohican Indians in a settlement called Tullihas on the west branch of the Muskingum River about twenty miles above its fork. Smith refers many times to various war songs and dances. For example, in one performance,

only one [warrior] sung at a time, in a moving posture, with a tomahawk in his hand, while all the other warriors were engaged in calling aloud *he-uh, he-uh*, which they constantly repeated, while the war song was going on.[4]

He waxed eloquent about "another sort of dance, which was a kind of promiscuous dance":

The young men stood in one rank, and the young women in another, about a rod apart, facing each other. The one that raised the tune, or started the song, held a small gourd or dry shell of a squash, in his hand, which contained beads or small stones, which rattled. When he began to sing, he timed the tune with his rattle; both men and women danced and sung together, advancing towards each other, stooping until their heads would be touching together, and then ceased from dancing, with loud shouts, and retreated and formed again, and so repeated the same thing over and over, for three or four hours, without intermission. This exercise appeared to me at first irrational and insipid, but I found that in singing their tunes, they used *ya ne no hoo wa ne &c.*,

like our *fa sol la*, and though they have no such thing as jingling verse, yet they can intermix sentences with their notes, and say what they please to each other, and carry on the tune in concert. I found that this was a kind of wooing or courting dance, and as they advanced stooping with their heads together, they could say what they pleased in each other's ear, without disconcerting their rough music, and the others, or those near, not hear what they say.[5]

He also described music-making associated with a game resembling the throwing of dice, which he observed during June 1756: "Some were beating their kind of drum, and singing, others were employed in playing on a sort of flute, made of hollow cane: and others playing on the jews-harp."[6]

A further observation of what Anglo-Americans overheard is that of Col. John May of Boston, who in his journal documenting a journey "to the Ohio Country" in 1788, described a sleepless night of August 1–2 in Marietta:

Here I was introduced to old Pipes, chief of the Delaware nation, and his suite, dressed and acting like the off-spring of Satan. They did not stay long before they went to their camp in the woods, and I crossed the river back to my lodgings [i.e., from west to east across the mouth of the Muskingum from Fort Harmar to Marietta itself]. Went to bed at 12, but got little rest. The Indians made one of their hellish pow-wows, which lasted till the hour of rising. I have no doubt psalmody had its origins in heaven; but my faith is just as strong, that the music of these savages was first taught in a place the exact opposite. About 2 o'clock I got some sleep, when I supposed the damnable music ceased.[7]

Shards of evidence dating from the turn of the eighteenth into the nineteenth century allow some insights into the musical practices of Ohio's early European settlers. A handful of literate colonists and other travelers kept diaries or journals detailing their adventures and experiences as they began the process of penetrating and taming what was for them a forbidding wilderness. These scraps of information allow only a minuscule view but do confirm a natural progression from purely practical, vernacular music making, by those whose initial goal was simply that of survival under rather rude circumstances, to pioneering efforts at presenting examples of cultivated art music, mirroring the arrival of sufficient stability and leisure to allow establishment of the accouterments of a culture left behind in the towns and cities of the eastern seaboard or in the more mature centers of the parent European cultures, forsaken but not forgotten.

For example, Fortescue Cuming, a well-traveled Englishman, crossed the state on Zane's Trace between August 6 and 19, 1807, from a point opposite Maysville,

Kentucky, through Chillicothe, Lancaster, and Zanesville to Wheeling, mainly as a pedestrian but also partly by stagecoach and on horseback. Between Manchester and Chillicothe he spent the night of August 10 in the house of a farmer named Marshon:

> Three of his sons play the violin by ear—they had two shocking bad violins, one of which was of their own manufacture, on which they scraped away without mercy to entertain us, which I would most gladly have excused, though I attempted to seem pleased, and I believe succeeded in making them think I was so.[8]

The following day he stopped at the home of an immigrant Irishman named Bradley, whose daughter had just married a young shoemaker named Irons. Cuming lingered to have his shoes mended and

> found a dozen of stout young fellows who had been at work repairing the road, and were now sheltering themselves from the increasing storm, and listening to some indifferent musick made by their host on a tolerably good violin. I proposed taking the violin while he repaired my shoes. He consented and sat down to work, and in a few minutes I had all the lads jigging it on the floor merrily; Irons himself, as soon as he had repaired the shoes, jumping up and joining them.[9]

A few days later Cuming arrived in what was then called New Lancaster, where he passed a most fitful night:

> I was soon awoke in torture from a general attack made on me by hosts of vermin of the most troublesome and disgusting genii. I started from the bed, dressed myself, spread a coverlet on the floor, and lay down there to court a little more repose, but I was prevented by a constant noise in the house during the whole night, beginning with church musick, among which some sweet female voices were discernible, and ending in the loud drunken frolicks of some rustick guests, who kept Saturday night until late on Sunday morning.[10]

John Melish, another British traveler, enjoyed the same sorts of serendipitous musical experiences. On September 3, 1811, in transit down the Ohio River between Marietta and Gallipolis, rain forced Melish and party to take shelter in the cabin of an Irishman who had emigrated to fight on the winning side during the Revolutionary War: "He was an excellent musician, and amused us with some tunes on the violin."[11] Approaching Cincinnati, Melish overnighted on the Kentucky side of the river in the home of a Scotsman named Kennedy. The following morning,

[b]efore we had finished our breakfast, Mr. Kennedy drew a fiddle from a box, and struck up the tune of Rothemurche's Rant. He played in the true Highland style, and I could not stop to finish my breakfast, but started up and danced *Shantrews*. The old man was delighted, and favoured us with a great many Scottish airs. When he laid down the fiddle, I took it up, and commenced in my turn, playing some *new strathspeys* that he had not heard before; but he knew the spirit of them full well, and he also gave us Shantrews "louping near bawk height," albeit he was well stricken in years.

He next played a number of airs, all Scottish, on a whistle; and then pulled out some MS. poetry, and read several pieces, which were highly humorous.[12]

Melish, after a Kentucky sojourn, also set out on Zane's Trace, but after Zanesville he turned north through Coschocton, New Philadelphia, and Canton to Cleveland, after which he journeyed along the shore of Lake Erie on his way to Buffalo and New York City via Albany. He and a traveling companion spent the night of October 22 in the home of a Squire Leet near the mouth of the Ashtabula River in "New Connecticut":

My fellow-traveller was acquainted in the family, and they were acquainted with his vocal powers. He sang an excellent song, but like other good singers, he was unwilling to make a display, and it was not till after a good deal of pressing from the ladies, that he would open the concert. He soon made ample amends for the delay, however. He sang a number of elegant songs, and having elevated the spirit of the company, we had songs and stories in abundance, till a pretty late hour. I was called upon, of course; but, as heretofore, I could do nothing except in Scottish songs, and I was doubtful how they would answer on the banks of lake Erie. However, I soon found that this was one of the most acceptable treats I could give the company. They were, in fact, enthusiastic admirers of Scottish music; Burns' songs were highly relished, and one of the company anticipated me by singing my favorite song of Muirland Willie.[13]

James Hall (1793–1868), an English judge, published his *Letters from the West* in 1828. Part of the adventure of his descent of the Ohio during April 1820 involved "Pappy" and his violin, "Katy." Old Pap (estimated to be about fifty years old) possessed "an affected gravity, a drawling accent, and a kind, benevolent manner, which accorded well with the paternal appellation given him by the boatmen, [and] marked him as an eccentric being":

He was a man of endless humour—a fellow of infinite fancy. While others worked, he would sit for hours scraping upon his violin, singing catches, or relating merry and marvellous tales. . . . If the boat grounded on a sand-bar, he was the first to plunge into the water; if a point was to be weathered, or a rapid to be passed, his was always the best oar; if a watch was to be kept at night who so wakeful as he? And on such occasions, he would fiddle and sing the live-long night. . . .

More than once he enacted chief musician at dances got up at the hovels along shore, near which we *lay by* for the night. Lady Morgan styles this amusement the "poetry of motion," and I assure you it was not the less poetic with the accompaniment of Pap and his musical Kate.[14]

Let us now turn to several of the first urban centers established in what became Ohio, since they soon offered the stability in which a more mature musical culture could flourish.[15] Naturally, these urban centers generated a more abundant fund of evidence, and their stories offer paradigms of similar tales spun elsewhere.

CHAPTER 2

Marietta

On April 7, 1788, associates of the Ohio Company landed at the juncture of the Ohio and Muskingum Rivers and established on the east bank of the latter a village first known as Adelphi, but soon renamed in honor of Queen Marie Antoinette of France, our ally in the struggle for independence from Great Britain. Across the Muskingum from Fort Harmar and its military garrison (dating from the summer of 1785) they laid out a community designed on the New England model that included Campus Martius, an imposing fortification designed to offer protection from Indian attacks.

On July 9 the inhabitants of Marietta joined soldiers from Fort Harmar in welcoming "with music" Gov. Arthur St. Clair to the Northwest Territory's first official settlement. Presumably the music was made by men attached to the garrison, its flavor akin to procedures of spring 1790, described by Col. Joseph Barker:

> It became my duty to keep a rool of every person amenable to Military duty, to attend at the place of Public Worship with my rool, Call every mans name, examine their Arms & Ammunition, see that every man was equip^d agreeable to Law, note down & report delinquencies, On sunday morning at 10 oclock, at which the Law made it their duty to appear for Inspection; [there were] those who staid through the service, and there generally was a pretty punctual attendance. The Clergyman was commonly preceded by Colo Sproat with his Revolutionary Sword & Sheriffs Wand, & he [was preceded] by a Drum & Fife at the Point, & by Genl Putnam & Genl Tupper at Campus Martius, & [by] Drum & Fife [they] marched to the place of Public Worship. Such Citizens as Chose fell into the procession. In the mean time the Citizen Soldiers having been inspected, all were ready to attend divine service.[1]

Col. Ichabod Nye (1763–1840), son-in-law of General Tupper, described a scene from the summer of 1788 delineating the parlous state of music making among these pioneers. At Sunday services

> there ware Some Singers under the lead of Capt. Lunt, . . . with him Capt. Grey, a Verry good Base Singer, and others. They rose to sing in Meeting[.] They started on the way a line or two & got lost. I struck in with them & continued on till I found all the congregation in a gaze at me; I felt Streeked enough (as the saying is) however I aided Lunt, untill he got his core under way again, and I gott off as well as I could.[2]

John May, who had been present at Governor St. Clair's arrival, described a ceremony held on July 20, 1788, that for the first time allows a specific insight into the kind of music the settlers favored:

> At 11 o'clock to-day a religious service. Mr. Daniel Breck began the observances by singing, praying, and preaching. The place of worship was our bowery, on the bank directly over my ship. A large number of people were assembled from the garrison, Virginia, and our own settlement—in all about three hundred; some women and children, which was a pleasing, though something unusual sight for us to see. Mr. Breck made out pretty well. The singing excellent. We had "Billings" to perfection. Governor St. Clair was pleased with the whole exercise.[3]

Despite the quotation marks, it can be presumed that May was referring not to a tune named Billings but to a work by William Billings (1746–1800), the best-known and most prolific of a substantial number of itinerant New England singing-school masters who during that period published their own pedagogical manuals, each of which included a generous helping of the teacher's own compositions. The best of this music has about it a vigorous, intentionally rough-hewn quality, and it is tempting to speculate that at least some of these transplanted New Englanders might actually have learned to decipher musical notation and lustily sing a fuging tune or two from Billings himself.

Barker left other anecdotes that hint at the musical accomplishments of these initial pioneers, as well as the nature of their existence at the edge of the wilderness. He recalled Maj. Anselm Tupper, a Revolutionary War veteran who was one of the first surveyors sent out from New England by the Ohio Company, a man who

> had genius & Capacity & taste for literary persuits, some specimens of which both in prose & poetry occasionally served, in the dearth of amusement, to while

away the monotonous hour amid the cares & labours incident to a new settlement. He delivered severel Public Orations on the 4th of July and 7th of April [1790], & furnished some very good patriotic songs. But as he wrote principally to amuse himself & those about him, a little sarcasm was a spice not to be left out of his compositions—nor too much extream delacacy to be admitted in.[4]

Barker also reminisced about the plight of a poor soul victimized by the Indians' practice of slaughtering too many deer and wild turkeys, and then piling the excess on the riverbank "like a rick of Hay," or leaving the carcasses lying about the forests, thus attracting wolves and panthers:

A man by the Name of Bagley, [a] fid[d]ler, coming from Wolf Creek, towards spring one Cold, Snowey, frozen Afternoon, was attacked by [a] large gang of Wolves who drove him up a Tree, where he had to sit & play the Fiddle for them until they saw fit to leave the next day.[5]

A pity that we will never know the tunes of Tupper's "songs" or learn whether poor, hapless Bagley was on his way to the village to play for one of the dances described as having taken place as early as December 1788.

Indeed, these early settlers brought with them many of the conventional social graces of the period. Samuel S. Forman, who spent the night of November 11, 1789, at Marietta, commented on the evening's diversion in what he decried as an otherwise "dreary place": "The young ladies were good singers, and entertained the officers awhile with their vocal music."[6]

However, both the social and cultural life of the place were considerably enhanced by the arrival in 1797 of Harman and Margaret Blennerhassett. Blennerhassett was a wealthy Irish aristocrat who in 1798 bought an island in the middle of the Ohio River fourteen miles downriver from Marietta and completed there in September 1800 what was surely the most imposing residence between the eastern seaboard and New Orleans.[7] Although the Blennerhassetts' Palladian-style Camelot stood in Virginia (the political boundary having been fixed at the northern waterline of the river), they were frequent visitors to Marietta and quite involved in its business, social, and cultural life, which they must have considerably enlivened with a large whiff of the Enlightenment.

Retiring in life, [Blennerhassett's] life was sedentary and studious; books and philosophical experiments possessing greater attractions than the gay and fashionable assemblies of the ball-room. Always entertaining, he never indulged in trivial conversation, but interested his audience in something calculated more to instruct than amuse their idle fancy. . . .

He was a connoisseur in music, and performed admirably upon the violin and violoncello. Many of his hours of recreation were whiled away with this delightful amusement; and, being an adept, pieces of his own composition were played with animating effect.[8]

Anecdotal evidence remains that Blennerhassett was a member of a string quartet in Marietta. Also, that he may have also played the bass viol and cultivated chamber music on his island as well as in the village: "The spacious hall of the mansion being constructed so as to give effect to musical sounds, the tones of his viol vibrated through it with thrilling effect, calling forth the admiration of his guests."[9] Of his purported compositions, only *Blennerhasset's March and Quick Step* is known, attributed to Herman [*sic*] Blennerhasset, arranged by William Cumming Peters, and published by Peters, Field, and Company in Cincinnati in 1847, with a view of the Blennerhassett mansion on its title page. While the published score asserts, "The Melody of the two following pieces is copied from the recollection of an Old Pioneer of the West, who was intimate with the family of Mr. Blennerhasset," one might suspect that Peters worked from a manuscript provided by the family of Lucy Wallace, to whom the arrangement is dedicated, since Peters stated that the Wallaces were "intimate with the family of Mr. Blennerhasset."[10]

If Harman Blennerhassett appeared as somewhat of a studious recluse, Margaret must have served as a striking antidote:

> History affords but a few instances where so much feminine beauty, physical endurance, and many social virtues, were combined with so brilliant a mind, in the person of a female. . . .
>
> Although she participated in the various amusements through the country, and was the ruling spirit in every assembly, she never neglected the ordinary duties of her household; every apartment received her personal attention, from the kitchen to the chambers, and was duly cleansed and arranged according to her direction.[11]

She was also reputed to be "passionately fond of dancing, and greatly excelled in this healthful and charming exercise, moving through the mazes and intricacies of the various figures, with the grace and lightness of the 'queen of the fairies.'"[12]

In short, this amazing pair must have brought to the fledgling community unprecedented standards of cosmopolitan refinement. An awed visitor of 1805 recorded that

> it was tea time. Refreshment was served and conducted with a propriety and elegance which I never witnessed outside of Britain. The main hall was wide

and spacious and adapted to respond to the harmonies with which the lady of the mansion by voice and harpsichord, in the evening hour often delighted the guests.[13]

Alas, this sylvan existence was short-lived, for Blennerhasset became involved with Aaron Burr's alleged scheme of creating a new country by severing the western regions from the original seaboard states. Blennerhasset subsidized the building of a fleet of riverboats for Burr near Marietta, but on November 27, 1806, President Jefferson issued a proclamation calling for the arrest of his former vice president (who probably was only intent on invading and settling land on the disputed border of Spanish Texas). In early December Ohio's Governor Tiffin ordered seizure of Burr's still-unfinished flotilla, and on the eleventh, Virginia militiamen invaded Blennerhassett's island, forcing the family to flee. The mansion's furnishings were later sold at public auction and the property left in the custody of the friend who was Fortescue Cuming's host in 1807. Cuming observed that he departed

> with regret that such a terrestrial paradise should be deserted by an owner who had taste to blend judiciously the improvements of art with the beauties of nature. Its fertility will always ensure its cultivation, but without a Horace it must cease to be a Tivoli.[14]

This New World Tivoli was completely destroyed by fire in 1811 but then reconstructed between 1984 and 1991 on its original foundations by the West Virginia Division of Natural Resources and now serves as the centerpiece of the Blennerhassett Island Historical State Park.[15]

In Marietta the organization of congregations and the construction of permanent houses of worship symbolized increasing stability and growth. Philander Chase was elected the first bishop of Ohio at the initial diocesan convention of the Protestant Episcopal Church held in Columbus during January 1818. He was finally consecrated in Philadelphia during February 1819 and made his way to Marietta in August 1820, a year during which he rode 1,279 miles on horseback, visiting the far-flung reaches of his realm. The bishop's son then paid the village a visit in 1822, but it was two years more before another Episcopal priest made his way to the mouth of the Muskingum.

In January 1826 a group of seven prominent citizens organized the Parish of St. Luke in a village with a population of barely more than one thousand. Arius Nye (1792–1865), son and grandson of two of the community's founders, was appointed lay reader, a position he held for seven years, during a period when Marietta was visited only irregularly by ordained clergymen. To put his responsibilities in perspective, during the period of 1827 to 1829 the parish rolls contained the names of only twelve families and ten communicants. Services were conducted in the Lyceum or Library Hall after its construction in 1831.

Scanty evidence remains as to how much music was employed during this period, although John Delafield, an officer of the parish, supposedly taught music in the Marietta Female Seminary, which had evolved from the Young Ladies' Department of the Marietta Collegiate Institute. Delafield was described as the son of a wealthy New York banker and a graduate of Columbia College, who had been shipped out to Ohio "with gun, fishing rods and artificial flies, books, musical instruments, and two Scotchmen 'to sow his wild oats,' . . . a fine musician, a good composer, and [one who] painted well in oil and water colors."[16] On his arrival he introduced himself to Nye as a student of Jonathan Mayhew Wainwright (1792–1854), co-compiler (with Augustus Muehlenberg) of *Music of the Church. A Collection of Psalm, Hymn, and Chant Tunes, Adapted to the Worship of the Protestant Episcopal Church in the United States* (first published in 1828 and so popular that it went through multiple editions until at least as late as 1856), apparently Nye's principal resource as worship leader of the young parish.

We do know that on Christmas Day 1832 the Reverend John Thomas Wheat of Wheeling, later St. Luke's first permanent rector, preached and created an ode of five strophes for the service that was sung to the tune of Vincenzo Pucitta's "Strike the Cymbals." The parish was incorporated the following month, and its first building opened on November 22, 1834, with an elaborate processional and service that involved the singing of at least parts of the liturgy and a hymn. A subscription drive to purchase an organ was initiated in 1836, but a five-hundred dollar instrument constructed by Johann Koehnken of Cincinnati was not installed until 1843. Charles J. Sheppard of Wheeling, later St. Luke's first trained organist, had originally recommended purchasing an instrument from George Jardine and Son of New York City, and the wisdom of his recommendation was apparently justified after a few years when some of Koehnken's "pipes[,] being made of soft lead, got out of shape and became useless." A six-stop instrument by Jardine costing six hundred dollars then served the parish for many decades.

Of course, we can only wonder about the consequences of the music-making of that period:

> When the church was built, Mr. Nye had his seat near the chancel and when a chant or hymn was to be sung he would step forward to the chancel-rail and with an unerring voice lead the congregation. He was very correct and rarely, if ever, failed to strike the right pitch. But very little anthem music was ventured on in the early days. Mr. Nye continued to sing after a choir was organized, and on one occasion an anthem was attempted which was somewhat beyond their ability to sing. Mr. Nye took the principal part and

when in the midst of it, being, like the chorister in Irving's Christmas, wrapt up in his own melody, he did not notice that the other voices dropped out one by one, and that he alone finished the anthem. He afterward remarked, "We got through that in very good style."[17]

Nye's passion for exercising his voice in song extended to the performance of ballads. He even assembled his own wordbook in December 1817, copying the lyrics of all twenty-nine verses of the "Battle of Muskingum or Defeat of the Burrites," a parody of "The Battle of the Kegs," attributed to Anselm Tupper, as well as four verses of "The Star Spangled Banner" and non-topical songs such as "Sandy and Jenny" and "When pensive I thought of my love."

Two other local personalities surely reflect other common kinds of quotidian music making. Several commentators detail the minisaga of Connecticut-born Beman Gates, who arrived by boat during the fall of 1837 in the company of an ill relative. Penniless and despondent, essentially stranded at the Broughy House, the nineteen-year-old Gates was accustomed to raising his spirits by playing the flute or singing. Overheard one night by the pastor of the First Congregational Church, Gates was recruited as that congregation's choirmaster in a structure dating from 1809, concurrently leading a singing school with considerable success:

> The stupidest could get the stir of the perfect time that he exacted. Voices that were merely loud were made to blend themselves with others, strident or off color voices were trained to harmonize with the choruses. Best of all was the finish with which his few picked singers learned to sing really good music.[18]

When the community celebrated, Gates served as the song leader, as at an April 7, 1838, commemoration of the arrival of the original pioneers, for instance. Other music that day was furnished by the College Band, led by Samuel Hall, a recent graduate of the institution.[19]

On November 6 of that same year Gates proposed to the Washington County School Association that the study of vocal music should be introduced into the public schools and buttressed his argument with further remarks on May 7, 1839, but to no avail since the systematic use of music in Marietta's schools was not introduced until 1892. Perhaps Gates's concern was fueled by his friendship with Daniel Gregory Mason (1820–69), a son of Lowell Mason, the patriarch of public school music in this country. The elder Mason purportedly urged Gates to consider a career as a professional singer and imported him for a Boston performance of Handel's *Messiah* during the spring of 1839. But Gates became a newspaperman and remained loyal to Marietta, although during the period of 1846 to 1855 he lived in both Columbus and Washington, D.C. Earlier, during the presidential campaign of 1840,

Gates, a partisan of the Whig candidate William Henry Harrison, organized a Marietta Glee Club, which then sang

> at towns as far as a hundred miles from Marietta[,] which meant hard driving over dirt roads, and at night much of the time. Stump speeches were made literally on stumps and songs were sung by the flickering light of torches or in the moonlight.[20]

A musician of a different sort is limned in the pages of a journal kept by Dennis Patterson Adams between September 3, 1845, and November 5, 1846. Adams was involved in the building of a sailing vessel on which he then traveled down the inland river system to New Orleans between February 11 and March 28, 1846, and on to Boston between April 8 and May 5. He then made his way back to Marietta overland via New York, Philadelphia, and Harrisburg, arriving on May 17.

His journal entries describe an amateur musician of multifaceted interests and abilities. Some excerpts:

> 6 [September 1845]–Worked 7 hours in the college and in the afternoon finished my *squirrel* cage and in the evening went to the point and then went and borrowed Baldwin's flute and went to the sing at Mr. Tylers and had a pretty good time.

> 7–Sunday–Went to church and played the Bass Viol all day tonight Sabath school too.

> 8–Worked in the shop all day and in the evening played the violin with Mr. Nales.

> 12–Worked in the shop near all day and in the evening went to the point and after loafing about for awhile went and *borrowed* a flute of Wilsom and Shipman and went to the sing at Mr. Temings staid till it was out. . . .

> 17-Worked in the shop all day and in the evening went to the point and loafed awhile and came home and wrote music all the evening and then went to bed tired.[21]

Adams's recital can become a bit monotonous, since almost every entry contains some reference to music making. For example, on the nineteenth he went to a sing, wrote music during the evening of the twentieth, played the violin at church on the twenty-first, and wrote music again during the evenings of the twenty-second, twenty-third, and twenty-fourth.

By October 8 he was in possession of his own instrument, since "Mr. Baldwin brought my flute up from *Cincinati* to day 8 keys." Seven days later he records having "played the flute with the *Orchastra*." Later that month, in addition to regular attendance at singing schools, he began to mention participation in choir meetings, although it remains unclear as to whether he actually sang on Sundays since the journal entries refer only to performances on the violine, violin, or flute.

All of this is interlarded among comments about hunting expeditions, being "*enitiated* as 2nd Librarian in the *Sabath* School," voting for the first time (as a Whig), gawking at General Tom Thumb ("he is about 30 inches high and well proportioned as any common slim man he is 22 years of age born at Boston admittance 12 1/2 cents"), drawing lessons "of Miss Nancy M. Wood at Mr. Sheldons," sleigh rides and ice skating on the Muskingum, plus temperance and abolitionist meetings. Yet music remained the guiding force of his kaleidoscopic existence—December 30 brought a "sing [that] is for a Concert to be given at the [Congregational] church to help pay for the organ"; on January 5, 1846, he "went to monthly concert"; on June 11 "in the evening Nort Jim Charley Nolcini and myself went serenading all over the stockade with a Bugle Trombone horne and I performed on the Tamborene got home at 10 oc."—and the coterie of other individuals involved in these activities suggests a rich tradition of music making deeply embedded in the lives of the citizens of Marietta.[22]

CHAPTER 3

Cincinnati

While chronological precedence must be ceded to Marietta, the settlement and development of Cincinnati followed almost immediately, and the village soon was defined as the Queen City of the West.

Its first settlers arrived during the waning months of 1788; a protective stockade was erected the following autumn, christened Fort Washington, and occupied by soldiers who came downstream from Fort Harmar.[1] Governor St. Clair moved to the adjacent village on January 2, 1790, designated it the capital of the Northwest Territory, and christened it Cincinnati, thus honoring the Order of Cincinnatus, an association of former Revolutionary War officers. By 1792 it was estimated that Cincinnati's civilian population totaled 750, sufficient to justify founding of the First Presbyterian Church, constituted in 1791 and initially housed in a log building. The *Centinal of the Northwest Territory*, the village's first newspaper, appeared on November 9, 1793. Renamed the *Freeman's Journal* in 1795, it persisted until 1800, when it was relocated to Chillicothe. It was joined in 1799 by a more influential periodical, the *Western Spy and Hamilton Gazette*.

Although Cincinnati was not incorporated until 1802, evidence of a rudimentary musical culture appeared there even earlier. On November 19, 1799, R. Haughton announced in the *Western Spy* that "having taught with great reputation in different parts of Pennsylvania and Virginia last winter and spring, and whose letters of introduction to this place and Lexington, are most respectable," he intended to open a school as soon as he obtained subscriptions from at least sixteen scholars. The classes were to be offered every morning at ten o'clock and also in the evening at seven o'clock for working gentlemen:

He teaches particularly, the Minuet Cotillion, Cotillion, French and English Sets, in all their various and ornamental branches—Exclusive of which, he teaches the most fashionable Country Dances and the City Cotillion, taught in New York, Philadelphia and Baltimore.—His terms are three dollars entrance, and five at the expiration of their quarter.

N. B. Mr. Haughton also teaches some favorite Scottish Reels.[2]

On December 27, 1800, readers of the *Spy* were advised,

Those gentlemen and ladies who feel disposed to patronize a SINGING SCHOOL, will please to convene at the Court house, to-morrow evening, at candle light. As it is proposed to have singing, they will please bring their books with them.[3]

The organizer of this venture cannot be identified, but in 1801 Levi McClean, a butcher by trade, advertised, "Subscriptions for singing lessons $1 for thirteen nights, or $2 a quarter. Subscribers will please bring their own candles."[4]

The Poor Soldier, the most widely performed English comic opera of the era, was staged near Fort Washington on September 30, 1801. It is probable that members of the garrison's band provided instrumental support and also may have afforded the local citizenry something akin to concerts. For example, on July 4, 1799, "Captain Miller furnished a piece of artillery which, with Captain Smith's company of militia, accompanied by martial music, made the woods resound to the toasts that were made." A few years later the fort's band celebrated Independence Day with a repertory of favorite tunes: "The President's March," "French Grenadiers' March," "George Washington's March," "Yankee Doodle," "Guardian Angels," "Rural Felicity," "Soldier's Joy," "Reveille," "Anacreon in Heaven" (the English drinking song later borrowed to support "The Star-Spangled Banner"), "Madam You Know My Trade Is War," "Fair American," "Love in a Village," "Goodnight be wi' you 'a,'" and "Flowers of Edinburgh."[5] Extant evidence suggests that in the years immediately preceding the garrison's removal to New Orleans in 1808, General Wilkinson, its commandant, maintained a band supposedly containing a number of French- and German-born musicians. On a river excursion for his officers, this ensemble "accompanied them with the harmonies of Gluck and Haydn, and the reports of the champagne bottles transported the guests from the wilds of the Northwestern Territory into the Lucullian feasts of the European aristocracy."[6]

The first formal public concert of record in Cincinnati was offered on April 26, 1810, at the Court House by the Harmonical Society as a benefit for William Wilkinson. The society was of recent creation, a brass band whose members played primarily for their own diversion. Their repertory that evening is unknown, but spectators paid twenty-five cents to support "a [young] gentleman generally believed to be worthy of public encouragement, in his laudable undertaking to instruct the youth of our community, in the elegant and refined science of Music." Wilkinson demonstrated a degree of ingratitude by leaving Cincinnati soon afterwards and expiring only three years later, in Alexandria, Louisiana.[7]

The society also attracted notice the following year for its participation in ceremonies marking the death of David Ziegler. German-born Ziegler (1748–1811) had achieved distinction as an officer in the Continental Army, followed by service in several of those campaigns during the early 1790s whose purpose was to eliminate American Indian control of their ancestral lands in the Northwest Territory. While in command of Fort Washington during early 1792, anti-German xenophobia led to charges of drunkenness and insubordination. Disgusted, Ziegler not only relinquished his command but also resigned from the Army on March 5. He subsequently became one of the settlement's most prominent citizens and was elected president of the village council, a de facto mayor, after incorporation in 1802. Merchant, Cincinnati harbor collector, and adjutant of the state militia, he was buried on September 26, 1811, with full military honors, "accompanied to the grave by the Harmonical society, who played on various wind-instruments during the procession, which was extremely numerous and respectable."[8]

The first itinerant entertainer arrived two years later, on October 25, 1813. An Irishman named Webster offered "The Harp of Erin," a collage of "Conversation, Anecdote, and Song," in the assembly room of the Columbian Inn. For seventy-five cents his auditors heard songs like "Sally Roy," "Fair Ellen," "Faithless Emma," "The Willow," "Paddy in a Pucker," "The Glasses Sparkle," "The Exile of Erin," "Honey and Mustard," "Saint Senanus," and "The Doldrum." Webster also advertised "a quantity of Music (particularly songs) all arrayed for the Piano Forte to dispose of; which will be highly advantageous to Ladies who play that instrument." On November 1 he offered an entertainment called "The Wandering Melodist," which included songs such as "The Harp That Once Through Tara's Halls," Thomas Moore's "Fly Not Yet," and Williams Shield's "Post Captain." The printed song lyrics were offered to the public gratis; sheet music was again for sale.[9]

The Harmonical Society surfaced again on February 3, 1814, in the Columbian Inn with what was billed as its "First Public Concert." Several similar events were presented during the autumn prior to the "Annual Concert and Ball" on December 21 in the concert room of the substantial former home of William Henry Harrison that was soon to be known as the Cincinnati Hotel.[10] Its repertory: "Hail, Columbia," "Life Let Us Cherish," "Will You Come to My Bower?" "Italian Waltz," "Monroe's March," "America," "Liberty or Death," "Masonic Dead March," "The Star-Spangled Banner," and something called "Haydn's Fantasy." The Harmonical Society apparently functioned until early 1823. We can only hope that its capacities were not related to an announcement by James H. Hoffman on December 15, 1815, that he was about to establish a musical academy with the goal of instructing players of military band instruments. His guarantee: he would teach, "in a scientific and comprehensive manner, a scholar thirteen tunes, at least, in eighteen lessons, or no compensation will be required." Apparently his students were to master one instrument per session to a maximum of nineteen; these included the Grand Oboe (or "Voice Umane"), fife, German flute, flageolet, bassoon, serpent, sacbut, hurdy-gurdy, cymbals, and bass drum.[11] In that same year a Mrs. Hopkins announced the opening of her Musical Academy on Main Street opposite the Columbian Inn.

The Cincinnati Euphonical Society had held meetings during 1811 and 1812, and there are references to an organization known as the St. Cecilia Society or Apollonian Society during 1816. The labels probably reflect a group of gentlemen amateurs and professionals who first assembled at the home of Frederick Amelung, a recent transplant from Pittsburgh, where he had earlier presided over that city's Apollonian Society. Although their purpose was the "cultivation of vocal and instrumental music," they apparently made music only for their own pleasure. They taxed themselves in support of their activities, and when membership ballooned to as many as forty-five, they moved their headquarters from Amelung's home to the Apollonian Gardens, one of Cincinnati's first beer halls.

Itinerants continued to find their way to Cincinnati during the second decade of the century. For example, on January 10, 1819, auditors were invited to the Presbyterian Church to hear "Mr. Myers, the converted Jew," who had astonished audiences in New York and elsewhere by singing in Russian. And in September of that year a group of "Caledonian Youths" presented a miniseason of nine concerts, including "a great variety of Scotch and American airs on the Scotch harp."[12]

The increasing musical sophistication of the community is also reflected in the appearance of instrument builders and music publishers. The community's first pipe organ was built in 1808 by Adam Hurdus, who had kept a dry goods store since 1806 and became a minister to the New Jerusalem Society. Pianos were manufactured by George Charters, Francis B. Garrish, and Aaron Golden, gentlemen productive enough that a visitor of 1816 noted that "pianos are counted by the dozen with no one to tune them," apparently unaware that the prior year Adolphus Wupper had recommended himself as a tuner and repairer of pianos as well as a teacher. By 1826 John Imhoff was offering musical scores and instruments to the public at the "Sign of the Violin."

Presumably Imhoff included among his wares the trickle of scores printed in Cincinnati. These included:

[Robert] *Patterson's Church Music* (Locker and Wallace, 1813)
John McCormick: *Western Harmonist* (Locker and Wallace, 1815)
Timothy Flint: *The Columbian Harmonist* (Coleman and Phillips, 1816)
Samuel Lytler Metcalfe: *The Kentucky Harmonist* (Morgan and Lodge, 1817)

Alexander Johnson: *Johnson's Tennessee Harmony* (Morgan, Lodge, and Company, 1818)

William Little and William Smith: *The Easy Instructor* (J. Pace, 1819)

Allen D. Carden: *The Missouri Harmony* (Morgan and Sanxay, 1820)

Seth Ely: *Sacred Music* (Morgan, Lodge, and Company, 1822)

W. C. Knight: *The Juvenile Harmony* (Morgan and Sanxay, 1825)

William Moore: *Columbian Harmony* (Morgan, Lodge, and Fisher, 1825)

Most of these publications were not authored by Cincinnatians (for example, Robert Patterson was a resident of Pittsburgh, and the Little and Smith volume had first appeared in Albany in 1798) and were intended by their compilers for use elsewhere on the frontier. However, that the proliferation of musical societies resulted in an expanded local market is suggested by an advertisement for the *Western Harmonist* inserted in the *Liberty Hall* of April 7, 1815: "The author having been nearly two years in the contemplation of the work flatters himself he will be able to furnish the different societies with the most useful tunes and anthems."

Collectively these volumes suggest that by 1830 Cincinnati was recognized as a significant publishing center; by the time of the 1850 census, the "Literary Emporium of the West" had become the country's fourth busiest publishing center, surpassed in output only by New York, Philadelphia, and Boston.[13]

The Queen City's increasing cultural maturity is reflected in the eleven public concerts given by the Haydn Society between May 25, 1819, and November 11, 1823. Its initial outing, mounted in Christ Episcopal Church only six weeks following the group's organization, was surely the most elaborate musical venture yet attempted west of the established seaboard cities. It was led by Philibert Ratel, a French native who had spent six or seven years in Philadelphia before deciding to relocate to Nashville. However, in transit during the summer of 1817, he was recruited as director of a Cincinnati theater ensemble, opened a dancing school, and soon became an active figure in the town's musical life. The 1819 program was a pastiche "taken from the most popular authors, with the exception of some original adaptations arranged by Mr. Ratel, whose taste and judgment entitled him to much applause."[14]

Part First

Overture	
Chorus, China	T. Clarke
Grand Chorus, The Marvellous Works	Joseph Haydn
Jehova Speaks	[Oliver] Holden
Chorus, Strike the Cymbals	[Vicenzo] Pucitta
Anthem, Our Lord Is Risen from the Dead	[Samuel] Arnold
Chorus, Cranbrook	T. Clarke

Part Second

Overture	
Chorus, Jabez' Prayer	[Thomas] Jarman
Overton	T. Clarke
Anthem, O Praise the Lord	Meinecke
Poland	[John] Husband
Chorus, New Year's Ode	T. Clarke
Hosanna Chorus	[Christian] Gregor
Duett and Chorus, Hail Judea	G. F. Handel

Somewhere between one and two hundred auditors were in attendance, and the evening netted one hundred dollars, at least part of which was devoted to purchasing an organ for the church. The critical response was generally laudatory. One commentator opined that the event had

> given very general satisfaction Indeed, yielding to the delightful emotions which sacred harmony must excite even in uncultivated minds, none other could be felt by an intelligent auditor when, in addition to the excellent selection, the execution would have reflected credit on our Eastern cities, and the melody in several instances was divine. This exhibition must have been highly gratifying to those who begin to feel proud of our city. It is the strongest evidence we can adduce of our advancement in those embellishments which refine and harmonize society and give a zest to life.[15]

Another observer reported that the event was "fully and fashionably attended," despite "the intervention of some unexpected impediments." He commented on "the solemn stillness and rivetted attention which prevailed among the spectators during the whole representation" and then ventured to suggest that

> It is not our intention to enter upon a minute criticism of the performance; as the task of judicious discrimination would be attended with delicacy, and might possibly wound, although unintentionally, the feelings of some individual concerned. Nor have we the right to *expect* from the amateur that perfection which may be *insisted* on from the professor. There were, at the same time, some deficiencies of a general character, the mention of which can give no offence, and may be of service, perhaps, hereafter; we allude to the occasional disproportion which the instrumental bore to the vocal parts; and in some pieces a lack of strength on the bass. . . . The little trifle from Gregor at the close, produced quite an exhilarating effect, and was well calculated to send the audience home satisfied with the divertissement and themselves.[16]

The society initiated a second season on October 19, 1819, with a repertory that included repetitions of the more popular items from their first venture as well as unnamed overtures by Handel and Haydn, an instrumental "Finale" by Ignaz Pleyel (1757–1831), a "Duett and Chorus" by Charles Burney (1726–1804), and a "Hymn and Chorus—Come hither all" by one B. Cuzens. The goal was to raise funds for the local Sunday schools and to purchase scores for the society's future use. While the critics were pleased, attendance was minimal. Under the misguided perception that the slight patronage was a fluke, the event was repeated on November 1 with minor changes in the agenda but to no avail. Obviously exasperated, the society vowed "to discontinue public exhibitions," lamenting that "the members of this laudable association have been at much expense and labour, under the conviction that their exertions would tend to the edification of our citizens and contribute to the purpose of benevolence. . . . Their anticipations, however, it seems, have proved fallacious and illusive."[17]

On March 16 and 23, 1820, a Mr. Garner, in transit from the eastern seaboard to New Orleans, gave two concerts in the ballroom of the Cincinnati Hotel. He presented songs by John Braham, Henry Rowley Bishop, Thomas Philipps, Thomas Moore, and others, while a "Full Band" under the direction of Ratel played overtures, and Ratel offered several sets of variations using both the "French Flageolet" and "Clarionet." An "Italian Waltz, with variations on the Clarionet" was offered by Josiah Warren, and Ratel and Warren participated in a trio for two flutes and bassoon, perhaps the first public celebration of chamber music in the city.

Encouraged by Garner's considerable success, the Haydn Society emerged from its self-imposed hibernation on May 4, 1820, with a program consisting mostly of recycled repertory allied with "new" works by Oliver Shaw and William Bradbury. Alas, this venture was again greeted by public indifference and a financial deficit, and the society disappeared from public view until a celebration at the First Presbyterian Church on July 4, 1821, to which its members contributed "some appropriate odes and anthems."[18]

Would-be choral singers had available alternatives to the Haydn Society. The Episcopal Singing Society had been organized in 1819; the Swedenborgians supported a New Jerusalem Singing Society for a decade beginning in 1820; and churches like the Second Presbyterian and Vine Street Methodist fielded their own choirs. Several of these groups combined with an ad hoc ensemble of instrumentalists and organist James W. Whittaker for a concert on July 18, 1821, that included first performances in Cincinnati of several works, most notably Handel's "Hallelujah" but also the *Messiah* air, "Thou shalt break them in pieces" and three items each from Oliver Shaw and Thomas Hastings.

Public indifference suggests a growing aversion to these all-sacred ventures, but the seemingly indefatigable Haydn Society rallied by November to prepare yet another "Concert of Sacred Music" in the First Presbyterian Church on December 20,

1821, in which Mr. Whittaker was to accompany "Songs and Duetts upon a fine toned *Organ.*" Again, the literature was mostly recycled but did include Haydn's "The Heavens are telling" from *The Creation.* Despite the lack of public response, the society reorganized and began to meet on alternate Sundays to rehearse and perform privately for its "subscribers." Active membership climbed to thirty-four, one hundred dollars worth of musical scores was purchased from the Handel and Haydn Society of Boston, and the society participated in dual celebrations of Washington's birthday in transit to a concert on April 29, 1822, of which no record remains. However, a local journalist recorded that on April 7 during a rehearsal of Handel's "He gave them hailstones for rain" from *Israel in Egypt,* "a violent storm of *hail,* wind, *thunder* and *lighting* arose, which accorded completely with the words and music of the chorus."[19]

The Haydners celebrated Independence Day of 1822 twice, including several odes accompanied by the Cincinnati Band, conducted by Josiah Warren. By October the Haydn Society announced a grand plan to present four oratorios a season. The following month the society was visited and rehearsed by a Mr. Lewis, who with his wife and five children, aged four to twelve, offered nine concerts at Colonel Andrew Mack's Ball Room between November 4 and 16. Apart from the spectacle of this gaggle of infant performers on various instruments, the Lewis clan brought to Cincinnati another first: a "Grand Overture [by Mozart], arranged as a Duet, with two performers on one Piano-Forte, with a Violincello accompaniment." The Lewis repertory also included a hackneyed bromide by Franz Kotzwara, leading one local journalist to suggest, "It is impossible to convey to the minds of those who were not present, any idea of the masterly manner in which they performed the celebrated 'Battle of Prague'; the imitations of the groans of the dying, on the Violin, were peculiarly striking."[20]

The Haydn Society's concert of December 19, 1822, with Mr. Whittaker presiding at Luman Watson's new pipe organ in the Episcopal church and an orchestral ensemble enlarged for the occasion, was announced as a "Select Oratorio." However, the program was again a mélange, including some of the group's signature works but also an organ voluntary by John Marsh, organist of Chichester Cathedral, an anthem by Samuel Webbe (1770–1843), a duet by Philippo Traetta ([1777–1854], born in Venice but active in Boston and Philadelphia after 1799), four diverse pieces by the Englishman Matthew P. King (1773–1823), and "The saffron tints of morn appear," a "chorus" by Mozart. Although the performers far outnumbered the twenty auditors, the society persisted doggedly and repeated the venture on December 27 to an equally limp response. A month later another "Sacred Concert" garnered only $9.25 in receipts. Two weeks later a local partisan huffed that

> The city of Cincinnati is already so celebrated for the failure of everything of public utility, that to produce the HAYDN SOCIETY as a new instance, is a circumstance, as disagreeable to the writer as it is disgraceful to our citizens....

[T]he fall of this Society, is an unexceptionable evidence of our total indifference to everything that characterizes a polished city. . . . I understand a dissolution of the society is in contemplation, and should it take place, it may reasonably be supposed that most of our citizens are still the "hunters of the backwoods," and that the few who pretend to be in any degree polished, are incapable of appreciating the value of music, when it is carried beyond the powers of a tambourine or a hand-organ.[21]

Apparently chastened or humiliated, the Haydners continued to rehearse in private. They entertained a touring Welsh tenor, Thomas Philipps, during March but declined participation in the 1823 Independence Day celebrations.

They had been joined in the local arena by an Euterpeian Society, which offered public concerts in February, May, and July 1823, apparently eliciting more public support through a policy of not selling tickets, instead soliciting donations at the door, and by offering their performances not in churches but in venues like the Cincinnati Hotel and Colonel Mack's Ball Room. However industrious and active (for example, it offered concerts to extensive audiences on both October 16, 1823, and January 9, 1824), the group survived only until 1825.

However, the Haydn Society soldiered on during its final season with weekly rehearsals begun on the last Sunday of September 1823. Cincinnati was besieged with visiting entertainers that autumn, and the success of one perhaps explains the Haydn's faltering fortunes. John C. Muscarelli, "From Italy, Professor and Composer of music," offered concerts followed by dances in Colonel Mack's Ball Room on October 30 and November 5. His first program surely mirrored the taste of the time:

Part I

Overture—Full Band
Imitations of the chirping and warbling of birds, violin, solo
Auld Lang Syne, with variations, solo
Italian Song, accompanied on the guitar, solo

Part II

Symphony—Full Band
Tyrolese Song of Liberty, with variations, violin, solo
Italian Waltz, on the guitar, solo
The Concert to conclude with an imitation of Dogs and Cats, solo, on the
     violin[22]

Before Professor Muscarelli had completed his brief run, the Lewis family returned to offer four concerts at Colonel Mack's between November 4 and 12. The Lewises also assisted the Haydn Society in their November 11 program, which included an overture to *Lodoiska* by Rodolphe Kreutzer (1766–1831) and a *Grand Overture* by Padre Giovanni Battista Martini (1706–84), presented by two players on the organ in the company of other instrumentalists. Alas, this attempt at dabbling in the secular realm proved fruitless since, although the society continued to meet until at least April 25, 1824, this was to be its final public performance.

The competing choral societies flourished intermittently and were joined by a New Apollonian Society, which made its début on December 5, 1823. For example, the Euterpeians offered a benefit concert on January 13, 1824, which raised $339 to aid the Greeks in their struggle for independence from the Turks. The *Liberty Hall and Gazette* opined that "[t]he music was fine and the ode written for the occasion was sung in good style and received by the audience with acclamations of applause."[23] The New Jerusalem Singing Society then offered a performance on March 30, 1824, with a familiar format: An overture by the "Full Orchestra" prefaced part 1, an organ voluntary part 2. The repertory was a potpourri of choruses and ensemble pieces for soloists by Oliver Shaw, Matthew King, Sir John A. Stevenson (1762–1833), Samuel Arnold (1740–1802), and Mozart. One observer complimented the group on its "judicious selection" of repertory, adding that

> the parts were performed with correctness of taste, hardly expected in this western section of our country, bearing in mind, as we do, the low state of the science of music in this city only four or five years ago. Confessing our surprise and pleasure while we listened to the charming performance . . . by those who but a short time since could hardly read music, we were forcibly impressed with the idea that the public cannot too highly appreciate the services of those modest and unobtrusive gentlemen.[24]

In May 1825, when the Marquis de Lafayette visited Cincinnati as part of a triumphal tour of the country, a grand procession through the city preceded an equally grand ball in the evening at Colonel Mack's establishment:

> All the celebrities of the city, with their guests, were therein assembled, and to the man in proud recognition of whom the occasion had been drawn they paid hardly more attention than to an almost beardless stripling, fresh from the Paris Conservatory and full to the brim with the fire and enthusiasm of a true musical nature. This youth was Joseph Tosso—how the mere mention of the name links the present [1888] with the past. He conducted the orchestra on that memorable evening and, whether especially brought here from the East for the purpose or not, here he lived, labored and died and his name is indissolubly connected with the rise and progress of the art in all its phases.[25]

This tale, often repeated with relish, needs a bit of redressing. Tosso (1802–87) had been born in Mexico City of an Italian father, a graduate of the University of Louvain who had made a fortune dealing in jewels. The elder Tosso arrived in Mexico during 1800, where he played violin in the orchestra of the national theater. Joseph (né Jose Anguel Augustin), a child prodigy, first studied the violin with his father, was taken to Paris at age six for more advanced work, and only two years later was admitted to the Paris Conservatory. In 1817 Tosso joined his family in Richmond, Virginia, where his father was playing in a theater orchestra. The father soon moved to Baltimore where he directed a singing society and played in a string quartet. In 1820 the Tossos migrated to Louisville after a brief stop in Cincinnati. In Louisville the son began to teach and concertize and married the woman with whom he would sire nine children. In 1824 he joined a horse troop being organized to escort the Marquis de Lafayette on his tour across Kentucky the following year. The general arrived in Louisville on May 11, 1825, and it seems probable that Tosso directed the music at that evening's "splendid ball." The Lafayette Guards then escorted their namesake to Frankfort, Versailles, Lexington (where Tosso played for the grand ball of May 16), Georgetown, and Blue Springs as the procession made its way to Cincinnati. Tosso recalled that Lafayette, disembarking on the nineteenth from the barge that had conveyed him across the river from Covington, disdained the carpet spread from the landing to the carriage that was to carry him to his lodgings, stating that he was quite content to walk on America's soil. But nowhere in Tosso's reminiscences or contemporaneous newspaper accounts is there is any mention of the visiting violinist's having any part in that evening's music making.

His relocation to Cincinnati was announced on September 8, 1827, concurrently with an advertisement that he was prepared to teach "Piano Forte, Violin, Viola, Violincello, Guitar, Harp, and also Vocal Music."[26] In addition to his own school, Tosso soon took on the role of professor at Dr. John Locke's Female Seminary (where he taught for twelve years), as well as at the French and English Boarding School of the Montaigniers. In addition he sold pianofortes and for four years directed the orchestra of the Cincinnati Theatre, creating at least fifty arrangements for its ensemble.[27] He also supplemented his income by performing at private parties and both played the organ and directed the choir at the St. Xavier Church. In April 1830 he and a partner named Pius opened a music and dancing academy in Mrs. Trollope's Bazaar. Pius was soon supplanted by Henry Guibert, proprietor of a rival academy and Tosso's brother-in-law, and these partners insinuated themselves into the cultural life of the city. As example, an ad for "the most splendid ballroom and the Most Classical Music for those refined amusements west of the mountains," surely to be patronized by those "who know how to appreciate these important advantages &c &c."[28]

Thus Tosso and Guibert had complete charge of the arrangements for an elaborate supper honoring Lafayette on November 25, 1830, during which a band under

Tosso's direction interspersed tunes ranging from the "Marseillaise" to "Hail, Columbia" and "Yankee Doodle" among the numerous toasts to the "great apostle of Liberty." Tosso figured prominently in a concert given for flood relief on February 23, 1832; his unnamed air with variations was juxtaposed with works by Handel, Haydn, Mozart, Beethoven, and Pucitta. This was one of many examples of his generosity, since he played numerous benefits for schoolchildren, orphans, needy musicians, and political refugees, as well as wounded soldiers and widows during the Civil War. He occasionally offered a benefit on his own behalf, such as that of March 4, 1833, in the Bazaar, assisted by local amateurs, singers Mesdames Montaganier and Mullon, and a Mr. Young, formerly of the Royal Marine Band, who afforded Cincinnatians their first sounds from a serpent (a musical instrument, rather than a reptile).

Later that year he found a new partner, so that it was Tosso and Winter who offered cotillion parties at the Bazaar, complete with refreshments, until 1839 when the building was sold, after which they opened the Cincinnati Assembly Rooms. In 1835 Tosso became associated with the Musical Fund Society and was still leading its orchestra in 1841.[29] In 1837 he announced a "Music & Fancy Store," offering scores, instruments, and nonmusical novelties. The following year a J. D. Douglas arrived from New York and set up his own musical instrument shop, but by 1839 the two had combined their resources as "Musical Instrument Makers and Importers of Musical Instruments," offering

Finest quality of Rose and Mahogeny Pianos; Guitars of Rose and Satin Wood; Cocoa Flutes with 12, 9 and 5 keys; French Horns with patent valves. Cornopeons with double slides, Ophiclydes with 3 valves; d[itt]o. with 11 keys; Clusecords, Accordians, etc., all warranted. T & D continue to manufacture Flutes, Clarionets, Bassoons, Obves [sic] and double and single Flageoletts [30]

Over the following decades Tosso seems to have participated in almost every musical event of any significance. For example, on February 16, 1847, he conducted the orchestra of the Philharmonic Society in the overture to Étienne-Nicholas Méhul's *Two Blind Mice of Toledo,* played an obligato to a polonaise drawn from Rodolphe Kreutzer's *Lodoiska* and Charles-Auguste de Beriot's "It Is the Hour," and then led the orchestra through the overture to Mozart's *Marriage of Figaro.* On September 14, 1848, Tosso was one of the locals who assisted Signor Natale Giamboni of Havana in a mixed concert inaugurating the new Apollo Hall. On February 16, 1849, "that prince of fiddlers and good fellows, the inimitable Tosso" led his cotillion band at the ball honoring President-elect Zachary Taylor in transit to his inauguration. During May 1850 Tosso's Queen City Quadrille Band was engaged for a grand soirée opening the Burnet House, an event that included a *Burnet House Polka* written for the occasion by "A. Mine" and published by W. C. Peters and Sons. Through the *Gazette* Tosso offered a soirée on March 30, 1854, at Melodeon Hall, at which he was assisted by several prominent local musicians such as the German-born violinist Henry Appy and French singer L. Corradi Colliere as well as his daughters Matilda and Louisa and what was titled "The Columbian Orchestra." He also taught ("Mons. J. Tosso" was noted in 1859 as Professor of Instrumental Music at Herron's Seminary for Boys)[31] and toured the Ohio River Valley and to cities as distant as Philadelphia, offering both dance music and more substantial fare.[32] Tosso remained an active performer as late as December 1886, only a month before his death on January 6, 1887. The headline in the next morning's *Cincinnati Commercial Gazette* read: DRAWN HIS LAST BOW. TOSSO AND HIS ARKANSAW TRAVELER HAVE GONE TO THEIR REST.

"The Arkansaw Traveler," on an instrument built by the illustrious Nicola Amati (1596–1684), one of the most renowned of Italian violinmakers? Tosso had apparently made the tune a signature piece as early as 1841, claiming authorship both of the music and supporting comic dialogue between a transient fiddler and a squatter from whom he successfully cajoles lodging for the night.[33] Tosso also devised original, albeit less popular, bits of musical entertainment, such as "A New Way to Give Music Lessons," "Music and Physic," and "The Story of John Anderson and His Tune." His remarkable eclecticism, a blurring of any distinct boundary between the cultivated and the vernacular, was certainly not unique during his era. Thus while some considered him the equal of concert violinists such as Ole Bull,

> He could take his violin from beneath his chin, place it against his breast, begin to sway rhythmically, and play a good backwoods tune with as much grace as he had the moment before played a classic. He composed dance tunes that set every foot tapping, he composed fantasies on familiar melodies, he played airs from the early operas with variations. He played to please his audience, for he thought it better to create and encourage a genuine love of music, even the simplest kind, than to discourage it by playing classics to unappreciative ears.[34]

This sort of cultural dichotomy surely fueled the discomfort of Mrs. Frances Trollope (1780–1863) during her Cincinnati sojourn between February 1828 and March 1830. Her goal was to create what would later be labeled a department store, but her Bazaar became a bizarre folly, a strange quasi-oriental architectural monument to ambition gone amok. Stocked with unsellable goods when it opened to the public on October 15, 1829, bankruptcy loomed almost immediately, and Mrs. Trollope slunk back to England where in 1832 she published her *Domestic Manners of the Americans*.

She considered Cincinnati "a place delightful to visit, but to tarry there was not to feel at home,"[35] for she desperately missed the refinements of English society.

Her patronizing manner quickly aroused the ire of her former American hosts, although her view was perhaps more balanced than their rage allowed them to admit. For example,

> Though I do not quite sympathise with those who consider Cincinnati as one of the wonders of the earth, I certainly think it a city of extraordinary size and importance, when it is remembered that thirty years ago the aboriginal forest occupied the ground where it stands; and every month appears to extend its limits and its wealth.[36]

Despite this backhanded compliment, she loosed a condescending diatribe:

> I never saw any people who appeared to live so much without amusement as the Cincinnatians. Billiards are forbidden by law, so are cards. To sell a pack of cards in Ohio subjects the seller to a penalty of fifty dollars. They have no public balls, excepting, I think, six, during the Christmas holidays. They have no concerts. They have no dinner-parties.
>
> They have a theatre, which is, in fact, the only public amusement of this triste little town; but they seem to care little about it, and either from economy or distaste, it is very poorly attended. Ladies are rarely seen there, and by far the larger proportion of females deem it an offence against religion to witness the representation of a play. It is in the churches and chapels of the town that the ladies are to be seen in full costume: and I am tempted to believe that a stranger from the continent of Europe would be inclined, on first reconnoitering the city, to suppose that the places of worship were the theatres and cafés of the place.[37]

Pretty strong stuff and sufficient to arouse a local patriot more than six decades later to claim that "she possessed as easy a conscience in the matter of allopathic lying as many of the commercial tourists of this after period."[38] Assuming that Trollope's sourness had been engendered by her failure as an entrepreneur and her exclusion from much of what passed for polite society at the time, he trotted out as an antidote the musings of Harriet Martineau (1802–76), another English author, who spent May through August of 1835 in Cincinnati and later reflected on that experience in her *Retrospect of Western Travel*.[39]

Although ignorant of the many antecedents of the event, her reflections made better copy for local chamber-of-commerce types:

> Before eight o'clock in the evening, the Cincinnati public was pouring into Mrs. Trollope's bazaar, to the first concert ever offered to them. This bazaar

is the great deformity of the city. Happily, it is not very conspicuous, being squatted down among houses nearly as lofty as the summit of its dome. From my window at the boarding-house, however, it was only too distinctly visible. It is built of brick, and has Gothic windows, Grecian pillars, and a Turkish dome, and it was originally ornamented with Egyptian devices, which have, however, all disappeared under the brush of the whitewasher. The concert was held in a large plain room, where a quiet, well-mannered audience was collected. There was something extremely interesting in the spectacle of the first public introduction of music into this rising city. One of the best performers was an elderly man, clothed from head to foot in grey homespun. He was absorbed in his enjoyment; so intent on his violin, that one might watch the changes of his pleased countenance, the whole performance through, without fear of disconcerting him. There was a young girl, in a plain white frock, with a splendid voice, a good ear, and a love of warbling which carried her through very well indeed, though her own taste had obviously been her only teacher. If I remember right, there were about five-and-twenty instrumental performers, and six or seven vocalists, besides a long row for the closing chorus. It was a most promising beginning. The thought came across me how far we were from the musical regions of the Old World, and how lately this place had been a cane-brake, echoing with the bellow and growl of wild beasts; and here was the spirit of Mozart swaying and inspiring a silent crowd as if they were assembled in the chapel at Salzburg![40]

Writing at some distance from the event, Miss Martineau must have attributed more historical significance than was warranted to the "First Grand Concert by The Music Fund Society," held at the Bazaar on Thursday, June 18, 1835. Earlier announcements had predicated a "Grand Concert of Vocal and Instrumental Music." Tickets were offered to the public at one dollar, while tickets for society members were distributed at Flash's Book and Music Store on Third Street on the eighteenth. Could the author's approbation have been nourished in part by Alex[ander?] Flash's announcement that he had available for sale at least eight of Miss Martineau's works? It is a pity that extant records contain no program or roster of performers.

Of course, Mrs. Trollope had fled five years before this event, and her building had been renovated for the use of individuals like Joseph Tosso. One wonders whether the "large plain room" entered by Martineau was the original ballroom, sixty by thirty-eight feet, intended to evoke the idiom of the Alhambra, as described in an 1829 directory:

Above the Bazaar is a magnificent ballroom, the front of which looking upon the street, will receive the rays of the sun, or emit rival splendors of its gas-illumined walls, by three ample arabesque windows, which give an unrivalled lightness and grace to the festive hall. The walls and the arched and lofty ceiling of this delectable apartment are to be decorated by the powerful pencil of Mr. Hervieu.[41] The rear of the room is occupied by an orchestral gallery whence dulcet music will guide the light fantastic toe in the mazes of the giddy dance.

Below the gallery there were niches containing figures of infants holding standards imprinted with patriotic epigrams, and over the windows loomed two female figures allegorically representing the muses of music and dance.[42]

One of the few individuals to arouse Mrs. Trollope's approval during her sojourn in Cincinnati was Timothy Flint:

> The most agreeable acquaintance I made in Cincinnati, and indeed one of the most talented men I ever met, was Mr. Flint, the author of several extremely clever volumes, and the editor of the *Western Monthly Review*. His conversational powers are of the highest order; he is the only person I remember to have known with first-rate powers of satire, and even of sarcasm, whose kindness of nature and of manner remained perfectly uninjured. . . . The pleasant, easy, unpretending talk on all subjects, which I enjoyed in Mr. Flint's family, was an exception to everything else I met at Cincinnati.[43]

Flint (1780–1840) received a degree from Harvard in 1800 and then taught and preached in Massachusetts before embarking on the missionary endeavors which brought him to Cincinnati in 1815, surely in part because an uncle Hezekiah, one of the original settlers of Marietta, had moved to Cincinnati sometime before his death in 1811. A son of the same name lived in the city until his death in 1843. After only a year, Timothy Flint continued westward, spending 1816 to 1826 in Missouri, Arkansas, and Louisiana, interrupted by brief trips to New England. After 1818 he attempted to sustain himself as a farmer and teacher. In 1826 he initiated a considerable literary career by publishing a series of autobiographical recollections and a novel, *Francis Berrian, or the Mexican Patriot*.[44] He returned to Cincinnati in 1827 and lived there until 1833, for three years editing the *Western Monthly Review* and churning out a veritable stream of books, including *A Condensed Geography and History of the Western States* (1828), *The Shoshonee Valley* (1830), *The Art of Being Happy* (1832), *The History and Geography of the Mississippi Valley* (1832), *Indian Wars of the West*, *Biographical Memoir of Daniel Boone* (whom he had met back in 1816), and *Lectures upon Natural History, Geology, Chemistry, the Application of Steam, and Interesting Discoveries in the Arts* (all in 1833), mostly published in Cincinnati, many by E. H[ubbard] Flint, his second son. Ill health dogged Flint for the rest of his life, much of it spent in long convalescent trips to Louisiana, Cuba, Canada, and elsewhere before death in his native Massachusetts.

However, none of his biographers[45] seems to have noticed his first publication, issued during that initial stay in Cincinnati: *The Columbian Harmonist: In Two Parts. To Which Is Prefixed a Dissertation Upon the True Taste in Church Music* (Cincinnati: Coleman and Phillips, 1816). While Flint served only as a compiler of its contents, it stands as another example of his pioneering spirit, since it was one of the first such didactic works to be published west of the Alleghenies.

A Timothy of another sort arrived in Cincinnati during June 1834 and had a considerable impact on its musical development during the next two decades: Timothy B[attelle] Mason (1801–61), seldom-noticed brother of the illustrious Lowell, had been appointed vocal professor of the Eclectic Academy of Music, organized by a group of influential citizens with the primary purpose of "promoting the introduction of vocal music as a branch of education throughout this country."[46] Chartered by the state legislature the following year, one announced goal was "to promote knowledge and correct taste in music, especially such as are adapted to moral and religious purposes."[47] Mason joined the William Nixons, who had in 1832 established a musical seminary and Piano Forte Saloon [*sic*] and advertised their advocacy of the Logierian method, based on the theories of German-born Johann Bernhard Logier (1777–1846), who invented, patented, and promoted the "chiroplast," a means of holding the hands in optimal positions while practicing.[48] As pedagogues, the Nixons joined William Nash, who since 1829 had operated a music academy, offering instruction in music theory (based on his own *Elements of Music*, copies of which were offered gratis to his students), voice, and various instruments. Tuition was five dollars per quarter. Thomas Hawkes then opened another music school in 1831, leading to some spirited competition. Nash, in an attempt to raise his profile, organized a Beethoven Society, railed against the ineffectiveness of the Logierian method in newspaper advertisements, and on October 13, 1833, presented his first (and last) Annual Musical Festival at Mrs. Trollope's Bazaar to showcase the skills of his students. The event began at four o'clock and resumed at seven after a supper break, concluding somewhere after ten o'clock. Whatever the audience response, it was the Nixons who eventually triumphed and remained prominent in Cincinnati musical circles for many decades, since Hawkes left the city soon thereafter, and Nash migrated to Tennessee three years later.[49]

Mason also periodically announced the organization of freestanding singing classes. For example, one such venture was held at the Unitarian Church beginning on January 22, 1840. Its students were to meet weekly for twenty-four sessions at a total cost of three dollars. "Illustrations and examples will be given in the Italian, German, and English style of performance," with examples by Rossini, Lanza,

Rodolphe, Bellini, and others. There was to be instruction in the singing of glees and, "if time permits, in thorough base and chanting."[50]

The *Western Messenger* of March 1839 presented an insight into the environment in which Mason worked. He had been attacked for employing a "Catholic text" in a concert at the Second Presbyterian Church back on December 12, including not only Latin phrases such as *Ave sanctissima* and *Ora pro nobis* but also a reference to "Sweet Mother." The anonymous diatribe (that had appeared earlier in the *Cincinnati Journal*) questioned how an admitted Protestant could "introduce into the Presbyterian Church the absurd superstitions and idolatrous worship of the Catholic," concerned about "the strenuous and unparalleled efforts of Catholics to make theirs the prevailing religion in this country." "If papists ever succeed in duping the people of this community to embrace Romanism, it will be by disguising its bloated and hideous form in the beautiful garments of poetry and music." Mason was asked to submit both explanation and apology, but "[u]ntil he does, no Protestant parent will be justified in placing a child under his tuition." A respondent suggested that Mason remain silent (which he apparently did, at least in print), since the music had been offered "simply as an expression of art, of beauty, of poetry, of music— not as a *hymn* or *prayer*," suggesting that because "the Presbyterian church does not relish the doctrine contained in this piece, are the walls of the building polluted and the faith of the audience endangered because heterodox *sentiments* are discovered under the veil of the music?"[51]

After Mason resigned from the academy in 1841 (one year before it expired) he continued to offer singing classes and conventions in Cincinnati and elsewhere in the region. For example, he and H. Auguste Pond presented a "Select, Progressive Singing Class" at the Second Presbyterian Church beginning on November 17, 1842, its principal goal the mastery of choruses from the standard oratorios but including "Solfeggios and exercises from the works of Rossini, Weber, Zingarelli, and others."[52] Conventions, an outgrowth of the singing-school movement, involved a concentrated period of instruction followed by a concert demonstrating the students' newly acquired prowess. Lowell Mason was a regular on the circuit and record remains of an 1854 Cincinnati convention led by Isaac B. Woodbury and Benjamin F. Baker, which fielded a chorus of 125 and an orchestra of thirty.[53]

Timothy Mason also maintained a shop on Walnut Street where he sold musical scores and Chickering and Gilbert pianos as the sole agent in Cincinnati for the former firm. His ad in the *Daily Gazette* of July 20, 1835, contained a list of the noted American professors of music willing to offer testimony that Chickering instruments were "superior to any other Pianos for sale in the Western market." Prices ranged from $275 to $450. Mason also had available a secondhand piano built by Clementi and Company of London.

In 1847 Mason was announced as director of a Handel and Haydn Society, surely modeled on the pioneering organization in Boston with which brother Lowell had long been associated.[54] On June 8, 1847, the society's vocal ensemble presented choruses by their namesakes, probably with William F. Colburn at the piano, while the orchestra of the Amateur Musical Society, directed by Victor Williams, presented overtures and perhaps supported some of the solo and ensemble numbers. The next extant reference to the Handel and Haydn Society mentions a "third illustrative exhibition of Sacred Music" at the Vine Street Congregational Church on March 27, 1849. The event was not considered a formal concert but merely a representation of anthems, chants, and hymns as "some of the various kinds of music which can be devotionally sung in public worship." A similar event, both comprising lectures by local clergymen, was held on May 1, 1849, after which the Handel and Haydn Society seems to have passed into oblivion.[55] Mason, however, remained in Cincinnati until his death in 1861. He allied himself with his longtime associate to create the publishing firm of Mason, Colburn, and Company in 1849. Five years later he surfaced again as a member of a two-man "Committee from the 'Kansas League,' of Cincinnati" (his associate was the Reverend Charles Brandon Boynton). The issue of slavery in the western territories had been only temporarily resolved by the Kansas-Nebraska Act of 1854, and Cincinnati abolitionists were intent on populating the area with those who would vote for "free soil." The result was the jointly written *A Journey through Kansas; with Sketches of Nebraska: Describing the Country, Climate, Soil, Mineral, Manufacturing and Other Resources. The Results of a Tour Made in the Autumn of 1854* (Cincinnati: Moore, Wilstach, Keys, and Company, 1855). Its preface designated the American Reform Tract and Book Society as joint sponsors of the expedition (Mason was listed in the 1855 and 1856 city directories as its treasurer), and while the volume can be read in part as a travelogue (with descriptions of "Indian Fighting," "A Mule Chase," and "An Indian Murderer"), its doctrine can easily be gleaned from the titles of the final three of twenty-eight chapters: "Great Importance of the Kansas Question," "Warning Voice," and "Christian Obligation—Christian Colonization."

Swedish-born Victor Williams arrived in Cincinnati during 1840, apparently via an eastern seaboard city, to become the instrumental professor of the Eclectic Academy between the Novembers of 1840 and 1841. During his tenure the academy orchestra of twenty-four members normally provided overtures at the outset of both halves of a concert and also, at its conclusion, works such as Mozart's to *Don Giovanni*, Louis-François-Marie Auber's to *Fra Diavolo*, and François-Adrein Boieldieu's to *La dame blanche* and *Le Calife de Bagdad*. However, sporadically Williams programmed symphonies, although it remains unclear whether entire works or only individual movements were heard. For example, the concert of March 9, 1841, contained the third and fifth symphonies of a Bruno Held, that of April 6 the Andante of Haydn's "Surprise" Symphony, and that of April 27 an unidentified symphony by Beethoven. The academy sponsored only two all-vocal concerts during 1842 before its demise, directed by a Mr. Wellington, since Mason had vacated his position as vocal director during 1841 perhaps in the aftermath of a semipublic professional tussle with Williams.[56]

However, soon after an academy concert for his benefit on November 2, 1841, Williams was named director of the newly formed Cincinnati Amateur Musical Society, whose first outing was a benefit for Joseph Tosso on December 9, 1841. Evidence suggests that the Amateur Musical Society was in fact nothing more than the Eclectic Academy's orchestra under a new label.

At least by May 3, 1842, Williams had become director of the choir at the Ninth Street Baptist Church, a position he was to retain until 1890. Their first outing included "choruses from the Oratorio of the Creation (accompanied by an effective orchestra), Anthems, Solos, etc."[57] Evidence suggests that the Ninth Street Baptists furnished the core of the Cincinnati Sacred Music Society, which offered the standard pastiches of oratorio choruses, solo songs, and ensembles in its four concerts between May 4, 1843, and May 7, 1844.[58] The choruses of the Amateur Musical and Sacred Music Societies were allied as the Cincinnati Academy of Music for a performance of Haydn's *The Creation* on October 5, 1843. However, this momentary bond was soon severed, for the two organizations were listed separately in announcements of a concert on April 4, 1844, dedicating as the Amateur Musical Hall what had been known as the Assembly Rooms.

Various commentators suggest that the Sacred Music Society's chorus swelled to as many as 150 voices during the 1840s and 1850s, offering multiple performances of not only *The Creation* but also masses of Haydn and Mozart as well as substantial portions of Handel's *Messiah* and *Judas Maccabaeus*. If one tale about a presentation of *The Creation* at the Universalist Church can be believed, Williams must have harbored the instincts of a showman, since,

> with the intention of enhancing the effect, [he] had the lights turned low during the progress of those portions leading up to the inspiring climax on the word "light!" He had posted a young man in the choir so that, at the proper moment, he might turn on the illuminating medium to the full. The scheme promised well; but alas! who can measure the grief of the leader, the dismay of the choir and the unaffected consternation of the audience when, instead of the sudden glory, they were immersed in darkness, deep and impenetrable. The agent, being seized with sudden confusion while nervously awaiting his cue, had thrown the connective valve in the wrong direction. From that time on he was held strictly to his duties as chorister, and history has it that it was absolutely his first and last appearance in a theatrical capacity.[59]

The Amateur Musical Society's final hurrah seems to have been a performance of Sigismund Ritter von Neukomm's *David* in its entirety on April 8, 1858, only five days after its composer's death, offered as a benefit for Williams, although "at this, their final concert, the society reaped more glory than money for their unselfish leader."[60]

Williams also supported himself by teaching voice, piano, guitar, and band instruments (he was noted as a Teacher of Vocal and Instrumental Music at the Cincinnati Female Seminary in 1859),[61] and after the Civil War he became actively involved in promoting music in the public schools. Obviously a crucial catalyst, "[a]s a musical pioneer he must be placed at the head of the honored list who so successfully shaped the artistic destinies of the Queen City of the West."[62]

But Williams's was not the only game in town. During the early 1850s Elisha Locke led the Morris Chapel Singing Society of one hundred voices that managed presentations of *The Creation* (with an orchestra of thirty-four and a quintet of soloists), Romberg's *Song of the Bell*, and Woodbury's *Absalom* and promised but was unable to deliver a *Messiah.*

German singing societies had sprouted during the 1840s, but Frédéric L. Ritter, when he appeared in 1856, organized a Cecilia Society, unique in the city's culture, since,

> [t]hough it was largely composed of cultivated Germans, it was not an organization representing one section of the inhabitants. Many of its chorus singers were Americans of culture: and the subscription list of the membership contained the names of the best families in the city—German, Irish and American.[63]

The first outing of this multicultural organization (on September 19, 1856) included Mendelssohn's *42nd Psalm,* an unidentified Mozart "cantata," and choruses from Gaspare Spontini's *La Vestale,* Haydn's *The Seasons,* and *The Last Judgment* of Friedrich Schneider (1786–1853). Ritter quickly organized a coordinate Philharmonic Society and with their combined strengths presented Cincinnatians a repertory previously unrivaled in its sophistication.

A variety of visiting performers also enlarged the city's cultural perspective during the decades immediately preceding the Civil War.

Henry Russell (1812–1900), the English-born presenter of his own luridly descriptive songs and lushly sentimental ballads, gave three concerts during September 1840, three more during the summer of 1841, and a pair in April 1844 followed by a full half dozen during late May and early June of that same year. His enormous popularity was explained by the *Republican*'s critic on June 24, 1841:

> The West can sympathize in his music, more heartily than the East, as our ears have not been tortured with the shakes and flourishes of those foreign

singers, whose only effort seems to be, to ascertain the amount of patience contained in the human ear. Plain, simple, unadorned, Mr. Russell's songs appeal to the heart, not head;—his style, is the good, old Ballad-style, in which the feelings of the People have always been expressed. . . . Those who like to feel the power of music,—who relish it in its simplicity, without cant or humbug will rejoice in the arrival of the "Prince of Vocalists."

Except for the chronology, one of those "foreign singers" might have been the English tenor John Braham (1774–1856), who came to Cincinnati for four concerts during July 1842 at the end of an extended American tour, assisted by son Charles, also a singer, relying heavily on his own songs. One of those events was witnessed by Mary Conclin, who wrote on July 29, 1842, to her friend Elizabeth Richards, daughter of a prominent Cincinnati businessman.

> Louisa [her sister] & myself attended a Sacred Concert given by Mr. Braham last evening at the Baptist Church. I do not admire his style of singing as much as that of Mr. Russel [sic], but some of his selections were beautiful, particularly "Jephtha's rash vow" [by Handel].[64]

The two most celebrated violinists of their time descended on Cincinnati mid-decade: the Belgian Henri Vieuxtemps (1820–81), accompanied by his sister Fanny at the piano, appeared on April 26, 1844 (billed in the *Atlas* that day as "The King of the Violin, VIEUX-TEMPS [Old Times]), and the Norwegian virtuoso, Ole Bull (1810–80), played four concerts between April 19 and June 3, 1845 (and was to return in the future, for example, during Christmastide 1852 in the company of eight-year-old soprano Adelina Patti). The youthful William Mason (1829–1909) appeared as cooperating pianist at concerts on November 2, 1847, and September 16, 1848, both ventures perhaps coordinated with father Lowell's periodic business trips to the city or simply with visits to uncle Timothy. Pianist Maurice Strakosch (1825–87), recalled today primarily as an impresario, played four concerts at the Melodeon Hall between May 5 and 17, 1848, assisted by "Madame M. C. Casini, the Prima Donna of the French Opera in New Orleans." The noted English soprano Anna Bishop (1810–84) sang four times at the Melodeon between June 28 and July 7, 1848, assisted by harpist Robert Nicholas-Charles Bochsa (1789–1856), for whom she had abandoned her husband, the composer Henry Bishop (1786–1855), a notable scandal of the period. During the following decade the Queen City was visited by other luminaries such as Swedish soprano Jenny Lind (1820–87) and German piano virtuoso Sigismond Thalberg (1812–71).

In response to another sort of taste, Cincinnati was invaded by at least fourteen blackface minstrel troupes during the 1840s.[65] Cincinnatians were also enamored of entertainers like the Rainer Family, billed as "The Celebrated Tyrolese Minstrels," who filled the hall during their two series of concerts during 1843 (January 9–20, and May 5–11), as well as their American offspring, most notably the Hutchinson Family, who offered an extended series of concerts between November 23 and December 28, 1848.

All of these ingredients can be construed as ingredients inherent in a complex stew of cultural influences and impulses from which master chefs would in the decades following the Civil War fashion the cuisine marking Cincinnati as one of the nation's dominant musical centers.

CHAPTER 4

Cleveland

Although Cleveland would later assume a notable ascendancy, its first decades were spent in relative somnolence.[1]

The chain of events leading to its founding date back to September 14, 1786, when Connecticut relinquished any claim to all of its western lands except a tract known as the Western Reserve or New Connecticut. In May 1792 some half-million acres of the western part of the reserve were set aside for citizens who had suffered losses to fire or other calamities during the Revolutionary War (hence the appellation of "Fire Lands" to modern-day Erie and Huron counties). Three years later the remaining three million acres were offered for sale and snapped up, sight unseen, by the forty-nine shareholders of the Connecticut Land Company.

One of these, Moses Cleaveland, was deputized as superintendent of a surveying party on May 12, 1796. His expedition reached the mouth of Conneaut Creek on July 4, and with considerable ceremony he christened the spot Port Independence. After establishing a headquarters the surveyors were split into several groups as a means of expediting the process. General Cleaveland himself led that portion of the company that proceeded southwestward on Lake Erie and entered the mouth of the Cuyahoga River on July 22. After returning to Port Independence on August 5 to prepare a report for the home office, Cleaveland rejoined his men, determined that the site later to bear his respelled name should become the capital of this new enterprise. He then returned to his Connecticut law practice, never again to set foot in the Western Reserve.

An "Original Plan of the Town and village of Cleveland [*sic*], Ohio" was prepared by October 1, and the first settlers arrived the following year. However, disease took its toll, and by 1800 only seven people inhabited what had become little more than a trading post. Growth was so sluggish that a decade later Cleveland's population totaled only fifty-seven. In fact, the census of 1820 ranked Cleveland as the thirteenth most populous settlement in the Western Reserve, less than half the size of Painesville (with 1,257 inhabitants).

Nonetheless, there is one bit of evidence that the intrepid few who persisted employed vernacular music at celebratory times of diversion from the toil of everyday life. The July 4th celebration of 1801 involved a ball in the double log house of Major Lorenzo Carter, a building that also housed the settlement's first store and distillery. The beverage of the day involved maple sugar, water, and whiskey; the master of ceremonies and "chief musician" was Maj. Samuel Jones: "The violinist, Mr. Jones, proceeded at once with spasmodic hand and listening ear to harmonize the strings of his instrument, and then struck up 'Hey Betty Martin,' the favorite dancing tune of that day."[2]

A library of "Scientific and Miscellaneous Books for general circulation" was established in July 1811; Trinity Episcopal Church was organized in November 1816 (although a minister had been posted to the frontier by the Connecticut Missionary Society in 1800 and religious meetings of various sorts announced as early as 1805); the first school building was erected in 1817; the first newspaper was published in 1818 (*The Cleaveland Gazette and Commercial Register,* a weekly, was joined and then superseded the following year by the *Cleveland Herald*); and a bookstore was opened in 1820, but the next record of music making occurs only in that year. During May 1820 the Blanchard Troupe turned Mowrey's Tavern into a theater of sorts with a repertory that included Samuel Arnold's *The Mountaineers,* a popular comic opera of the period. There is also passing mention of a concert of sacred music offered on May 10, 1821, at P. Mowrey's Assembly Room, the first report of formal music making by local citizens.

Although not a Clevelander, Jonathan Hale (1777–1854) had moved to the Western Reserve in 1810 from Glastonbury, Connecticut, bringing with him the tradition of the New England singing school as well as several of the tunebooks then in general use. Hale, who also played the violin, taught music along the upper reaches of the Cuyahoga, and his extensive papers, housed at the Western Reserve Historical Society, include comments about music in his own hand, as well as two tunebooks of his own devising. One is dated January 12, 1819, from Bath, the other November 2, 1832. Both contain a variety of standard literature from the tradition for three or four voices.[3] The first record of comparable activity in Cleveland itself dates from about 1824, when one Elijah Ingersoll offered singing lessons at various locations. One participant later reminisced that the master "lined and we sang, and the woods rung with the melody."[4]

The First Presbyterian Church was incorporated in 1827 (and the first "Stone Church" opened in 1833), but the next extant reference to music making dates only from 1830, when, "A concert will be given by the choir at the Episcopal church on Apr. 1st. Also a lecture on sacred music will be delivered by the Rev. M. Lyster."[5] Other than the Trinity Choir, the earliest musical organization seems to have been the Cleveland Musical Society, its advent announced in June 1832 through a notice that its members "are requested to meet at the Cleveland Recess, on every successive Monday & Tuesday evening at 7 o'clock P. M. By order of the President, A. S. Sanford." Although a resident of Painesville had owned a piano since 1824, it was only six years later that Mr. Bennet, the town's brewer, imported Cleveland's first piano. In 1833 John Ross and Joel P. Davis announced that they would offer a series of weekly concerts of both vocal and instrumental music "assisted by several gentlemen amateurs of this village, who have kindly volunteered their services." Listeners were charged twenty-five cents.

The Trinity Choir offered yet another concert of sacred music in 1835, and the Cleveland Sacred Music Society met for the first time in February 1836, only weeks before Cleveland, with a population of about five thousand, was declared a city and elected its first mayor. This group, which functioned until at least 1842 under the direction of George W. Pratt, sang at Trinity Episcopal Church and may well have been constituted mainly of Trinity Choir members, buttressed with some outsiders.

The earlier trickle of musical activity turned into a veritable torrent during the waning years of the decade. Ross and Davis announced another series of Monday-evening concerts during 1837. The Cleveland Harmonic Society, organized in 1835, made its first public appearance two years later. This group comprised seven amateur instrumental performers, two of whom, Jarvis F. Hanks and Silas Brainard, became crucial catalysts in the development of a musical culture in Cleveland, while a third, Theodoric Cardeno Severance, bore a family name prominent in the community to the present. A fourth, H. J. Mould, was reportedly organist of Trinity Episcopal Church and most certainly the partner of Silas Brainard, joint dealers in musical scores and instruments, with a shop at 34 Superior Street.

The First Baptist Church had been organized in 1833. On March 23, 1837, its choir, under the direction of George W. Pratt, offered a concert of sacred music with the assistance of the Harmonic Society. The program was a pastiche of songs, hymns, and choral pieces, many of them unidentifiable, others by composers whose names provoke no flicker of recognition today such as Chapple, Milgrove, Dixon, and Dutton. But Puccita's omnipresent "Strike the Cymbal" served as the curtain raiser and was eventually followed by Haydn's "Now elevate the sign of Judah" and Samuel Arnold's "Our Lord is risen from the dead." The *Herald and Gazette*'s reporter the following day pronounced the event "agreeable" and "highly creditable," "one that sufficiently proves that musical taste exists in the young and busy cities of the West, as well as among the old and leisure-like communities of the East." However, he had some reservations, especially about the balance between voices and instruments:

> Frequently, a thrum of the piano, or a twang of the bass strings drown the most delicate strain of the vocalist. And while acting critic for a moment, we

would suggest a fact which those who participate in the performance may not observe or appreciate, which is that the opening strains are often struck *too heavily*. It creates a harshness, especially when many voices unite. Softness and distinctness are the charm of music. When a choir commence a clause with a crash, they are frequently obliged to continue it in a howl, and end with a screech. If the space is confined, the grating of sounds is increased, especially when instruments accompany the voices. Performers, we fear, in the excitement of the moment, lose sight of these things.

The Harmonic Society ventured forth independently on June 28, 1837, with an evening that included works by Boieldieu and Cimarosa arranged by Silas Brainard for the society's "Full Orchestra," as well as an exotic delight by one H. Herz, involving H. J. Mould as piano soloist: *Grand Variations for the Piano Forte, La Parisenna March Nationale, accompanied by the Orchestra, "Executee au Concert donna a l'Hotel de Ville au profit des victims des 27, 28, et 19 Suiller* [*Juillet*] *1830*."[6]

In April 1837 banker Truman P. Handy was elected president; Hanks, vice president; Severance, treasurer; and the ubiquitous George W. Pratt, conductor of the Cleveland Mozart Society, its goal the "promotion of Musical Science and the cultivation of a refined taste in its members, and in the community." The Mozarteans' first concert took place at the Baptist Church on November 10, 1837. A second more ambitious venture occurred on February 16, 1838, and was repeated three days later. It involved eleven instruments—piano, organ, three flutes, violin, viola, cello, double bass, and two horns—played primarily by members of the Harmonic Society using arrangements made for them by Silas Brainard. Pratt led the program, each of whose halves opened with a Boieldieu overture. Part 1 continued with an anthology of songs and anthems by Chapple, Webb[e], Bradbury, Kent, and Shaw, as well as a cantata by Webb[e].[7] It concluded with a chorus from Haydn's *The Creation*, and part 3 included another chorus and three solo movements from that work, sung by William Carpenter Webster (1813–82) and Mary Clark Cushing Webster (1812–1905), who, although only briefly residents in Cleveland, as educators had a considerable impact on its musical development as well as four solo movements and the "Grand Hallelujah" from Handel's *Messiah*. The *Cleveland Herald and Gazette* remarked in its edition of February 20 that

> The concert last evening was all the Mozart Society and audience could wish. The large Church was well filled, and the look of satisfaction beaming on every countenance, expressed a high encomium on the merits of the exercises. To the Mozart Society our citizens are indebted for much of the musical taste that now distinguishes Cleveland, and we were glad to see the obligation so well cancelled.

Brainard played flute in consort with T. C. Severance and his younger brother, John Long Severance, while Erasmus Darwin Severance, their elder sibling, sang a Haydn recitative.

Jarvis F[rary] Hanks (1799–1853), the ensemble's single violinist, was resident in Cleveland from 1825 until 1828 and then from 1835 until his death. Trained at the National School of Design in New York, he established himself initially as a painter, ready to "execute Portraits, Signs, Landscapes, Military Colors &c, on the shortest notice and on moderate terms." Later, when he titled himself both as "Painter and Professor of Music," Hanks was forced to remind his constituency, "Let it not be forgotten, that I will paint signs, as cheap as any man can afford to do them, and that they shall be correct and beautiful, and completed at the time promised." He taught vocal music privately (claiming in a *Cleveland Herald* announcement of July 27, 1840, "above 20 years experience in giving instruction in this delightful art") and in the public schools and was appointed director of the orchestra of the Mendelssohn Society in 1850. One oft-repeated anecdote about this colorful personality: Hanks was one of the elders and Sunday school superintendent of the First Presbyterian Church of East Cleveland. One Sunday, while the Presbyterians were still borrowing the sanctuary of a sister church prior to occupying their own space, Hanks played his violin during the singing of the hymns. Some conservative members of the congregation were outraged at the practice, but Hanks silenced them by explaining that both he and his violin had been converted, and thus it could do no harm.[8]

Henry Russell presented two of his entertainments during 1837 as part of his first foray through this country. By June of the following year Henry Erben of New York had installed in the Stone Church the city's first pipe organ, an instrument of eight hundred pipes on two manuals that cost $1,800.[9] The first reference to paid musical staff dates from April 7, 1841, when "Mr. Knowlton was appointed to take care of the singing at two hundred dollars per annum; Edwin Cowles to blow the organ at twelve dollars per year." A $3,300 instrument by Jardine and Company of New York was placed in a new structure during 1856.

The Mozart Society, briefly directed by George Tolhurst, a founding member of the Harmonic Society, concertized at the Stone Church during June 1838. In November of that year they presented an unnamed oratorio twice and in early 1839 sponsored a singing school under the direction of Silas L. Bingham (another charter member of the Harmonic Society), described both as conductor of the society and a professor of music:

> Those desirous of attending to the study of music, will do well to embrace the present opportunity of preparing themselves to sustain that essential part of divine worship, the music in our churches. Terms—$2 per scholar, for 18 lessons. The first two evenings gratis.[10]

New Hampshire–born Bingham had first appeared in Cleveland during 1838 but later disappeared to unidentified environs only to be enticed back (according to the *Cleveland Herald* of September 14, 1841) "in compliance with the urgent solicitations of his friends. . . . He offers his professional services to the several choirs in this city and vicinity, and will also teach schools and societies in the different kinds of vocal Music from the juvenile to the highest character of Sacred Oratorios."

Clevelanders apparently responded with enthusiasm to this ad since in addition to his work at the Stone Church Bingham taught music at Mrs. Hamilton's English Academy, Miss Ludlow's School, and other such institutions. He conducted the Cleveland Sacred Music Society from 1842 to 1843 and became director of the Handel Society of Western Reserve College in 1844. He moved to Pittsburgh in 1847 but returned to Cleveland in 1852, where he played a seminal role in the establishment of music instruction in the public schools.

By 1840 Clevelanders could buy pianos made locally by John Schneider, a German immigrant, and could choose their scores, instruments, and supplies from the lavish stocks offered by three emporia. Brainard's Music Store stocked "superior bass viols of Italian and German Manufacture." The Bazaar had for sale not only hundreds of bundles of strings for violins but also "360 violins, 20 dozen violin bows, one dozen guitars, four trumpets, six bugles, six bass drums, and one pair Turkish cymbals." N. E. Crittenden advertised an assortment of instruments that included flutes, clarionetts, drums, fifes, flageoletts, trumpets, horns, bugles, pianos, trombones, cornopeons, and accordions—all of this for a metropolis of some 7,650 people.

The potential market expanded significantly with the formation of at least four new bands, joining the Cleveland City Band of nineteen members, which dated from 1837. The Cleveland City Guard, an independent military company, had been organized in 1837; adoption of a new uniform on June 7, 1838, prompted a change in denomination to the Cleveland Grays. This organization's armory was later to serve as one of the city's principal concert venues. The Grays' band presented its first concert on May 28, 1840, under the direction of Balthasar B. Schubert, a nephew of the Austrian composer,[11] and was soon joined by competing bands in 1841 and 1842 and a Cleveland Brass Band in 1843.

While the choral societies mentioned earlier seem to have languished during the 1840s, various church choirs remained active, particularly that of the Stone Church, directed by Silas L. Bingham between 1841 and 1845. With Professor Long at the organ, Bingham and his charges offered a concert of "select pieces of sacred music" in late 1842. Bingham's ensemble then presented a repertory of anthems, duets, and solos on March 23, 1843, and again on May 9, 1844. Organ voluntaries prefaced each half, followed by odds and ends from *The Creation,* Lowell Mason's *Carmina Sacra* of 1841, *The Intercession* of Matthew Peter King (1773–1823), John Braham (who with his son had sung a concert at the church in 1842), Shaw, Whitaker, Dr. Madan, Nägeli,

Deveraux, Moran, and others.[12] The earlier event included "The Old Church Clock," a song by Long, and the first performance of his *Grand Cantata* provided the core of a concert given at the Baptist Church in December 1848, the proceeds of which were devoted to the purchase of a new organ. Long presided at the keydesk, providing the "Organ Extempore, and Introduction" to the cantata, which "will occupy a full half hour in its execution." The second half of the evening was devoted to works by Haydn and Rossini, as well as by Bayley and Stegmann.

The Cleveland Mendelssohn Society was organized in December 1850 with Jarvis F. Hanks leading its orchestra and the ubiquitous Professor Long as organist. With a chorus of one hundred and an orchestra of twenty-five, the infant organization performed *The Creation* at Melodeon Hall on April 10, 1851, the first presentation in Cleveland of more than snippets of Haydn's masterwork. The piece was repeated the next spring with J. P. Holbrook as conductor, following presentations of Neukomm's *David* in February and again in March. A description of the society in an 1853 business directory promised *The Seasons* of Haydn during the winter of that year, although that apparently never came to fruition. *The Creation* was offered again in October 1853, after which the group faded from notice until 1868, when on December 10 in association with the Germania Orchestra it again essayed Haydn's familiar war-horse.

Other musical societies made fleeting appearances during the 1850s, including a Cleveland Philharmonic Society, a Cuyahoga County Sacred Musical Society, a Cleveland Musical Union, and (in the early 1860s) a Cleveland Choral Union, conducted by J. P. Holbrook, as well as the Zion Musical Society, founded by Gustave M. Cohen in 1861 when he arrived in Cleveland as cantor of the Anshe Chesed Congregation, which was very possibly the first Jewish musical society in the country. Little is known of the society's activities beyond a first concert of vocal and instrumental music in Melodeon Hall on March 8, 1862. It was associated with Anshe Chesed and probably remained active at least until Cohen left his position there in 1873.

In addition the Cleveland Musical Society surfaced again to present on January 9, 1857, a "grand vocal and instrumental concert . . . comprising a large chorus of male and female voices, a glee club, and a complete orchestra, under the direction of Mr. Abel."[13] Mr. Abel is presumably the Fritz Abel who conducted the *Gesangverein,* a German singing society dating from 1854 that supplanted Cleveland's earliest such society, the *Frohsinn,* organized in 1848. A few years later F. X. Byerly, organist of the Catholic cathedral, became conductor of the Musical Society and presided over events on May 1, 1860, and January 16, 1861, the latter involving an orchestra of thirty-one and guest pianist Alfred H. Pease (1838–82), a Cleveland native who later enjoyed a considerable concert career and wrote a piano concerto, as well as other works for orchestra and songs. Byerly's own forces at the cathedral had presented Haydn's *Mass in D Minor* (usually known as the "Lord Nelson") on the first day of

1860 and also offered a concert of varied sacred music in August of that year, assisted by outsiders.

Cleveland also attracted a variety of visitors during the 1840s and 1850s. Some were simply entertainers, such as Ralph Loomis, a Henry Russell clone who presented five recitals during the summer of 1841 and then returned two summers later, employing not only Russell standards, but some of his own compositions and other popular songs of the period. A writer for the *Herald* reported on June 8, 1841,

> We were delighted with the performance of Mr. Loomis last evening. Though not quite the Russell in vocalization, he much excells him in many things that make up the popular singer, and executes many of the songs of Mr. R. with a sweetness and power scarcely less irresistible. His "Maniac" is perfectly thrilling, and in several of his songs Mr. L. leads his listeners captive at will.

Two Junes later the paper's editor waxed rapturous:

> Reader, never lose a good opportunity either for improvement or pleasure. Be sure to hear Loomis sing this evening, and if you are not perfectly satisfied after hearing the "Ship on Fire" and the "Revellers," we will agree to quit forever the corps editorial, throw aside our pen, turn pettifogger and leave a disconsolate world miserable forever. Come shell out the "rocks," take a lady on each arm and give Loomis a bumper.[14]

Other popular entertainers, such as the Hutchinsons and similar family groups appeared from time to time, and Clevelanders were periodically lured by the bizarre, such as a Signor Martinez, who announced in the *Herald* of August 27, 1842, that during his concert he would "play a Duett himself on two guitars, one in each hand." Later that year a "Miss Hughes, only three years old, (designated by the southern press as the 'Eighth Wonder of the World,')" presented "several airs on the Welsh Battle Harp" and sang some songs accompanied by that harp.[15] Another youthful exhibitionist was

> Master S. L. Sage, four years old [who] performs upon the melodian in a manner that is truly astonishing. He is emphatically the greatest wonder of the age. He has no knowledge of music except by intuition, still he never performs, without playing two, three, and four parts and often singing with perfect calmness.[16]

These blatantly popular events at least periodically were complemented by the more staid. For example the *Herald* of November 8, 1842, noted that a Rev. Mr. Parsons of Massachusetts had lectured at the Stone Church on "the history, principles, powers and effects of sacred and social music." "A Grand Vocal and Instrumental Concert" of May 10, 1843, featured Mr. deFleur, an itinerant pianist, who was assisted by Brainard, Long, and Mould as well as a local Quartet Club. Violin virtuoso Ole Bull arrived that same year and then returned in 1846, 1854, and 1856. Madame Cinti Damoreau of the "Grand Royal Opera, Italian Opera, and Opera Comique, Paris" appeared in May 1844, and a Manvers Operatic Company arrived in May 1849 with Bellini's *La Sonnambula* and Donizetti's *Daughter of the Regiment.*

Jenny Lind dazzled Clevelanders on November 11, 1851, in a program shared with a company of fourteen, as was the custom of the period. She offered an aria from *The Creation,* as well as "John Anderson," "My Jo," a "Gypsy Song," a "Norwegian Echo Song," and her signature piece, the famous "Bird Song." Kelley's Hall had been rearranged to accommodate 1,125 spectators at prices ranging from two to four dollars. Some young male admirers, apparently lacking the price of admission yet eager for a glimpse of their idol, climbed to the roof and caused the collapse of a portion of the skylight, but Miss Lind apparently continued the "Bird Song" unperturbed, thus restoring calm.

Various touring opera troupes invaded the city during the 1850s, beginning in 1852 with one based in New Orleans, successful enough that it returned five years later. Luigi Arditi's Italian Opera Company was among those that followed, initially with the perennial standards but then in 1859 with Bellini's *Norma* and Verdi's *Ernani.* During that same year the Cooper Opera Company offered Clevelanders their first hearing of Rossini's *Barber of Seville* and Weber's *Der Freischutz.*

Other celebrities arrived, including pianist Sigismond Thalberg, who appeared several times in 1857. At the second concert Thalberg was joined at a second piano by his impresario, Maurice Strakosch. Thalberg returned during the following season in the company of violinist Henri Vieuxtemps.

Two years later Adelina Patti caused a stir, joined in the effort by her sister and two male singers. A most unusual notice of the event was penned by Charles Farrar Browne (1834–67), who wrote satire under the pseudonym of Artemus Ward for the *Cleveland Plain Dealer* for three years, beginning in 1857, after which he became editor of *Vanity Fair* in New York. Browne observed in his daily column, "City Facts and Fancies,"

> The moosic which Ime most use to is the inspirin stranes of the hand orgin. I hire a artistic Italyun to grind for me, payin him his vittles & close, & I spose it was them stranes which fust put a mossical taste into me. Like all furriners, he had seen better dase, having formerly been a Kount. But he aint of much akount now, except to turn the orgin and drink Beer, of which bevrige he can hold a churnful, *easy.*

While a regulation critic might have been pilloried for commenting on his subject's appearance, Browne admitted to being smitten:

> Miss Patty is small for her size, but as the man sed abowt his wife, O Lord! She is well bilt & her complexion is what might be called a Broonetty. Her ize is a dark bay, the lashes being long & silky. When she smiles the awgince feels like axing her to doo it sum moor, & to continner doin it 2 a indefnit extent. Her waste is one of the most bootiful wastisis ever seen. When Mister Strackhorse led her out I thawt sume pretty skool gal, who had jest graduatid frum pantalets & wire hoops, was a cumin out to read her fust composishun in public. She cum so bashful like, with her hed bowd down, & made such a effort to arrange her lips so thayd look pretty, that I wanted to swaller her.

He was bold to proclaim, "Other primy donnys may as well throw up the spunge first as last. My eyes don't deceive my earsite in this matter." But he did have one bone to pick:

> Miss Patty sung suthin or ruther in a furrin tung. I don't know what the sentimunts was. Fur awt I know she may hav bin denouncin my wax figgers & sagashus wild beests of Pray, & I don't much keer ef she did. When she opened her mowth a army of martingales, bobolinks, kanarys, swallers, mocking birds, etsettery, bust 4th & flew all over the Haul. . . .
>
> Miss Patty orter sing in the Inglish tung. As she kin do so as well as she kin in Italyun, why under the Son dont she do it? What cents is thare in singing wurds nobody dont understand when wurds we do is jest as handy? Why peple will versifferusely applawd furrin langwidge is a mistery. It reminds me of a man I onct knew. He sed he knockt the bottum out of his pork Barril, & the pork fell out, but the Brine didENT moove an inch. It stade in the Barril. He sed this was a Mistery, but it wasn't misterior than is this thing I'm speekin of.[17]

Pianist William Mason also created a favorable impression, but his father Lowell, intent on a different sort of mission, had preceded him. During September 1846 Mason and his associate George J. Webb held a "Teachers' Institute, or Convention of Teachers of Vocal Music, Choristers, and Singers," during which they shared their methodology and literature with 130 singing school teachers and church choristers from across Ohio and adjacent states. Webb disciplined the assembled chorus, while Mason lectured on topics like "The Cultivation of the Voice," basing his advice on "the Pestalozzian or inductive method of teaching." He also delineated the sorts of sacred music he found appropriate, as well as the "deportment of those so engaged" in its presentation.

Mason and Webb returned the following two years and again in 1850 (the hiatus occasioned by Mason's illness), while in 1851 Clevelanders were allowed to imbibe the wisdom of another team active in the movement fomented by Mason: Thomas Hastings and William Bradbury. This pair then returned in 1855 for another convention, the climax of which was a performance of *The Creation,* obviously Cleveland's favored oratorio of the period.[18]

When juxtaposed directly with Cincinnati (a city of 161,044 in 1860, compared to Cleveland's 43,417), Cleveland's pre–Civil War development appears laggard and sluggish, but a framework was gradually constructed on which later musicians would construct a major edifice, fueled by the city's exponential growth during the period 1865 to 1900 and beyond.

CHAPTER 5

Zanesville

Zanesville[1] was named after Col. Ebeneezer Zane (1747–1812), one of the founders of Wheeling, (West) Virginia, in 1770. Following the Revolutionary War he amassed wealth as a major landowner, property that included not only Wheeling but also Wheeling Island and a strip of land on the right bank of the Ohio River that stretched from present-day Martins Ferry to Bridgeport. At the time the river, still in a natural state, proved an often unpredictable and precarious means of transport, ranging from a raging torrent during times of considerable precipitation to a bare trickle during dry seasons. Zane conceived the idea of creating an overland route through the territories of the recently vanquished Indians, one that would prove both quicker and cheaper than that offered by the Ohio. On May 17, 1796, he was authorized by Congress to establish a road from Wheeling to Limestone (now Maysville), Kentucky, with ferries across the Muskingum, Hohocking, and Scioto rivers, a task completed during the summer of 1797.[2] His recompense: 640-acre tracts of lands at those crossings that would eventually become the cities of Zanesville, Lancaster, and Chillicothe. The result, blazed by his brother Jonathan and son-in-law John McIntire, was at first little more than a footpath, but it did open the interior to settlement. For their efforts and one hundred dollars, Colonel Zane deeded them the tract at the point where the Licking River converges with the Muskingum.[3] They settled in what was first called Westbourne in 1799, a community that began to grow and prosper only after Zanesville was named the Muskingum County seat in 1804.

Zanesville's first identifiable musician was "Black Mess" Johnson, a runaway slave whose freedom was purchased from his Maryland master by John McIntire for $150. In addition to his duties as cook and valet, Johnson furnished the music at celebrations like that of July 4, 1800, where after a reading of the Declaration of Independence toasts and a meal, whose centerpiece was a pig roasted in a clay and straw oven, the dancing commenced during the afternoon and lasted until four o'clock the following morning. Earlier, Louis Phillipe, the future king of France, lingered at the log tavern of the McIntires for several days during 1798 and "listened to the strains of the sweet music from the violin of the negro as it floated out over the waters and the wooded hills."[4] Later Johnson was joined by one Thomas Dowden, and "these two worthies played together, and furnished the music for the Terpsichoreans."[5]

The next amateur musician of note was Dr. Increase Mathews, who opened a medical practice in 1801. He built a substantial stone house west of the Muskingum in what became known as Putnam, where he supposedly played the cello for his own enjoyment. His name is attached to an advertisement that appeared in the *Muskingum Messenger* of September 3, 1816:

A gentleman who can come well recommended as a good character, and who is adept in teaching sacred music, will find encouragement for teaching young ladies and gentlemen of Zanesville and Putnam the principles and practice of church music. Application may be made to the Rev. James Culbertson, Dr. Mathews, or to Messrs. Convers, Chambers, Adair or Findlay.[6]

The fledgling town's first instrumental ensemble was organized in 1820 under the leadership of Charles Hill, whose "band" consisted of a clarionetist, three violinists, a cellist, a bassoonist, a "triangler," and a drummer. Hill's example was followed in 1829 with the organization of the Zanesville Harmonic Band under Jackson Hough; Hough fielded even more modest resources—clarionet, violin, flute, piccolo, bugle, and drums. The Harmonic Band expired in 1835 but was superseded the following year by Thomas Launder's Mechanics' Band, a fourteen-man ensemble that performed widely during its decade of existence, including the Muskingum College commencement exercises of 1841. Other bands marched across the mid-century decades: (Alonzo D.) Atwood's Brass Band, organized in 1847 and then reconstituted in 1855 as (John) Bauer's Band,[7] and (Louis) Heck's Band, almost a family operation in 1856 since it included Heck's four sons on its roster as well as five outsiders, including Mr. Atwood.

Leonard P. Bailey, a cabinetmaker, emigrated from Pittsburgh in 1820 but soon turned his attention to the manufacture of keyboard instruments. During the summer of 1822 he constructed what was described as a "parlor pipe organ," consisting of two stops, at a cost of three hundred dollars. An object of much curiosity and even suspicion, "it was conjectured to be of various strange pieces of machinery, until one day when the 'diapason' stop was adjusted. Mr. Charles Hill, (the jeweler,) sat down and played 'Old Hundred;' then the secret was out."[8] Two years later Bailey produced a second organ for the jeweler, at a cost of two hundred dollars, an instrument later sold to St. James Episcopal Church. He was still making organs as late as 1846 when he built an instrument of twelve stops for the First Congregational Church of Marietta; with a case of mahogany and cherry, it cost all of eight hundred dollars. Bailey constructed the first of his purported 162 pianos in 1833. In 1882 he was reported in possession of one of his seven-octave instruments, built in 1854, "on which he plays favorite airs with a power and pathos very rare, notwithstanding his age."[9] Bailey claimed to have created a manner of overstringing his instruments, which he intended to patent. However, before doing so, he made the error of showing his diagrams to piano maker Robert Nun at an exhibition in New York City, after which Nun appropriated the invention and patented it under his own name.

The first vocal music of note emanated from a Handel and Haydn Society, which sang unspecified literature before the Lodge of Amity for a St. John's Day celebration on June 25, 1821, repeating the practice the following year. On February 27, 1824, the ensemble appeared on a benefit program to raise funds for the Greeks in their quest for independence. The unnamed singers perhaps formed the nucleus of the church choirs that began sprouting during the same period.

"Memory," an anonymous correspondent to the Zanesville *Courier* on March 15, 1875, reminisced about the choir of the First Presbyterian Church of 1835:

> The gallery was large, running around three sides, and opposite the pulpit stood that grand old organ, and around it a few years later I was seated with the choir [who are then named].
>
> We often had concerts there, and I remember a singing master by the name of Little Jones. At one of his concerts the church was lighted with colored wax candles and tumblers filled with water of different colors with a light in each, and so arranged as to form the word Harmony over the pulpit.[10]

Memory's comments belie the fact that instrumental music, especially that involving the organ, generated considerable opposition, even consternation, especially among those weaned on John Calvin's injunctions forbidding the use of instruments within the confines of a church. Leonard P. Bailey built an organ in 1827 for a buyer who then reneged on his commitment. A group from the First Presbyterian Church arranged for its purchase as well as the necessary modifications to the gallery to accommodate its bulk. But then,

> On the first Sabbath, after this new organ was placed in the gallery of the church, it was not used. There it stood silent, many looking in blank astonishment at it. It was a new idea and many objected. On the second Sabbath it was played during the gathering of the Sunday School children. A week or two later it was played as the congregation was dispersing and it was some

months before it accompanied the singing of hymns. The congregation received its organ music in homeopathic doses.[11]

Several decades later Professor Horace Dwight Munson faced even more perilous circumstances. Munson, a Connecticut native who had studied with Lowell Mason in Boston, appeared in Zanesville in 1846 after teaching in Hartford, Pittsburgh, and several towns in Illinois over the span of a decade. He was hired to supervise music in the Putnam Ladies' Seminary (which had been founded in 1835 and occupied its own quarters in 1838). He also opened a music store in 1850, offering an assortment of instruments (according to an announcement in the city directory of 1851, these ranged from pianos and melodeons to guitars, banjos, violins, cellos, flutes, fifes, accordions, and tambourines) and sheet music and also taught vocal music in the community (and in neighboring towns such as Cambridge, Athens, and Newark, as well) to both children in the public schools and adults. He offered concerts with his young charges at several halls in the community, including one at the seminary in 1848 that included his ballad, "The Child's Wish." Through these juvenile concerts he "convinced the skeptical that children could sing, and then public sentiment demanded that they should be taught systematically."[12] Records remain of a concert by Munson's young charges at the Market Street Baptist Church during November 1852, prompting the editorial observation that "the deep interest taken by Mr. Munson in the musical education of our children, all of which has been done as a gratuity, should prompt our citizens to turn out and reward him in their smiles of approbation and a crowded house."[13] There is also knowledge of a concert of June 1857 in the Odd Fellows' Hall involving some three hundred children under Munson's guidance.

However, Munson faced a challenge of a different sort at the church where he had been hired to train a choir. Its pastor, a cultivated musician, suggested a kind of stealth operation: on a designated Sunday the choir members would suddenly appear and occupy assigned seats. However, the conservative opposition got wind of the plot, and when the pastor and choir assembled, they

found those seats were occupied by the opponents of this "new fangled singin," determined to "hold the fort," in spite of all the pastors and young folks in creation! And before the choir could get the "pitch," off started old Brother B., in the "amen corner," with his own tune, and the choir could only follow at a respectful distance. The full force of this difficulty will be realized, when it is remembered that at this time it was customary for men to take the leading part in singing. Ladies had not been convinced that they could carry the "air," or soprano part, and this also explains the difficulty experienced in organizing choirs. The result being that the first part was over-burdened by a class of singers who made more noise than music, and great effort was required to convince the gentlemen that their assistance was not needed, and the ladies that it could be dispensed with.[14]

Concordia, an all-male German singing society, was formed in 1854, followed by a Männerchor in 1859. Neither survived the Civil War, but both were progenitors of similar organizations that appeared during the remaining decades of the century. During the autumn of 1857, Professor V. C. Taylor, a visiting New Yorker, held a widely attended musical convention, which concluded with a grand concert in the Odd Fellows' Hall by a chorus of over one hundred voices. Apparently this sparked interest in the local church choirs and also generated the formation of a Harmonic Society the following year. This too failed to survive the Civil War but can be considered the parent of later choral societies.

Completion of the National Road westward through Ohio (it reached Zanesville in 1830), improvements to navigation on the Muskingum River allowing regular steamboat service during the 1830s, and the arrival of railroads during the 1850s facilitated contact with the outside world. Actually, the first known concert by a visiting professional was announced on the final day of 1825:

> This evening in the long room of Mr. Stewart's the lovers of vocal music will have the opportunity of being gratified with the performance of Miss Green, an eminent vocalist, who has exhibited her talents in various places with much applause.[15]

Most of the other itinerant professionals who reached Zanesville during the first half of the century were as acclaimed as Miss Green. Violinist Julius Herman played several events during November 1839, his repertory—*Variations on "Rosin the Bow," Oceana Quadrilles,* and *Weber's Last Waltz*—surely reflecting the tastes of his auditors. R[alph?] Loomis appeared at Stacey's Saloon on May 12, 1846, in a program that mixed works for the piano (particularly various sets of cotillions) with songs such as "The Rover Afloat," "The Indian Hunter," "The Irish Emigrant," and "The Prairie and Death of Warren." A "blind minstrel" named W. Van Deusen appeared as pianist and singer at Stacey's on September 13, 1848, carrying with him similar repertory: "I'll Tell My Ma," "Neil Gow's Farewell to Whiskey," "Texas" (with variations), "A Wet Sheet and a Flowing Sea," "Rory O'Moore," and others. Other visitors included a group of Swiss bell ringers (playing in part on tuned sea shells), druid horn blowers, and Mason's Metropolitan Serenaders. However, violin virtuoso Ole Bull played before enthused residents in 1853 and again the following year on the second floor of the Odd Fellows' Hall (receipts at the first concert totaled seven hundred dollars), and concert pianist Sigismond Thalberg appeared at Nevitt's Hall on May 1, 1857 (seats at either $1.50 or $1.00), supported by singers Teresa Parodi, Amalia Patti Strakosch (wife of impresario Maurice Strakosch and elder sister of the more famous Adelina Patti), a Signor Nicola, and a Herr Mollenhauer. Strakosch imported a Chickering piano for the event, and Nevitt's was "thoroughly freshened up and embellished for the occasion." Visitors of lesser note, such as Madame Anna de la Grange (May 28) and Professor Anton, a violinist from the Pittsburgh and Wheeling Academies of Music (July 14), had to be satisfied with L. P. Bailey's instruments.[16]

Zanesville also attracted educators of increasing distinction. One Actavous La Serre announced on September 3, 1836, that he intended to offer class and private instruction on the flute. Six years later Professor Charles B. Bosbuy set up shop in Putnam and on December 9 announced that he was capable of organizing amateur bands, tuning pianos, teaching the violin, and offering lessons in "the most fashionable style of dancing, including quadrilles, Polish mazurkas, gallopades, waltzes, Spanish dances, cotillions, country dances, Pas seul, Pas de deux, etc."[17]

Alonzo Attwood had arrived in town as leader of a touring circus band during the summer of 1846. The circus then wintered in Zanesville; Attwood married a local woman and made Zanesville his headquarters until his death in 1887. He traveled with his circus band during the summers, but, in addition to his own local band, he announced on April 9, 1847,

> The undersigned proposes to open in about ten days, if a class can be formed, a school for instruction in instrumental music, in this place. He will teach the proper use of all brass instruments, the clarinet and the flute. He will not only give instruction, but will aim to make his pupils good players. At the boarding house opposite the Presbyterian church.[18]

H. D. Munson became the town's principal musician after his arrival in 1846, his influence as a teacher and music retailer persisting until his death in 1897. He was joined in 1851 by William Lilienthal, born in Baden and educated in Mannheim. Lilienthal went first to Cleveland in a fruitless search for family members and then walked to Zanesville, where he painted railroad cars for one dollar per day while mastering English. He then became a church organist, first for the Unitarian Universalist congregation and then at First Presbyterian. He also began to concertize as a pianist and to teach both the piano and organ, at first charging twenty-five cents per lesson. While Lilienthal eventually was able to claim advanced students who could deal with works from the standard literature in a satisfactory manner, he recalled an incident from the 1850s that perhaps suggests the mixed cultural values he confronted at first:

A gentleman informed him that he had heard of his reputation, and wished him to give his daughter some instruction in singing, remarking that she was a good performer on the piano. He accompanied the gentleman home, and the daughter was invited to play a good piece, "Old Lang Syne," which she did, without regard to time, and in a manner that rendered it difficult of recognition, while the father was in ecstasy over it, saying it was splendid![19]

While Munson and Lilienthal may have had a major impact on the local culture, the Zanesville musician who achieved at least momentary national note was an amateur, Alexander Coffman Ross (1812–83). A son of the first local gunsmith, Ross was apprenticed at age seventeen to watchmaker and bandleader Charles Hill. Perhaps it should be inferred that Ross imbibed both his trade and at least a bit of musical knowledge from the mentor; it is known that Ross sang in local church choirs and played the clarinet in the Harmonic Band. He studied watch making in New York City during 1831 and 1832 and then returned home to open a store from which he sold not only watches and clocks but also jewelry, perfumes, powder flasks, snuff and tobacco, chess and backgammon boards, and musical instruments.

He achieved some notice in 1839 by concocting his own equipment and producing what was deemed the first daguerreotype made west of New York City,[20] but the mantle of fame was draped on his shoulders during the presidential campaign of 1840. Incumbent Democrat Martin Van Buren was pitted against the Whig candidate, William Henry Harrison. Harrison, son of a Virginia governor and victor over an Indian force near the Tippecanoe River during his tenure as governor of the Indiana Territory, was then serving as clerk of courts in Hamilton County. In a picturesque gesture, he had built a sixteen-room mansion around the core of a log cabin in North Bend, giving rise to his opponents' gibe that he would be more comfortable in that log cabin with a barrel of hard cider at his side than in the White House. The Whigs turned this snide observation on its head, rallying partisans of "Old Tippecanoe" in what became known as "The Log Cabin and Hard Cider Campaign."

The Zanesville Whigs started planning in January for a major rally on July 4 and asked Ross for a campaign song. Ross recalled a deluge of inspiration in the midst of a dreary Sunday sermon; band leader Thomas Launder suggested that the resulting lyrics could be fitted to a tune known as "Little Pigs." Ross performed the resulting amalgam at a local Whig meeting in the courthouse and was greeted by enthusiastic cheers and yells: "Next day, men and boys were singing the chorus in the street, in the workshops, and at the table."[21] In September Ross, while on a buying trip to New York City, attended a Whig rally and responded to public demand for a song. Although greeted with skepticism, the young Buckeye had his fellow partisans singing lustily by the third (of ten) verse of "Tippecanoe and [John] Tyler Too!" A sample, consisting of the first verse and chorus:

Oh what has caused this great commotion! Motion! Motion!
    Our country through!
It is the ball that's rolling on
    For Tippecanoe and Tyler too!

For Tippecanoe and Tyler too,
    And with them we'll beat little Van,
Van, Van, Van is a used up man,
    And with them we'll beat little Van.

Hardly the stuff of literary immortality, but

"Tippecanoe and Tyler Too" was in the political canvass of 1840 what the "Marseillaise" was to the French Revolution. It sang Harrison into the presidency. Through the half-martial, half-rollicking melody the pent-up feelings of a people whose banks were suspended, whose laborers were out of work, who were pinched by hard times and to whom the Whigs had promised "$2 a day and roast beef," had found expression and the song was sung throughout the country as if by madmen.[22]

Recall that Harrison's triumph was virtually as brief as Ross's fame, since he contracted a cold on his inclement inauguration day and was dead within a month,

Part Two

Education

CHAPTER 6

The Singing School

Speaking of Ohio in his "Recollections" of 1826, Timothy Flint asserted,

> It is generally denominated in the western country the Yankee state. Although
> I should not suppose, from my means of observation, that the greater pro-
> portion of its inhabitants were actual emigrants from New England, it is
> clearly the last region, in advancing west, where the institutions of that coun-
> try seem to have struggled for the ascendancy. The prevalent modes of liv-
> ing, of society, of instruction, of association for any public object, of think-
> ing, and enjoying, among the middling classes, struck me, generally, to be
> copies of the New England pattern.[1]

Infant Ohio as a cultural colony of New England? Nowhere in this study is that
relationship more apparent than in the realm of education.

In fact we must turn to New England of the seventeenth century in order to
locate the roots of music education in Ohio. Most New Englanders then lived in a
theocracy where the practice of metrical psalmody was the principal means of
musical expression. An earlier assumption that these immigrants, faced with the
necessity of establishing themselves on the fringe of the wilderness, brought with
them a standard of musical literacy that was gradually abandoned has been dis-
proved by more recent studies demonstrating that two methods of performance
were imported, side by side. The "regular way" involved reading from the page; the
"old way" assumed musical illiteracy, and was based on the process of "lining out."
A precentor, or song leader, would set the pitch and then lead the congregation
through the tune, phrase by phrase.

Remaining records suggest that by the end of the century performance standards had deteriorated badly. Congregations maintained a precarious repertory of

only a handful of tunes (to which they fitted the various metrical versions of the psalms), and often the precentors proved so unfit that they would start one tune and inadvertently wander into another.

By the early eighteenth century a handful of divines determined to correct what they found a shameful situation. The Reverend John Tufts proposed a solution in his *Introduction to the Singing of Psalm-Tunes*[2] that was announced in the *Boston News-Letter* in January 1721 as "a small Book containing 20 Psalm Tunes, with Directions how to Sing them, contrived in the most easy Method ever yet Invented, for the ease of Learners, whereby even Children, or People of the meanest Capacities, may come to Sing them by Rule."

Tufts abandoned conventional round note heads and placed on the staff in their stead the first letters of four traditional solmization syllables: F(a), S(ol), L(a), and M(i). Fa, Sol, and La represented the first three notes of the scale, after which the whole set was employed to signify the fourth through the seventh pitches. Time values were indicated by dots after the letters. Letter notation had been used in Europe for more than a century, and four-note solmization systems have been identified in Europe, but it is possible that Tufts thought he had stumbled on something utterly novel.

In 1720 the Reverend Thomas Symmes asked in *The Reasonableness of Regular Singing; or, Singing by Note,*

> WOULD it not greatly tend to the promoting [of] *Singing Psalms* if Singing Schools were promoted? . . . Where would be the *Difficulty*, or what the *Disadvantages*, if People that want *Skill* in *Singing*, would procure a *Skilful Person* to *Instruct* them, and meet *Two* or *Three* Evenings in the Week, from *Five* or *Six* a clock, to *Eight*, and spend the Time in Learning to Sing?[3]

Tufts apparently acted on that resolve, traveling about Massachusetts, organizing singing schools, and sermonizing about the matter. For example, the *New England Courant* of September 30, 1723, recorded that "on Thursday last a Singing Lecture was held here, when the Reverend Mr. Tufts of Newbury preach'd."[4] From these pioneering efforts at reform arose a singing school movement that gradually penetrated the original eastern seaboard colonies (states) and eventually western states such as Ohio.

The itinerant singing master of the late eighteenth century set up shop wherever he could find an appropriate space—church or meeting house, school, or even tavern—and advertised his presence via the local newspapers and posted broadsides. The classes were held in the evening as many as five times a week and lasted for days or even weeks, culminating in some sort of "concert" through which the "scholars" flaunted their newly acquired skills.

The students were expected to purchase a text, or tunebook, from the teacher. Oblong in shape (often called "end-openers"), these volumes included an extensive pedagogical section laying out all the rudiments as well as suggestions for proper vocalization and vocal health, followed by exercises and a healthy dose of music of various sorts, at least some of it written by the singing master himself.

Virtually all of this late-eighteenth-century repertory was printed using conventional European notation. However, in 1798 William Smith and William Little copyrighted a volume they called *The* Easy Instructor, *or a New Method of teaching* Sacred Harmony, *containing the Rudiments of* Music *on an improved Plan.* The volume, which finally appeared in 1801 and went through multiple editions until 1831, was entirely conventional, except that Smith and Little visually reinforced the four-syllable solmization system by representing fa with a triangle, sol with an oval, la with a square, and mi with a diamond. This fasola system, with its shape, patent (although not legally so), or buckwheat notes (the latter term alternately one of affection when applied by advocates, of derision when used by detractors of the whole tradition, although it originally was meant only to reflect the diamond-shaped mi), became virtually universal during the following decades (although it eventually was expanded to a seven-shape system), and is still employed today by groups in the South, many of which rely on recent editions of *The Sacred Harp,* first printed in Philadelphia in 1844.[5]

The Singing School in Ohio

This tradition was gradually abandoned in the eastern urban centers after a change of taste that triumphed by the third decade of the nineteenth century. Capitulating to new standards of musical propriety, the New England–born tradition simply migrated and found fertile ground elsewhere.

Before that metamorphosis, at least three early emigrants to Ohio brought with them handwritten tunebooks designed for their personal use, all notated in the letter notation introduced by Tufts. All three scribes created a repertory that has much in common both with Tufts and with Thomas Johnston (1708–67), a Boston publisher who printed a collection of fifty-one psalm tunes in 1755 designed to be employed with the standard Psalters of the day, and then five years later reissued the collection in letter notation, again intended as a mate for otherwise tuneless metrical Psalters. About 1763 he extended the anthology to seventy pieces, but reverted to conventional notation.[6] Surely Robert Barns, James English, and John Kerr must have had some contact with Tufts's widely circulated primer or with Johnston's publications, although it remains impossible to establish any specific correlation.

A page from the *Musick Book* of James English. Ross County Historical Society.

Unfortunately, nothing is known about Robert Barns beyond his songbook, which was acquired by the Western Reserve Historical Society in 1922. The initial inscription, "Robert Barns / His Book / Jan. 20th 1768," is followed by more than thirty tunes (nine of them found in Tufts), a concluding "Robt. Barns / His Hand and Book / March 6th 1778," and an extended poem, "The Musick Song," whose final stanza reads:

> Now to Conclude these Lines of mine
> I wish that Musicks Art may shine
> Through Africa and Asia . . .
> Through Europe and America. . . . .

Visually the least interesting of the three, Barns placed the texts on the left hand pages facing their designated tunes, outlining the latter with a simple border in both black and red ink.

James English (1768–1844) had been born in Pennsylvania, was licensed to preach in the Methodist Episcopal Church in Virginia as early as 1804, and arrived in Chillicothe from Charles Town, [West] Virginia by March 2, 1806. Since Thomas Worthington and Edward Tiffin had also emigrated from Charles Town, and English served as a pallbearer for both, it can probably be inferred that there was a mutual friendship prior to English's appearance in Chillicothe. He was authorized to sermonize in the Scioto Circuit, but was also a plasterer and carpenter and eventually a solid citizen of the community as a lumber dealer and bank director. English brought with him his "His Musick Book Made by Him, in the Year, of our Lord, One Thousand Seven Hundred and Ninety."[7] Again, about a third of the thirty-three tunes copied by English can be found in Tufts; twenty-four of them are identical to those of Barns.

English, however, was apparently not content to sing these tunes with only their original metrical psalm texts, since he included substitute verses, many of them blatantly secular. For example, "Newtown" was fitted with this quatrain:

If my love was a red, red, rose
Upon yon castle wall,
And I myself a drop of dew,
I on my love would fall.

"Bedford" could be sung to a query—

I hope, my dear you won't deny
The question I will ask.
The question is whether you love me
Or your father best?

—whose answer was attached to "St. Michails" [*sic*]:

My father's love I do adore,
And yours I don't deny.
Come sit you down by me awhile.
I'll tell you by and by.

Even more charming is a stanza written by brother John English for use with the tune "Willington":

There is a young man in the house
He has a spring'e mare,
And when that lad does get a wife,
The britches she will wear.

We know quite a bit about John Kerr, since the Western Reserve Historical Society owns letters, account books, field notes, records of business and literary associations, his certificate of naturalization, a diary of a trip from Pittsburgh on the Ohio and Hocking Rivers in 1800, and a diploma from the Scioto Masonic Lodge dated 1811, among other items. Born in Ireland, Kerr lived in Franklinton and was active in the movement to make Columbus the state capital. He served on the first Columbus City Council in 1816 and was the city's mayor (1818–19). He had been an agent for a Columbus land syndicate (1813–15) and was a Justice of the Peace and Associate Judge of the Court of Common Please of Franklinton in 1823, the year of his death. He also left the "Vocal Music Book: Brought to a Conclusion May the 10th in the Year of our Lord 1792." Visually elaborate, each tune name is boldly decorated in a definitive manner (and marked "tune tenor," acknowledging a melody that could have been surrounded by an additional two or three vocal lines), as are the beginning and end of each staff. These intricate abstractions seem akin to medieval illuminated manuscripts, although on a much more modest scale. Kerr's repertory demonstrates considerable commonalty with that of his fellow emigrants. Of his forty-five tunes, eleven can be found in Tufts; twenty-six were also copied by English.

We must assume that each of these gentlemen had mastered the letter notation first promulgated by Tufts either as autodidacts or as students of New England singing masters committed to the Tufts approach. Also, that the contents of these handwritten volumes were copied from some combination of the publications of Tufts and Johnston and then employed for their owner's personal edification and enjoyment.

But what about the singing-school movement in frontier Ohio? As noted earlier, announcements of singing schools in Cincinnati appeared as early as 1800. Their existence was acknowledged in pioneering publications like Timothy Flint's *The Columbian Harmonist* (1816) and W. C. Knight's *The Juvenile Harmony, or A Choice Collection of Psalm Tunes, Hymns and Anthems, Selected from the Most Eminent Authors, And Well Adapted to All Christian Churches, Singing Schools and Private Societies,* first issued in 1825 and popular enough that its sixteenth edition appeared in 1836. Typical of the genre, its three- and four-part tunes (which include both "Ohio" and "Cincinnati"), presented in shape notes, were preceded by "The Rules of Singing, And an Explanation of the Rules and Principles of the Ground Work of Music."

Their manifestation elsewhere in Ohio is charmingly described in William Cooper Howells's *Recollections of Life in Ohio, from 1813 to 1840* in language that ought to seem familiar by now. In the fall of 1825 Howells opened two grammar schools near the family farm in Jefferson County, near Steubenville. However, he noticed that singing schools held in the area were much more attractive to the young people,

> as the music was more generally interesting, and those who attended to take part in them [did so] without much study. Indeed, the science brought into use at these schools was very limited, and consisted mostly in a few of the crudest rules of notation, with practice in singing, which was nearly all by ear; while the music produced was entirely church music, such as they hear at all places of public worship. The principles of music were never learned by many who sung tunes from the books in use. The singing was either in words of hymns where each note had its syllable printed under it, or, as they called it *by note*, which consisted in singing in unison the notes of the tune by the syllable *me, faw, sol, law*, for at that time *do, re, mi*, were not used in English

psalmody. As it was very difficult to fix these syllables to the right notes, the books were printed in what they called patent notes, or, in ridicule, *buck-wheat* notes. Instead of having the note-heads round, they were made of different shapes, the seven notes of the scale being made up by repeating three of the notes.

With this arrangement they could sing slow tunes very readily, and as for rapid ones, they managed it by ear. There was nothing but vocal music taught at that time. They had no pianos out of the large towns, and the violin was played by ear; playing the fiddle was a rather sinful affair, at best.

The attraction to the singing schools was the social one of the young men and women getting together and having a pleasant time, for it was understood that the girls, who could generally come out with their brothers or family friends, would accept the company of some young man to go home, as an escort. In this way they made acquaintances and sometimes matches, as well as having a pleasant time.[8]

Although derogatory about the outcome of the process, Howells thus confirmed that the singing school culture had been transported intact to the frontier.[9]

A slightly different pattern can be discerned from a diary kept by John M. Roberts (1833–1914) beginning in 1853. Roberts, who eventually became a rural schoolteacher in Madison County, peppered his account with references to singing schools held weekly, with a series of sessions lasting about three months. Here again the singing school seems to have fostered social interchange as much as musical literacy. As witness, an entry from April 14, 1854:

I was at singing school last Tuesday & had a refreshing time, a decidedly invigorating, truly enchanting, felicitously endearing [time]. I had the good luck to fall in with Miss Lydia Robinson, who by the by is a buxom lass of 24 & weighs 180 lbs. avoirdupoise. Well, I went over to old Auntie Barbara's & found Mr. Charlie Burke, a young man excessively verdant, waiting to escort Damoiselle to the singing school. She was not at home at the time of our arrival, & Allen Anderson, Mr. Burke, [and I] all started to the singing school, when who should we meet but Madamoiselle going home. Of course we stopped & went back with her; when Mr. Burke clinched her & we all started, she & he leading the crowd. . . . Well, by & [by] the singing school broke up & Mr. Burke stood around & kept Madamoiselle waiting. She got tired & started & said ["]Come along, John.["] Of course I was not going to back out, so I just goes up & clinches, expecting her to give me the mitten & take her partner, but he got miffed and off he went full drive. So home I goes with Damoiselle, & talk to me about tall sparking, will ye? [10]

On New Year's Eve 1858 Roberts pondered a social problem of a different sort:

> Some time since, Mr. G[iles] A. James from near Charleston in Clark Co., who is teaching school in the Botkin s[chool]house, proposed to teach a class in singing at this s[chool]house for the sum of $20 for 13 lessons. He came over about 3 weeks ago and we soon made up the money. There was an understanding, however, . . . that no spectators were to be admitted. Well, Messrs. Wilsons, Turners, & others from Clark County were very much put out about the matter. They came on the next evening after we had made up our class and wanted to sing. . . . They went away swearing deadly vengeance against the singing school & its friends. . . .
>
> On last Monday we had another sing, I being doorkeeper at the time. They had threatened to knock me down if I was at the door when they came. They had several of the class on their side of the question, and these . . . went out at recess and led the rest in.[11]

A distraction of another sort was described on June 20, 1859:

> We had quite a time here at our Saturday evenings sing. Wm. Opret was here drunk as a loon. He came up to the window on the outside of the house and commenced swearing roundly at the singing teacher. I went to him and civilly requested him to be still. He immediately commenced cursing me and pulling off his coat. I was sorely tempted to knock him down. He was so drunk, however, that he could not stand still. . . . Some persons keep selling him whiskey in London, & I am in hopes that they may be jerked up for it and fined severely. . . . I do wish that liquor laws were ten times more stringent than what they now are.[12]

Elsewhere Roberts talks about basket or picnic sings, including one in early June 1859 near Midway that included the "London brass band. . . . The Midway & Newport choirs were singing to see who could excel." These ventures must have been popular, since on September 24, 1859, Roberts mentions that Mr. James was mentoring a class of fifty. "The house was crowded to its utmost capacity." Nonetheless, our diarist on September 13 had admitted that

> I must try and come during this present quarter and see if I cant learn something. I have been coming for some time and have not as yet learned much; in fact, nothing. It is my own fault, however, as James always did his best and has very sensibly advanced the singing class in this neighborhood.[13]

Several singing teachers who were active on the east coast eventually found their way to Ohio, but only at the end of their careers. Stephen Jenks (1772–1856), born in Rhode Island, but active mostly in Connecticut, compiled ten tunebooks between 1799 and 1818 (some of joint authorship) containing 125 of his own compositions. The first of these was titled *The New-England Harmonist,* the last, *The Harmony of Zion; or, Union Compiler.* Jenks appears to have done little composing after 1811; in fact most of his works in *The Harmony of Zion* appear to have been written prior to 1810. Perhaps he sensed that his idiom was increasingly considered old-fashioned. In September 1827 he abruptly abandoned New England for Thompson in Geauga County, deep in the Western Reserve. He bought a forty-acre farm north of the village in 1833, although he retired from its active management two years later. He is supposed to have taught singing schools in Thompson and neighboring communities, and anecdotal evidence suggests that he may have manufactured drums and tambourines during the late 1830s and 1840s. Between 1847 and 1850 he assembled a manuscript copybook containing 102 compositions. Several are undated and a few had previously been published, while others are annotated as having been written between 1798 and 1823. However, about three-quarters of the corpus are dated between 1828 and 1850, the vast majority in 1847, meaning that Jenks actually wrote eighty-two pieces after his arrival in Ohio. At least three of the tune names suggest their Ohio provenance: "Painesville," "Thompson," and "Solon." The Newberry Library in Chicago has owned *Stephen Jenks's Book* since 1891. Four of its tunes, all of them from 1847 (along with "Mount Calvary," which had first been printed in the *American Compiler* of 1803), were published in *The Shawm,* compiled by William Bradbury and George F. Root, with the assistance of Thomas Hastings and Timothy Mason, and issued by the Mason Brothers in New York in 1853. Although it must be assumed that "Bright Glory," "Spread Thy Wings," "Invite," and "Will You Go" (renamed "Traveling Home") were issued with the composer's assent, it is difficult not to wonder whether he realized that they would be extensively revised by these advocates of the "scientific" music movement who had earlier routed the idiom Jenks practiced. In fact, "Spread Thy Wings" is even presented as having been "Arranged from Stephen Jenks" (while "Bright Glory" is attributed to "Stephen Jenks, of Thompson, Ohio").[14]

Lucius and Amzi Chapin might seem peripheral to this study, given their brief residence in Ohio. However, even though neither of these brothers issued his own compilations, tunes attributed to the Chapins inhabit virtually every nineteenth-century tunebook, including many of those published in Ohio. Their legacy survives to this day in the tune named "Twenty-Fourth," which was included in *The United Methodist Hymnal* of 1989 (No. 658) to words by Isaac Watts; the same tune, mated with other language, appears twice in the *Lutheran Book of Worship* of 1978 (nos. 122 and 126).

Lucius Chapin was born in Springfield, Massachusetts, in April 1760 and served as a solider in the Revolutionary War from 1775 until 1780. During much of that time he acted as a Fife Major, although without a regular appointment to that role. After learning the trade of clothier, he taught singing schools in New England from 1782 until 1787 before migrating to Lexington, Virginia. He managed a clothing business and taught singing schools in that region beginning in 1789 before relocating to Kentucky in 1797.

Amzi Chapin was also born in Springfield, in 1768, and may have been an apprentice cabinetmaker to his brother Aaron. He probably lived in both Hartford and New Haven before joining Lucius in Virginia in 1791. Having apprenticed under his brother, he struck out on his own in 1792 as a singing master in North Carolina, where he taught until 1795, when he also moved to Kentucky and established singing schools in Lexington and environs. He built a sawmill near the present town of Washington, as well as a home he named "Vernon," after Mount Vernon.

The two apparently founded singing schools, as well as teacher-training sessions for singing masters. Tension arose between the two brothers and Amzi departed for Pennsylvania in 1800, leaving Lucius his property and the mill, although the older brother apparently had little business acumen. Amzi married and became a farmer. He taught his last singing school in 1828, retired from active farming at age sixty-three and moved to Northfield, midway between Cleveland and Akron, in October 1831. He reestablished himself as a farmer in Ohio, although he left the heavy work to his two sons. His health declined, and he died in February 1835.

Lucius made a singing master of his son, Amzi Philander, and both taught singing schools in the Lexington, Kentucky, area, although by 1817 the son was on his own, teaching in Warren County near Bowling Green, Kentucky. The oldest son, Lucius Rousseau, also became a singing master and worked in Columbus during 1817 and 1818. Concurrently, father Lucius taught in Chillicothe (and may have been in Ohio earlier than January 1818). A letter dated August 1819 remarks, "About 18 months ago Mr. Chapin taught in this town the Harmonic Companion and at the close of his schools was able to afford the best Music we had ever heard." The addressee was New Englander Andrew Law, whose *Harmonic Companion* of 1807 had become the principal text employed by the Chapins. During November 1831 Lucius joined Vicissimus (his fourth son) and family in Breckenridge County, Kentucky. Vicissimus died in 1835, and sometime during 1836 or 1837 Lucius and wife Susan joined a daughter and son-in-law in Walnut Hills, near Cincinnati, where he lived on a soldier's pension until Christmas Eve of 1842. He was interred in Cincinnati's Spring Grove Cemetery.[15]

While most of the active Ohio singing masters remain unidentifiable, the activities of both James S. Warren Jr. (1829–1905) and Alexander Auld (1816–98) can be documented. Warren's grandparents lived in Shirley, Massachusetts,[16] but William and Hannah Warren migrated to Ohio with their nine children sometime during

1814, settling first in Marietta (they were to produce five more offspring after arriving in Ohio). About 1817 they moved twenty miles north to what became Olive Township in Noble County, and carved out a farm on a large tract of land bisected by a small stream still known as Warren's Run. One of their sons, James Sullivan Warren, Sr., who had been born in Maine in 1805 while his parents were on a visit there, purchased his own land in South Olive as early as 1826, and not only farmed but also taught school in neighboring Brookfield Township. He married Huldah Tuttle of Washington County in January 1826; that union produced nine children, including James S. Jr.

Anecdotal evidence suggests that father James imbibed some musical training from his parents and imparted that knowledge to son James; also that they jointly taught a singing school in South Olive. The father's culture is perhaps suggested by his 1886 obituary, which contains a six-verse dirge written by the deceased and sung to the tune "Liberty Hall," the second item in *Warren's Minstrel*. There is little specific information about the son's activities as an itinerant singing master other than a statement in a manuscript genealogy that he "taught vocal music in Noble and adjoining counties." However, unlike most other rural counterparts of the period, he possessed sufficient skill and industry to publish his own tunebook: *Warren's Minstrel: Containing a Plain and Concise Introduction to Sacred Music: Comprising the Necessary Rudiments, with a Choice Collection of Tunes, Original and Selected*, published by J. H. Riley and Company of Columbus in 1856, with a second, slightly expanded edition a year later. Warren's short preface was dated September 1855 from Olive.

Of the 141 items in the second edition, many are borrowed from New England or European sources. Most are designed for three voices—soprano and bass with the melody, as is normal in the inherited New England tradition, in the tenor. The continuity of that tradition is palpable in the number of borrowings from New Englanders like William Billings and Timothy Swan, but also indirectly in Warren's admission that he took the tune "Funeral Hymn" from *American Harmony*, Oliver Holden's first collection, issued in Boston in 1792. However, the author attributed thirty-six pieces to himself; nine appear to be entirely original, eighteen are arrangements, while another nine have simply been harmonized. William Putnam Warren (1837–1930), a younger brother, was, according to his obituary, "an ardent lover of music" who "taught vocal music for a number of years beginning at the age of nineteen, and later harmonized a number of selections." Assuming that the three tunes in the *Minstrel* by "W. P. W." can be attributed to him, he must have been somewhat precocious, since he could have been no more than eighteen when the volume appeared. Two other pieces were attributed to "J. M. W.," who may possibly have been Justice N. Warren, an older brother who was a doctor by profession. Thus, fully forty-one items in the collection were claimed by family members as original compositions or arrangements.

The volume was of the typical oblong format, with a concise pedagogical section preceding a variety of idioms, ranging from simple folk hymns to more elaborate anthems. A few of the tune names suggest Ohio connections, for example, "Cincinnati" (pages 32–33, unattributed) and "Olive" (page 135, harmonized by the compiler). Despite the title, the volume concluded with secular pieces. "The Old Arm Chair" (page 149, supposedly an original work of Warren) boldly appropriated the saccharine poetry of Eliza Cooke immortalized in the 1840 ballad of Henry Russell, asserting above the printing of succeeding verses on page 152 that the "exquisite" lyric had been "embalmed in song by the talented and much admired composer, Mr. HENRY RUSSELL." "Ben Bolt" (pages 150–51, harmonized by Warren) was presented as a "pathetic ballad," "composed by Mr. NELSON KNEASS, the popular and pleasing vocalist" (page 152). This pair was preceded on page 148 by "The Dying Californian," a sort of sacred ballad in sixteen verses, "harmonized" by Warren (which amounts to the addition of a bass line, since it is couched in only two parts). This popular, topical, parlor ballad was added to the second edition, perhaps because of the experience of several of Warren's neighbors who had joined the Gold Rush to California in 1852 only to return to their Olive farms in 1857.

Although Warren did not acknowledge its origin, the music was presented in the seven-shape system created by Alexander Auld and first employed in *The Ohio Harmonist* of 1847. Auld claimed the system as his "property" and proscribed its use "without my permission," from which it can be inferred that either Warren was a bold and fearless pirate or that the two were acquainted, since they lived and worked in the same part of the state and shared a Columbus publisher.

Auld had been born in Milton, Pennsylvania, but his family moved to a farm near Deersville in Harrison County in 1822.[17] He began teaching school in 1832 but after one year went east to Carlisle, Pennsylvania, where he studied music for two years. In 1835 he bought a farm six miles northwest of Deersville and commenced a teaching career which lasted until his death in 1892. Surely the most active and influential of the rural singing masters in Ohio, he compiled four published collections: *The Ohio Harmonist* (1847, 1848, and 1852), *The Key of the West: or The Ohio Collection of Sacred Music* (1856), *The Farmers' and Mechanics' Minstrel of Sacred Music* (1863, 1866, and 1867) and *The Golden Trumpet* (1863 and 1878). *The Key of the West* became the model for its successors, their contents largely identical.

The Ohio Harmonist was by far the most successful of this quartet, eventually selling close to 55,000 copies. Account books show that the volume was shipped throughout Ohio, as well as to West Virginia, Kentucky, Indiana, Illinois, Iowa, Michigan, and Pennsylvania, states in which Auld taught on a rather regular summer circuit. *The Ohio Harmonist* was initially self-published from Washington [Court House], Ohio (although printed in Cincinnati); a second "enlarged and revised" edition (234 pages vs. 160 in the original) was printed both in Cincinnati and Pittsburgh in 1848 and again by J. H. Riley and Company of Columbus in 1852. The volume is in the typical oblong shape with the introductory pedagogical section, including a glossary of terms, followed by a variety of music.

While the first edition of the *Harmonist* contained only five arrangements by its compiler, the "enlarged" version included seventeen original pieces and an equal number of arrangements (of an eventual total of forty original works and twenty-one arrangements and harmonizations).[18] The other identified composers were mostly from the urban, genteel European tradition, whose advocates waged war on the rural shape-note tradition: Lowell Mason (including a tune named "Ohio"), William Bradbury, and Thomas Hastings, as well as truncated and simplified arrangements of Handel, Haydn, and Mozart.[19] One oddity: "Yamuna (A Hindu Tune)," a bilingual thing whose "air" had supposedly been "sent to the United States by the Reverend J. Wilson of Allahabad" and then harmonized by a New York organist, information furnished by a compiler who attributed Loys Bourgeois's "Old Hundred" to Martin Luther.

This inclusiveness is matched by an apparent knowledge of schoolbook music theory and terminology: Auld wrote of "clefs" rather than the typical "cliffs" and major and minor rather than the more common sharp and flat keys. However, the first edition of the *Harmonist* demonstrates a continuity with earlier tunebooks, not only in its terminology but also in the language employed by Auld, on page ten of his "Rudiments of Music," to suggest proper performance practice. A few of his rubrics could have been plucked from many of the rural tunebooks:

In tuning the voice, let it be as smooth as possible, neither forcing it through the nose, nor blowing it through the teeth with the mouth shut. . . .

A genteel pronunciation is one of the greatest ornaments of music. Every word should be spoken clear and distinct as possible. It is this, that in a great measure, gives vocal music the preference to instrumental, by enjoying, at the same time, the sweets of harmony, together with the sense of what is expressed in these harmonious strains.

Let the base [*sic*] be sung bold and majestic, the tenor firm and manly, the treble soft and delicate.

Notes should be struck abruptly, like the report of a smith's hammer; but should begun and ended soft, swelling gently as the air of the tune requires. . . .

Decency in position of the body, and in beating time, are strictly to be adhered to. Likewise a becoming seriousness, while singing sacred words, adds dignity to the performance, and renders it at once respectable and solemn.

Everything was presented in the customary three voices, often disfiguring works conceived in four voices, made crude when their alto parts were simply eliminated (although Auld turned to the increasingly prevalent four voices in subsequent collections). The voice parts were not labeled, and while tradition would mark the tenor, or middle voice as most important, Auld's examples and explanations often suggest the soprano part as the "air." Auld was largely self-taught, and his rather rough-hewn idiom smacks of the frontier, marked by moments that defy academic convention.

Regardless of origin and idiom, everything was couched in Auld's unique seven-shape system. He announced that

> the principal design of the Compiler . . . is to offer the public a book that will assist them in acquiring a knowledge of the Seven Syllables in Music, without a resort to the tedious and never-ending study of the Round Note System.
>
> The author believes that the Patent Note plan is as much better than the Round Note plan, to give an easy and correct understanding of Music, as a well-painted landscape is to give a clear and correct idea of scenery than a meagre written description.[20]

Cocksure of the efficacy and potency of his approach, in a postscript to the revised edition Auld proposed "A New and Cheap Plan of Writing Music" using the seven shapes on, above, or below a single line, indicating each of three octaves. Clef and time signatures would appear on a slice of the normal five-line staff at the very beginning, but key signatures were to be eliminated, replaced by simple prescriptions, such as "Key of F." His readers were informed that

> the author has discovered that the notes are so perfect in their nature, that they will express the Seven Primary Sounds, without the usual five lines and four spaces, and in order to give more music in the same book, with two tunes more on a page, or nearly so, the following plan is proposed for the candid consideration of his worthy patrons.[21]

At the end of *The Key of the West*, Auld proposed a further refinement of his system, "containing a new style of writing music, which brings music, words, and all the parts, under the eye of the learner at the first glance, and also gives more music on the same page." Clef and time signatures were to be replaced by numerals indicating the number of beats in a measure and a letter indicating the key, while ledger lines would suggest various octaves. Auld ranted against the "absurdity" of conventional notation, the "[u]seless and unmeaning signs of the key, such as flats and sharps." In both cases this radical approach was illustrated with only a few examples, rather than applied to the entire contents of the volume.[22]

The only composition of Auld to escape eventual oblivion was "The Hills of Ohio," a work that first appeared in *The Key of the West*, was then included in the

THE HILLS OF OHIO.

1. The hills of O - hi - o, How proud - ly they rise, In the wild - ness of gran - deur To blend with the skies;
2. The streams of O - hi - o, That roar as they go, Or seem in their still - ness But dream - ing to flow;

3. The home of O - hi - o, Free, for - tuned and fair, Full man - y hearts treas - ure A sis - ter's love there;
4. God shield thee, O - hi - o, Dear land of my birth, And thy chil - dren that wan - der A - far o'er the earth;

With fair a - zure out - line, And tall an - cient trees, O - hi - o, my coun - try, I love thee for these.
Oh, bright glide the sun - beams They march in the seas, O - hi - o, my coun - try,

E'en more than thy moun - tains or stream - lets they please, O - hi - o, my coun - try, I love thee for these.
My coun - try thou art, where - e'er my lot's cast, Take thou to thy bos - om My ash - es at last.

Alexander Auld's "The Hills of Ohio," as found in *The Farmer's and Mechanics' Minstrel*, 1863. Ohio Historical Society.

two subsequent collections, and has by some in the past even been proposed as an official state song. Although Auld did not claim the piece as his own, tradition and some commentators ascribe both words and music to him, claiming that its senti-mental poetry reflects the homesickness of an itinerant singing master temporarily marooned either in Michigan or Indiana, depending on the narrator. However, it seems likely that Henry Howe's assertion that "the words are not original with Mr. Auld, but were set to music and largely sung by emigrants in the early years of this century"[23] comes somewhat close to the reality, since Auld could not have truth-fully claimed Ohio as the "dear land of my birth," as the poet does in his fourth verse. Unlike its companion pieces in the three collections, it is set in three rather than the four parts that had become Auld's norm, and the tune lies in the top rather than the tenor line.

Today a vibrant tradition of shape-note singing is maintained in the Southeast, particularly Tennessee, Georgia, Alabama, and Mississippi. Employing materials and methodology that would seem familiar to their forbears, modern-day shape-note singers congregate primarily in social groupings, even though the repertory they sing is still mainly religious. Although poorly documented and ephemeral, an offshoot of that tradition was transported to Ohio early in the twentieth century via the mass migration of southern blacks to the industrial Midwest in search of employment.[24]

These African American transplants to Ohio relied on a seven-shape system con-tained in volumes that were vertical rather than horizontal in format. They organized themselves in "classes" sometimes affiliated with a Baptist or A.M.E. church, but just as often functioned as independent associations. The classes usually met weekly to prepare hymns for presentation at a church service or at regularly scheduled gatherings on "Union Sundays." Each class leader was responsible for inculcating the rudiments contained in the didactic section of the volumes from which they sang, in addition to setting the pitch and tempo, teaching new repertory, and generally overseeing the quality of the performances, which were apparently pretty much straightforward, heavily accented, and marked by at least some spontaneous embellishment. True to the larger tradition, each hymn was and is sung through first on syllables. Many of the class leaders continue to rely on a textbook authored by Adger M. Pace and W[illiam] B[urton] Walbert, *Vaughan's Up-to-Date Rudiments and Music Reader Revised and Enlarged. A Progressive Course of Plain Statements of the Elementary Principles of Music and Musical Notation Together with a Graded Series of Exercises for Sight-Singing.* (Cleveland, Tenn.: James D. Vaughan, 1951. This edition is a revision of the original 1937 edition, of which G. T. Speer was also a coauthor), issued by the same publisher who supplied many of these classes with collections of hymns, all employing Aiken's system of seven shapes.[25]

At afternoon Union Sunday gatherings, devotions were followed by a "union" hymn, sung by all. After a business meeting and a collection whose proceeds were used to buy materials, subsidize the expenses of officers at conferences, and assist members with some special need, the individual groups sang hymns for one another in a mildly competitive atmosphere. As one participant noted: "They really worked hard to outdo each other. Sometimes two different classes sang the same song (claiming not to know the other class was singing the song). The second class making every effort to do it better!"[26]

Most of the classes belonged to one of two formal organizations: the Ohio, Michigan, Indiana Vocal Singing Convention, which dates from 1923, or the Ohio Incorporated Singing Union, probably formed in 1932. Sometimes individual groups hosted annual meetings to mark their own anniversaries (for example, the East End Glee Class, which gathered eight other Columbus groups in early October 1969 to mark its fifty-first birthday, or a three-day conclave at the Mount Calvary Holy Church in Columbus during March 1978 to mark the thirteenth anniversary of the Eveready Vocal Class (which attracted nineteen groups from Columbus, Cincinnati, Dayton, and Toledo), or simply to honor the recently deceased (for instance, a 1976 gathering hosted by the Unity Vocal Chorus at Zion Benevolent Baptist Church in Cincinnati for seventeen guest groups from Cincinnati, Columbus, Dayton, Springfield, and Indianapolis, the twenty-first such "Memorial Service").

The annual conventions of the formal associations were more involved affairs. For example, the Ohio Incorporated Singing Union met at the Pleasant Green Baptist

Church in Columbus for three days during August 1977. Business was conducted, reports delivered, and sermons preached, with "convention songs" performed at some sessions. However, on the final Sunday afternoon fourteen classes strutted their stuff, each group singing one selection and then returning later with another hymn.

Only remnants of this tradition remain, since many of the classes active earlier in the century have been dissolved, as has the Ohio Incorporated Singing Union. However, despite their depleted numbers, members of the Ohio, Michigan, Indiana Vocal Singing Convention have continued to gather on the fourth weekends of May and August. The 74th Annual May Day Session was convened at the Mount Period Baptist Church in Columbus on May 24 and 25, 1997, hosted by the four local groups collectively known as the Columbus Vocal Singing Union (the Christian Joyful Singers, Harmony Force, Highway Chorus, and Hosack Baptist Singers), joined by Greater New Hope, Greater New Light, and Revelation from Cincinnati, as well as two ensembles from Indianapolis and one from Detroit. As has been customary, song services intermingled with devotions, remarks by the host pastor, a business meeting, and socializing; however, the viability of the practice appears tenuous, since most of the current groups consist of only a handful of practitioners, many of them in their seventies.[27]

Auld's was not the only Ohio-born attempt at a novel and efficacious method of musical notation. In fact, an even more radical approach had been broached by the Reverend Thomas Harrison in his *Music Simplified: or A New System of Music, Founded on Natural Principles; Designed Either for Separate Use, or as an Introduction to the Old System, and Intended Chiefly for Educational and Religious Purposes: To Which Is Added a Collection of Christian Melodies.* Harrison's preface was dated November 1, 1839, from Springfield; the volume was printed concurrently there and in Cincinnati. On October 26 he had been awarded United States Patent Number 1,383 for his numeral notation system.

Harrison informed his readers that since, "[o]f those who have attended 'singing schools,' perhaps *not one in fifty* can make any sense of a new piece of music," he had thus "endeavored to forget the old system entirely, and to represent the principles of music *precisely as they exist in nature*."[28] He was later to remark in his preface to *The Juvenile Numeral Singer* of 1852 that "[n]umerals are what all are acquainted with, counting being one of the first mental acts of a child,"[29] and claimed in his initial publication that it was not his "design to introduce a *one-two-three* system, in contradistinction to the *fa-sol-la*, or *do-re-mi* systems," but rather "to inculcate the *practical study of the seven primary tones*."

An objection will probably be raised to the figures being placed on a straight line. When the author first thought of publishing an introductory work to the study of music, it was his intention to place the seven numerals on the *staff* of the old system. The thought struck him, however, that that would be but an *imaginary* rise and fall, and not *real*. He, therefore, simply placed them on a straight line; and from experience, he finds it is perfectly natural for the voice to rise from a less to a greater number, and to fall from a greater to a less.[30]

However opaque his logic (and he admitted to expecting some negative response, although, if the system was to "be the means of causing two tunes to be sung where only one has been sung before, [the author] will consider it a glorious counterbalance to all the opposition with which he may meet"), his system used Arabic numerals from 1 to 7 to define the basic pitches. "S" and "F" before a numeral stood for a sharp or flat, thus raising or lowering a pitch by a semitone. The "primary" octave was indicated between two parallel horizontal lines, with upper and lower octaves correspondingly above and below. Rhythm was created by punctuation marks: A period preceding a numeral created a "double tone" (or a half note), while a single comma under a numeral led to a "half tone" (or eighth note), multiple commas indicating further subdivisions. The conventional dotted note was represented by a horizontal line following the numeral, making it "half-lengthened"; "P" marked a "Prolong" ("After the proper beat has been given, the beating by the hand is suspended, and the sound continued, extra beats being made with the thumb"). Rests were signified by the letter "R," their length defined in the same manner as the pitches. The music was written in four parts, defined from top to bottom on the page as C (for counter, to be sung by low female voices), D (for double air, sung by high male voices), A (for air, that is, the melody, sung by high female voices), and B (for the "base, or foundation part," sung by low male voices). Harrison's "Principles of Music" in *The Juvenile Numeral Singer* run a full and terribly dense thirty-one pages. He also concerned himself with "Modes of Intonation," discriminating what he labeled an "organ tone" ("resembling that of an organ, which is begun, continued, and ended, with an equal degree of force," and was represented by a horizontal line) from an "eolian tone" ("resembling that of an eolian harp, which is commenced softly, gradually increased in force, and then gradually decreased," represented by what look suspiciously like traditional crescendo and decrescendo marks).[31]

In addition to the two collections already mentioned, Harrison published *The Sacred Harmonicon* in 1842 and *The Sacred Melodeon* four years later. He also headed the Cincinnati Numeral Music Association, giving "instructions in the more advanced parts of the science besides superintending the vocal exercises." A broadside dated August 20, 1844, and signed by five members of the Committee of Arrangements informed its readers that Harrison's system was "worthy of all confidence, and that we recommend it to all those who are desirous of acquiring a practical knowledge of

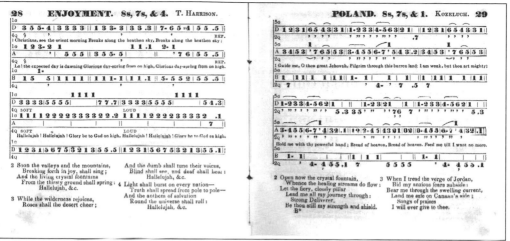

Two pages from Thomas Harrison's *The Sacred Melodeon*, 1846. Ohio Historical Society.

the science, as a system complete in itself, and of much easier acquisition, in a much shorter time, than any other we are acquainted with."[32]

This self-serving hype was premised on the use of *The Sacred Harmonicon*, but others also commented on the success of Harrison's system. A writer in *The Western Christian Advocate* of September 1841 noted,

> We, in this place, as well as hundreds more in other places, have had a practical proof of the efficiency of the system, the author having delivered twelve lessons to a senior class, and as many to a junior, by which numbers of the junior class were so far advanced as to be able to transpose keys with great facility, while several of the senior composed original pieces without violating a single rule of composition.[33]

The Ohio Historical Society's (OHS) copy of the Numeral Music Association's broadside has appended to it a handwritten minibiography of Harrison, furnishing what little is known about the man. The unidentified writer pictured Harrison as "a local preacher, a teacher of Latin and [illegible] English branches at New Carlisle, O [west of Springfield], and Moores Hill, Ind. [in the very southeastern part of the state, west of Cincinnati], and was for some time assistant editor of the Western Christian Advocate. He led the singing at the dedication of the Wesleyan Cemetery of Cincinnati in 1843."

The Ohio Historical Society's copy of *Music Simplified* has an unidentified appended newspaper clipping describing this "musical curiosity of local historical interest," then in the hands of Frank G. Bartholomew of Springfield (the OHS received the volume in 1929):

The author seems to have taught his new system in Springfield over 65 years ago. His work contains some original compositions by his pupils, W. B. Smallwood, Miss A. S. Smallwood, Miss M. H. Williamson of Springfield, Miss L. J. Nealey of New Carlisle and Miss R. Scudder, Miss J. Widney and Miss A. Kayt of Piqua. This work is written in quaint style and is of great interest.

The efforts of these youthful students were presented in an unpaginated second appendix to *Music Simplified,* preceded by a prefatory statement from their mentor dated February 1, 1840, in which he compared his system as "being to the old system what simple Arithmetic is to Algebra or Geometry." He also stated that in the three months since publication of the volume "[u]pwards of thirty new tunes have already been composed, some of which were entirely free from mistakes: they were sung, at the end of the term, in public concert." Seven of the results were presented on pages fifty-three and fifty-six. Mr. Smallwood's "Perseverance" was published by way of encouragement to the young: the "Air was composed, without a single error, by a youth only fourteen years of age."[34]

Harrison's collections include a high incidence of his own compositions, as well as pieces borrowed from a variety of sources, ranging from Drs. Arne and Arnold to Mozart, Pleyel, and other, utterly obscure Europeans, Holden's "Coronation," family members R. Harrison and P. Harrison ("Springfield"), and A. D. Fillmore.

Among those who adopted Harrison's system was Augustus Dameron Fillmore (1823–69), patriarch of a family dynasty that was to found a major publishing house and flourish as writers and practitioners of both sacred and band music. Fillmore settled in Cincinnati some time during the early 1840s after a stint as a frontier preacher in Illinois. A fairly prolific composer, he also assembled several collections, including *The Christian Psalmist* (1847), the *Temperance Musician* (1853), *The Universal Musician: A New Collection of Secular and Sacred Music Designed for Schools, Musical Associations and Social Music Parties; with a New and Comprehensive Plan of Instruction, Embracing the Various Systems of Notation* (a twelfth edition appeared in 1859), *The Nightingale* (1856), and *Fillmore's New Nightingale; or Normal School Singer: Designed for Schools, Home Circle, and Private Practice, on a Mathematically Constructed Plan of Notation* (1857), *Fillmore's Christian Choralist* (1864), and *Fillmore's Harp of Zion* (1865; compiled jointly with son James Henry).

The Christian Psalmist (compiled jointly with Silas W[hite] Leonard [1814–70]) was presented as *A Collection of Tunes and Hymns of Various Metres, Original and Selected: for the Use of the Church of God, Bible Classes, and Singing Societies. Embracing the Round Note, the Numeral, and the Patent Note Systems of Notation.* Fillmore embraced the three systems his customers might have desired, the repertory divided notationally into almost equal segments. He borrowed not only Harrison's system (acknowledging Harrison as its "inventor and patentee") but also a considerable number of pieces by both the Reverend and Mrs. Harrison. The *Psalmist*'s repertory is a true mélange, with pieces by both the compilers, Chapin, Ely, Timothy B. Mason ("We acknowledge our indebtedness to Mr. MASON for some splendid Tunes from the first and second volumes of the Sacred Harp"), Billings ("Savannah" in shape notes), and Holden ("Coronation" in numerals), plus truncated pieces from various Europeans (Mozart's "Fraternity" and Pleyel's "Germany" in numeral notation). That origin did not dictate the system in which the piece was notated is confirmed by Fillmore's "Cincinnati," presented in Harrison's numerals.

In his preface to *The Universal Musician* Fillmore explained that he had designed the volume

for everybody. The style of expression is in common plain English, so that it may be adapted to the capacities of all, instead of simply pleasing the fancy of the few, who are already thoroughly versed in science and literature. And if, on the one hand, the ear of the fastidious is a little shocked, the brown critic made to croak, and the slow professor (who spends months in imparting instruction which should be given in a few hours), is heard to complain; and on the other, if the fireside of the humble cot is made happy; the home of the industrious made joyous, and the "million" whose circumstances do not allow that years of their time should be devoted to the study of music— if they are in some degree profited by being made acquainted with the "Universal Musician," the anticipations of the author will be fully realized.

Some have already given their sentence of condemnation, because they understood that the work would not be devoted to the advocacy of one particular system of notation. To all such we would say, judge nothing before the time. An explanation of all the principal systems of notation is given, for the purpose of supplying all with such information in a single volume, without the trouble and expense of supplying themselves with a great number of books."

Consumers of the volume were then introduced to "The Guidonian, or Round Note System," the normal four-shape patent system, as well as those of Andrew Law, J. B. Aiken, and Alexander Auld, the numeral systems of Harrison (in which the book's music is couched), Day and Beall (*The Boston Numeral Harmony*, 1845), E. Pease (*The Youth's Musical Lamp*, 1854), Dutton and Hall, and a letter system of C. S. Peck. Fillmore also mentioned a system of which he had only read in the *Phonetic News*, published in London in 1845: sequentialism, devised by one W. A. Wallbridge Lynn.

In later editions of *The Universal Musician* Fillmore presented yet another approach, one he had introduced in *The New Nightingale*, a "Mathematically Constructed Plan of Notation," perhaps actually conceived by his brother, Comfort Lavius Fillmore. This plan substituted numerals for noteheads in otherwise utterly conventional notation, "1" always representing the tonic of the prevailing key. Again, as with Harrison, the conventional musician's eye is titillated reading Fillmore's "Sun, Moon, and Stars" (a solo with keyboard accompaniment), "Washington's Grave" (melody and bass line only, adorned with an engraving of the subject), the six verses of "The Indian's Farewell" (in three voices), "The Telegraph" (melody and bass only, beginning, "Along the smooth and slender wires, The sleepless heralds run, Fast as the clear and living rays, Go streaming from the sun"), or "Father Is Coming" (melody and bass, its seven verses by Mary Howitt) in *Fillmore's New Nightingale.* Son James Henry (1849–1936) added a new wrinkle in his collections from the 1870s and 1880s, such as the "Figure Note" edition of *Praise and Rejoicing* (1884), by overlaying numerals on normal oval noteheads, calling the result "combined notes."

It must be evident that notation defined the products of two warring camps—the rugged, quasi-folk idiom presented in various kinds of nontraditional notation, versus the products of the urban advocates of a "scientific," derived idiom presented in traditional garb. However, accommodation, even capitulation, can be seen in the employment of seven-syllable solmization systems, as well as in diverse anthologies encompassing everything from the works by New Englanders to folk and revival hymns, temperance songs, and abbreviated arrangements from European masters, as well as pale imitations of such by their American-born advocates. Surely one urge toward such inclusiveness was purely mercantile, an attempt to tempt as broad a clientele as possible.

Timothy Flint, only a year after his arrival in Cincinnati from New England, defined the battle lines forthrightly in *The Columbian Harmonist: In Two Parts. To Which Is Prefixed a Dissertation Upon the True Taste in Church Music,* issued in 1816. Flint's ire was provoked particularly by the fuging tune, an idiom ultimately borrowed from England but practiced with great eagerness by the New Englanders. Flint admitted in his preface,

> Young people, whose taste is yet crude and uninformed, almost universally prefer the rapid and fuging music of American composuists, to such airs as compose this selection. But, as their taste becomes more delicate, their relish more just, and their judgment better informed, much of the former class becomes cloying and insipid; and having passed through the different grades of improvement, the feelings and the ear rest with the greatest delight on tunes like York, Quercy, Old Hundred and Canterbury.[36]

In his *Dissertation* Flint deplored

> a day of innovation and experiment, [in which] young and gay men, novices in the art, and their fancies and memories stored with merry airs and marches,

leagued their exertions, and produced a memorable and very different era in church music. Innumerable composuists, scarcely versed in the first principles of psalmody, sprung up on every side. The press groaned under the burden of their ponderous productions, and of "making music books there was no end." To copy the air of a march, or a song, in the middle of the tune to have one part fall in after another, and have four divisions of the choir repeating different forms of words at the same time, and thus produce a Babel-confusion. . . .

We admit that all the music of our country has not been of this stamp. We are slow to believe that the western world cannot give birth to as much taste and genius as the eastern. Set us on the right track, give us motive and an object, and there is no degree of improvement, in any art, or science, to which our countrymen may not aspire. Wherever our masters of music have formed themselves on the sublime models of true taste, their productions have been excellent, and worthy of being retained. Unhappily, there have been but very few instances of the kind. Some prevailing fashion generally rules the age. The models of our music were almost universally faulty in the extreme. Few had the courage to emancipate themselves from the thraldom of the prevailing fashion. Flighty and fuging music became the common taste. Books of another stamp could not be sold; and all our collections of music were moulded in one form. The simple and solemn airs of the reformation were banished, and in their place we had a music, certainly not sacred, and yet we hardly dared call it profane.[37]

Flint's ponderous diatribe concluded, despite evidence to the contrary, that

A more chastened and correct taste began to prevail. . . . The slow and solemn tunes of the great masters of music of old time resumed their reign. Luther and Pleyel, and Handel, and Arne, and Arnold, and Boyce, and Madan, and Purcel [sic], once more furnished us music for our songs of praise. . . .

The population and improvement of the western country are rapidly advancing. Towns and villages, and the spires of frequent temples, we joyfully anticipate, will in a few years emerge from the wilderness, and gladden the whole region from the river to the lake. . . . Let the inhabitants strive with a laudable anxiety to bring early to their embryo institutions, both civil and sacred, correct principles, and a just taste.[38]

After this weighty pontification, it should come as no surprise that the bulk of Flint's material originated with the composers whose names he had evoked, as well as others of lesser repute. However, the informed consumer might have experienced considerable consternation in stumbling across at least a handful of works by those "composuists" of "rapid and merry airs," although none is represented by a fuging tune: Oliver Holden ("Paradise"), William Billings ("Jordan"), Timothy Swan ("Poland"), and Daniel Read ("Winter").

Furthermore, the collection was presented in conventional shape-note notation, a prime symbol of the enemy camp. Flint announced in his preface that he faced "conflicting claims of the patrons of this work," but that the

> much larger proportion, were desirous of having the patent notes. The compiler fears, with the former class, that the patent notes tend to form superficial singers. . . . The attention which is requisite in order to read music in the old way, learns the beginner the power of the notes, and the intervals of sound between one note and another. But, patent notes were in general use in this quarter; the people were attached to them: and to amend the public taste, and introduce classical music, it was thought best to pay this deference to general opinion, and to adopt them.[39]

Thus the battle lines were as clearly etched in Ohio as they had been earlier on the eastern seaboard. For example, in the 1840s one Augusta Brown thundered in Cincinnati's *Musician and Intelligencer* that

> The most mortifying feature and grand cause of the low estate of scientific music among us is the presence of common Yankee singing schools, so called. We of course can have no allusion to the educated professors of vocal music, from New England, but to the genuine Yankee singing masters, who profess to make an accomplished amateur in one month, and a regular professor of music (not in seven years, but) in one quarter, and at the expense, to the initiated person, usually one dollar. Hundreds of country idlers, too lazy or too stupid for farmers or mechanics "go to singing school for a spell," get diplomas from others scarcely better qualified than themselves, and then with their brethren, the far famed "Yankee Peddlars," itinerate to all parts of the land, to corrupt the taste and pervert the judgement of the unfortunate people who, for want of better, have to put up with them.[40]

Timothy Battelle Mason (1801–61), brother of the illustrious Lowell Mason, surely a prime example of Miss Brown's "educated professor of vocal music," arrived in Cincinnati from Boston in June 1834, intent on reforming musical taste in the west. Only months later this professor of the Eclectic Academy of Music issued *The Sacred Harp, or Eclectic Harmony: A Collection of Church Music, Consisting of a Great Variety of Psalm and Hymn Tunes, Anthems, Sacred Songs and Chants, Original and Selected; Including Many New and Beautiful Subjects From the Most Eminent Compos-*

ers, *Harmonized and Arranged Expressly for This Work* (Cincinnati, 1835). While the volume was ascribed to both brothers, surely in an attempt to capitalize on Lowell's reputation, the preface was dated September 1834 from Cincinnati. The Mason credo, in the guise of a "Publishers' Advertisement":

> The "*Sacred Harp*" was undertaken at the request of many highly respectable individuals, who have long felt the importance of the introduction of an elevated style of Sacred Music arranged on the immovable basis of science and correct taste. It has been prepared with special reference to the wants of the West, and it is believed will meet with approbation, and supply a deficiency the lovers of sacred song have long experienced, and receive such a share of patronage as it shall be found to merit
>
> It contains, in addition to the most favorite and useful tunes in common use, a great variety of new and valuable music, much of which has been procured from Europe, and has been written expressly for the Editors, and furnished in manuscript, by English and German composers. It also contains a variety of beautiful subjects from the works of Haydn, Mozart, Cherubini, Naumann, Marcell, Méhul, Hummel, Winter, Weber, Rosini [*sic*], and other celebrated authors; all of which have been arranged and harmonized *expressly for this work*, and are now for the first time published. A great number of very beautiful compositions have been taken, *by permission*, from the Handel and Haydn Society Collection; Choir or Union Collection; Lyra Sacra, and other musical publications of the senior Editor.
>
> Most of the music in this work is flowing, melodious, and tasteful in its character—of a style perfectly simple and intelligible, so as to be easily sung. Simple and natural harmony is vastly better adapted to impress the heart, and promote devotional feeling, than the most highly wrought pieces of scientific skill. The most sublime and the most pathetic are always the most simple. Sacred music should be like the gospel, which commends itself by its simplicity and sublimity, alike to the learned and unlearned.[41]

The volume contains much by Lowell Mason, but also a sprinkling of pieces by the disdained "Yankee Pedlars," including Holden's ubiquitous "Coronation" and Billings's "Jordan." Ironically, the Cincinnati "Proprietors of 'Mason's Sacred Harp' have (contrary to the express wishes and view of the authors) prepared and stereotyped an edition of the Harp of 232 pages [versus the advertised 360 pages of the round-note edition], in PATENT NOTES, under the belief that it would be more acceptable to singers in the West, and South, where patent notes are generally used."[42] Customers were advised to specify which edition they wished when ordering. Thus, as with Timothy Flint, commercial considerations led to this project being presented in a notation representing the traditions the Masons were determined to vanquish. However, the patent note version was eventually abandoned and the volume reissued with standard notation in numerous new editions until at least 1859.

It was joined by Timothy Mason's *Sacred Harp, or Beauties of Church Music. Volume II* in 1841, a collection that also enjoyed multiple editions. This "New Collection of Psalm and Hymn Tunes, Anthems, Motetts, Sentences and Chants, Derived from the Highest Sources of the Musical Talent of Europe and America, . . . Constituting a Work Probably Combining as Much Beauty and Utility as Was Ever Published," contained 120 pages of new material, including a fair number of pieces by the compiler. While some of the early editions contain no pedagogical section ("The Elements of vocal music have been omitted, because they are quite full and complete in the first volume; and it is thought that the same space occupied by music, would be more acceptable."), later issues contain as many as forty-two pages of didactic material borrowed from Volume I, perhaps to make its sequel more attractive as a free-standing item.

Mason's initial admonition:

> The teacher should first direct his attention to the location of the pupils in the school room. They should be placed at one end of the room, arranged in two divisions, males and females, separated by a narrow *aisle*, each division as compact as possible with comfort. When they are properly seated, their minds should be called to the following ELEMENTARY PRINCIPLES, which may be taught either in familiar lectures, the teacher using his own language and confining himself only to the order of arrangement here laid down, or by requiring each pupil to study the various chapters successively. Whichever method the teacher may pursue, however, he must RECAPITULATE *over and over again*, until by questions, in every possible form, he is perfectly sure that the pupils not only *remember* the explanations, but that they also *understand* the subject, and the uses of all the characters in their various forms and positions.[43]

This language aptly mirrors the pedagogical principles of the early public school music instructors, and an endorsement from the Eclectic Academy of Music's Committee on Musical Publications (commending the two volumes of *The Sacred Harp* as having been "arranged on the immovable basis of science of correct taste, as one of the very best means of introducing a pure and elevated style of Sacred Music") makes it clear that the Academy and two *Harps* were intimately linked elements in the Mason campaign.

Mason's subsequent pedagogical volumes included *Mason's Young Minstrel: A New Collection of Juvenile Songs* (Cincinnati: Truman and Smith, 1838); *The Harp: A Collection of Choice Sacred Music, Derived from the Compositions of About One Hun-*

dred Eminent German, Swiss, Italian, French, English, and Other European Musicians;
Also Original Tunes by German, English, and American Authors, Many of Them Having
Been Arranged or Composed Expressly for This Work, compiled jointly with brother
Lowell (Cincinnati: Moore, Wilstach and Baldwin, 1841); and *Mason's Juvenile Harp:*
Containing a Large Number of New and Beautiful Melodies and Hymns (Cincinnati:
William T. Truman, 1844).

Another Ohio compiler conflicted as to notation was J. J. Fast, an Evangelical
Lutheran pastor in Canton as early as 1831, who issued *The Cantica Sacra; A Collec-*
tion of Church Music, Embracing, Besides Some New Pieces, a Choice Selection of German
and English Chorals, Set Pieces, Chants, etc. in 1854. Fast asserted in his preface that

> I was long undecided whether I should use the round (or uniform) notes, or
> whether I should adopt a peculiar shape for each note of the scale. Finally I
> decided upon the latter, after being satisfied, that the shaped notes would
> meet more general approbation than the round. I have but this remark to
> add: Any one, who designs to learn the art of reading music, either with the
> shaped or the round notes, must not expect to accomplish it without much
> study and practice; and whilst the shaped notes may be of advantage to him,
> who cannot bestow the requisite attention upon the art, those, who can do
> so, will find it no more difficult to read them than the round notes.[44]

The same insight is available in the German *Vorrede* (preface), for the entire volume
is bilingual, the prose of the pedagogical section and elsewhere in parallel columns
on the same page. Fast, by the way, used a seven-shape system of his own devising,
with only four shapes identical to those of Aiken.

The volume contains a generous sampling of traditional German chorales borrowed from the *Kern des deutschen Kirchengesangs* of one Dr. F. Layriz, most of them
with texts in German only. Fast explained that this "Kernel of German Church Song"

> contains a rich treasure of Protestant Church music of the sixth and seventh
> century [a mistranslation of the German "sixteenth and seventeenth centu-
> ries"], and it therefore affords the church of the present day the opportunity
> to acquire a familiarity with the style of the Church music of our forefathers
> at the time of the Reformation.[45]

The polyglot volume also contains a generous sampling of American composers,
ranging from Daniel Read and Stephen Jenks to William Bradbury, Amzi Chapin,
Thomas Hastings, and both Masons, with a sprinkling of identifiable Europeans
like Lotti, Nägeli, Arne, Handel (the complete "Hallelujah Chorus" in shape notes),
Haydn, Mozart, and Weber. One peculiarity: Felice de Giardini's "Italian Hymn,"

which normally supports the text beginning "Come, thou almighty King," carries Samuel Smith's words beginning with "My country, 'tis of thee," an accommodation also suggested in *The United Methodist Hymnal* of 1989. Fast also included a generous sampling of Anglican chants and an Altar-Service, recognizing that congregational responses "to the prayers and recitations of the minister, which were spoken or sung before the altar, [common at the time of the Reformation, are] now again attracting the attention of the church."[46] A majority of the pieces set only German words, a few appear only in English, while the rest are bilingual. The writing is predominantly in four voices, the soprano and bass on the bottom pair of staves, alto and tenor above.

While these various pedagogues were creating weighty, even ponderous, multisectioned introductions to the rudiments of music, W. A. Williams of New Athens presented *The Science of Music in a Nutshell*, perhaps in 1840. He assumed that everything one needed "to learn to read the notes" could be reduced to both sides of a 7 x 5 inch card costing only ten cents. His all-encompassing graphic compilation of pitches, key signatures, dynamic markings, meter signatures, tempo markings, etc., and his terse, relatively no-nonsense prose stand in diametric opposition to the normal practice of the period, aptly fulfilling his promise of *Multum in Parvo*, or "Much in Brief."

A final tribute to the singing school, rendered peripheral with the advent of music instruction in the public schools: An epitaph for "The Good Old Singing School," published in *Brainard's Musical World* of March 1874 (vol. 11, no. 123):

Lost! $100 Reward!
Somewhere between 1854 and 1874 the old-fashioned singing school. Had on when last seen a striped blackboard and checkered attendance. Walks with measured pace, and is a little crotchety [crotchet = quarter note] in deportment. Leans hard on the staff, but often beats even time. Honors all notes at sight, and would not impress the public as a "swell" or "dead beat." Well versed in certain branches of hardware—as scales, keys, bars, etc. Frequents country school-houses, halls, etc. No airs to speak of.

Any person giving information as to the whereabouts of the aforesaid will greatly oblige the anxious undersigned, who will also receive the above reward for his services at the time and place agreed upon.

Pro Phundo Basso

CHAPTER 7

Public School Music

Public School Music in Cincinnati

Lowell Mason (1792–1872) settled in Boston in 1827, where he established himself as choirmaster of Dr. Lyman Beecher's Bowdoin Street Church and was elected president of the Handel and Haydn Society, although he resigned the latter position in 1832 in order to gain more time for the teaching of music to children.[1] He issued his first children's music book in 1829—*The Juvenile Psalmist, or The Child's Introduction to Sacred Music*—and capitalized on its success with *The Juvenile Lyre, Hymns and Songs, Religious, Moral and Cheerful for Use of Primary and Common Schools* in 1831. Two years later, in association with other local musicians, Mason founded the Boston Academy of Music, dedicated to employing the educational principles of the Swiss theorist Johann Heinrich Pestalozzi (1746–1827). The academy was an instant hit, offering free instruction to as many as fifteen hundred children and adults in its first year, two hundred more the following year.

One of Mason's goals was "the introduction of vocal music, as an ordinary branch of study, into common schools—not only those under private patronage, but public schools generally as an important object to be aimed at in its labors."[2] In 1836, prodded by various petitions, the Boston School Committee appointed a special panel to study the possibility of introducing vocal instruction into the curriculum. Having investigated the work of the academy and queried the principals of five private schools already offering music instruction, the panel in August 1837 recommended that for reasons intellectual, moral, and physical, vocal music should be introduced on an experimental basis in four schools under the supervision of the academy staff. The report was approved in September, but the city's common council refused to fund the program. Mason returned from Europe the following month after a period of imbibing Pestalozzian principles and volunteered to teach gratis at a single school in South Boston. Several observers expressed satisfaction with Mason's work, and an August 14, 1838, exhibition concert with his young charges convinced the school committee that music should be formally introduced to the curriculum, the first such example in this country.[3] A motion of August 28 led to Lowell Mason's appointment as superintendent of music, also a first. He was authorized to hire assistants, and by 1844 he was personally teaching in six schools and supervising ten assistants serving an equal number of schools.

That this pattern was replicated in Cincinnati[4] should come as no surprise, since the catalytic figure was Lowell's younger brother, Timothy. The Eclectic Academy of Music was organized in the spring of 1834, only a year after its spiritual parent in Boston:

> A society has been formed . . . at Cincinnati, with two objects in view; first to promote the introduction of *vocal music as a branch of school education*, throughout this country; second to promote improvement in church music. . . . The Trustees express their conviction, founded on the entire success of the plan abroad, and the happy results of the experiments in Boston and Philadelphia, that it is *practible* to make it a branch of *common school education*. They hope to convince the public of its importance, and eventually to secure the proper instruction of teachers in this art. . . . We cordially hail every kindred institution; and hope that music thus early implanted, may become one of the rational recreations of the rising West.[5]

An April 16 announcement in the *Cincinnati Daily Gazette* stated:

> Timothy B. Mason, Esq. of Boston (brother to Lowell Mason, President of the Boston Academy of Music) has been elected Professor in the academy, and has accepted the appointment. Mr. M. is a competent musician, and a gentleman with whom the instruction of children in this highly important branch of education, may be entrusted with the utmost confidence. His arrival in this city is expected daily, when friends of education will be afforded an opportunity to bestow upon the institution, the patronage and countenance it may deserve.

Mason finally arrived in June and held his first classes—"strictly elementary and conducted upon the Pestalozzian system"—in the Second Presbyterian Church. The location was certainly not by happenstance, since the Second Presbyterian pulpit was occupied by Lyman Beecher, enticed to the Queen City in 1832 to become president of the relatively new Lane Seminary.[6]

Imagine then, what must have been the feelings of the elder Dr. Beecher, . . . [pastor] where L. Mason presided at one of the best organs in the country, assisted by the best-trained, and, perhaps the most effective choir in America at that time. In addition to this, the doctor was a great lover of music, besides considering it an essential aid in the promotion of religion.

He could not endure that this part of worship should be thus neglected and marred. He soon sent to his friends in Boston, saying, "Come over the mountains and help us;" or (to use the language of Billings) our "nerves will be rent asunder" with discordant, unmeaning singing in church.

The voice was heard and heeded; and Mr. T. B. Mason, brother of the professor, was selected as the man to supply the place. He was received with joy by those who knew how to appreciate good music; and he soon commenced his labors, assisted by the influence and action of many of the principal characters of the city.[7]

Another catalytic organization in the process of establishing public school music in Cincinnati was the Western Literary Institute and College of Professional Teachers, a group of educators from as many as fifteen western and southern states and territories. Dating from 1829, although a constitution was not formally adopted until October 3, 1832, as many as fifteen hundred members gathered for about four days each October, mostly in Cincinnati. Local pedagogue William Nixon addressed the fourth such gathering on October 10, 1834, presenting an "Address on the History and Moral Influence of Music." One relevant passage:

Did time permit, I should dwell on the importance of making *pure taste* the first object, where music is brought into the general schools; since it is obvious, to those who understand the subject, that a very good attempt at *reading* music might be made by such as could make but a very poor nasal attempt at singing it; and equally obvious to all, that a smattering of rules, and book discipline can be obtained and taught, by those who have had no opportunity of devoting their attention to good models of musical taste. And if children be so instructed, we may predict, without any gift of prophecy, that instead of the present taste being improved, it will only become more generally confirmed in the corruption it should endeavor to remove.[8]

Three years later, the seventh annual meeting heard two reports that had a major impact. Calvin E. Stowe, professor of biblical literature at Lane Seminary, had traveled in Europe during 1836, studying various school systems.[9] His "Report on the Course of Instruction in the Common Schools of Prussia and Wirtemberg [sic]" included the assertion:

The method of teaching music has already been successfully introduced into our own state, and whoever visits the schools of Messrs. Mason or Solomon, in Cincinnati, will have a much better idea of what it is than any description can give; nor will anyone who visits these schools entertain a doubt that all children from six to ten years of age, who are capable of learning to read, are capable of learning to sing, and that this branch of instruction can be introduced into all our common schools with the greatest advantage, not only to the comfort and discipline of the pupils, but also to their progress in their other studies.

He also informed his listeners that he had asked various teachers whether they encountered children who were incapable of learning to sing or draw:

> I have had but one reply, and that was, that they found the same diversity of natural talent in regard to these as in regard to reading, writing, and the other branches of education; but they had never seen a child who was capable of learning to read and write, who could not be taught to sing well and draw neatly, and that too without taking any time which would at all interfere with, indeed which would not actually promote his progress in other studies.[10]

Stowe had also been commissioned by the Ohio General Assembly to study current European practices and describe anything that could prove useful in improving the condition of public education in the state. He delivered his message to that body, which then authorized the printing of ten thousand copies of his *Report on Elementary Public Instruction in Europe.* These were distributed to every school district in the state, and the document was reprinted by the legislatures of Massachusetts, Michigan, North Carolina, Pennsylvania, and Virginia.[11]

Among those who received Stowe's report to the thirty-sixth General Assembly was Caleb Atwater (1778–1867), a member of the House of Representatives since 1821.[12] Atwater, an alumnus of Williams College in his native Massachusetts, after a multifaceted career in the East had settled in Circleville in 1815, where he practiced law and became the local postmaster in 1817. A passionate advocate of an adequate system of public education in his adopted state, Atwater chaired the commission that prepared the bill of 1825 setting aside lands for public schools, mandating the creation of school boards, and creating a system of taxation in support of education.

In 1838 he published *A History of the State of Ohio, Natural and Civil,* the first such study, which included a description of the Western Literary Institute, demonstrating his awareness of the influence of Nixon, Stowe, and others.[13] Three years later he issued *An Essay on Education* (of 123 pages), which in passing vigorously argued the case for music education in the public schools, including the assertion that "every teacher should understand vocal music well and be able to teach that branch of learning."[14] Atwater stated several times that the practice of vocal music could have a "re-animating" impact on the physical health of well-rounded children, for example, by strengthening their lungs. He evoked the Germans as an object example, reasoning that they were "so seldom afflicted with pulmonary complaints," due "in a measure, to their study and practice of vocal music; these being universal, prove a universal antidote, among that people, to that appalling disease," and added:

> If education be the development of all the powers of our bodies and all the faculties of our minds, musical powers being one of them, they must be improved and developed, by studying its theory and practising on its principles. Are there any powers or faculties given to us in vain? We say no. Then we should all learn and practice vocal music in early life.[15]

In fact, he attributed enormous power to music, extending far beyond its use as "a relaxation from severer studies, and as an innocent and elegant amusement," since

> it rises in dignity still higher, when we consider its benevolent effects on the mind, the heart and soul of man. It softens care, enlivens mirth, lulls the angry passions into rest, awakens all our sympathies towards those who suffer pain, either physical, mental, or moral, and it turns into harmony and love every discordant feeling. It can ennoble, dignify, and exalt into ecstasy, almost divine, all our moral feelings. It can raise all our desires from earth to heaven, and transport us, in all our feelings, so that our souls can join that high, holy, happy, and innumerable throng of saints and angels, who, with their golden harps and heavenly voices, continually sing the praises of God and of the Lamb, that was slain for us.[16]

Having decisively demonstrated utter lack of modern concern for separation of church and state, Atwater fussed about songs that were "immoral and of wicked tendency" that "will be pressed into the service of the devil." After all, "[w]hat mighty armies have rushed on death, and crimsoned the earth with human blood, moved by martial music?"[17]

However, he also suggested, as did other contemporaries, that music had the utilitarian capacity to focus the wandering attention of school children through his description of daily life at the German Immigrant Friend's Society School in Cincinnati, a privately supported institution that enrolled some two hundred children. Mr. Salomon, its principal, mandated that each day began and concluded with the singing of a verse or two of a hymn, followed by recitation of the Lord's Prayer. Then,

[a]ll the scholars stand up, the teacher pointing with the long staff to the gammut [*sic*], or notes of music, plainly printed on the ceiling or a board, which is in full view of every scholar. There also are several full tunes printed on the same board. The teacher sounds the proper note, at which he points, and every pupil follows the instructer [*sic*], singing through the eight notes backwards and forwards, until he strikes off into some tune, which is sung, first by note, then by the words set to it. This exercise having occupied but a few minutes, in the morning, the pupils all go to their several studies, but as soon as the teacher discovers that listlessness and languor prevail, calling them off from their several pursuits, he rises, and his staff points to the gammut board again. All the pupils arise at once upon their feet. The eight notes are sung, and soon two hundred voices are heard, singing with cheerfulness, life and glee—"Germany, sweet Germany," or some other song, that re-animates every soul, crimsons every cheek, and lights up every little sparkling eye in the school-room.[18]

Atwater also observed,

One defect in mental education exists, in passing through studies without thoroughly fixing in the mind all the important ideas belonging to such studies. One wretched pretender follows another, over our country, offering to teach writing, reading, arithmetic, book-keeping and grammar in a few lessons! Even those teachers who are in some sort located among us, teach their scholars, like parrots, to repeat answers to a number of questions. The end of the term arrives; the questions are asked; the pupil, parrot-like, answers them; medals and ribbons are distributed; a display is made; the parents are enraptured; the pupil's vanity is flattered; but, in one short month's space, all the knowledge acquired at school is gone, and gone forever.[19]

Those gathered in 1837 for the Western Literary Institute also heard a "Report on Vocal Music, as a Branch of Common School Education," prepared by Timothy Mason and Charles Beecher, son of the preacher, who had as a committee of two labored over the project for a year.[20]

Their motivation was "the question [that] is daily assuming more importance in the minds of thinking men, 'Ought not music to receive a place among the regular studies of our common schools.'" The response to that overarching query was for them yet another question: "Can all men [*sic*] learn to sing?" They assumed three necessary conditions: the powers "to understand the characters used in written music," "to appreciate the distinctions of musical sounds," and the possession "of vocal organs requisite for the production of a given compass of sounds." They reasoned that any child conversant with the alphabet could master musical notation, since "*The power of learning the shape, name, and uses of one set of characters, is the power of learning the same of any, or of all characters.*" They then assumed that the users of spoken language, particularly poetry, could discriminate loud or soft, long or short, high or low sounds, making it "evident, therefore, that they possess the constitutional adaptation for discriminating them" in the study of music also. And "[s]ince in all men, the vocal machinery is the same—since in conversation we have shown men do, by inflexions [sic], pass through all the requisite compass of sounds, and which require only to be separately dwelt on, to constitute singing,—it cannot be doubted, that they have the organic power of uttering the same sounds in the prescribed manner." Assuming that they had convinced their listeners that all possessed "the constitutional endowments requisite for the study of vocal music," they admitted that

> there will be differences in degree of talent, on this, as on all subjects. Neither must every man expect, that because he can learn to sing, that, therefore, he can be a Mozart, Haydn, or Rossini. All men are qualified to study arithmetic, algebra, and geometry; but not every man can be a Euclid, a La Place, or a Newton.[21]

To investigate the "expediency of the introduction of vocal music" in the common school curriculum, they decided to inquire as to its physical, intellectual, and moral effects on children.

They assumed that all were "aware of the deleterious effects upon the young, of long continued confinement, and silent application to study. . . . [T]hat whatever over-wearies the mind, and exhausts its powers, injures the brain, and through it, entails upon the entire physical system, a catalogue of ills." Therefore,

> [w]hen in the school-room, the minutes drag heavily by; the minds of the scholars begin to weary and flag; spirits droop, and confinement becomes irksome, and study a pain;—let the teacher strike the strain of some well-known juvenile song. How electric the instantaneous flash of renovated life in every bosom! The physical system is awake; casts off its drowsiness; the mental powers, before over-taxed, rest, and give place to the musical faculties; and when the half hour is over, the school is as fresh, and as well prepared for study as at morn.[22]

They argued that studies in music required considerable mental discipline,

> beneficial in this respect, exactly in proportion as they require close attention, abstraction, and discriminating analysis. In respect to the degree in which the education of the musical faculties demands these three things, we can say, with

certainty, not only that it is not a whit less than is required for arithmetic, geography, etc., but that these last studies are far inferior to music. We know of no study, not even the mathematics, more beautifully systematic in its analysis, or requiring more vivid energizing of intellect in its attainment.[23]

Intrepid and apparently oblivious of any offense they might have proffered colleagues in other disciplines, they tackled the matter of moral education broadside:

Look through our land, and ask what has been hitherto the moral influence of our public schools, academies, and colleges, particularly in the larger cities. Let those who know the deep penetralia of college dissipation, say! Let those declare, who know the withering blight of a promiscuous public school of boys, fastening upon aught pure coming into its midst, with the scorching influence of the blast of the desert! Do we not know these things? Have not our eyes seen them? And have not teachers, in despair, lamented the evils which were utterly beyond their powers to resist or counteract?[24]

They then evoked authority figures of the stature of Plato and Martin Luther to solidify their thesis that "the study of music does refine and ennoble," that it "teaches obedience, and habits of order and discipline."

In another argument they asserted,

Without discipline as rigid as the military drill, no class can become proficient in music. They must all concentrate thought and action into simultaneous obedience to the word of command of their instructer [*sic*]. . . . Now in this land of republicanism, we are in no danger of too much subordination, or rigid discipline, either in school or out. It might possibly be highly beneficial, if the reins could be drawn upon us a little tighter. Certainly they ought upon the young, whose greatest danger is, that untrammelled freedom will become unbridled licentiousness.[25]

The authors assumed that proper pedagogy

requires in the teacher, not only the perfections he [*sic*] would communicate, so that he himself may be to the eye of his pupils a living and ever present model of his teachings,—but it requires talents of winning affection, engaging confidence, and in a word, power of fascinating the whole being of his pupils.[26]

What more efficacious way of achieving these goals than through the use of music, since:

What can so charm the young as music? What is there, that all children every where [*sic*] love so passionately? feel such noble ardor in acquiring? engage in with more unwearied perseverance and more rapid progress? What that gives more to one individual, of a power over the entire being and sympathies of many young hearts, almost magical?[27]

How to achieve this pedagogical paradise, given the diversity and conditions of common schools of that era and the lack of trained teachers, as well as any sense of either "a refined national taste" or a "national music"? They assumed that qualified teachers, armed with appropriate materials, could override the other deficiencies, and asked that teachers "be convinced of their ability to qualify themselves." Then,

> if ever the period arrive, when in any way, either by national or by state legislation, or by public convention, a system of universal education can be framed, which as a second constitution shall embrace our whole land, to guard and rear its destinies to good; then let us be assured that MUSIC—DIVINE MUSIC will stand high, very high, in the scale of importance in that system.[28]

Mason and Beecher based their prognostication on the success of the twenty-three graduates of the Boston Academy of Music who had fanned out across the country to parts as distant from Boston as South Carolina and practiced their profession with success. They also mentioned, "We are aware of two teachers of public schools [in Cincinnati], who have been successful in introducing the study [of music] into their schools, with gratifying results, merely by having attended two courses of lessons of the Eclectic Academy, and by studying to keep in advance of their pupils."[29] In other words, Timothy Mason had already provided the Cincinnati school system with two teachers who had retooled and were offering formal instruction in music to school children in the Queen City a year before such study was available in Boston.

Virtually no information survives detailing Mason's specific pedagogy at the academy, although on April 15, 1835, in the Second Presbyterian Church he presided over a "Juvenile Concert; by the Second and Third Classes of the Eclectic Academy of Music," which apparently consisted of didactic songs demonstrating the children's proficiency with solfege syllables and scales. A ceremony commemorating the fiftieth anniversary of the founding of the city, held on December 26, 1838, in the First Presbyterian Church, included contributions by both "Professor Timothy B. Mason's Eclectic Choir and the Buckeye Band." Anecdotal evidence also suggests that Mason may actually have worked in the public schools in 1837 and 1838, including a public performance.

However, the pair of Eclectic Academy graduates cannot be identified. The annual report for the year ending June 30, 1838, merely mentioned that music has been taught and practiced in several of the Schools—not by any request of the Board of Trustees, but as a means of rational amusement. A majority of the Board think that the pupils have not only made proficiency in acquiring a knowledge of this science, but that it has been a useful auxiliary in the promotion of good order where it has been introduced.[30]

When the College of Professional Teachers convened again in October 1838, "several select pieces were sung by a large number of pupils of the Common Schools, led by Mr. Mason."[31] However, music did not immediately become a regular branch of instruction, but for several years was offered at the discretion of the regular teacher, with voluntary participation by the students.

William F. Colburn was apparently a student of Lowell Mason during the 1838 convention in Boston and had been teaching in Louisville before his appearance in Cincinnati during the early 1840s. The report for the school year ending June 30, 1844, concluded,

> During the past year, Mr. W. F. Colburn, an efficient instructor in Music, has given gratuitous lessons to a large number of pupils of most of the Public Schools. The result has been in every respect, satisfactory, and has, in some measure been the means of inducing the Board, as well as the public to come to the conclusion, that Music ought to be introduced into the Schools, as a regular branch of instruction.
>
> In whatever light we view it, whether as a means of social enjoyment, or moral influence, or intellectual improvement, [music] seems to have a happy effect upon the pupils. The Board have accordingly appointed a committee to report a place, by which, hereafter, music may be regularly taught . . . and we trust that our successors may enjoy the privilege of adopting a plan by which music may be regularly taught to all the youth in our schools whose parents desire it.[32]

In fact, a special committee of the board had on June 3 issued a ringing clarion call:

> Let taste and skill in this beautiful art be diffused throughout our public schools, and every family will have a new resource of pleasure, every home a new attraction. Social intercourse will be more pleasant and cheerful, and an innocent and unfailing source of amusement will be rendered accessible alike to the humblest and wealthiest members of society. A wise and benevolent Creator has placed unbounded stores of enjoyment within the reach of all, by surrounding us with an atmosphere which can be the means of producing sweet sounds capable of being combined in an endless variety, and of

being made to minister in the highest degree to a refined moral and intellectual taste. Then shall not the guardians of public instruction in this city permit all the youth to have access to this fountain of pleasure[?][33]

Activation of the fountain was entrusted to two teachers of vocal music: Colburn, at a salary of forty-five dollars per month (identical to that of school principals of the day), and Mrs. Elizabeth K. Thatcher, paid only twelve dollars a month (three dollars less than that of full-time female teachers at the bottom of the salary scale). This pair began their labors on August 12, 1844; Thatcher taught until June 1846, Colburn until February 1848. The disparity in compensation was not based on gender; Colburn worked in seven district schools, three Anglo-German schools, and the orphan asylum, meeting his charges twice a week for forty-five minutes, while Thatcher was assigned to only three schools, where she ministered twice a week for an hour, later reduced by fifteen minutes. These specialists were transients, whose work was supplemented in the lower grades by regular classroom teachers who offered whatever instruction they were capable of.

Thatcher was succeeded by Elisha Locke and Solon Nourse, appointed in July 1846. Both had apparently been associated with Lowell Mason in Boston prior to their appearance in Cincinnati during 1845. Locke joined the staff of the new Central School, the city's first high school, in November 1847, and after he was succeeded in that position by Charles Aiken in 1850 taught in other schools until 1866; Nourse resigned in 1850.

Their predecessors had employed as texts William B. Bradbury's *The School Singer, or Young Choir's Companion* (1841) and Timothy B. Mason's *Juvenile Harp* (1846). Locke and Nourse, however, produced *The School Vocalist, Containing a Thorough System of Elementary Instruction in Vocal Music, with Practical Exercises, Songs, Hymns, Chants &c., Adapted to the Use of Schools and Academics.* The authors presented the volume to their board of trustees during the fall of 1848; it was adopted for use in the system in March of the following year. The twenty-page pedagogical section contains a discussion of the nature of sound, music theory (including scale degrees couched in both numbers and syllables), voice ranges, and the nature of singing, all copiously interlarded with questions designed to test the students' comprehension of the material. Thirteen pages of exercises are followed by sixty-seven songs, eight rounds, eighteen hymns, and three church chants. The majority is in three parts, although in some cases the part defined by the bass clef is obviously meant as an instrumental line. The preface announced that the volume "contains a choice selection of songs from German, English, and American authors. Much of the poetry has been written expressly for this work." Among the Americans were Nourse ("The Snowflakes Are Merrily Flying," "A Dirge for the Beautiful," "The Spring Time," and "Be Kind to Each Other!") and Locke ("Song of Freedom," "Summer Night," "The Streamlet," and "The Picnic"). The duo also published *The School Melodist: A Songbook for School and Home* in 1854. This eclectic collection, some of it again by the compilers, was adopted for use in the intermediate schools the following year.

Accountability was dictated by the board of trustees to these pioneer educators with enormous specificity. For example, early in 1856 the board adopted a "Classification and Course of Study in Music," which mandated that what we would call third-graders were to learn "the staff, cleffs [*sic*], letters, bars, measures, methods of reading from the lines and spaces, and scales. Pupils in this class must be able to name the letters from F below the staff to C above the staff." These micromanagers also demanded that fourth-graders learn transpositions, dynamics, and accents, while those in what we would call the sixth grade were to be taught minor and chromatic scales.[34]

The most crucial figure during this formative period was Charles Aiken (1818–83), an 1838 graduate of Dartmouth College, who settled in Cincinnati in 1839 only to journey almost immediately to St. Louis, where he spent three years directing the choir of the Second Presbyterian Church. He returned to the Queen City in 1842 and graduated from the Lane Seminary five years later, addressing his fellow students that June 9 on "Music as Adapted to Devotion." He taught singing schools in the basement of the Sixth Presbyterian Church, thus serving as mentor to Colburn, whom he then succeeded. He also taught Latin and Greek at Herron's Academy, a responsibility he retained after his first five years as a half-time public school teacher. He had served as a coexaminer at the semiannual examinations in 1848, replaced Locke at the Central School in 1850, and one year later was appointed to the faculties of the new Hughes and Woodward High Schools, where he remained until 1878, one year before his retirement because of ill health. When the office of music superintendent was created in 1871, Aiken was the first to fill it. Prior to that appointment, he had overseen the preparation of the five hundred to six hundred intermediate and high school students who participated in a benefit concert for the public library at Pike's Opera House with Carl Barus and the Philharmonic Society, so successful that a second performance was arranged to satisfy those turned away, an event repeated the following year. Eight hundred children then sang another benefit at Mozart Hall on December 26, 1863, as part of the Great Western Sanitary Fair, and some one thousand performed at the dedication of the Tyler-Davidson Fountain in 1871. Aiken also prepared large choruses of Cincinnati school children for the first two May Festivals in 1873 and 1875, initiating a practice that has persisted to the present.[35]

Many decades later Aiken's son recalled that initial festival, which involved a total of twelve hundred youngsters:

First came the choir of eight hundred voices of the Intermediate schools singing in three parts, unaccompanied by instruments and with overpowering volume. The theme was passed over to four hundred basses and tenors of the high schools and then given forth by the combined forces of the different choirs. It was all over in two or three minutes but away down on the stage musicians were wiping their eyes, some had risen to their feet. A feeling of awe had come over them. Tremendous applause greeted this childish effort. They had won recognition in the great world of Music. And how did this all happen a half century ago? It came about in this wise. There were teaching in our schools, men and women who . . . understood the art of stimulating children so that they delighted in the exercise of real power. Their text books were not constructed just to please the young learner, but to make the child pleased with his own labor in the soul-trying effort to learn.[36]

Other similar ventures included concerts to raise money for extensions to Music Hall in 1878 and various expositions, including the opening of the Cincinnati Industrial Exposition in 1879 in the Music Hall before Generals Sherman and Sheridan, as well as President Rutherford Hayes, who, according to the official report of the board of commissioners, "led the well-merited applause by a healthy clapping of his honest ungloved hands."

During Charles Aiken's eight-year tenure,

the study of music, even technically, [was extended] through all the grades of the public schools, not even the primary being excluded; the requirement of a general knowledge of music and ability to impart elementary instructions in the same upon the part of all candidates for teachers' positions in the schools; and the establishment of annual and semi-annual examinations, for testing the practical character of the work of both pupils and teachers. These examinations were personally superintended and conducted by Professor Aiken; and the results thereat obtained of clever work done, even by teachers outside the corps of music masters, and the facility exhibited by pupils of all grades in reading exercises at first sight were so remarkable, as to compel the notice and praise of school officials in many other and older quarters.[37]

The charts of exercises prepared by Aiken from which students sang at sight during oral examinations held in December and June of each year furnished the core of exhibits prepared by the Cincinnati school system for expositions at Philadelphia in 1876 and Paris two years later, both of which attracted widespread attention and a pair of medals in Paris. The advanced approach to music theory and the demanding vocal exercises contained in the publications about to be described suggest a level of music literacy approaching what would be considered collegiate today.[38]

Despite his emphasis on theory and sight singing, Aiken was also concerned with what he termed "tasteful expression" and vocal culture. The annual report for the 1871–72 school year observed that Aiken was

> endeavoring to correct the one fault that has hitherto characterized the singing of our schools, particularly in the lower grades—the overstraining of the voice by too loud singing. Much has already been done in this direction, and we may confidently expect that through his exertions the evil will entirely disappear within a short space of time.[39]

Aiken must have been an effective teacher, because a year later the general superintendent observed that "the quality of the singing voice of the pupils was greatly improved, the piercing, harsh tones having been to a great extent discarded. Good progress was also made in general expression and in the enunciation of the words of the songs."[40]

Aiken was also vital in the preparation of several textbooks prepared for use in the Cincinnati system. *The Young Singer: A Collection of Juvenile Music, Compiled (at the Request of the Board of Trustees) for the Cincinnati Public Schools, by Messrs.* [Luther Whiting] *Mason,* [D. H.] *Baldwin, Locke and Aiken, Teachers of Music in Those Schools* was issued in 1860. Part 1, designed for the primary schools, emphasized the rote learning of simple songs in two or three voice parts as a means of musical understanding:

> The following Songs, designed for the youngest class of pupils, are taught by rote. The manner in which this is done is deemed a matter of great importance.
>
> The utmost care should be taken from the first attempt at singing, to avoid bad habits. Let the pupils be taught to regard a noisy, heedless or careless manner of singing in the schoolroom, as they would rude or disorderly conduct.
>
> While the children are learning these and similar songs by rote, they may also be taught by imitation to sing the scale and short musical phrases, designed to enable them to distinguish between high and low, long and short, soft and loud tones, and thus lay the foundation for future instructions.[41]

Actually, the students were introduced by diagrams to the staff, clefs, scales, intervals, and so forth, preceding twenty-seven pages of "Practical Exercises in Reading Music" in various keys. An appendix contained German words for many of the songs, rounds, and hymns by Locke and Nourse, as well as by Europeans ranging from Tallis, Mozart, Haydn, Beethoven, and Weber to others with names like Glaser, Hurlbut, and Nathersius.

Part 2, intended for the intermediate schools, contains an elaborate pedagogical section dealing with the elements of music (extending as far as descriptions of ornaments like the trill and turn). This is followed by sixteen pages of exercises, including canons at various intervals. The songs are mostly in three-part arrangements (soprano, alto, and baritone), drawn primarily from European composers ranging from Handel, Haydn, Mozart, Beethoven, and Schubert, to Boieldieu, Méhul, Bellini, and Verdi, and also both Locke and Nourse. Again, reflecting Cincinnati's bilingualism of the period, "Selections also from the German, with original words at the end of the volume, will, it is believed, prove acceptable to a large class of singers."

In 1866 the board authorized preparation of *The Young Singer's Manual* by Aiken, Alfred Squire, J. P. Powell, and Victor Williams, a volume used until 1882. The *Manual's* introduction to the rudiments was followed by two-part exercises in various major keys, while the second part of the volume contains "solfeggios" and songs in three and four parts." Aimed at "the higher classes of Graded Schools, where Music is regularly taught," its consumers were cautioned,

> As the reading of music, at sight, is an art which can be accomplished only through diligence, all should "hasten slowly" in their elementary studies, especially in the solfeggios in *two parts*, where a practical knowledge of the time-table and of harmony is requisite. If these exercises be thoroughly mastered, each part separately, the accompanying songs, in *two* or *three parts*, which have been selected from [Friedrich] Silcher, [Guillaume-Louis] Wilhelm, [John Pyke] Hullah, Rossini, and others, will afford delightful recreation.[42]

Although his name was not formally attached to either volume (since he was "not worthy of sitting at the table of contents with Handel, Haydn, and Mozart"), Aiken also published two anthologies of choruses for use in high school classes: *The High School Choralist* in 1866 and *The Choralist's Companion* in 1872. Both contained glees, anthems, and choruses from the standard operas, oratorios, and masses by the predictable European composers intended for use at festivals, conventions, and graduation ceremonies.

With all these accomplishments,[43] it should come as no surprise that a substantial marble bust was commissioned from Preston Flowers of Florence, Italy, and installed in the vestibule of Music Hall a year after Aiken's death.[44] In his dedicatory address, Noble K. Royse, after likening the hall to a shrine—music's "consecrated Temple"—asserted that "it is eminently proper, then, that in the vestibule of this temple we should be tangibly reminded of one, who, in his day, rendered signal service before the high altar—who himself did much toward suitably preparing the minds and hearts of many now ministering there, and who aided largely in attuning the ears of the vast auditory to the appreciation of the splendid service."[45]

Of course, there were bumps on the road Aiken traveled. For example, after a thorough study of the music program, a report included in the April 25, 1859, minutes of the board of trustees and visitors of common schools noted,

> It is with very great pleasure that the Committee can speak of the improvement observable in the character of the Music now sung in our Schools, as compared with that which, a few years since, greeted the ears of the listeners. Formerly, at the opening of the Schools, the reading of the Scriptures, in which, perhaps, was depicted the Christian life, was followed by the Negro melody "Jordan Is A Hard Road to Travel;" or it may be, an interesting biography from the Bible was succeeded by "Old Dan Tucker;" or when the duty of all to "watch" was inculcated, the children would be called upon to sing "Old Dog Tray's Ever Faithful." Now we can hear God's word read and succeeded by the solemn Chant, beautifully rendered, or an appropriate hymn adapted to the very best music. In years not long gone by, to pass one of our School Houses during a singing exercise one could readily imagine himself in the vicinity of Bedlam, such was the racket, "confusion of Tongues" and roaring of voices. To be inside the Building at such a time as this, was a matter of pain instead of pleasure. Those days have happily departed. One may now listen to music from the best composers, sung with sweetness and taste, the words beautifully and distinctly enunciated, the time perfectly kept, and altogether rendered in such a manner as to produce the most pleasureable emotions.[46]

Smug about the purification of the musical literature practiced by Cincinnati school children, the committee members did note that the music specialists had not received full cooperation from all the classroom teachers, with a corresponding lack of accomplishment. They called for the creation of texts that would allow uniformity of instruction throughout the system, resulting in *The Young Singer*, but were rebuffed when they sought mandatory daily music instruction, although such a regimen was introduced in grades D and C the following year.

Several of Aiken's colleagues deserve at least passing notice. *The Young Singer* introduced us to yet another transplanted Mason. Luther Whiting Mason (1818–96), perhaps a distant relative of Lowell, at least studied with the patriarch. He had been teaching in the public schools of Louisville for three years before accepting a position in Cincinnati in 1856. Before departing during October 1864 to become Instructor of Music in the primary schools of Boston (leading eventually to an international reputation), he achieved what one journalist termed "astonishing" success teaching primary students in the Queen City. He became an advocate of the methodology of Christian Heinrich Hohmann (1811–61) and borrowed exercises and songs from the works of that German pedagogue. These were integrated into *The Young Singer*, while Mason employed Hohmann's *Practical Course in Singing* in his teaching, and then prepared "Music Charts" derived from Hohmann publications for use in the D, E, and F grades.[47] This Mason must have had a bit of showbiz in his blood, for on June 8, 1860, he directed a "Grand Floral Concert and Mythological Exhibition" in Pike's Opera House featuring five hundred performers, a garden with functioning fountains, and the coronation of a "Queen of the Day." If an account in the *Cincinnati Daily Gazette* of June 27, 1856, can be believed, his popularity must have been almost instantaneous, for his pupils in the Second District School gave him a rocking chair only six months after he had arrived in town, since "[t]his active and excellent teacher was never seen to sit down while teaching and his pupils wished him to enjoy a little rest, in an easy chair, during the vacation."[48]

Pennsylvania-born D[wight] H[amilton] Baldwin (1821–99) attended the preparatory department of Oberlin College before serving as a singing school teacher in Kentucky and then in Ripley, upriver from Cincinnati. Baldwin was first hired on a part-time basis in August 1857 and elevated to full-time status the following June. He collaborated with Mason in preparing the "Elements" section of the first part of *The Young Singer* and also wrote some songs for the publication. He resigned in spring 1864 and became a dealer in pianos and organs and the eventual founder of the Baldwin Piano Company.

The dominant figure during the final two decades of the century was German-born G[ustavus] F[rederick] Junkermann (1830–1906). After early training in his native land, he seems to have arrived in Cincinnati in 1849, a refugee from the revolutionary upheavals of that period. Various accounts suggest that he first worked in a tannery and as a bricklayer and played in theater ensembles as well as for dances and parties. While seeking teacher certification, he taught German, drawing, and arithmetic, served as a clerk in a homeopathic pharmacy, and as a bookkeeper for the city's first homeopathic physicians,[49] and led the choir in a Jewish temple. He accepted his first teaching position in 1855 and subsequently was appointed principal of schools in nearby Corryville and Camp Washington, teaching music concurrently, "although not engaged to do so, and says [now] that he would not now teach, or act as Principal of any school where music is not in the curriculum, because of its wholesome influence over the mind and physique of the children."[50] Other accounts suggest that Junkermann continued to play in theater orchestras after becoming a teacher, and during an interim period lived in St. Louis, Memphis, and New Orleans, where he served as a cellist in the opera orchestra, returning to Cincinnati during 1872.[51]

He joined the Cincinnati system on a temporary basis in April of that year, became a permanent member of the staff in 1873, succeeded Aiken at the Hughes and Woodward high schools in 1878, and then followed Aiken as superintendent a year later, a position he held until June 1900. Hardly an innovator, Junkermann continued to stress acquisition of the rudiments of music (and regular written examinations of such) and the ability to sing at sight with ease; the school children of Cincinnati during his reign constantly impressed listeners with their facility in various venues, such as the May Festivals, Sängerfests, expositions, and other public ceremonies.

Junkermann cannot be credited with creation of *The Cincinnati Music Readers,* a series that attracted national attention, since the first edition had been issued in 1875 at the suggestion of Charles Aiken. However, he wished to have available volumes appropriate for the various age levels of his students, so the board of trustees resolved on February 8, 1875, that there be

> two books of not less than 48 pages each of songs and musical exercises, one to be used in the D and E grades, and the other in the F, G, and H grades, with the proviso that the books shall be furnished to pupils at a cost not to exceed ten cents per copy and that . . . the teachers shall not share in any part of the profits arising from such publication.

This mandate was followed almost literally, although the two "books" were bound as a single volume. The forty-eight pages destined for the H, G, and F grades contained twenty-nine pages of exercises and twenty-seven unison songs. The texts of many of the latter appear to have been selected by the teachers who participated anonymously in the process with the intent of inculcating moral truths about justice, charity, obedience, and the like; there were also various kinds of seasonal lyrics. The book designed for the older students consisted of thirty pages of more advanced exercises, as well as twenty songs, everything in two voice parts. Each contained folksongs of various sorts, as well as songs attributed to composers ranging from the noted to the obscure, all predominantly German in origin. A slight majority of the songs were provided with German translations of their texts.[52]

A revision of 1882 included more challenging exercises and songs in the existing book intended for the lower grades, as well as a third book for the intermediate schools, billed as "A Supplement to the 'Young Singer's Manual.'" Its 256 pages contained the usual section dealing with the rudiments of music (presented in a question and answer format), as well as a section of suggestions about posture, breathing, mouth shapes, and enunciation, plus 361 exercises and 94 songs in two-, three-, and four-voice parts, all of it rigorously and systematically organized.[53] Junkermann's caveat in the revision:

> This book has a true face, it needs no other face, and, therefore, has no preface. I only wish to state that nearly all the music teachers of the Public Schools of Cincinnati have furnished exercises and songs for it, that many of the ex-

ercises and songs prepared by the former superintendent, Mr. Charles Aiken, have been adopted, and that most of them are made up from the latest and best works in use in the schools of Europe and this country, and that special thanks are due Messrs. [Walter] Aiken, [J. L.] Zeinz, and [Henry J.] Brusselbach for their valuable assistance in preparing and selecting both exercises and songs.[54]

Junkermann and Zeinz[55] took credit for the five-part revised and enlarged edition of 1893.[56] Part 1, designed for the youngest children, was prefaced by this credo:

It is the belief of the revisers of the present edition that a love for music can be created in the children as they enter School by teaching them songs by rote, containing sentiments that are in accordance with what children think and talk about, rather than by teaching Music systematically from the beginning.

To form a love for a soft flowing melody, to teach them how to produce a pleasant tone from an open mouth and thus strengthen them physically and morally is all that should be attempted for a year or two. . . .

The pages of this edition have been filled with songs and exercises, instead of words directing the music teachers or pupils how to proceed. Any intelligent person will see from the nature of the exercises and songs when and how to present them to the children, and where that ability does not exist, the work would better not be undertaken until a teacher can be obtained who is prepared for his work. The voices of children are delicate and therefore require gentle treatment towards development, and unskilled persons should not be permitted to experiment with them.[57]

Continuing precedent, twenty-seven of the songs in this volume were furnished with German words.

Part 2 was intended for those eight years old in grade three and emphasized rote singing, although the exercises were "arranged to train the child to become a reader of music." Fully thirty of the fifty-one songs were furnished with German words. Part 3 was destined for use in the fourth grade and assumed some degree of sophistication since two-part singing was introduced, and it was suggested that those assigned the lower line "be given a chance to sing their part frequently by note and without hearing the first part." Part 4, for fifth and sixth graders, aged ten to thirteen, included exercises and songs by Mozart, Cherubini, Mendelssohn, and others,

embrac[ing] nearly all the major and minor keys in common use. The words of the songs are such as can be understood and appreciated by children of that age, because they treat of matters and things that naturally engage their thoughts, and, combined with music will form the means of inspiring them with a desire for what is good, pure, and true in life.[58]

Part 5, intended for seventh and eighth graders, contained songs for three- and four-part treble voices, as well as three- and four-part mixed voices,

> since quite a number of boys are already possessed of a bass voice at this age. Care should be taken with voices during the time of mutation, force should not be attempted, and any tone that is liable to break into the higher octave, should not be insisted on at the time. Pupils at this age should be encouraged to sing by note, using the syllables or vowels before singing the words of the songs, and to practice individual and class sight singing.[59]

Junkermann also published *Vocal Selections for High Schools,* part 1, in 1880, and part 2 two years later. Nonetheless, the Union Board of High Schools decided to continue relying on *The Choralist's Companion.*

Although during his first year as an administrator Junkermann continued to spend four days in the classroom, by 1895 virtually his entire time was devoted to administrative tasks. Although he evidently never inspired the same sort of affection as his predecessor, a testimonial benefit concert was held in Music Hall on February 21, 1901, and to mark his passing, the flags at all city schools were lowered to half-mast on February 6, 1906.

He was succeeded by Walter H[arris] Aiken (1856–1935), son of Charles and a product of the Queen City's music tradition. He had attended Woodward High School but chose not to graduate, electing instead to assume the role of music teacher in Middletown during 1874. He taught there and in Hamilton for five years before returning to the Cincinnati system, where he served in various primary and intermediate schools until 1895, when he was appointed to the Woodward High School faculty, a position he retained until he became superintendent. His thirty years in that role witnessed the evolution of a broader program of instruction that will begin to seem familiar to modern-day educators.

While singing remained the principal activity, the scope of the repertory was expanded considerably. Aiken adopted publications in general use but also edited *The Jennings* [later, *Willis*] *Collection of Supplementary Songs for Public Schools,* several operettas and cantatas (under the Willis imprint, for example, Andreas Romberg's *Lay of the Bell* [1911]), plus *Aiken's One Book Course, Melody Studies for Primary Grades* (1908), *For High Schools: Part Songs for Mixed Voices* (1908), and *First Studies in Two-Part Singing* (1911, all from the American Book Company).[60] While student-organized, single-sex glee clubs based on collegiate models had existed at various times during the late nineteenth century, it was only about 1910 that they were granted official status, directed by music teachers but rehearsing after the close of the school day as an extracurricular activity. Academic credit was not awarded until 1914. And while records remain of a student-organized mixed chorus at Woodward High School in 1914, other such groups did not appear until the mid-1920s, when rehearsals were finally scheduled during regular school hours.

The earliest mention of instrumental music in the Cincinnati schools dates back to 1855, when a benefit concert raised funds for the purchase of a grand piano, supplemented by the gift of a bass viol from piano dealers Colburn and Field. There is passing mention of a string quintet at Woodward High School in 1872, and six years later the Union Board of High Schools granted the staff of Hughes High School its request for "6 music stands and 10 chairs for Amateur Orchestra." In December of that same year an "orchestra" of three violins, bass viol, cornet, and piano presented a concert at Woodward. Sporadic references to orchestras during the waning decades of the century remain (for example, an ensemble under Junkermann performed at the Founders' Day program at Woodward High School in March 1894), but silence about such activities in official reports suggests that they were not considered a formal part of the instructional system. Thus, permanent high school orchestras were not established until 1910, followed shortly by orchestras in the primary and intermediate schools (in 1912), joined gradually by piano classes (in 1915), drum corps, bands (the first seems to be that of Hughes High School in 1918, transformed into a marching band in the fall of 1925), and clubs celebrating the mandolin, guitar, ukulele, and auto-harp.

Aiken also introduced courses in voice, harmony, dictation, and the history of music. By 1911 he had created a vocational music course, which allowed students to major in music and even receive academic credit for work done outside the school, provided that they enrolled in music theory courses and successfully passed examinations judging the success of their external study and practice.

Attempts to cultivate informed listeners date back as far as January 1854, when according to newspaper accounts a visiting soprano performed for students of the high schools and upper grades of the district schools at the National Theatre, after which the children reciprocated by singing under the direction of Charles Aiken and Elisha Locke. During March 1857 the Philharmonic Society gave a free concert for the teachers and students of the intermediate and high schools, and a year later opened a rehearsal to school children, who had discussed the literature to be played with their teachers beforehand. In a reminiscence of 1924 Aiken wrote about those concerts and suggested that they were "the first of the kind that were ever played, in so far as we know, for young folks." As support, he offered a March 14, 1857, review of the first of the pair in *Dwight's Journal of Music:*

The audience numbered nearly 500 (living) heads. They seemed spell bound in listening to the heavenly strains of the greatest of all music masters; there was not a whisper, hardly a breath. As yet the latest New York fashion of handing around chocolate and ice cream has not been adopted in Cincinnati. Think of the Pastoral Symphony and the whole of St. Paul given but a few days ago in the Western backwoods.[61]

Walter Aiken also concentrated on developing a listening public; in 1908 he instituted classes in what came to be called music appreciation, first with the use of the reproducing piano (perhaps better known as the player piano), later the phonograph. He prepared the *Music Appreciation Series* of eight pamphlets discussing the masterworks, eventually coordinated with concerts being offered school students by the Cincinnati Symphony Orchestra. A rich relationship between the orchestra and the city's schools apparently dates to 1908, since the 1908–09 annual school report recognized,

> With the reorganization of the Cincinnati Orchestra this year, a remarkable series of concerts has been given. The programs have been obtained in advance, and the various numbers analyzed and discussed with high school classes and their attendance upon the concerts encouraged in order that they might be familiarized with classical compositions and be taught to recognize the style of the different composers. The future of music depends as much upon well trained listeners as upon performers.[62]

In March 1915 the symphony offered an educational afternoon that included demonstrations of the various instruments; during the following season one hundred elementary school children heard Friday afternoon concerts at a season price of two dollars, having attended an hour-long discussion of each program beforehand. The first Young People's Concerts were offered during February 1920; the following year these were coordinated with the music appreciation curriculum of the schools. Recordings of the repertory to be presented were employed to prepare the students, and Aiken encouraged local radio stations to broadcast these recordings so as to broaden the outreach of his efforts. While assistant conductors were responsible for these concerts during Aiken's tenure, Eugene Goossens took charge during the 1931–32 season, and coordination between the orchestra and school system became even more intimate. Program notes were prepared in advance and sent to the teachers, committees of whom even suggested repertory for Goossens's consideration.

Aiken reached mandatory retirement age in 1927 but was persuaded to extend his tenure for another two years. A new general superintendent then requested that he remain on temporary assignment yet another year, resulting in a daunting fifty-six years of service and a commendation of great appreciation of Mr. Aiken as a musician and teacher, a lover of children and of all the gentle things of life, and as a noble citizen. The city owes him a debt of gratitude that it will never be able to repay. His reward must be in the consciousness of work well done. He is loved and respected, not only by the pupils and teachers, but by the entire city.[63]

Aiken was succeeded by Ernest G. Hesser, whose six-year tenure was hampered by the financial exigencies of those Depression years. Hesser, the first director not drawn from the incumbent staff, arrived with ample credentials: With undergraduate degrees from Winona College and Butler University and work at the New School of Methods in Public School Music in Chicago, he also had received two graduate degrees from the Cincinnati Conservatory, where he had studied under Walter Aiken. He had taught public school music in California and New York State and had served as director of music at what was then Bowling Green State Normal College. He resigned to accept a professorship at New York University.

He oversaw the creation of more comprehensive courses of study in both elementary and high schools and pressed for greater correlation of music and social studies, thus urging forward the tendency inaugurated by his predecessor to make the study of music something more stimulating that the mere mastery of technical skills. He attempted to foster greater professionalism in his staff by publishing a departmental periodical called the *Music Bulletin* and by organizing a teachers' chorus at the Teachers College of the University of Cincinnati, where he taught during the summer. Members enjoyed not only the advantage of earning university credit for this activity, but the chorus created a forum in which they could study repertory and conducting techniques.

It remained for Hesser's successor, Francis C. Biddle, to complete the evolutionary process begun under Walter Aiken, thereby transforming the Cincinnati program into something thoroughly modern. West Virginia–born Biddle was also hired from outside the Cincinnati system, although he held degrees from both the College of Music and the University of Cincinnati. He had also studied at the Carnegie Institute of Technology; had taught in Rochester, New York, and Asheville, North Carolina; and came to the Queen City from Wilkinsburg, Pennsylvania, where he had been director of music.

After a year of studying the system he had inherited, Biddle in 1937 issued a report that must have challenged any complacency among those who assumed that Cincinnati remained in the vanguard. He questioned the adequacy of the texts then in use, the time allotted for music instruction, the confusing role of the general classroom teacher, the irregularity in goals and procedures among his staff, and the status of instrumental music instruction in the lower grades.

By the 1939–40 school year, new texts were in use that effectively applied the methodology of language teachers. One hundred minutes of music instruction per week became the standard, and resident, rather than itinerant, music specialists taught in grades four to eight, while the general teachers had responsibility for the instruction of younger children. The compulsory vocal music that had been a hall-mark of the Cincinnati approach since 1847 was abolished in the high schools in favor of elective, five-times-a-week courses, which included not only chorus, band, or orchestra, but what Biddle called, in a letter dated December 7, 1937, "appreciational" experiences. A high school student could still major in music, but such a curriculum no longer required study outside the school system.

To supplement this activity and to assure increased opportunities for those able and eager, Biddle gradually organized various city-wide choral and instrumental groups, festivals, and sings, such as that of May 1946, when seventeen hundred junior high school children performed sixteen songs that they had mastered in their classrooms. Much of this was dependent on an expanded system of instrumental instruction in the elementary grades. Summer classes and clinics by recognized teachers led gradually to a formal course in instrumental study by 1946 and even a two-year class piano course the following year. Amidst all this activity, Biddle maintained the school system's intimate relationship with both the May Festival and the symphony and made an arrangement by which sixth- and seventh-graders could attend opera performances at the Cincinnati Zoo.

Thus Biddle completed the metamorphosis tentatively begun by Aiken, an approach that in many ways repudiated the method that had made Cincinnati an exemplar for much of the preceding century, motivated by his belief that "music education should start with thrills and then proceed to drills and skills."[64] One statistic might suffice to symbolize this transformation: In 1936 Biddle inherited a staff of fourteen music specialists. A decade later, that staff had more than tripled in size, to forty-eight.

The ideas and attitudes of the music supervisors obviously had the most profound influence on the evolution just traced. However, attention needs to be paid to at least one remarkable teacher: Joseph Surdo (1876–1956). A Cincinnati native and 1889 graduate of Woodward High School, Surdo studied with Frank Van der Stucken and Edgar Stillman Kelley at the College of Music and began teaching in the public schools in 1891, even before his college graduation four years later (the college was also to confer an honorary master's degree on him in 1926). He worked in various elementary and high schools before being assigned to the new Withrow [East] High School in 1919, where he taught until retirement in 1938.

His work there elicited much admiration, including a halo-like encomium from his general superintendent. Randall J. Condon had witnessed an evening showcase of Withrow's ensembles and then announced to his profession, any man who can direct the musical education of these children in such a way as to have such a symphony as this is making one of the biggest and best contributions to the education of young people. It is far beyond the value of the education which comes from mathematics, science, or English, or anything else . . . for I don't care how valuable others may be, this man has done more for the education of these young people than any other teacher.[65]

Surdo also served as a church musician, taught privately, and after forty-seven years in the Cincinnati system worked on a temporary basis for school systems in northern Kentucky following formal retirement.

He also achieved considerable renown as a composer, and not just for utilitarian music destined for the use of school children. He did write *Our Lincoln, an Ode for One, Two, and Three Equal Voices*, with words by Dr. W. C. Washburn, in 1908 and conducted it with a chorus of 750 children and orchestra. He also wrote *Woodward: Past, Present and Future. A Cantata for the Dedication Exercises of the Woodward High School Building, October 24, 1910*, with words by Alice Williams. Earlier he had written for the 1899 Sangerfest a *Flag Song* and *96th Psalm*, the latter another chorus for children's voices. Mentor Frank Van der Stucken conducted his *In Flanders Field* and *The Viking* at the 1923 May Festival, and *Enter Pauline* was first heard at the Cincinnati Zoo Opera in July 1929. He also left two operettas, *The Crowning of the Gypsy Queen* (1903) and *Prince Charming* (1907), as well as both sacred and secular solo songs[66] and some church music.

CHAPTER 8

The Foundations of Public School
Music in Oberlin, Zanesville,
Cleveland, and Columbus

While it seems appropriate to have spent an extravagant amount of time in Cincinnati, given the Queen City's precedence and prominence in any history of public school music in this country, as well as the abundance of documentary evidence, the introduction of similar instruction in Cleveland and Columbus needs to be considered as well, since neither lagged far behind, and at least a mention needs to be made of Oberlin and Zanesville, since both may have taken chronological precedence over the Queen City.

Scant evidence remains, but a report of 1842 suggested that music was part of the agenda offered youngsters in Oberlin. The subject was apparently offered by generalist, since references were made to the employment of music professions only in 1869.

In Zanesville, a "system of organization" for the graded schools was approved and enacted in September 1842. They were divided into Male and Female Seminaries, each with junior and senior departments. Students in the junior departments were to be taught "spelling, reading, and the elements of arithmetic and geography; and the scholars shall be allowed to attend lessons in singing and writing." There was to be a designated teacher of writing and vocal music who "shall occupy the room at each building appropriated to his use; and the scholars shall attend his instruction in such classes and under such arrangements as he, with the sanction of the Board of Education, shall think proper." This teacher of writing and music was also to serve as general superintendent of the female seminary and "shall reside in the building and protect it and premises from injury."[1]

Although official records prior to 1845 were destroyed by fire, it seems that Zanesville's first specialized teacher of writing and singing was probably Capt. Jesse P. Hatch. Hatch, who had studied at Captain Partidge's Military School in Norwich, Vermont (later Norwich University), may also have served as drillmaster of the Putnam Greys, across the Muskingum River in neighboring Putnam. He was teaching penmanship as early as December 1840, and a report printed in a local newspaper dated September 17, 1842, to the board of education suggests that Hatch was even responsible for seeing that fires were being made in the morning and then "secured at night, so as to insure the safety of the building," for which extra services he received his lodging quarters gratis. He spent the mornings with his female charges, his afternoons with the males, all for a salary of $400 per annum, the same compensation he received three years later, at a time when his principal text was reported to be "Mason's Sacred Harp." Unfortunately, the chronology of all this remains fuzzy, since the 1842 newspaper article implies a mature system in September 1842, while other sources state unequivocally that this arrangement was instituted only three years later.

Hatch resigned his position in April 1848. Mr. O. L. Castle, principal of the male seminary, then taught writing and singing to his charges, while Miss Adaline Parker, a teacher in the female seminary, became its principal. It isn't clear whether or not she taught writing and singing as well, but in January 1849 Mr. L. P. Marsh was imported from Delaware, Ohio, to offer the two subjects. No information remains as to why his tenure was so brief, but he resigned in October 1850 and was succeeded by Captain Hatch. Hatch persisted this time around until 1856 or so, since by January 1857 Professor Horace D. Munson was identified as the high school music teacher, although he was either replaced or assisted by Miss Lucy Abbott in 1860.

Whoever was in charge must have been doing a credible job, since the "Report of the Board of Education and Superintendent of the Zanesville Public Schools for the Year Ending August 1 1858," announced:

It is rare to find a child who does not love music, and equally as rare to find one who cannot learn to sing. If care is not taken to teach children proper music, with appropriate words, many of them will pick up the low and vulgar songs of the street, and sing them to their own degradation and the pollution of those with whom they associate. Singing adds wonderfully to the interest of the school; it is a relief from the fatigue of study and recitation, and a powerful aid in governing and managing children. It keeps both pupils and teachers better natured, and greatly cheers them in their monotonous labor. The children have taken hold of this exercise with commendable zeal, and have made great proficiency. Almost every pupil in the Primary and Second Schools has learned to sing; and some of them with an artistic skill quite wonderful for the time they have been practicing.[2]

The first mention of communal schooling in Cleveland dates from 1802, when "Miss Ann Spafford . . . made effective use of the well-known 'front room' of Major Carter's, where she gathered perhaps a dozen youngsters of the settlement, and taught them the simplest forms of book knowledge."[3] Another school was opened by Asael Adams in 1806. In 1816 a group of citizens constructed a frame schoolhouse, which a year later was purchased by the village council and made available without charge to teachers. Five years later a brick building known as the Cleveland Academy was constructed by popular subscription, its title held by a group of shareholders. Various private primary schools dotted the community during this period, tuition to some degree subsidized from public funds. In April 1836 Cleveland was incorporated as a city and on June 9 the new council "Resolved, That a committee be and is hereby appointed to employ a teacher and an assistant, to continue the Free School to the end of the quarter, or until a school system for the city shall be organized at the expense of the city."[4] The "Free School" was a mission or charity school that had been in operation for several years.

The next step in the establishment of tax-supported public schools did not occur until July 7, 1837, when the city council authorized its School Committee to purchase appropriate buildings or rooms, to furnish them with the necessary equipment, and to hire instructors. The first term was to last only four months, from July 24 until November 24, and the State Superintendent's Report for 1838, while commending the city for having based her schools "on principles which, if carried out to the extent demanded in that flourishing place, will distinguish her on the list of free school cities,"[5] noted that tight finances blessed each teacher with fifty to eighty children. Cleveland offered only primary education until 1846, when the Board of Managers opened the first public high school in Ohio.

Concern for the musical education of Cleveland youngsters seems to have surfaced toward the end of that first school term in 1837. On November 23 the *Ohio City Argus*, a weekly published in what was then an independent community west of the Cuyahoga River, asked,

> Why then, is there so little attention given to this subject? We allude more particularly to *vocal music*. The main reason undoubtedly is, that it is considered of secondary importance. Should the science of vocal music be introduced into every school and every child capable of understanding the subject be required to study it, there would be an entire revolution in this department in less than ten years.

The first identifiable singing school in Cleveland had been held by Elijah Ingersoll about 1824, but the well-informed *Argus* editorial was surely sparked by the arrival in Cleveland of William Carpenter Webster (1813–82) and Mary Cushing Webster (1812–1905). After a preliminary notice on December 29, 1837, Mr. Webster on January 10, 1838, announced a singing school "designed for those who have acquired some information of the science, and are desirous of obtaining a more thorough knowledge by study and practice. A correct style of singing as well as a good theoretical understanding of it, will be given to his pupils, thereby rendering them useful in sustaining that important part of divine service so essential in our churches."[6] Gentlemen were to be charged three dollars per quarter, ladies a dollar less.

Two weeks later Mrs. Webster notified the public of a "Juvenile Singing School" that would commence on February 3. "The Pestalozzian system of instruction, which has been so fully tested in other cities in schools of this character will be adopted in this." The charges for twenty-six lessons: two dollars, or five dollars for a family ticket admitting three or more. Another fortnight later Mr. Webster, "late of the Boston Handel and Haydn Society," announced the organization of a Union Singing School, beginning on February 12. No record remains of Mr. Webster's success with his enterprises, but the newspapers of the day tracked his wife's activities in lavish detail.

She presented her juveniles to the public for the first time on May 15, an evening that elicited "unqualified praise":

> "Viva La Musica," that is, long live music, and long will it live while our children are taught to lisp in melody. The concert last evening was one of the most interesting exhibitions that I have ever witnessed. Some sixty boys and girls from fourteen years down to six, stood up before a large audience, and with no leader, and no accompaniment but the pianoforte, sung [sic] in perfect harmony, a great variety of tunes and songs, with a correctness and precision that would do credit to older and long practised musicians. . . . I know not by what magic (if it be magic) Mrs. Webster has instructed these children in the short space of three months, not only to sing, but to sing in perfect harmony with the most distinct pronunciation; but by note, so that every one evidently understood what they were doing, and did it from knowledge.[7]

The concert evoked not only critical acclaim but also a letter to the editor of the *Cleveland Herald and Gazette* of June 28 from "Agnostos" that asserted:

> We long to see music become a branch of education, and considered and viewed in the light which its importance demands. We hope soon to see it introduced into our schools, public and private, and that parents will feel as anxious that their children should possess a knowledge of music as of Geography, or Arithmetic. . . . It is almost the only branch of study, the direct tendency of which is to improve and cultivate the feelings.

Mrs. Webster offered public programs on August 16 and November 22, 1838, the second of which sparked a colloquy in the *Herald and Gazette* about the merits of universal music education, as well as the observation that the concert had been "an entertainment as we venture to assert cannot be equalled in any city West of the mountains, and reflected the highest credit on that lady and her eighty pupils."

Mrs. Webster announced a concert by the just-created Cleveland Juvenile Musical Society on March 21, 1839, in the Stone Church. The program, a typical mélange of solos, rounds, choruses, exercises, and a single anthem (listed by title only), was treated as a benefit by some 150 "Young Men of the City of Cleveland," anxious

> to express to you in some manner their high estimation of your professional attainments—the grateful sense in common with the whole public they feel for your almost gratuitous exertions during the past winter in the Common Schools of this city—their esteem for your private worth, and their anxiety that a liberal public should sustain you in your profession.[8]

An even more affective tribute was delivered by one of her young charges, purportedly about nine years of age:

> Whenever we see you coming, our countenances are lighted up with a bright and a sunny smile, and join with our whole heart in the delighted amusement your instructions afford. We may have for others the tear of sympathy, and the affections of the heart, but our smiles and happy feelings must ever be yours.
>
> What shall we say to our dear teacher for the unwearied pains she has taken to prepare us for usefulness here and happiness hereafter[?] But this is not all; she has allowed us the delightful privilege of smoothing every step we have taken up the rugged hill of science with the sweet variety of song. If she could read our hearts, she would know our grateful feelings, but we cannot express them. Wherever we may be in after life, whether in joy or sorrow, we shall look back to this winter, as *one* bright spot in the morning of life.[9]

In addition to the public concert of August 16, 1837, Mrs. Webster's children sang at a meeting earlier that month in which the state Superintendent of Common Schools addressed the local citizenry on various matters related to public education. Samuel Lewis was reported (according to the *Herald and Gazette* of August 10) to have rendered "an eloquent tribute to the musical skill of the choir of children," and then to have appealed to parents to cultivate "the minds, the morals, the tastes, the voices of their children." Mrs. Webster's juveniles scored another triumph in their concert of November 22, eliciting an editorial comment in the *Herald and Gazette* two days later that the event should have impressed on "the attention of our leaders, the great importance of parents attending to the musical education of children."

Webster also had an impact on the annual meeting of the Ohio Education Convention, which opened on December 26, 1838, in Columbus with eighty leading educators from all sectors of the state in attendance, including notables like Calvin E. Stowe and William H. McGuffey (he of the *Readers*). Dr. J. D. Weston, a member of the Cleveland delegation, read a letter from Webster "on the introduction of Normal Music into our Common Schools." The letter itself has not survived, nor was it read into the record, but newspapers across the state reported that her thesis was greeted with enormous enthusiasm. Two resolutions were introduced the following day:

> *Resolved*, 1st, That we regard the Education of children and youths in the theory and practice of vocal music, as constituting an important part of a *system* of Physical, Mental and Moral discipline, designed to prepare them for the duties and enjoyments of life, inasmuch as it tends to promote health, strengthen and enlarge the mind and to soften and elevate the affections.

> *Resolved*, 2nd, That we hail the introduction of Sacred Music into our primary and higher Schools, as an important and promising era in the history of Education in our Country, and that we highly recommend its introduction into Common Schools, Academies and higher Seminaries of Learning in this State.[10]

Strenuous discussion must have ensued, since these resolutions were tabled after a first reading and then returned to the floor on four subsequent occasions during the afternoon. The result, adopted the following day, must have disappointed the absent Mrs. Webster and her allies:

> *Resolved*. That experience has shown that the practice of vocal music in our schools so far from encroaching on the time of the pupils, by promoting cheerfulness and activity of mind, renders their progress in all other respects more rapid and certain.[11]

One account of Dr. Weston's presentation of Mrs. Webster's letter to the convention delegates (in the *Herald and Gazette* of January 4, 1839) suggests that during the 1838–39 school year Webster must have been teaching music in at least one public school in Cleveland, the first documented evidence of such instruction in the city. According to Dr. Weston, visitors to "the city of the Lake, may hear her [Webster's] pealing tones in the Gloria Patriae of the Church, or the softer melody of her voice, in the Common School House at the foot of the hill."

A few weeks later Mrs. Webster was campaigning before members of the Cuyahoga County Common School Association. The January 31, 1839, *Herald and*

Gazette reported that "Mrs. Webster having been invited, attended with her juvenile singing school, and performed sundry pieces of music, in an interesting and appropriate manner which added much interest to the proceedings of the meeting. All appeared to appreciate the labors of Mrs. W. in her efforts to cultivate vocal music, and were delighted with the performances." Although without immediate tangible result, the Association resolved to "recommend the introduction of vocal music into our common schools, as an important part of the system of Education to be pursued in them."

Alas, despite sustained public success and those multiple expressions of support, J. A. Briggs, the commissioner of insolvents, announced on September 18, 1839, that he would on October 4 sell at public auction "a lot of personal property, consisting of household stuff, &c. (assigned to me by W. C. Webster, an application, &c.)."[12] The Websters surfaced later in Boston, Brooklyn, Rochester, and Buffalo, although they both died in Ohio; he in Canton, where he was listed as a music teacher in the local directory as late as 1880; she in Wooster.

During the early 1840s a number of private schools allowed young Clevelanders the possibility of musical instruction. The most important and active of their proprietors were "Professors" Jarvis F. Hanks and Silas L. Bingham.[13] Although extant records are scanty, the painter-musician Hanks supposedly petitioned the city council in 1840 to include music in the city's educational scheme, and offered his services "at so small a salary that it almost amounted to a gratuity," an offer refused with the observation of one member "that dancing with equal propriety might be introduced into the schools, and of the two, he should prefer to have dancing taught."[14] It was only in the spring of 1846 that Silas Bingham was engaged to teach for a few months on an experimental basis for the sum of one hundred dollars. Despite the enthusiasm of Hanks and others (he was quoted in the *Cleveland Herald* of August 11 as praising "[t]he managers of public schools in Cleveland [who] have done one of the wisest acts in furnishing *musical* instruction in addition to that in other branches"), the "experiment" proved short-lived, and Cleveland's public school children had to await the 1848–49 school year to enjoy the fruits of music instruction. Nonetheless, during his brief tenure Bingham was able to amass a choir of 250 children for a July 4 performance at a meeting of the National Jubilee of the Young People's Washington Total Abstinence Society.

One J. H. Clark announced in the *Cleveland Daily True Democrat* of April 3, 1848, that he would offer classes in the basement of the Baptist church. By August 30 he was able to assert in the same newspaper that, "from the encouragement he received the past season in his vocation, [he] begs leave to inform his friends and the community generally, that he has established himself permanently in this city as a teacher of vocal music." Permanency apparently came to mean only two years, after which Clark disappeared from the local scene, but the "Annual Report of the Board of School Managers" of March 17, 1849, stated:

> Mr. J. H. Clark in Vocal Music, at a salary of $250 has devoted three fourths of an hour every other day during the year to each of the five higher schools. Many of the scholars under him have become familiar with the elements of musical science. In all the schools, with a single exception, singing has been a daily exercise. This popular branch may be considered as re-established in all the departments.[15]

The report's reference to the reestablishment of musical instruction perhaps suggests predecessors of whom there is no knowledge, but Clark's success led the board to suggest extending the benefits of musical instruction to the primary schools.

In October 1851 Lowell Mason delivered a lecture to school officials, teachers, and others on the matter of music in the public schools, proclaiming (according to the *Daily True Democrat* of October 13):

> A low estimate of the advantages and designs of music in schools, may be comprised in these; it amuses, it interests, it promotes good nature. In a higher view, it improves the voice, the musical taste, the moral character, when the music is accompanied by language of sentiment; it contributes to general vocal cultivation, and has a very beneficial influence on health.

Boilerplate rhetoric from the patriarch himself, but it may have strengthened the resolve of Clevelanders anxious to install music as a permanent part of the school curriculum, since Jarvis Hanks was hired to teach at the Central High School, and in 1852 Silas Bingham was reemployed and embarked on a six-year tenure, one that attracted national attention to the Cleveland program. His and Hanks's sense of security could hardly have been buttressed by the "Sixteenth Annual Report of the Board of Managers," dated March 14, 1852, which concluded,

> We have always wished to encourage the idea that the lighter exercises and accomplishments of the school room, such for example as music and special declamation, which last is at best of questionable utility, should occupy a place most thoroughly subordinate, on all occasions, to the more solid displays of mental culture and acquirement.[16]

Nonetheless, by October 1, 1853, the *Daily True Democrat* could proclaim, in a chauvinistic and misinformed compliment, that

[t]he progress in vocal music is well deserving of a passing remark. A year ago this was unknown as a branch of tuition in our schools. Now it is receiving more attention than in any other city in the Union. The teachers and others conversant with the great success of Prof. Bingham, unanimously concur in pronouncing him the best teacher of vocal music that the country affords. Cleveland is the only city in the state employing a teacher of vocal music.

In fact, Cleveland did achieve national renown following the appointment of N[ewall] Coe Stewart (1838–1921) as supervisor of music in 1869.[17] During a thirty-eight-year career as supervisor of music he received considerable national attention. However, almost nothing is known of Stewart prior to his appointment. One source claims him as a student of Lowell Mason, but circumstances suggest that such study might have consisted only of the six-week normal institute that Mason mounted in Wooster during July and August of 1862.

Stewart initially held a concurrent appointment in Akron, but in 1872 he resigned his responsibilities there to Nathan L. Glover, who remained in that position until his retirement in 1921. Assisted by Glover, Stewart led a six-week normal institute in Akron in 1871, surely modeled on similar ventures by Lowell Mason. Stewart served as choral director and assembly singing leader at Central High School in Cleveland, and also oversaw classroom music instruction in the elementary schools, at one point instructing and supervising 160 teachers. He also organized exhibitions of singing by the elementary pupils, and led student choruses of sixteen hundred at the 1874 Sängerfest in Cleveland and four thousand at a similar event in 1893 (at which he also conducted a performance of Haydn's *The Creation*). He organized a Central Musical Association in 1881 and led its chorus until 1887. During the 1890s he developed the Star Course, a concert series hosting ensembles like the New York Symphony, each event prefaced by an introductory lecture. In 1894 he led a large chorus of school children at the dedication of the Soldiers and Sailors Monument.

He also published three didactic volumes between 1872 and 1875, all of them issued by S. Brainard's Sons in Cleveland: *The Singing School Echo; A New Collection of Music for Singing & High Schools, Classes, Conventions, etc.* (1872, with James W. North); *Merry Voices; A Collection of Songs, Duets, Trios, Choruses, etc. Especially Adapted for the Use of Schools, Seminaries, and Juvenile Classes* (1873); and *The Crown King; for Singing and High Schools, Conventions, Musical Societies, Choirs, and Social Gatherings* (1875, again compiled jointly with North).

Each of the oblong volumes begins with the predictable didactic material (Stewart was a mainstream Pestalozzian, insisting on a rote-note path to musical literacy, with lots of drill on patterned exercises), presented in question and answer format between teacher and pupils in the two joint publications, and concluding with an especially detailed discussion of vocal training. The musical material consists of psalm tunes and other liturgical music, anthems, hymns, and children's songs (many written by Stewart and North, fewer by Nathan L. Glover), as well as a few examples from the standard literature.

Stewart was active in several national professional associations, most notably the Music Teachers National Association. The idea of such an organization was first broached by Theodore Presser (1848–1925), later founder of *The Etude* and the publishing house that still bears his name but in 1875 a teacher of piano at the Female Seminary in Delaware, Ohio. (He supposedly spent nine years in Ohio, teaching not only in Delaware at what is now Ohio Wesleyan University, but also at Mount Union and Ohio Northern Colleges and at a conservatory in Xenia.) During the summer of 1875 Presser convened a group of those attending a normal music institute being held in East Greenwich, Rhode Island, under the direction of Eben Tourjée, one of the founders of the New England Conservatory of Music. Two of those involved in the discussions were also Ohioans: Stewart and William Henry Dana. All three were also among those who gathered in Delaware during December 1876 when the MTNA was formally organized and Tourjée elected its first president. Stewart presented a paper at this initial gathering and at several subsequent meetings, and served as president of the association during the 1895–96 academic year.

By 1929 Russell V. Morgan, Supervisor of Music, was able to report in *The Fine Arts Guide of Ohio: Season 1929–1930* a pattern of "Music in the Cleveland Public Schools" that ought to feel a bit familiar to music educators more than seven decades later. Morgan's credo was:

> The first philosophy of the music department of the Cleveland Public Schools is that every child have a maximum opportunity for becoming sensitive to beauty in musical art. This involves the activities in both listening and performance. No complete response to music is possible from the student alone. Some conception of the problems of performance is essential; on the other hand, training in performance does not insure the result wished for. It is essential that the performance have, as a corollary, intelligent and discriminative listening as it is necessary for the highest result to have some performance at least as a corollary to the definite program of listening (so called appreciation).[18]

Morgan had at his command about 250 music teachers spread across the system. Elementary-age students enjoyed seventy-five mandatory minutes of instruction in general music each week, could also participate in glee clubs or orchestras, and were offered classes in piano, violin, and other orchestral instruments. Junior high students spent ninety minutes per week in general music instruction and also had available girls' and boys' glee clubs (one for unchanged, another for changing voices), mixed chorus, orchestra, band, instrumental ensembles, and class instruction on orchestral instruments, plus music theory and literature classes. General music classes were not offered at the high school level, although the same array of activities and classes was continued. High school administrators must have been granted a bit of flexibility, since some apparently required chorus participation in the tenth year, others through all three years. Several even offered a music major, and one provided "a very complete vocational course in professional music training."

The whole system benefited from an extensive series of children's concerts offered by the Cleveland Orchestra. These were coordinated with rigorous classroom preparation in advance of each event, "so that no child attends a concert without being familiar with the sound of the composition, and certain instructional points that are within his grasp." The orchestra also offered a music memory contest each spring at which teams nominated by their schools competed. More importantly perhaps, orchestra players taught in tandem with regular faculty members at Saturday morning sessions in two different locations, with the goal of increasing the facility of the city's orchestras and bands. In addition, "[f]rom this instruction there have been a number of students showing enough talent to be encouraged to do professional work by the symphony men and there are now nine or ten of these young men in the Orchestra whose training was largely received as a result of the Saturday schools."[19]

Of the state's three largest cities Columbus is the youngest. Lucas Sullivant, during the process of surveying the Virginia Military Tract, became attracted to land near the juncture of the Scioto and Olentangy Rivers, bought a substantial tract of property west of the Scioto, and in 1797 laid out a town he called Franklinton. Joined by fellow Virginians, he eventually built a residence at the corner of what became West Broad and Sandusky Streets. In the course of extended discussion as to where to locate a permanent seat of state government, a quartet of Franklinton citizens in 1810 offered the General Assembly land they owned on the east bank of Scioto, a gift accepted in February 1812. By June the town had been platted, the promised property conveyed to the state, and the sale of lots to the public initiated.

Musical culture arrived quickly in the infant capital. A Handel Society was organized in 1821, a Haydn Society three years later. The latter group apparently offered a concert at the State House in 1825 celebrating authorization of a portion of the canal system, and may eventually have merged with the older society. A. C. Parker announced a school of sacred music at the Columbus Academy in October 1828. A pipe organ built by the Thomas Appleton firm of Boston was installed in the First Presbyterian Church during 1831, concurrent with mention of a "Columbus Band," which participated in various celebrations that year. The Franklin Harmonic Society, open to "all those interested in the cultivation of Musical Science," appeared in 1832, the same year that the Washington Artillery Company organized its band. A short-lived Columbus Sacred Music Society appeared in 1845 and the venerable Columbus Männerchor three years later.[20] The city began to attract visiting artists such as the Christy Minstrels in 1844, Ole Bull the following year, and Jenny Lind in 1851. G. Machold and Brother's "Pianoforte and Music Saloon," housed in the Columbus Insurance Building on High Street, advertised in the 1848 city directory a stock of "Trombocellos, Opheclides, Trumpets, Concert-Horns, Trombones, Post-Horns, Bugles, Cornopeons, Clarionetts, Flutes, Flageolets, Fifes, Violincellos, Violins, Accordeons, Guitars, Piano Fortes," as well as bows, strings, reeds, mouthpieces, and so forth. By 1850 what had become the G. and F. B. Machold "Piano Forte & Music Store" was located on State Street and had been joined by the "Boston Piano & Music Store," at the "Sign of the Harp, 4 doors north Neil House," advertising Chickering and Gilbert pianos in various new styles, including the "Boudoir, Louis XIV, Æolichord, Æolian Attachment," priced from $200 to $650.

While the first private school was organized in 1814, and the first publicly supported school dates from 1826, a stable system was established only in 1845. Dr. Asa D. Lord (1810–74), appointed superintendent in early 1847, had became principal of the Western Reserve Seminary in Kirtland at age twenty-three. While there he received a degree in medicine and also organized the first teachers' institute in the state in 1843. In Columbus he completed a course in theology and in 1863 was licensed to preach by the Presbytery of Franklin. After serving the public schools until 1856 (with the exception of an interim year, during which he worked as an agent of the Ohio State Teachers' Association), he became superintendent of the Ohio Institution for the Blind in Columbus, and three years later took a similar position in Batavia, New York, where he died.[21]

In 1836 a committee appointed by the General Assembly to study the possibility of a state school for the blind concluded that "it is desirable also, that as early as practicable, musical instruments may be procured, and the necessary arrangements may be made for teaching music, not only as a solace and a pleasure to the blind in their disconsolate condition as strangers to sight, but also as a means of contributing to their own support in the school, and afterward also."[22] After its establishment the following year, public concerts were offered periodically by its students. For example, in a review of "a most gratifying exhibition at the Asylum" on March 2, 1854, a reporter for the *Ohio State Journal* noted that, "With regard to the musical exercises, we must say that the pupils never appeared to so good advantage—particularly as to music as a science. Professor Nothnagle is very thorough and effective in his system, and his 'drill' will bring out all that nature has bestowed."

In the public schools of Columbus, Lord soon organized a formal course of study that included music throughout the nine years of elementary school and the four of high school.[23] At the elementary level "singing by note" was one of the required "exercises for the ear and the voice," and all the schools "shall be opened daily with singing, reading a portion of scripture, or prayer, and shall be closed with singing." One of the high school departments was labeled "Reading, Declamation, and Music," and by 1851 Lord was able to state that, "In our High School, music is now taught as a regular branch of study."[24]

In fact, Lord's concern was demonstrated almost immediately with the publication of *The School Song Book* under his name, its preface dated August 1847. This pocket book contained words only, directing the teachers to other publications, but "if they are not at hand, or the music is not known to the teachers, many of the songs can be sung to other music."

As was done elsewhere, Lord employed music making in his efforts to publicize and popularize public education. His first such effort seems to have been mounted during September 1847. The *Ohio State Journal* of September 29 announced:

> *Juvenile Concert.*—The pupils belonging to the Public Schools in the North School Building, will give a free Concert of Vocal Music at the New Methodist Church, on the evening of Thursday of the present week. Doors open at a quarter before 7. Citizens, and all interested, are respectfully invited to attend.

The paper then reported on October 6 that the singing by about one hundred children had been "executed in a manner highly creditable to all concerned." The evening also included demonstrations of the children's skill in geography and arithmetic.

Two days later the *Journal* reported on a concert by pupils of the Middle School Building, an article that also included considerable comment about the moral and social values that could accrue to the practitioners of vocal music:

> The pieces sung consisted of Sentences, Rounds, and Semi-Chorusses and Chorusses, and were sung by classes, a single [classroom] or by the whole choir [180 strong] which was composed of three [classrooms]. The singing was interspersed with exercises in Geography, Reading and Mental Arithmetic, all of which were executed in a very satisfactory manner, and spoke well for the course of instruction pursued in our public schools.

These and other similar events allowed Lord in his annual report of July 1848 to observe that the Juvenile Concerts "have generally been given in the largest churches in the City[,] which have often been filled to overflowing, and through the addresses made in connection with them and the school exercises introduced, have furnished to many, who might never have visited the schools, an opportunity to become acquainted with the system and to feel a deep interest for its success."[25]

Music apparently became part of the public examinations that concluded each quarterly term, although no record remains as to the repertory employed until 1851, when a selection of "Songs and Glees" to be sung in March of that year was issued in

The High School Magazine, a modest publication of the "Male and Female Departments of the High School." Columbus high school students were asked to perform songs with titles such as "Fair Is Our Native Land," "Be Kind to Each Other," "Land of Our Fathers," and "The Rock of the Pilgrims." Earlier that year Lord had enumerated the holdings of the high school library, a collection that included a dozen copies of Locke and Nourse's *The School Vocalist,* used in Cincinnati since March 1849.

The first identifiable musician in this mix is Elan Dryer, listed in city directories as early as 1848 as a "music teacher." One historian recalled Dryer from the vantage point of 1905:

> In the early fifties Elan Dryer was a choir leader and teacher of old-fashioned singing schools. He was long, and somewhat lank, in body, and his bass voice was as rough as a cross-cut saw; but he was good-natured and kind-hearted, and old men and women in Columbus today could testify that he made the boys and girls sing.[26]

The nature and duration of Dryer's employment remains unclear. However, a March 1851 newspaper account of a high school exhibition refers to him as teacher of the choir, and a December 23, 1852, account of a high school recitation asserted, "Under the direction of Mr. Dryer, they are making efficient progress in the science of music. There are several fine voices, and the general effect of the whole choir, when singing together, is very pleasing." Dryer then led his high school students in a repeat of their ambitious program at City Hall the following evening:

Part I

1 Sound our voices long and sweet	Chorus
2-In the valley I would dwell	Chorus
3-Mountain Song	Chorus
4-When night comes o'er the plain	Chorus
5-"Thy will be done"	Chorus
6-Farmers Song	Chorus
7-Gentle thoughts, O, give me them	Quartette
8-'Tis well to have a merry heart	Chorus

Part II

1-We roam through forest shades	Solo and Chorus
2-See our Bark	Trio
3-The Alpine Echo	Chorus
4-Hark! A low and soulful Anthem	Trio
5-Dream on	Chorus

| 6-I've wandered in dreams | Duett |
| 7-Lutzow's Wild Hunt | Chorus |

The schoolchildren of Columbus must have been kept busy that December, since two of what were labeled "grand music festivals" were presented under the direction of E. Pease, a singing schoolteacher from Pittsburgh who had arrived in Columbus from Sandusky only the month before. Shortly thereafter he offered a public lecture on his new "numeral" method of music notation (published as *The Youth's Musical Lamp* in 1854), as well as a course of lectures, "Music for the People." The Pease festivals were apparently not sponsored by the school system, but a mix of students from both private and public schools as well as the Columbus Institution for the Blind presented "Choruses, Semi-Choruses, Glees, Songs, &c., with Piano accompaniment." The proceeds were "appropriated to defray the expenses of the pupils' education." Pease must have drifted on south almost immediately, since he is noted as having taught music in the lower grades of the Eleventh District School in Cincinnati the following spring, perhaps on a gratuitous basis.

The *Ohio State Journal* of June 29, 1854, described the annual high school exhibition, during which "the audience were entertained at intervals with music from the female members of the school, which was appreciated by them. The 'Star Spangled Banner' and the 'Farewell Anthem' of the graduates were fine pieces of music."

There is no indication of who was responsible for preparing this repertory, but the August 19 minutes of the board of education noted that J. Suffern had been hired as a special music teacher, thus assuring the practice of music in the public schools of Columbus on a continuing basis, although Suffern resigned in October of the following year. In fact, Osman Castle Hooper listed in his *History of the City of Columbus, Ohio* of 1921 a succession of musical specialists and superintendents.[27]

Momentary stability was achieved during the tenure of Karl Schoppelrei from February 1866 to February 1870. Public concerts under his direction received rave reviews;[28] the apex certainly was a "Grand Vocal and Instrumental Concert" at the Opera House on December 3, 1869, at which his high school students were joined by several soloists, an "Orchestra from Columbus and Cincinnati, composed of Thirty of the best Performers in the West," and the Columbus Männerchor, of which Shoppelrei was director (1865–66, 1869–71, 1875, and 1879–81). The ambitious program, a benefit for the high school library:

Part I

1. Overture—William Tell, by Rossini. Grand Orchestra.
2. Chorus—"Hark! Younder Swelling Strain," Armorer of Nantes, by [Michael William] Balfe. By the Pupils of the High School with Orchestra accompaniment.

3. Piano Solo—Polonaise in E flat Major, by Chopin. Herr Karl Walter.
4. Duo—Cheerfulness (for Soprano and Alto). Miss Lully Galloway and Miss Lucy Ziegler.
5. Chorus—How Bright and Fair, from William Tell, by Rossini. By the Pupils of the High School, with Orchestra accompaniment.

Part II
Gymnastic Exercises —By Pupils of the High School.

Part III
1. Battle of Spirits—by Kretschman [*sic*; perhaps Kretschmar?]. Columbus Maennerchor and Orchestra.
2. Steam Waltz—by Canthal. Grand Orchestra.
3. Double Chorus from Tannhauser [*sic*]—by R. Wagner. By the Pupils of the High School, Columbus Maennerchor and Grand Orchestra.
4. Grosses Duo, for Violin and Piano—by DeBeriot. Herr Geo. Brand and Herr Karl Walter.
5. Quartette and Chorus—Soldiers for France abounding, from Il Puritani, by Bellini. By the Pupils of the High School with Orchestra accompaniment.

Soon after this triumph, Herr Schoppelrei was forced to resign because of complaints about "faithfulness in the performance of his duties." In fact, the board of education adopted a resolution at its meeting of February 8, 1870: "That no one occupying the place of a Teacher of Music in our schools be permitted to be or act as leader or instructor of any society or corporation whatever, that he be not allowed to play in places of public amusement but that he be hereby instructed to devote his entire attention and labor to the Public Schools."[29] Schoppelrei remained in Columbus until at least the turn of the century as a private teacher and conductor not only of the Männerchor but also of the Amphion Glee Club, Columbus Liederkranz, and the Germania Singing Society.

Despite the board's resolve, Herman Eckhardt, who served from February 1870 until October 1873, was also forced to resign following an investigation into accusations that he was devoting insufficient attention to his public school duties. Eckhardt, a violinist, had been trained in his native Germany and had directed the Boston Museum Orchestra before arriving in Columbus during 1859. He became director of the DeBariot Club in that year and of the Columbus Philharmonic Society a decade later. He also served as director of the Columbus Männerchor during four periods between 1872 and 1893, and led other organizations, such as the Columbus Liederkranz, the Orpheus Club, and the Columbus Opera Club. In 1873 he organized a string quartet (sometimes expanded to a string ensemble of as many as fourteen players), which functioned until his death in 1896. Despite a controversial tenure (that included complaints about methodology and lack of rapport with colleagues), Eckhardt participated in the creation of a complex course of study, derived from Luther Whiting Mason's *National Music Course*, which was adopted late in 1872.[30]

The article about Columbus in the *Historical Sketches of Public Schools in Cities, Villages and Townships of the State of Ohio* (1876) suggests that the road was not without some bumpy stretches. The anonymous author states (on page 15 of the article in an otherwise unpaginated volume):

> The appointment of Col. Scarritt changed the whole course of instruction in this branch which had heretofore been exceedingly unpopular with the board, teachers and pupils. The progress made during the year in music, drawing, botany, and physics was unparalleled in the history of the schools.

James A. Scarritt, sometimes referred to in official reports as "Superintendent/Supervisor of Music," held the position from December 1873 until June 1886. A native of New Hampshire, he had arrived in Columbus as early as 1855 and had conducted the choir of the Westminster Church and taught vocal music at the Ohio Institution for the Blind until 1864, when he resigned to become a clerk in the adjutant general's office. By 1870 the colonel had risen through the ranks to become an assistant adjutant general, a position he relinquished when he accepted the appointment offered by the board of education.

Scarritt, who assembled a chorus of two thousand school children to welcome former President Grant to the rotunda of the State House in 1878, was popular enough that his pupils planted a tree in his honor during the Arbor Day celebrations of 1884. He had been joined in 1880 by Miss Mary H. Wirth, who took charge of music in the high school for the next six years.

Scarritt was succeeded in 1886 by William H. Lott, who served until 1904, when he moved to Los Angeles. Like Scarritt, Lott had previously enjoyed a multifaceted career: freight agent and supervisor for the Hocking Valley Railroad, examining clerk with the Ohio State Insurance Department, and chief clerk and manager of the Sunday Creek Coal Company. However, he had apparently directed church choirs as early as the 1860s, and conducted the Republican Glee Club much of the time between 1872 and 1902, including a performance at the White House before President Grant in 1873. Lott put Columbus squarely in the pedagogical mainstream by adopting Luther Whiting Mason's *New National Music Course* of 1883 as the basis of a revised curriculum. He was also directed by the board of education to offer instruction to every teacher who was unable to teach music satisfactorily, a preface to the Board's ruling that every teacher in the system had to be qualified to offer instruction in music.[31] In 1888, the same year that his annual salary was raised to $2,000, he directed a chorus of one thousand in a celebration of the centennial of the first settlement of Ohio. According to the superintendent's annual report to the board of education in August 1905, Lott's resignation "at the close of the fall term was greatly regretted by teachers, officials, and all who were connected with the schools. He carries with him to his new field of labor the best wishes of a host of friends."[32]

CHAPTER 9

The Cleveland Music School Settlement

Although not unique in its structure or goals, the Cleveland Music School Settlement[1] attracts national attention as the largest community music school in the country. From an initial enrollment of about fifty in 1912, the institution grew to encompass at one point more than five thousand students, with several branches and affiliated organizations.

Its founding matriarch was Almeda C. Adams, born in Pennsylvania in 1865, but as the daughter of an itinerant clergyman soon resident in Ohio. Having lost her sight at the age of six months, she first studied at the Ohio School for the Blind in Columbus. She then learned of an offer by the *Ladies Home Journal* of a scholarship to the New England Conservatory of Music in exchange for a substantial number of new subscribers to the magazine. Miss Adams embarked on a statewide crusade, but met with final success only in Cleveland, where considerable local support led to the accumulation of twenty-five hundred subscriptions, allowing her two years of study in Boston. Although the conservatory originally accepted her only on a probationary basis upon learning of her handicap, she proved a star student, and in 1895 moved to Nebraska, where for five years she taught at what was then called Lincoln Normal University, as well as at the Nebraska School for the Blind. After a year of advanced study in New York City, she abandoned her hopes of a singing career and returned to Cleveland to care for an ailing mother. She also taught voice and conducted a choral class at several of the Cleveland settlement houses.

The settlement movement dates from 1884 in the Whitechapel district of London. Toynbee Hall was named for Arnold Toynbee, the English social reformer and economist, who had an abiding concern for that poverty-stricken area, generated by his interest in the needy and a desire to become personally aware of their circumstances. The university graduates who staffed this first venture were intent on participating in the life of the neighborhood and improving the existence of its inhabitants by offering counseling, as well as various areas of study and gratis programs of music and other sorts of self-entertainment. The idea spread quickly, leading to the establishment of the Neighborhood Guild in New York in 1886 and Chicago's Hull House three years later.

Miss Adams's inspiration was the distinguished violinist and conductor, David Mannes (1866–1959), whose passion for spreading the benefits of music education to the young and underprivileged led to his founding in 1894 of the Music School Settlement in New York City and in 1912 of the Music School Settlement for Colored Children in Harlem. After a visit to New York, Miss Adams presented the idea of a specialized settlement school to Adella Prentiss Hughes, certainly the most powerful figure in Cleveland musical circles. Mrs. Hughes shared the idea with fellow members of the Fortnightly Club, who on February 7, 1912, established a committee to assist Miss Adams in her quest. These prominent Clevelanders moved expeditiously: the Cleveland Music School Settlement was incorporated on April 25 and an executive board held its first meeting on May 6. A decision was made to finance the school by a membership plan, with gifts from one thousand dollars or more down to five dollars allowing the donors the status of founders, patrons, or associates. Three rooms in the Goodrich House at St. Clair Avenue and East 6th Street were leased, and Miss Linda W. Sampson, a nurse rather than a musician, was imported from the east coast at the suggestion of one of the trustees and appointed superintendent; Almeda Adams was named head of the voice department, Walter Logan of the violin department, and Mrs. Gertrude Kemmerling of the piano department.

The school was formally inaugurated on October 1, 1912, and by the end of its first month enrolled 111 students. In April of the following year Miss Sampson reported to the National Association of Music School Societies that enrollment had reached 207 and that during its first six months of operation 780 lessons had been offered in piano, violin, cello, cornet, and voice, with class instruction available in sight-reading, harmony, and music history. Fees were twenty-five cents per lesson, although soon those over eighteen and gainfully employed were charged double that amount, in part to subsidize those from poverty-stricken families struggling to pay tuition. Miss Sampson was also able to report that eighteen nationalities were represented on the school's roster.

At the beginning of the second academic season Walter Logan was appointed dean. Logan, an Oberlin graduate who had studied further in Chicago, taught at Northwestern University, played with the Chicago Symphony Orchestra, and was later to become a founding member of the Cleveland Orchestra. Lyric soprano Emma Eames (1865–1952), who had abandoned her glittering opera career in 1909, offered a benefit concert in the Statler Hotel Ballroom in March 1914, an event managed by Mrs. Hughes, who also served as Madame Eames's accompanist, and David Mannes paid a ceremonial visit the following month. Entertainment at a lavish reception was furnished by a quartet from the settlement, as well as James H. Rogers, who played the private home's Aeolian pipe organ. Mannes gave a spirited pep talk, including an admonition:

> When a physician takes up his residence in a city he says, "In what hospital can I give my services?" Every serious-minded musician in Cleveland should look upon the Music School Settlement here as the local music hospital. He ought to offer some of his services. There is no better place to prepare the musical soil in Cleveland, with its large foreign population. . . . Musically, the Settlement work ought to be the greatest thing here.[2]

In October 1914 the trustees conferred on Almeda Adams the honorary title of Founder and two months later Walter Logan proposed that his Young People's Symphony Orchestra become affiliated with the settlement. This amateur ensemble was constituted of wage-earning young men and women who rehearsed once a week at the school. Logan's suggestion was accepted with the proviso that the orchestra's one concert a season (later expanded to three) would not entail any financial obligation on the part of the trustees. This wariness was no doubt engendered by the school's precarious financial situation. In fact, at the October board meeting a decision had been made to reduce the paid faculty members to six hours of teaching, the resulting slack filled by able but unpaid volunteers. A novel money-raising plan was undertaken that December: groups of children from all over the metropolitan area were recruited and trained and on Christmas Eve sang carols before every home with a lighted candle in its window, after which donations were solicited from the residents. The program raised more than thirteen hundred dollars, assuring its continuation.

Financial concerns persisted, despite the Musical Arts Association's support of an increasingly active Young People's Symphony Orchestra (YPSO). However, the orchestra, which had earned two hundred dollars for a concert presented at the Hippodrome Theatre in January 1917, incurred a deficit of $1,100 in a series of five Sunday afternoon concerts presented in Grays' Armory at popular prices ranging from ten cents to twenty-five cents. Nonetheless Logan arranged another pair of Armory concerts during January 1918, and the YPSO participated in the settlement's spring concert in consort with the school's senior, junior, and elementary orchestras, an event that also included some chamber music, as well as excerpts from Almeda Adams's operetta, *A Modern Cinderella*.

Miss Sampson resigned in April 1918 and was replaced by Mrs. Catherine Saunders of the Boston Music School Settlement. By August of that year the settlement had leased a property at 7033 Euclid Avenue. The house provided more spacious quarters for its four hundred students, and an adjacent barn was remodeled to provide a rehearsal hall for the orchestra and chorus as well as ballet classes. The following year witnessed assimilation of the YPSO as an integral part of the curriculum, reorganization of the music library, publication of a bulletin for subscribers and other interested friends, and the resignation of Almeda Adams. Miss Adams had just returned from a year's sabbatical, during which she studied at the Mannes School. She was to have assumed responsibility for the settlement's chorus. However, its repertory was to be chosen not by the director but by the various heads of departments, a caveat that Miss Adams apparently found unacceptable.

During 1920 a decision was made to join what was first known as the Community Fund (later, the Community Chest, United Appeal, and today United Way Services), replacing reliance on a system of subscribers. Mrs. Saunders's account to her new benefactors in May 1921 reported a staff of thirty-five; instruction in piano, violin, cello, oboe, clarinet, trumpet, percussion, and voice; classes in theory, solfeggio, chorus, dancing, and orchestra training; and pupils' recitals on the first Sunday of each month and on alternate Saturdays. Some fourteen thousand individual lessons had been given to that point, while 375 individuals were currently enrolled.

Walter Logan had resigned in September 1920, miffed that the annual salary promised to him on the condition that he vacate his position in the Cleveland Orchestra was considerably less than he expected. Despite the departure of all three of the pioneers, the settlement prospered, and in October 1922 the trustees made a decision to purchase a "permanent" home at 1927 East 93rd Street. The building was refurbished and occupied during October of the following year; a new recital hall was dedicated in January 1924. Fees were raised to fifty cents for children and seventy-five cents for adults in order to provide salary increases for the faculty. By 1929 a decision had been made to augment income by renting the recital hall to outside organizations, and fees were raised again: those who could pay more than the regular one dollar were asked to contribute an extra half dollar.

With the advent of the Great Depression, officials of the Community Fund in 1930 questioned whether the settlement deserved continued support. The school had earlier established several outreach programs and in April 1931 announced that it would spearhead a program to meet the needs of the community's various social service organizations; also, that the settlement would institute the study of folksongs of the various nationalities represented in Cleveland's social fabric and would develop a training school for social workers and musicians. In the midst of this fray, Mrs. Saunders, director since 1918, retired and was replaced by Mrs. Martha Cruikshank Ramsey.

By January 1932 Mrs. Ramsey was able to report an enrollment of 621, including those in the various extension programs. She also mentioned a new activity—the therapeutic use of music in various mental hygiene programs: "The Settlement has been cooperating with the Child Guidance Clinic, Mount Sinai Clinic, and the Psychiatric Clinic of Lakeside Hospital in planning treatment programs for unadjusted personalities."[3] Another Ramsey innovation was a 1932 summer session of ten weeks that proved successful musically and financially. Nonetheless, by that fall economic circumstances led to various barter arrangements with both students and faculty and the necessity of borrowing funds to keep the school operating through December. Even with that expedient, the faculty worked without salaries during the latter part of that month. A 1933 bank holiday left the school without operating funds and a deficit of $900, despite an enrollment of 519, many of whom, however, required financial assistance.

Mrs. Ramsey resigned in June of that year and was replaced in November 1933 by Emily McCallip, who had been associated with the Settlement Music School in Philadelphia from 1916 until 1924 and subsequently with the Curtis Institute of Music. McCallip quickly recognized that her school's collaboration with the various settlement houses across the city in their music programs required specialized teachers, and by January 1936 she had organized a sixteen-week course meant to train those intent on teaching music in those settlement schools and other social agencies.

The settlement's silver anniversary was celebrated in October 1937, with benefit appearances by the Curtis String Quartet and violinist Samuel Duskin ([1891–1976] for whom Stravinsky had written his *Violin Concerto* in 1931), and in August of the following year the school moved to its present site—an elegant forty-two-room mansion at 11125 Magnolia Drive in what has become known as the University Circle area. During this period the settlement's voice department cooperated with Garfield House in an experimental program to help correct the speech of hard-of-hearing children through vocal instruction. In 1938 the school inaugurated a series of musicianship classes for preschool children, a program that by 1943 had blossomed to include kindergartners and first-graders, as well as older students up to thirteen years of age. A semester-long regimen of fundamentals was intended as a prerequisite to formal study of an instrument or voice. In 1944 an experimental approach allowed children aged nine or older to study an instrument after only a month of basic musicianship. Faculty were now required to present at least one free public recital a year, a series adorned with new additions to the roster, among them cellist Leonard Rose (1918–84) and Boris Goldovsky (1908–2001), head of the settlement's piano department from 1940 until 1942,[4] concurrent with his more familiar role as head of the adjacent Cleveland Institute of Music's opera department.

The war years depleted the ranks of both students and faculty. By February 1942 the school had been asked to institute a song-leader training course, on the theory that group singing might prove a means of maintaining morale in the community. By June it was decided to schedule one of the summer recitals during the late morning, allowing defense workers on afternoon or evening shifts to attend. The settlement continued to mount an active series of public concerts throughout the years of conflict, most of which drew good audiences and thus indirectly contributed to the war effort.

Miss McCallip (who had become Mrs. Lawrence Adler) resigned in 1945 and was replaced by violinist Louise Palmer Walker, who had been her assistant. By 1946 enrollment totaled 1,721 and the school fielded a Settlement Chamber Orchestra, since what had been the senior orchestra had been merged with that of Western Reserve University back in 1936. The following year saw the appointment of Cleveland Orchestra concertmaster Joseph Gingold (1909–95) as head of the violin department and the resignation of Miss Walker for reasons of health. By February 1948 she had been succeeded by Howard Whittaker, a composer who held the position until 1984. Whittaker, a 1943 graduate of the Cleveland Institute of Music, had taken an advanced degree at Oberlin after Army service, followed by additional work at the Eastman School of Music and with composer Herbert Elwell. Since he believed that "music education should contribute to the students' freedom of expression, and that discipline was one of the joys and qualifications of art,"[5] Whittaker quickly reorganized the curriculum, emphasizing group participation in classes and ensembles, which now included a student string quartet and a string orchestra. He restructured the music theory program into preparatory work for children under the age of eleven, a four-year program for those twelve to seventeen years of age, adult programs comparable to those at professional schools, and advanced work in orchestration and composition on an individual basis. He also issued the school's first catalog, took a personal hand in assuring that the public programs held both focus and interest, and hired Leonard Shure (1910–95) as head of the piano department. Shure and Gingold became headliners, for example, in a program of Brahms violin sonatas in May 1949. The following year the settlement cooperated with Western Reserve University in a series of six concerts, marking the two-hundredth anniversary of the death of Bach, as well as presentations of Stravinsky's *L'histoire du Soldat* and Menotti's *The Medium* in conjunction with Karamu House, celebrating the opening of its new theater. Founding spirit Almeda Adams died at age eighty-four.

A new library funded by Mr. and Mrs. Elroy J. Kulas was opened in the former coach house of the Magnolia Drive estate in January 1951. Later that year the settlement presented a series of concerts in the auditorium of the Museum of Art celebrating American composers; the first event was devoted to the music of Roy Harris (1898–1979), who traveled to Cleveland for the affair, accompanied by his pianist and wife, Johanna, who participated in the program. In 1953 the Cleveland Foundation granted five thousand dollars in support of the settlement's plan to service all ten neighborhood settlement houses, as well as the Jewish Community Center. Richard Kauffman of the St. Louis Institute of Music was hired to direct this expanded extension program. Instant success led to a festival during the spring of 1954, which included twenty-five music clubs from the various settlements totaling 263 participants.

In October 1954, faced again with the lack of space, the trustees decided to buy an adjacent house, which would allow the addition of eleven new studios, as well as what director Whittaker called

> a new children's music workshop, especially designed to meet the needs of the pre-school child, four and five years of age. This program is planned as a kind of musical nursery school, which will include rhythm band, singing, musical games, and listening to develop the child's musical instincts as well as appreciation for music. In combining the two fields, music and nursery school, we have approached the beginning of a new phase of musical training for the pre-school child.[6]

The Kulas House was dedicated in February 1955 with a concert that included a new piano sonata in A by Whittaker (dedicated to Mrs. Kulas), a group of four songs by Herbert Elwell, and the Beethoven Piano Trio, opus 1/1, performed by Gingold, cellist Robert Ripley, and Shure.

Shure resigned in 1957 and was soon replaced by another eminent pianist, Theodore Lettvin. A West Side branch of the settlement was established in 1958 and quickly enrolled 150 students in its Saturday program. In 1959 the settlement participated in a May Festival of Contemporary Music, with a program including works by Prokoviev, Arthur Shepherd, Whittaker (Sonata for Cello and Piano in F), and Starling Cumberworth, head of the settlement's theory program (Sonata for Violin and Piano, played by Gingold and Lettvin). Such repertory reflects an institutional commitment to new music, including performances during that decade of such works as Benjamin Britten's *The Rape of Lucretia* (1946), Bartók's *Bluebeard's Castle* (1911), and Stravinsky's *Cantata* (1951–52).

In November of that year Josef Gingold announced that he was relinquishing his positions at the Cleveland Orchestra and the settlement to join the faculty of Indiana University. A major drive to fund a viable endowment culminated in May 1962, during a yearlong celebration of the school's fiftieth anniversary. This included a recording that presented works by four settlement composers—Cumberworth, Elwell, Bain Murray, and Whittaker—prefaced with remarks by Boris Goldovsky.[7] Goldovsky also participated in an extended series of recitals by former and incumbent faculty and students. These included a program by violinist Jaime Laredo (a Gingold student) and his first wife, pianist Ruth Meckler, as well as Theodore Lettvin's performance of Howard Whittaker's new Sonata No. 2 in D.[8] Nadia Boulanger conducted two master classes and was fêted at a reception. Burton Garlinghouse elected early retirement from a distinguished career on the Baldwin-Wallace College faculty to become head of the settlement's voice department.

A new South Side branch was opened in the fall of 1963, and the basement of the main building was converted to allow the addition of ten new teaching studios as well as a ballet classroom. During the 1950s, Richard Kauffman, director of the extension program, had become interested in music therapy and, with the assistance of volunteers, had established links with programs at the Cleveland State Hospital and the Mental Development Center of Western Reserve University. A pilot program funded by the Cleveland Foundation was undertaken in January 1965, involving a professional whose time was divided between the Mental Development Center and the nursery school of the Parents Volunteer Association for Retarded Children. By September 1966 music therapy was officially embedded in the settlement's curriculum.

During October 1966, protracted negotiations were finally concluded with the Rainey Institute, located on East 55th Street near Superior Avenue, in a racially diverse area. This unique affiliation led to equally unique programs devised to meet the challenges offered by Rainey's clientele, for example, guitar for teenaged juvenile delinquents. During April 1968, two additional buildings on Mistletoe Drive were added to the settlement's campus: The Lucile and Robert Hays Gries House contained the nursery school and teaching studios, while the Margaret Rusk Griffiths House accommodated the extension program, including its music therapy component. During the fall of 1970 the West Side branch was closed, a void filled the following year when the Koch School of Music in Rocky River became an affiliate institution. In that same year, Burton Garlinghouse retired, the nursery school program was converted into a preschool program now called the Early Childhood Department, and a six-month internship program was approved by the National Association for Music Therapy.

During the decade in which the school celebrated its sixtieth birthday, further methods of outreach were evolved: jazz was added to the curriculum; a cooperative program in urban studies with several area colleges and universities allowed their students to work for a semester studying the innovative methods of the preschool program; a University Circle Center for Community Programs, designed to make the activities of the various Circle institutions available to residents of the contiguous neighborhoods, led to a new series of Sunday afternoon concerts; Dalcroze Eurythmics instruction was offered to children at the Cleveland Society for the Blind; and music teachers were sent to several public elementary schools that lacked music programs of any sort.

The Cleveland Music School Settlement, with its University Circle campus, Maple Heights branch, and various neighborhood centers, schools, group homes, and other locations, remains "dedicated to the continual search for the best ways to serve the Greater Cleveland community in bringing together persons of different racial, religious, and economic backgrounds. It has been demonstrated to us time and time again that a most powerful force to achieve this is through the media of the arts."[9]

The Professional Collegiate Schools

During the nineteenth century, Ohio's landscape blossomed with private music schools, whose self-anointed professors offered training in every conceivable medium, surely with vastly diverse degrees of expertise and success. Even though most of these have disappeared without a trace, two remain worthy of note before we limn the histories of the three most significant of Ohio's collegiate schools of music.

CHAPTER 10

The Lane Conservatory of Music

The Lane Conservatory of Music's 1899–1900 prospectus presented Professor Leasure Porter Lane as:

THE FOUNDER OF THE FIRST VIOLIN SCHOOL IN ZANESVILLE, IN 1890—THE ORIGINATOR OF THE LANE THEORY OF MUSIC, IN 1892— THE FOUNDER OF THE FIRST KINDERGARTEN MUSIC SCHOOL IN ZANESVILLE, FEB. 17–1899—THE FOUNDER OF THE FIRST CONSERVA- TORY OF MUSIC IN ZANESVILLE, INTRODUCING CLASS SYSTEM.

With unabashed self-adulation Lane presented himself as a teacher in the theory and string departments and of German, French, and English descent, even though he had been born on a nearby Muskingum County farm in 1849, and elsewhere claimed to have first offered himself as a teacher in Zanesville as early as 1879:

[N]ature seemed to give through him the three nation's characteristics, namely music, technic [sic] and literature. His musical gifts are too well known throughout the state to be commented upon here. His power to concentrate the student's mind is wonderful. His self convincing systems have inspired both the dullest and brightest minds. His pedagogical work is something re- markable as he has shown in his kindergarten work, by teaching the child of four years to understand music. Besides his wonderful energy and enthusi- asm, he evinces characteristics essential to the successful teacher in his abil- ity to inspire his pupils with the necessary enthusiasm and to win and hold their confidence and esteem.[1]

Lane's "Class System" (a not uncommon approach during the period) promised "technically better students, more practical students, broader minded students, consequently better musicians,"[2] who could enroll in the departments of violin, viola, violoncello, contra bass [sic], piano, organ, theory, harmony, guitar, mandolin, flute, cornet, clarionet, voice culture, elocution, and French. Tuition fees varied, based on the number of students involved. For example, in the string department, for two lessons every week of a ten-week term, each pupil paid twelve dollars with two per class, ten dollars with three, but only eight dollars with four. The length of a lesson was determined by the number enrolled in the group: An hour for two, and an extra fifteen minutes for groups of three and four. Private lessons were available in any department at a cost of fifteen dollars per term.

An unidentified commentator suggested that Lane's faculty numbered as many as fourteen at one point, but only four are presented in the prospectus. Besides the director the roster included his two children: Ora Delpha Lane Folk, depicted as widely known enough to have won the sobriquet "the natural violinist," and Bronson R. Lane, also a student of his father, who taught violin, mandolin, and guitar and led the Conservatory Orchestra, "a position for which he is gifted by nature." Mrs. H. L. Jones was pictured as a teacher of piano, and readers were promised that Dr. L. R. Culbertson "will lecture on the ear, as to how it is affected by sound waves." Professor Lane was also to offer free lectures on the "interpretation and conception of music," "the educational plan," and "devitalization of muscles." Students at the Conservatory were promised appearances at periodic recitals; performances could be furnished on demand by the Lane Family Concert Company.[3]

Lane's stab at immortality, *Tone, Silence and Time*, was issued in 1907. The covers of two of his three published pieces—*Storms of May. Concert Waltz*, a programmatic work for piano, and a song, "Loved Though It Be," both of 1910[4]—tout the Lane Time-Mark and Whole-Measure-Note (asserting that such were employed in all his compositions, although these two are couched in utterly conventional notation), and suggest that the reader send for an "Illustrated Time-Mark Card. Size 18 x 14." If totally baffled, one could turn to

"TONE, SILENCE AND TIME," (just out), which also gives the 26 newly invented characters—including the whole-measure note, the MOVABLE REST, etc., etc., etc.

TONE, SILENCE AND TIME is a MASTER work on teaching music. Its notation, etc. shows what causes music to exist, where it comes from, and how it should be taught. The work is new and logical, it contains a deep and true philosophy of music. It is the best for PUBLIC SCHOOL WORK.

TONE, SILENCE AND TIME further instructs all teachers, all beginners, doctors, all musicians and critics.

INDORSED BY LOGICAL TEACHERS and the BEST MUSICIANS.[5]

Lane's tome was subtitled "A Comprehensive and Logical Treatment of the True Meaning of Characters That Represent Music" and "A True Guide to the Art of Timing." Each of the volume's major sections is plainly delineated: "Tone by a red colored page; Silence by a black colored page, and Time by a blue colored page, and thus are Tone, Silence and Time presented plainly to the eye, as are the treatment and study of each of them to the conception of the mind."[6]

Any attempt to ferret out something of revolutionary import from what appears in the main a rather routine presentation of the rudiments of music is surely deflected by Lane's dense, virtually opaque prose. In fact, he appears a master of obfuscation, routinely capable of taking pages to describe what others might accomplish in a few sentences. One example of his style:

> The custom of measuring the length of time indicated by one time-character and of guessing at the time indicated by others, will not do and should never be permitted. The law of measurement demands that all characters which indicate length of time in either tone or silence shall be measured. Hence, if the length of time of each tone and length of time of each silence is to be felt, (which it is), then the *feeling* must be measured. Therefore, the length of time indicated by each time-character must be measured, and not measured by the law only, but by the natural and true feeling of length of time, governed by the timing senses, which senses should be tutored by the inward spirit and developed by intelligent execution.[7]

A specific example of his methodology, with its utterly bewildering presumption: After taking a considerable number of pages introducing his readers to the staff and the three principal clefs (that are to be "tuned" to the staff), Lane posited "THE NEW SYSTEM FOR LEARNING THE NAMES OF THE LINES AND SPACES." He mated the pitches by letter and number, running successively from 1 to 7 and A to G, and then demonstrated at length how 4 corresponds to D, 6 to F, etc. His seemingly illogical conclusion, despite all evidence to the contrary: "This system is easily acquired and easily remembered by the following phrases: UP on the STAFF, DOWN on the ALPHABET; DOWN on the STAFF, UP on the ALPHABET."[8]

He created a timetable of note values, ranking them as first through seventh (what would in common parlance be named whole through sixty-fourth notes), wrote at length about their different colors (black or white) and forms (with stems or not, the stems either plain or modified with "hooks" or "bands" linking groups of fourth [eighth] through seventh [sixty-fourth] notes), and then evolved for his students a mind-numbing system of manifesting rhythm by patting ("striking the floor with the foot"), beating ("a motion of the fore-arm"), and counting ("speaking the number of parts of a measure"), tantamount to a mental and physical gymnastics exercise.

His discussion of silence (that "is not produced; it exists. Silence is felt; it is not seen, smelt, heard or tasted. Silence must therefore, be realized by the *feeling-minded* senses of man, there being no other faculties by which it can be recognized")[9] produced new characters for whole and half rests, essentially imposing over the traditional symbols partially blackened versions of whole and half notes.

Finally, in part 14, Lane announced his unique replacement for the traditional time-mark (what is normally called a meter signature, thoroughly diagnosed earlier in the volume). He presumed that he had convinced his readers of the "inappropriateness, insufficiency and absurdity" of the existing system.

> It now only remains to provide a true, useful and convenient time-mark which shall obviate the distraction of attention that results from presenting to the mind of the inquirer mathematical perplexities, gastronomic suggestions, or any other mental pictures foreign to the subject. For this purpose, and, as the culminating, distinctive excellence of this system, the Author gives a simple, appropriate and truthfuliy accurate time-mark, that cannot be confounded with any other character used in music, can suggest nothing extraneous to its intent, and which will appeal with reason to composers, music-typographers, and to musicians, as being convenient, intelligible, easily taught and easily learned.[10]

He proposed as his framework a semicircular band that he likened to "a segment from the disc of the sun-dial—that ubiquitous outgrowth of the earliest device suggested by man's ingenuity for indicating the passage of time, whose universality in the infancy of all nations and races of mankind shows it to be the first natural means of expression of time-measurement, and whose recent adaptations recognize its pre-eminence over all other devices as a reliable and universally applicable time-indicator,"[11] a theory that must have come as a shock to watchmakers in Switzerland and elsewhere. Nestled in the apex of the disc was the note value, or count-note, an indicator "called the *gnomon*, [which] rises from the face of the dial, and intercepting the sunlight, thus throws a distinct line of shadow on the marked margin of the disc."[12] Inside the disc the composer then placed as black dots the number of count-notes for each measure. Thus, a quarter note as the indicator and two dots in the disc would be equivalent to the traditional 2/4 meter, an eighth note as the indicator and six dots in the disc the normal 6/8 meter. "It must now be evident that the time-mark herein presented is a perfect one and meets every requirement that a time-mark should for any musical composition."[13]

Lane's pursuit of immortality through such bombast obviously perished with his death in 1913.

CHAPTER 11

The Dana School of Music

Dana's Musical Institute (DMI)[1] was founded in Warren in September or October 1869 by William Henry Dana (1846–1916), a native who had been educated in the Warren public schools and the Williston Academy in Easthampton, Massachusetts. He also spent several crucial years at the Allegheny Academy of Music in Friendship, New York, having during the interim served in the 171st and 196th Ohio Volunteer Infantry during the Civil War, first as a field musician and then as a staff member for several generals. Dana's enterprise was originally housed in several rooms atop downtown commercial buildings with a pair of rented pianos and as additional faculty a pianist and vocalist who had been student peers in Friendship. Dana advertised, "A Hack at all trains to care for students and their baggage."[2] He then boasted in the *Western Reserve Chronicle* of June 1, 1870, that the school had "opened with three teachers, two rooms, two instruments, and one pupil. It now numbers eighteen rooms, eighteen instruments, and between fifty and sixty pupils; and its prospects daily improving."

Dana asserted in his 1870–71 catalog:

The study of Music is not the mere accumulation of ideas and facts which may be obtained from books, or which may be taught or learned in any other way. Neither is it the acquiring of the ability to thump off the notes on the piano, or to place the throat and mouth in certain positions and scream out a piece of vocal music "according to the rules." The study of *essential* music is the cultivation necessary to produce musicians capable of filling places of trust. To procure, successfully, this cultivation, it is necessary that students should be placed—not where they might take one or two lessons a week, and practice to suit themselves, but where their exercises can be carefully supervised every day; where they can hear music discoursed and also performed;

where their attention can be called to the faults and virtues of others, and thus cultivate a critical ear.[3]

His regimented daily plan of study involved class lessons on the student's chosen instrument, classes in theory, solfeggio, and music history, and participation in the band, orchestra, or chorus "with four hours of practice in the school's buildings." Students and faculty were involved in weekly concerts, at first on Tuesday evenings, later on Wednesdays, presented in the City Hall, in one of the local churches, or even alfresco.[4] Originally the school year consisted of three twelve-week terms, but was soon expanded to four ten-week sessions. At first the students boarded with private families. Dana maintained a very explicit code of conduct, including daily chapel exercises at 9:00 A.M., a prayer meeting at 7:00 P.M., and mandatory church attendance on Sundays: "Seats have been procured in the various churches in the place, and it is expected that students will attend at least one service on the Sabbath." Students were not allowed to attend dances or the theater, "calls from gentlemen" were permitted only with the joint approval of the woman's parents and Dana, and women were required to send and receive mail at the Institute rather than the official post office.

The core of the curriculum was a two-year program that nominally prepared students for careers as teachers, even though most male Dana students aspired to become members of professional concert bands or orchestras. Admission standards were virtually nonexistent and attrition rates high, so that the 1870–71 catalog listed thirty students enrolled in the Secondary Department (the first-year program) but only eight in the High School Department (the second-year program). There was also a Primary Department, which catered to would-be musicians with minimal experience until they were proficient enough to enter the Secondary Department. Advancement from one level to the next was determined by weekly (later, bimonthly) Wednesday examinations. This classification system was further confused by the gradual grouping of studies into church music, parlor music, orchestra music, and brass (later military) band departments.

Dana's enterprise was underwritten in large part by his father Junius (1822–1906), a prominent local banker who also played the bass viol and later the cello. Junius paid three thousand dollars for the four-story American House Hotel on Warren's central square, a structure that, beginning with the summer of 1870, became home to the institute for more than four decades. The ground floor housed an office, a library (that also offered musical scores for sale), a reception room, a "Teacher's Study," and a room for the voice and thorough bass classes; the second floor contained a piano classroom, piano practice rooms, and the Pythagoras Society's room; the third housed a theory classroom and organ practice rooms; the top floor contained a ballroom, which also served as a rehearsal space for band and orchestra.

DANA'S MUSICAL INSTITUTE
———— WARREN, OHIO ————

Established
in
1869
by
William H.
Dana

Send
for
Special
Catalogue
and
Blue Book

JUNIU'S COTTAGE   DANA HALL   MARTHA POTTER HALL

The oldest Military Band and Orchestra School in North America. Lessons daily and private on all Instruments, Theory, Solfeggio, History, etc. Superior advantages for the study of Clarinet and other Reed Instruments.

———————— ENSEMBLE CLASSES DAILY ————————

Chorus, 10 a. m.   Military Band, 4 p. m.   Orchestra, 5 p. m., in Dana Hall

———— CONCERT EVERY WEDNESDAY NIGHT, 7:30 ————

Fine Dormitories for the Pupils, with all modern conveniences. Two large brick buildings devoted exclusively to Practice and Recitation.

———— Address LYNN B. DANA, President, Drawer "MG," Warren, Ohio————

SUMMER TERM OPENS JUNE 26th AND CLOSES AUGUST 4th, 1916

An advertisement for Dana's Musical Institute found in the *Musical Messenger*, June 1916. Ohio Historical Society.

Inherited balconies adorned the building's façade; a brass band gave weekly ser-enades from the third floor.

After almost a decade of pedagogy, Dana departed in June 1879 to burnish his skills in Berlin with organist and theorist August Haupt at Theodor Kullak's *Neue Akademie der Tonkunst* and, after a visit home, at the Royal Academy of Music in London, returning to Warren in April 1882.

In 1884 Dana instituted a four-year course of study, although few completed the curriculum. By 1890 he began acknowledging students with a certificate at the end of their first year, bronze and silver medals at the conclusion of their second and third years, and a diploma at the conclusion of their fourth year, certifying the re-cipient as an Associate of the College of Music. By the 1890s the institute fielded a faculty of ten (most of them DMI graduates) and as many as seventy students. The Wednesday evening concerts featured the institute's orchestra (and its band after 1905), as well as student or faculty soloists and chamber ensembles; the one thou-sandth such concert was presented on November 7, 1894. An addition to the main building, which contained twenty-eight practice rooms as well as the Dana Concert Hall seating three hundred, was dedicated in January 1897; private instruction replaced the class lessons (and were correspondingly reduced in length from an hour to thirty minutes); Dana's military band attracted considerable notice with its off-campus performances, as well as Sunday afternoon concerts that, however, aroused the ire of some pious locals intent on maintaining the tranquility of the Sabbath.

Early in the new century, DMI for the first time offered dormitory housing to its students with the construction of Martha Potter Hall, a women's dormitory named in honor of the founder's mother and first occupied in 1906. Emma (Mrs. W. H.) Dana was named "matron" of the new facility the following spring; she and her husband took up residence, allowing transformation of their former home (renamed Junius Cottage) into a men's dormitory, this at a time when enrollments barely exceeded fifty students. The former American House had been condemned in 1905 but was not replaced until 1912 by the new five-story Dana Hall adjacent to Martha Potter Hall, providing an auditorium seating three hundred and housing a two-manual pipe organ, offices, a library, three classrooms, fifteen teaching studios, and sixty-nine practice rooms.

Earlier the DMI had been incorporated and in November 1903 was chartered by the state, including authority to award the degrees of Fellow and Master in the Art of Music, although Dana retained his traditional approach, conferring these degrees only on distinguished alumni. Earlier the school on its own volition had awarded diplomas signifying the recipients as a bachelor of music, teacher of music, or even professor of music. A new state charter in 1911 "enlarged the course of study and included degrees in other lines of intellectual work."[5] Although little seemed to change, the institution was now legally identified as Dana's Musical Institute and College of Music.

The Dana Music Company was organized in December 1903 and until 1906 issued a monthly *Music Times,* a vehicle for announcements of concerts, correspondence from alumni, and general articles by DMI faculty and graduates that was revived briefly during the early months of 1918.

William Henry Dana was a prolific author, publishing *Dana's Practical Thorough-Base (The Art of Playing Church Music)* (1875); *J. W. Pepper's Practical Guide and Study to the Secret of Arranging Orchestra Music, or, The Amateur's Guide* (1879, 1891, 1906); *Amateur's Guide in Arranging for Military Bands* (1880); *Dana's Practical Harmony* (1883); *Dana's Practical Counterpoint* (1885); *The National School for Cornet* (1890); *The Modern Arranger for Band* (1906); and *The Essentials of Musical Knowledge* (1915). Many of theses volumes were self-published and employed as texts by Dana faculty. As a composer, he left an orchestrated *De Profundis,* as well as motets, songs, and works for piano, such as a series of *Sunshine Waltzes* (1873) and *The Circuit Riders' Gallop* (1878). In addition, *The Students' Collection of Choral Music,* issued as an appendix to the thorough-base treatise, contained four-voice hymns by Emma T. Dana, his first wife, as well as a motet, keyboard voluntary, and several hymns by the patriarch (one was named "Warren," the other "Junius"). He was active in the founding of the Music Teachers National Association in Delaware, Ohio, in late December 1876, and presented the first of his several lectures to conclaves of the organization, "The Coming Music Teacher." Dana also became an active lecturer to the larger world, an avocation that by the late 1890s blossomed into summer-long tours on the Chautauqua circuit. For example, during the summer of 1897 he traveled about seven thousand miles to deliver twenty-three lectures in eight states on subjects as varied as "Beauties of the Bible," "Church Music," "On Foot and Rail through Ireland," and "Woman Suffrage."

At his death in 1916 he was succeeded by his son, Lynn Bordman Dana (1875–1941), a pianist who had studied with several noted teachers, including William H. Sherwood, and who had in fact assumed considerable control more than a decade earlier. The younger Dana was a DMI graduate of 1897 who had moved to Lima that year, established his own piano and theory school, and by late 1898 had become director of his own Dana's band. By summer 1900, he had returned to Warren and was appointed a teacher of piano and director of the chorus of his father's Institute. He became active in the Ohio Music Teachers Association and was to serve a three-year term as its president, beginning in 1914. He conducted several local choruses and was also appointed assistant musical director of New York's Chautauqua Institution in 1905. As a composer he supposedly left marches and novelty numbers written for his Lima band, a violin sonata, a piano trio, a piano concerto, a symphony, songs, anthems ("As Moses lifted up the serpent" [1904] and "Thou wilt keep him in perfect peace" [1909]), choruses for male voices, an oratorio (*The Triumph of Faith*, written for the dedication of the McKinley Memorial in Niles, and performed there by a chorus of 350 and orchestra of eighty on October 5, 1917), and *The Challenge*, a "Pageant of American Music" (1933).

Under the son's leadership the full-time faculty was expanded to as many as eleven and the full-time student body numbered between eighty and one hundred (plus as many as six hundred enrolled in the Junior Department). The younger Dana fostered a choral program in which a mixed chorus as well as single-sex glee clubs joined flourishing orchestra and band programs. During the 1920s these vocalists were involved in the annual presentation of fully staged Gilbert and Sullivan operettas, as well as "Frolics" presented by the DMI Minstrels, productions often carried to nearby towns as well. By 1925 the institute was operating its own low-power radio station, which broadcast the Wednesday evening concerts as well as Sunday morning services from the First Methodist Church. Dana also embarked on an expansion that added to the piano, voice, orchestra, military band, and theory departments those of Expression (that offered, for instance, a class called "Elocution,

Expression, and Dramatic Reading") and Public School Music. The three-year, public-school curriculum included courses in English, French, or Italian, and psychology, and de-emphasized performance, since its students were not required to participate in ensembles (excepting the chorus in their third semester) or to present a graduating recital.

The Fifty-seventh Annual Catalogue, issued in 1926, promised students a whole array of social occasions, ranging from an acquaintance party to the commencement reception and ball. It was noted, "[w]hile it is not insisted upon, young men pupils of the school will find full dress the rule at these affairs." Would-be students were told of the various professional ensembles that numbered Dana graduates among their ranks and were also informed of the "Institute Call," a short motive stolen from a Haydn symphony and overlaid with the mantra, "Where Is Papa Dana," performed when grandfather Junius, who played his cello in the orchestra, was late to a rehearsal of the work because of a meeting at his bank. According to the catalog it gradually became the equivalent of a signifying handshake. At the close of the opera season in Chicago, "an operatic leader stepped to the curbstone on crowded Dearborn Street and whistled the call. Immediately six persons responded and joined him—all former Institute pupils. Another, as a matter of curiosity, whistled it in a mining camp of Colorado, and immediately got a response from an assayer, who was at one time a member of the school."[6]

The catalog proudly and chauvinistically portrayed the institute as

an "American School" taught by Americans who are intelligent in matters musical and otherwise and where every good feature of our colleges and other institutions is incorporated. Avoiding all commercialism, avoiding all compromise with unworthy standards, all facile and adventitious success, the school has gained its world-wide reputation by right of conscientious control and unflagging industry.[7]

Nonetheless, the Great Depression dashed hopes for new facilities on the almost sixteen acres Dana had purchased on the banks of the Mahoning River, and enrollment dropped precipitously. New guidelines adopted by the state Department of Education led to the loss of accreditation, invalidating the institute's public-school program. Temporary affiliations with Hiram College in 1933 and later with what is now Kent State University through their Warren branches allowed the awarding of formal degrees by those institutions, but statistics tell of continued decline: Sixty bachelor of music degrees were conferred between 1930 and 1935 but only twenty-eight during the four years beginning with 1937.

For much of its history the school had operated virtually as a nonprofit organization, furnishing instruments gratis to its students and maintaining tuition rates considerably lower than competing institutions. In a meeting with his fellow citizens in 1894 William Henry Dana had stated,

> For evidence that the school is run not for the purpose of making money, I will tell you that in the twenty-five years the school has run it has sunk not less that $28,000. Father [Junius] has supplied this deficiency. At the end of the year, he only asks, "Has any one been made happier and better prepared to go out into the world this year?" Upon answering yes he always says "Well, the school is worth all it has cost." It might have been made a paying institution, had it been run like the conservatories of music.[8]

Since such patriarchal philanthropy had long since disappeared, salvation was afforded by a merger in 1941 with nearby Youngstown College. This assimilation was negotiated by Lynn Dana Jr. (born 1911), since his father had suffered a serious heart attack in 1938. Formally designated as Dana's Musical Institute of Youngstown College, the new entity was to be headed by Dr. Henry V. Stearns, the single full-time faculty member of Youngstown's Department of Music when it was organized in 1930 (Stearns had taught the seven classroom courses while eight part-time instructors offered practical instruction), with Lynn Dana Sr. as dean emeritus and Lynn Dana Jr. as registrar (although he left that position shortly after the United States entered World War II). Tenure for full-time Dana faculty had been incorporated into the agreement, and four made the move to Youngstown, one of them remaining active until 1951.

The Dana Institute of Music of Youngstown College opened on September 14, 1941, with a full-time faculty of seven and an enrollment of nearly one hundred (including almost forty transfers from Warren). One week later Lynn Dana Sr. died in his Warren apartment. While World War II had a major impact, by 1950 the Dana Institute enrolled more than 150 students taught by a full-time faculty of twelve. A quest for membership in the National Association of Schools of Music was granted that same year, with the stipulation that the name of the school be refined to the Dana School of Music of Youngstown College.

Youngstown College became a University in 1955 and in 1967 joined the state system as Youngstown State University, the same period during which a graduate program was initiated. Expanding enrollments during the 1970s led to the completion of Bliss Hall in 1977, which provided a new home for the still-flourishing Dana School of Music, since 1974 a unit of the College of Fine and Performing Arts.

CHAPTER 12

The Oberlin College Conservatory of Music

The practice of music at Oberlin College[1] followed a trajectory typical of Ohio's many small, private (but usually church-related), liberal arts colleges: a pastiche of performing ensembles was, during the decades following the Civil War, gathered administratively into a conservatory of music, that designation based on the venerable premise—still maintained in Europe and to some degree in the Ivy League schools—that the mere practice of music (in distinction to study or writing about it) should be quarantined in its own professional "school." With only a few exceptions (Baldwin-Wallace College is another example in Ohio), the formal distinction has gradually been eliminated, as conservatories metamorphosed into departments of music, often left with a principal mission of educating and nourishing consumers, rather than practitioners of music. Oberlin's Conservatory, however, has persisted, recognized internationally for the quality of its students, faculty, and facilities.

Oberlin College dates its founding to December 3, 1833, when twenty-nine young men and fifteen young women enrolled in what was initially an academy preparing its charges for collegiate work. In February 1834 the Oberlin Collegiate Institute was chartered by the state. In 1835 the Reverend Elihu Parsons Ingersoll, a graduate of both Yale College (1832) and Seminary (1835), was appointed professor of sacred music, the first such position in an American college. The title, however, was apparently somewhat of a misnomer, since Ingersoll was also director of the preparatory department. A later commentator asserted that "the musical instruction given at this time, was limited to the training of classes in singing; and this instruction was free to students in all departments. . . . Instruction in music formed no definite part of the course."[2]

Ingersoll left for Michigan after only one year, so that Oberlin's musical legacy during its first decades can be attributed almost solely to George Nelson Allen, a Bostonian who had arrived in 1836 as a collegiate and later a seminary student. During the fall of 1837, Allen, still a student, was appointed a "Teacher of Sacred Music" in the institute, a position confirmed and extended in September 1838. In 1837 Allen had helped to found and direct the Oberlin Musical Association, later and still known as the Musical Union, one of the longest-lived musical societies in the country. By 1839, Allen, a disciple of Lowell Mason and his associates, had nearly one hundred students in his classes; two years later the number totaled almost 250. His fruitful labors were acknowledged by the board of trustees, which on August 27, 1841,

> Resolved that George N. Allen be duly appointed to the Professorship of Sacred Music in this Institution. . . . Resolved that it is the sense of the Trustees in this appointment of Mr. Allen that the style of sacred music in this Institution be in accordance with what is understood to be the style of the Manhattan Collection of Thomas Hastings.[3]

This example of micromanaging would obviously be found indefensible today, but the Oberlin trustees had adopted as their model a leading advocate of "scientific" music, whose principles New York–based Hastings (1784–1872) had expounded in his *Dissertation on Musical Taste* (1822). His six hundred or so hymns were issued in tunebooks like *Musica Sacra* (1815) or the *Manhattan Collection* (1836). Hastings served as guest conductor of the Musical Association's commencement concert in August 1845. These events had become a regular feature of campus life as early as 1841. At first they consisted of individual sung items, perhaps accompanied by a small instrumental group, but by 1860 the chorus was supported by an orchestra of five violins, a single viola, two celli, a string bass, two flutes, and two horns. Sometimes the concert was an assembled pastiche grandly labeled as an "oratorio." For example, *The Oratorio of Absalom*, heard in 1852, contained a potpourri of music from Beethoven, Handel, Haydn, Rossini, and Andreas Romberg (1767–1821) assembled and arranged by Isaac Woodbury (1819–58), plus a recitative and aria contributed by George Allen. Allen also assembled Oberlin's first hymnal, *The Oberlin Social Sabbath School Hymn Book,* issued in 1844, with later editions called *The Social and Sabbath School Hymn Book* (at least by the fifth edition in 1854) and, finally, simply *Hymns for Social Worship* (the seventh edition was perhaps the last, in 1868). This was a pocket volume containing more than 250 hymn texts without tunes. Allen's hymn tune "Maitland" remains current, usually supporting words beginning "Must Jesus bear the cross alone?"

Allen, who played both the piano and violin, encountered resistance in his attempts to introduce instrumental music into the community. The trustees passed a resolution in 1841 "that it is not expedient to introduce piano music as a branch of Instruction in the Institution," and as late as 1846 a trustee resigned in part because "a vast amount of time and money had been expended for fashionable amusements and accomplishments, such as Piano Music, Dress, etc."[4] In fact, as early as 1839

Allen had begged for the purchase of a piano as an instructional aid, and soon managed to assemble a ragtag ensemble of perhaps six or eight instrumentalists to accompany the chorus. In 1841 he collected funds for a music hall, which consisted of a single large room housing classes, chorus rehearsals, and meetings of the various literary societies. A decade later a melodeon was donated to the Musical Association by a Buffalo firm, and in 1855 a pipe organ of twenty-nine stops was installed in the Oberlin Meeting House. This imposing structure, still extant, housed the local Congregational (now United) Church of Christ. At the time of its completion in 1844, it was the largest hall west of the Alleghenies, seating 2,500. George Allen conducted its choir, peopled essentially by members of the Musical Association.

The 1849–50 Oberlin catalog announced that "Instruction in Instrumental Music can also be had at moderate charges" and four years later that

> ample facilities are here afforded with extra charge, to those who wish instruction in instrumental music. In this department special pains have been taken to provide suitable instruments for practice, and to procure thoroughly competent teachers, while at the same time the terms are as moderate as can possibly be afforded.[5]

A department of instrumental music was finally authorized in 1855, although its offerings remained extracurricular. Allen was appointed "superintendent to provide instruments and teachers." Students paid him eight dollars per term for lessons, as well as for the use of instruments and instructional materials. From this income Allen was expected to remunerate his teachers and buy equipment. He complained at one point that he was losing money on the venture and persuaded his staff to accept a reduction in pay. Music competed for Allen's attention. He served as principal of the preparatory department from 1841 until 1864 and as professor of geology and natural history from 1848 until 1871.

One other instructor from this period, Charles H. Churchill, an 1845 graduate of Dartmouth College, had come to Oberlin to study theology in 1849. He apparently taught piano and organ, played the cello, conducted in Allen's absence, and taught some of the formal classes. He is reputed to have built a small pipe organ in 1851 that was used until the appearance of the larger imported instrument in the meeting house four years later. He left Oberlin in 1852 for a position at Hillsdale College in Michigan but returned four years later to succeed Allen as professor of sacred music and superintendent of the department of instrumental music.

Allen had resigned from those positions in 1855 in a snit over questions about his financial management and curricular control. Churchill lasted a single year, after which he accepted a professorship in the department of mathematics, astronomy, and physics. In fact, his onerous responsibilities had included not only complete oversight of all the vocal and instrumental music practiced both on the campus and in the meeting house, as well as public concerts whose income was to provide part of his salary, but he was also to teach in mathematics "an amount equivalent to one recitation per day."

The music position remained vacant for a year, after which Allen was persuaded to reaccept responsibility rather than see the program collapse. He retained this dual role until 1864, when he again resigned the music position, although he taught natural history until 1871. He died six years later at age sixty-five.

In 1865 two of his students, both of them Oberlin natives, announced an Oberlin Conservatory of Music. John Paul Morgan, son of a professor of theology, had taught privately in the Cleveland area before advanced study at the Leipzig Conservatory between 1863 and 1865. George Whipple Steele, son of one of the village physicians, stayed at home and advertised that he would offer instruction in the "Cultivation of the Voice, Musical Elocution, Elementary Principles of Notation, Harmony, Thorough Bass, Piano and Organ." Morgan took responsibility for the 1865 commencement concert and also offered the fruits of his German sojourn in the Grand Organ Concert. A local reporter noted that many were baffled by some of the "inexplicable German productions" but were enamored of "the beautiful execution of the Overture to William Tell and the Variations on the Last Rose of Summer."

Morgan presented himself as president and principal of the department of sacred music, Steele as principal of the department of secular music. Professor John M. Ellis was to serve as part-time lecturer in music in relation to intellectual and aesthetic culture; Charles H. Churchill was a lecturer on the laws of sound.

While the conservatory was a strictly private school, certain of the college buildings were made available for instruction. However, its two directors were responsible for collecting fees, from which they paid their operating expenses. Although it is not clear whether the fledgling institution was capable of meeting the grandiose claims of its prospectus, Morgan and Steele promised a three-year course in music theory based on Leipzig theorist Ernst Friedrich Richter's *Lehrbuch der Harmonie* of 1853 (known in translation as the *Manual of Harmony*), periodic lectures on varied musical subjects, free access to a "large and carefully selected Library of Standard Music," as well as instruction on the organ, piano, stringed and other orchestral instruments, solo and chorus singing, solo playing with accompaniment, and ensemble playing and directing. The classes in choral singing were available without fee to all students in both conservatory and college, but private lessons cost twelve dollars for two lessons per each of the twelve weeks in a term. Students were expected to furnish or rent their own instruments, the latter at the cost of two to three dollars per term for one hour a day.

Morgan departed the new enterprise after only a year to become organist of Trinity Church in New York City; Oberlin conferred an honorary master's of arts degree on him in 1870. The president's report to the trustees in August 1867 noted that more than one hundred students were enrolled in the conservatory, and suggested that the "College assume the work of giving instruction in music, appointing a professor to have charge of the department." A resolution of August 26 then ordered that the conservatory "be brought into connection with Oberlin College." Steele was appointed professor of music, responsible for superintending the new department of music, offering four hours of vocal classes and two hours of harmony per week, teaching private students two hours daily, leading the music at prayer services and lectures, and assuming responsibility for the annual commencement music.[6]

Steele, intent on advanced study in Leipzig, was given a leave of absence and replaced by John Comfort Fillmore (1843–98), an Oberlin graduate of 1866 who had just returned from his year of study in Leipzig. Fillmore (no relation to the Fillmore clan of Cincinnati) left after only a year for posts at Ripon College, the Milwaukee College for Women, Milwaukee School of Music, and Pomona College. He was one of the first musicologists to take an interest in the music of American Indians and also wrote several widely circulated textbooks, including *Lessons in Musical History* (1888). Steele returned from Germany during the summer of 1869 and immediately recruited to his faculty Fenelon Bird Rice, a professor of music at Hillsdale College, his alma mater (he had also studied at the Boston Music School with Benjamin F. Baker), and his wife, Helen Maria Libby Rice, a graduate of the Maine State Seminary (later Bates College), who taught French and music at Hillsdale, where she was also principal of the ladies' department. The Rices had visited Oberlin during the summer of 1862, when they participated in the commencement concert, guest conducted that year by Professor Baker. They had become acquainted with Steele during two years of study in Leipzig and were then invited to participate in the 1869 commencement event, Rice as organist and his wife as soprano soloist in Heinrich Proch's "Concert Variants" for coloratura soprano and flute obligato, as well as the "Inflammatus" from Rossini's *Stabat Mater*.

Steele, however, was not allowed to offer Rice a normal salary, and the two gentlemen were "given jointly, the option of assuming the entire financial responsibility of the Department of Music, and receiving by way of compensation whatever [they] could make of it." The president's annual report for 1870 noted "the advantages of the position, thus saving the College from any pecuniary outlay for the music."[7] But friction soon developed between the pair, and a July 31, 1871, resolution of the board of trustees clearly favored Rice. Steele withdrew in a huff and on January 15, 1872, incorporated a rival Oberlin Conservatory of Music, housed in private quarters in the building that is now home to the Oberlin Co-op.

Rice, faced with the challenge of providing instructors for his students, succeeded in attracting several, including Lucretia Celestia Wattles, a former student of John Morgan and a graduate of the Leipzig Conservatory, who was to teach at Oberlin for forty-four years. But both conservatories suffered financial difficulties. Rice petitioned the trustees to reassimilate his as a college department but was rebuffed, although they noted the existing "special circumstances" and voted him a stipend sufficient to bring his annual compensation to $1,200.

On April 13, 1872, Rice and Steele reached an agreement, which included the stipulation that Steele would as of May 11,

> cease giving instruction in music in the Village of Oberlin, and that from that time henceforth he will never in any way engage in the business of teaching music in any of its branches in the said Village, or be in any way whatever connected or interested with any other person or persons in such business in said Village.[8]

For $1,830.50 Steele sold to Rice "1 Organ, 1 Piano, 3 Stoves with the pipes and Zincs belonging with them, 108 Chairs, 2 Busts and Brackets, 1 wash-stand and the furniture belonging thereto, . . . 3 Music Stands, 1 Blackboard, 2 Wood boxes, Shovel, 7 Tongs, and 1 Ash bucket."[9] Thereupon, the vanquished Steele left for the Hartford Conservatory of Music, where he taught until his death in 1902.

Rice moved his conservatory into the rooms vacated by Steele and embarked on a period of almost continuous growth. He also found time to assemble another Oberlin hymnal: *Sacred Songs for Social Worship* appeared in 1875 and in 1880 became *The Manual of Praise for Sabbath and Social Worship*, edited jointly with Hiram Mead. After several editions the volume in 1901 became the *New Manual of Praise*, its preface signed by Professors Rice and Edward Dickinson, as well as G. Frederick Wright. With a faculty that usually numbered only about half a dozen, enrollment grew from 263 in 1870, to 346 in 1874, to almost 500 a decade later. Rice maintained total fiscal responsibility for the enterprise and in 1881 purchased with his own funds a house on the northwest corner of North Professor and West College Streets known locally as the "Morgan Home," since it had been the home of the professor whose son was one of the cofounders of the conservatory.

The challenge of adequately housing the conservatory's activities was finally met in June 1883 by Dr. and Mrs. Lucien C. Warner. Warner, an Oberlin graduate of 1865, had made his fortune manufacturing ladies' foundation garments and became a member of the Oberlin Board of Trustees in 1878. The conservatory catalog of 1884 breathlessly announced the Warners' gift:

> The building is to be constructed of stone and will stand when completed about one hundred and fifty feet on Professor Street by about one hundred and twenty feet on College Street, and will be in its central part about four stories high. The interior of the building will furnish ample accommodations

for the school in the way of offices, library, lecture, lesson, and practice rooms, with a fine concert hall. It will be warmed by steam and thoroughly ventilated. The walls and floor are all to be deadened to prevent sound from passing from one room to another. The exterior of the building will be of a medieval style of architecture; its round tower with conical top and gothic gables, reminding one of Holyrood Castle. When completed it will unquestionably be the finest building ever erected for the use of a school of music, either in this country, or so far as we know in Europe.[10]

The Norman Gothic structure, when finally completed in 1905 (and demolished sixty years later) at a total cost to the Warners of more than $100,000, contained everything promised, including 105 practice rooms, twenty-eight teaching studios, and a concert hall, later remodeled to accommodate a three-manual, forty-stop organ originally built by the Roosevelt brothers of New York City for a private residence in Rochester.

Three years later Finney Chapel was dedicated, erected by his son as a memorial to Charles Grandison Finney, the spellbinding evangelist who was lured from New York's Broadway Tabernacle to Oberlin in 1835 to head the infant institution's theology department, and who then served as pastor of the First Congregational Church from 1837 to 1872 and as Oberlin's president from 1851 until 1865.[11] One of the stellar moments in a series of dedicatory events during 1908 was a performance of the Beethoven Ninth Symphony by the Musical Union and the Cincinnati Symphony, conducted by Leopold Stokowski. Modified Romanesque in idiom, Finney's 1,960 seats accommodated the large audiences attracted to artist and commencement recitals. In 1914 it was equipped with a four-manual, seventy-eight-stop organ constructed by Ernest M. Skinner of Boston (his opus 230), an instrument rebuilt by the Aeolian-Skinner Company in 1955 and removed in 1999; its replacement is a three-manual, 76-rank mechanical action instrument in the late Romantic French symphonic style by the C. B. Fisk firm, dedicated in a season of inaugural events beginning on September 28, 2001.[12]

Another seismic shift had occurred in 1885 when Rice negotiated an agreement transferring fiscal responsibility for the conservatory to the college. He obviously operated from a position of strength, since he owned the property on which Warner Hall was being built, as well as most of the equipment that was to be moved into the new structure. Consequently he was able to insist that "no part of the income derived from the tuition paid by students in this department or from other sources should ever be used for any other purpose than for the uses of the conservatory."[13] His salary was fixed at $1,800 per annum, where it remained until his death in 1901.

Rice's early hires were mostly Oberlin graduates who then studied in Leipzig before returning to their alma mater. Frank M. Davis, contracted in 1875 principally to teach piano, became the conservatory's first violin instructor, using as the basis of his instruction the Ferdinand David methodology that he had imbibed in Leipzig. Calvin Cady (1851–1928) had received a diploma from the Oberlin Conservatory in 1872, and after two years of study under the revered Ernst Richter in Leipzig returned to teach piano and theory until 1879, when he left to become the first director of the University of Michigan School of Music. Of these pioneers, only George Whitfield Andrews (1861–1932) enjoyed a long tenure (since Davis also departed in 1879). Andrews studied with Rice as a youngster, graduated from the conservatory at age eighteen, and then joined its faculty three years later. He did further study in Leipzig, Munich, and Paris; became a nationally recognized recitalist; was named organist and later director of the Musical Union and also of the Conservatory Orchestra; and was duly honored by Oberlin with a master of arts degree in 1900 and an honorary doctorate three years later.[14]

It should come as no surprise that Leipzig became the model for Oberlin. Instruction was by the class method, which persisted at Oberlin in diluted form until about 1930. The required curriculum was simple and straightforward: piano, three years of theory, and an elective instrument. The choices gradually extended to include not only voice and organ but also a considerable number of string and wind instruments. To receive a diploma the students had to demonstrate that they had completed studies in nonmusic courses equivalent to those provided by the best high schools of that era, had successfully completed the sequence of theory courses, and had passed the requisite examinations in piano and their elective instrument. While no academic courses were required, the conservatory catalog acknowledged the proximity of the college—"Students can frequently devote a part of their time to literary studies, and where their circumstances will permit we advise them to do so"—although evidence suggests that only the voice students were encouraged to study foreign languages and oratory. No specific residency was specified, although it was expected that a normal student might require anywhere from three to five years; most, however, apparently studied for a term or a year, not aspiring to full certification.

Unlike Leipzig, students were bound by college regulations, which required church attendance twice on Sundays (a considerable reduction, however, from the stipulations of the 1860s and 1870s, which mandated daily morning devotions with the families with which the students boarded, daily afternoon prayers in the college chapel, and attendance at a weekly religious lecture by a faculty member), as well as abstinence from tobacco and intoxicants. Furthermore, would-be students were required to bring "testimonials of good moral character," and no student was "allowed to visit one of the other sex in a private room, except by special permission in case of severe illness." Attendance was required at the weekly "Student Rehearsal," actually a recital, and a visiting artist series was initiated in 1878, a tradition that has continued to the present.

During the 1890s the curriculum was extended considerably. Arthur E. Heacox (1867–1952), a graduate of 1893, was "retained" to offer a new two-term course in ear training (appended to the existing four terms in harmony and six terms in counterpoint), a retention that lasted until his retirement in 1935. He also studied at the Leipzig Conservatory and from 1909 to 1910 with Vincent d'Indy at the Schola Cantorum in Paris. He eventually taught all aspects of music theory and achieved national renown through a large handful of texts, including *Ear Training* (1898), *Lessons in Harmony* (1904, with a revised edition as late as 1931), *Keyboard Training in Harmony* (1917, and as late as 1961), and *Harmony for Eye, Ear and Keyboard* (1922).

The three-term, one-year course in analysis was taught by Charles P. Doolittle, who was hired in 1885 as an instructor in violoncello and flute and lecturer on musical form. Doolittle offered a set of lectures on music history during the 1888–89 school year and then a scheduled course on the subject in 1891 as part of the theory curriculum.

However, it was Edward Dickinson who established music history as a legitimate form of inquiry at Oberlin. Dickinson (1853–1946) received both a bachelor of arts (1876) and a master of arts (1881) degree from Amherst College and had studied musicology in Berlin with the eminent Bach scholar, Philipp Spitta, after which he had in 1882 become director of music at Elmira [New York] College. He delivered a series of guest lectures at Oberlin during January 1891 and, after another year of work with Spitta, joined the Oberlin family in the fall of 1893. The faculty had in March 1891 voted unanimously to hire Dickinson "to teach mostly piano at first, with the expectation of his doing gradually more work in history and analysis." In fact, Rice had at first to defend his employment of a specialist, but Dickinson gradually established a national reputation as a pioneer in methods of teaching both music history and "appreciation." He never considered himself a specialist, and became a passionate advocate of music as an integral facet of the liberal arts. In 1905 he offered the first conservatory course aimed exclusively at college students. His appreciation of music course was "a course in the art of listening to music in the broadest sense of the term," designed for those who "wished to obtain the culture and refinement of music, but who had no time for the technical study of any musical instrument." His concern was manifested in his published works, including *Music in the History of the Western Church* (1902), *The Study of the History of Music* (1905), *The Education of a Music Lover: A Book for those who Study or Teach the Art of Listening* (1911), *Music and Higher Education* (1915), and *The Spirit of Music* (1925).

William Treat Upton (1870–1961) was another Oberlin music historian who attracted national attention. He eventually possessed four Oberlin credentials (a bachelor of arts degree in 1896, a bachelor of music degree in 1904, a master of arts degree in 1924, and an honorary doctorate in 1945) and had done further piano study with Theodor Leschetizky in Vienna and Josef Lhévinne in Berlin. He taught piano at Oberlin from 1897 until 1936 but became a pioneering Americanist with his *Art-Song in America* (1930), biographies of Anthony Philip Heinrich (1939) and William Henry Fry (1954), and especially his revision and expansion of Oscar Sonneck's *Bibliography of Early Secular American Music* in 1945, most of this accomplished during his post-Oberlin association with the music division of the Library of Congress.

At the dedication of Warner Hall Fenlon Rice had enunciated the credo that had governed his stewardship during these seminal decades:

> Music excites, regulates, and relieves the life of emotion, and life is rich mainly in proportion to the fullness of its emotional activity; and it is noble almost in proportion to the strength and balance of emotion. It is this power which music possesses that raises it, when properly used, into a higher realm where it becomes a moral agent.[15]

That vision hardly perished with his death in 1901, but the appointment of Charles Walthall Morrison as his successor signaled the advent of a new era. The same resolution anointing him director of the conservatory reorganized its faculty in a manner analogous to that of the college, with the Conservatory Council constituted of all its full professors, a committee on appointments, an annual budget submitted to the trustees, and so forth. (Morrison was later to invite broader participation in conservatory governance with committees on curriculum, the library, artist series, and social activities.) This action presaged further integration of conservatory and college, a process fostered by both Morrison and President Henry Churchill King.

Morrison had graduated from the conservatory in 1880 and was immediately appointed an instructor in pianoforte, although he later replicated the typical Oberlin pattern by studying in both Leipzig and Berlin between 1882 and 1885 and again during the 1894–95 academic year. The King-Morrison alliance made an initial attempt at further integration on October 2, 1912, when King appeared before the conservatory faculty to request their participation in the general affairs of the college. He claimed,

> The Conservatory is not simply, first, a school of Music, but a musical department of a great College, with a much larger and richer life just on that account, and second, the Conservatory may well be urged to see and feel the full opportunity and responsibility involved in that relation and so to take your share in the larger life to which you belong.[16]

Despite President King's assurances of his appreciation for their contributions to the life of the college, his listeners took considerable umbrage, and the first tangible symbol of intimacy occurred only during the fall of 1914, when the conservatory opted for the semester calendar that the college had adopted in 1901. Concurrently the conservatory faculty accepted a system of semester credit hours similar to that used in the college, thus quantitatively equating conservatory and college courses and facilitating the exchange of students between the two.

In 1903 the conservatory faculty had decided to award a bachelor of music degree. At first its requirements differed only slightly from those already in force, and for two more years diplomas were granted to those who had not met the admission standards of the college. Furthermore, in 1905 the faculty decided to confer the newfangled degree retroactively on alumni who offered "satisfactory evidence of creditable post graduate work in music, such evidence to consist of study for a sufficient period, either in this country or abroad; successful teaching; or other active musical work."[17] A special committee granted the honor to seventy-one earlier graduates; each candidate paid a five-dollar fee.

As of 1907 full-time conservatory students had to meet the same requirements for admission as college students, and by 1910 those requirements were specified: fifteen units in English, mathematics, foreign languages, history and civics, and the sciences. Morrison boasted in his annual report of 1910, "It would be difficult to find anywhere in the world so large a body of music students with so high an average of general culture." Even though the 1903 catalog had announced an English literature course in the novel, "intended exclusively for such conservatory students as are, for any reason, unable to pursue the courses in musical theory, and are at the same time not prepared to carry advantageously an English course in the college or in the Academy,"[18] no college courses were required of the conservatory students until 1930, although voice majors after 1913 studied either French or German for two years, the second year replaced later by a course in dramatic expression and training for the speaking voice.

Morrison soon faced a critical shortage of space for his burgeoning enterprise. Several of the large spaces in Warner Hall were compartmentalized to create more practice rooms, and in 1910 Rice Memorial Hall was dedicated. Named in honor of Morrison's predecessor and his wife (an endowed professorship bearing the name of the former had been created back in 1901), the new four-story, $75,000 structure was located immediately to the west of Warner. It contained 114 practice rooms, six classrooms, and an orchestra rehearsal hall. In addition, it was considered fireproof and was "thoroughly lighted with electricity, heated with steam, and equipped with an Otis elevator."

Between 1903 and 1929 the Musical Union provided a focus for annual May Festivals. Their pattern was typical of the era: An imported professional orchestra (those brought to Oberlin came from Boston, Chicago, Cincinnati, Pittsburgh, and, after its founding, Cleveland) performed a matinee concert under the baton of its own conductor, and also collaborated with the Musical Union at two evening events. (At this point the MU also sang an annual *Messiah* during December.) In 1916 the Chicago Symphony and MU presented the Beethoven Ninth Symphony under the baton of Frederick Stock, while Professor Andrews conducted Ermanno Wolf-Ferrari's cantata *La Vita Nuovo,* opus 9 (1901). The next afternoon Stock led his orchestra in the overture to Wolf-Ferrari's *Il Segreto di Susanna* (1909), the Brahms Fourth Symphony, one of Adrien François Servais's Fantasias for Cello and Orchestra, and the Tchaikovsky overture, *Francesca da Rimini.* That evening Andrews conducted the combined forces in the Verdi *Requiem.* During that academic year Oberlin students had been provided an equally dazzling Artist Recital Series, including programs by pianists Percy Grainger and Ossip Gabrilowitsch, organist Joseph Bonnet, violinist Jacques Thibaud, the Flonzaley String Quartet, and the orchestras of Philadelphia (with Leopold Stokowski on the podium and his then-wife, Olga Samaroff, as soloist), New York (the symphony, conducted by Walter Damrosch), Cincinnati (led by Ernst Kunwald), and Chicago (with Stock conducting the Mahler Fourth Symphony).[19]

Morrison retired in 1924 after forty-four years of service. During his tenure the conservatory faculty had increased from twenty-eight to forty members. Morrison made several critical appointments, including James Husst Hall, a graduate of both the college (1914) and conservatory (1915), a disciple of Dickinson who succeeded his mentor upon the latter's retirement in 1922. Morrison also organized a faculty string quartet in 1916 and, early in the next decade, a faculty piano trio, which concertized widely and made a series of network radio broadcasts from WTAM in Cleveland.

William Jasper Horner, a college graduate of 1896, had been hired as an instructor in singing, harmony, and ear training after receiving a conservatory diploma in 1900. He attended the School of Methods summer course in Chicago in 1901 before offering Oberlin's first public-school music courses the following year. He supposedly developed an immediate aversion to this new assignment and after a year of advanced voice study in Berlin taught only voice until his retirement in 1937. The two public-school music courses were then taught by part-time instructors until the arrival of Karl Wilson Gehrkens (1882–1975) in 1907. Gerhkens had enrolled in the college in 1900 as a premedical student but gradually turned toward school administration or teaching as a vocation. He also took some conservatory courses but without any intention of becoming a professional musician. After graduation in 1905 he taught algebra and German at the Oberlin High School and became conductor of its chorus. In 1907 he was hired both as instructor in the conservatory and supervisor of music in the Oberlin schools, inheriting fifteen students (considered by many as rejects from more rigorous programs) and a two-term course. Gehrken's vision and energy led by 1913 to the Supervisor's Training Course in Public School Music of three terms (coupled to prerequisites in harmony and ear training). A year later the course work entailed four semesters in the classroom and a class in string teaching, supplemented five years later by wind instrument classes. The course was extended to three years in 1917, and, fortified by Gehrkens's seminal work within the Music Supervisors National Conference and the Music Teachers National Association, the conservatory faculty in November 1921 approved (although not without vociferous opposition) a four-year bachelor of school music degree, the first such program in the country.[20]

Gehrkens had threatened to resign if thwarted, but he remained at Oberlin until retirement in 1942 and became a widely published author. He served as music editor of the second edition of *Webster's New International Dictionary,* edited the *School Music Monthly* from 1917 until 1939, wrote for periodicals such as *Educational Music Magazine* and *Etude,* and published several influential books, including *Music Notation and Terminology* (1914, his master's thesis at Oberlin, issued in a revised edition as late as 1942), *Essentials in Conducting* (1919), *An Introduction to School Music Teaching* (1919), *Fundamentals of Music* (1924), a *Handbook of Musical Terms* (1927), *Music in the Grade Schools* (1934), *Music in the Junior High School* (1936), and *The Teaching and Administration of High School Music* (joint authorship, 1941).[21]

Morrison chose his successor, Frank Holcomb Shaw, who was to serve as director until 1949. Shaw had graduated from Oberlin in 1907, spent 1912 to 1914 studying the piano in Paris and Stuttgart, and had taught briefly at Monmouth College in Illinois before appointment as director of the Conservatory of Music at Cornell College in Iowa. For his achievements at Oberlin, he was awarded honorary doctorates by Syracuse University in 1929 and Cornell College a year later.

Shaw determined to strengthen the conservatory's string and wind programs. Consequently, expanded numbers of both faculty and students allowed the creation of all-student string ensembles, an orchestra of symphonic proportions (conducted by violinist Maurice Kessler), and a band program directed by Arthur Williams from 1928 until 1957. An Aeolus Cornet Club had been mentioned as early as 1880, and by 1903 it included twenty members, including student trombonist Frank Shaw; in 1911 the director of athletics purchased uniforms in order to encourage the ensemble's presence at various sports events. Williams organized the Men's Marching Band and two years later the Oberlin College Concert Band. These ensembles were complemented by a Women's Band, dating from 1929, directed by George Waln as of 1930. Following Williams's retirement, the college band became a feeder ensemble for the Oberlin Wind Ensemble, conducted for many years by Kenneth Moore.

Olaf C. Christiansen was imported in 1929 to establish a viable choral program. He organized a sequence of conducting classes, a madrigal group, and the sixty-voice A Cappella Choir, which achieved considerable recognition through its spring vacation tours of the Northeast and Midwest. Christiansen departed in 1941 to join his father, the legendary F. Melius Christiansen, at St. Olaf College in Minnesota, leaving a void filled only by the Musical Union (that was directed by Professor Kessler until his retirement in 1954) until the arrival of Robert P. Fountain (1918–96) in 1948. Under his direction the Oberlin College Choir achieved national prominence, especially following its State Department–sponsored tour of the Soviet Union and Romania in 1964, a venture that included forty concerts in fifty-five days. Fountain was succeeded by conductor and composer Daniel Moe in 1972.

In 1932 Shaw also hired the young composer Normand Lockwood (1906–2002), straight from work with Ottorino Resphigi and Nadia Boulanger, as well as several years as a fellow of the American Academy in Rome. Lockwood, during a tenure that lasted until 1943, managed to elicit some interest in the larger world of modern composition through visits by Boulanger, as well as composers of the stature of Roy Harris and Bela Bartók.

Oberlin became a charter member of the National Association of Schools of Music (NASM) in 1924. Five years later NASM adopted a requirement that all bachelor of music candidates in its member institutions complete a minimum of eighteen credit hours in academic coursework. The Oberlin faculty begrudgingly responded to this mandate, finally approving a plan of action in 1932. No attempt had been made to coordinate conservatory and college curricula, so that the college curriculum was structured around courses offering three hours of credit, while those in the conservatory offered only two. Consequently, advanced music history courses were allowed to satisfy the new requirement, as were conservatory-taught offerings in dramatic expression, introduction to the arts, and the physics of musical sound. A special two-hour English course could substitute for the more rigorous three-hour college offering, and in 1944, after a decade of persuasion, the college faculty created three-hour (rather than five-hour) language courses, which were compulsory for voice majors.

Oberlin was a pioneer in the introduction of Dalcroze Eurythmics, that unique system evolved by Emile Jacques-Dalcroze (1865–1950) intended to develop an awareness of musical rhythm by coordinating music with physical movement. An experimental course was first introduced in 1937; three years later the faculty required conservatory women to make Dalcroze a major part of the required Physical Training program, a requirement extended to men in 1941. While available as an elective, the mandatory requirement was eliminated in 1956.

No major construction occurred during Shaw's term, but he succeeded in purchasing an enormous number of pianos, organs, and orchestral and band instruments. The Warner Concert Hall organ, rebuilt by Ernest Skinner in 1927, was replaced in

1950 by one designed on "classic" lines by Cleveland's Walter Holtkamp. That instrument was later removed to the new Warner Concert Hall and then replaced in 1974 by an even more ascetic one by the Dutch builder, Dirk Flentrop.

Frank Shaw retired reluctantly in 1949 at age sixty-five and was succeeded by the first director who was not an alumnus or pianist: David Ritchie Robertson. Robertson held degrees from Drury College and the State University of Iowa, had served as a violinist in the NBC Symphony under Toscanini, had founded the State Symphony of Arkansas in Little Rock, and came to Oberlin from the University of Wichita, where he headed the orchestra department and served as concertmaster and associate conductor of the Wichita Symphony. Robertson stipulated that his role would include directing the Oberlin Orchestra, and he quickly increased its rehearsals from two to five times weekly, raising it to the professional standards that attracted national attention during its frequent tours.

During his twelve years of leadership he presided over major revisions in the undergraduate curriculum (most noticeably a "core" of integrated courses for first-year students, but also new majors in composition and sacred music), and in 1957 succeeded in terminating the graduate program, which since 1926 had awarded 173 master of music and three master of arts diplomas. In 1958 he oversaw the introduction of the Suzuki method of string pedagogy in this country. He also pressed for a mandatory junior year in residence at an Oberlin-in-Salzburg program housed at the Mozarteum. This venture was devised in part to allow a proportional increase in the total number of enrolled students to 540, with 420 resident in Oberlin. While the program attracted considerable attention, a substantial minority of the faculty, concerned about the disruptions it caused, especially to the continuity of the various ensembles, and aware that the year abroad seriously impinged on the coherence of the students' training, succeeded in 1960 in avoiding indefinite extension of the program, limiting it to another three-year trial period, ending in 1964.

Robertson also initiated a three-day, four-concert series of works by Oberlin faculty, students, and alumni, which soon evolved into the annual Festival of Contemporary Music, over the years anchored by visiting headliners such as Peter Mennin, Aaron Copland, Wallingford Riegger, Luigi Dallapiccola, Leon Kirchner, Roger Sessions, Milton Babbitt, and Igor Stravinsky. He also fostered opera in Oberlin with the creation in 1952 of the Opera Laboratory, which offered a staged performance of *The Bartered Bride.*

Robertson presided over planning for new facilities to replace Warner and Rice Halls. The Detroit firm of Minoru Yamasaki was designated to design a complex of interconnected structures at the southeast intersection of West Main and South Professor Streets facing the College Square. The principal unit contains administrative offices, classrooms, and teaching studios. Immediately to the south is a wing encompassing choral and instrumental rehearsal halls, a recital hall seating 150, the library (considerably extended in 1988), and the new Warner Concert Hall, seating six hundred, donated by Mr. and Mrs. Seabury Cone Mastick (Mrs. Mastick was the daughter of the Lucien C. Warners) and renovated acoustically in 1983. The southernmost unit contains 173 practice rooms. While construction was authorized in 1957, the initial buildings were not dedicated until October 31, 1964, with ceremonies that included an address by conductor George Szell.

Robertson had spent the spring of 1961 in Salzburg, attempting to strengthen the program he had nurtured and thus immunize it against the attacks of its critics. It was there that he suffered a heart attack; he died in Paris on July 12 on his way home. His assistant became acting director and was succeeded in 1963 by Norman Lloyd, with the title of dean. Lloyd, a theorist, composer, and pianist, had been on the staff of the Juilliard School and returned to New York after only three semesters to head the Division of the Arts of the Rockefeller Foundation. Perhaps wary at this point, the Oberlin Conservatory faculty again became introverted in its search for leadership, turning to its own ranks to choose as its next three deans choral conductor Robert Fountain (1965–70), pianist Emil Danenberg (1971–75, at which point he was appointed president of the college, a position he held until his death in 1981), and organist David Boe (1976–91) before electing music educator Karen L. Wolff, hired away from the University of Minnesota in 1991. Wolff in turn was succeeded in 1999 by Robert Dobson, dean of the Conservatory of Lawrence University in Appleton, Wisconsin. Dodson left his post in 2004 to become provost of the New England Conservatory of Music and was succeeded by David H. Stull, Dodson's assistant at Oberlin and, earlier, at Lawrence.

The one-hundredth anniversary of the conservatory was celebrated from 1966 to 1967 with a series of eight faculty and ensemble concerts in New York City, as well as a series of master classes by the likes of organist André Marchal, violinist Ivan Galamian, pianist Alfred Brendel, and singer Gerard Souzay. Robert Shaw served as guest conductor of the Musical Union, Rudolf Serkin played the Beethoven "Emperor" Concerto at a benefit concert to establish a scholarship fund in his name, and composer Aaron Copland was in residence for five days during May. A series of "Music from Oberlin" programs was syndicated and broadcast over more than thirty FM stations across the country, a venture later to reach as many as 125 outlets.

During July 1967 the Teaching Performance Institute linked 205 high school teachers from thirty-five states with guest composers Richard Hoffman, Donald Erb, Ross Lee Finney, and Easley Blackwood for a month of orchestra, wind ensemble, chorus, and chamber ensemble rehearsals and performances. Fall 1968 brought a new course, An Introduction to Ethnology: Negro Music in the United States, the genesis of what became a substantial ethnomusicology curriculum. A pioneering program in electronic music inaugurated in 1969 led by 1973 to a major in technology in music and related arts and in 1986 to one in electronic and computer music.

The noted summer Baroque Performance Institute was created in 1972; a Collegium Musicum was organized the following year, leading to a historical performance program in 1986. Jazz studies, earlier proscribed as unworthy of notice by the Oberlin faculty, became a program in 1973. Major festivals in 1985 were devoted to the tercentenary of the birth of Bach and the centenary of the birth and fiftieth anniversary of the death of Alban Berg.

Then-president S. Frederick Starr, a noted expert on the Soviet Union and a practicing jazz musician, sparked the most audacious venture of recent decades. During the summer of 1988, Oberlin cosponsored with the American Field Service Intercultural Program (Nancy Reagan was its honorary chairwoman) the 110-member American Soviet Youth Orchestra. After two weeks of rehearsal in Oberlin during late July, the ensemble, conducted by Oberlin's Larry Rachleff and Leaned Nikolayev of the Moscow State Conservatory (and guest conducted by Zubin Mehta in Washington and New York) embarked on an extended tour of eleven concerts ranging from San Francisco to Milwaukee, Trenton, Moscow, and Leningrad, playing literature by Ives, Copland, Prokoviev, Shostakovich, Tchaikovsky, and Mahler, as well as commissioned pieces by Libby Larsen and Edison Denisov. A projected 1989 sequel was postponed a year because of the lack of funding from the Soviet Union. However, the 1990 venture, sponsored by Oberlin and the Moscow State Conservatory, with Barbara Bush and Raisa Gorbachev as honorary chairwomen, involved one hundred young performers and violin soloist Joshua Bell, conducted by Leonard Slatkin of the St. Louis Symphony, Catherine Comet of the American and Grand Rapids Symphonies, and Alexander Lazarev of the Bolshoi Theater. The concerts, played in twenty-one cities across this country as well as in the Soviet Union, the German Democratic Republic, Denmark, Italy, Holland, and Switzerland involved a commissioned work by Charles Wuorinen and pieces by Barber, Copland, Joseph Schwantner, Tchaikovsky, Borodin, Moussorgsky, Beethoven, Dvořák, and Sibelius.

All of this would seem to substantiate the credo enunciated by then assistant dean Thomas E. Cramer more than three decades ago: "Education in music at Oberlin attempts to lead the student to become an enlightened citizen of the world of music—a citizen who has special skills and talents which are developed to their highest potentials. He [sic] must ultimately be a musician who combines in himself the performer, the creator, the teacher, and the discriminating listener. Above all, he must be aware of his responsibility to the art of music, since he will be part of the generation that will become the musical leaders of the future."[22]

CHAPTER 13

The Conservatory and College of
Music of Cincinnati

The Conservatory of Music[1] was founded by Clara Baur in 1867. The College of
Music was organized in 1878 by a coterie of important citizens who hired conductor Theodore Thomas as its first musical director. The two merged in 1955 and were
then assimilated by the University of Cincinnati in 1962, thriving to the present
under the ungainly label of the College-Conservatory of Music of the University of
Cincinnati.

Conservatory of Music, 1867–1955

Clara Baur (1835–1912) was born in Bartholomew, Württemberg. Educated at home
by her father, a Lutheran pastor, she was eventually sent to Stuttgart to study piano. In 1848 her brother Theodore immigrated to Cincinnati and became a banker;
the following year he was joined by Emil, the other Baur male sibling. Clara was
persuaded to join them, and spent several years serving as Theodore's housekeeper
and as a private teacher of voice and piano, having undertaken studies in the former
after her arrival in Cincinnati with the dramatic soprano, Caroline Rivé. A notice in
the *Cincinnati Commercial* of March 15, 1866, suggests that she flourished: "The vocal and instrumental concert given on Tuesday evening the 13th, at Mozart Hall by
Miss Baur and some of her pupils . . . was a success. Miss Baur may well be proud of
her pupils. The tenorist deserves much credit, and the amateur instrumental quartet finished the complete success." Such activities evidently fueled a desire to establish a formal school based on European models, and in 1867 Baur visited the Stuttgart
Conservatory for a look at its methodology. She also studied the piano there and
then journeyed to Paris to work with a Mme. Winter Weber and in the Italian bel
canto manner with a Mme. Maroncelli.

She returned to Cincinnati in October 1867 and two months later opened Clara Baur's Conservatory of Music in a single room rented from Miss Clara Nourse in her School of Young Ladies at 87 West Seventh Street. The initial faculty of four included Baur's former mentor, Caroline Rivé, cellist Michael Brand, and pianist Henry Andres, all among the most notable musicians of the city. At the outset Baur made housing and boarding arrangements for students from outside Cincinnati, unique at the time. To maintain continuity through the customary summer lull, she established a summer session in 1868. She also fostered beneficial links with various civic and religious organizations, as well as with local music retailers.

During the second year the voice faculty was expanded to three, seven instrumentalists offered instruction in piano, violin, and flute, and a theory department of two was created. Classes were offered in both the afternoon and evening in order to meet the needs of a growing and diversified clientele. In 1869 the school was renamed the Cincinnati Conservatory of Music. Since Bauer insisted on a broad curriculum that did not isolate music from the other arts and larger culture, the school's growing offerings included courses in Italian, French, and German. Annual spring concerts were also instituted in 1869, as was the practice of public examination of the progress of students. The faculty continued to expand with the addition in 1871 of Philadelphian William Wallace Gilchrist (1846–1916), who for one year only taught voice, theory, and composition. Violinist Jacob Bloom of the Stuttgart Conservatory arrived in 1873, initiating a tenure lasting twenty-five years.

Three years later the conservatory took possession of its own quarters, a four-story brick structure at Eighth and Vine Streets, at the east end of Garfield Place on the present site of the Public Library of Cincinnati and Hamilton County. The ground level was occupied by retail merchants, while the school functioned on the remaining floors, including a supervised dormitory for young women. However, the appearance of rival institutions (particularly the College of Music in 1878) led to the defections of several faculty members, declining enrollments, and serious financial difficulties.

Stability was regained during the early 1880s with the addition of outreach programs for young children and adults (the latter in the form of a Cincinnati Conservatory of Music Society). Saturday afternoon musicales presented by faculty and students throughout the season and demonstration student concerts at the conclusion of the school year attracted wide attention. By 1881 a certification program was established for those judged competent to teach, and four years later a "Normal Department" was instituted with the purpose of training would-be teachers.

The conservatory's viability was again threatened during 1884 by a devastating flood in January and a smallpox epidemic that affected several students and sent boarders fleeing to their homes. Miss Baur resolutely responded by expanding the school on a site at 140 Broadway across from the Scottish Rite Temple, where concerts and recitals were staged. By 1885 the faculty totaled twenty-three; the annual catalog segmented instruction into three departments (preparatory, normal, and artists) and five "branches" (vocal, instrumental, theory, elocution, and languages). The repertory offered by students became more varied and challenging, so that a program of June 30, 1885, presented by students of Baur and pianist George Magrath (Brooklyn-born but a Stuttgart Conservatory graduate, who had joined the faculty in 1883 and also developed the Conservatory Chorus) consisted of a Chopin Nocturne and Polonaise, a Liszt Hungarian Rhapsody, arias by Bellini and Weber, a song by Beethoven, and an aria from the Rossini *Stabat Mater.* An imposing keyboard program of February 11, 1886, included a set of variations by Mozart, the first movements of concerti by Mozart and Ignaz Moscheles, the "Wanderer" Fantasy of Schubert, and the Ballade in G minor, opus 23 of Chopin. Faculty presented solo performances and a faculty string quartet offered an annual series of four programs. Their 1886 season included works by Mozart, Haydn, and Schubert, was well as the Piano Quartet in E-flat, opus 38, by Jacob Rheinberger, and the Piano Quintet in D minor, opus 7 by Charles-Marie Widor. Faculty and students traveled outside of Cincinnati to present programs (faculty soon had a contractual obligation to perform in neighboring states), and the conservatory furnished music departments for both the Cincinnati Wesleyan College and the Mount Auburn Institute.

All this increased activity stretched the Broadway facility beyond its capacity, and in June 1888 the conservatory occupied new quarters at Fourth and Lawrence Streets. A handsome four-story mansion, with a large drawing room converted to a recital hall, was complemented by a four-story addition of fifty rooms providing both teaching studios and sleeping rooms for the boarding students. During the 1888–89 season, the conservatory presented more than thirty public programs, including those by a men's chorus conducted by George Magrath, soon to be joined by a boy's chorus, which presented an annual Christmas Carol program that has survived to the present as the popular Feast of Carols.

Clara Baur had from the start hosted visiting dignitaries in the conservatory facilities, and a notice in the *Commercial Gazette* of May 8, 1890, suggests the graciousness of the hospitality proffered these visitors to the Queen City:

> Miss Clara Baur gave a most delightful reception yesterday from 2 to 5 o'clock, in honor of the artists of the Boston Symphony Orchestra, Madame Steinbach-Jahns, Herr Arthur Nikisch, Herr Anton Hekking, Herr Franz Kneisel. A crowd of pretty girl pupils of the Conservatory, their faces beaming with pleasure, formed an animated background for the receiving line. Miss Baur received in a handsome black velvet gown, with decoration of duchesse lace. . . . The presentations were made by Mr. Magrath, who made a most gracious master of ceremonies. . . . Madame Steinbach-Jahns speaks

no English, but the company was deterred by no limitations of language in doing honors to the artists.[2]

The final decade of the century was one of enormous expansion. By 1894, students from every state were enrolled; the roster totaled eight hundred by the following year, when sixty-one students received diplomas or certificates. More than forty public programs were presented, among them two by the conservatory's string quartet and pianist Frederic Shailer Evans. The first included the Beethoven Quartet in E-flat, opus 74, the Grieg Violin-Piano Sonata, opus 8, and the Quintet in E minor, opus 5, for piano and strings by Christian Sinding. The other included the Schumann Piano Quintet in E-flat, opus 44, what was billed as the first performance in the country of the César Franck Violin Sonata in A, and Grieg's Quartet in G minor, opus 27.

Only a few years later, the commencement examination recitals lasted a full two weeks. Baur made an unsolicited suggestion to the founders of the new Cincinnati Symphony Orchestra that the ensemble's concertmaster be offered a faculty slot at the conservatory, a goal realized in 1895 when Josef Marien began to teach violin and coach ensembles. Other additions to the faculty included German-born pianist Theodor Bohlmann (1865–1931), a student of Eugène d'Albert and Moritz Moszkowski, and violinist Pier Tirindelli (1858–1937), a composer of operas and songs who had previously taught at the Liceo Benedetto Marcello in Venice and became conductor of the conservatory orchestra.[3] In 1898 the two began a sonata series that included all the Beethoven violin-piano sonatas; they later organized the Bohlmann-Tirindelli Concert Company, touring widely in this country. In February 1900 the Cincinnati Symphony Orchestra presented the first performances of Tirindelli's Concerto in G minor, with the composer as soloist. In addition to the concerts and recitals, illustrated lectures on history and general musicality were offered by faculty members and guests like John Van Cleve, a local music critic.

Baur was intent on providing a home-away-from-home for her students, and the conservatory social season became both elaborate and formal. A Thanksgiving dinner served over the span of four hours was a highlight. The menu for the feast of November 29, 1894, suggests the seriousness of the occasion: blue points, *dindon rôti à l'américaine, pommes de terre à la crème, petits pois français,* olives, *celeri, huîtres, sorbet aux oranges, salade de poulet à la mayonnaise, tourte d'émincé, cidre nouveau, fromages et biscuits secs, glaces au tutti frutti, gâteaux,* fruits, raisins, *noix,* and *café.* Students were expected to dress formally; toasts and poetry recitations accompanied the repast. The Feast of Carols marked the beginning of the holiday season; a formal dance greeted the students' return in the new year. Commencement week was marked by numerous parties and a boating picnic on the Ohio River. Teas and other parties were scheduled, as were weddings, including a few between faculty and their students.

Burgeoning enrollments (858 students in 1897, only fifty-three of them male) fostered plans for an enlarged facility, including a large recital hall and an opera theater, but the available land could not accommodate this ambitious project. Miss Baur's desire to provide something approximating a domestic environment for her students led in 1901 to the purchase of an estate on fashionable Mount Auburn, despite the advice of bankers, who assumed that removal from the business center of the city would lead to decreased enrollments. The elegant mansion, at the corner of Oak Street and Highland Avenue, conceived in an idiom described as Elizabethan Renaissance,[4] had been occupied by merchant John Shillito on its completion in late 1866. Situated on five acres of elegant landscaping, spacious lawns, and gravel drives, it required virtually no alteration, although the Shillito's dining room was transformed into an organ studio.

Architect Samuel Hannaford devised a new five-story structure to the south of the mansion. Its ground floor contained classrooms, teaching studios, and offices, while the upper stories housed 185 students and an infirmary. And,

> the teaching studios and the living apartments [were] separated from each other by hollow tile partitions carried on steel beams, in order to secure the minimum transmission of sound. The floors of the rooms were so constructed that no beam or flooring board was continuous under any adjoining rooms.[5]

An auditorium seating 640 was constructed to the east of the main building, behind which were situated a dining hall and kitchen; a gymnasium and laundry were constructed in the former carriage house:

> the new buildings were constructed for permanency. Fireproof qualities and sanitary arrangements were also taken into consideration. The three main buildings were connected by corridors. The corridor floors were built of "armoured concrete." No wood was used. The surface of the floors was finished with "Venetian Mosaic" and was intended to be fire and sound proof. The rooms were arranged to give the advantages of air and light to the teaching studios and to the living quarters of the students. Every room was provided with hot and cold water, and with gas and electricity. The entire school was heated by steam. The elevator in the main building, and the two large pipe organs were run by electricity.[6]

The move into these facilities was accomplished during the morning of February 1, 1902. Breakfast was taken downtown; lunch was served atop Mount Auburn. Despite the dire premonitions of Miss Baur's bankers, enrollment reached one thousand, ministered to by a faculty of thirty. In 1910 another addition, in brick and

Jacobean in style, added sixty rooms, including nine teaching studios. In April 1917 a building on the adjoining Durrell estate was purchased, adding a residence of eighteen rooms and a new home for Miss Baur. In 1921 the Miller estate across Highland Avenue was purchased; its two structures became Auburn Hall, a men's dormitory, and Opera Hall, housing classes in opera, theater, and ballet. The following year the remainder of the Durrell property was added, although the house it contained was destroyed by fire in 1932 and never rebuilt.

From 1867 until her death in 1912 the conservatory was the personal creation and possession of Clara Baur, although in 1878 her niece Bertha joined the staff and gradually assumed many of her aunt's administrative responsibilities. A nephew, George, became the head bookkeeper in 1892. But Miss Baur was able to tell a reporter from the *Cincinnati Times-Star* on December 24, 1903, "There are not many that live to see their dreams come true; there are not many that worked and see the work come out as they have planned. But it was so with me, that as I dreamed, the hopes of all my life came true one bright, bright day."

The dedication ceremony involved the rector of Christ Episcopal Church in full clerical regalia consecrating the facilities to the study of music in the name of the Triune God. Miss Baur's conviction that music was the handmaiden of religion manifested itself in various writings about her religious ideals, as well as in the behavior demanded of her charges. After breakfast in the dormitory dining room she would read passages from the Bible; she led prayer meetings in the drawing room on Wednesday evenings; attendance at Sunday morning worship services was required; and no music-making of any sort was allowed on the Sabbath. Miss Baur also organized the Conservatory Missionary Society, functional for several years in support of activities in India and China, as well as a Young Women's Christian Association, also short-lived.

An attractive woman of irrepressible energy and slight stature, she at one point was teaching 124 lessons a week. Her workday was interrupted by a set of special breathing exercises undertaken before lunch, to which she attributed her excellent physical condition. Multilingual and well read, she aspired to publish a method detailing the vocal pedagogy she evolved across an extended career, but the work remained in manuscript at her death. Apparently astute as a financial manager, she left an institution without debt. She never accepted a salary, appropriating from the school's income only what was necessary to maintain her modest lifestyle. She was far more interested in attracting the finest faculty available and in aiding students, even to the point of subsidizing foreign travel and study. She took a personal interest in the lives and accomplishments of the conservatory students, insisting not only on their development as musicians, but also that good deportment, social etiquette, and a wide knowledge of literature were integral to that success. Her devotion to the conservatory was perhaps asserted most cogently in a speech delivered on the annual Tree Day, April 1, 1911, shortly before her death:

By faith in God the Cincinnati Conservatory was planted as "a grain of mustard seed" growing continuously, by His Grace, until it shall be like a great tree with more and more outspreading branches, that bear blessed fruit for life and eternity.[7]

Responsibility for that great tree passed into the hands of Bertha Baur (1858–1940), who had served thirty-four years of apprenticeship as secretary and associate director of the school. More active in civic and professional organizations than her aunt, she perpetuated Clara's tradition of treating faculty as members of an extended household, and presided over an active social calendar for the students, including teas, monthly dances, periodic smokers for the males, a Halloween masquerade party, Christmas dinners, and taffy pulls for those unable to return to their homes for the holidays.

An astute financial manager, she nonetheless faced a changing environment. For years she had been her aunt's emissary in almost yearly forays to Europe in search of talented teachers. However, those artists demanded increasingly high salaries. The expense of expanded facilities and the necessity of granting large scholarships to talented but needy students placed unseemly burdens on a privately owned, unendowed institution. Furthermore, the opera program established in 1915 (headed by Ralph Lyford beginning in 1916), despite patronage by several wealthy Cincinnatians who pledged substantial scholarships to attract students of merit, became a financial drain because of its annual performances of fully staged works in Emery Auditorium. While the bulk of the repertory consisted of standard works, the conservatory also presented the first American performances of Gustav Holst's *Savitri* (of 1908, but not performed until 1916), Ralph Vaughan Williams's *Riders to the Sea* (of 1932), and Arthur Benjamin's *The Devil Take Her* (of 1931).

The conservatory was incorporated in 1920, with several prominent citizens of the city as shareholders, Bertha Baur as president and treasurer, and George Baur as secretary. Several classes of stock were issued and the assets of the conservatory sold to the new "Company." Incorporation led to financial security, but Bertha Baur retained control of the institution, and the other investors took no active part in its administration. In fact, their last formal meeting apparently took place on May 16, 1921.

The following year the conservatory was granted authority by the state to offer degrees in music, rather than the diplomas conferred to that point. Curricula leading to both the bachelor of music and master of music degrees were established, and five such degrees were conferred in the spring of 1923. The state also authorized the awarding of honorary doctorates and later expanded that authority into new fields, including a bachelor of letters in theater degree in 1927.

A department of normal instruction in public-school music became a feature of summer sessions after 1905 and, under the direction of George E. Leighton,[8] of the regular winter sessions after 1909. This eventually led to an affiliation with the College of Education (later Teachers College) of the University of Cincinnati in 1923, established in tandem with the Cincinnati College of Music. Aligning the faculty and facilities of the three institutions offered a more efficient means of meeting state certification requirements, so that the music courses were taught by college and conservatory faculties, while the education courses were offered at the University, which assessed the same fees normally charged University of Cincinnati students. The bachelor of science in public school music (later, in music education) degree was conferred after four years of study, the bachelor of education degree after an additional year of work. Practice teaching for fifth-year students was at first confined to elementary schools but extended to high schools in 1926. Graduate study in music education was initiated in 1932, and during that decade an interchange of faculty among the three institutions developed.

The conservatory was actively involved in another type of accreditation when, in 1924, Burnet C. Tuthill,[9] a choral conductor who also served as general manager from 1922 until 1929, met at the conservatory with the administrators of six professional institutions to organize what became the National Association of Schools of Music. Their purpose was to create curricular standards for their various degree programs. The organization flourished and, beginning in 1928, became the country's principal agency accrediting music schools and determining norms for the training of musicians.

During the latter 1920s the conservatory's financial situation became more complex. Competition from newly created professional schools (the Eastman School of Music in Rochester in 1921, the Juilliard Graduate School [created from an endowment left by Ohio-born Augustus D. Juilliard] in New York and the Curtis Institute of Music in Philadelphia, both in 1924) as well as the publicly supported institutions (a particular threat in the field of music education), exacerbated by the general financial collapse of 1929, led to decreased student enrollments. Bertha Baur, intent on assuring the future viability of her conservatory, reincorporated it on November 28, 1930, as a nonprofit institution and transferred its assets to the Cincinnati Institute of Fine Arts.

The institute had been created in 1927 by Mr. and Mrs. Charles P. Taft, intent on furnishing financial stability to the Taft art collection and the Cincinnati Symphony Orchestra. The Tafts' $1 million gift was quickly matched by another $2.5 million raised by subscription, allowing the institute to assume its role of furthering "the musical and artistic education and culture of the people of Cincinnati." A letter of July 8, 1930, from Miss Baur had offered to convey all the conservatory stock to the institute, with the stipulation that she was to be provided an income of ten thousand dollars per year and her cousin three thousand dollars per year for the remainder of their lives, an obligation assumed by Mrs. Taft.

Miss Baur retired and was succeeded in March 1931 as director of music by Frederic Shailer Evans, a member of the piano faculty since 1889.[10] Evans retired the following January and was eventually succeeded by singer Herbert Witherspoon in the fall of 1932 (his title was changed to director of the conservatory), who was succeeded the following year by singer and choral conductor John A. Hoffman, who enjoyed a considerably longer tenure.[11] The number of faculty members was reduced (for example, in 1929 there were thirty-two people teaching piano, sixteen in 1934, and twelve in 1939; the voice faculty was slimmed from fourteen to eight between 1929 and 1936), and those who remained were compensated on a joint salary and commission basis.

A required yearlong course in Dalcroze Eurythmics was added to the curriculum, a graduate program in musicology was instituted under the direction of Thomas J. Kelly in 1931, and the band program was expanded to meet the needs of the music education students, this under the direction of Frank Simon (1889–1967), who had achieved national renown as director of the Armco Band, headquartered in nearby Middletown and who was to serve on the conservatory faculty until 1953. Conservatory programs had been broadcast over WLW since 1923 (for instance, a program of December 8, 1929, by the Conservatory Symphony Orchestra, conducted by Vladimir Bakaleinikoff, that included Leo Sowerby's *Overture—Comes Autumn Time*, single movements from piano concerti by Hummel and Grieg, an *Andante Cantabile* by Tchaikovsky, and the Wagner prelude to *Die Meistersinger*), and a series of weekly programs over the Columbia Broadcasting System was inaugurated in 1934. Hundreds of such programs featured faculty soloists and various ensembles but most prominently the orchestra, by then under the direction of Alexander von Kreisler.

The seventieth anniversary of the conservatory's founding was celebrated with great ceremony during April 1937. Highlights included presentation by the Cincinnati Symphony of the new *Symphony No. 1, Gulliver: His Voyage to Lilliput*, opus 15, by Edgar Stillman Kelley, who had taught theory and composition at the conservatory from 1911 until 1934; Kelley's *Israfel*, presented by the Cincinnati Mothersingers under the direction of John Hoffman; and *The Songs of Songs*, a cantata by C. Hugo Grimm, who had taught at the conservatory since 1930 (the last was also heard on a national broadcast by the Cincinnati Symphony). There was other music-making, plus proclamations and receptions galore, honoring not only Miss Baur as president emeritus, but also the Kelleys, the Hoffmans, and Eugene Goossens, incumbent conductor of the Cincinnati Symphony. Despite her titular position, Miss Baur remained a presence in the quotidian life of her beloved conservatory, especially its social calendar, until her death on September 18, 1940. Her utter devotion to the institution was manifested in a will bequeathing all her property to the conservatory upon the death of the remaining members of her family.

World War II inevitably had an impact on the conservatory, but by 1949 enrollment reached 531; 117 degrees were conferred. A music therapy curriculum was added in 1951, and in that same year WKRC installed a radio station on the campus, later extended to include television broadcasting. However, by the following year, enrollment had declined to 235, with only 83 degrees conferred. Faculty pay was decreased, teaching loads increased. The financial predicament became evermore dire, to the point that the Cincinnati Institute of Fine Arts had to deal with a deficit of twenty thousand dollars at the conclusion of the 1954–55 academic year. How to deal with the crisis?

The College of Music of Cincinnati, 1878–1955

Good private teachers had always found appreciation in the Queen City, but there was no musical atmosphere such as is produced by a large concourse of professors and students of the various branches of music. There were no facilities for instruction in normal classes, solfeggio classes, ensemble classes, prima vista classes, or orchestral classes, and no opportunity for the critical study of harmony, composition, or orchestration. For the study of the organ, the noblest of instruments, there were no advantages whatsoever.[12]

Clara Baur surely would have taken offense at this retrospective assessment of Cincinnati in 1878, found in the minutes of a meeting of the Board of Trustees of the College of Music of Cincinnati on January 19, 1895. Nonetheless, it perhaps explains what motivated Reuben R. Springer and George Ward Nichols, creators of the world-class May Festival and Music Hall, to extend their reach with an equally potent pedagogical institution. A "Preliminary Circular of Information" proclaimed,

It is the aim of the College to impart instruction, theoretically and practically, in all branches of musical education. The plan of instruction adopted is intended to give to the student who wishes to become a professional musician, a methodical, scientific, and complete education, and is of great advantage to the amateur who wishes to learn one or more special branches of the art and science of music. While this most advanced and thorough instruction will be given in the College, it is intended also to take young girls and boys, or any person who has never been taught the art of music. Teachers will be employed, who are able to execute as well as teach.[13]

A meeting of stockholders (virtually the same group that controlled both the May Festival and Music Hall) was held at Pike's Opera House on August 16, 1878, at which articles of incorporation were filed, with capital of fifty thousand dollars, shares at fifty dollars each. Colonel Nichols read a letter to be sent to Theodore Thomas, offering him the post of musical director of the school and stressing, "We recognize your special fitness for a trust so important, and believe, if you accept, that you will be taking another step forward in the noble work of musical education, to which your life has been so successfully devoted."[14]

Several weeks earlier Nichols had laid the groundwork. In a letter dated July 22 he inquired of Thomas, "Are you not tired of carrying the weight of that orchestra? Will you accept the opportunity of firmly fixing yourself for life in a position which you can if you choose make distinguished and successful?"[15]

On July 29, lacking a response from Thomas, Nichols pressed his case further, asserting that, "we can build up a school as complete and efficient as any in Europe. We are geographically well placed. Living is very cheap here." He assured Thomas,

> With the number of good musicians here you would have an orchestra you would not be ashamed of. Just how much of your Eastern life and work you could keep is a matter for consideration. You are strongly wedded to New York, and your reputation is more or less identified with it, but you may be sure that in Cincinnati we shall contend for musical supremacy. We will make this the musical center of the United States. . . . I want you to come here and work with me to organize *a complete and brilliant musical university*. If you can't come I will go to Germany for Raff, Joachim, or some other big fish whose name and experience will give us the prestige which assists success. But I know you can and ought to come.[16]

Thomas had penned a response that very day, which Nichols acknowledged on August 2, admitting the existence of unresolved questions, but suggesting "a fixed income of say from $8,000 to $10,000 a year guaranteed to you for five or more years."[17]

The college was to be governed by a board of seven directors, who would manage the business affairs of the institution, while the musical director was to have full responsibility for the courses of study, nomination of the faculty, and other such matters. In contrast to the conservatory, the founding directors of the college were all lay people, prominent businessmen intent on the success of the enterprise because of their deep involvement with music as an avocation. That very afternoon they elected Colonel Nichols as president, Peter Rudolph Neff as treasurer, and Jacob Burnet Jr. as secretary.

Thomas accepted the position in a letter dated August 20, 1878, and two days later signed a five-year contract brought to New York by Nichols. It insisted that he must "give his entire professional services solely to the said College," although he was allowed an annual vacation of at least six weeks. One stipulation that surely must have rankled: He was allowed to involve himself in outside events but had to remit to the college 20 percent of any compensation derived from such activities.[18]

The college was formally opened on October 14, slightly less than two months after its incorporation. Its activities were housed in Dexter Hall, part of Music Hall. Thomas had recruited a faculty of thirty-one, who dealt with a student body of almost three hundred. Miraculous as all of that appears, Thomas's forces then managed during their first season to mount a rather astounding series of twenty-four orchestral and twelve chamber music concerts. The third orchestral event, conducted by Thomas in Music Hall on December 19, 1878, consisted of the Beethoven overture to *Leonore* No. 3, the first movement of the Paganini D major Violin Concerto (with visiting virtuoso August Wilhelmj as soloist), the Schumann Fourth Symphony, the *Hungarian Airs,* opus 22, by Heinrich Wilhelm Ernst, and the Weber Overture to *Euryanthe.* On March 20, 1879, Thomas led his forces in the Mozart G minor Symphony, Schubert's *Psalm 23,* with the female voices of the college choir, and the Rossini *Stabat Mater,* sung by a chorus of 150 voices. He had organized and trained the college choir, beginning in January (it soon totaled two hundred singers), taught some classes, attended to his responsibilities with the May Festival Association, and once a month traveled east to rehearse and conduct the Brooklyn Philharmonic Society.

The dynamo also actively participated as principal violinist in the chamber music programs heard in College Hall, although the press of his administrative duties eventually forced him to relinquish that role. The first of these (on November 14, 1878) included quartets by Mozart and Beethoven, as well as the Cello Suite, opus 16 of Saint-Saëns. That of December 5 contained quartets by Haydn and Schumann, as well as the Beethoven "Archduke" Piano Trio, opus 97. The eleventh event in the series, on May 8, 1879, programmed the Beethoven Serenade in D, opus 25, for flute, violin, and viola; the Piano Quartet in F, opus 37 of Xaver Scharwenka (from 1877); and the Beethoven Violin Sonata in A, opus 47.

Most of the twenty-five faculty performers were European immigrants whose names provoke no recognition today. However, Thomas had recruited violinist Jacob Bloom and pianist Henry Andres from the faculty of Clara Baur's conservatory. Otto Singer, the Thomas protégé and assistant who served ably as the May Festival chorusmaster, taught piano and theory, as did Arthur Mees, another May Festival associate. Although he stayed only a few years, George E. Whiting (1842–1923) was brought from Boston to head an organ department and offered recitals in Music Hall on Wednesday and Saturday afternoons. In addition to the orchestral and vocal departments, the college offered piano, theory, history of music, lectures on musical subjects (particularly the literature being offered in the public concerts), score playing and conducting, foreign languages, elocution, and "Concert-room Deportment, Dramatic Expression, etc."[19] Enrollment reached five hundred by the conclusion of the first year.

Heady stuff, indeed, but by early March 1880 Thomas had submitted his resignation. Apparently a contest of wills developed almost immediately between two imperious personalities, both intent on the same goals.[20] During the spring of 1879 Nichols had announced a plan to have students serve local churches as vocal soloists and organists, their wages remitted to the college. Henry Andres protested by resigning from the faculty and critic Henry Krehbiel was fired when he criticized the practice in print, as had other local musicians whose livelihood was threatened by the practice. The firestorm of protest forced Nichols to rescind the plan within a few weeks.

It was reported that Thomas had attempted to resign only six weeks into his tenure, but the final crisis was precipitated by a letter addressed to the board during February 1880, recommending that the school year be segmented into two terms of twenty weeks each, thus entailing less time evaluating would-be students desiring entrance to the school; that a fund of five-to-ten thousand dollars be established to guarantee a permanent orchestra, which would be administered independently; and that Thomas be granted exclusive control over all operations of the college, especially admissions, since students were apparently being enrolled regardless of talent by faculty intent on inflating their incomes.

The board, however, preferred four terms (the first of five weeks, the remaining three of ten each), fearing that the seemingly larger fees would lead to a decline in enrollment. They were less concerned with the fluid personnel roster of the orchestra, feeling that Thomas's enormous success under the existing circumstances obviated the need for such an expenditure. Thomas, in a letter of March 1, stated that he could manage as president of the institution with the assistance of a secretary and a clerk. However, the board asserted in a letter dated the following day,

> Your present powers far exceed those ordinarily exercised by such officers. It is not common for the Board of Trustees to appoint professors on the sole recommendation of the director, as we do upon yours. It is not common for a director to dispense with faculty meetings, and conduct and direct the whole scheme of study in all departments as you do. Your powers, as exercised, are more nearly autocratic than those at the head of the instruction department of any college of the country, and we have recognized the propriety of this in the organization of the College of Music.[21]

The nasty mess quickly became a public scandal. An unidentified musician was quoted in *The Cincinnati Enquirer* of March 4:

> The cause of all the trouble is Mrs. Thomas' dislike of Cincinnati, and an impatient desire to get back to New York. He said that for several months Mr. Thomas had been complaining of his health and that of his family. The

musician also stated that a heavy pressure had been brought upon Mr. Thomas by his friends in New York, urging him to return to that city, that the Steinway piano folks were willing to pay him almost any price to get him back again, for commercial reasons.

Thomas had formally submitted his resignation that same day (effective the following October, although on April 8 the board voted to terminate his contract immediately) and exposed the power struggle to public view in an interview published in the *Enquirer* on March 5:

> The whole secret of the business, [said Thomas] and I have said as much to Mr. Nichols, is that he ought to be satisfied with the honor of having inaugurated the school and being President of the school and a member of the Board of Trustees, but his ambition does not allow him to be content with that sphere, and it is impossible for me to conduct the school with his constant interference in matters that properly belong only to the Musical Director.

Nichols also submitted his resignation, although it was refused by the board. On March 9 he was humiliated at a rehearsal of the May Festival Chorus when a demonstration of gratitude to Thomas for his work with the ensemble quickly turned into denunciations of Nichols, complete with shouted invective and crashing chords from the Music Hall organ, courtesy of George Whiting, accompanying cheers of support for Thomas. The *Commercial* reported the following day, "The answering shout would have put a Democratic convention to shame." In full retreat from his opponent's enclave, Nichols quickly resigned from the May Festival Association Board, as did Peter Neff and Jacob Burnet, his colleagues on the College Board. Major opera festivals from 1881 to 1884 sponsored by the college were surely intended by Nichols and his associates as a very public rebuff of Thomas and his May Festival forces. But Thomas exacerbated the acrimony by unceremoniously firing Otto Singer on the Friday evening of the 1880 festival, replacing him with Arthur Mees as resident conductor. Singer's sin of disloyalty had been to remain on the college faculty, while Mees had resigned in protest.

One point of contention between Thomas and his erstwhile employers had been the lack of any significant endowment for the college, forcing Thomas to rely on tuition income. Springer, who had earlier given five thousand dollars, from whose interest annual medals were given to superior students, gave the school railroad stock valued at sixty thousand dollars in November 1882. Two years later, it was his donation of fifteen thousand dollars worth of stock in the Cincinnati Gas, Light, and Coke Company that allowed Colonel Nichols to build the Odeon at Grant and Elm Streets, the first real home of the college. Dedicated on October 28, 1884, the building contained a concert hall seating fifteen hundred, with a two-manual pipe organ on its stage, as well as twenty-four practice rooms. Peter Neff then bought the adjoining property on Grant Street and constructed the Lyceum, a performance space seating four hundred designed especially for chamber concerts, lectures and examinations, with another pipe organ on its stage. By 1892 the college required housing for the increasing number of out-of-town students, so three residential properties on Elm Street were leased and remodeled as a dormitory for women. Since this solution soon proved inadequate, in 1902 J. E. Schmidlapp, then treasurer of the college, constructed as a memorial to his wife a four-story dormitory residence, also on Elm Street. However, on September 6 of that same year a fire destroyed both the Odeon and Lyceum and also did considerable damage to the Horticultural Hall of Music Hall. Temporary quarters were quickly improvised, and concerts were presented in Greenwood Hall of the Ohio Mechanics Institute.

From 1880 until 1897 the college functioned without a musical director, guided only by the officers and board. Nichols died in 1885 and was succeeded as president by Peter Neff, who resigned in 1898, succeeded by then–vice president William McAlpin. McAlpin died in office the following year and was succeeded by Julius Fleischmann, concurrently mayor of Cincinnati.

Frank Van der Stucken, the first conductor of the Cincinnati Symphony, who had joined the college faculty in 1895, was appointed dean in 1897, a position that evidently offered him full control of both the musical and financial affairs of the college. Winthrop S. Sterling, the first recipient of a Springer medal and the third graduate of college, was appointed assistant dean (with responsibility for musical matters), and Arnold J. Gantvoort was named assistant director (with responsibility for financial matters). That administrative structure was simplified in 1901, when Van der Stucken's schedule forced him to resign as dean, although he was granted honorary status and retained control of the orchestra, chorus, and opera classes. Sterling succeeded him as dean, and Gantvoort was named manager. In September of the following year, Mrs. Frederick H. Alms (who in 1918 was to fund Alms Hall, a dormitory adjacent to Schmidlapp Hall on Elm Street) offered both $100,000 and a plan by which the college would affiliate with the University of Cincinnati, but that union was to be postponed for six decades, in part because of a provision that the college endowment would revert to the St. Joseph Orphanage if it were to lose its identity.

The silver jubilee of the college was celebrated with a series of seven concerts presented at Robinson's Opera House between February 24 and 28, 1903. Van der Stucken conducted two performances of Ignaz Brüll's *The Golden Cross*, a two-act romantic opera of 1875, as well as an orchestral concert featuring faculty member Albino Gorno in a Mozart piano concerto, faculty violinist Josef Marien in works by Johan Svendsen (1840–1911) and Tividar Nachez (1859–1930), Mendelssohn's incidental music for *Midsummer Night's Dream* with the college chorus, soloists and narration by Jennie Mannheimer (who headed the dramatic department), plus Nicholas J. Elsenheimer (1866–1935), a member of the faculty since 1891, in a performance of the Beethoven C minor Piano Concerto. There was also something called *The Amazons,* a "farcical romance in three acts," and a final orchestral concert with the college chorus and younger faculty members presenting works by Saint-Saëns, Lalo, Benjamin Godard, Handel, Tchaikovsky, and Thierot.

The 1907–08 financial depression and the country's later involvement in World War I both had a serious impact on the financial condition of the college. Severe winter weather and a coal shortage even forced the holding of classes in the dormitory for two weeks following the Christmas respite. The 1918 influenza epidemic further decimated the student body, depleting the orchestra of virtually all its male members.

On December 18, 1918, Julius Fleischmann announced his resignation as president after a tenure of eighteen years and was succeeded by Nicholas Longworth.[22] In 1920 Gantvoort was succeeded as business manager by J. H. Thuman, a college alumnus who served as music and theater critic of the *Enquirer,* editor for the Willis Music Company, manager of the May Festival, and impresario of an active booking agency that imported celebrated ensembles and soloists to the Queen City.[23] Forsaking some of those activities, Thuman presided over a period during which various shareholders forsook their ownership of the college, so that by January 15, 1926, the institution actually owned the ground on which its buildings stood. During the 1922–23 school year a public-school music department was organized as the college and conservatory jointly entered into the reciprocal arrangement with the University of Cincinnati discussed earlier. In 1923 the college was authorized by the State Department of Education to grant degrees and joined the fledgling National Association of Schools of Music the following year.

The school's tenuous financial situation and Thuman's inability to devote as much time to the college as originally envisioned led to an administrative reorganization in early 1925. The office of business manager was abolished, and Adolph Hahn was named the school's director.[24] He presided over a period of phenomenal growth: 480 students when he assumed his position, 1,325 by 1928.

The 1927–28 golden-jubilee season was marked by the opening of a new administration building, which still stands on Central Parkway. The three-story structure contained offices, studios, reception, and classrooms; four organ practice studios; a library; and an assembly hall for dance and physical culture classes, complete with locker rooms and showers. The college orchestra offered a series of five concerts; the College Choral Club of over one hundred voices prepared John Henry Maunder's *Bethlehem;* the Children's Theatre Company offered a series of one-act plays, and the Players' Guild was organized within the department of drama; the Heermann Quartette and Trio gave a series of Twilight Concerts; and much attention was lavished on a program of excerpts from *La Traviata* and *Il Trovatore* presented in Emery Auditorium by students coached by Italo Picchi,[25] the orchestra conducted by Hahn. The Fiftieth Annual Commencement was held on June 8, 1928, in Music Hall before a crowd of 4,500, who witnessed the conferring on the largest class ever of fourteen bachelor of music degrees, as well as numerous diplomas, certificates, and Springer medals. The formal exercises were preceded by a concert involving a chorus of over three hundred and an augmented orchestra of one hundred led by Frederick Stock (conductor of the Chicago Orchestra and conductor-elect of the May Festival), Hahn, and Albino Gorno, dean of the faculty. Stock presented the "Gloria" from the *Missa Lautreutica*, opus 10 (1925), by college alumnus Martin G. Dumler, and "Thanks Be to God" from Mendelssohn's *Elijah*. Hahn conducted Liszt's *Les Préludes;* Gorno played the Beethoven Funtasia, opus 80, for piano, chorus, and orchestra; and Hahn led an organ and orchestra version of Marcel Dupré's *Cortège et Litanie,* opus 19 (1921).

The resulting euphoria must have been short-lived, since the financial crisis of 1929 and beyond had an immense impact on the college: enrollment was almost halved, to 721. Hahn's health began to fail during the spring of 1930, and, although he lived until 1934, he retired from active duty in December 1930. He had been succeeded in July as acting director by Sidney C. Durst, theorist, composer, and organist and a member of the faculty since 1923. As director from 1931 to 1934, Durst presided over a period of further decline (enrollment had shrunk to 365 by the end of his tenure). Orchestral concerts were reduced in number from five to three and plays from fifteen to seven. Print advertising was severely curtailed, but a high public profile was maintained by monthly broadcasts over WLW, and weekly programs over WCKY and WFBE.

Discussions were held in 1930 and again two years later about a potential merger with the conservatory, but to no avail. An affiliation with the Athenaeum of Ohio, mentioned as early as September 1931, was brought to full fruition only in April 1935, whereby courses in Gregorian chant, liturgy, polyphony, the history and appreciation of church music, and boy's voice and choir training offered at the Athenaeum were accepted by the college as fulfilling work toward the bachelor of music degree, while certain college courses could be used to fulfill requirements for the Atheneum's bachelor of science degree. A similar exchange program with Xavier University became effective in July 1936.

Durst presided over only a portion of this activity, since he was succeeded as director in 1934 by no less than J. H. Thuman, who held the office until 1941, when he was in turn succeeded by David Frederick (Fred) Smith, appointed with the title of managing executive. After a varied career, much of it in Europe, Smith had settled in Cincinnati during 1921 and a year later became associated with the Crosley Radio Corporation and WLW, its signature station. A pioneer, he adapted many classic plays for radio presentation and dramatized the first radio serial. In 1928 he had moved to New York City and joined the staff of *Time,* where he conceived the idea of radio news syndication, providing the news by air mail and special delivery to as many as seventy-five stations. He also, on March 16, 1931, had originated the *March of Time* program. His only apparent connection to the world of music was his marriage in 1924 to a concert pianist of some repute.

Smith appeared on the scene five years after a radio curriculum had been established at the college. The first collegiate department of radio—officially the Radio Extension of the College of Music of Cincinnati—had been formed in 1936, headed by Uberto Neeley, a staff musician at WLW and part-time violin instructor at the college. During the first year of its existence the department originated fifty-one thirty-minute broadcasts over WLW, as well as a single fifteen-minute program over the Blue Network of NBC. There was also a series of thirty half-hour music appreciation programs (expanded to forty the following year), modeled on a concept originated by Walter Damrosch, called *Music of the Masters,* as well as a series of ten thirty-minute broadcasts over WSAI collectively titled the *Odeon Radio Workshop.*

On October 12, 1941, Mrs. Helene V. B. Wurlitzer assisted in dedicating in honor of her mother the Henriette Billings Studios, thoroughly modern broadcast facilities located on the first two floors of the Alms Building. The inaugural program, heard nationally on the NBC Red Network, featured the college orchestra. Guest Eugene Goossens, conductor of the Cincinnati Symphony, presented Beethoven's Overture to *Egmont,* after which its regular conductor, Walter Heerman, assumed the podium for songs by Schubert and Beethoven sung by Madame Lotte Leonard and movements from a Mozart piano concerto played by John Quincy Bass, another college faculty member. Although it hardly dissolved all of the college's problems, the new facilities provided a boost, since enrollment in the radio curriculum reached fifty-five in 1942, twenty more the following year, and fully 100 by 1947. A bachelor of fine arts in radio education degree was authorized by the state in 1945, and television equipment was installed in Dexter Hall during the summer of 1950. By 1952 what was called the radio-TV arts department had a faculty of twenty-two, offering more than sixty different courses.

But overall enrollment was shaky (489 in the 1953–54 academic year; 507 the following year) and costs were outpacing income as the school celebrated its seventieth birthday in 1953. A merger with the conservatory was proposed to the board of trustees during February 1954, and trustee committees from both institutions were established, leading to a joint meeting of both boards in May 1955. It was determined that the merged college-conservatory would operate on the conservatory campus in Mount Auburn, although the radio and television department of the college would remain downtown. The conservatory endowment would be placed in the hands of the College Corporation, to avoid negating the college's endowment. The college properties were to be sold to liquidate existing debt and then to become the core of a new endowment; the Schmidlapp estate agreed that the dormitory bearing the family name could be sold and the proceeds employed to construct a new residence on the conservatory campus. The trustees embarked on a quest for an endowment of one million dollars and the Cincinnati Institute of Fine Arts pledged to grant the new institution twenty thousand dollars for each of the following years, a sum expected to meet any accrued deficits. The books of the College of Music were officially closed on July 31, 1955.

College-Conservatory of Music, 1955–1962

Thus two proud and venerable institutions submerged their increasingly parallel personalities in a marriage that many had considered inevitable. Initially the new College-Conservatory of Music absorbed both parent faculties (some had in fact taught at both premerger schools), but both college dean Eugene J. Selhorst and conservatory dean William S. Naylor resigned, supplanted by conservatory professor of composition Scott Huston as acting dean.

However, financial problems continued to plague new Dean J. Laurence Willhide and the trustees. The physical plant was sadly overused and in need of considerable repair and expansion. Even though, for example, there were no retirement benefits for faculty as late as 1959, the school lost $25,000 in 1956; $29,000 the following year; and a grand $467,000 in 1960, after registering a modest profit of $7,737.40 in 1958. In 1956 the State Department of Education refused to accredit the College-Conservatory of Music's master of music degrees because of the lack of a supporting endowment, and in 1959 the National Association of Schools of Music announced that it was considering refusing accreditation to professional schools that were not members of the North Central Association of Colleges and Secondary Schools. Clearly, short of a miracle, another merger loomed as inevitable. Negotiations with the University of Cincinnati were undertaken during April 1959. Again money became the nettlesome issue, especially the College-Conservatory of Music's indebtedness to the Cincinnati Institute of Fine Arts, but on August 1, 1962, the College-Conservatory of Music became the fourteenth college of the University of Cincinnati.

The tenuous nature of what had clearly been an interim solution was aptly summarized in the January 1961 issue of *Opus No. 1*, the journal of the Cincinnati Musicians' Union: "The merger of the College of Music and the Cincinnati Conservatory of Music in 1955 did not result in the strengthening of music and music education in Cincinnati as everyone had hoped. Perhaps this merger with the University of Cincinnati will mark the beginning of a real Renaissance in the musical life of our community."[26]

Dean Willhide resigned in 1961, succeeded temporarily by Marjora Shank, and in 1963 by Jack Watson. Watson, a conservatory graduate who held a doctorate from Columbia University, had been a contract actor in Hollywood and had sung with the likes of Harry James and André Kostelanitz and on *The Kate Smith Show*. By the time he was lured back to Cincinnati, this protégé of Bertha Baur had become head of graduate studies at the School of Music of Indiana University. Most grant Watson solo credit for the institution that evolved during his nine-year tenure, inevitably tapping variants of the bromide about "the house that Jack built."

The first challenge was that of physical facilities. The goal was to complete new structures on the University of Cincinnati campus by 1965 while the College-Conservatory of Music continued to inhabit its inherited buildings nearby. However, by the following year the new quarters had still not been completed and the Cincinnati Board of Education took possession of the Oak Street property, which it had bought as the site of a new junior high school. Thus the College-Conservatory of Music was forced into improvised spaces scattered hither and yon for a full academic year. Watson had mobilized a handful of benefactors, principally J. Ralph and Patricia Corbett, so that the new complex comprised Mary Emery Hall, housing teaching studios, classrooms, and practice facilities, as well as the Corbett Center for the Performing Arts with a major auditorium, plus a Radio and Television Wing funded by the Crosley Foundation. The Corbetts also gave fifty thousand dollars a year to burnish the College-Conservatory of Music orchestras with scholarship students and imported noted English recitalist Peter Hurford for a year in order to showcase the substantial Harrison and Harrison organ installed in the auditorium. The Clara Baur Memorial Fountain, dating from 1914, was relocated to the plaza fronting Emery Hall.

The Corbetts underwrote the week of dedication events in late November and early December 1967. These included a performance of Borodin's *Prince Igor; Proud Music of the Storm*, for chorus, brass, and organ, commissioned from Norman Dello Joio; new pieces by faculty composers Scott Huston (a cantata, *The Path and the Praise*) and Felix Labunski (*Intrada*); the Cincinnati Civic Ballet in a new work choreographed by David McLain,[27] and a concert by the Cincinnati Symphony, conducted by Max Rudolf (who had been named a Distinguished Professor of Music at the College-Conservatory of Music in 1966), with tenor John Alexander of the Metropolitan Opera (a College-Conservatory of Music alumnus) and Suzanne Farrell, principal dancer of the New York City Ballet (an honorary lecturer on ballet and an alumna of the College-Conservatory of Music preparatory program), assisted by Jacques d'Amboise and Arthur Mitchell. The week was also touted as a celebration of the College-

Conservatory of Music's centenary, commemorating that December in 1867 when Clara Baur had opened her Conservatory of Music in a single room downtown.

The Patricia Corbett Pavilion—the third unit of the complex—was opened in 1972. Its centerpiece is a four-hundred-seat theater, but it also houses the dance program, rehearsal and studio spaces, and offices. The dedication ceremonies included Francesco Cavalli's 1651–52 opera *Calisto* and a restaging of *The Beloved*, a ballet by Lester Horton, by James Truitte, a faculty member who had been a principal dancer for Horton.

During this period the acclaimed LaSalle Quartet (in residence since 1953) continued to attract international attention through its concerts and recordings (and especially through its espousal of twentieth-century literature); what is now known as the Percussion Group became another resident ensemble. Jazz was gradually introduced into the curriculum, although jazz and studio music was declared an official major only in 1976, and a musical theater program began to evolve toward its nationally acclaimed status. In 1984 a department of theater in the university's College of Arts and Sciences was incorporated into the College-Conservatory of Music as one facet of an expanded division of opera, musical theater, drama, and arts administration.

Watson was succeeded in 1974 by Eugene Bonelli, Alan Sapp, and several others, including Joseph Polisi, whose brief tenure led to his appointment as president of the Juilliard School. Stability returned only with the appointment of Robert J. Werner as dean in 1985; Werner was succeeded in 2000 by Douglas Lowry, previously associate dean of the School of Music of the University of Southern California.

Bonelli procured a substantial grant from the Starling Foundation, which not only provided scholarship funds for outstanding violin students but also allowed a yearlong residency by the renowned pedagogue, Dorothy DeLay. Bonelli also saw the University of Cincinnati assimilated into the state system in 1977.

It was Polisi who fostered an appearance by the Philharmonia Orchestra under Gerhard Samuel at New York's Carnegie Hall in March 1985; the orchestra subsequently traveled to Paris four years later for an appearance at a Mahler festival. Among the most noted of a plethora of similar outreach programs was a staged performance of Mozart's *Zaide*, K. 336b, at Lincoln Center in New York. The school has also attracted notice by the addition to its faculty of several superstars: Dorothy DeLay was appointed Dorothy Richard Starling Visiting Professor of Classical Violin, dividing her schedule between the College-Conservatory of Music and Juilliard. James Tocco was named Artist-in-Residence and Eminent Scholar in Chamber Music, the latter distinction based on a grant from the Ohio Board of Regents. In 1987 the acclaimed Tokyo String Quartet was hired as an ensemble-in-residence.

The school has responded to constantly changing circumstances in the professional world by installing five state-of-the-art electronic labs and reconfiguring the broadcasting division into one encompassing all the electronic media, including not only radio and television but also computers, film, and telecommunications. Courses in non-Western music, practical pedagogy, and "performance stress management" have broadened the curricular offerings considerably. A seven-year, $93 million program of renovation and expansion of facilities was completed in 2000, one noticeable addition being the Dieterle Vocal Arts Building, housing voice teaching studios as well as the choral and opera programs.

Certainly the Baurs and the rest of that large family of persons involved in the evolution of both conservatory and college (perhaps even Theodore Thomas himself) would enthusiastically commend the present-day offspring of their labors.

CHAPTER 14

The Cleveland Institute of Music

Although younger by several generations, the Cleveland Institute of Music[1] was conceived under circumstances analogous to those that gave birth to the College of Music in Cincinnati, where a group of wealthy aristocrats funded an institution meant to attract instant attention through the considerable reputation of its leader.

Although the city already possessed a respectable number of music schools (for example, the Cleveland School of Music [1885], the West Side Musical College [ca. 1900], and the Hruby Conservatory of Music [1918]), in April 1920 a group of prominent local citizens, led by Mrs. Franklyn B. Sanders, each contributed one thousand dollars toward a goal of establishing a "school of music where every type of student could find opportunity for the best musical education." Temporary quarters were established in the Hotel Statler. The eminent Swiss-born composer, Ernest Bloch (1880–1959), was named the Cleveland Institute of Music's first musical director, while Mrs. Sanders served as executive director. The institute officially opened on December 8, 1920, in a converted residence on Euclid Avenue, with a faculty that included several members of the Cleveland Orchestra, including its concertmaster and principal cellist. Costs for a twenty-four-week term ranged from $150 to $500; the curriculum offered instrumental study, theory, composition, and both vocal and instrumental ensembles. The initial enrollment of seven had ballooned to two hundred at the outset of the second year and more than four hundred by its conclusion. For that second season the pioneers were joined by pianist Beryl Rubinstein, organist Edwin Arthur Kraft, and composer Roger Sessions.[2] In 1922 the institute moved to more commodious quarters in another converted residence at 2827 Euclid Avenue. A preparatory division was established, and a two-year course in Dalcroze Eurythmics became a requirement for all students. The school also became a charter member of the National Association of Schools of Music.

Bloch, who arrived in this country in 1916 and had been teaching privately in New York City and, after 1917, at the Mannes School of Music, had proclaimed, "Musical education, in addition to the thorough study of technique, ought above all else, to develop qualities of appreciation, judgment and taste, and to stimulate understanding and love of music."[3] A radical in the realm of pedagogy, he proposed eliminating such traditional tools as grading, examinations, and textbooks in favor of a more immediate and direct musical experience, teaching directly from the scores of the master composers. He also insisted on the efficacy of the European solfège system, lacked the temperament of a fundraiser, and disdained the requisite social functions of his position. Asked to resign in 1925, he was immediately named director of the San Francisco Conservatory of Music. Sessions was later to conclude,

> Cleveland's rejection of Bloch was a rejection precisely of the best that he had to give. His very geniality, his ironic laughter—his richness of temperament and culture, in other words—stood in his way. The city which had summoned him, at first, disarmed by his magnetism into partial capitulation, took alarm before the full impact of his personality. It was not, in the last analysis, an individual, a style, or an aesthetic that went down to defeat in Cleveland; it was rather just those disinterested and human conceptions which form the indispensable background for artistic creation of any kind.[4]

The most durable legacy of the twenty-one works Bloch completed during his five-year stint in Cleveland was the Concerto Grosso No. 1 for string orchestra and piano, first heard at the Statler Hotel on May 29, 1925; the composer conducted the institute orchestra in the concluding gesture of his tenure at the Cleveland Institute of Music.[5]

This performance followed by only a week a blaring headline on page one of the *Cleveland Press* of May 22: INSTITUTE HAS ROW; BLOCH OUT. Bloch was quoted as believing that his departure for San Francisco would allow him to broaden his activities as "lecturer, conductor and pedagogue. I owe to myself more time for my creative work, which has more or less suffered in expending too much energy in purely administrative affairs." However, he betrayed his true feelings in a letter to Romain Rolland, written in July:

> The 12th of May, three weeks before the end of the season, my Committee "showed me the door" politely, and without looking me in the eyes . . . because they had hired me for another year, 1925–26 as early as January. But, after five years of cordial relations and mutual confidence—and having absolute faith in the work of "Chairman" of the Executive Committee, Sheldon Cavy, whom I held in high esteem—I had on my own, not demanded a *writ-*

ten contract! The long intrigues against me were finally successful . . . and I found myself in the street with my family after five years of hard work and devotion to this institute, that I created.[6]

A threatened lawsuit was settled out of court.[7]

Mrs. Sanders succeeded Bloch as director, pianist Arthur Loesser joined the faculty in 1926, and the first of what would become four preparatory branches was opened in Cleveland Heights the following year. Beryl Rubinstein succeeded Mrs. Sanders in 1932, and the school migrated to yet another residence on Euclid Avenue. The faculty came to include legendary Cleveland Orchestra harpist Alice Chalifoux, as well as composer Herbert Elwell. Rubinstein and a cellist colleague were allied with violinist Josef Fuchs, concertmaster of the Cleveland Orchestra, as the Cleveland Trio.

Elwell substituted for Rubinstein during the latter's sabbatical in 1935, by which time the school fielded a faculty of forty, serving six hundred students. The following year Boris Goldovsky was appointed founding head of an opera department, a position he held until 1942; he inaugurated that tenure with Mozart's *The Marriage of Figaro*, followed by Puccini's *Gianni Schicchi* in early 1937.[8] The Cleveland Institute of Music migrated again in 1941 to yet another converted residence on Euclid Avenue; a recital hall named for Willard Clapp, the institute's first president, was constructed (joined by a Martha Sanders Hall, a converted carriage house, in 1950). The following year the National Association of Schools of Music authorized the Cleveland Institute of Music to offer graduate work.

World War II inevitably led to major adjustments. The noted two-piano team of Rubinstein and Loesser was temporarily disabled when both men became Army captains. Theorist Ward Lewis succeeded Rubinstein as interim director. Violinist Joseph Knitzer also went off to war, but several noted performers joined the faculty, including Leonard Rose, principal cellist of the Cleveland Orchestra from 1939 until 1943, and pianist Leonard Shure.

In September 1945 the Cleveland Institute of Music celebrated its silver anniversary with a special concert featuring Beryl Rubinstein playing the Chopin Scherzo in C-sharp minor, opus 39, a work heard at the school's opening concert a quarter-of-a-century earlier. Enrollment swelled with the return of peace. Ten faculty members were added in 1946, including theorist and composer Marcel Dick and the Cleveland Orchestra's noted flutist, Maurice Sharp. The physical facilities were expanded with the addition of teaching studios, classrooms, and practice rooms, as well as a library. By the beginning of the 1949–50 academic year the Cleveland Institute of Music could boast of a faculty of fifty-one and a student body of 919.

Rubinstein died in December 1952 and was eventually succeeded by pianist Ward Davenny in April 1954. Davenny became Arthur Loesser's new duo-piano partner and presided over planning for a new structure on East Boulevard in the heart of the University Circle area. At its dedication in September 1961, it contained thirty teaching studios, eleven classrooms, twenty practice rooms, a library, and a 525-seat concert hall. The Cleveland Institute of Music's concert season was inaugurated by a new director, pianist Victor Babin (1908–72), and his two-piano partner and wife, Vitya Vronsky. Babin presided over a decade of considerable growth before his premature death. Composer (and alumnus) Donald Erb attracted national attention and supervised the installation of an electronic music studio. Le Pavilion, a more intimate recital hall, was completed in 1966. A major capital funds drive was undertaken in quest of an endowment that would allow financial stability. The University Circle Training Orchestra was created and first entrusted to James Levine; the Cleveland Quartet, actually formed at the Marlboro Festival in Vermont in 1968, the following year became quartet-in-residence at the Cleveland Institute of Music, where its first violinist, Donald Weilerstein, was already a member of the faculty, a relationship that lasted for two years.

Babin was succeeded in 1973 by yet another renowned pianist, Grant Johannesen (b. 1921), first as a consultant and advisor, as director the following year, and from 1977 as president. He announced his resignation in 1984 and was succeeded the following year by violinist David Cerone. The stewardship of these two men saw the introduction of programs confirming the school's significance: Cleveland Chamber Music Seminars, instituted by Cerone in 1974; the Robert Casadesus International Piano Competitions, dating from 1975; and, during the following decade, a new audio-recording program, a graduate program in Suzuki pedagogy, the creation of a contemporary music ensemble under the direction of Donald Erb, the biennial Art Song Festival (inaugurated by soprano Elly Ameling in 1986), appointment of the Cavani String Quartet as Artists-in-Residence, and, more recently, in partnership with Case Western Reserve University, a technology learning center.

Much of the dazzle can be attributed to the Cleveland Institute of Music's proximity to Severance Hall and the high incidence of Cleveland Orchestra members on its faculty. Many of the Cleveland Orchestra's distinguished guests have traveled that short distance down East Boulevard to offer master classes or benefit programs, for instance, Mstislav Rostropovich in consort with the Cleveland Institute of Music Orchestra in 1973 and André Watts in 1988.

Once can only assume that this richness of opportunity surely has satisfied the dreams of its founders, intent on providing opportunities "for the best musical education."

Part Three

Art Music

CHAPTER 15

Art Museums and a Hall of Fame

Of Ohio's notable art museums, those of Toledo and Cleveland have most obviously established connections between the worlds of music and the visual arts. In Toledo that relationship is manifested in the Peristyle, an elegant neo-Grecian concert hall, which houses a large organ by Ernest M. Skinner of 1926 (opus 603) and is home to the Toledo Symphony and a venue for touring artists and ensembles.

The Cleveland Museum of Art, however, not only sports an auditorium with an imposing organ by the local Holtkamp Company, but also a Department of Musical Arts, with its own staff and three self-generated concert series.[1] This arrangement dates from 1921 (only five years after the museum opened to the public), when a Massachusetts educator, Thomas Whitney Surette (1861–1941), was appointed curator. Surette conducted adult "sings" and children's music hours, gave illustrated lectures on musical subjects, sponsored chamber music programs, and developed a young people's orchestra. He also planned the installation of an Ernest M. Skinner organ (opus 333), which was dedicated in March 1922 with a recital by Harvard's Archibald T. Davison (who had been a consultant for the project), and was subsequently installed on a balcony in the museum's Garden Court after the original location in an attic space above a sub-skylight between the court and the rotunda did not prove felicitous. The relocated instrument was dedicated in 1924 by the noted Belgian-born recitalist, Charles Courboin. The instrument represented one-fifth of a $250,000 gift made in honor of P. J. McMyler, a Cleveland industrialist.

Surette departed after only a year and was succeeded by his assistant, composer Douglas Moore (1893–1969), who left to join the faculty of Columbia University in 1925. Moore continued the educational practices of his mentor but also began emphasizing live performances of music, including a series presenting all the string quartets of Beethoven, a two-season venture initiated in 1923. Moore was succeeded by organist Arthur Quimby, a member of the Western Reserve University faculty.

Quimby and his friend, Cleveland native Melville Smith, were soon offering local listeners literature not in common practice at the time. In 1930 André Marchal, the eminent French recitalist, played a series of all-Bach programs, and the following year Smith offered five recitals that explored then-unknown music from the sixteenth and seventeenth centuries. During 1933 and 1934, Quimby and Smith partnered to present the complete organ works by Bach, a series that provoked the installation of an experimental neo-Baroque *rückpositiv* division built by Walter Holtkamp, the first of its kind in this country, and a considerable revelation to those who heard it. Holtkamp then incorporated its pipes in his complete rebuilding of the instrument during 1946.

Quimby was succeeded in 1941 by Walter Blodgett (1907–75). Blodgett graduated from Oberlin and had done advanced study at the Juilliard School of Music in New York. He arrived in Cleveland in 1931 and held a series of church positions, most obviously for a quarter-of-a-century at St. Paul's Episcopal Church, where he developed a noted choir. Blodgett not only played about twelve hundred organ recitals during his tenure; he also assisted in the design of the museum's Gartner Auditorium and the rebuilding and resituating there of the P. J. McMyler Memorial Organ in 1971.

He also presided over a distinguished concert series but realized that the McMyler Musical Endowment of 1920 was no longer generating sufficient income to support those events. Consequently, in 1946 he organized the Musart Society, whose members provide the funds that today underwrite the Musart Mondial Series of evening programs, and Musart Matinée, a series of Sunday afternoon chamber-music programs (a tradition dating from 1979) and numerous organ recitals, for a total of about fifty events each season. The society has also purchased several musical instruments for the museum, most recently a harpsichord built by Bruce Kennedy of Amsterdam, dedicated in September 2000.

An interest in new music dates back to the early years of the museum's history, with concerts and lectures by Ravel, Bartók, Bloch, Tippett, Messiaen, Stockhausen, and others (for example, in 1928, radical Hans Barth, who played on a two-keyboard quarter-tone piano of his own invention). In 1959 Blodgett initiated the May Festival of Contemporary Music, featuring literature by local composers as well as that of visitors like Phillip Glass and Steve Reich. Under Blodgett's successor, since 1974, the Czech-born organist Karel Paukert, the Department of Musical Arts in 1977 undertook a biennial festival of new music called AKI, the Japanese word for autumn. After hosting Steve Reich and Musicians, the Philip Glass Ensemble, Elliott Carter, George Crumb, Mario Davidovsky, and many other notables, funding difficulties led to a hiatus in 1985. However, AKI was revived in March 1999 with a series of eleven concerts containing music by twenty-five different composers.

A proud heritage indeed, especially when considering that, according to an archival document, Mr. Blodgett's Department of Musical Arts chartered the Cleveland Guild of Page Turners as well as the Society of Professional Organ Recital Technicians (or SPORTs).[2]

Cincinnati has recently become the home of the American Classical Music Hall of Fame. The heady dream of a local pharmacist, this infant pantheon, for the moment, is little more than a program book and a storefront operation on West Fourth Street, a mini-museum housing graphic presentations of its honorees, as well as displays of appropriate artifacts and a small recital hall on the second floor.

Founded in September 1997 with the intent of "honoring the great figures of our musical past and present" and graced with both a National Artistic Directorate of individuals and a Professional Artistic Advisory Council of organizations, the American Classical Music Hall of Fame inducted its first honorees in a Music Hall ceremony on May 24, 1998, featuring the United States Marine Band. This first "class" contained not only the Marine Band itself (as "America's oldest professional music organization") but also a full range of conductors (among them, John Philip Sousa, Arturo Toscanini, Serge Koussevitzky, Robert Shaw, Theodore Thomas, Fritz Reiner, and Leopold Stokowski, the last four all with Cincinnati connections), composers (such as Barber, Bernstein, Copland, Hanson, Ives, John Knowles Paine, Sessions, Schoenberg, and Stravinsky), soloists (Leontyne Price and Isaac Stern), and others whom a purist might consider crossover artists (Duke Ellington, George Gershwin, and Scott Joplin). A second group of inductees was honored at a Cincinnati Symphony Orchestra concert in Music Hall on April 24, 1999. It included an institution (the Music Division of the Library of Congress), a musicologist (H. Wiley Hitchcock, a pioneering guru of studies in American music), composers (Béla Bartok, Amy Cheney Beach, George Whitefield Chadwick, Charles Tomlinson Griffes, William Grant Still, and Edgar Varèse), singers (Marilyn Horne and William Warfield), a violinist (Jascha Heifetz), and two conductors (Max Rudolf, maestro of the Cincinnati Symphony from 1958 until 1970, and Dimitri Mitropolous). The April 2000 inductees included the Metropolitan Opera Company, philanthropist Elizabeth Sprague Coolidge, composers Edward MacDowell, Walter Piston, and then-seventy-seven-year-old George Walker (who holds an undergraduate degree from the Oberlin Conservatory of Music), soprano Beverly Sills, pianists Leon Fleisher and Rudolf Serkin, and conductors Eugene Ormandy and George Szell (who presided over the Cleveland Orchestra from 1946 until 1970). The class of 2001, inducted in a ceremony at the University of Cincinnati in April, proved equally polyglot, and without direct Ohio connections: composers William Billings, George Crumb, Antonin Dvořák, Paul Hindemith, Sergei Rachmaninoff, and Virgil Thomson; conductors Frederick Fennell and Arthur Fiedler; violinist Itzhak Perlman and pianist Van Cliburn; plus the Juilliard String Quartet and New York Philharmonic.

Orchestras

Ohio is the home of fine regional orchestras in Akron, Canton, Columbus, Dayton, Toledo, and Youngstown, as well as an abundance of community ensembles, paraprofessional groups in collegiate schools of music, and public-school orchestras of varying sizes and capabilities. Nonetheless, prudence suggests that we restrict our attention to the pair of ensembles that have achieved international recognition: the Cincinnati Symphony Orchestra, which made its formal appearance in Pike's Opera House on January 17, 1895, with Texas-born Frank Van der Stucken on the podium (the fifth such ensemble to appear, preceded only by permanent orchestras in New York [the Philharmonic Society in 1842 and the Symphony Society in 1878], Boston [1881], and Chicago [1891]), and the Cleveland Orchestra, first identified as Cleveland's Orchestra, which made its début in Grays' Armory on December 11, 1918, under the baton of Russian-born Nikolai Sokoloff.

CHAPTER 16

The Cincinnati Symphony Orchestra

Independent orchestras (orchestras other than those employed in the theater pits) appeared in Cincinnati as early as 1835,[1] when the Musical Fund Society was organized. Its announced purposes included "the cultivation of musical taste, by the encouragement and improvement of professional and amateur talent, and the establishment of a musical academy, by means of which pupils may be instructed in the theory and practice of music," plus the gathering of money with which to aid musicians in distress, as well as their widows and children in the event of their fathers' deaths. Little evidence of the society's activities remains, although it appears that violinist Joseph Tosso[2] led its orchestra, perhaps through 1839, and that from the autumn of 1840 until the summer of 1841 the composer and publisher William C. Peters was in charge. A typical concert under his baton included opera overtures such as Mozart's to *The Marriage of Figaro*, Méhul's to *Two Blind Men of Toledo* (*Les deux aveugles de Tolède*), and Rossini's to *An Italian Woman in Algiers*, as well as solos, duets, and so on, their accompaniments arranged by Peters.

After five concerts during the 1841 season, the Musical Fund Society disbanded and was superseded by the Amateur Musical Society, whose first concert of note was held on December 9, 1841, as a benefit for Tosso. Led by Swedish-born Victor Williams, this organization soon fielded an orchestra of about thirty, constituted of amateurs and their professional "assistants." Williams followed the Peters' programming paradigm, with operatic overtures bracketing a mélange of less substantial music. For example, a concert of April 27, 1842, opened with Mozart's overture to *The Abduction from the Seraglio*, followed by a Thomas Moore song, a flute solo, an unidentified glee, another song, and Rossini's overture to *The Barber of Seville*. Part 2 began with the Mozart overture to *Don Juan* [*sic*], followed by vocal and piano duets and yet another song. In 1844 Williams leased the Assembly Rooms at Pearl and

Walnut streets as a concert site, a space briefly identified as Amateur Musical Hall. A typical season of four concerts extended from December until spring.

The Philharmonic Society, a similar organization, was announced on February 6, 1847, with Peters as conductor and treasurer. The group's announced goals ought to sound familiar, with one notable exception: "[T]he cultivation of an elevated and refined musical taste in the community; the improvement of amateur talent; and the encouragement of professional musicians, by paying them for services rendered." The concluding stipulation surely betrays the increasingly dense cultural fabric of the city. The Philharmonic Society's first concert took place on the sixteenth, conducted by Tosso, Williams, Peters, and others. It included overtures by Méhul (*Les deux aveugles de Tolède*) and Gluck (*Iphygenie* [*sic*]), a set of waltzes by the omnipresent Joseph Labitzky, a polka by Brulon, songs (including an excerpt from Topliff's *Ruth and Naomi* presented by Peters), plus flute and violin solos. Although five concerts were projected, only three were presented, including one on March 5 as a benefit for those starving in Ireland. After a May 15 performance at Melodeon Hall, then the city's principal concert space, the society seems to have evaporated.[3]

When Frédéric L. Ritter arrived in the city in 1856, he organized the Cecilia Society of eighty singers, as well as a subsidiary Cincinnati Philharmonic Orchestra. During his five-year tenure, the two ensembles independently and collectively essayed a considerable swath of literature.[4]

The first of three subscription concerts was heard at Smith and Nixon's Hall on February 19, 1857. It included Mozart's Overture to *The Magic Flute* and Weber's to *Der Freischütz*, the complete Beethoven Sixth Symphony (that supposedly held the audience "spellbound in listening to the heavenly strains"), vocal solos from Rossini and Delsarte, two movements of a Beethoven piano quartet, and an excerpt from Rossini's *Semiramide*, arranged as a duet for clarinet and bassoon. The orchestra consisted of twenty-seven players, among them the most prominent of the city's German-born musicians. Although a note on the program suggests three hundred subscribers, only 145 are listed by name, but these include prominent musicians like piano pedagogue William Nixon and Victor Williams. The society's directors appealed to their public for continuing support: "To execute well such masterly works as the Pastoral and other symphonies by Beethoven, requires a much greater amount of labor and perseverance than is generally supposed. OLD Societies must rehearse such works for MONTHS[;] how much more difficult, then, must their performance be for a NEW Society[?]" Claiming those three hundred subscribers, the directors stated that

> twice as many would hardly remunerate the members of the Orchestra for the great expenditure of time and energy involved in this undertaking; and they would earnestly request the true friends of music to use their influence

in interesting others in it. A society, like this, which aims at the advancement of Instrumental Music, and at the cultivation of a general musical taste among us, can be placed on a safe and permanent basis only by a very widely extended interest of the public. Unless audiences of about a thousand persons may be expected, Orchestral Concerts of a high character cannot be relied upon in future seasons.[5]

On April 23 in Melodeon Hall, Ritter presided over a concert presented for his benefit that included the Mozart Overture to *The Marriage of Figaro,* the slow movement of the Second Symphony of Beethoven, Niels Gade's overture *Nachklänge von Ossian,* and Part 1 of Mendelssohn's *St. Paul.* On June 5 the final concert of this first season (that also included informal entertainments mounted for the particular pleasure of the associate, that is nonperforming, members, as well as a public rehearsal every other Saturday) encompassed two movements of Mozart's final symphony, as well as excerpts from Weber's *Euryanthe,* Wagner's *Lohengrin,* and Haydn's *The Seasons.*

The highlight of the second season was the presentation of a complete *The Seasons* on April 6, 1858, while the third season concluded on June 16, 1859, with Part 1 of Mendelssohn's *Elijah* and Gade's cantata *Comala* of 1846. The fourth season included major portions of Handel's *Messiah* on January 25, 1860. Ritter abandoned Cincinnati the following year in favor of New York, where he conducted two German choral societies until 1867, when he was appointed professor of music at Vassar College. He wrote a considerable amount of music for various media, as well as many essays and the first attempt at a comprehensive survey of music in this country. He and his several significant contemporaries constructed the platform from which were launched the astounding achievements of the waning decades of the century and beyond, for they worked "at a fortuitous moment, [when] the people were ready to gratefully acknowledge the receipt in full of compositions of which they had hitherto been given but a taste."[6]

Prior to leaving Cincinnati Ritter conducted a "Grand Concert Symphonique" on April 12, 1861, which must have haunted both its participants and auditors. The program was ambitious: the Beethoven Overture to *Prometheus,* a violin concerto by Charles-Auguste de Bériot (1802–70), the Mozart G Minor Symphony, an *Overture de Concert* by Johann Wenzel Kalliwoda (1801–66), Weber's *Konzertstück* for piano and orchestra, and Mendelssohn's March from *Athalie.* The Weber had not been heard in Cincinnati and was to be played by Henry G. Andres, a newly arrived resident of the city. As it began people near the doors were seen leaving the hall. By the middle of the work the exodus had become more general, so the conductor halted the performance to essay what was happening. Baffled, conductor and soloist decided to continue, but had to abandon the piece when a virtual stampede left the hall empty. Fort Sumter had been fired on, ushering in the Civil War.[7]

After Ritter's departure in 1861 both ensembles were entrusted to Silesian-born Carl Barus, who maintained the nucleus of the orchestra intact, in part to collaborate with the Harmonic Society, an English-language singing society he founded in 1864. Barus had arrived in Cincinnati in 1851 and across three decades directed various of the local German singing societies, served several churches (two Catholic and one Methodist) and a synagogue as organist and choir director, and headed the music department of the Wesleyan Female Academy for twenty-two of those years. The Philharmonic barely survived the Civil War period, but beginning in 1866, underwritten by Lewis C. Hopkins, a wealthy dry goods merchant who even built his own seven-hundred-seat concert hall at the corner of Fourth and Elm Streets in 1867, what became the twenty-five-man Hopkins Hall Orchestra presented thirty-seven orchestral programs during three seasons of subscription concerts, a rich diet that included five symphonies by Beethoven, three of Mozart, four of Haydn, and single symphonies by Schubert, Mendelssohn, and Gade. However, financial reverses led to the loss of Hopkins's support after the first two seasons, and substantial deficits caused the demise of this ensemble in the spring of 1869. Perhaps more than symbolically, the final concert of the second season included Haydn's "Farewell" Symphony, in whose final movement the performers depart the stage one-by-one.[8]

Theodore Thomas brought his touring, New York–based orchestra to Cincinnati for the first time in December of that year, and announced his pleasure in discovering "excellent choral societies there, and an orchestra superior to that of any city west of the New York."[9] Thomas may have been alluding to the short-lived Orpheus Society Orchestra, substantial enough to have as its core a string section of eighteen. Although his five concerts drew small audiences, Thomas was to pay annual visits to Cincinnati and eventually had a considerable impact on the cultural life of the city.

However, he was not the first to bring an orchestra of touring professionals to the city. The Germania Musical Society visited Cincinnati in both 1853 and 1854, and the showman Louis Antoine Jullien led his orchestra at Smith and Nixon's Hall on February 2, 3, 4, and 6, 1854, and then returned for another series of farewell concerts on April 23, 25, and 26, immediately preceding the Germania's farewell cycle.

Jullien's February 2 program offered a considerable dose of his own works (a *Quadrille "Californian"*; a waltz, *La Prima Donna* [with cornet solos and cadenzas by Herr Koenig]; a *Quadrille National; The American,* with twenty solos and variations; the *Sleigh Polka*; and a galop, *The Target,* "descriptive of a grand field day") as well as an Auber overture, sung bits from Donizetti and Meyerbeer, a song from Thomas Arne's *The Tempest,* a violin duet by the Mollenhauers, and a clarionet solo by M. Wuille. This pattern (with some of the same repertory) was repeated in the subsequent concerts. On February 9, 10, 11, and 13 Kunkel's Nightingale [Ethiopian] Opera Troupe, capitalizing on the flamboyant maestro's success and idiosyncrasies, offered Cincinnatians, "for the first time, The Great Burlesque of JULLIEN."

Victor Williams's Amateur Musical Society collaborated with the Germania Musical Society in *Morning* by Ferdinand Ries (1784–1838) and *The Power of Song* by Andreas Romberg (1767–1821), both conducted by Williams,

> Mr. [Carl] Bergmann resigning the desk in his favor. Before departing the band presented him with a heavy silver punch ladle, bearing the inscription: "To Victor Williams; from the Germania Musical Society;" and on December 29th, 1854, forwarded to him from Boston a handsomely executed picture of the members, posed as for rehearsal.[10]

Frank Tunison dated this collaboration to 1854, but advertisements for the Germania's "five successive vocal and instrumental concerts" offered between May 2 and 6 of that year, assisted by vocalist Caroline Lehmann, as part of their farewell tour, contain nary a reference to the Amateur Musical Society. The initial three potpourris contained works by Auber, Donizetti, Flotow, Mendelssohn, Verdi, Wagner, Weber, and others and featured soloists drawn from the ensemble, such as flutist Carl Zerrahn. However, Friday evening brought to Cincinnati Mendelssohn's incidental music for *Midsummer Night's Dream,* the vocal parts "sustained" by Miss Lehmann, the words of Shakespeare recited by Miss Kate Saxon, billed as "a highly accomplished Reader and Lecturer, who has gained a great reputation in England where she has read repeatedly before audiences of two or three thousand listeners." "By general desire," the Mendelssohn was repeated the following evening, marking Germania's swan song to the Queen City.

However, in the initial announcements for this series, its members "tender[ed] their sincere thanks to the musical inhabitants of this city for the liberal patronage bestowed on them on their last visit." This occurred during the previous season, when the ensemble presented four concerts in Smith and Nixon's Hall (April 26, 28, and 30, and May 3), assisted by pianist Alfred Jaëll (1832–82) and "The Youthful Violinist," Camille Urso (1842–1902). Again, the programs were pastiches containing pieces by many of the same composers (but also conductor Bergmann's *Festival March* and *Love Polka*). However, the "Fourth and Last Grand Instrumental Concert" opened with the entire Sixth Symphony of Beethoven. The Germanians then lingered for what was billed as a "Grand Musical Festival" on May 5, presented "with the very valuable assistance of the CINCINNATI AMATEUR ASSOCIATION." This one-night festival was initiated with Verdi's Overture to *Nabucco,* after which the locals presented *The Morning.* Urso performed Hubert Léonard's *Souvenir de Grétry,* a Mr. Wetherbee sang Schubert's "Der Wanderer," the orchestra played a "Torch Dance" and the Overture to *Les Huguenots* by Meyerbeer, and Jaëll offered Rudolf Willmers's *The Bird Song—A Danish Canzonette* prior to the Amateur's presentation of *The Power of Song.*

Announcements in the *Cincinnati Daily Gazette* described the Amateur's second concert of the following season in Smith and Nixon's Hall on January 5, 1854. The group was to be joined by violinist Henry Appy and singer Signor Corradi Colliere, and "with the fine choruses, duets, &c., by the lady and gentlemen amateurs of the Society, we may look for a rich performance." The third and final event of their season was offered on April 8 as a benefit for Williams. With several guest artists and "full" orchestra, auditors were offered excerpts from Neukomm's *David*, snippets from Haydn, Calcott, Verdi, and others, plus a set of waltzes by the popular Joseph Labitzky. The finale was a rendering of the *Marseilles Hymn* by M. Colliere, supported by chorus and orchestra.

In 1872 Louis Ballenberg and George Brand organized the forty-two-member Cincinnati Grand Orchestra, committed to a winter series of six concerts in Pike's Opera House. Brand departed midseason for Boston and was succeeded by his younger brother Michael, who had left a position as principal cellist in the Theodore Thomas Orchestra. The Grand Orchestra lost money and subsequent seasons were reduced to five concerts, but the ensemble did present twenty-seven complete symphonies during its six years of existence (1872–78) and at the time was the only permanent orchestra west of the Atlantic coast.[11]

In late 1871 Thomas, in town for one of those eleven visits his orchestra paid between 1869 and 1878, met with Maria Longworth and George Ward Nichols to plan what became the first May Festival, held in 1873 to national acclaim. Most of Thomas's 108-member orchestra were New Yorkers, buttressed by local players. The biennial festivals led to the construction of Music Hall in 1878. That same year the Cincinnati College of Music opened in rented space on the third floor of Music Hall, with Thomas as musical director. Part of Thomas's responsibility was the creation of a professional orchestra, albeit one supported and marketed by the college. The result: a sixty-man ensemble, essentially the Grand Orchestra melded with various members of the college faculty, which presented a total of twenty-four concerts during its 1878–79 season. During the winter it offered substantial literature, including the first performances in Cincinnati of the first two Brahms symphonies, but it perhaps attracted more attention through a series of twenty-six concerts at the Highland House during the summer of 1879, the last of which was attended by dignitaries in town for the opening of an industrial exposition. These included President Rutherford B. Hayes and Generals William T. Sherman and Philip H. Sheridan, all of them Ohio natives. Thomas had presented a similar series with his touring orchestra two years earlier: twenty-three concerts that became so popular that railroads created excursion packages for out-of-town tourists.[12]

Thomas's precipitous resignation as director of the college in 1880 fractured the musical community and led to the temporary demise of the college orchestra. Lucien

Wulsin, president of the Musical Club and a partner of Dwight H. Baldwin, then initiated an attempt to provide a series of five concerts with the Cincinnati Grand Orchestra under Michael Brand but by December had not succeeded in soliciting a viable number of subscriptions. However, on Christmas evening, Thomas conducted the first of six annual presentations of *Messiah* with the May Festival Chorus and Cincinnati Grand Orchestra (having done so with College of Music forces in 1878 and 1879). The 1881 performance involved Thomas's New York Orchestra and superstar Adelina Patti. About four thousand tickets had been sold in advance by auction, and, according to the *Commercial,* it was estimated that seven thousand auditors overwhelmed Music Hall. Louis Ballenberg then attempted to resuscitate the Grand Orchestra in both 1882 and 1883 but without success. However, during the summer and fall of 1884 Wulsin and Peter R. Neff, soon to become head of the College of Music, reconstituted the Grand Orchestra as the Philharmonic Orchestra, under the direction of Michael Brand. This fifty-man ensemble presented a series of five concerts in the twelve-hundred-seat Odeon Hall, a gift to the city by Reuben R. Springer. However, internecine struggles led to Brand's resignation and an 1885–86 season of six concerts whose leadership was shared equally by violinists John A. Broekhaven and Henry Schradieck.

During the following two seasons the College of Music sponsored six pairs of concerts presented by an orchestra constituted mainly of former Philharmonic players under the baton of Schradieck, a member of the college faculty. However, public support for this venture faltered, and during 1889 and 1890 Ballenberg underwrote parallel series of symphony concerts in the Odeon and Sunday afternoon popular concerts in Music Hall with Brand leading a regenerated Grand Orchestra. *The Cincinnati Musical Directory, 1886–87,* published under the aegis of the Cincinnati Wesleyan College for Young Women, contains an advertisement for the Cincinnati Grand Orchestra and Reed Band, both of them conducted by Michael Brand: "The Management are prepared to Furnish Music for All Legitimate Entertainments, Symphony Concerts, Oratorios, Festivals, Operas, Theatricals, Commencements, Dancing, etc. Also make a specialty to furnish first-class CHAMBER MUSIC and ensemble performances. Only first-class musicians are engaged in the above organizations."[13] Only the inexpensive Sunday events survived under Brand's baton until 1895, after January 1891 attracting an average attendance of three thousand with an ensemble named the Cincinnati Orchestra Company.

Members of a Ladies' Musical Club, organized in September 1891, originally intended to devote themselves "to the study and practice of music and the promotion of a higher musical taste and culture" through performances by their own active members, as well as sponsorship of visiting artists and ensembles. However, on April 11, 1894, these women, under the leadership of president Helen Herron

(Mrs. William Howard) Taft, incorporated the Cincinnati Orchestra Association Company with the express purpose of establishing a permanent, indigenous ensemble, and quickly raised the necessary funds.

A May letter soliciting potential contributing members by appealing to them as "patriotic citizens" asserted,

> The benefits arising to our city from such an orchestra can not be overestimated. The fact that it would be and remain distinctly a Cincinnati affair, should enable it to receive support here and from the towns tributary to us; and to the business interest, the fact that the money spent in support of a permanent orchestra would remain and be spent here, should be a matter of no small import. An orchestra harmoniously supported on the lines indicated would give us yearly a series of concerts of a high degree of artistic excellence, which, with the aid of distinguished soloists, would form also a most attractive feature of social life. [14]

Having announced that their goal would "require a director of the highest talent," the club's board of directors solicited recommendations from Thomas (by then firmly ensconced in Chicago), Henry Krehbiel ([1854–1923] perhaps the most influential music critic of his time, at this point appearing in the columns of the *New York Tribune* but from 1874 until 1880 on the staff of the *Cincinnati Gazette*), Charles Ellis (manager of the Boston Symphony), and Walter Damrosch (conductor of the New York Symphony). They eventually settled on two equally unrenowned candidates: Henry Schradieck and Frank Van der Stucken (1858–1929), a native of Fredericksburg, Texas, whose family had emigrated to Antwerp in 1866. He trained there and in Leipzig before appointment as *Kapellmeister* of the Municipal Theater in Breslau. He had returned to this country in 1884 to succeed Leopold Damrosch as conductor of the Arion Society, a German-language male choral society in New York City. He conducted several German singing society festivals and achieved a bit of recognition as an advocate of American music: In 1889 he had led an all-American program at the Paris Exposition, which included works by George Whitefield Chadwick, Arthur Foote, and John Knowles Paine, as well as Edward MacDowell's Concerto in D minor with the composer at the piano. Schradieck, violinist and erstwhile local conductor, had apparently relocated to Europe about 1889 but at this point was living in New York actively seeking employment.

A majority of the board preferred Van der Stucken, while a preponderance of the local orchestral musicians apparently favored the known quality. Complex negotiations with Van der Stucken during the summer of 1894 foundered in part over financial considerations, in part over the Orchestra Association's unrequited desire to have its conductor take charge of the May Festival. Thus the Cincinnati

Symphony's initial season was initiated on January 17, 1895, with responsibilities divided among Van der Stucken, Schradieck, and Anton Seidl (1850–98), a Hungarian-born Wagnerian who had succeeded Leopold Damrosch as principal conductor of the Metropolitan Opera in 1885 and Theodore Thomas at the New York Philharmonic in 1891. Each was to preside over a series of three concerts on three consecutive days. Seidl, whose programs were presented in February, apparently had no interest in a permanent position, and general enthusiasm for the Texan led to a six-year contract authorized two days before his local competitor took the podium on April 11.

Michael Brand's Grand Orchestra furnished the nucleus of the forty-nine-person ensemble (Brand, who had earlier declined to be considered a candidate, served as principal cellist and Van der Stucken's assistant). The initial Cincinnati Symphony roster suggests the dominance of local Germans resident in the Over-the-Rhine District, as well as the ubiquity of the Brand clan: Albert served as a second violinist and percussionist, Arthur as violist, Louis and George as trombonists, and Leo as timpanist. Concertmaster Henry Schmitt had been imported from New York. Harpist Mrs. A. T. Lawrence was the solitary female of the contingent.[15]

Van der Stucken's ample initial concert on that January day in 1895 in Pike's Opera House included the Mozart Symphony in G minor, two overtures (Beethoven's to *Coriolan* and Weber's to *Euryanthe*), and the Schumann Symphony No. 4, as well as an aria from *The Creation* of Haydn and songs of Schubert and Mendelssohn presented by soprano Lillian Blauvelt. The following day offered an all-American matinee, including Edward MacDowell in a performance of his Second Concerto, Arthur Foote's Symphonic Prologue, *Francesca da Rimini*, overtures by Chadwick (*Melpomene*) and Horatio Parker (*Robert, Count of Paris*), three movements from a Victor Herbert Serenade for strings, and songs by Victor Harris and Ethelbert Nevin sung by Mrs. Julie L. Wyman. This initial whirlwind concluded with an evening concert on the nineteenth based on shorter, more popular works, including Wagner's prelude to *Die Meistersinger* and movements from the Grieg *Peer Gynt* suites, as well as songs by Van der Stucken performed by Wyman.

The orchestra's first two seasons were heard in Pike's Opera House, but an ensemble enlarged to sixty-three players appeared in a remodeled Music Hall beginning in 1896. Soloists of international stature were soon hired, including pianist Teresa Carreño, who presented the "Emperor" Concerto of Beethoven in March 1897; violinist Fritz Kreisler, who played the Bruch Concerto in G minor during January 1901; contralto Ernestine Schumann-Heink; pianist Josef Hoffman; and others. A first tour was undertaken during the 1897–98 season, with concerts in Detroit; Louisville; and Columbus, Dayton, and Delaware, Ohio. An even more successful venture concluded the 1901–02 season, with eleven concerts in three states, and by the 1905–06 season the orchestra was playing twenty-one out-of-town engagements. A series of programs featuring works by Americans was presented during the summer of 1899 to those attending the twenty-first annual convention of the Music Teachers National Association. Richard Strauss conducted his *Don Juan* and *Tod und Verklärung*, as well as four songs with his wife as soloist on April 8 and 9, 1903, and Van der Stucken led the first American performance of Gustav Mahler's Symphony No. 5 on March 24 and 25, 1905. The 1906–07 season included appearances by Camille Saint-Saëns and Alexander Scriabin performing their own piano concerti, violinist Maud Powell with the Sibelius Violin Concerto, and George Whitefield Chadwick conducting his symphonic poem, *Cleopatra.*

Van der Stucken had also become head of the College of Music in 1895. In October he was described as a "consulting director"; by January 1896 he had been designated as dean and de facto musical director. In the fall of 1901 he was relieved of his burdensome administrative duties, while retaining responsibility for the school's opera program, orchestra, and chorus but in February 1903 unexpectedly announced that he would resign all those responsibilities at the end of the school year. In 1906 he fulfilled the initial desire of the Orchestra Association's board with his appointment as director of the May Festival following Theodore Thomas's death in January 1905. Van der Stucken continued in that position until 1912, even after relinquishing the Cincinnati Symphony Orchestra podium during 1907, and returned in future years to conduct both during the regular orchestra season and as director of the festival.

Financial and labor difficulties led to two dormant seasons from 1907 until 1909. The Orchestra Association Company presented pairs of concerts by five visiting orchestras during the 1907–08 season (the Theodore Thomas Orchestra under Frederick Stock, the Russian Symphony Orchestra under Modest Altschuler, the New York Symphony under Walter Damrosch, the Boston Symphony under Karl Muck, and the Pittsburgh Symphony under Emil Paur) and then devoted the following season to the creation of a guaranty fund of $50,000 for each of five years.

A seventy-two-member Cincinnati Symphony Orchestra was then resurrected under the baton of Leopold Stokowski on November 26, 1909. English-born Stokowski (1882–1977) had arrived in New York in 1905 as organist and choirmaster of St. Bartholomew's Episcopal Church. A fledgling conductor with limited knowledge of the repertory but with a notable capacity for self-promotion, the twenty-seven-year-old was offered the orchestra's helm principally on the basis of a concert of Russian music he had conducted in Paris in May 1908 with the noted Colonne Orchestra and Olga Samaroff as piano soloist. During his three-year tenure the orchestra roster was expanded to seventy-seven (he immediately began to experiment with unorthodox seating arrangements to gain the ideal sounds he envisioned), a series of five popular concerts was scheduled during the 1910–11 season (thus establishing a tradition), and the following season was extended to twelve pairs of regular concerts. Thirty-two road performances were scheduled during the 1910–11 season, taking the orchestra as far afield as Buffalo, Wichita, and Omaha, and the following year found the orchestra in cities like St. Louis and Chicago, featuring the conductor's new bride, Olga Samaroff-Stokowski, as soloist. Major soloists were imported, among them pianist Sergei Rachmaninoff, who on January 21 and 22, 1910, performed his own Second Piano Concerto. The orchestra also found a new home on January 6, 1912, in the recently constructed 2,211-seat Emery Auditorium (its capacity more akin to the orchestra's constituency of the day than the 3,623-seat Music Hall), where it played until 1936.[16]

However, Stokowski became embroiled in an ugly public dispute with board president Mrs. Christian R. Holmes and others over management of the ensemble. A letter of March 23, 1912, from Stokowski refers to "the unfortunate friction which has existed between us for some time, owing to our inability to agree regarding the affairs of the orchestra." The board's response: "Your recent behavior and repeated aspersions upon members of the Board of Directors of the association, and your unfounded reflections upon the musical public of Cincinnati, have destroyed your usefulness to the Cincinnati Symphony Orchestra Association Company."[17] His resignation was accepted on April 13, 1912. On June 12 he signed a four-year contract with what was then called the Philadelphia Symphony Orchestra and marched off to apparent immortality.

Stokowki's successor was Austrian-born Ernst Kunwald (1868–1939), since 1907 conductor of the Berlin Philharmonic. On April 25 he was offered a two-year contract at $10,000 per annum and by late May was westward bound across the Atlantic. Kunwald's experience and disciplined approach to his considerable repertory provided an abrupt contrast to his flamboyant predecessor. In an interview published in the *Enquirer* on October 31, 1912, he spoke of a desire "to present the music purely, nobly, humanly and sincerely." Of his initial offering, an all-orchestral program on November 15 conducted from memory, J. Herman Thuman, critic of the *Enquirer* and a persistent detractor of Stokowski, reported that Kunwald "does not find it necessary to resort to vaudeville stunts to gain the acclaim of the crowd."

Early success led to his appointment as director of the May Festival in 1914 (at which time the Cincinnati Symphony Orchestra replaced the Chicago Symphony as the official festival orchestra, a role that had been relinquished to the visiting ensemble in 1908, 1910, and 1912, when it had been known as the Theodore Thomas Orchestra), and Kunwald attained triumphs with performances of the Bach Mass in B minor, the Verdi *Requiem,* and the Beethoven Ninth Symphony. A ten-day eastern tour in January 1917 included concerts in Boston's Symphony Hall and New York's Carnegie Hall, as well as a two-day recording session that same month for the Columbia Graphophone Company (the third American orchestra to do so) involving nine pieces, only four of which were eventually released (Johan Halvorsen's

Triumphal Entry of the Bojaren, "Waltz of the Hours" from Léo Delibes' *Coppelia,* an abridged version of the Strauss *On the Beautiful Blue Danube* waltz, and the "Barca-role" from Offenbach's *Tales of Hoffmann*). The *Times-Star* informed its readers that the orchestra had given "a series of concerts in negligee attire on Saturday and Sun-day, with an audience consisting of Business Manager Kline Roberts of the orches-tra, three phonograph operators and a pair of office boys. The concerts were given in the laboratory of the Columbia Phonograph company in Thirty-eighth street."[18]

The orchestra also hosted famed soloists like tenor Enrico Caruso, cellist Pablo Casals (the first of his six appearances with the orchestra), and pianists Leopold Godowsky and Josef Lhévinne. Caruso's appearances in Music Hall on May 1, 1917; Toledo on May 3; and Pittsburgh on May 5 were his first "concert" ventures with an orchestra. He was paid as much as $7,000 for each event at which he presented three popular operatic arias as well as a small host of encores.

Kunwald's tenure in Cincinnati was terminated by our entry into World War I on April 6, 1917, and the resulting anti-German hysteria. On November 22 pressure by members of the Daughters of the American Revolution caused Pittsburgh's pub-lic safety director to forbid Kunwald's appearance with his orchestra at a concert in that city. On December 8 he was arrested and detained overnight in Dayton; two days later the board accepted his resignation, and in January he was arrested again and interned at Fort Oglethorpe in Georgia for the duration of the conflict. The remainder of the twenty-third season was led by guest conductors, including Henry Hadley, Victor Herbert, Ossip Gabrilowitsch, Edgard Varése, and Eugene Ysaÿe.

Belgian-born violin virtuoso Ysaÿe (1858–1931) had become a familiar figure in Cincinnati. He made his American début on November 16, 1894, playing the Beethoven Violin Concerto with the New York Philharmonic, and appeared with the Cincinnati Orpheus Club only six days later. He had since soloed with the Cin-cinnati Symphony five times, including its inaugural season. His success with the orchestra on April 5, 1918, as well as at the subsequent May Festival, led to his ap-pointment as its music director.

Ysaÿe's first concerts in that capacity occurred on November 22 and 23, opening with the national anthems of Great Britain, Italy, Belgium, France, and the United States to mark the armistice signed just eleven days earlier (the hefty program con-tinued with Saint-Saëns's *Marche Héroïque,* the Mozart E-flat Violin Concerto with Jacques Thibaud, the Beethoven Fifth Symphony, Felix Borowski's *Paintings,* Ysaÿe's *Chant d'Hiver* for violin and orchestra, the *Introduction and Rondo Capriccioso* of Saint-Saëns, and Chabrier's *España*). The orchestra toured extensively, including its first foray into the South in January 1919, with eight concerts in Nashville, Atlanta, and New Orleans; a similar venture the following year included concerts in those cities as well as Memphis, Birmingham, Shreveport, Houston, Chattanooga, and smaller communities. October 22, 1919, saw a special concert in honor of the visiting king and queen of Belgium, including the Franck Symphony in D minor, the conductor's signature work, his *Exile*, a *Marche Héroique* of Saint-Saëns, a movement of the Delibes ballet suite *Sylvia*, and, as a violin solo, Vieuxtemps's *Polonaise*, a favorite of the queen.

The Cincinnati Symphony made the first "national" radio broadcast by such an ensemble from the University Armory in Madison, Wisconsin, on November 1, 1921. In fact, the concert, initiated by the University of Wisconsin's radio station and physics department, was audible to listeners as far east as Pennsylvania, as far south as Florida, and as far west as the Dakotas. A dispatch to the *Enquirer* dated that same day declared, "[t]his is the first experiment of its kind here with 'broadcasting' orchestral music, and the university station declares that the uniform volume and music and tone made the experiment an interesting success." Later that month the orchestra returned to the Columbia studios in New York while on tour and in three sessions recorded works by Massenet, Rubinstein, Rimsky-Korsakov, Mendelssohn, Delibes, Offenbach, and Chabrier, as well as Eduard Lassen (1830–1904), Aimé Maillart (1817–71), and others. In February 1920 the orchestra also initiated a tradition of "Concerts for Young People," conducted by first trombonist Modest Alloo.

The 1921–22 season included twenty-eight subscription concerts, ten popular concerts, four young people's concerts, a unique program at which Vincent d'Indy conducted his own works, and sixty-two road concerts in fourteen states, ranging from Oshkosh, Wisconsin, to Syracuse, Washington, D.C. (with Vice President Coolidge and Chief Justice Taft in the audience), Wilmington, North Carolina, and New Orleans.

Ysaÿe's health faltered under the increasing demands of his position. He resigned in May 1922 and was succeeded by Hungarian-born Fritz Reiner (1888–1963), conductor at the Royal Opera in Dresden since 1914. Reiner imposed on the orchestra his since-legendary insistence on discipline and expanded the ensemble's repertory, as well as its season (to twenty pairs of concerts by 1926) and size (101 strong by 1929, after which reductions were made for budgetary reasons). Igor Stravinsky made the first of his three appearances with the orchestra on March 6 and 7, 1925, conducting his own works (*Song of the Volga Boatman*, *Scherzo Fantastique*, and suites from *The Firebird*, *Pulcinella*, and *Petrushka*). Ottorino Respighi appeared on February 5 and 6, 1926, as pianist and conductor in his Concerto in the Mixolydian Mode (with the orchestra's associate conductor Ralph Lyford, who had been appointed to this new position at the beginning of the season, primarily responsible for direction of the popular and young people's concerts) and *Pines of Rome*. George Gershwin played his Concerto in F and *Rhapsody in Blue* on March 11 and 12, 1927, described in one prominent headline as "Jazz in Polite Society" (and supplemented by Beethoven's Seventh Symphony and the Strauss *Till Eulenspiegel*). Béla Bartók, one of

Reiner's mentors, performed his First Piano Concerto on February 24 and 25, 1928, surrounded by an early Haydn symphony and the Richard Strauss *Don Quixote,* having presented the first American performance of the work at an acclaimed Carnegie Hall concert on February 13, complemented in that instance with works by fellow Hungarians. Vladimir Horowitz offered the Rachmaninoff Third Piano Concerto on March 2 and 3, 1928, and the Tchaikovsky Concerto the following October.[19] The orchestra also continued to tour extensively, including concerts during early 1927 in Cleveland, Philadelphia, Pittsburgh, Toronto,[20] and Washington, where they paid a visit to the White House and received individual handshakes from President Calvin Coolidge.

Despite these successes, some disenchantment surfaced over Reiner's reliance on new music by the likes of Paul Hindemith, Kurt Weill, Ferruccio Busoni (the first American performance of his Piano Concerto), John Alden Carpenter, Roger Sessions, Aaron Copland, and Hans Barth (his Concerto for Quarter-Tone Piano and Strings on an instrument constructed by the Baldwin Piano Company), as well as his increasingly frequent absences to guest-conduct elsewhere (for example, Victor de Sabata, music director of the Monte Carlo Opera, was engaged for the first eight pairs of concerts during 1927 and 1928, while Reiner substituted for Stokowski in Philadelphia and Eugene Goossens and Respighi guested in early 1929 while Reiner worked with the New York Philharmonic). However, the decision not to renew his contract was precipitated by Reiner's divorce in January 1930 from his wife of eight years (on grounds of "cruelty and neglect") and his marriage only three months later to Carlotta Irwin, an American-born actress ten years his junior.

He was succeeded in 1931 by English-born Eugene Goossens (1893–1962), conductor of the Rochester Philharmonic since 1923, who had proved a hit as director of the 1931 May Festival.[21] A prolific composer for a wide variety of media, he programmed his own works (one example being a Symphony, opus 58, dedicated "To My Colleagues of the Cincinnati Symphony Orchestra," on April 12 and 13, 1940), as well as those of British moderns like Frederick Delius, Arnold Bax, Ralph Vaughan Williams, William Walton, and Benjamin Britten; he also championed the work of Prokoviev, Shostakovich, Poulenc, Kodály, and others.

For the wartime 1942–43 season, Goossens commissioned from a small galaxy of eminent composers a series of fanfares to be heard at the opening of each concert, following the playing of the national anthem. His letters of invitation suggested the imposition of a title and that each become a "stirring and significant contribution to the war effort." Morton Gould furnished a *Fanfare for Freedom,* Howard Hanson a *Fanfare for the Signal Corps,* and Roy Harris a *Fanfare for the Forces.*[22] However, the most enduring result of this effort was Aaron Copland's ubiquitous *Fanfare for the Common Man.*

The Cincinnati Symphony Orchestra and conductor Eugene Goossens on the stage of Music Hall in an undated photograph from the late 1930s. Courtesy Cincinnati Symphony Orchestra Archives.

By way of contrast, Goossens reintroduced an appealing series of Sunday evening Pops concerts, commenting in his unpublished memoirs, "They helped to win over literally hundreds of new subscribers for whom the tariff and atmosphere of the rather exclusive symphony concerts had hitherto held little appeal."[23] However, the financial exigencies of the Depression forced a reduction of the 1933–34 season to sixteen pairs of concerts, coupled to salary cuts of one-third for conductor and players. The opening weeks of the following season included Paul Hindemith's brand-new *Mathis der Maler*, Gustav Holst's *The Planets*, the two symphonies of Edward Elgar, and Maurice Ravel's *Concerto* for the Left Hand, played by its dedicatee, pianist Paul Wittgenstein. Goossens then presided over the orchestra's return to a remodeled Music Hall in 1936 as well as two seasons of staged opera (four of the Wagnerian canon during 1935 and 1936, followed by *Carmen, Tosca, The Marriage of Figaro*, and *Salome*, after which the experiment was abandoned because of the costs involved). Australian-born pianist and composer Percy Grainger played concerti of Saint-Saëns and Delius in March 1937 and then returned in both 1940 and 1942 for programs that included his orchestral suite, *In a Nutshell*.

During those dark years of Nazi ascendancy, Goossens also had to deal with the reality that Cincinnati was home to a significant Jewish population and that he presided over an orchestra whose roster included both Jews and Germans. On the very day in March 1938 when Hitler's Germany annexed Austria, the orchestra was presenting a concert that included not only Ernest Bloch's *Schelomo*, "A Rhapsody for

Cello and Orchestra on Hebrew Themes," but also Richard Strauss's *Till Eulenspiegel.* Goossens recorded in a letter of March 12, 1938, to his parents back in England,

> All the Jews in the orchestra played *Schelomo* as though it were their swan-song, the Germans meantime preserving rather glum set looks. But when it came to *Till*, the Germans let go with a vengeance and gave a virtuoso performance such as probably has never been equalled by any orchestra. Both numbers were received with proportionate enthusiasm by a very mixed audience. Both scored an ovation, but one could easily tell that in both cases it arose from rather racial sources.[24]

Despite the onslaught of war, the orchestra made recordings for the first time since 1919. The new Walton Violin Concerto (with Jascha Heifetz) and the Second Symphonies of both Vaughan Williams and Tchaikovsky were committed to vinyl in late February 1941, the first of ten issues on the RCA Victor label under Goossens; subsequent releases included works by Schumann, Grieg, Stravinsky, Richard Strauss, and Respighi.

The 1942–43 season of fanfares included the Fifth and Seventh Symphonies of Shostakovich, an all-Gershwin program with pianist Oscar Levant, Virgil Thomson conducting his Second Symphony (revised in 1941), Artur Rubinstein playing the Piano Concerto (1936) of Aram Khachaturian, and Vaughan Williams's "Pastoral" Symphony in recognition of the composer's seventieth birthday. The following season a budding Gunther Schuller (b. 1925) was appointed principal horn (and was to play the first performance of his Horn Concerto with the orchestra before departing for the Metropolitan Opera Orchestra in 1945), and pianist José Iturbi played the first performance of Goossens's Phantasy Concerto, opus 60, on February 25, 1944.

Goossens presided over the ensemble's golden jubilee during the 1944–45 season. One facet of that celebration was a national competition, whose prize was a $1,000 war bond. William Grant Still's *Festive Overture,* one of thirty-nine entries, was selected by Goossens; composer, author, and commentator Deems Taylor; and conductor Pierre Monteux and was first heard on January 19, 1945.[25] Goossens also invited Ernest Bloch, Aaron Copland, Paul Creston, Anis Fuleihan, Howard Hanson, Roy Harris, Walter Piston, Bernard Rogers, William Schuman, and Deems Taylor to contribute variations on a theme of his own invention. In addition, the jubilee was manifested in an array of visiting luminaries: pianist Alec Templeton playing the Rachmaninoff Second Concerto and improvising; violinist Zino Francescatti with the Tchaikovsky Concerto; Morton Gould conducting an all-American program, including three of his own works; Jascha Heifetz playing the Louis Gruenberg Concerto and Chausson *Poème*; Artur Rubinstein performing the Rachmaninoff

Rhapsody on a Theme of Paganini; pianist (and radio personality) Oscar Levant in the Grieg Concerto and Gershwin *Rhapsody in Blue;* Fritz Kreisler playing the Mozart Fourth Violin Concerto; soprano Marjorie Lawrence in works by Handel, Purcell, and Richard Strauss; pianist José Iturbi ("Known to Millions through Motion Pictures") with a Mozart concerto; Lauritz Melchior, "Greatest Living Interpreter of Wagnerian Heroes," portraying some of those figures in an all-Wagner evening; basso Ezio Pinza with works by Verdi, Mozart, and Moussorgsky; and pianist Alexander Brailowsky in the Tchaikovsky Concerto. Patrons contributed funds for ten thousand tickets, which were distributed to members of the various armed forces.

That November Goossens had spent time in Chicago conducting Debussy's *Pelléas et Mélisande.* In a letter to his parents on the fifth he wrote,

> I always enjoy trips to the "Windy City," which after the rather sedate pomposity of Cincinnati strikes me as stimulating and virile. Young Leonard Bernstein [1918–90], a gifted New Yorker who is enjoying a vogue something similar to the one I enjoyed in the early twenties, took over the Cincinnati orchestra for a week.[26]

Bernstein conveyed his gratitude in a letter of November 21.

> I want to send you my warmest thanks for the privilege of conducting your fine orchestra. The men were wonderful to work with. It was a great pleasure to get to know you better and I can't tell you what a pleasure it was to know a conductor who carries out that often heard, but seldom executed, promise of playing contemporary music.[27]

Goossens's sixteen-year tenure ended with his resignation in December 1946 and a move to Sydney, Australia, where he was to conduct the Sydney Symphony and head the Conservatorium of Music. His successor was Wisconsin-born and American-trained (the Universities of North Carolina and Michigan) Thor Johnson (1913–75). Johnson's eleven-year stint (1947–58) witnessed the introduction of Neighborhood Family Concerts, as well as an increased number of outreach programs, especially those heard in area elementary and junior high schools.[28] An active propagator of new music, he conducted some sixty-one performances during his period at the helm, many of which he commissioned. The Cincinnati Symphony and Johnson also recorded for both London and the short-lived Remington label, including such unusual works as the Henry Brant Saxophone Concerto (with Sigurd Rascher) and Robert Ward's Third Symphony. Johnson left to direct the conducting program at Northwestern University.[29]

He was followed by German-born Max Rudolf (1905–95), who had been associated with the Metropolitan Opera since 1945. Under Rudolf, the orchestra was increased in size, the season extended, the number of children's and school concerts expanded, a long-term recording contract with Decca Records signed (that led to issues of standard literature, as well as works by Carl Nielsen, Franz Berwald, William Schuman, Peter Mennin, Anton Webern, and Luigi Dallapiccola), and the weeklong Exposition of Contemporary American Music mounted in consort with the University of Cincinnati College-Conservatory of Music in May 1965. Beginning on August 2, 1966, the orchestra embarked on a ten-week globe-circling tour under the aegis of the Department of State. With pianist Lorin Hollander as soloist and associate conductor Erich Kunzel sharing podium responsibilities, the orchestra presented forty-two concerts in Greece, Turkey, Lebanon, Israel, Yugoslavia, Switzerland, India, Malaysia, Singapore, Hong Kong, the Philippines, Taiwan, Japan, and South Korea over a period of sixty-eight days, traveling more than 33,000 miles. Kunzel also initiated his remarkable recording legacy with issues on Decca of substantial works by and with jazz pianist and composer Dave Brubeck (*The Light in the Wilderness, The Gates of Justice,* and *Truth Is Fallen*), as well as three discs with Duke Ellington, all during 1970.[30]

Rudolf served as music director of the May Festival after 1963 but resigned both posts in 1970 to become head of the opera and conducting departments of the Curtis Institute in Philadelphia.[31] His successor, Thomas Schippers (1930–77), born in Kalamazoo, Michigan, the orchestra's third native-born music director, had been trained as a pianist both at Curtis and Yale University. Encouraged by his teacher, Olga Samaroff-Stokowski, he turned to conducting. With a seemingly natural bent for musical theater, he soon constructed a considerable career in association with several important Americans. He was in the pit for Gian Carlo Menotti's *The Consul* and the first televised performance of that composer's *Amahl and the Night Visitors* (and was later appointed musical director of Menotti's Festival of Two Worlds in Spoleto, Italy), for the first performances of Aaron Copland's *The Tender Land,* and for Samuel Barber's *Anthony and Cleopatra* when it inaugurated the new Metropolitan Opera House in 1966. He also enjoyed an active association with Leonard Bernstein and the New York Philharmonic and was widely considered a possible successor when Bernstein was anointed Conductor Laureate in 1969. However, the position was awarded to Pierre Boulez, and Schippers arrived in Cincinnati the following year. Tragedy soon interfered: His wife died of cancer in 1973, and Schippers himself succumbed to lung cancer four years later.

Prague-born Walter Susskind (1913–80), who had served as conductor of the Toronto Symphony from 1956 to 1965 and the St. Louis Symphony from 1968 until 1975, was then appointed the orchestra's music advisor. He presided over the orchestra's eighty-fifth birthday party in 1979, as well as a seventeen-day tour that concluded with a Carnegie Hall concert. He was succeeded in 1980 by Michael Gielen (b. 1927), a native of Dresden who had received his early training in Argentina after his family fled Nazi Germany in 1939. Gielen, earlier associated with the Royal Opera in Stockholm and the National Orchestra of Belgium, maintained his role as general music director of the Frankfurt Opera concurrently with the post in Cincinnati. A composer himself, he aroused considerable initial anxiety among Queen City listeners through his championing of composers such as Arnold Schoenberg and Witold Lutoslawski and his introduction of works like George Crumb's *Variazioni*.

The orchestra had offered alfresco Concerts in the Parks since 1947, had presented a six-concert Summerfest in the University of Cincinnati's Nippert Stadium during the summer of 1967, and had initiated a series of Fountain Square concerts downtown in 1982. However, those traditions were dwarfed by the opening of the Riverbend Music Center, an outdoor amphitheater owned by the orchestra and designed by architect Michael Graves that hosts during the summer not only conventional and pops concerts but also imported freestanding events, ranging from country to rock. The facility was inaugurated on July 4, 1984, with Erich Kunzel conducting Copland's *Lincoln Portrait* (with then-Senator and retired astronaut John Glenn as the speaker), two groups of pop songs with Ella Fitzgerald, and the Tchaikovsky *1812 Overture*.

While concerts of the light classics and popular music date back to the Stokowski era, the Cincinnati Pops Orchestra was formally created only in 1977 with Kunzel as its conductor. Kunzel, first associated with the Cincinnati Symphony in 1965, has been dubbed the Prince of Pops, a Midwestern Arthur Fiedler with a far-flung career still centered on Cincinnati. Kunzel and the Cincinnati Pops have issued more than one hundred recordings, of which more than eight million copies have been sold. His youthful associate, Keith Lockhart, who joined the Cincinnati Symphony staff in 1990 and assumed responsibility for the Young People's Concerts, the Lollipop Family Concerts, and the Casual Classics, proved so adept that he was selected to succeed John Williams as conductor of the Boston Pops in 1995 and has since been named music director of the Utah Symphony.

Gielen returned "home" in 1986 to become conductor of the Southwest German Radio Orchestra, at which point Spanish-born Jesús López-Cobos was appointed the Cincinnati Symphony Orchestra's eleventh music director. Having served in a similar capacity with both the German Opera in Berlin and the Spanish National Orchestra, López-Cobos maintained the momentum of his predecessors with a thirty-day tour in 1990 (the orchestra's first international outing since 1966), consisting of nineteen concerts in eleven cities in Japan and Taiwan. The orchestra also made its first West Coast foray during the 1991–92 season—a five-city event. In 1988 the orchestra also initiated a Cincinnati Symphony Orchestra Chamber Players series in the restored Beaux Arts Memorial Hall that neighbors Music Hall and continued to add to its discography, now on the Telarc label. In December 1998 Maestro López-Cobos announced that he would not seek renewal of his contract but was asked to remain on the podium through the 2000–01 season during the search for his successor, after which he would assume the role of music director emeritus. Having enjoyed the second-longest tenure of any of the orchestra's music directors, conducted 564 concerts (including fourteen times in Carnegie Hall), and issued a total of twenty-six recordings, he was succeeded by Estonian-born Paavo Järvi, a member of a distinguished family of orchestral conductors headed by his father, Neeme Järvi, current music director of the Detroit Symphony.

With such a distinguished history, firmly launched into its second century, it can only be presumed that Mrs. Taft and her fellow female directors would be fully satisfied that the dreams enunciated in their May 1894 letter of solicitation have been more than accomplished: "In view of the many benefits to be gained by the establishment of this [permanent] orchestra [of high standard] in our midst, we appeal to you to help our cause by a subscription, which will be repaid you many times in the benefits financial, social and artistic, which will accrue to Cincinnati."[32]

CHAPTER 17

The Cleveland Orchestra

Cleveland grew much more slowly than Cincinnati and was overshadowed for many decades by the Queen City; however, the period following the Civil War proved a period of enormous growth and rapid cultural maturation.

Orchestral ensembles[1] had been assembled on an ad hoc basis earlier in the nineteenth century. For example, the orchestra of the German-dominated St. Cecilia Society offered a rather substantial program in January 1853: the overture to Mozart's *Marriage of Figaro; Die Industrielle* of Joseph Labitzksy; a violin-cello duet by one of the Rombergs; the *Kathinka Polka* of Johann Strauss; the Overture to Bellini's *Norma;* a string trio of Beethoven, the *Sophien Mazurka* of Lumpe; and Labitzky's "Elfen" Waltzes.[2]

However, ensembles with more than a momentary shelf life appeared only during the century's waning decades. Thus, the organization of a Cleveland Philharmonic Society was mentioned in December 1860, and during March 1867 the group's twenty-five members were reported to be rehearsing a Haydn symphony under the direction of Otis Boise, organist of the Euclid Avenue Presbyterian Church.

The Germania (or, German Concert) Orchestra first surfaced in February 1868 with a performance of the Rossini *Stabat Mater.* Constituted entirely of ethnic Germans and apparently without a regular conductor, it seems to have functioned into the 1880s as what is often called a "utility" orchestra, hiring itself out particularly to the various singing societies in need of a collaborating ensemble. However, records remain of polyglot programs of vocal and instrumental solos interlarded with overtures by Rossini, Weber, and others, as well as Haydn symphonies; the Germania also offered fluffier programs during the summer months.

Pittsburgh native Alfred Arthur (1844–1918), educated in Boston and Europe, arrived in Cleveland in 1871. He soon opened a voice studio and in 1875 founded the Cleveland School of Music, which was later managed by his son until its demise in

1938. Arthur, certainly the city's most influential choral conductor of his era, founded the Cleveland Vocal Society in 1873 (and led it until 1902), which he showcased at May Festivals he organized from 1880 until 1886 and again from 1895 through 1897. He also conducted the Sacred Music Society, the Cleveland Oratorio Society, and the East End Choral Society. A composer of songs and operas, all unpublished, he did issue at least one pedagogical work: *Seventy Lessons in Voice Training* (Cleveland: J. H. Rogers, 1892). He also formed a collaborating orchestra for his choral ventures and conducted some purely orchestral programs at Brainard's Piano Ware Rooms in 1872, soon after his appearance in the city.

A freestanding orchestra was organized by Ferdinand Puehringer (1841–1930)[3] in 1881: the Cleveland Amateur Philharmonic Society of thirty-six players, the amateurs laced with a few professionals, an ensemble that may have evolved from the Germania Orchestra. Puehringer was succeeded in short order by Müller Neuhoff, Franz X. Arens, and Czech-born Emil Ring (1863–1922), who had arrived in this country to become principal oboist of the Boston Symphony Orchestra but who left that post after a single season and moved to Cleveland in 1888.[4] What became known as the Cleveland Philharmonic Orchestra had matured to the point that in April 1882 it could host Eduard Reményi in a presentation of two movements of the Mendelssohn Violin Concerto. By March 1886 it was able to essay a program that included Beethoven's *Prometheus* Overture, the Mendelssohn Fourth Symphony, a pair of movements from Bellini's *La Sonnambula,* and the prelude to Act 3 of Wagner's *Lohengrin.* Under Ring the Philharmonic presented four concerts a season, employing substantial literature in addition to collaborating with the Cleveland *Gesangverein* (of which Ring was also conductor); it also appeared during the summers at Haltnorth's Gardens, a German beer garden located at Woodland Avenue and what is now East 55th Street. Although the Philharmonic played alfresco at Haltnorth's, light opera was presented by a stock company in a theater seating six hundred to eight hundred auditors. An ensemble of about fifty-five had become capable during the 1893 Sängerfest of presenting the overtures by Beethoven to *Egmont,* Berlioz to *Benvenuto Cellini,* and Weber to *Der Freischütz,* as well as Mozart's final symphony, a Liszt symphonic poem, and the ballet music from Anton Rubinstein's *Feramors.* However, financial difficulties befell the Philharmonic, and it was dissolved in 1899 after having been reorganized in 1894.[5]

Ring and Johann Heinrich Beck (1856–1924) led orchestras of brief tenure early in the following century: a Cleveland Symphony Orchestra[6] from 1900 to 1901, what was known as the Cleveland Grand Orchestra from 1903 to 1909, and the Cleveland Symphony Orchestra again from 1910 to 1912. During the years 1913 to 1915, Dutch violinist Christiaan Timmner led the ensemble, directly supported by the city and thus renamed the Cleveland Municipal Symphony Orchestra, whose library was bequeathed to the soon-to-be-hatched Cleveland Orchestra.[7]

Beck, despite his name, was Cleveland-born, although educated in Leipzig and of a distinctively Germanic bias. He returned home in 1882 to become one of the city's most influential musicians (although he spent the 1895–96 season conducting an orchestra in Detroit).[8] His short-lived Cleveland Symphony demonstrated considerable aspirations. Its first offering, in the Cleveland Grays' Armory on January 16, 1900, included the Beethoven Overture to *Leonore* No. 3 and two movements of Beethoven's Second Symphony, a cello concerto by Jules de Swert (1832–1910), Borodin's orchestral suite, *The Steppes of Central Asia*, the conductor's Overture to Bryon's *Lara*, and an excerpt from Wagner's *Lohengrin*. A February 20 program encompassed Mozart's Overture to *The Magic Flute*, Mendelssohn's Fourth Symphony and Violin Concerto, ballet music from Cherubini's *Ali Baba*, and the *Slavonic Fancies* by Clevelander John Zamecnik. Beck hired high profile soloists, such as soprano Lillian Blauvelt in an excerpt from Ambroise Thomas's *Hamlet* in November 1900, Fritz Kreisler in the G Minor Concerto of Max Bruch the following month, and pianist Ossip Gabrilowitsch in the Schumann A Minor Concerto in January 1901. He also continued to spice his programs with music by local composers: an excerpt from his own *Skirnismal* in November 1900; an overture to *As You Like It* by Charles Davis Carter of Pittsburgh, and an Intermezzo and Prayer from *Nada* by Clevelander Harry Lawrence Freeman in March 1901; Cleveland-born Charles Sommer's symphonic poem *Hero and Leander*, as well as the final chorus from Beck's own cantata, *Deukalion*, at the orchestra's final appearance, on May 28, 1901.[9] The allure of competing musical events (such as a concert by a Viennese orchestra under the baton of Eduard Strauss on February 6, 1901) and the lack of any sort of guarantee fund led to bankruptcy after only two seasons.[10]

After a hiatus of almost two years, another ensemble was organized and presented on Sunday afternoons what were labeled Citizens "Pop" Concerts (although the literature presented was distinctly highbrow) and then, after 1910, what were called People's Symphony Concerts in Grays' Armory between 1903 and 1912, with Beck and Ring alternating as conductors and with the periodic renaming of the ensemble mentioned earlier.[11]

The first event, on January 4, 1903, consisted of the Weber Overture to *Euryanthe*, Borodin's *Steppes of Central Asia*, excerpts from Bizet's *Carmen*, and Mendelssohn's incidental music for *A Midsummer Night's Dream*, as well as noted pianist William Sherwood with the Liszt Concerto in E-flat. Ring and Becker, as before, interlarded the standard literature with works by locals like Charles E. Burnham, Fanny Snow Knowlton, Charles Sommer, James H. Rogers, Charles Rychlik, Patty Stair, and Wilson G. Smith. The event of February 5, 1911, was thus initiated with H. Biringer's *March, Cuyahoga County Centennial*, followed by the first movement of the Mendelssohn Fourth Symphony, the Chopin F Minor Piano Concerto, the Overture to Glinka's *A Life for the Tsar*, a suite of dances by Anton Rubinstein, an excerpt from Massenet's *Le Roi de Lahore*, and the prelude to Wagner's *Die Meistersinger*.

They also relied heavily on local soloists, many of them women. For example, pianist Katherine Pike, a student of Wilson G. Smith, played a Benjamin Godard concerto on March 18, 1908, and returned on February 13, 1910, with the first movement of Anton Rubinstein's Fourth Concerto. Clarice F. Balas had returned to Cleveland in 1908 after study in Vienna with Theodor Leschetizky, and on January 23, 1909, still a teenager, performed Ferdinand Hiller's F Minor Concerto. Mrs. Sol Marcosson played the Liszt E-flat Concerto exactly a year later.[12] Numerous local singers collaborated both as soloists and members of ad hoc ensembles, as did local choruses such as the two hundred voices of the Harmonic Club, which sang movements by Handel and Edward German at the fourth event of 1911. Another local chorus, the Jewish Orphan Asylum Children's Chorus, directed by Emil Ring, contributed a group of German folksongs, an excerpt from Verdi's *La Traviata,* and somebody's lyrics to Sousa's *Stars and Stripes* at the ninth concert that year.

Christiaan Timmner had been concertmaster of the Concertgebouw Orchestra in Amsterdam before emigrating in 1911. After a single year with the St. Paul Symphony, he arrived in Cleveland and, although totally inexperienced with the baton, was named conductor of a reorganized Cleveland Symphony Orchestra in December 1912. He led a new series of nine Sunday afternoon concerts initiated during January 1913 in Engineer's Hall, a venue at the corner of St. Clair Avenue and Ontario Street opened on October 1, 1910, by the Brotherhood of Locomotive Engineers. Timmner's first offering included Weber's overture to *Oberon,* Mozart's *Eine kleine Nachtmusik,* and the ballet music from Gounod's *Faust* but ended with the Johann Strauss *Emperor Waltz* and Elgar's *Pomp and Circumstance,* that ubiquitous "Military March." It was Wilson G. Smith, composer and influential newspaper critic, who played a major role in the ousting of Beck and Ring and who then facilitated the city's support of what was soon renamed the Cleveland Municipal Symphony Orchestra. This incarnation of the ensemble played substantial programs on the stage of B. F. Keith's Hippodrome Theater between November 1913 and March 1915 (there were sixteen concerts during that first 1913–14 season, the average attendance seventeen hundred, admission charges of twenty-five cents, fifteen cents, and ten cents) and appeared on Sunday afternoons in city parks throughout the summer. However, whatever his capacities as a violinist, Timmner's authority was weakened by charges early in 1915 that he was, in effect, selling positions in the orchestra to his private students; the resulting scandal, coupled with a crisis in the city's finances and fiscal mismanagement by its conductor, led to the collapse of the ensemble. Timmner debarked to California and a career as a chamber musician.[13]

The Cleveland Orchestra of today owes its genesis in large part to the imagination and energy of one woman: Adella Prentiss Hughes. Born in Cleveland in 1869 of New England emigrants, she graduated from Vassar College in 1890, after which she indulged in the customary grand tour of Europe, plus six months sopping up culture in Berlin. Back home in 1891, she joined the Friday Morning Musical Club, functioned as a piano accompanist for various local and visiting singers, and by 1898 had seized on her true vocation, that of impresario.[14] Her first effort was a ten-city tour she arranged for a vocal quartet (that included noted baritone David Bispham), singing Liza Lehmann's 1896 song cycle *In a Persian Garden*, with Prentiss at the piano.

In 1894 and 1895 the Fortnightly Musical Club, which held its first meeting in February 1894, sponsored twelve afternoon programs given by members, as well as three evening events by visiting professionals and two concerts by the Chicago Orchestra. The succeeding season included four concerts by that ensemble, which apparently stretched the club's resources. The outcome of these ventures was appointment of Miss Prentiss as corresponding secretary, with full responsibility for all public concerts. Her first major project was the Fortnightly's sponsorship of the second biennial festival of the National Federation of Music Clubs during May 1901. Miss Prentiss considered the local orchestra inadequate for her purposes and hired the Pittsburgh Symphony under Victor Herbert for a series of three concerts in Grays' Armory featuring soloists, including the illustrious contralto Madame Ernestine Schumann-Heink and pianist Fannie Bloomfield Zeisler.

Success led to nineteen seasons of subscription concerts by visiting orchestras (a total of 162 concerts by eleven orchestras under the batons of twenty-one conductors), under the aegis of the Fortnightly Club until 1909, after which the events were managed independently by Mrs. Hughes (she married baritone Felix Hughes in 1904, a union that resulted in divorce during 1929, but in the interim made her the sister-in-law of writer, critic, and composer Rupert Hughes [1872–1956]) until she organized the Musical Arts Association, incorporated on October 5, 1915. Initially a for-profit venture, capitalized at $10,000 through the sale of two hundred shares worth fifty dollars each, the association's announced purpose was to further "the interests of music in the community, accepting and administering trust funds and guaranty funds for musical purposes and acquiring, holding and operating property to promote the efficiency of musical enterprises."[15]

The 1902–03 series was extended to five concerts, with the Cincinnati Symphony under Frank Van der Stucken presenting the additional programs. On March 10, 1904, Richard Strauss, as part of his first American tour, led a Pittsburgh Symphony augmented by sixteen players in a program that included the Beethoven Seventh Symphony, two of the composer's principal symphonic poems, *Till Eulenspiegels lustige Streiche* and *Tod und Verklärung*, and three of his songs sung by his wife with Strauss at the piano. Afterward, the Strausses were entertained at a reception in the Hollenden Hotel, involving an impromptu concert by some three hundred members of the local German singing societies, which included Stephen Foster's "My Old Kentucky Home," sung in German. During that same season Miss Prentiss allied the Pittsburgh orchestra with the Oberlin Musical Union and local soloists for a performance of *Messiah* directed by Oberlin's George W. Andrews.[16]

The Chicago Orchestra under Frederick Stock, in his first season as Theodore Thomas's successor, first visited Cleveland in 1905 with pianist Rudolf Ganz as soloist and became the core of the series by the 1909–10 season, during which Mrs. Hughes imported the 228-voice Mendelssohn Choir of Toronto and its director, A. S. Vogt, for a pair of programs, replicating a practice well-established in Chicago. The Boston Symphony under Karl Muck appeared for the first time in January 1907; the New York Philharmonic with Gustav Mahler arrived on December 6, 1910, only months before his death (the program included a Bach "Suite" arranged by Mahler, which Mahler conducted from the keyboard, the Beethoven Seventh Symphony, and a second half of Wagner excerpts); the Russian Symphony of New York under Modest Altschuler performed for the first time in 1911 (in a staged performance of Shakespeare's *Midsummer Night's Dream* by a company of thirty-five with Mendelssohn's complete incidental music for the work, recognizing the centenary of the composer's birth). The Minneapolis Symphony under Emil Oberhoffer and the Philadelphia Orchestra under Carl Pohlig appeared the following year, and in January 1916 Walter Damrosch, as educator, the Leonard Bernstein of his day, with the New York Symphony (that had first appeared on the Hughes series in 1910) manifested his considerable skills at an illustrated afternoon concert for children, during which he discussed the music to be played and members of the orchestra demonstrated their instruments for the youngsters.

Mrs. Hughes also sponsored in April 1913 a celebration of the centenary of Wagner's birth with three concerts involving the Chicago Symphony, Stock, one of the local German singing societies, the Singers Club, and an ad hoc women's chorus trained by William Treat Upton of the Oberlin College faculty for the Flower Maidens' scene from *Parsifal*. Hughes explained, "To further the interests of the public, and contribute to its full enjoyment of this forthcoming Wagner Festival, the Extension Section of the Fortnightly Musical Club"[17] mounted five series of eight lectures each given in various parts of the city over a period of two months. In March 1916 Serge Diaghilev's Ballet Russe visited Cleveland during its first American tour under the aegis of the new Musical Arts Association. Eleven works were seen in four programs over the space of three days in the Hippodrome, all with conductor Ernest Ansermet in the pit. Stravinsky's *Petrushka* and *Firebird* coexisted with *Cléopâtre* (music by Anton Arensky, choreography by Fokine, décor by Bakst), *Sheherazade, Les Sylphides,* and *Afternoon of a Faun.*

On June 22 of that same year Hughes presented in League Park (then home of the recently renamed Cleveland Indians) a touring production of Wagner's *Siegfried,* starring Madame Ernestine Schumann-Heinck. She negotiated the addition of adequate lighting for the grandstands and an agreement with the Cleveland Railway

Company that during the performance passing trolleys would move slowly and not sound their gongs. However, despite her plea that the stage be set within the diamond, she was forced to place it behind second base. A local paper screamed,

SIEGFRIED IN BOX, WAGNER AT BAT—PLAY BALL!
HOW OPERATIC FANS WILL YELL WHEN THE FIERY
DRAGON DIES ON FIRST![18]

She also imported the Boston Grand Opera Company for five performances in November 1916 (including the city's first *Andrea Chénier* and Maggie Teyte in both *Faust* and *Hänsel und Gretel*) and then again in January 1917 for three standard works of Puccini and an *Aida* involving one hundred Case Institute and Western Reserve University students as extras. Her orchestra series that season included three appearances by the Chicago Symphony under Stock, two by Cincinnati and Ernst Kunwald, a pair by Damrosch and the New York Symphony, Boston with Muck, Philadelphia with Stokowski, and the New York Philharmonic with Stransky.[19]

But Mrs. Hughes, chagrined at having to import an orchestra from Minneapolis, a younger and smaller city, was determined that Cleveland should have a permanent resident orchestra, and finally managed that feat in the aftermath of World War I.

Violinist Nikolai Sokoloff (1886–1965) had been born near Kiev, but his family emigrated to this country in 1900. After study at Yale, he joined the Boston Symphony at age seventeen, where he came under the influence of a colleague, Alsatian-born violinist and composer Charles Martin Loeffler (1861–1935), and visited Cleveland for the first time with the Boston Symphony Orchestra during the 1906–07 season. Sokoloff then became concertmaster of the Russian Symphony and in that role visited Cleveland again in 1911, featured in two solos: the "Meditation" from Massenet's *Thaïs* and Saint-Saëns's *Le Déluge*. After further European study, he began to develop facility with the baton, and after conducting incidental music at a repertory theater in Manchester, England, he moved to California, where he briefly led the People's Philharmonic Orchestra in San Francisco. A series of coincidences during 1918 then made him the Cleveland Orchestra's founding conductor.

Mrs. Hughes and Sokoloff met briefly in January in New York, to which he had recently returned from entertaining American troops in Europe with sixty recitals given in YMCA recreation centers, and where he was several months later to lead an orchestral concert of French music in Carnegie Hall. Gregarious and charming, Sokoloff made a lasting impression on Hughes, fortified by social occasions in late February in Cleveland, which he visited as part of a campaign to raise funds to support impoverished French musicians. Their paths then crossed again in June. Mrs. Hughes was attending a meeting of the Ohio State Music Teachers Association in Cincinnati, where Sokoloff was a guest of the Cincinnati Symphony, conducting a series of popular concerts in the zoo pavilion. She heard him talk, was equally impressed by a concert for children from the local orphanages, especially by the manner in which Sokoloff introduced the music to his young guests, and recalled especially his query, "How will there ever be an American conductor if no one entrusts him the tools with which to ply his trade?"[20] She also heard performances by students from the Cincinnati public school system, which convinced her of the necessity of making similar opportunities consistently available to the youth of Cleveland.

During the summer of 1918 she approached Cleveland school officials with a proposal that the Musical Arts Association finance the hiring of an individual who would survey the reigning circumstances, outline a program of instrumental music instruction, and organize an orchestra to play concerts in schools and community centers. Sokoloff had proposed an orchestra of fifty that would require five rehearsals for each of three programs. These would be presented in November, January, and March at five locations across the city. Mrs. Hughes cajoled her close friend, John L. Severance, into paying Sokoloff's $6,000 salary. Before their agenda could be put in motion, the catastrophic flu epidemic of that year closed the schools and precluded any sort of public gathering.

A predicament of a different sort intervened to place her new protégé in the public eye. The Chicago Symphony was scheduled to open the Hughes series on October 29, but Frederick Stock was abruptly declared a German national in wartime America, since he had neglected to complete his naturalization papers, even after twenty years of residency. He was forced to step aside in favor of his assistant, Eric DeLamarter. Mrs. Hughes insisted that DeLamarter was not sufficiently known to assure success in Cleveland and suggested Sokoloff as a substitute. As a preface to its Cleveland appearance, the Chicago Symphony engaged Sokoloff for a successful pair of concerts in Chicago on November 29 and 30, prior to a triumph in Grays' Armory with a program that included the Sibelius First Symphony, the Saint-Saëns Fourth Concerto with Brazilian pianist Guiomar Nováes, and slighter works by Borodin and Glazunov.

Eight days earlier Sokoloff had conducted the first concert by what was at first dubbed Cleveland's Symphony Orchestra. Father John Powers of St. Ann Church in Cleveland Heights had proposed a fundraising concert for his parish, featuring his own Irish tenor in various songs and ballads. Powers sang with the support of piano while the orchestra offered Victor Herbert's *American Fantasy,* an orchestral suite from *Carmen,* two movements of the Tchaikovksy Fourth Symphony, Anatol Liadov's *Enchanted Lake,* and Liszt's *Les Préludes.* St. Ann's was charged six hundred dollars for one rehearsal and the concert; Mrs. Hughes, to assure the success of the venture, had the Musical Arts Association invest another six hundred dollars in rehearsal time; Sokoloff claimed that Mr. Severance agreed to fund yet another seven rehearsals, leading to a total of ten sessions, so as "to groom an untried group

The earliest known photograph of the Cleveland Orchestra with conductor Nikolai Sokoloff on the stage of Grays' Armory, November 13, 1919. Courtesy Cleveland Orchestra Archives.

into a respectable orchestra."[21] The December 11, 1918, concert was a decided success. Wilson G. Smith, writing in the *Plain Dealer*, proclaimed,

> Cleveland has at last a symphony orchestra.... We have in the past heard much of our orchestra nucleus and its possibilities under favorable circumstances. Those favorable circumstances seem to have arrived in the person of Nikolai Sokoloff.... He has first of all, musicianship that analyzes, a personal magnitude that impels response from his players, the temperament of artistic conception and consequent artistic finish and nuance. What I particularly like about him is a certain grace in batonic manipulation and an emotional control that, while impelling, does not degenerate into tempestuous noise.

With Weber's overture to *Der Freischütz* replacing an absent Father Powers, the concert was repeated on December 22, assuring perpetuation of the fledgling ensemble. The remainder of this first, improvised season consisted of a total of twenty-seven appearances, including three formal evening concerts (the first of these on January 30, 1919, featured Sokoloff as soloist in the Vieuxtemps Concerto No. 4), as well as six concerts for the board of education, five sponsored by the American Steel and Wire Company for 12,500 of its employees, collaborations with the Harmonic Club and Mendelssohn Club of Pittsburgh, supplanting the Chicago Symphony for the three concerts of the Oberlin May Festival, and appearances in Akron, Kent, and Pittsburgh. Sokoloff also organized the Cleveland String Quartet and for two years functioned as its principal violinist. This group's success at a June 2 benefit led to a contract guaranteeing them independent engagements and extra compensation; they spent eight weeks of that summer performing in California.

For the 1919–20 season, the orchestra was expanded to seventy-two players, who presented sixty-one events over twenty-eight weeks, including seven pairs of subscription concerts (with celebrated soloists like cellist Pablo Casals and pianist Jacques Thibaud), plus twelve popular Sunday afternoon programs (with local soloists), all in the new Masonic Hall.[22] Arthur Shepherd was named Sokoloff's assistant (although he did not assume the position until October 1920), and the ensemble traveled to Berea, Canton, Dayton, Elyria, Lakewood, Mansfield, Youngstown, Pittsburgh, Buffalo, and Chicago. To raise its profile, the orchestra played in high school auditoriums using local soloists, and Sokoloff programmed works by locals like Johann Beck and Charles Rychlik. The National Lamp Works of the General Electric Company supported a benefit concert on December 19, offering tickets to its employees only, resulting in a standing-room-only crowd; all the proceeds were returned to the orchestra's Maintenance Fund. One anomaly was that construction delays forced the Masons to postpone the formal dedication of their new edifice, so the Cleveland Orchestra returned to Grays' Armory for a concert that included music by Goldmark, Liadov, Borodin, and Berlioz, plus the Saint-Saëns G Minor Concerto with Harold Bauer performing in absentia via the Duo-Art reproducing piano (a feat later repeated in Buffalo).

The following years were ones of almost exponential growth. The 1920–21 roster was expanded to eighty-five, and in February 1921 the young ensemble traveled as far as Washington, New York, and Boston, with concerts in seven other cities. Mrs. Hughes recalled that of the season's 104 events, forty-seven occurred on the road.[23] The American Steel and Wire Company purchased three more concerts for its employees. The 1921–22 series was extended to sixteen pairs of concerts (of the 139 played between October and May, which included an appearance at the formal opening of the Public Auditorium before thirteen thousand auditors on April 15), and by the eighth season subscribers were offered twenty weeks of performances. In addition to the formal subscription concerts, the orchestra continued to mount Sunday afternoon popular concerts, the latter shamelessly hawked in language that would do credit to present-day hucksters. Take, for instance, a 1924 pronouncement that "next Sunday at Masonic Hall you can hear ninety artists for the price of a ticket to a movie. Don't you want to hear a Strauss waltz, familiar opera selections, a lovely soloist, and a gorgeous orchestral piece that describes a battle? All of this is yours for fifty cents."[24] Hoopla of this sort triumphed in an October 11, 1925, concert in the Public Auditorium before ten thousand people, which concluded with both the *William Tell* and *1812* overtures.

A women's committee was organized in 1921, one of whose goals was to present children's concerts under the direction of assistant conductor Arthur Shepherd in conjunction with what were called Music Memory (later, Memory and Appreciation) Contests. The children studied the music to be heard and then were asked to produce as much factual information as they could about each work; points were given not only for correct answers but also for neat penmanship. This outreach program was extended in 1929 when Lillian Baldwin (1887–1960) was hired by the Cleveland Board of Education as supervisor of music appreciation (she was dubbed consultant in music education for the Cleveland Orchestra by the Musical Arts Association). As the liaison between the orchestra and public school system Baldwin gradually developed the Cleveland Plan, based on the concept of what she termed "Musicianly Listening," which allowed students to prepare in a systematic fashion for the experience of the Educational Concert Series at the end of each semester, relying on pamphlets she prepared (including "Manners Rhymes for Young Listeners," which were probably partly responsible for the restrained deportment of the children, which amazed observers) and, after 1953, *Musical Sound Books for Young Listeners*, recordings issued with the support of the Kulas Foundation.[25] The Baldwin approach became a model for similar programs across the country and earned her wide recognition, including an honorary doctorate from Western Reserve University in 1948.[26]

The orchestra played in Canada during 1922 and by the 1923–24 season had traveled as far west as Kansas City. Sokoloff felt confident enough to program tone poems of Richard Strauss, Stravinsky's *Firebird* Suite, and a version of the Rachmaninoff Second Symphony revised by the composer at Sokoloff's request, which was presented in Carnegie Hall on January 23, 1923, to considerable acclaim; Rachmaninoff himself then appeared in Cleveland, playing his Second Piano Concerto twice during late March. Weekly one-hour radio broadcasts over WJAX had been initiated on November 16, 1922, and a first recording appeared during the sixth season—an abridged version of the Tchaikovsky *1812 Overture* on Brunswick, the first of several releases over the next several years on that label, most notably 1928's revised Second Symphony of Rachmaninoff, the first complete symphony recorded by any orchestra.[27] Tours of the southeast from 1926 to 1928 were extended to include three concerts in Havana.

During his fifteen-year tenure Sokoloff slighted the classical and early romantic standards in favor of works by late romantic and neo-romantic Frenchmen and Russians. His repertory included many of the better-known works of Dukas, Franck, Debussy, and Ravel. Sokoloff particularly favored the *oeuvre* of his teacher Vincent d'Indy: *Saugefleurie*, opus 21, in 1919; a movement from *La Légende de Saint Christophe*, opus 67, the following year; the Second Symphony, opus 57, in 1923; the *Symphonie sur un chant montagnard français,* opus 25, with Alfred Cortot as soloist in 1925; and the *Istar Symphonic Variations,* opus 42, in 1929. He also programmed a substantial number of pieces by his Boston friend, Charles Martin Loeffler: *A Pagan Poem,* opus 14, in 1920; *La Mort de Tintagiles,* opus 6, in 1922; *La Villanelle du Diable,* opus 9, the following year, and *Memories of My Childhood* (dedicated to "my friends, Mr. and Mrs. John L. Severance") in 1925. Sokoloff was also generous with the music of Swiss-born Ernest Bloch, who spent the years 1920 to 1925 in Cleveland as the first director of the Cleveland Institute of Music: the Symphony in C-sharp Minor in 1920, the *Trois Poèmes Juifs* during the fourth season, the *Psalm XXII* in 1923, *Schelomo* in the tenth season, *America* the following year, and the Suite for Viola and Orchestra during the twelfth season. Nor was the work of the orchestra's assistant conductor slighted, since Clevelanders heard Arthur Shepherd's Fantasy for Piano and Orchestra in 1920, Overture to a Drama in the sixth season, and *Horizons, Four Western Pieces for Orchestra* four years later. Sokoloff's adventuresome programming perhaps reached some sort of extreme in late 1929 when the Cleveland Orchestra presented both in Cleveland and New York the first performances of the First Airphonic Suite, opus 21, by Ukrainian-born Joseph Schillinger (1895–1943). Schillinger, recalled today primarily for the idiosyncratic compositional system he was to share with George Gershwin, chose as his solo instrument the theremin, a creation of Russian Leon Theremin (1896–1993), a device consisting of oscillators, antennas, and loudspeakers, notable in that its performer doesn't actually touch the instrument but controls pitch and volume by moving his hands in the air. The eerie sounds generated by this prototype of later electronic instruments were on these occasions activated by the inventor himself but likened by the *Herald Tribune*'s noted critic Lawrence Gilman to "a slightly adenoidal saxophone."[28]

Noted composers presented their own scores. In February 1924 Ernst von Dohnányi (1877–1960), grandfather of a later conductor of the Cleveland Orchestra, played his *Variations on an Old Nursery Song* and conducted his Suite in F-sharp Minor. Later that year Georges Enesco introduced his Symphony No. 1 in E-flat, opus 13, and his Roumanian Rhapsodies. Igor Stravinsky evoked both hurrahs and hisses with a February 1925 program that included his *Fireworks, Chant du Rossignol,* and the suite drawn from *The Firebird.* Ottorino Respighi appeared in February 1927 and then again in 1929 with *Belfagor, The Birds,* Concerto in the Mixolydian Mode (with the composer at the piano), one of the suites of *Old Airs and Dances for the Lute, The Pines of Rome,* the Toccata for Piano and Orchestra (again with Respighi as soloist), and *Church Windows.* During January 1928 Maurice Ravel lectured at the Museum of Art and conducted Cleveland premières of *Valses Nobles et Sentimentales, Rhapsodie Espagnole,* and *Sheherazade.* Sergei Prokofiev arrived two years later to play his First Piano Concerto and conduct his suite from *The Steel Step.*

During the 1925–26 season Sokoloff acknowledged Cleveland's swirling ethnic mix with a special series, Music of Many Lands. Several of the local national singing societies joined the orchestra in their own musics. During March of that same season the orchestra presented an all-American evening: Henry Hadley's *Lucifer*, principal violist Carlton Cooley's *Song and Dance* (with the composer as soloist), Howard Hanson's *Lux Aeterna*, Ernest Schelling's *Victory Ball*, and Cleveland-native Emerson Whithorne's *Aeroplane*.

At the end of the season Arthur Shepherd resigned as assistant conductor due to his increasing responsibilities at Western Reserve University, although he remained program annotator for several more years. Rudolph Ringwall, who had been a colleague of Sokoloff's in the Boston Symphony and had also directed the house orchestra of the Hotel Cleveland, succeeded Shepherd in a tenure lasting until 1956. One of Ringwall's first assignments was the 1927 summer season of Open Air Concerts at the Edgewater and Gordon Parks, funded by the city, the success of which was replicated the following summer with a series of thirty-one Cleveland Civic Summer Concerts, including seven Nationality Night programs.

Masonic Hall, even with its seating capacity of 2,260, ample stage, and pipe organ, had proved a less-than-ideal home. With a dry acoustic and uncomfortable seats sometimes too numerous to fill, the orchestra was little more than a tenant and was often forced to tour when displaced by Masonic activities. Thus, both astonishment and relief greeted a surprise announcement by Dudley S. Blossom, Severance's successor as president of the Musical Arts Association, during a concert at the Public Auditorium on December 11, 1928, celebrating the orchestra's tenth birthday, that John and Elisabeth Severance would contribute one million dollars toward construction of a new concert hall if other friends of the orchestra would furnish a $2.5 million endowment fund.

Western Reserve University donated a plot of land facing the juncture of Euclid Avenue and East Boulevard, and Blossom quickly raised more than $3 million from only eleven families, including $250,000 from John D. Rockefeller Jr.[29] Mrs. Severance died the following January, and her widower made the new hall a memorial to her, eventually tripling his original pledge.[30] Ground was broken on a rainy day in November 1929, with the orchestra playing the overture to *Leonore* No. 3 of Beethoven. The 1,832-seat hall was opened on February 5, 1931, with *Evocation*, a work commissioned from Charles Martin Loeffler for a mammoth "modern" orchestra, including saxophones and vibraharp, as well as a four-part women's chorus. Loeffler chose to invoke Pan and his pipes with excerpts from J[ohn] W[illiam] Mackail's *Select Epigrams of the Greek Anthology*. The core of this apt invocation: "Breathe music, O Pan that goest on the mountains, with thy sweet lips, breathe delight into thy pastoral reed, pouring song from the musical pipe, and make the melody sound in tune with the choral words." The following day the 424-seat Reinberger Chamber Music Hall was dedicated with Sokoloff and a twenty-five-piece ensemble playing Wagner's *Siegfried Idyll* and Robin Milford's Suite for Chamber Orchestra. The following month a large organ by Ernest M. Skinner (opus 816) in the main auditorium (funded by the children of David Z. and Mary Castle Norton in their parents' memory) was dedicated by University of Michigan organist Palmer Christian.

Designed by Fritz Walker of the local firm of Walker and Weeks, the building's opulence denied the national economic catastrophe that accompanied its construction. In what is usually described as a Georgian idiom meant to reflect existing structures in the area, its outer walls are of Indiana limestone, with an elaborately sculpted façade. Marble was employed lavishly, and the Grand Foyer, conceived in the Egyptian Revival idiom popularized by the discovery of the tomb of King Tutankhamen in 1922, is defined by twenty-four columns of red jasper, which rise a full two stories. There originally was an automobile entrance allowing as many as fifteen cars to load or unload simultaneously on the ground level inside the building. The air was "conditioned" by the best available technology of the day, an elaborate elevator system allowed access to all levels of the structure, backstage facilities included those for recording and radio broadcasting, and a lighting system hailed as the most elaborate of its time allowed some four thousand different light plots in the hall and on the stage. In fact, one of the goals was its programmed ability to flatter the appearance of the ladies of the audience, with more blue in the afternoons to highlight their makeup, more yellow in the evenings to blend with their formal wear. Among the other unusual design elements, new-fangled aluminum was employed extensively in various wall, ceiling, and door panels, as well as for pieces of furniture custom-designed for the structure.

The hall, with its striking ceiling, covered in silver leaf in a lace-like pattern said to replicate that of Mrs. Severance's wedding dress, was designed with a proscenium arch, so as to be transformable into an opera house, with footlights and a substantial pit under a portion of the stage and a bit of the audience space that could be raised and lowered on massive screw jacks. There was a permanent cyclorama, or sky dome, with its own lighting system behind the roofless orchestra shell, which was made of lightweight plywood. These properties, mated with the deep carpeting and richly upholstered seats, led to a distressingly dry acoustic and a sense that much of the orchestra's sound remained trapped behind the proscenium. Many were frustrated by this environment and the orchestra was forced back to the Masonic Hall for recording sessions during the early 1950s. All of this was alleviated in 1958 with a design by Heinrich Keilholz, then chief recording engineer for Deutsche Grammophon Gesellschaft. The new design banished sound-absorbing fabrics in favor of reflective terrazzo floors, sealed the organ pipes in their chamber above the stage and vainly attempted to carry their sound to listeners through large speakers, and imposed a hefty roofed shell designed to disperse the orchestra's sound into the hall. However, the sleek Scandinavian design of the shell was hostile to the Art Deco environment on which it was imposed.[31]

Even though the acoustical deficiencies of Mr. Severance's temple have been remedied, the Cleveland Orchestra still plays in the smallest hall occupied by a major American orchestra. While the original capacity has been expanded to 2,101 seats and one can revel in the relative intimacy between performers and auditors, there have been periods when demand far exceeded supply, meaning that only subscribers had access to the orchestra. In March 1998 a $36.7 million renovation was begun (in part the result of a $100 million capital funds drive initiated during 1996 under the banner, "Our Legacy to the 21st Century: The Campaign for the Cleveland Orchestra"), eventually forcing the orchestra's temporary relocation to the Allen Theater downtown for the end of the 1998–99 season, as well as for concerts presented the following fall prior to completion of the project in January 2000. The interior was painted for the first time since 1931. A five-story addition at the rear of the building added storage space, a loading dock, a canteen, dressing and rehearsal spaces for the performers, revised pedestrian patterns, and doubled restroom facilities for concert patrons. The restaurant housed in the original motor entrance was replaced by a permanent facility; a new stage shell stunningly incorporates the decor of the hall, and the 6,028 pipes of the E. M. Skinner organ were moved from their loft above the stage to a new chamber at the rear of the stage, while the original space, emptied of pipes, has become the Resonance Chamber.[32]

Dissatisfaction with Sokoloff surfaced as his fifteenth season approached, and when Artur Rodzinski, the orchestra's first guest conductor who was not also a composer, created an enthusiastic uproar on December 29, 1932, with a program mating standard favorites with Stravinsky's *Petrushka*, it was only a matter of weeks before he was announced as Sokoloff's successor. Sokoloff concluded his tenure (encompassing 1,608 concerts) with an all-Brahms event in April, marking the centenary of the composer's birth; his retirement coincided with that of Mrs. Hughes as the orchestra's manager, concluding the professional career of this unusual dynamo, who had been noted by *Fortune* magazine in November 1931 as combining "the artistic perceptiveness of a musician with the efficiency of a locomotive."[33]

Rodzinski (1892–1958), born in Split, Croatia, of Polish parents, arrived in this country in 1925 and had served as conductor of the Los Angeles Philharmonic since 1929, having earlier been Leopold Stokowski's assistant at the Philadelphia Orchestra. It became his destiny to transform the Cleveland Orchestra into an ensemble of national stature over the next decade, a period some now identify as its first Golden Age. Despite the reality that the Great Depression had forced reduction of the ensemble to eighty players and a season of only twenty-four weeks, Rodzinski considerably expanded its repertory and also utilized Severance Hall's dual personality to house five seasons of fully staged operas. This experiment was initiated with Wagner's *Tristan und Isolde* in November 1933 (with a cast including Cleveland-born Rose Bampton), followed by Ermanno Wolf-Ferrari's *The Secret of Suzanne* in March. Rodzinski's second season offered not only eighteen pairs of regular subscription concerts, but six operas as well, also in paired performances (opening with *Die Walküre* and closing with *Die Meistersinger*). Standard works stood in antithesis to the first performances outside the Soviet Union of Dmitri Shostakovich's year-old *Lady Macbeth of Mzensk*. With a cast of Russian émigrés living in New York, the production was also taken to the Metropolitan Opera under the aegis of the League of Composers.[34]

Financial restraints reduced subsequent opera seasons to four works (beginning with a *Der Rosenkavalier* starring Lotte Lehmann and concluding with *Parsifal* during Eastertide), two weeks (concluding with *Elektra* of Richard Strauss, a Rodzinski specialty), and for the 1937–38 season, only one. Actually, Rodzinski had no role in the January 1938 performances of *The Sleeping Beauty,* a new opus by Beryl Rubinstein, director of the Cleveland Institute of Music, in a production initiated at the Juilliard School of Music in New York and conducted by Alfred Stoessel. For the 1935–36 season Rodzinski had hired as his assistant the young Boris Goldovsky (1908–2001), who had been in Philadelphia serving in a similar capacity to Fritz Reiner. Goldovsky's assignment was to coach the solo singers, prepare the choruses, and play for the piano rehearsals.

However, only days before the February 27 opening of *Die Fledermaus,* the mercurial Rodzinski abruptly withdrew from the project, deputizing Goldovsky to complete the rehearsal process and conduct the three performances. When the 1937 opera schedule was severely curtailed, Rodzinski asked his assistant to organize a 250-voice Philharmonic Chorus, whose immediate challenge was participation in performances of the Beethoven Ninth Symphony and Verdi's *Requiem.*[35]

Rodzinski also insisted on leavening his concert programs with heavy doses of new music in what were sometimes described as unhealthy portions by Severance Hall patrons. His initial season included John Alden Carpenter's *Skyscrapers* (completed in 1924 but first heard only in 1926), Arthur Honegger's oratorio *King David* (1921), the Prokoviev "Classical" Symphony (1916–17), Zoltán Kodály's *Háry János* Suite (1927), and the Bartók Rhapsody No. 1 (1928), with Joseph Szigeti as violin soloist. The 1934–35 season introduced Cleveland to the Strauss *Also sprach Zarathustra* and Stravinsky's *Le Sacre du printemps* and included an all-American program (Werner Josten's Serenade for Orchestra, as well as works by Toledo native David Stanley Smith [a brand-new overture, *Tomorrow,* opus 66/2] and Cleveland-born Emerson Whithorne [his Symphony No. 1 in C minor, opus 49]). The following year included a seventeen-city tour in January, as well as Paul Hindemith's *Mathis der Maler* (of 1934), Mahler's Symphony No. 2 (the "Resurrection"), and the Symphony No. 4 of Ralph Vaughan Williams (also completed in 1934).

The Great Lakes Exposition was held downtown during the summer of 1936. Rudolph Ringwall organized a Great Lakes Symphony Orchestra (constituted largely of Cleveland Orchestra players) for a series of concerts in a shell on the Sherwin-Williams Plaza, assisted in the enterprise by guest conductors such as Hans Kindler and José Iturbi:

> In Sherwin-Williams Plaza, the concerts of the Great Lakes Symphony proved almost too popular for the taste of guest conductor Jose Iturbi, who laid down his baton one evening to lecture the audience on the impropriety of munching hot dogs in the presence of Bach, Beethoven, and Brahms. He must have made an impression, for hot dogs became known as "Iturbis" for the remainder of the exposition [36]

Rodzinski was off that same summer earning laurels at the Salzburg Festival under the aegis of his mentor and friend, Arturo Toscanini.[37] Upon his retirement as conductor of the New York Philharmonic in 1936, Toscanini proposed that Rodzinski and Wilhelm Furtwängler be named his joint successors, but the German was found politically unacceptable, so manager Arthur Judson's candidate, the Englishman John Barbirolli, was appointed. Toscanini then nominated Rodzinski as assistant conductor of the new NBC Symphony Orchestra. The disciple was authorized to select its personnel, undertake its preliminary training, and conduct three of its trial-run broadcasts during December 1937 (an earlier three were led by Pierre Monteux). Rodzinski caused some consternation in Cleveland when several of the orchestra's principal players were recruited to the new orchestra. Despite his crucial role in establishing this novel ensemble, Rodzinski was restricted to four of the ten concerts he expected to lead during the 1938–39 season, and a breach with Toscanini fomented by a bizarre misunderstanding on the part of the Italian maestro resulted in the termination of Rodzinski's role with the NBC Symphony after a New Year's Eve performance.

Back in Cleveland, the Cleveland Orchestra's nineteenth season included Beryl Rubinstein in his own Piano Concerto, Samuel Barber's Symphony in One Movement, William Walton's *Façade*, the first American performance of Karol Szymanowski's ballet-pantomime *Harnasie*, opus 55, and Georges Enesco playing the Beethoven Violin Concerto and conducting his own Orchestral Suite No. 2, opus 20. The 1938–39 season, the orchestra's twentieth and Rodzinski's fifth, included a first performance of Arthur Shepherd's new cantata, *Song of the Pilgrims*, and the orchestra's first bout with Bruckner (his Seventh Symphony). It concluded with a

Bach St. Matthew Passion in Severance Hall[38] and, as a gift to the city, a gratis performance of the Beethoven Ninth Symphony in Public Hall on April 22.

The orchestra resumed recording the following December, now on the Columbia label. *Finlandia* of Sibelius and Rimsky Korsakov's *Sheherazade* were followed by standard literature from the pens of Beethoven, Berlioz, Mendelssohn, Richard Strauss, Debussy, and Ravel, as well as the First and Fifth Symphonies of Shostakovitch, Jaromir Weinberger's *Under the Spreading Chestnut Tree* (of 1939, with Boris Goldovsky as pianist), and the Alban Berg Violin Concerto (with Louis Krasner, who had played its first performance in 1936).[39]

The following years witnessed a continuing stream of scores either brand new or at least new to Cleveland ears: the William Walton Violin Concerto (with Jascha Heifetz); Bartók's Second Violin Concerto (with newly anointed concertmaster Tossy Spivakovsky) and in December 1940 the composer in his own Second Piano Concerto; in 1939 the Ravel Concerto for the Left Hand with Paul Wittgenstein, the pianist for whom it had been written; the Hindemith Violin Concerto; the Poulenc Concerto for Two Pianos and Orchestra (with locals Beryl Rubinstein and Arthur Loesser); the Shostakovich Seventh Symphony; Berlioz's *The Damnation of Faust,* opus 24, last heard in Cleveland in 1886; Mahler's *Das Lied von der Erde;* the Strauss *Symphonia Domestica,* opus 53; and Prokoviev's *Peter and the Wolf.*

During the Depression years the Federal Music Project had been formed to foster the work of American composers, and Rodzinski responded eagerly to the challenge with varying degrees of popular success. He presented pieces by relatively unknown composers (such as David Van Vactor's Symphony in D, a prize-winning composition first played by the New York Philharmonic), as well as works by those more established: the Second Symphony of Arthur Shepherd, the Third Symphonies of Howard Hanson and Roy Harris; the Fourth Symphony of William Schuman, William Grant Still's Symphony in G Minor, Samuel Barber's Violin Concerto (with Arthur Spalding) and First Symphony, John Alden Carpenter's Violin Concerto, Aaron Copland's *Billy the Kid* Suite, Walter Piston's *The Incredible Flutist* Suite, Gian Carlo Menotti's *Amelia Goes to the Ball* Overture, Bernard Rogers's *The Dance of Salome,* Gershwin's *American in Paris* and Piano Concerto (with Oscar Levant), and Jerome Kern's *Scenario for Orchestra on Themes from* Show Boat, a work commissioned by Rodzinski that he often programmed when on tour and the Columbia recording of which became a bestseller for the orchestra.

However, Clevelanders also feasted on standard literature. For example, the 1938–39 season contained all the Beethoven symphonies (six of them conducted by Rodzinski), as well as several of the piano concerti with Artur Schnabel as soloist. On January 8, 1939, Rodzinski and the orchestra were joined by Wagnerian soprano Kirsten Flagstad before an audience of ten thousand at the Public Auditorium, the flavor of the evening perpetuated the following season with a series of All-Star Popular Concerts in the same space featuring superstars like Lauritz Melchior, Fritz Kreisler, Marjorie Lawrence, and Lily Pons.

Rodzinski was clearly a maestro with a mission. He was quoted by the *Plain Dealer* in 1936 as saying, "The problem of the moment is to make the great mass of people conscious of the progress which is being made in music. . . . There is no reason for sticking to the classics simply because they are 'safe' and everyone will recognize their names. . . . Never condemn music at the first hearing. . . . Music is a living art, and we must keep up with it." Yet he also wished to preclude the work of the orchestra being perceived as a luxury and the domain of Cleveland's aristocracy: "I hope all working people who can will come. Let them come in their working clothes, their overalls if they like, and they will be most highly welcome. Severance Hall is not just for the rich. It is for all who love music. . . . It doesn't matter what one wears," the latter phrase amplifying an earlier populist assertion, "You can come in a silk hat or none at all. Let the music lover come in any garb, but let him come."[40]

John L. Severance died during January 1936, and Dudley S. Blossom in the fall of 1938.[41] Rodzinski had just signed a five-year contract, but increasing friction with a board impatient with their temperamental and unpredictable conductor (to whom they refused the extra string players he felt essential for the ensemble of his imagination) surely sullied the time immediately prior to his departure for the helm of the Philharmonic-Symphony of New York in the fall of 1943. In order to choose a replacement, Rodzinski suggested the orchestra use guest conductors for a period of time, which would create a pool from which the strongest candidate could be culled. Rodzinski offered the then-radical suggestion that orchestra players be polled by secret ballot in order to determine the most popular conductor and their decision heeded by management. With twenty-two players serving in the various armed forces, there was talk about reducing the ensemble to a chamber orchestra or even suspending activity altogether. Others felt that the orchestra needed an American-born conductor, with Albert Stoessel their prime candidate, although Rudolph Ringwall also had his share of advocates. It is interesting that the list of proposed candidates submitted to the board in February 1943 contained two conductors of the Metropolitan Opera, one of them named George Szell. It is also interesting that the third annual Pension Fund concert in the Public Music Hall on March 14 was conducted by a thirteen-year-old prodigy named Lorin Maazel; composer and critic Herbert Elwell observed in the *Plain Dealer*, "His work is already mature enough to claim serious attention and it has many signs of great promise."[42]

However, in March 1943 a committee of the Musical Arts Association, with the support of seventy-three-year-old Adella Prentiss Hughes, announced the appointment of Erich Leinsdorf (1912–93), Austrian-born and only thirty-one years old. He had come to this country in 1937 as an assistant conductor at the Metropolitan Opera and was in Chicago on tour with the company when the announcement was made. Although he had never made music with the Cleveland Orchestra, Leinsdorf had become a familiar figure to Clevelanders through the annual visits of the Met.

Leinsdorf was to conduct sixteen weeks of subscription concerts, with the assistance of notable soloists such as Rudolf Serkin, Yehudi Menuhin, Artur Rubinstein, Efrem Zimablist, Josef Hofmann, and Helen Traubel. The Mutual Broadcasting System and the United Broadcasting Company contracted to air live broadcasts on Sunday evenings, which would reach not only Mexico but also, by short-wave transmission, Europe, South America, and the South Pacific and, via recorded rebroadcasts, military forces overseas. However, the reigning euphoria was interrupted by Leinsdorf's induction into the army during January 1944. Ringwall, Frank Black (music director of NBC), Sir Thomas Beecham, Vladimir Golschmann, Eugene Goossens, Fritz Reiner, and George Szell served as guests until Leinsdorf's return in April 1945 for the final concert of the season, a program that included the Bruckner Fourth Symphony and Copland's *El Salón México*. His initial offering before entering the service had concluded with Morton Gould's *American Salute*, and during the few months prior to his transformation into Corporal Leinsdorf and a consequent period of what he called "enforced idleness" at Fort Lee, Virginia, he spiced traditional literature with works such as Randall Thompson's Second Symphony and Brazilian Francisco Mignone's Symphonic Poem, *Four Churches*. To initiate the orchestra's second quarter century, E[lroy] J. Kulas, a major patron of the arts in Cleveland, had offered a $1,000 prize for a new orchestral work. A blue-ribbon panel selected Estonian-born Nikolai Lopatnikoff's *Opus Sinfonicum*, and Leinsdorf conducted its première on December 9, 1943.

Fifteen months later he returned to lead twelve of the twenty subscription weeks of his third and only complete season. In tandem with conventional repertory, he introduced Clevelanders to the Second Symphony of Walter Piston, the Fourth Symphony of George Antheil, Bohuslav Martinů's Violin Concerto (with Mischa Elman), two works of Prokoviev (the Second Violin Concerto and the Second Suite drawn from the ballet score for *Romeo and Juliet*), Aaron Copland's *Appalachian Spring*, and William Walton's Overture, *Portsmouth Point*. Recordings on the Columbia label from 1946 suggest that Leinsdorf achieved credible musical results with a somewhat decimated ensemble.[43] However, some of his players considered him more than a bit detached and aloof, in dramatic contrast to the warm ebullience of his predecessor, and some more traditional members of the board were horrified by what they saw as the brashness of his relative youth.

Those factors alone might have denied him a long tenure in Cleveland, but at least one observer considered Leinsdorf's fate as having been determined on November 2, 1944, "when George Szell walked on the stage and put the orchestra through its paces with a commanding force that had never been surpassed in the memory of the audience."[44] Szell made his impact with scores by Mozart, Beethoven (including an all-Beethoven evening in December 1945, with Rudolf Serkin playing the "Emperor" Concerto), Brahms, Tchaikovsky, Rachmaninoff, Stravinsky, and others, but he also introduced Cleveland to the Hindemith *Symphonic Metamorphosis on Themes by Carl Maria von Weber* (dating from 1943 and eventually one of Szell's signature pieces) and the Bartók Concerto for Orchestra (first heard under Koussevitsky in Boston in December 1944).

Leinsdorf recalled considering asking for release from the final year of his contract,[45] but he chose instead to resign at its conclusion, allowing the uncontested appointment of forty-nine-year-old Szell as his successor in January 1946, effective at the beginning of the following season.[46] In another equally significant rite of passage, Adella Prentiss Hughes resigned her remaining position as secretary of the Musical Arts Association on July 6, 1945. Despite her unparalleled contributions to the cultural life of the community over some five decades, there were some who considered her a manipulative busybody (most recently because of her shameless lobbying on behalf of Leinsdorf). One member of the board confided to his diary, "It took 5 or 6 big strong men to oust one lone woman, aged 75, but we did it and a great victory was the result."[47]

Born in Budapest and raised in Vienna, George Szell (1897–1970) emigrated in the autumn of 1939 (although he had made his first American appearance with the St. Louis Symphony in 1930) and gradually amassed a reputation after his début with the NBC Symphony during March 1941. Guest stints with other orchestras (including five summers with the Chicago Symphony at the Ravinia Festival) dovetailed with work at the Metropolitan Opera beginning in 1942. Presaging his fabled reputation as a meticulous disciplinarian and absolute perfectionist, on his arrival in Cleveland he demanded and was granted an additional eight players and soon replaced many of the musicians he inherited (for a total of eighty-four changes of personnel during his first five seasons).[48] He also demanded a salary of $40,000, fully $10,000 more than the compensation bestowed on Sokoloff and Rodzinski and a humiliating $12,000 more than that earned by the hapless Leinsdorf; he also demanded the title of music director and conductor, suggesting a higher degree of control over the enterprise. He insisted on five rehearsals per week before the paired Thursday and Saturday concerts and also was granted nine preseason sessions before his official début on October 17, with a program consisting of what became signature parts of his repertory: the overture to Weber's *Oberon*, Debussy's *Prelude to the Afternoon of a Faun*, *Don Juan* of Richard Strauss, and the Beethoven Third Symphony.

He gradually transformed the Cleveland Orchestra into a virtuoso ensemble, a gigantic string quartet consistently ranked among the best in the country, if not the world. His credo:

I personally like the complete homogeneity of sound, phrasing and articulation within each section, and then—when the ensemble is perfect—the proper balance between sections plus complete flexibility—so that in each movement one or more principal voices can be accompanied by the others. To put it simply: the most sensitive ensemble playing.[49]

While the Cleveland Orchestra continued to present an abundance of new music during Szell's tenure, some of this literature was relegated to associates and guests, since he believed,

I cannot be an advocate of a work with which I cannot identify myself, in which I cannot do justice to the composer—although the difficulties may lie in my shortcomings rather than his. There is a body of literature for which I am a pretty good advocate. Many of the other conductors of my generation are dead. My task during the last years of my life, professional and otherwise, is to hand over a tradition—to keep it alive and in good shape. My colleagues identify more readily with some of these newer styles. I do what I think I do best.[50]

Consequently, his repertory included the Germans, from Mozart and Beethoven, through Mendelssohn and Schumann, to Bruckner and Mahler; the French from Berlioz through Debussy to Messiaen; Czechs from Smetana through Dvořák to Janácek; Sibelius and various of the Russians; and Englishmen from Elgar through Vaughan Williams and Walton to Britten. However, he also introduced to Cleveland works by Americans like Copland (the Third Symphony), Paul Creston (*Two Choric Dances*, opus 17b), David Diamond (*The Enormous Room*, Fourth Symphony, and *Music for Shakespeare's* Romeo and Juliet), Herbert Elwell (Ode for Orchestra, Pastorale for Voice and Orchestra, and *The Forever Young*, "A Ritual for Solo Voice and Orchestra"), Alvin Etler (Passacaglia and Fugue), Howard Hanson (Second Symphony and the *Merry Mount* suite), Gian Carlo Menotti (Piano Concerto), Walter Piston (Toccata), Bernard Rogers (*Three Japanese Dances*), Arthur Shepherd (*Fantasy on Down-East Spirituals* and Theme and Variations, a Cleveland Orchestra commission in its thirty-fifth season), William Schuman (Third and Fifth Symphonies), and Bernard Wagenaar (*Song of Mourning*).

Guest conductors included Ernest Ansermet, Dimitri Mitropoulous, Pierre Monteux, Leopold Stokowski, Sir Thomas Beecham, Heitor Villa-Lobos, Carlos Chávez, Igor Stravinsky, Sixten Ehrling, Lukas Foss, and Pierre Boulez, the conductor-composers largely presenting their own works. For its fortieth anniversary, the orchestra commissioned works from an eclectic group of ten prominent composers: Boris Blacher (*Music for Cleveland*), Creston, Henri Dutilleux, Gottfried von

Einem, Etler, Hanson, Martinů, Peter Mennin (a Piano Concerto written especially for local legend Eunice Podis, who on February 27, 1958, made her fiftieth appearance with the orchestra), Robert Moevs, and William Walton. Other new works continued to dot the regular programming, such as the Copland Clarinet Concerto, George Rochberg's Second Symphony, and Witold Lutoslawski's Concerto for Orchestra. Clevelander Donald Erb's *Christmasmusic* and the Frank Martin Cello Concerto (with Pierre Fournier) were heard for the first time during the orchestra's 1967–68 golden anniversary season.

The orchestra continued its tradition of major outreach programs to public school children through various series of educational concerts, most of them in Severance Hall. In 1956 it initiated a subscription series in the Lakewood Civic Auditorium for the West Side of the metropolitan area and in 1965 established a presence in the southwest suburbs with a series in the Parma High School Auditorium. With Szell's advent, pedagogy of a different stripe was undertaken with the aid of the Kulas Foundation, which had been established in 1937 with the express purpose of supporting the arts in northeastern Ohio. An apprentice program was established, allowing young conductors a wondrous laboratory in which to acquire their craft under the guidance of a master mentor. One of the first three apprentices was Louis Lane, who was named an assistant conductor in 1956 and associate conductor four years later. Another prominent apprentice was James Levine, who also served as an assistant conductor from 1964 until 1970. The orchestra mounted two-week conducting workshops in 1954, 1955, and 1956 and with the support of the Kulas Foundation initiated a fellowship program for budding conductors that allowed them full access as observers to all the orchestra's activities.

Throughout its history the orchestra had presented choral works. In fact, one of Arthur Shepherd's announced responsibilities was the establishment of a Cleveland Orchestra Chorus. However, that ensemble had led a fitful existence, and the orchestra often relied on imported groups. Thus, in 1952 a Cleveland Orchestra Chorus was reintroduced, making its début in the spring of 1953 with performances of the Verdi *Requiem*. Two years later, Robert Shaw (1916–99) was appointed associate conductor with specific responsibility for the chorus and its offspring, a chamber chorus. In addition, he was to direct four pairs of subscription concerts and to share with Louis Lane responsibility for a Sunday afternoon series and the orchestra's educational concerts. Shaw's appointment unfortunately coincided with a controversial decision to terminate sixty-five-year-old Rudolph Ringwall's thirty-year association with the orchestra, which provoked the resignation of Lillian Baldwin, matriarch of the ensemble's children's programs since 1929, who was suspicious of Szell's commitment to the Cleveland Plan. Shaw survived the resulting furor and, prior to his departure to become music director of the Atlanta Symphony in the spring of 1967, led performances of standard choral works by Bach, Mozart, Haydn,

Berlioz, Brahms, Verdi, and Stravinsky, as well as rarer items like the Bartók *Cantata Profana, Belshazzar's Feast* by William Walton, Hindemith's *When Lilacs Last in the Dooryard Bloomed,* and the première of Russell Smith's Magnificat.[51]

The orchestra recorded extensively on both the Epic and Columbia labels under Szell, Lane, and Shaw, as well as with guests like Pierre Boulez, Igor Stravinsky, and Robert Craft.[52] It resumed national broadcasts on the CBS network in November 1957, toured the breadth of this country, and traveled to Europe in 1957 (twenty-two cities on both sides of the Iron Curtain), 1965 (forty-four concerts over ten weeks in the Soviet Union, Scandinavia, Poland, Berlin, Prague, London, and the Netherlands), 1967 (eleven concerts at the Salzburg, Edinburgh, and Lucerne Festivals, including two performances guest-conducted by Herbert von Karajan), and to East Asia in 1970.[53]

In a tradition dating from 1939, Louis Lane conducted a summer pops series in the Public Auditorium, except in 1953 when the concerts became part of Cleveland Indians' baseball games while the auditorium was being air-conditioned. Discussion about a permanent summer home for the orchestra had been initiated during 1965, partly as a means of assuring year-round employment for the players. Various sites were considered, and Szell's dream was finally realized on July 19 and 21, 1968, when he conducted the *Consecration of the House* Overture and Ninth Symphony of Beethoven in the Blossom Music Center. Named in honor of a family that had proved indefatigable in its support of the orchestra, the Blossom Music Center was built in a natural amphitheater on a bluff above the Cuyahoga River north of Akron, now incorporated into the city of Cuyahoga Falls. The dramatic pavilion, conceived by Peter van Dijk of the firm of Schafer, Flynn, and Van Dijk, with an acoustical design by Christopher Jaffe and Heinrich Keilholz, is the centerpiece of an eight hundred-acre reserve adjacent to the Cuyahoga Valley National Park and seats 5,281, with space for an additional 13,500 auditors on the sloping lawn. During late 2001 it was announced that van Dijk had been hired to oversee extensive renovations, including another one thousand seats inside the pavilion, which received a new roof and upgraded stage lighting. Additional restrooms, increased access for the handicapped, and enhanced landscaping are also part of the $14 million project, completed during 2003.

The programming format involves a core of conventional concerts led by the summer festival's director (the designation was conferred on Leonard Slatkin in 1990 and Jahja Ling in 2000, although predecessors like Pierre Boulez and James Levine had performed a similar function), as well as guests and the orchestra's music director and resident conductors. These are accompanied by various kinds of rock, jazz, country, and pops events (beginning in 1990 presented under the management of MCA Concerts and since 2000 by House of Blues), stints by guest ensembles such as the Boston Esplanade and Cincinnati Pops Orchestras, and even dance compa-

The Blossom Music Center. Photograph Roger Mastroianni.

nies prior to 1985. Modeled on the Berkshire Music Center in Massachusetts, a summer school operated in conjunction with Kent State University offers intensive study under the tutelage of members of the orchestra and its staff and guests, although Szell's dreams of a separate campus for the school have never been realized.[54]

Alas, Szell did not have long to enjoy the Blossom Center since he died on July 29, 1970, soon after the orchestra had begun its summer series there, only weeks after a strenuous tour to the West Coast, Korea, Japan, and Alaska, during which Szell's declining health became evermore apparent. Pierre Boulez, who had been named principal guest conductor in 1968, was anointed musical advisor; he and Louis Lane shared much of the responsibility In the interim until Lorin Maazel arrived in 1972 (making his début on November 24 with the Verdi *Requiem*). After Maazel's departure a decade later for the Vienna State Opera, guest conductors (including Erich Leinsdorf) staffed the two seasons prior to the arrival of Christoph von Dohnányi, effective in 1984.

The hiring of Maazel (b. 1930), who had since 1965 enjoyed a joint appointment as artistic director of the *Deutsche Oper* and music director of the Berlin Radio Symphony Orchestra, was initially opposed by a majority of the orchestra personnel (who favored Hungarian István Kertész), an attitude fortified by the new conductor's decision to replace eighteen incumbents.[55] However, a kind of stability was eventually established, and Maazel widened the orchestra's repertory still further with Music of Today and Great Composers of Our Time Series, including new works (many of them commissioned) by Jacob Druckman, Morton Gould, Donald Harris, Salvatore Martirano, and Charles Wuorinen, as well as the American premières of eleven pieces, including Luciano Berio's *Coro*. He also revived the Rodzinski tradition of staged opera and toured with the orchestra to Hawaii, New Zealand, and Australia prior to the opening of the season in 1973 (although most of the concerts were led by Eric Leinsdorf and Stanislaw Skrowaczewski); Japan in May 1974 (twelve concerts, preceded by appearances in Spokane, Seattle, and Portland); Latin America in April and May 1975 (fifteen concerts over a three-week span, prefaced by a pair of Florida appearances); and western Europe (twenty-one concerts in September 1975 and again in September 1979, with twenty concerts in twenty-six days) and made more than thirty recordings on various labels, including a critically acclaimed, complete *Porgy and Bess*.[56] Concerned with outreach, Maazel also initiated a popular Friday Early Matinee Series in 1972, took the orchestra back to the Public Auditorium downtown, and during the 1978–79 season created a Pops at the Palace (Theater) series in what was to become the Playhouse Square development. With the following season the position of director of educational activities was in effect reinstituted, leading to a cadre of trained volunteer docents who prepared students for the educational concerts, which included events at the Public Auditorium featuring mass choruses drawn from area schools. A concerto competition for young musicians was established during the 1980–81 season, the winners offered the opportunity to play with the orchestra at educational and family concerts.

Christoph von Dohnányi, Maazel's German-born successor, who had been music director of the Hamburg *Staatsoper* prior to his advent in Cleveland and who retired at the conclusion of the 2001–02 season (and was succeeded by Austrian-born Franz Welser-Möst, music director of the Zurich Opera, and earlier of the London Philharmonic Orchestra), continued to nurture all facets of the tradition he inherited, other than staged opera,[57] maintaining the high standards of a universally admired ensemble. He also indulged in adventuresome programming. For example, the third program of his 1984–85 inaugural season included Arnold Schoenberg's unfinished oratorio *Die Jakobsleiter,* and it was followed by works like Carl Ruggles's *Men and Mountains,* Charles Wuorinen's *Movers and Shakers,* and Hans Pfitzner's Violin Concerto. The Great Composers of Our Time tradition was continued with guests such as Hans Werner Henze and Pierre Boulez, who returned in November 1986 after a fourteen-year absence. Educational outreach programs were extended with a Musical Rainbow Series for pre-school children, Young People's Concerts especially designed for high school students and, beginning with the 1997–98 school year, a Learning through Music program through which orchestra musicians visit selected partner schools as part of an interdisciplinary program created by the classroom teachers in tandem with the orchestra's staff. The Cleveland Orchestra Youth Orchestra was established in 1986, the Cleveland Orchestra Youth Chorus four years later. Under Dohnányi's baton, the orchestra traveled to Europe seven times between 1986 and 2000 and to East Asia four times between 1987 and

1997, in addition to annual East Coast tours, appearances at the Tanglewood Festival in 1984 and again in 1991, and a tour of the West in 1991. The 1990 journey included a highly lauded performance at the Salzburg Festival, which led to another novelty: the Cleveland Orchestra became the first American ensemble offered residency at this most prestigious of summer gatherings, this in 1992, 1994, 1995, and 1996. The seventy-fifth anniversary season was initiated in the fall of 1993 with a Beethoven Festival in Severance Hall, followed by a trip to Japan, where all the Beethoven symphonies (plus two of the piano concerti) were performed in Tokyo's Suntory Hall. The Cleveland Orchestra performed in the People's Republic of China in May 1998 (including a concert at the Great Hall of the People in Beijing before an audience of almost ten thousand, which included President Jiang Zemin) and inaugurated the Canary Islands Music Festival in January 1999 (that was followed by performances in Spain and Paris). During the summer of 2000 the orchestra played in Vienna and Cologne, as well as at the Edinburgh International Festival. The 2000–01 season was followed by a South American tour. Dohnányi and Cleveland recorded much of the standard nineteenth-century literature on the Telarc, Teldec, and London-Decca labels, as well as more arcane material by Busoni (the Piano Concerto with Garrick Ohlsson) and Lutoslawski;[58] the ensemble also recorded with Oliver Knussen, Pierre Boulez (exclusively on Deutsche Grammophon), and former principal guest conductor Vladimir Ashkenazy.

We certainly can accept the continuing validity of George Szell's belief that he had

put the American orchestra's technical perfection, beauty of sound, and adaptability to the styles of various national schools of composers into the service of warmhearted, spontaneous musicmaking in the best European tradition.

It is not surprising that this has produced an ensemble of a unique type, an orchestra that, although based in the Great Lakes region of the North American continent, appeals to the basic musical sensitivities and satisfies the sophisticated demands of audiences in many different countries of widely divergent musical traditions. It gives me satisfaction to think that the Cleveland Orchestra does not reflect any national school but a deeper, more universal relationship to the fundamental spirit of music itself.[59]

Opera

Cleveland, Columbus, Dayton, and Toledo host regional opera companies, presenting limited seasons, using primarily imported soloists, allied to local choruses and orchestras, while several of the major professional schools of music in the state field substantial opera programs.

The Metropolitan Opera first visited Cleveland in 1886, sporadically thereafter (for instance, in both 1910 and 1911, during the latter visit with Arturo Toscanini in the pit for three of four performances), after which the city became a regular stop on the Met's post-season tours, appearing in the Public Auditorium under the aegis of the Northern Ohio Opera Association. That of 1976 was billed as the fiftieth such annual visit, although the New York company had stayed home in 1975 and was a decade later to abandon the practice of routine touring altogether. The Met also paid regular visits to Cincinnati between 1896 and 1911.

The Ohio Light Opera, an enterprise of a different stripe, in residence during the summers since 1979 at the College of Wooster, has attracted international attention with its diet of operetta from the halcyon decades of that form's history. Founding Artistic Director James Stuart (who moved to emeritus status after the 1998 season) initially focused on his deep affection for and wide experience with Gilbert and Sullivan, whose works remain the core of the company's repertory. However, aficionados assemble from the four corners to relish works by Offenbach, Strauss, Herbert, Romberg, and Friml, as well as other hits from the past consigned to oblivion spun from the imaginations of Leo Fall (*The Dollar Princess* [1907]), Edward German (*Merrie England* [1902] and *Tom Jones* [1907]), Richard Heuberger (*The Opera Ball* [1898]), Emmerich Kálmán (*Sári* [1912], *The Gypsy Princess* [1915], and *Countess Maritza* [1924]), Carl Millöcker (*The Beggar Student* [1882]), and Carl Zeller (*Der Vogelhändler* (1891]), a total by 2002 of eighty-one works by thirty-four composers. Stuart also stepped gingerly outside the mainline tradition with pieces such as Emmanuel Chabrier's *L'Étoile* (1877), Noel Coward's *Bitter Sweet* (1929), Kurt

Weill's *The Firebrand of Florence* (1945, with lyrics by Ira Gershwin), and Robert Ward's *Lady Kate*; the 2000 season departed a bit further from the mainstream repertory with a production of Lerner and Loewe's hit from 1960, *Camelot*, followed in 2001 by Rodgers and Hammerstein's *Carousel* of 1943 and Lerner and Loewe's *Brigadoon* of 1947 in 2002. The troupe has also issued nineteen recordings, including Victor Herbert's *Eileen, Naughty Marietta,* and *The Red Mill;* Emmerich Kálman's *The Bayadere, Sári,* and *Autumn Maneuvers;* Thomas Breton's *La Verbena de la Paloma;* André Messager's *Véronique;* Oscar Straus's *The Chocolate Soldier;* Lionel Monckton's *The Arcadians;* Gilbert and Sullivan's *Princess Ida, Utopia,* and *The Grand Duke;* as well as Johann Strauss's *A Night in Venice* and Jacques Offenbach's *The Brigands,* all on the Newport Classic label.

Such a unique operation seems destined to garner continued notice and success. However, the state's most established musical theater organization, the second eldest opera company in the country, has flourished in Cincinnati since the summer of 1920, recognized in no small part because of its initial venue, a remodeled band shell in the Cincinnati Zoological Gardens.

CHAPTER 18

Opera in Cincinnati

Musical theater has been an important part of the city's cultural life virtually since its founding. In fact, a performance of *The Poor Soldier*, a comic opera with words by John O'Keeffe and music by William Shield, was presented by the amateur Thespian Corps in a shed in the artificer's yard near Fort Washington on September 30, 1801. The work, basically a spoken play with inserted songs, had first been heard in London in 1783 and made its way to New York two years later. An enormous hit, said to be a favorite of George Washington, the piece was a natural choice for performance on what was then the raw frontier, the first known example of theater in the Northwest Territory,[1] No information remains as to the identity of the players or how much music was actually employed. The company was surely an amalgam of soldiers and civilians; the ad hoc instrumental ensemble was probably drawn from the garrison's band, with "orchestrations" concocted from the keyboard reduction of the score.

The Cincinnati thespians mounted *The Poor Soldier* again on January 1, 1802, in tandem with Samuel Arnold's *Peeping Tom of Coventry*, and then essayed Arnold's *The Agreeable Surprise* (its words by O'Keeffe) and the following month a ballad opera, *The Mock Doctor*, which was a piece of the same ilk but with music borrowed from the folk realm and fitted to new words.[2] The next musical theater of record appeared in 1805 and 1806 with amateur performances of Arnold's *The Mountaineers* and Charles Dibdin's *The Padlock*. In June 1811 a William Turner Company of eight professionals arrived and played twice a week with a repertory that included Stephen Storace's comic opera, *The Prize*.

Parallel streams of performances by local amateurs and touring pros can be traced through the first half of the century. The repertory was primarily English or adaptations of Italian and German works, these usually by the prolific Henry Rowley Bishop (1786–1855), recalled today mainly for his authorship of the song, "Home,

Sweet Home." This British orientation is hardly surprising, since the personnel of the touring stock companies were mostly English-born, at least at first. Pit orchestras were initially constituted of local amateurs. Eventually the theaters maintained small ensembles to service the traveling troupes. For example, in 1836 the orchestra of the Third Street Theatre consisted of four violins, one cello, a double bass, pairs of clarionets [sic] and trombones, plus a flute.[3]

One of the most prominent visitors during the pre–Civil War period was English-born Mrs. Edward Knight. She performed widely in this country between her arrival in New York in 1826 and her return home in 1849. She first appeared in Cincinnati on December 30, 1828, in Thomas Arne's *Love in a Village* and achieved her greatest triumphs during the summer of 1833 when she and James Caldwell's New Orleans Company presented Bishop's adaptation of *The Marriage of Figaro*, his *Guy Mannering, or The Gypsy's Prophecy*, *Rob Roy*, and *Home, Sweet Home! or, The Ranz des Vaches*, as well as a lavish production of Michael Kelly's transformation of Rossini's *La Cenerentola* into *Cinderella; or, The Little Glass Slipper* and an English version of Carl Maria von Weber's *Abu Hassan*. *Cinderella* had been touted as a production "in a style of superiority never paralleled in this city," and an ad in the *Daily Cincinnati Gazette* of August 12, 1833, announcing that evening's benefit for the diva described the eight-day run of August 5–12 as

> decidedly the most splendid treat ever witnessed in this city. The managers to show the estimation in which *they* hold this sweet vocalist, have, with a generosity unparalleled, allowed her the *last* representation of this magnificent spectacle, the producing of which has cost them considerably over $3,000. Need we say more to insure her an overflowing house?

An observation in the same newspaper on January 6, 1829, might, however, serve to remind us that Cincinnati was at this period still a bit rustic. It describes an altercation that intruded on one of Mrs. Knight's songs during the previous evening's performance of *Guy Mannering*, a presentation "marred by some blackguard in the second tier, fighting for a seat. But they [sic] were politely invited by the police officers to take but one step, and that was from the top to the bottom of the stairs, and did not return again that evening."

Another English diva important in Cincinnati's operatic annals was Mrs. Thomas Bailey, who made her American début at Niblo's Gardens in New York during 1834 and arrived in the Queen City in August 1837. During that visit and one the following year, she and her troupe presented mostly English comic operas and Bishop's adaptations of Mozart, Rossini, and Donizetti. However, from September 2 to 11, 1837, she starred in *La Bayadère*, an adaptation of Daniel-François-Esprit

Auber's *Le Dieu et la Bayadére* of 1830, and in October 1838 presented Carl Maria von Weber's *Der Freischütz* of 1821.

During her visits, there was increasing recognition that Cincinnati was entertaining the same performers and enjoying the same literature as the more mature East Coast metropolises. An anonymous critic for the *Daily Cincinnati Republican* wrote on August 25, 1837, that the city's support of opera "will ultimately draw attention to our most beloved and beautiful city from all parts of the Union: and our taste will not be sneered at, nor our judgment slighted by the dilettantes of any of our Eastern cities." That same writer demonstrated his informed perceptions on August 28 by lacerating the orchestra for its sloppy playing, even naming the individual offenders, and then on September 4, in a commentary on *La Bayadére*, noted,

THE ORCHESTRA PERFORMANCE WILL IMPROVE. Mr. Cooke has a good deal to attend to in this piece and has hardly had time to make himself quite so perfect as he will be. The Indians, who were present on this occasion, kept the yelling scamps who visit the pit more quiet than they generally are. These latter gentry were shamed, by such an example, into proper behavior.

Despite such concerns about slovenly playing in the orchestra pit and rowdy behavior by the audience, a certain sophistication must have been insinuating itself into Cincinnati culture, if "An Amateur," whose letter was published in the *Daily Cincinnati Republican* on June 9, 1838, is to be believed. After lamenting the slender crowds that had greeted Mrs. Bailey's return visit, he observed: "As an opera can not be performed without a good orchestra, we would only say, that we do not recollect of having heard a better one in this city, nor in the East; for each of the performers may be said to be master of his instrument, and excellent in the orchestral performance."

In June 1843 Edwin Hickman brought from New Orleans a company of about thirty singers of the Havana Opera in transit to a New York season. Over a period of three weeks they presented seven performances in the National Theatre, including Bellini's *Norma* and *I Puritani*, Donizetti's *Gemma di Vergy* of 1834, and *Lucia di Lammermoor* of 1835. These Italians were followed almost immediately by the English Opera Company of Arthur Edward Sheldon Seguin (1814–88) and his wife, Anne Child Seguin (1809–52), the first of their several visits to the Queen City. The couple had emigrated in 1838 and soon created their own touring troupe. They presented four works to the local populace during the first two weeks of July 1843, all of them sung in English: Bellini's *La Sonnambula*, Bishop's bowdlerization of *The Marriage of Figaro*, Donizetti's *The Elixir of Love*, and Auber's *Masaniello; or, La Muette de Portici*, renamed *The Love Spell*. While the visitors' performances were lauded, attendance was scant and a letter to the editor of the *Cincinnati Daily Gazette* on July 1 raised the issue of presentation in the vernacular rather than the original language in combative terms:

> The English Operas are superior to the Italian. Anyone will see this by making the contrast. I like English; it is our mother tongue; and whatever is said or sung, I want to hear said or sung in English. The Old Saxon idiom's soft enough for any music, as we know it to be strong enough for any human speech. . . . It will be seen that the English Opera will be much more acceptable to our community than the Italian, for the sufficient reason that we can not only understand the words of the song, but by being made acquainted with the story of the play as it progresses, feel an interest in the *denouement*.

The Seguins returned to the National Theatre in June 1851 with some of their earlier repertory, plus Michael William Balfe's *The Bohemian Girl,* Auber's *Fra Diavolo,* and a lush production of *Cinderella*—Rossini through the prism of Bishop—said to have cost more than $4,000. Two years later, Anna Thillon, an English soprano who had married a Frenchman (formerly Jullien's concertmaster and now her conductor) and performed mostly in Paris, brought her troupe to Cincinnati with a work supposedly written expressly for her: Auber's *Les Diamants de la couronne; or The Crown Diamonds.*

Later that summer the city was visited by Luigi Arditi's Artists' Association Italian Opera Company, arguably the most significant such group yet, since it included singers like Filippo Colletti, a favorite of Verdi; correspondingly, this group presented *Ernani* (1844), the first Verdi to be heard in the city. Arditi (1822–1903), who was later to enjoy a considerable career in London and elsewhere in Europe, was from 1846 until 1858 attached to the Teatro Imperiale in Havana but toured this country during the summer months. Consequently, the troupe with which he returned to Cincinnati in July 1854 included many from the Havana company. They presented Bellini, Donizetti, Rossini, and a Cincinnati first: Mozart's *Don Giovanni.* At least the anonymous critic for the *Cincinnati Enquirer* was sufficiently impressed to posit on July 16,

> The first production here of Mozart's great masterpiece is an event which marks the progress of art and taste among a people who now occupy that fair portion of the earth which was so recently possessed by the red men of the forest. Its brilliant reception was at the same time complimentary to the audience, and gratifying to the performers.

Several minor English troupes arrived sporadically during these years (particularly the Pyne and Harrison Opera Company, which presented sixteen performances of eight operas at the National Theatre, December 10–29, 1855),[4] their importance eclipsed by Signor Corradi Setti's Grand Italian Opera Troupe, which appeared for two weeks in July 1857 with three works by Verdi in their repertory. These included *Il Trovatore,* with prima donna Felicita Vestvale, the contralto who had sung the role of Azucena at La Scala and then presented it for the first time in America during May 1855.

Perhaps more important was the inauguration of Samuel N. Pike's Opera House with a festival ball attended by two thousand people on February 22, 1859. The hall, considered one of the finest and most opulent theaters in the country, lauded by the local papers as "a temple to the Muse of Song," was said to have cost $500,000. Its stage was fifty-eight by ninety feet, the auditorium ninety-two feet square and eighty-two feet high. There were thirteen separate entrances and a spacious lobby in marble that ran the entire width of the building and opened into reception rooms and a grand promenade, which was made over into a concert hall seating eight hundred in 1861. The main auditorium's ceiling was defined by an octagonal dome, whose murals were illuminated by three hundred gas jets. The five-story façade was ornamented with allegorical representations of music, poetry, agriculture, and astronomy, as well as bas-reliefs of Shakespeare and Mozart.[5]

Two weeks later the building was formally inaugurated with appearances by Maurice Strakosch's Italian Opera Company. Strakosch (1825–87) had arrived in this country during 1848, married Amalia, the eldest of the Patti sisters, in 1850, and had managed his first season of Italian opera in New York in 1857. The tour, which brought him to Pike's Opera House for a month's worth of twenty-four performances, was the last before his return to Europe, where he became preoccupied with managing his famous sister-in-law, Adelina Patti. Although there was considerable public dismay over the decision to bless the new hall with Flotow's *Martha,* a capacity crowd of three thousand flocked to the opening night and then thronged to ensuing performances of *Don Giovanni, Norma, La Traviata, Roberto il diavolo* (the Italian version of Meyerbeer's *Robert le diable*), and other works performed by perhaps the finest singers available to American audiences at the time.

To remain competitive, the managers of Cincinnati's older theaters were forced to undertake renovations. Consequently, when Teresa Parodi, a prima donna with the Strakosch company, arrived in August 1858 with her own troupe, she was booked at first into a newly remodeled and expanded Wood's Theatre but soon transferred to Pike's for widely acclaimed but poorly attended performances of *Norma,* as well as two works new to Cincinnati: Donizetti's *Poliuto* (1848) and Verdi's *Rigoletto* (1851).

Homegrown opera reappeared in April 1860 when the Cincinnati Männerchor mounted a full production of Albert Lortzing's *Zar und Zimmermann* at the German Institute with such success that the work was transferred to the National Theatre for four additional performances, and then an additional two evenings at Pike's. Such a venture was certainly impressive for an organization that had resulted from an amalgam of three male singing societies only three years earlier and in 1858 had chosen as their conductor Carl Barus, who was to become one of the city's most prominent musicians. Except for the principal female role, assumed by an imported diva, all the parts were taken by male singers of the Männerchor; several commentators noted that the orchestra was one of the best and largest yet heard in the city. The following year Barus mounted a miniseason, alternating the Lortzing with Flotow's *Alessandro Stradella.* The Flotow featured Bertha Johannsen, who had made her New York début at the Academy of Music back in 1856, singing the same role; the chorus, including women, was 120 strong.

Although Cincinnati never directly felt the brunt of the Civil War, its onslaught led to a temporary paucity of touring troupes so that Barus and company were left to slake the thirst of the locals during the resulting draught: Weber's *Der Freischütz*[6] and Conradin Kreutzer's *Das Nachtlager von Granada* in April 1862, and Auber's *La Muette de Portici* the following two years. The Auber was joined in revival by *Stradella* and François Adrien Boieldieu's *La dame blanche,* or *Die weisse Dame. Zar und Zimmermann* was then revived, accompanied by Lortzing's *Undine,* which was then revived the following season in the company of Weber's *Oberon,* perhaps for the first time in this country. An impressive repertory, especially when considering that each work was presented at least several times. In 1864 discussion over whether to continue the production of opera caused a disgruntled faction to bolt from the Männerchor and found the Cincinnati Orpheus. By 1868 that group was mounting three performances each of Ferdinand Hérold's *Zampa* and Lortzing's *Der Wildschütz,* followed the next year by Auber's *Gustavus III* (commonly titled *The Masked Ball*), which was heard three times in Cincinnati and traveled to Dayton as well. It was revived the next year, joined by Peter Winter's *Das unterbrochene Opferfest* (*The Interrupted Sacrifice,* a work of 1796, its plot set in an Inca village). Orpheus produced at least seven more operas, including such unorthodox choices as Johannes Schenk's *Der Dorfbarbier* (*The Village Barber,* a 1796 *Singspiel,* or comic opera with spoken dialogue) and *Martha,* a comic operetta by Hermann Kipper (1826–1910).

Sufficient economic stability had returned by 1863 so that Jacob Grau, uncle to the more famed Maurice, brought his Italian Opera Company to Pike's for a season that included Fromental Halévy's *La Juive,* Meyerbeer's *Dinorah,* and Rossini's *Mosè in Egitto.* The *Enquirer* crowed on June 13, "Twenty-four successive operatic entertainments is as much, even more, than our egotistic Eastern neighbors can often boast of, and we have cause to be proud of the musical taste of our city." Grau returned twice during 1864 with performances of Meyerbeer's *Les Huguenots* and Gounod's *Faust* (sung in Italian). The impresario announced that the latter piece had been in rehearsal for over two months, that its costumes had cost more than a thousand pounds, and that he had employed the forty men of Horne's Brass Band to add extra oomph to the Soldiers' Chorus in the fourth act. Grau reappeared soon after conflict's end with new singers (including American Clara Louise Kellogg), Donizetti's final opera (*Dom Sébastien, roi de Portugal*), Auber's *Fra Diavolo*, and Verdi's *La Forza del destino*, which Cincinnati heard only three months after its first performances in New York. The *Enquirer*'s reaction on May 30, 1865 was, "This opera has fewer of the airs and more of the blasts than is usual even for Verdi, and this will suggest an opinion of it as a work of art. We will not analyze it, nor praise it, nor condemn it, nor dislike it: it is enjoyable though unhappy, and pleasurable though tragic."

Grau returned in early 1866 with two more novelties: Giovanni Pacini's *Saffo* (1840) and Meyerbeer's posthumous *L'Africaine*, which had surfaced in Paris only a year earlier and aroused considerable ire in Cincinnati since it was new to the company's repertory and apparently still in what today might be considered a preview stage.

While Barus and his charges continued their annual productions, professional German opera first appeared in Cincinnati during early 1865. Leonard Grover's Grand German Opera Company, resident at the Chestnut Street Theater in Philadelphia, promised first-class singers and the gifts of prominent conductor Karl Anschütz (1815–70), who had arrived in this country during 1857. While delivering one novelty, Beethoven's *Fidelio*, Cincinnati was denied its first taste of Wagner when Anschütz became ill and *Alessandro Stradella* was substituted for *Tannhäuser*.

Touring companies of various sorts and fortunes drifted in and out of the city during this period, complicated by the burning of Pike's Opera House on March 22, 1866,[7] temporarily leaving only Mozart Hall in the German Institute and the National Theatre to house any kind of full-scale productions. Noted impresario Max Maretzek (1821–97) appeared during early 1868 with a company singing works in both Italian and German (as well as a bilingual *Fra Diavolo*) and a young Minnie Hauck (1852–1929), who would become one of the reigning divas during the latter half of the century.

A new animal appeared on the local scene that spring of 1868 with performances of various examples of comic opera by Jacques Offenbach, followed by his brand-new *La Grande-Duchesse de Gérolstein* in September. Grau, attempting to capitalize on a growing rage for the frothy French idiom, brought to Cincinnati in the spring of the following year a troupe gathered from New York's Théâtre Français. While their performances of the latest hits by Offenbach, Hervé (aka Florimond Ronger), and Charles Lecocq elicited critical admiration, and crowds flocked to see the "lively French girls," a streak of Puritanism surfaced in the *Enquirer* on May 12, 1869:

> We are sure the majority of those present had but a faint conception of the story the lively French girls were sputtering out with so much vivacity. They heard without a blush a nastier, filthier narrative than any man in England or America has dared to offer any audience but those that gather in a concert

saloon. . . . If fashion countenances such a work, self-respect at least should condemn it. . . . For the drama is not above suspicion, and so far as Opera Bouffe is concerned, suspicion is the only prudent course.

But the fervor for things French still allowed for other passions, so that in January 1872 brothers Maurice and Max Strakosch brought Swedish soprano Christine Nilsson to town for five performances of Italian opera. The legendary diva warranted the highest prices ever envisioned in the city—season tickets for fifteen dollars—but the hall was crowded, even standing-room-only for *Il Trovatore.* The Strakosches mined their initial success by returning at the end of the month with five more performances, including Cincinnati's first *Mignon,* and then again on February 7 for opera excerpts at a Grand Gala Farewell.

An unusual troupe appeared in April 1873—a company organized by Pauline Lucca and Clara Louise Kellogg, both noted sopranos. Their repertory was planned and scheduled so as to allow the prima donnas to appear on alternate nights—Lucca in *La Favorita, Faust,* and *Fra Diavolo,* Kellogg in *Martha* and *Il Trovatore.* Both were required for *Mignon.* Apparently the actual performance proceeded without visible tension, but then Kellogg refused to accept the final applause on the same stage as Lucca and took her bows from one of the boxes. Needless to say, this joint venture was short-lived, and Kellogg returned in November as *prima donna assoluta* with her own company.

Max Strakosch reappeared with Christine Nilsson in tow during the waning days of 1873, but three months later Cincinnatians abruptly transferred their affections to Hungarian-born Ilma di Mursak (1836–89), who had only recently emigrated to this country from London, where she had been based for the preceding eight years. Apparently she won the hearts of local listeners at least in part with what seems today like a shameless stunt: the notoriously demanding Queen of the Night aria from Mozart's *The Magic Flute* presented as an afterpiece to *Martha.* The *Enquirer* noted on March 28, 1874,

> The little warbler was soon pirouetting with the utmost ease among the high notes. . . . With perfect accuracy she struck the notes that seemed to be impossible, and then descended to the common plane with a volume of sound which showed that the effort was not exhaustive. More than once the audience interrupted her with applause, and at the close a ring of "bravo," "encore," called her again before the curtain, and she repeated the most difficult part of the aria. . . . It is true, it was not sung as advertised, in the original key, but in a key one tone lower . . . [,] but the brilliancy of delivery and distinctness and purity of the intonation were unparalleled by anything we have ever heard.

Slightly later that spring, local forces collaborated to present what was touted as the first opera created in what was then still considered the West. Unfortunately, little is known about *Alidor,* written by Signor Jannotta, a local voice teacher, and heard on May 12, 1874. Soloists (perhaps the maestro's students), a chorus of sixty-five, and an orchestra presented only the overture and the first act, after which the piece was swept off the stage into oblivion. More attention was paid to performances of Verdi's new *Aida* by the Strakosch Grand Italian Opera Company on May 20 and 22. The *Enquirer* noted on the twenty-first that the production had been "placed on the boards with a lavish disregard of expense, with all the splendor of its rendition at the Academy of Music in New York" and with many of the same singers who had sung the work's American première only months earlier.

Over the following years Cincinnatians were entertained by familiars like Clara Louise Kellogg, who opened the new Grand Opera House in November 1874. Her appearances concluded with a benefit organized by a committee of admirers so successful that it occasioned half-price railroad tickets; trains were held until 11:45 P.M. to facilitate homeward travel by patrons. French comic opera continued in popularity, presented both in translation and the original language. Yet another novelty surfaced in March 1877, when Tomasi's Grand Juvenile English Opera Company presented a week's worth of Luigi Ricci's *Crispino e la comare* at the Grand Opera House. In November of that year, Kellogg, now fronting her own company, presented *Carmen* to Cincinnatians only a month after New Yorkers first heard it. On November 7 the *Enquirer's* critic made one of those predictions which must haunt journalists entrusted with making such judgments: "This opera, however, will not be likely to take high and enduring rank. . . . [It is] a charming novelty[,] . . . pleasing to the world for a time, but it will probably perish before the Pyramids."

Colonel James Henry Mapleson (1830–1901), whose career as an impresario of opera dated back to 1861 and who was prominently connected with Her Majesty's Theatre in London, mounted several American tours between 1878 and 1886. He arrived in Cincinnati for the first time during early February 1879, with Luigi Arditi in the pit, Minnie Hauk as Carmen,[8] and Hungarian soprano Etelka Gerster, often touted as Adelina Patti's chief rival, as Lucia.

The Queen City, in concord with the rest of the country, was then struck by "Pinafore Fever," a malady inflicted universally by W. S. Gilbert and Arthur Sullivan's first unalloyed triumph as a team. *H. M. S. Pinafore* had been heard first in London on May 25, 1878, and created an instant vogue. So many pirated performances cropped up in this country that impresario Richard D'Oyly Carte decided to take his authentic production to New York, a visit that also included the brand-new *Pirates of Penzance,* which enjoyed its first hearing at the Fifth Avenue Theatre on December 31, 1879.

The first local amateur rendering of *Pinafore* was mounted at the reconstructed Pike's by the Unity Club of the First Unitarian Church. This was followed by a variety of other productions, including that of a Juvenile Pinafore Company, whose September performances involved fifty Cincinnati school children. However, the most unusual essay was by the New York English Opera Company, a venture with premonitions of what was to transpire forty-one summers later. Its stage was the deck of a real ship anchored in a lake at the Zoological Gardens. Unfortunately, the substantial public that gathered for the first performance was forced to wait while management dealt with the logistical problems of ferrying the cast to its floating stage. The D'Oyly Carte Company arrived in Cincinnati with *Pirates* on February 23, 1880, and Gilbert and Sullivan themselves joined the troupe on the twenty-seventh, the penultimate day of the run.

In September of that year impresario Max Maretzek arrived as head of a new opera department at the College of Music and initiated a two-year experiment in December with a production of Rossini's *La Cenerentola* that elicited scant public support and public queries as to whether the work exceeded the capacities of its young performers.

However, the rift between George Ward Nichols, founder of the college, and Theodore Thomas, which had precipitated the latter's resignation as its musical director in the spring of 1880, led to a major opera festival at Music Hall in 1881. Its goals were to raise money for the college and to thumb its nose at Thomas and his May Festival. Colonel Mapleson was hired to organize and promote seven performances in a space not originally designed as a theater. Hence, a proscenium 112 feet wide and 84 feet high, as well as boxes decorated in satin and gold, were hastily added. Otto Singer groomed a chorus of three hundred (although some never made it to the stage since Mapleson had not provided a sufficient number of costumes), and an imported orchestra was augmented by players from the college, eventually totaling one hundred. Season tickets were offered at auction in the hope of goading public-spirited citizens into contributing in excess of the stated tab. It was reported that during the first two days, 1,521 seats were auctioned for nearly $25,000. Some 5,336 auditors purportedly jammed the hall for *Lohengrin,* and subsequent performances of everything but Boito's *Mefistofele* provoked the same enthusiastic response (the other repertory was *The Magic Flute, Lucia di Lammermoor, Aida, La Sonnambula,* and *Faust*).

Despite some grumbling about the quality of the performers, plans were laid immediately for a sequel the following year. Adelina Patti was to be one of several headliners, but her company was managed by one of Mapleson's rivals, Henry A. Abbey,[9] so that both companies were engaged concurrently, certainly a perilous arrangement. Patti was to present two varied concerts, each involving a single act from a Verdi opera, as well as individual arias and favorite sentimental ballads of the period. The off-stage comedy that resulted from this collation of egos remains titillating. One of Mapleson's principal singers was injured toward the close of *Les Hugue-nots,* and then the impresario arrived at his hotel to find a message from Abbey that Patti had a cold and would not be able to appear the following day. Suspecting a trick, Mapleson, with a doctor in tow, went to Patti's hotel only to discover that the diva was certifiably sick. Her first performance was postponed twice, leading to lots of juicy public gossip as to the truth behind the formal announcements. Then Minnie Hauk, halfway through *The Magic Flute,* claimed that she too was stricken with a sore throat and refused to continue with her next aria, even though she had just (as was the custom of the time) broken Mozart's continuity with an encore. She, how-ever, recovered quickly enough to portray Elsa in the following day's *Lohengrin.* Hauk also again electrified Cincinnatians in the title role of *Carmen,* at that point only seven years old, and, as noted earlier, laggard in attaining favor. Patti finally rallied enough to present her first concert on February 18, the concluding day of the festi-val, and lingered to present its companion the following Monday.[10] Audiences ap-proaching seven thousand at both events assured yet another sequel.

The third festival, in early February 1883, again involved both Mapleson and Abbey, but as rivals. Patti's company was no longer managed by the latter, so Ab-bey rented Robinson's Opera House and presented Christine Nilsson in concerts of opera excerpts, creating a notable clash of titans. While Patti was his principal draw, Mapleson had assembled other noted singers, creating enough furor that two per-formances were added to the announced schedule. Patti appeared in *La Traviata, La Sonnambula, Semiramide,* and *Don Giovanni* and concluded the event with a sig-nature gesture, substituting "Home, Sweet Home" for a final duet. According to the *Commercial Gazette* of February 7, "Applause and shouts and waving of handker-chiefs were in order, and six times the diva was called before the curtain." Sumptu-ous settings and the addition of Currier's Grand Military Band to the chorus of two hundred and orchestra of one hundred assured the commercial success of *L'Afri-caine, William Tell,* and *Lohengrin.* A profit of $65,000 was realized, divided between the impresario and the college, and Mapleson was given the keys to the city at a banquet in his honor.

Mapleson assumed that he had been contracted to mount the Cincinnati opera festivals in perpetuity, but Nichols and the college board hired Abbey's company for the 1884 event, perhaps impressed that he was to manage the first season at the new Metropolitan Opera House in New York. In revenge, Mapleson announced that his company would mount its own season at the new Hauck's Opera House concurrently with the festival. But Mother Nature became the ultimate avenger, in the form of the historic flood of 1884. Abbey's company arrived to find the city under water and in darkness, since the gas works had been submerged. Mapleson sent word that his visit was to be postponed until late March, leading to public taunts about his virility in the face of "a little water." In an act of penitence he staged a benefit in Chicago for flood victims, but this act of contrition apparently did not suffice since the Courthouse Riots forced cancellation of the March visit as well.[11]

However, Abbey was already in town with Christine Nilsson and Polish soprano Marcella Sembrich as his stars, so he improvised, using gas supplies borrowed from a nearby hospital, plus a few new-fangled electric lights. Twelve performances were presented over a period of two weeks, including a benefit on February 17 at which $6,000 was raised to alleviate the suffering of the local citizenry. Nilsson, who replicated her recent success in New York with Amilcare Ponchielli's *La Gioconda,* won the hearts of the local populace by venturing out in a boat to view the ravages of what had become the most devastating flood in the city's history. But conditions were such that the festival proved a financial disaster, and since the college was forced to meet Abbey's guaranty, the series was terminated.[12]

A year later, Walter Damrosch, who had just assumed responsibility for the Metropolitan Opera on the death of his father, Leopold, brought the company to Cincinnati with an all-German repertory as part of a national tour. The Metropolitan was not to return until March 1896, when it appeared with Anton Seidl in charge, superstars Emma Calvé and Jean and Edouard de Rezke, and a diverse standard repertory ranging from *Carmen* and *Faust* to *Aida* and *Siegfried.*

During the summer of 1885 a group named the Milan Italian Opera Company presented two weeks of Italian opera in a pavilion at the Highland House, which had been constructed in 1877 to house a series of twenty-three concerts by Theodore Thomas and his orchestra,[13] and by 1897 Cincinnatians could again enjoy light opera at the zoo with something called the McKay Opera Company, while the Boston Lyric Opera Company held forth with "grand" opera in English at a new outdoor opera house in Chester Park, a venture that moved indoors in late September, first to Music Hall and then to the Odd Fellows' Temple.

Rather than attempt a chronicle of the plethora of visiting companies that passed through the city during these years, presenting an enormously diverse literature in various venues, both in- and outdoors, let us fast-forward to 1910 and mention of a handful of local firsts.

The College of Music had resurrected its opera program and on May 24 offered, in English, what was claimed to be the first performance in this country of Mozart's *Così fan tutte.* This "first" was followed by the announcement that the board of directors of the Ohio Valley Exposition, to be held that fall, had commissioned *Paoletta,* with a libretto by Paul Jones, a local writer and artist, and music by Italian-born Pietro Floridia (1860–1932), who had taught at the College of Music from 1906 until 1908 before settling in New York. David Bispham, one of the leading baritones of the day, sang some of the first performances, but he and other imported singers were double cast with locals since the piece was to be presented every day for almost a month, beginning on August 29. The chorus totaled 140, the corps de ballet (imports from New York) numbered fifteen, and the orchestra consisted of fifty-three members of the Cincinnati Symphony.[14] Bursting with pride over the event, the *Enquirer* on August 30 acclaimed "the first grand opera written in English and given under civic auspices" but was forced to admit that "no more could be understood than if a foreign tongue were used."

In March 1920 the Chicago Grand Opera Company returned to Cincinnati after a seven-year hiatus. With virtuosi like Mary Garden, Amelita Galli-Curci, and Tita Ruffo on its roster, its work dazzled and allowed the *Enquirer* to claim on March 20 of the opening night's *Lucia di Lammermoor:* "Cincinnati has not enjoyed a more magnificent opening of an opera season since the opera festivals in the 80's."

However, an event of greater import occurred that summer when Ralph Lyford organized a seven-week repertory season at the zoo, employing a mix of imported and local solo singers, a local chorus, and thirty-seven members of the Cincinnati Symphony.[15] A graduate of the New England Conservatory of Music, Lyford (1882–1927) had then studied under Arthur Nikisch in Europe and worked with several minor opera companies before he was hired to organize an opera department at the Conservatory of Music in 1916. He had already staged student operas at Emery Auditorium and by the summer of 1919 was furnishing student opera scenes to complement orchestra concerts at the Cincinnati Zoological Gardens.

The format was a complex amalgam of full operas, orchestral concerts under the direction of Modest Alloo, and mixed evenings in which the orchestra furnished half the event, a single opera act the other. Intermissions at the hybrid ventures lasted a full forty-five minutes so as to allow patrons to partake of the zoo's other attractions, especially a professional ice-skating show at a small arena adjacent to the Opera Pavilion, which was hastily concocted from the existing bandstand. With the exception of Ermanno Wolf-Ferrari's *The Secret of Suzanne* (1909), the season's repertory was standard: *Martha, Il Trovatore, Rigoletto, Faust, The Barber of Seville, Il Pagliacci, Don Pasquale, Carmen,* and *Hansel and Gretel.* With one anomaly, the names of the imported soloists evoke no immediate recognition: John Jacob Niles (1892–1980), who had studied at the Cincinnati Conservatory in 1919 and was later to achieve fame as a collector, arranger, and performer of Appalachian folk music, sang several minor roles and served as a general backstage factotum for Lyford. Success was instantaneous, with crowds that exceeded all expectations, creating the enormously positive problem of accommodating auditors, divided between those who had paid for reserved seating and those who wished to claim the less desirable free spaces on the peripheries. It was estimated that more than 100,000 people attended the 42 performances that summer, and the *Cincinnati Times-Star's* critic claimed after opening night, "All doubt as to the interest of the Cincinnati public in high-class music as a summer attraction was dispelled Sunday night by the prolonged applause and the record breaking attendance."

The 1921 season proved even more ambitious. It was to last eight weeks, the number of solo singers was expanded to twenty-six and the chorus to as many as forty-two (for *Lohengrin*), ballet was added to the menu (including a *divertissement* paired with *Cavalleria Rusticana*), the pavilion was furnished with a balcony and a row of box seats, and a box office was established downtown to facilitate the purchase of reserved seats. While Lyford responded to his public's apparent taste for "grand opera," he also programmed Offenbach's *The Tales of Hoffmann*. A different sort of fan surfaced during the second act of *Lucia di Lamermoor* on June 27 when a nearby peacock insisted on accompanying tenor Mario Valle every time he sang, apparently with a less-than-complementary timbre.

By the third season storm curtains had been installed to protect listeners from the elements. The repertory included works of substantial dimensions, such as *La Gioconda, Aida, Samson and Delilah* (with a chorus of sixty-five), and *Mefistofele*. Saturday evenings were devoted to full-length ballets and vocal solos by the visiting stars. In 1924 twenty-four members of the Metropolitan Opera chorus were hired as the nucleus of the Cincinnati ensemble, and the first American performance of a complete three-act *Coppelia* by Léo Delibes was mounted on July 4. By 1925 Lyford had been appointed associate conductor of the Cincinnati Symphony under Fritz Reiner, and an ambitious season had been announced, including six works new to the zoo's repertory. But by May a labor dispute with stagehands and a rift between Lyford and Charles G. Miller, business manager of the zoo, led to cancellation of the opera season and its replacement with eight weeks of orchestral concerts.[16]

From 1926 until 1933 the company was led by Isaac Van Grove, during the first year as conductor, thereafter in total control as general manager. A Philadelphia native, he had graduated from the Chicago Musical College and was music director of the Chicago Civic Opera Company, from whose chorus he drew twenty-four singers as the core of his Cincinnati Zoo Opera ensemble. The novelties of his first season were *The Love of Three Kings* (1913) of Italo Montemezzi and the first performance of Van Grove's own *The Music Robber* on July 4.[17] The 1927 season saw live radio broadcasts, initiated with a performance of *Carmen* over WLW on June 24, as well as a couple of novelties: Wolf-Ferrari's *The Jewels of the Madonna* (1911) and *The Jewess* (1835) by Fromental Halévy. Since it was considered light opera, Michael William Balfe's *The Bohemian Girl* (1843) was offered August 14–20 as a postscript to the regular season.

That same pattern was followed during 1928, an ambitious season that concluded with weeklong runs of *The Mikado* and *The Bohemian Girl*. Vladimir Bakaleinikoff, the new associate conductor of the Cincinnati Symphony, led two full-length ballets, and an ambitious production of *Die Meistersinger*, with as many as 109 people onstage, involved members of the May Festival Chorus and an expanded orchestra. The ninth season introduced as postscripts Victor Herbert's *Naughty Marietta* and Reginald

DeKoven's *Robin Hood,* as well as Umberto Giordano's *Andrea Chénier,* Meyerbeer's *Dinorah,* and *Parsifal,* whose performances began at 5:30 P.M., with a ninety-minute dinner break à la Bayreuth. The utter novelty was another first performance, this one homegrown: *Enter Pauline, A Lyrical Romance in Two Chapters and a Frontispiece,* with a libretto by Clark E. Firestone, associate editor and theater critic of the *Times-Star,* and a score by Joseph Surdo, music director at Withrow High School. Firestone's paper described the première on July 27 as the "biggest night of the year, its opening performance crowding the pavilion, populating its aisles, and quadrupling the size of the audience predicted by hard-boiled Zoo officials." In August the entire company traveled to Asheville, North Carolina, to present at that city's Opera Festival Week six operas and a ballet set on John Alden Carpenter's *Krazy Kat.*

The Great Depression had a noticeable effect on attendance at the ten-week 1930 season, and fireworks were added to the ice show as an enticement. The summer's novelties: the company's first performances of *Don Giovanni,* Mascagni's *Iris,* and week-long runs of Rudolf Friml's *The Firefly* and Robert Planquette's *The Chimes of Normandy.* The 1931 season saw the addition of *The Bartered Bride, Fidelio, The Masked Ball,* and Vincent Youmans's *Wildflower* to the repertory, as well as Sunday evening Zoo Opera Presentations, described in the *Times-Star* of June 15 as "a sort of glorified vaudeville, which included dancing, opera, solos and ensemble music by the band—In this event gentlemen of the Cincinnati Orchestra—and a jazz-ballet." The resulting $70,000 deficit was assumed by Mrs. Anna Sinton Taft, but by April 1932 zoo officials announced that financial constraints would force the park's closing at sundown, except on weekends, that the ice-skating would be discontinued, and that some sort of external underwriting would be needed to mount an opera season. Funds were raised, and Van Grove managed a traditional ten-week run that added *Norma, The Magic Flute, La Forza del Destino,* and Johann Strauss's *The Gypsy Baron* to the regular repertory, with Sidney Jones's *The Geisha* and *H. M. S. Pinafore* as its two week-long supplements. Control of the zoo itself then shifted to the city government, and it became clear that private financing would be necessary to maintain the company. A Zoo Civic Opera Association finally managed to locate enough money to support a curtailed six-week season in 1933 (one that introduced *Thaïs* and *The Girl of the Golden West* to the company's repertory), followed by two weeks of Gilbert and Sullivan. But attendance faltered, and the summer generated a deficit of $18,000.

Futile efforts to overcome this inertia, coupled with the general economic climate, led to a five-week season the following summer in the University of Cincinnati's Nippert Stadium on a temporary proscenium stage with limited lighting and seating. The polyglot programs were tripartite in structure: a band concert, a symphonic concert, and a condensed version of a popular opera. Fausto Cleva (1902–71), who had served as chorus master and assistant conductor at the zoo in 1927 and was later to achieve a larger renown at the Metropolitan and San Francisco Operas, had charge of a company of fifty (many imported from New York) and an orchestra of sixty-five. Supported in large part by the local musicians' association, eager to find work for otherwise unemployed instrumentalists, as well as gifts allowing free admission to other unemployed individuals, attendance ranged from nine hundred to over two thousand. Soon thereafter a new start was envisioned with the incorporation of the Cincinnati Summer Opera Association.

Although financial instability persisted, with Cleva at the helm summer opera returned to the zoo in 1935 and has been maintained in Cincinnati without interruption to the present. Although the basic repertory remained generally familiar and predictable, Cleva extended it with the introduction of Meyerbeer's *L'Africaine* and Deems Taylor's *The King's Henchman* (1926–27) in 1936 and *Boris Godunov* in 1948. With soloists such as Ruth Page and Paul Draper, the ballet company flourished in works like *Bolero, American in Paris* (a first performance, which Gershwin was asked to conduct but declined in order to complete work on *Porgy and Bess*), and *Nocturne and Dance,* with a score by Cincinnatian John W. Hausserman Jr. Major artists joined the roster and then became regulars, including Cleveland-born Rose Bampton, who sang Leonora in *Il Trovatore* in 1938, Gladys Swarthout in her first *Carmen* on July 25, 1939, Jan Peerce and Robert Weede presenting Verdi's Duke and Rigoletto on July 3 that same summer, and Leonard Warren portraying Amonasro in *Aida* the following year. Risë Stevens appeared as Ambroise Thomas's Mignon in 1942, while Lawrence Tibbett played Scarpia in *Tosca* and Zinka Milanov portrayed Aida in 1943; Licia Albanese, Alexander Kipnis (as Mephistofeles in *Faust*), and conductor Thomas Beecham made their débuts the following summer; Martial Singher and Jeanette MacDonald, a singer of a different ilk as Gounod's Juliet, appeared in 1945; Ezio Pinza assumed the role of Mephistopheles during the twenty-fifth anniversary season, and polio-stricken Marjorie Lawrence sang Amneris seated on a throne the following summer. In late June 1946 the Cincinnati Summer Opera Orchestra, led by Cleva, recorded thirteen sides for Decca, of which eleven were released but only in 1953. The idea was to celebrate the twenty-fifth anniversary of the organization with familiar works by Debussy, Liszt, Gounod, Offenbach, Verdi, and others, with the additional hope of generating income. The literature was rehearsed in Cincinnati before the season opened, but the actual recording was accomplished in Decca's Chicago studios.[18]

Financial problems surfaced periodically, in particular during 1949, the same year that a subscription plan replaced the time-honored system of guaranty loans. Attendance was down, the third week of the agenda was maintained only with support from the Crosley Broadcasting Corporation, and on July 10 the management announced termination of the season on the sixteenth, since losses had mounted to $30,000. However, prominent citizens and the musicians' union responded to the need and rescued a company that only a decade earlier had produced a surplus of $20,000.

In 1950 new management instituted a pattern that prevailed throughout most of the following decade: a more modest scheme of four weeks established in advance, with a normal week's extension, the contents of which were announced only after the season was underway. In 1951 *Aida* and Johann Strauss's *Rosalinda* were presented in the Cincinnati Gardens in a vain attempt to discover an indoor environment with a larger seating capacity. However, sorry acoustics and high levels of humidity caused by the hockey ice resting immediately under the temporary flooring led to the conclusion that the zoo facilities were superior to that venue. That summer also marked the Cincinnati débuts of Roberta Peters as Gilda in *Rigoletto*, Jerome Hines as Gounod's Mephistopheles, and Robert Merrill as Rossini's Figaro. Eleanor Steber arrived the following summer as Violetta in *La Traviata*.

Sunday evening radio broadcasts aided in spreading the reputation of the company, and by 1953 branch ticket offices had been opened in fourteen cities across the tri-state area of Ohio, Kentucky, and Indiana; three hundred more seats were added to the pavilion in 1954, increasing its capacity to three thousand spectators.[19]

Although he increasingly shared conducting responsibilities with others, Fausto Cleva remained the company's guiding force as musical director and in 1958 was presented a silver tray at a special ceremony marking his quarter century of service.[20] Elinor Ross met a different sort of roar of approval when the neighboring lions added their approbation during her Cincinnati début as Leonora in *Il Trovatore* on July 24.

By the summer of 1959 the Cincinnati Summer Opera Association had employed its first year-round staff and had hired Dino Yannopoulos, a stage director at the Metropolitan Opera. The following year Yannopoulos was named artistic director and by 1961 was appointed general manager as well. The 1959 season was graced with Carlisle Floyd's *Susannah* (1954), a work that not only introduced conductor Julius Rudel and singers Phyllis Curtin, Richard Cassilly, and Norman Treigle to Cincinnatians, but also allowed ample manifestation of Yannopoulos's sense of opera as vivid theater. The summer also saw the first appearances in Cincinnati of Giuseppe Di Stefano as Giordano's Andrea Chénier and the Chevalier des Grieux in the company's first production of Puccini's *Manon Lescaut*. The fortieth anniversary season was expanded, allowing the presentation of nine works, including three new to the company's repertory: Verdi's *Macbeth,* Bellini's *La Sonnambula*, and Britten's *Peter Grimes*. The following summer Cleva was named musical advisor and Carlo Moresco musical administrator, James King arrived in Cincinnati for the company's first go at Richard Strauss's *Ariadne auf Naxos,* and Roberta Sue Ficker, later known as Suzanne Farrell, made her first appearance as a solo dancer, although she had been a member of the corps for several seasons.

However, artistic success did not necessarily lead to financial stability, and the 1961 season generated a deficit of about $80,000. During the messy turmoil that ensued, Yannopolous resigned and was replaced by Tito Capobianco as artistic and stage director, titles he retained only through 1965. Cleva agreed to return as musical advisor for an abbreviated season of four weeks based on standard favorites. According to an article in the *Post and Times-Star* of July 16, 1962, Cleva personally paid the costs of overtime rehearsals for the season's triumph, Richard Strauss's *Salome,* with Phyllis Curtin in the title role. What might be labeled downsizing today led to complaints about constraints on rehearsal time and various tensions between conductors and stage directors, which spilled into the public press and led to Cleva's departure. Some sense of stability was achieved in the near term through reliance on safe repertory and restricted budgets. Of the conductors imported to replace Cleva, Anton Guadagno achieved the greatest longevity, appearing in the pit intermittently over the next three decades.

In 1964 Cincinnatians were introduced to Sherrill Milnes as the Count di Luna in *Il Trovatore* and to both Martina Arroyo and Ara Berberian in *Aida.* The following summer brought Beverly Sills to town in a generous production of Offenbach's *Tales of Hoffmann,*[21] as well as an offstage event of enormous significance: *La Forza del Destino,* the season opener, was underwritten by a gift from Patricia and J. Ralph Corbett, philanthropists whose generosity has had an ineffable impact on the Queen City's arts community over the subsequent decades.

In 1966 they supported a new production of *Faust,* as well as Rossini's *Cinderella,* new to the zoo repertory, while Mildred Miller and Placido Domingo wowed locals as the fated lovers in *Carmen.* While Lili Chookasian as Madame Flora in Gian Carlo Menotti's *The Medium* arrived in the city for the first time in 1967, attention was riveted on Elisabeth Schwarzkopf in her two appearances as the Marschallin in *Der Rosenkavalier.* Despite the excitement generated by the Strauss, attendance was down again, fomenting a sense of crisis. Talk about a move to Music Hall, which had first surfaced in 1966, was coupled to new promotional strategies, such as research into potential audiences. Perhaps the most significant decision was the hiring of Ohio-born James M. de Blasis as production manager and director of three of the 1968 productions. A judgment was made to rely on star appeal, and that summer was certainly studded with major singers: Richard Tucker, Roberta Peters, Frank Guarrera, Beverly Sills (in a new production of *Lucia di Lammermoor,* paid for by the Corbetts), Norman Treigle, Placido Domingo, Felicia Weathers, and Anna Moffo in her Cincinnati début as Violetta in *La Traviata.*

The following summer was prematurely announced as the company's last in its alfresco location, and a special gala on July 12 brought a small brigade of vocal celebrities to the summer's forty-ninth and purportedly final year at the zoo. Partnered with this premature eulogy were the company's first performances of Bellini's *Il Pirata* with Monserrat Caballé in her company début, complicated by the diva's illness, which forced a postponement of the second performance. By January 1970 it had become obvious that the lack of funding (while the Corbett Foundation had given the seed money, matching funds were slow to appear) and construction delays in the renovation of Music Hall meant that the fiftieth-anniversary season would be celebrated at the zoo. Its highlights were Louis Quilico as Verdi's Iago and Shirley Verrett, who triumphed both as Saint-Saëns's Delilah and Bizet's Carmen. The company then initiated its second half-century at the zoo with Beverly Sills as a dazzling Lucia but also ventured a production of Carlisle Floyd's *Of Mice and Men*, which had first been heard in Seattle during January of that year. The composer directed many of the original cast with Emerson Buckley in the pit and sets borrowed from the Kansas City Lyric Opera. Although the season nominally closed with a pair of performances by the Vienna State Opera Ballet, the final opera performed at the Cincinnati Zoological Gardens was Rossini's *The Barber of Seville*, directed by de Blasis, with native son James Levine in his pit début.

Following a commemorative ceremony, destruction of the pavilion began on November 16, 1972, but the fifty-second season had already been completed, initiated with a gala performance in air-conditioned Music Hall of Boito's *Mefistofele* with Norman Triegle in the title role and Julius Rudel as conductor. The production had originally been mounted by the New York City Opera in September 1969, designed for joint presentation by the Cincinnati Summer Opera. The entire venture, including the New York performances, was underwritten by the Corbetts, who had also contributed $2 million for the refurbishing of Music Hall and directed that all proceeds from the Cincinnati performances be employed to create an endowment fund for the company. They also supported *The Marriage of Figaro*, which was accompanied by *Die Fledermaus*, *Turandot*, *Madame Butterfly*, and a new production of *La Traviata* as a vehicle for Beverly Sills.

James de Blasis was named general director of the company the following summer, having accepted a role as advisor to the Corbett Foundation a year earlier. He chose to shun total reliance on the standard war-horses by scheduling Puccini's *La Rondine* and Donizetti's *Daughter of the Regiment* in 1973, Donizetti's *Roberto Devereux* and Offenbach's *La Périchole* in 1974, and Puccini's *Il Trittico* (*Il Tabarro, Suor Angelica*, and *Gianni Schicchi*) and Wagner's *The Flying Dutchman* in 1975. The company's first season in Music Hall was marked by a luxurious production of *Aida* with King, Arroyo, and Quilico, fifteen members of the May Festival Chorus, and eight extra dancers added to the normal chorus of thirty-six and corps of twelve, scads of supernumeraries and enough live animals (a parrot, cockatoo, peacock, snake, tiger, chimpanzees, and an elephant) to suggest that the zoo had now come to the opera, rather than the reverse.

The new general director aspired to year-round operation and realized that this would require an expanded audience pool. To this end, he began to present more of the repertory in English and also established the Young American Artists Resident

Training Program, staffed by gifted apprentices who could profit by association with the experienced pros as they sang minor roles but who also undertook various outreach programs, such as previews preceding each performance. The Cincinnati Summer Opera became the Cincinnati Opera Association in 1975. The following year brought a slightly new twist with the Cincinnati Opera Ensemble, young singers who prior to the summer season gave demonstration performances across the community, particularly in the schools. That summer also brought Portsmouth, Ohio–born, College-Conservatory-of-Music-trained Kathleen Battle back to town for Mozart's *Così fan tutte*, first performances in Cincinnati of Douglas Moore's *The Ballad of Baby Doe* (1956), and an obvious attempt to attract an extended clientele with four performances of Jerome Kern's *Show Boat*.

The remainder of the decade was marked by other highlights: Renata Scotto's arrival in town as Bellini's Norma and Frank Loesser's *The Most Happy Fella*, both in 1977; Catherine Malfitano's Cincinnati début as Donizetti's Lucia; Romberg's *The Student Prince* and the statewide broadcast of *Die Walküre* on public radio the following summer;[22] the postseason studio taping of de Blasis's production of *The Elixir of Love* and its eventual national broadcast over PBS on January 5, 1980; and the introduction to the company's repertory in 1979 of Francesco Cilea's *Adriana Lecouvreur* and Verdi's *Attila*. In an increasingly common pattern, production costs were shared with companies in Edmonton, Philadelphia, and Washington.

While *Hansel and Gretel* had been staged in December 1978 in collaboration with the Cincinnati Symphony, a decisive transition toward year-round operation occurred with performances of *La Traviata* on March 5 and 9, 1980. Following the five-week Summer Festival, the new season was initiated with *Carmen* in November, *Faust* in April, and a traditional six-week Summer Festival, which included *Aida, Das Rheingold, Don Pasquale, Tosca, H. M. S. Pinafore,* and four performances of *South Pacific*. This pattern was maintained for a half decade, spiced with a handful of novelties: Franco Alfano's *Resurrection* (1902–03) in June 1983, Leoncavallo's *Zazà* (1900) in April 1985, and Jaromír Weinberger's *Schwanda, the Bagpiper* (1927) in March 1986. SurCaps, with their simultaneous translation of the language being sung into English above the proscenium, were tentatively introduced in the spring of 1984 and then made permanent the following year.

However, increasing competition for the affection of audiences distracted by new sources of summer entertainment led to whopping deficits and a decision to return to a compact summer season in order to concentrate and thus reduce costs. So the experiment begun in 1980 concluded with two performances of *Turandot*, starring Martina Arroyo, in November 1987. With a revised management structure, new fundraising strategies, and aggressive, hip advertising in place, James de Blasis and his company in the 1990s settled into a stable pattern of presenting paired performances of four works each monthlong summer season, relying mostly on standard literature and the city's favorite singers but occasionally adding to the traditional repertory, for example, Mozart's *The Abduction from the Seraglio* in 1992, Massenet's *Werther* in 1993, and Jake Heggie's *Dead Man Walking* in 2002. After twenty-eight years at the helm, during which he directed one hundred productions,[23] de Blasis announced his retirement and was succeeded on August 1, 1996, as artistic director by Nicholas Muni, a widely experienced stage director who formerly held the same title with the Tulsa Opera.

With its unique, fascinating, sometimes turbulent history, now more than eight decades old, this novel troupe seems destined to enjoy an equally illustrious future.

Festivals

Ohioans produce a staggering diversity of festivals, hallowing everything from the bratwurst to the dulcimer and beyond, but two demand our attention: Cincinnati's May Festival, dating from 1873, and the Baldwin-Wallace College Bach Festival, first mounted in 1933. Another on a path toward prominence is the Lancaster Festival, held during the final two weeks of July, which celebrated its fifteenth anniversary in 1999. Now built around its own Festival Orchestra and Chamber Orchestra, which present classical, pops, and Young Peoples concerts with soloists ranging from violinist Joshua Bell to the Manhattan Transfer, daytime hours are filled with a non-stop cornucopia of events, from chamber music (by established ensembles as well as ad hoc groups drawn from the resident orchestra) to jazz, polka bands, community sings, and beyond in a variety of venues. The festival sometimes has sponsored a composer-in-residence, ranging from the prominent (William Bolcom) to the up-and-coming (Augusta Read Thomas) and in 2000 organized a competition for new orchestral works involving both a read-through of pieces by the finalists and a re-hearsed performance of the winning work, Michigander Anthony Iannaccone's *American Jubilee*.

CHAPTER 19

May Festival

The Cincinnati May Festival[1] was born through a conflation of events and person-alities. The most crucial of these were the seventeenth Sängerfest of the North American Sängerbund, held in Cincinnati June 15–19, 1870, and the impact of Theo-dore Thomas and his touring orchestra.

The Sängerfest preceded by only three months the Industrial Exposition mounted by the local board of trade, chamber of commerce, and Ohio Mechanics Institute in an effort to attract attention to the city. A decision was made to construct a build-ing compatible with the needs of both festivals. Thus, the exposition authorities contributed $5,000 toward construction of the Sängerfest-Halle Exposition Hall at the corner of Fourteenth and Elm Streets. The wooden structure encompassed a room 250 by 100 feet, seating three thousand performers and ten thousand specta-tors, surrounded by galleries allowing ample exhibition spaces. Wings were later added to house the Power Hall (displaying the latest in steam age technology), the Fine Arts and Music Hall, and the Mechanics Hall (for the newest contrivances in the manual arts). Annexes were later built in Washington Park for subsequent ex-positions and connected to the parent structures by a bridge over Elm Street, even-tually allowing four-and-a-half acres of floor space. Exhibits from twenty-four states attracted 300,000 visitors between September 21 and October 22.

While not as blatantly commercial, the Sängerfest was marked by considerable civic boosterism. Eighteen hundred singers from sixty-one Midwestern German sing-ing societies were supported by an orchestra of seventy-five, and auditors swelled the roster of "strangers" to perhaps thirty thousand. The *Cincinnati Commercial* pro-jected on May 21, "This will be a big advertisement to our city, and of much benefit to our hotels, restaurants, boarding-houses, dry goods stores, places of amusement and entertainment, brewers, and saloon keepers—the two latter in particular." On the first day, the local German consul led a procession of participants through a series of triumphal arches on Fourth and Vine Streets; Governor Rutherford B. Hayes delivered the opening address.

German-born Theodore Thomas (1835–1905) had emigrated with his family to New York in 1845 and, having played in various orchestras, including that of the French showman Louis Jullien in 1853, joined the first violin section of the New York Philharmonic the following year. In 1855 he and pianist William Mason initiated a series of chamber music concerts at Dodworth Hall. His first conducting opportunity came in 1859, and the baton gradually became his principal means of expression. He was appointed conductor of the Brooklyn Philharmonic in 1862, initiated a personally funded symphonic series in Irving Hall in 1864, and the following year began offering enormously successful, lighter programs during the summer, first in Terrace Garden and then in Central Park. Emboldened by his success, he engaged forty German American musicians on a full-time, year-round basis, and in November 1869 the Theodore Thomas Orchestra embarked on the first of its numerous far-flung tours.

The genesis of the May Festival can be pinpointed with considerable accuracy. On either October 29 or November 5, 1871, Thomas met informally at her home with Maria Longworth Nichols, who proposed that Cincinnati undertake a music festival featuring major choral and orchestral masterworks, taking as its model the Birmingham, England, festival she had attended a year earlier.

Mrs. Nichols was the daughter of Joseph Longworth, a highly respected and successful landowner and producer of wines. Her husband, George Ward Nichols, became a principal figure in Cincinnati's musical development. Born in New England and educated in both Boston and Paris (where he studied painting), he served as a staff officer to General William Tecumseh Sherman and in 1865 published a book detailing his experiences during the Great March. After the war he worked as art editor of the *New York Evening Post* before moving to Cincinnati in 1868. After taking as his bride the nineteen-year-old Maria, thus precluding the necessity of any obvious employment, he assumed the role of cultural leader in the Queen City, manifesting an interest in music through his membership in the Harmonic Society. An organization typical of the period, it consisted of both active and associate members. The actives constituted a mixed-voice chorus, while the associates served as the audience at periodic private concerts. Nichols, an active bass, served as the Harmonic Society's president from 1873 until 1878.

Thomas immediately assented to Mrs. Nichols's vision, recalling that

> a young married lady, who was a member of one of the leading families of the city, laid before me a plan for a large Musical Festival. She proposed that I should be the conductor of it, saying that if I would be responsible for the artistic side, she would find the men who would take charge of the business

details. I soon found out that this lady was not only very talented herself in many ways, but that her taste was not amateurish in anything, and I readily consented to undertake the work she wished me to do. Some of the programmes were sketched at her house.[2]

The Nicholses recruited various prominent citizens to their board (whose president was Mr. Nichols), raised a guarantee fund of $30,000 by October 1872, and sent invitations to choral societies everywhere inviting their participation in a festival, whose object was "to elevate and strengthen the standard of choral and instrumental music, and also to bring about harmony of action between the music societies of the country, and more especially of the West." Scores were furnished by the board, but the 1,250 members of thirty-six societies, thirteen of them local (initially trained by Carl Barus), the others from as far away as Des Moines, Milwaukee, and Titusville, Pennsylvania, rehearsed on their own until April 1873, when Otto Singer, Thomas's assistant, arrived to rehearse the combined forces.

Singer (1833–94), a protégé of Thomas and a student of Liszt, Moscheles, and others, had come to this country in 1867 to teach piano in the conservatory established by Thomas and William Mason in New York City. He was universally admired for his ability to discipline his massed forces, so that at least one commentator believed, "Not a little of the success of [the 1873] festival was due to his ability and untiring energy, and as a chorus master he covered himself with glory."[3] Singer remained in the city until his retirement in 1892, composing, lecturing, teaching, and conducting at various times the Harmonic Society, Männerchor, Musik-Verein, several festivals of the North American Sängerbund, and the Dayton Philharmonic Society.

The initial concert of the first Cincinnati May Festival was heard on May 6, 1873, in the Sängerfest-Halle Exposition Hall. Its principal components were the Handel *Dettingen Te Deum* (supposedly its first American performance) and the Beethoven Fifth Symphony. The 108-man orchestra consisted half of Thomas's own players, the others added ringers from the region, including thirty-five members of the Cincinnati Grand Orchestra. Pairs of concerts were then presented on each of the next three days, the evenings dominated by substantial works like the Beethoven Ninth Symphony, Schumann's Second Symphony, Mendelssohn's *The First Walpurgis Night,* and Liszt's symphonic poem *Tasso,* while the afternoon events consisted of conglomerations of shorter pieces. The third matinee featured a chorus of local school children, supported only by local instrumentalists, conducted by Michael Brand. Plenteous refreshment was offered during the half-hour intermissions, and the hall was decorated "with long festoons of evergreens between columns." There was also "an immense pyramidal display of hothouse plants and flowers, twenty feet in diameter at the base and rising to a height of twenty feet or more, probably the finest display in the country."[4]

His widow was later to comment,

A few years later in his career, Thomas would not have used the name "Festival" to designate a series of programmes of such a popular and miscellaneous character. . . . but in 1873 he did not as yet dare to make even his festival programmes in New York and Cincinnati, or his symphony programmes in Boston, without the sugar-coating of a Strauss waltz to make the public swallow the symphonic pill. . . . [I]t was a fundamental principle of Thomas, throughout his life, to make his programmes always as much in advance of the popular taste as the people would stand. In doing this, however, he had to feel his way very carefully, because, as he had no private resources to fall back upon, it was essential for him to make programmes which, in managerial parlance, would "draw."[5]

"Draw" they did, for success was instantaneous, and it was reported that on the final evening more than six thousand people crowded the hall. Following the Beethoven Ninth the audience

rose en masse and went wild with enthusiasm. People mounted their seats, and hats and handkerchiefs were waved. Cheer upon cheer rent the air; and they were not all masculine voices either. Thousands of shouts for "Thomas!" "Thomas!" "Thomas!" went up all over the great hall, until Thomas appeared, and again and again bowed his acknowledgements. . . .

My eyes unconsciously filled with tears, and I was not alone. Was it unmanly? If so, I plead that you have not heard the Ninth Symphony as I heard it last night. Utter strangers grasped each other by the hand and exchanged congratulations. Friend clasped friend, and said: "Wasn't it glorious!" and the warm responding pressure told volumes that words could not utter. Cincinnatians were jubilant, gloriously jubilant, over the musical success, and the financial aspect, good or bad, seems to be entirely forgotten for the time being.[6]

The writer need not have worried about finances, since, remarkably, all expenses were met with box-office receipts, and the guarantors suffered no losses. Nichols had from the stage asked the final audience about a future festival and received a resounding affirmative. A petition signed by various prominent local aristocrats was presented, virtually demanding a sequel. Nichols accepted the challenge and by January 1874 had incorporated the Cincinnati Musical Festival Association, which sold one hundred shares of stock at twenty dollars each.

The 1875 festival, like its antecedent, featured a massive chorus of public school children assembled and trained by Walter Aiken. The conscious dichotomy of heavier evenings and lighter afternoons was maintained so that the nocturnal listeners heard the Beethoven Seventh and Ninth Symphonies, Mendelssohn's *Elijah*, and excerpts from *Lohengrin, Die Meistersinger,* and *Die Walküre,* as well as what was touted as the first American performance of the Bach *Magnificat in D* (rescored for the standard nineteenth-century orchestra by the German song composer Robert Franz [1815–92]). The city was resplendently decorated, including triumphal arches and even a mammoth poster of a battle scene with Liszt, Schubert, and Wagner pouring

> a destructive fire of musical notes upon the assailants below. . . . [These] are exploding in every direction. Theodore Thomas, mounted upon a prancing steed, is leading up a solid phalanx of fiddlers to the assault, and a heavy battery of trombones and ophicleides is hurling bass notes into the forts.[7]

The opening concert was delayed for thirty minutes by a powerful storm, whose downpour on the tin roof and wooden walls made it impossible to continue. In fact, if one can believe Rose Fay Thomas, the weather must have played a major role in the week's events. She recalled that the city had been suffering under a long drought, and all during the day of the second concert storm clouds had been gathering. Just as the performers were about to launch into Mendelssohn's setting of "Thanks Be to God, He Laveth the Thirsty Land," the rain descended in torrents:

> Nothing inspired Thomas so quickly as a display of the forces of nature, and, entering instantly into sympathy with the storm, and the feeling of public thankfulness for the coming of the rain, he gathered all his forces —chorus, orchestra, and organ—in one sublime outburst, harmonizing with and rising above the tumult of the elements without.[8]

The fortunate consequence of these incidents was an immediate decision by Reuben R. Springer, a wealthy merchant and real estate speculator, to envision a more permanent home for the festival. He offered $125,000 toward construction of a new Music Hall but with several crucial conditions. First, that the city-owned lot on which the Exposition Hall stood be conveyed tax-free in perpetuity to a society formed for the specific purpose. Second, this conceptual pioneer of a modern fund-raising approach demanded that his gift be matched by subscription dollar-for-dollar by his fellow citizens. The nonprofit Cincinnati Music Hall Association was incorporated in 1876, its board and fifty stockholders numbering representatives from the May Festival organization, the board of trade, the chamber of commerce, and the Ohio Mechanics Institute. The articles of incorporation insisted on the multipurpose nature of the building, a structure "for holding Musical Festivals, concerts, expositions of industry and art and also for holding such conventions, fairs, public meetings and entertainments of a kind not prohibited by Law." The principal donor asserted in the *Daily Gazette* on June 8, 1875,

> Music at the time being in the ascendant, the name was naturally adopted to make it more popular with the public. . . . But, from the first, the Industrial Exposition always had a prominent place, and the intention was never lost sight of, in the construction of the hall, to adopt it for Exposition purposes, as well as for music and other great public needs.

Springer contributed $50,000 toward the addition of a pair of wings to the central core of the building, these intended for exposition duties, stipulating a public response on a two-to-one basis. He then increased his original donation by $20,000 on the condition that the public subscribe an extra $105,000, all of which was accomplished by November 17, 1875.[9] The Exposition Hall was sold by bid for $2,105 and demolished during the fall of 1876. Construction of Music Hall was begun that winter but completed only in time for an 1878 festival, purposely postponed to await a habitable new home.

Samuel Hannaford of the local firm of Hannaford and Procter was awarded the design contract.[10] The imposing result manifested what was at the time described as "modified, modernized Gothic; the material bright-colored pressed brick, with sunken joints; the ornaments of stone, tile, and colored brick." Of the 372-foot span fronting Elm Street, ninety feet were devoted to each of the flanking exposition wings (that to the south designated as the Horticulture [later, Art] Hall, that to the north as the Power, or Machinery Hall, neither of which was completed until 1879), 178 feet to the focal core. Springer Hall towered three stories above the sidewalk, and its 150-foot pinnacle was shown in preliminary engravings as surmounted by a massive figure of a winged goddess, which was never installed. The idea was to link the three buildings through bridges connecting their upper stories, allowing their use either separately or concurrently.

The main auditorium spanned 192 by 112 feet and with its horseshoe gallery could accommodate nearly five thousand spectators. The massive performance platform was 112 by 56 feet, sufficient to house almost seven hundred choristers and an orchestra of one hundred. Unlike ornate structures, such as Pike's and the Grand Opera House, the interior walls and ceiling of Springer Hall were simply paneled with oiled yellow poplar or tulip wood, resulting in widely admired acoustics. While ten stained glass windows at the gallery level allowed in natural light during the day, the hall was illuminated at night by large gas lamps in the ceiling. The back of the stage platform was dominated by a 6,237-pipe organ built by Hook and Hastings of Boston (their opus 869) at a cost of $26,000, $10,000 of which had been donated by

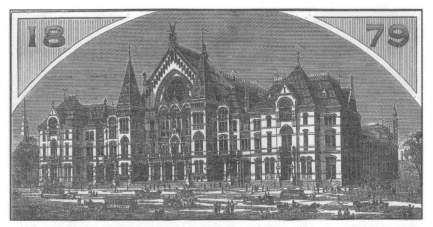

A vintage view of Music Hall, from *Report of the Board of Commissioners of the Cincinnati Industrial Exposition*, 1879. Public Library of Cincinnati and Hamilton County.

Springer. With ninety-six registers and four keyboards, it was at the time of its installation the largest instrument in the country and, depending on the source, anywhere from the second to the fifth largest in the world. Its framing case in wild cherry was designed by Robert Rogers and then carved by 112 local female students from both the School of Design, directed by Benjamin Pitman, and another school of carvers supervised by Henry Fry; elaborate floral designs had various composers' names embedded in them.[11] No trace of the original instrument remains today, a process begun with the its relocation twelve feet upstage to accommodate alterations imposed beginning in 1896, this followed by "modernization" of the instrument by the Austin Organ Company in 1923, replacement by a Baldwin electronic in 1975, and another electronic instrument by the Allen Organ Company in 2003.[12]

The room originally did not contain a proscenium arch, which then became the focus of 1896–97 renovations, when the organ was moved, the interior surfaces redesigned in plaster, and most of the upholstered seats for 4,200 placed on a slightly pitched main floor, which could, however, be removed to reveal the permanent flat surface. Electric lighting and steam heat were also part of this $100,000 project. The hall lacked boxes for housing the local elite, so the association's officers were confronted with the dilemma of assigning seats to wealthy guarantors without violating social protocol. To avoid charges of favoritism, they decided to auction the choice of seat location to season-ticket holders, the highest bidder given priority. The practice proved wildly successful (and was perpetuated until 1960), and the more than $28,000 raised from the selling of 2,242 seats included about $5,700 in auction profits (defined as premiums). In fact, the 1878 event realized a net profit of $32,000, of which $5,000 was distributed among the singing societies that constituted the 650-voice chorus.

Storming the Works. Cartoonist Will P. Noble's view of the 1878 May Festival. Of unidentified origin. Courtesy H. Perry Mixter.

Music Hall was dedicated on May 14, 1878, in a preintermission ceremony on the opening night of the third festival, which included a brief address by Springer as well as the Beethoven Third Symphony and Otto Singer's *A Festival Ode,* written for the occasion and inscribed to Springer.[13] Its concluding paean, in the words of Frederick Alfred Schmitt's "Hymn of Dedication":

> Rejoice, ye mighty choirs, rejoice,
> And dedicate our noble halls!
> Let songs of mirth ring to the skies
> Within their sacred walls!
> This temple be your dearest spot;
> May purest art this place adore—
> Ye graceful muses, leave it not
> For ever—evermore!

The festival repertory also included the Ninth Symphony of Beethoven, Wagner excerpts, portions of Gluck's *Alceste,* and the "Dramatic Symphony," *Roméo et Juliette* of Berlioz.[14]

By then Thomas had become a Cincinnati resident as a result of Nichols's creation of the College of Music with Thomas as its director, followed by their rupture over policy and the conductor's resignation from his college post in March 1880.

Impatient with the practice of attempting to meld choristers, whose qualifications were determined by the directors of their individual societies, into a coherent whole during the final stages of the rehearsal process, for the 1880 festival, Thomas organized the May Festival Chorus, the proficiency of whose members was determined on an individual basis by him. Despite considerable opposition from the vested powers, Thomas prevailed; he and Singer prepared more than six hundred singers for the daunting challenges of the Beethoven *Missa Solemnis*, perhaps its first performances in this country. Supposedly the local Orpheus Club had to be recruited at the last minute to bolster the Thomas-Singer forces, but the result met with universal approbation. J. R. G. Hassard of the *New York Tribune* even claimed that "there never had been anything like the chorus in America and no better chorus singing can be heard in the world."

The Beethoven work was actually offered twice during the standard format of four evening and three afternoon concerts. The series opened with the Bach Cantata No. 80, *Ein feste Burg*, adapted by Thomas and with an imposed organ prelude furnished by George E. Whiting. The Festival Association had also offered a $1,000 composition prize for a large work for chorus and orchestra, a competition open only to American-born composers, although four of the five jurors had been born in Germany. The result was Dudley Buck's *Scenes from Longfellow's Golden Legend*, although in a procedure weirdly akin to present-day phenomena like beauty pageants, the winner's name was not printed in the program but drawn from an envelope and announced at the performance.[15] Handel's *Messiah* had been offered as an integral part of the 1878 Festival and was then presented during six consecutive Decembers with the support of the Cincinnati Grand Orchestra as a means of maintaining the continuity of the May Festival Chorus.

The 1882 festival saw dedication of the statue of Reuben Springer by Preston Powers, which still stands in the foyer of Music Hall (Springer was to die in 1884), what was proclaimed as the first complete Bach *St. Matthew Passion* to be offered on this side of the Atlantic, the introduction of another prize-winning composition, Philadelphian William Wallace Gilchrist's *Psalm 46*, and as an addendum the Thanksgiving Choral Concert on the following November 30. In 1884 the format was altered to include only two matinees across the span of five days, and the repertory included increasingly heavy doses of Wagner, the first hearing in Cincinnati of Handel's *Israel in Egypt*, and Gounod's *The Redemption*, with prima donna Christine Nilsson as soloist. Financial disaster ensued when the auction sale of seats coincided with the confusion and turmoil engendered by the Court House riots of late March (that had followed the equally disastrous flood of the previous month). Consequently, only 712 season tickets were auctioned, and the resulting deficit of almost $19,000 absorbed the accumulated profits of earlier festivals.

Public grumbling ensued, based on the perception that Thomas and his imported orchestra and stars were grossly overpaid and glorified, while the local singers and players were by comparison badly compensated and ill-treated. In fact, Thomas had received his usual $5,000, diva Nilsson $6,000, and the ninety New York orchestra musicians an aggregate of $11,700, plus travel expenses, while the thirteen resident players hired to augment the orchestra received only $663. Even more dissension surfaced in 1886, and the controversy produced a $7,200 deficit, despite the richness of the musical offerings: *The Creation* of Haydn, the Third and Seventh Symphonies of Beethoven, both *The Damnation of Faust* and *Symphonie Fantastique* of Berlioz, and the Second Symphony of Schumann. Wagnerian soprano Lilli Lehmann was received with plaudits, but portions of an incomplete Bach *Mass in B Minor* were considered a bore, and the critics lambasted Thomas for what they considered arbitrary and ill-considered tempi that had the effect of undermining the work of the chorus. In fact, some even suspected that Thomas was attempting to sabotage the work of chorusmaster Arthur Mees, who was never called to the stage to accept public acknowledgment of his work and resigned immediately afterwards.

But the festival board demonstrated continuing loyalty to Thomas, who directed the sixteen festivals that preceded his death in 1905. For example, board president William N. Hobart, in his address to the stockholders on June 21, 1886, lauded Thomas and asserted that contrary to the chauvinistic civic boosters who increasingly derided what they viewed as a personality cult, "any attempt to give the Festivals with an ordinary orchestra or soloists of insufficient ability would simply belittle the value of the chorus, lower the entire standard, and drop the character of the performances."[16]

The Centennial May Festival of 1888 marked the city's centenary with a commissioned work by John Knowles Paine of Harvard University—a cantata, *Song of Promise,* opus 43, based on "My Country," an ode by George E. Woodberry that had been published in the *Atlantic Monthly* of July 1887. While the celebrants were also presented the Fifth and Sixth Symphonies of Beethoven and Mendelssohn's *St. Paul,* the Paine was not the only "new" work of the season. Dvořák's "dramatic cantata," *The Spectre's Bride* (first performed in 1885); Anton Rubinstein's "sacred opera," *Paradise Lost* (1875), and *Russia,* a symphonic piece for orchestra and organ (1882); as well as Camille Saint-Saëns's Third Symphony, for orchestra and organ (1886), posed so many challenges for listeners of that era that they were encouraged to attend chorus rehearsals as a means of comprehending these contemporary idioms.

Messiah was sung again at the 1890 festival and its "Hallelujah" chorus detached and repeated at the conclusion of the final concert, a regular practice since 1950, although recent audience members are presented a score "so that you may sing along, follow along or simply marvel as it resounds through Music Hall as in years past." Two years later the chorus was reorganized and each member required to reaudition for chorusmaster W[illiam] L. Blumenschein of Dayton.[17] Dvořák's *Requiem* was sung only months after its first hearing at the Birmingham Festival in October 1891. In 1894 three men's choruses, the Apollo and Symphony Clubs and the Dayton Philharmonic Society, were imported to augment the festival chorus in a repertory that included Horatio Parker's *Hora Novissima* (first performed in New York only a year earlier) and the Berlioz *Requiem,* plus the first American performances of Anton Rubinstein's *Moses* (a "sacred opera," first performed in Prague during 1892) and Rubin Goldmark's orchestral *Sappho* (written in 1893 and first heard in Berlin earlier in 1894).

In 1895 civic pride in the new Cincinnati Symphony Orchestra and its founding conductor, Frank Van der Stucken, led to renewed grumbling about Thomas and his reliance on imported performers, likening the situation to "a Chicago Festival given in Cincinnati." César Franck entered the festival annals in 1898 with his symphonic poem *Les Éolides* (1877). Patriotic fervor engendered by the Spanish-American War was reflected in a *Festival March and National Hymn on "The Star-Spangled Banner"* by Hugo Kaun (1863–1932), German-born but resident in Milwaukee from 1887 until 1901.

The festival of 1900 introduced new works by three Americans and two Englishmen: Edward MacDowell's symphonic poem *Lancelot and Elaine* (1888), Horatio Parker's symphonic poem *A Northern Ballad* (1899), Louis Victor Saar's *Ganymede,*[18] Samuel Coleridge-Taylor's *The Song of Hiawatha* (1898), and Charles Villiers Stanford's ode, *East to West* (1893). Contralto Ernestine Schumann-Heink made the first of her eight May Festival appearances in Mendelssohn's *St. Paul* at the opening concert and in Wagner excerpts to conclude the festival. A season ticket that year cost a grand total of twelve dollars.

The first event of the new century two years later introduced into the tradition Franck's *The Beatitudes* (1891, his Symphony in D minor of 1889 had been heard at the prior festival), as well as the first of nine subsequent festival performances of the complete Bach *Mass in B Minor.* Critic Henry Krehbiel, never a fan, carped at "Thomas' absurd jigging and mad tempo." The festival of 1904, the last of the Thomas era, served up a full diet of blockbusters—a repeat of the Bach Mass, both the *Missa Solemnis* and Ninth Symphony of Beethoven, as well as Edward Elgar's new oratorio, *The Dream of Gerontius.*

Following Thomas's death, Van der Stucken and the Cincinnati Symphony Orchestra were engaged for the 1906 festival, thus resolving the tension and resentment generated for decades by the ascendancy of a person considered by many little more than a carpetbagger who had become increasingly devoid of imagination. However, Thomas unwittingly provoked a bit of posthumous controversy when the May Festival Chorus engaged the Thomas Orchestra for a memorial concert in

March without the knowledge of the board, which then forbade the event and even threatened to disband the chorus. In a magnanimous gesture, Van der Stucken opened the seventeenth May Festival with the Bach Cantata 106, *God's Time Is Best*, which was dedicated to the memory of Thomas. In another savvy move, he incorporated the traditional children's chorus into mainline works, instead of relegating it to the presentation of shorter, less substantial pieces. Thus, almost one thousand youngsters sang Belgian Peter Benoit's *Into the World* and the conductor's own *Pax Triumphans, a Festival Prologue*, opus 26. Sir Edward Elgar became the festival's first guest conductor by reprising his *Dream of Gerontius* in a week that also contained another of his oratorios, *The Apostles* (1903), as well as an overture, *In the South* (1903–04), and the *Introduction and Allegro* (1904–05), for string quartet and string orchestra. Elgar was paid the princely fee of £1,500, ungraciously observing in private, "My *feelings* are dead against coming here but my pocket gapes aloud."[19] His presence attracted considerable attention and an intense social schedule, but any discomfort he was suffering was surely exacerbated at the performance of *The Apostles* on May 2, when the audience insisted on applauding after each scene. His pique was recorded in an interview immediately afterwards:

> "Why," asked Sir Edward, somewhat irritated, "why ruin the dignity of the performance by applause between the episodes?"
> "But aren't you satisfied with Cincinnati's enthusiastic greeting?"
> "I know nothing about it," replied the composer. "I walk to the desk, take up my baton, and set about my work. I am merely an artist, and as an artist I'm satisfied with nothing on earth."[20]

The equanimity resulting from reliance on local forces was shattered by the labor problems that led to temporary dormancy for the orchestra. Thus, while Van der Stucken directed the festivities of 1908 and 1910, the Festival Association was forced to hire the Theodore Thomas Orchestra from Chicago (soon to be rechristened the Chicago Symphony Orchestra), by then under the baton of Frederick Stock, who had been Thomas's assistant. The 1910 festival brought President William Howard Taft and the German ambassador to dedicate the statue of Theodore Thomas by Clement J. Barnhorn, which stood for many decades in the Music Hall foyer. The musical work of the evening was Handel's *Judas Maccabeus* in a version by Van der Stucken; local journalists considered its basic themes of patriotism, liberty, and ultimate justice appropriate to the occasion.

Ernst Kunwald, newly anointed Cincinnati Symphony Orchestra conductor, enjoyed an unmitigated triumph as the festival's music director in 1914. Kunwald had endeared himself to the chorus with a December 1913 performance of *Messiah* and, thanks to the munificence of Mrs. Charles P. Taft, the festival orchestra was expanded to more than one hundred players. Kunwald enjoyed a full four weeks of rehearsals, including twice a week with both chorus and orchestra. Enthused by the association's reliance on local forces, patrons jammed Music Hall for Berlioz's *The Damnation of Faust,* which involved both Ernestine Schumann-Heink and the festival's children's chorus. The following evening's *Mass in B Minor* of Bach was witnessed by ex-president Taft, and the rest of the week contained both the Verdi *Requiem* (not heard since 1890) and the Beethoven Ninth Symphony (its tenth appearance). Almost 21,000 attended the six concerts and a net profit of almost $10,000 was realized. Henry Krehbiel gushed in the *Enquirer* of May 9,

> The Twenty-first Festival has shown itself the peer of the best of its predecessors in all the essential things, and that the policy of the Festival Association in enlisting the aid of the Cincinnati Orchestra and placing the baton of authority in the hands of Dr. Kunwald has been triumphantly vindicated.

The 1916 festival included Mendelssohn's *St. Paul,* the Brahms *Requiem,* Gabriel Pierné's oratorio *The Children's Crusade* (with a chorus of seven hundred children drawn from the public schools), and a repeat of that earlier marathon that must again have strained at least a few voices: back-to-back performances on the same program of the Beethoven *Missa Solemnis* and Ninth Symphony, which lasted until nearly midnight.

The season's novelty was the American premiere of the Richard Strauss *Alpine Symphony,* which had been first performed on October 28, 1915, in wartime Dresden with the composer at the helm. Several American orchestras vied for the distinction of introducing the piece to American ears, a process complicated by the British naval blockade of Germany and their control of trans-Atlantic cable communication. Influential Cincinnatians working with their congressman and embassy officials in Berlin prevailed, and the Strauss score and parts arrived on April 4, allowing festival officials to announce a May 4 performance. The reigning euphoria was shattered by a late April announcement that Leopold Stokowski planned performances of the piece in Philadelphia on April 28 and 29. Outraged by what they considered a major impropriety on the part of their former darling-turned-nemesis, the Cincinnati crew retaliated with a trick of their own. Kunwald and the Cincinnati Symphony Orchestra managed to play through the piece in its entirety for the first time at a rehearsal on April 25. Two days later, an announcement appeared in the local papers inviting May Festival patrons to a performance of the Strauss that very noon. Despite the shortness of the notice, some two thousand people assembled to hear Kunwald conduct from memory a score he had seen for the first time only three weeks earlier. Stokowski had been vanquished by a margin of slightly more than twenty-four hours, but the board then faced the dilemma of justifying this preseason performance in light of their proscription against repeating works during a single festival. Their transparent rationale, issued in the *Enquirer* on April 28, was that "so many music-lovers requested an opportunity to hear the work twice."

After the United States entered World War I and Kunwald became a victim of anti-German hysteria,[21] Eugene Ysaÿe, his successor with the Cincinnati Symphony, took command of the next two festivals. The festival of 1918 was packed with patriotic symbolism, including "The Star-Spangled Banner" (not yet our official anthem) as a rousing curtain raiser and Alfred Hartzell, chorusmaster since 1908, in military uniform. The "homeless" Belgian violin virtuoso also conducted a first performance of his *Exile*, opus 25 (a "Poem for String Orchestra without Basses"), and had the orchestra stand during their playing of the *Marcia funèbre* of the Beethoven Third Symphony to honor the war dead. Friday evening saw another first performance: Edgar Stillman Kelley's "Musical Miracle Play," *The Pilgrim's Progress*. Kelley, a teacher of theory and composition on the Conservatory of Music faculty from 1911 to 1934, dedicated his opus 37 to the Charles P. Tafts. The week also included a Bach *St. Matthew Passion* (that began at 5:00 P.M. and was interrupted with two dinner intermissions) and concluded with another dose of humanism, Ermanno Wolf-Ferrari's *The New Life*, built on Dante's *La Vita nuova*, followed by the communal singing of "America." The festival's $2,500 profit was divided between the Red Cross and YMCA.

While the 1920 festival proved a financial success, there was considerable disappointment in a repertory that included numerous repeats from the orchestra's regular seasons, although it did introduce Igor Stravinsky to patrons through the orchestral suite from *The Firebird*. Furthermore, public dissatisfaction with a conductor never noted for his attention to detail surfaced and led to a rupture with the May Festival Chorus. According to a dispatch in the *Musical Courier*, Ysaÿe had been "in a fitful mood on several occasions during the festival and did not treat his assisting forces or the audience with all the consideration and courtesy due them." The chorus supposedly sent a petition to the board asserting that Ysaÿe had not allowed them sufficient rehearsal time, since he had been in New York giving recitals, and that, consequently, they would not consent to sing until he had been replaced. The chorus disbanded during the 1920–21 season, and the board postponed the next festival until 1923, ostensibly as a means of accurately marking the festival's first half century, a decision that gracefully allowed the turmoil to subside.

By November 1921 Frank Van der Stucken had been engaged to train the chorus, beginning in October of the following year. He was also to conduct the four evening concerts of the Golden Anniversary jubilee, while a guest, presumably the orchestra's musical director, would take charge of the pair of afternoon concerts. Van der Stucken, still beloved of the locals, became the center of attraction:

Mr. Van, as the chorus called him, looked older than his 60 years—a gold watch chain emphasized his generous girth, his bald dome had a halo of short gray curls, his blue eyes squinted a twinkle through his small, gold-rimmed glasses and even when he was angry he had a benevolent look about him.[22]

In a Music Hall graced with its "new" instrument by the Austin Organ Company, as well as updated wiring and plumbing, Van der Stucken introduced Henry Hadley's *Resurgam*, opus 98, written for the event, and presided over Cincinnatian Joseph Surdo's *In Flanders Fields*, as well as the fourth festival presentation of Mendelssohn's *Elijah*. Fritz Reiner, Ysaÿe's successor, electrified listeners with programs pairing Wagner excerpts with the Saint-Saëns's Symphony No. 3 (as a showcase for the organ) and the Beethoven "Eroica" Symphony with Richard Strauss's *Ein Heldenleben*.

While the Van der Stucken–Reiner partnership appeared satisfactory in 1923, an impasse developed over Reiner's future relationship to the festival, since the orchestra board obviously wanted their man to take control. Consequently, Van der Stucken individually commanded his sixth and seventh festivals, those of 1925 and 1927. The former added to festival annals the Bach *St. John Passion*, Pierné's oratorio *St. Francis of Assisi*, and the first performance in this country of *Young America*, a "Children's Cantata" by the Belgian Lodewijk Mortelmans (1868–1952). Edgar Stillman Kelley conducted his *The Pit and Pendulum*, a "Symphonic Suite after Poe," and Frederick Stock, his *Symphonic Variations*. Van der Stucken was the sole conductor of the 1927 event, including an all-Bach program, containing what was announced as the first American performance of *Cantata aug. Maglog Appeased*.

A rapprochement between the May Festival and orchestra boards was initiated soon thereafter, in part precipitated by Van der Stucken's declining health (he was to die in August 1929). Their newfound rapport was demonstrated in a triumphant November 18, 1928, performance of Gustav Mahler's Symphony No. 2, "The Resurrection," by the orchestra and May Festival Chorus, under what was described as Reiner's "generalship."

However, the geniality engendered by this collaboration did not extend to naming Reiner music director of the May Festival, since Frederick Stock (who had been associate director of the 1908, 1910, and 1912 festivals) was appointed. Stock enjoyed a relationship with Cincinnati sufficiently cordial that his silver anniversary with the Chicago Symphony was celebrated in part by bringing 250 members of the May Festival Chorus to Chicago by chartered train in 1930. But he reneged on his obligation to the 1931 festival and was replaced by Eugene Goossens, who, after some awkward negotiations, was relieved of his contract with the Rochester Philharmonic and succeeded Reiner as conductor of the Cincinnati Symphony Orchestra at the beginning of the 1931–32 season. He was to direct the next eight May Festivals during his sixteen years in the Queen City and electrified the community in 1931 by introducing them to coloratura soprano Lily Pons and Mahler's Symphony No. 8, the "Symphony of a Thousand." The opening concert featured the Brahms *Requiem,* presented in memory of Van der Stucken; during the intermission a bronze portrait plaque of the beloved maestro by Clement J. Barnhorn was unveiled and dedicated in the Music Hall foyer.

Despite financial difficulties during the 1930s, the festival managed to field a formidable array of noted soloists, including Ezio Pinza in 1933. A diet of familiar literature was spiced with novelties like first performances of Cincinnatian Martin G. Dumler's *Stabat Mater* and the American premières of Granville Bantock's *Atlanta in Calydon* (a "Symphony for Chorus" of 1911) and Cyril Scott's *La belle dame sans mercie* (1916) in 1935, African American R. Nathaniel Dett's *The Ordering of Moses* ("A Biblical Folk Scene") in 1937, and, two years later, the first performance of *Watchman, What of the Night?* an oratorio by James G. Heller, a local rabbi.[23] Goossens's own one-act opera, *Judith,* opus 46, was heard in 1937.

The onslaught of World War II led to a three-year hiatus before the 1944 festival, abridged to three concerts and a slender printed program occasioned by the shortage of paper. Haydn's *The Seasons* (last heard at the 1918 festival) was preceded by both "The Star-Spangled Banner" and "Hallelujah" Chorus. The second concert was truly novel: Frank Loesser's "The WAC Hymn," a recruiting song whose performance included a fifty-member WAC chorus from Fort Campbell in Kentucky, preceded a first performance of *The Passion,* an oratorio by Bernard Rogers of the Eastman School of Music. This mini-festival concluded with Ernest Bloch's "Epic Rhapsody," *America.* What was dubbed the "Victory Festival" of 1946 included the Roy Harris "Folksong" Symphony No. 4, with five hundred high school students in costumes divided into broad swaths of red, white, and blue, as well as the first performance of Martin Dumler's *Te Deum* and the American première of Frederick Delius's *A Mass of Life.* A special tribute was paid to Alfred Hartzell, who had recently died after serving as chorusmaster for thirty-seven years.

After Goossens's departure for Australia, the festival board turned again to an outsider, German-born Fritz Busch (1890–1951), who had left Nazi Germany in 1933 and during the 1940s conducted opera both in South America and at the Metropolitan Opera in New York. Perhaps his most notable additions to the festival repertory were Prokofiev's *Alexander Nevsky* and Benjamin Britten's "Spring" Symphony of 1949, both in 1950. That same year much of the festival was recorded by the Voice of America for broadcast and subsequent distribution to embassies and consulates across the world.

Busch's death in September 1951 forced the board to appoint three guest conductors for the 1952 festival: Austrian-born Fritz Stiedry (1883–1968), then at the Metropolitan Opera; French-born Jean Morel (1903–75), then at the New York City Center Opera; and American-born Thor Johnson, incumbent conductor of the Cincinnati Symphony Orchestra. Morel introduced Arthur Honegger's *Joan of Arc at the Stake* to the festival tradition, with Vera Zorina as the narrator in a special setting designed by Philip R. Adams, director of the Cincinnati Art Museum.

As a permanent successor to Busch the board chose yet another outsider, Austrian-born Josef Krips (1902–74), who had just been appointed conductor of the Buffalo Philharmonic. Krips, however, made frequent use of Thor Johnson as a "guest conductor" of his own orchestra. This duo leavened the traditional repertory of their four festivals with a fair number of novelties: the American premières of *The Book with Seven Seals*, an oratorio by Austrian Franz Schmidt in 1954, whose first performance Krips had conducted in Vienna back in 1938; *Images of Youth*, a cantata by Cincinnatian Feliks Labunski, Britten's *Glorianna*, *Voices of the Night*, opus 27, a cantata by Franz Reizenstein, a German-born Englishman, and the first performance of Wallace Berry's *Spoon River Anthology*, featuring soprano Leontyne Price and her then-husband, baritone William Warfield, all in 1956; and Cincinnatian Jenö Takacs's *The Chant of Creation*, as well as Ogden Nash narrating Saint-Saëns's *Carnival of the Animals* in 1958.

The 1960 event added Lukas Foss's *Parable of Death* to the festival repertory with Felicia Montealegre, Leonard Bernstein's wife, as narrator; Basil Rathbone served in the same capacity with Arthur Honegger's *King David*. The use of Nash and the Saint-Saëns two years earlier reflected an attempt to combat the dwindling audiences of the Krips era with more easily digestible edibles. Krips apparently quibbled about including the *Carnival* but drew the line in 1960 at personal involvement with the *Queen City Suite*, a forty-five-minute work for children's chorus, narrator, and solo baritone, written by a relative of a board member, Margaret Johnson Bosworth, a popular radio and nightclub entertainer known professionally as Corky Robbins. Critics decried the suite's Broadway pop idioms, and one was outraged that cuts had to be made in the Berlioz *Requiem* to accommodate its presentation.

Drastic reorganization of the board ensued, which led to a three-year interval before the next festival. Max Rudolf, conductor of the Cincinnati Symphony, was engaged as music director, and he persuaded Leopold Stokowski to return as a guest for the first time in a half century in the city he had left in such a considerable dudgeon. The most notable musical event of their 1963 festival was the first performance of Gian Carlo Menotti's "Dramatic Cantata," *The Death of the Bishop of Brindisi*. That same May the festival structure was changed to two pairs of performances on consecutive weekends.

Two years later Rudolf was preoccupied with an upcoming around-the-world tour by the orchestra, so the board appointed as guest conductors Stanislaw Skrowaczewski of the Minneapolis Symphony and Robert Shaw, then associate conductor of the Cleveland Orchestra. Skrowaczewski was in charge of a first performance of *The Song of Terezin* by Franz Waxman (1906–67), a German American better known for his film scores, while Shaw led the festival's first presentation of an antiwar statement of an entirely different stripe, Britten's *War Requiem.*

Beginning in 1967 the festival became an annual event. Max Rudolf directed those of 1967 to 1970, albeit with the support of guests like George Szell and Eugene Ormandy, as well as Robert Shaw, who became a regular with thirteen stints over the next three decades. Julius Rudel, noted for his tenure at the helm of the New York City Opera, succeeded Rudolf for the festivals of 1971 and 1972; that first year brought to town both the Joffrey Ballet and his own company's production of Handel's *Julius Caesar,* starring Beverly Sills and Norman Treigle. For the centenary celebration, Leonard Bernstein was dubbed Honorary Music Director, assisted by Shaw and James Levine, the Cincinnati boy who had made his Metropolitan Opera pit début in 1971 and was named the company's principal conductor during 1973. Levine became music director the following year and was succeeded in 1979 by James Conlon, another American, who had made his reputation in Rotterdam (the Philharmonic), Cologne (as general music director of the city and chief conductor of the opera), and as of 1996, Paris (music director of the opera).

While recycling festival standards like the Beethoven Ninth Symphony and *Missa Solemnis,* laced with heavy doses of Wagner, the festival has continued to challenge its patrons with new ideas: a first performance of Hans Werner Henze's *Moralities* in 1968; a first performance of Peter Mennin's "Cantata de Virtute," *The Pied Piper of Hamelin* the following year; a first performance of Wilfred Josephs's *Mortales,* opus 62, in 1970; the Bernstein *Mass* in 1972. (This controversial "Theatre Piece for Singers, Players, and Dancers" is another rare example of a staged work at the festival, although the Pennsylvania Ballet had been imported for a dramatic representation of Carl Orff's *Carmina Burana.*) Krzysztof Penderecki's *The Passion and Death of Our Lord Jesus Christ According to Luke* initiated the centenary celebration in 1973; Ohio-born Donald Erb's *New England's Prospect* received its first hearing in 1974; Scott Joplin's opera, *Treemonisha,* was presented in concert form in 1988 in a performance conducted by Gunther Schuller; and the tradition of May Festival commissions was continued with Alvin Singleton's *PraiseMaker* (marking the festival's 125th anniversary), David Brewbaker's *Cincinnatus Psalm* in 2000, and Paulus's *All Things Are Passing* in 2004.

William N. Hobart, who became president of the May Festival Association in 1884, asserted, "We are reasonably safe in being able to retain the Festival as a permanent institution of the city, if we take no steps backward or downward."[24] More than a century and a quarter after its founding Mr. Hobart's aspirations for the country's oldest continuing choral festival seem to have been realized in full. The May Festival Chorus has become a year-round operation with its own Carolfest concerts in December, as well as frequent appearances with the symphony during the regular season, both in Cincinnati and occasionally in New York. Yet the core of its responsibility remains with its namesake festival. As the 1886 program book claimed,

Great soloists and a great orchestra can always be commanded, though only a great occasion can make their engagement possible, by bringing together great audiences and as a result, great sums of money. A great chorus, however, is the result of much unselfish labor on the part of hundreds of individuals.

Sylvia Kleve Sheblessy, in her 1973 overview of the festival, concluded with an observation that seems an apt assessment: "In music, as in life, styles change; new works are produced and old ones forgotten; but an institution that is a part of the life of the people, if it deserves to survive, may aspire to perpetuity."[25]

CHAPTER 20

Baldwin-Wallace College
Bach Festival

The Baldwin-Wallace College Bach Festival owes its origins to Albert Riemenschneider (1878–1950), distinguished organist, conductor, teacher, editor, and bibliophile.[1]

Riemenschneider was born on the campus of what was then known as German Wallace College to a professor of ancient languages, who was soon to be named the college's vice president and then president. Riemenschneider studied piano and theory with James H. Rogers in Cleveland, and at age nineteen, as a senior pursuing a B.A. degree, was asked (without the knowledge or connivance of his father) to head and reorganize the college's department of music. Having done so, he spent the 1902–03 academic year studying in Vienna and then resumed his responsibilities in Berea for a year. After marrying Selma Marting, daughter of the college treasurer, in July 1904, the newlyweds sailed for Paris, where the groom studied organ with Alexandre Guilmant and theory with Charles-Marie Widor, while the bride, a singer, coached with Mathilde Marchesi. Although he was later to make other trips abroad to study, particularly with Widor (whom he often assisted or substituted for at the great organ in the church of St. Sulpice and who was, with Albert Schweitzer, to coedit five volumes of the organ works of Bach between 1912 and 1914), Riemenschneider concentrated his attention on what became Baldwin-Wallace College in 1913, when German Wallace merged with Baldwin University. At first he taught organ, piano, and theory (and also maintained a private piano studio in downtown Cleveland for many years) but gradually was forced to restrict himself to the organ and administration. He also served three different Cleveland churches as organist and music director between 1911 and 1930. Active as an organ recitalist, both in Berea and elsewhere, including a series of twenty programs in 1927 devoted to all the known works of Bach, he meticulously edited several of the important Bach organ anthologies (the *Orgelbüchlein* [that he called *The Liturgical Year*], the

Six Organ Chorales [*Schübler*], the Eighteen Large Chorales, and the *Clavierübung,* Part III) as well as a volume of *371 Harmonized Chorales* and *69 Chorale Melodies with Figured Bass,* seminal publications in their time. He retired from teaching and administration in 1947 but briefly served as B-W's acting president in 1948. Two years later, having planned for retirement in California, Riemenschneider died just weeks short of his seventy-second birthday.

During multiple visits to Europe, he began to collect manuscripts and rare editions, most of them by or related to Bach. Edwin Riemenschneider reminisced in 1979 about his father's methodology of buying at auctions or from booksellers during the 1920s and 1930s, a propitious time for a collector, since many European owners had become impoverished and were forced to sell items that had not been on the market for years. "At the end of each trip, a series of specially made valises would always be delivered to the hotel room," filled with what became a personal collection of over twenty-five hundred volumes, about a tenth of those extremely rare.[2] These included original imprints of five of the handful of Bach's own publications (the *Clavierübung,* Part I, the "Goldberg" Variations, *The Musical Offering, Canonic Variations on "Vom Himmel hoch,"* and *The Art of Fugue*), as well as novelties like a manuscript copy of *The Well-Tempered Klavier* made in 1725 by Heinrich Nicholaus Gerber, a student of the Leipzig master.

The collection was willed to Baldwin-Wallace, partially cataloged, and then stored in the college library, available only by appointment. In 1960 Baldwin-Wallace was the recipient of a collection of rare music scores amassed by Mrs. George Martin, including a first edition of Brahms's *Ein deutsches Requiem* with generous conductor's annotations in the composer's own hand, Beethoven's own orchestral parts for his first piano concerto, and first editions owned and signed by Schumann, Richard Strauss, Wagner, Franck, Debussy, and Massenet. This too joined the Riemenschneider trove in secure seclusion. In 1968 Julius Herford of Indiana University, Harold Spivacke of the Library of Congress, and Elinore Barber, then of Hastings College in Nebraska, were assembled and asked to determine how better to dispose of the Riemenschneider collection. The result was the Riemenschneider Bach Institute, which opened for business in the fall of 1969 with Dr. Barber as its director. In April of the following year the college purchased the library of the late Hans T. David, an eminent German-born musicologist who had been Dr. Barber's major professor at the University of Michigan. It contained over nineteen hundred volumes, including rare imprints of works by Corelli, Handel, Haydn, and John Gay (*The Beggar's Opera*), plus important eighteenth-century treatises on both theory and performance. The cumulative result is a collection that has come to number more than nine thousand items, of which more than eight hundred are considered rarities, and that is an important destination for scholars and students of seventeenth- and eighteenth-century music.

In January 1970 the institute initiated publication of its elegant quarterly, *Bach*. Widely circulated, it contains scholarly articles and announcements germane to anybody involved with Johann Sebastian Bach or the music of his period. In 1985 and 1986, the institute issued two volumes of profusely annotated facsimiles of its most important Bach manuscripts; it has also sponsored lectures and symposia that have added to our knowledge of the period.

A handsome legacy indeed, but Albert Riemenschneider also bequeathed Berea and the world the annual Bach Festival, which he founded in 1933. Enamored of the venerable Bethlehem (Pennsylvania) Bach Festival, which dates from 1898, and the work of its founding conductor, J. Frederick Wolle, Riemenschneider determined to share his knowledge of and affection for Bach with residents of the greater Cleveland area. The resulting annual event has since then presented well over 450 of the master's works.[3]

Several of the founder's prescriptions have remained fairly constant to the present. In 1934 he decided that a compact, two-day event with four (sometimes five) principal concerts would be optimal and that Bach's major choral masterpieces ought to be presented in a four-year cycle, so that every undergraduate could enjoy a chance to perform or hear the two Passions, the *Mass in B Minor,* and the *Christmas Oratorio.* In addition, the festival forces have performed all the motets; eighty-eight of the cantatas; the *Magnificat in D Major* and *Easter Oratorio; The Art of Fugue;* the four orchestral overtures; the "Brandenburg" Concerti and many of the concerti for harpsichord, violin, and other instruments; multiple sonatas, partitas, and suites; and a major chunk of the organ literature. But the festival's focus has not remained exclusively on Bach, for its patrons have heard a variety of music by some seventy other composers, including members of the Bach clan, as well as Vivaldi, Scarlatti, Buxtehude, Handel, Telemann, and others, primarily from the eighteenth century.

Regulars have also enjoyed contact with a distinguished roster of performers, many of them local or regional, and others whose names do not resonate today but include singers Adele Addison, Betty Allen, Arlene Auger, Ara Berberian, Helen Boatwright, Phyllis Bryn-Julson, Lili Chookasian, Jan DeGaetani, Jon Humphrey, Lois Marshall, John McCollum, and Seth McCoy; as instrumentalists, lutenist Suzanne Bloch, recorder virtuoso Frans Brueggen, harpsichordists John Challis, Ralph Kirkpatrick, and Rafael Puyana, pianists Arthur Loesser and Rosalyn Tureck, organists Heinrich Fleischer, Peter Hurford, Robert Noehren, Arthur Poister, and Carl Weinrich, violinist Sergiu Luca, violist Paul Doktor, flutist Paula Robison; and as lecturers Olin Downs, Hans T. David, Karl Geiringer, Julius Herford, Paul Hume, Paul Henry Lang, Arthur Mendel, William H. Scheide, and Christoph Wolff.

Various choruses have served as the backbone of the festival—the Festival Choir, the College Choir, the Motet Choir—some of them all-student, some mixtures of town and college. In recent seasons, in addition to the ad hoc festival orchestra, the festival has employed the Ohio Chamber Orchestra, a professional ensemble based in Cleveland (whose founding music director was Dwight Oltman, now the group's laureate conductor), and the Cleveland San Jose Ballet Orchestra. Riemenschneider served as music director until 1948; he was succeeded by George Poinar and in 1975 by Professor Oltman.

A couple of other idiosyncrasies of the tradition bear noting. Riemenschneider from the very beginning funded his festival by inviting the participation of guarantors, whose contributions awarded them seats at the festival concerts, but whose generosity in turn allowed free admission to students and others. The 1933 Berea Bach Festival was underwritten with three $100 gifts, but in 1934 a larger club of guarantors was asked to contribute $10 each. By 1957 the tab had risen to $15 and then to $25 in 1961. Naturally, inflation has intruded so that the fee had doubled to $50 by 1996, with two people admitted at the bargain rate of $90.

One other constant has been the use of Bach chorale harmonizations played by a brass choir prior to each concert, usually from atop the Marting Hall Tower. Audiences have at times been invited to join in the singing of the chorales embedded in the cantatas and passions, replicating the role of the congregation in Bach's time.

However, certain of the founder's ideas have been modified. His festival chorus soon blossomed to about one hundred voices, and his orchestras ballooned from forty to seventy-five; the choral works were usually sung in English. Dwight Oltman's advent as music director led to a greater concern for purer performance practices with reduced performing forces, and the vocal pieces are now presented in their original languages.

Albert Riemenschneider in the 1933 program booklet quoted Robert Schumann as claiming, "To Bach music owes almost as great a debt as a religion owes to its founder." Riemenschneider certainly subscribed fully to that credo throughout his long and fruitful career, and countless lives have been enriched by the various outcomes of his proselytizing.[4]

Part Four

Religious Music
and
Singing Societies

CHAPTER 21

Protestant and Jewish Hymnals

Despite its title, Thomas S. Hinde's *The Pilgrim's Songster, or, A Choice Collection of Spiritual Songs, from the Best Authors, with Original Pieces, Never before in Print* contains words only. His preface addressed "To the friends and pilgrims of Zion" describes his sources: John Wesley's collection, John Newton's collection ("composed by himself and Mr. *William Cowper,* called 'Olney Hymns'"), poems by William Cowper and Hannah Moore, collections from Baltimore, Philadelphia, and New York, as well as the

> excellent collection of Mr. *Stith Meade.* of Virginia—and the original printed selections of our two western bards, Mr. *John A. Granade.* and Mr. *Caleb J. Taylor.* These two poets composed their songs during the great revivals of religion in the states of Kentucky and Tennessee about the years 1802, 3 and 4. They appear to have been written in the midst of the Holy Flame—and have since been printed and published all over the continent, and are to be found in some form or other almost in every collection of songs of every order, till at length they are now so *garbled* that they scarcely bear any resemblance to the original. The peculiar turn of these two interesting poets, the former of whom has gone to receive his reward, the latter nearly ripe for it, is very particularly adapted to the minds of dispositions of the western people. Their language is that of the church in the wilderness, flourishing and triumphant—bursting through heathen darkness and the power and dominion of sin, to behold the full blaze of Gospel day![1]

Hinde then mentions borrowings from "Mr. T," other unnamed manuscripts, and his own collection, which had been published in 1810. Many of the 114 hymns are subtitled, and those whose authorship can be identified include an author's initials or an asterisk designating anonymity, while other writers, like Dr. Watts, are named. In only a few instances is a tune suggested.

Some hymnals were generated by or for specific denominations, for example, *The Christians' Duty; Exhibited in a Series of Hymns, Collected from Various Authors, Designed for the Worship of God, and for the Edification of Christians. Recommended to the Serious of All Denominations. By the Fraternity of Baptists.* A fourth, "improved" edition of this volume was issued in Canton in 1822 by Jacob and Solomon Sala, although its May 18, 1791, preface had been written in Germantown, Pennsylvania. Demonstrating Ohio's polyglot culture, Jacob Sala und Sohn the year before had issued both *Das kleine Lust-Gärtlein, oder schöne auslesener Gebeter und Lieder, zum Gebrauch der Jugend, sowohl in der Schule als zu Hause (The Little Pleasure Garden, or Beautiful Selected Prayers and Songs for the Use of the Youth, Both in the School and at Home)* and a first edition of *Das neu-eingerichtet Evangelisch-Lutherische Gesangbuch, bestehend aus eine Sammlung Lider, zum Gebrauch des offentlichen Deutschen Gotteseligten, in dem Staat von Ohio, and den angrenzenden Staaten (The New Official Evangelical Lutheran Hymnal, Consisting of a Collection of Songs, for the Use of the German Parishes in the State of Ohio and Adjacent States).* Ohio's German communities generated other collections, such as *Herzens Opfer, eine Sammlung geistreicher Lider aus den mehrsten jetzt üblichen Gesangbücher gesamelt; zum öffentlich und privat Gebrauch für Liebhaber des göttlichen Lebens (Offering of the Heart, a Collection of Spiritually Rich Songs Assembled from Many Practical Songbooks; for Public and Private Use by Lovers of the Godly Life),* copyrighted in 1815 and published the following year by Eduard Schäffer in Lancaster for the United Brethren in Christ.

Joseph Muenscher's *The Church Choir: A Collection of Sacred Music: Comprising a Great Variety of Psalm and Hymn Tunes, Anthems, and Chants* (Columbus: I. N. Whiting, 1839; Boston: Oliver Ditson, 1851) was a denominational collection of a different sort. Muenscher (1798–1884), a Rhode Island native, had graduated from Brown University and served several parishes in Massachusetts and Maine before being appointed "Professor of Biblical Literature in the Theological Seminary of the P[rotestant] E[piscopal] Church, Gambier, Ohio," in 1833. He resigned that position in 1841 to become rector of St. Paul Protestant Episcopal Church in nearby Mount Vernon, although he continued to teach Hebrew in Gambier for two more years. Kenyon College conferred an honorary doctorate on Muenscher in 1849, as did his alma mater three years later. He retired from St. Paul's in 1855 (having presided over the installation of an organ in 1842) and "remained without any particular charge" for the rest of his life, during which he issued several tomes more reflective of his profession (the *Manual of Biblical Interpretation,* self-published from Gambier in 1865; *The Book of Proverbs in an Amended Version,* printed at the Western Episcopalian Office in Gambier a year later; and *An Introduction to the Orthography and Pronunciation of the English Language,* published for the author by Bosworth,

Chase, and Hall of Mount Vernon in 1870). His musical anthology was surely intended to serve multiple purposes and might be more properly considered a didactic work, since it was issued in the familiar oblong shape and opens with a section detailing the "Rudiments of Vocal Music," beginning with rhythm and concluding with solmization, admitting the prevalence of the four-syllable system but advocating the "Italian method" with its seven syllables. Muenscher's editorial preface stated that it was "his aim to furnish our Churches with as great a variety of tunes, composed in different styles, and adapted to the various occasions of public worship, as the limits of the work would permit." While the literature is mainline, meant to be "sufficiently copious for all the ordinary purposes of public and social worship," the notation has a peculiar twist to it. Often tenor and alto lines during this period were printed above those of soprano and bass, suggesting that a keyboardist could thus more easily play the top and bottom parts, filling in the inner parts with the aid of numerals indicating the implicit harmonies or simply furnishing them by instinct. This editor, however, must have found his fellow "Episcopalians of the West" a bit deficient, since,

> Instead of a figured base [sic], the music has all been carefully arranged for the Organ or Piano-Forte, from the conviction that many performers on those instruments have not had the opportunity to perfect themselves sufficiently in the science of music, to play the harmony with facility, even of plain psalmody, from figures.[2]

Consequently, sopranos and basses were left to ferret out their pitches from the keyboard score, and the words were printed only between its top staff and the alto part, a seemingly confusing arrangement.

Hymnals were issued from virtually everywhere, for example, Barzillai H. Miles's *The New Christian Hymn-Book*, designed for "the use of the Church of Christ" and published for the author by A. G. Brown of Athens in 1827, or *The Christian Hymn-Book*, compiled by Matthew Gardner, an elder in the Church of Christ, its eighth edition "corrected and enlarged," published by D. Ammen in the Brown County community of Georgetown in 1829, or John Secrest's *A Selection of Psalms, Hymns, and Spiritual Songs, Carefully Examined and Improved*, published in St. Clairsville by Horton J. Howard in 1832. Naturally, many similar volumes were issued from Cincinnati, for instance, *The Sunday Scholar's Companion*, printed for the Wesleyan Sunday School Society of Cincinnati by Looker, Palmer, and Reynolds in 1821, or *Hymns for the Use of the New Church, Signified by the New Jerusalem in the Apocalypse* (Looker and Reynolds, 1826).[3]

The fifth edition of *Die Kleine Lieder-Sammlung, oder Auszug aus dem Psalterspiel der Kinder Zion's (The Little Collection of Songs, or Selection from the Psalter of the Children of*

Zion)[4] was printed by Heinrich Kurtz (1796–1874)[5] in the Stark County village of Osnaburg in 1835. German-born Kurtz had emigrated in 1817 and served as a Lutheran pastor in rural Northampton County, Pennsylvania, and Pittsburgh from 1819 until 1826, when he resigned after generating dissent in his Pittsburgh congregation by fervently advocating the establishment of a Christian communal settlement based on the second chapter of Acts. Kurtz had described this "German Christian Industrial-Community" (later, simply "Concordia") in August 1825 and in September began to publish a monthly magazine called *Das Widergefundene Paradies (Paradise Regained)*. By early autumn 1826, meetings in Greensburg, Pennsylvania, and Springfield, Ohio, led to the pledging of some capital, the discovery that some thirty families were ready to enter Concordia, and the decision to locate the community on the Tuscarawas River near New Philadelphia. All of this coincided with the rupture in Pittsburgh, and by January 1827 Kurtz had moved to Stark County, where he published *Der Friedensbote von Concordia (The Peace Messenger from Concordia)*. However, the community remained a dream, and by April 1828 Kurtz had renounced Lutheranism and was baptized anew by an elder of the German Baptist Brethren (now the Church of the Brethren). Two years later he was elected a "free minister" of the Brethren (salaried pastors did not become a Brethren practice until many decades later) and in 1841 took charge of the Mill Creek Church in Mahoning County, where he was to serve for three decades. In 1842 he moved his family to a farm near Poland, so as to avoid a forty-mile horseback ride to his responsibilities, and two years later was ordained an elder, the highest church office in the Brethren structure.

Kurtz published extensively: a primer for young students, theological works, Martin Luther's translation of the New Testament, a medical guide, bilingual minutes of the yearly Brethren meetings, and beginning in 1851, *The Gospel Visitor*, a denominational journal that is still being issued. However, his first publication was *Die Kleine Lieder-Sammlung (The Little Song Collection)*, a pocket-sized collection of 169 hymn texts, each with an inferred melody specified by name. First printed in Hagerstown, Maryland, in 1826, it was issued three years later by Solomon Sala in Canton. Later editions (there were at least eight), such as the one mentioned earlier, were printed by Kurtz himself after he secured his own press. In 1830 he published from Osnaburg, *A Choice Selection of Hymns, from Various Authors, Recommended for the Worship of God*, a volume that eventually contained 293 hymn texts, delineated only by generic titles and poetic meter. It became the hymnal of choice for Brethren congregations in the Midwest and went through at least seven printings, the last in 1844 when an "enlarged" edition was issued from "Summer's Place, near Poland, Trumbull County, Ohio."

As his publishing ventures became more extensive, Kurtz found Poland inconveniently isolated and moved to the town of Columbiana in 1857. His last undertaking was as chair of a committee charged with compiling yet another Brethren hymnal, the *Neue Sammlung von Psalmen, Lobgesangen und Geistliche Lieder (A New Collection of Psalms, Songs of Praise and Spiritual Songs)* with 303 texts (still without tunes), published by James Quinter of Covington (near Piqua) during 1870.[6]

While the Brethren sang hymns, they were leery of instrumental music and proscribed its use in church. It is strange, then, that such a prominent figure in the denomination owned a modest three-rank organ that had been built in 1698 by Johan [*sic*] Christoph Harttman of Nürtingen, a village near Stuttgart. This lapsed Lutheran carried the instrument with him during his westward migration and employed it in the privacy of his home. A former printer's apprentice recalled an encounter in Columbiana:

> Brother Kurtz was quite a musician, vocal and instrumental, and had an organ in the house, but rarely used it. I shall long remember one occasion on which I heard him perform and sing one of his favorites. I went to the house, where the editorial sanctum was, on business connected with the office. After entering the hall, I heard music, and finding the door ajar, I stopped and listened till the hymn was completed, much delighted with the strains. When I complimented him on his success, he explained that he had been tired of reading and writing, and had sought recreation and solace in the music.[7]

Even more exotic than these various Christian hymnals are two collections by Gustave M. Cohen (1820–1902): *The Sacred Harp of Judah: A Choice of Collection of Music for the Use of Synagogues, Schools, and Home. Part I. Sabbath Liturgy* (1864) and *The Orpheus, or Musical Recreations, for the Family Circle and Public Worship* (1878) German-born Cohen, perhaps the first trained Jewish cantor to work in this country, emigrated in 1844 and was appointed chazan (cantor) of Temple Emanu-El in New York, where he organized that congregation's first choir and introduced organ music into the services. In 1856 he moved to Chicago and then to Cincinnati before arriving in Cleveland during May 1861. An Israelitic Society had been formed there in 1839, and a secessionist group of thirty Orthodox German Jews had organized the Anshe Chesed Society (now the Fairmount Temple) in 1842. The two merged on May 15, 1846, and dedicated Cleveland's first synagogue on August 7. A rabbi was hired in 1850, but after just a few months he departed with a group of dissidents to found the Tifereth Israel Congregation, a group that met in private homes until completion of its temple in 1855.

On his arrival, Cohen became cantor and spiritual leader of Anshe Chesed and also organized the Zion Musical Society. The Anshe Chesed congregation had careened back and forth between rigid orthodoxy and the modern reform movement. An orthodox rabbi had been hired in April 1860, but only months later plans were announced to enlarge the Eagle Street building to include an organ and space for a choir. The organ was actually to have been installed during December, but in November the rabbi stormed out, to be replaced by Cohen as spiritual leader the following spring. By 1863 both choir and organ were in use, and mixed-gender seating had been introduced. Tension between the opposing factions surfaced again two years later, when a group of liberal Anshe Chesed members petitioned Tifereth Israel for membership, with the caveat that Cohen be hired as cantor. Initially rebuffed, the offer was accepted in 1866, but Cohen was associated with the Tifereth Israel congregation for less than a year, since its core members wanted a true rabbi as their spiritual leader. Cohen then briefly served a congregation in Milwaukee but soon returned to Anshe Chesed, where he worked until 1873 when again he was replaced by a rabbi. Thereafter he enjoyed a multifaceted career as a music teacher, grocer, bailiff, and insurance agent.[8]

The Sacred Harp of Judah was one of the first collections of Jewish music published in this country.[9] Depicted on its cover as "The Result of 25 Years' Experience and Gleanings," Cohen promised two subsequent volumes, should "this Part meet with a favorable reception," a goal apparently never accomplished. In his preface Cohen remarked that after he pioneered the use of a choir in New York more than two decades earlier, they now existed "almost, as a necessary auxiliary to worship, in every Synagogue of our principle [*sic*] cities of this country." However, Cohen's goal was to allow the involvement of the congregation in worship, since,

> They listen to the Choir as they would to the feat of concert singers. The *ear* alone is tickled, but the deep recess of the heart is left dormant. It needs something to arouse their *hearts* and lift them on high, as by the finger of God. The glorious gift of music is confined to the Choir alone, and the Congregation is obliged to remain *silent* during the service. They catch the inspiration in a degree, but the glowing rapture of the soul is chained by the dread silence . . . In such [a] service, order and decorum is observed, but devoid of true devotion.[10]

He asserted that the music available to the synagogue musician at the time was

> too complicated, and designed only for well drilled Choirs and competent Solo Singers. Besides this, such works are too expensive for general use, and the fact of their being copied by hand, necessarily makes them too expensive to be brought *into general use*.[11]

His intent was to provide responses for the congregation, thus allowing their active participation in the principal prayers and liturgical songs, which he did for much of the volume, with "recitatives" for the "minister," unison responses for the congregation, and four-part settings for the choir (sometimes joined by the congregation). The language is mostly Hebrew (spelled phonetically according to the Ashkenazi pronunciation), although two pieces are in German, and the collection includes an elaborate duet and a solo setting of Psalm 150, both in English.

Cohen's announced goal of additionally providing music for school and home devotion was reflected in a succinct, totally traditional, didactic section inculcating the "Elements of Vocal Music," complete with several pages of exercises. After all,

> Parents are delighted to hear their children sing and execute Waltzes, Polkas, and Marches on the Piano. But how would their hearts glow with rapture, as the holy Sabbath-day approaches, to hear them sing the songs of ancient Hebrew lore, as composed by the fondly remembered bard of Israel?[12]

Cohen's bard was surely King David, but he attributed nothing in the volume, making it impossible to understand how many of the thirty-four entries were gleaned from borrowed sources and how much of the outcome, if any, was original with Cohen. Perhaps at least some of the melodies were appropriated from the repertory Cohen would have assimilated in Germany; whatever their source, they were then supported by the conventional harmonic garb of the day.

He presented himself on its title page as the sole composer of the forty-nine works contained in *The Orpheus*, although he qualified that claim by marking with two asterisks his own compositions; furthermore, several of the melodies were labeled as "traditionelle" [sic] and several pieces were attributed to Halévy, Naumburg, Salomon Sulzer (1804–90), and Edward Weber. Sulzer may have provided Cohen a model, since, as cantor of the main synagogue in Vienna from 1826 until 1881, he attempted to wed traditional Jewish cantillation with mainline western European musical idioms, even borrowing actual compositions from the giants of the Viennese classical tradition, such as Schubert. His anthology, *Schir Zion (The Heart of Zion)*, first appeared in 1839. *The Orpheus* contains everything from solos and duets to fairly substantial anthem-sized pieces involving interplay between soloists and chorus, often with the support of piano or organ. A few of the texts are in German, but English predominates, even in a series of confirmation songs and in works such as a "Hannucca-Hymn" [sic]. In his preface Cohen admitted to borrowing English texts from collections such as the *Hymns of the Congregation Beth Elohim* and mentioned that "I have added Psalms of most prominent composers of Hebrew melodies, and have given them the English translation, which has never before been accomplished, and for the first time becomes the property of the musical world at large." Perhaps Cohen betrayed his level of competence by acknowledging "Prof. L. Shehlman, a modest but thorough musician, to whom I am indebted for his kind assistance in harmonizing a number of pieces for this work." [13] It should be noted that Cohen's

"Musical Recreations" initiate the collection. "Song should stir the heart within us Like a patriot[']s friendly blow" is followed by "On the swinging branches Of the apple tree, Bobolink is sitting, Peeping down at me" and others in a similar vein.[14]

CHAPTER 22

The Mormons

Members of the Church of Jesus Christ of Latter-day Saints, or Mormons, established their headquarters in Kirtland, Ohio, between 1831 and 1838, a sojourn during their extended migration from upstate New York to a final sanctuary in Utah. Mormon missionaries began proselytizing the Western Reserve soon after Joseph Smith Jr. founded his church in April 1830, and their success, plus the absence of persecution of these new converts, convinced Smith to move his flock. Soon after their arrival in early 1831, plans were made for construction of a temple to symbolize their escalating presence (as many as 1,500 members in fifteen congregations by the end of that year, perhaps a peak of around 3,200 before the westward move was continued). Actual construction of the imposing edifice began only in 1833, and the building was finally dedicated in 1836, not long before dissension and economic woes led to the departure of Smith and most of the Mormons in 1838.[1]

During that period the first Mormon hymnal was published in Kirtland. The founder's wife, Emma, "selected" *A Collection of Sacred Hymns, for the Church of the Latter Day Saints,* printed by F. G. Williams and Company in 1835. Mrs. Smith's preface to her pocket-sized collection of ninety hymn texts stated that the collection was created so that the Mormons could "sing by the Spirit" hymns

> adapted to their faith and belief in the gospel.... Notwithstanding the church, as it were, is still in its infancy, yet, as the song of the righteous is a prayer unto God, it is sincerely hoped that the following collection, selected with an eye single to his glory, may answer every purpose till more are composed, or till we are blessed with a copious variety of the songs of Zion.[2]

The tiny volume contains no suggestions of the tunes to which the hymns were to be sung, although it is easy to infer the melodies appropriate to familiar texts, beginning

"From Greenland's Icy Mountains," "Joy to the World!" or "O God, Our Help in Ages Past." There is a high degree of correlation between Mrs. Smith's hymns and those represented in another early Mormon hymnal, *A Collection of Sacred Hymns, for the Use of the Latter Day Saints,* "selected and published by J. C. Little and G. B. Gardner" from Bellows Falls, Vermont, in 1844 (and reissued in facsimile by the Mason County History Project of Havana, Illinois, in 1990). This slender volume contains forty-eight hymns, thirty-one of them furnished with music in two parts— the melody and a supporting bass line. At least a few of these mate the text and tune that might be expected today (for example, Oliver Holden's "Coronation" with "All Hail the Pow'r of Jesus' Name" and Lowell Mason's "Missionary Hymn" with "From Greenland's Icy Mountains"), although the compiler presented no attributions of either writers or composers.

However, the March 27, 1836, service of dedication of the Kirtland Temple fills in a few of the blanks.[3] The Sunday program began at 9:00 A.M. and lasted until about 4:00 P.M. (broken only by a single twenty-minute intermission), witnessed by a crowd estimated at one thousand in a space that could nominally contain half that number, with others turned away and promised a repeat ceremony the following week. It contained scripture readings, prayers, an address by Smith, communion, testimonies, and six hymns. All but one of these can be found in Mrs. Smith's collection. The words of one were by Isaac Watts, another by Parley Parker Pratt, one of the four missionaries who had pioneered Mormonism in Ohio, the other four by W. W. Phelps, editor of the local church newspaper, the *Messenger and Advocate.* Phelps also contributed one of the tunes (all listed by name in the program), while two were from the pen of Ralph Harrison (1748–1810), presumably taken from the two volumes of his *Sacred Harmony* of 1784 and 1791, and another by Aaron Williams (1731–76), yet another Englishman, who issued collections of church music between 1766 and 1775, several of which enjoyed American editions. Hardly "the copious variety of the songs of Zion" envisioned by Mrs. Smith, but a significant first step for the Mormons.

CHAPTER 23

The Shakers

The United Society of Believers in Christ's Second Appearing, more commonly identified as Shakers, was a utopian society founded by "Mother" Ann Lee (1736–84) in Manchester, England. She emigrated in 1774 with eight followers and created a community in New York State. The Shakers believed in a dual God, male and female, Father and Mother, and that their founder was the female incarnation of the Gospel prophecy of Christ's Second Coming. To assure themselves of salvation, they remained celibate and led reclusive, gender-separated, communal lives devoted to work and prayer. By 1845 Shaker membership peaked at between five and six thousand, gathered in eighteen communities ranging from Maine and New York through Ohio to Indiana and Kentucky. Celibacy contributed to the decline of the movement, so that by 1910 perhaps no more than a thousand Shakers remained, and most of the communities were closed by the 1920s. While Ohio's last Shaker expired in 1928, the last active Shaker at the Canterbury Village in New Hampshire died in 1992 at age ninety-six (having lived in the community for eighty-five years), and a handful of the faithful (including a few younger converts) still inhabit the Sabbathday Lake Village in Maine. These and a few of the other communities (including those in Hancock, Massachusetts, and Pleasant Hill, Kentucky) remain as museums portraying the Shakers' unique lifestyle and work ethic.

The introverted Shaker communities were centered on the meetinghouse but included dormitory residences, barns, workshops, and other such structures. The settlements were completely self-sustaining, since the inhabitants grew their own food and made their own clothing and furniture. They also made commerce with the outside world by selling seeds, herbal medicines, cattle, brooms, and labor-saving inventions, like the washing machine and clothespins, as well as their distinctive furniture.

Four principal Shaker communities were founded in Ohio: Union Village, four miles west of Lebanon (1805–1912); Watervliet, six miles southeast of Dayton (1806–1900);

North Union, now Shaker Heights (1822–89); and White Water, in northwestern Hamilton County and southern Butler County (1824–1916). Physical remnants of two of these communities remain. The grounds of the Lebanon Correctional Institute and Otterbein-Lebanon, a United Methodist retirement community, represent Union Village, since the entire property (including 4,005 acres) was purchased by the United Brethren Church in 1912 with the purpose of establishing an orphanage and related home for adults. Although in degraded condition, since 1991 the Hamilton County Park District has owned twenty-three of the original White Water buildings, including the two-story 1827 meetinghouse (the only extant Shaker meetinghouse built of brick), as well as the 1823–33 North Family dwelling, the 1855 Trustee's Office (also in brick), plus various shops and farm buildings.[1]

While many recognize the simple, functional Shaker furniture, few realize that the Shakers collectively left a legacy of perhaps as many as ten thousand religious songs, only one of which achieved universality after being appropriated by composer Aaron Copland for *Appalachian Spring*, written for Martha Graham in 1944.[2] Major collections of Shaker musical materials exist at Miami University, the Shaker Historical Society Library in Shaker Heights, and the Western Reserve Historical Society Library in Cleveland.

Scholars have classified the Shaker repertory in minute detail.[3] Suffice it to say that their music was organically related to ritual and work. What was created before about 1870 consisted of melody only, while multivoiced settings became more common later, sometimes even supported by piano or organ. The earliest Shaker melodies were wordless, sung with vocables. It is assumed that such pieces were equivalent to "mouth music," meant to provoke movement in the absence of instruments, which had been proscribed by Mother Ann. Members of other sects during the era also marched, danced, or shook as they worshiped, but the ritual dancing of the Shakers, intended both as catharsis and praise of the Divine, took on an especial character. Seen at first as "a perpetual scene of trembling, quivering, shaking, sighing, crying, groaning, screaming, jumping, singing, dancing and turning,"[4] the choreography gradually evolved into various kinds of square, circular, chain, and ring dances.

Texted songs reflecting these activities began to appear in the early nineteenth century. Many of the melodies to which these words were sung were at first borrowed from a wide range of sources. The texts often referred to matters of faith but also at times described the choreography that they were meant to provoke or narrated actual events in Shaker history. As the repertory increased, so did the importance of perpetuating it in notation and creating a musically literate populace. "Singing meetings" were organized, their procedures and structure remarkably similar to those discussed earlier. At first conventional round- and shape-note notation was employed, but experiments began in the community at Harvard, Massachusetts, about 1816, using letteral notation. What gradually evolved was a system in which a capital letter indicated a whole note and lowercase letters with various graphic additions the smaller rhythmic values. The standard staff was sometimes employed but was at times absent or replaced by a single line, the letters above or below it suggesting their relationship. Several manuals of instruction appeared, the most important of them Isaac Newton Youngs's *A Short Abridgement of the Rules of Music, With Lessons for Exercise, and a few Observations* (New Lebanon, N.Y., 1843 and 1846).[5] The first printed volume with both text and music (in letteral notation), *A Sacred Repository of Anthems and Hymns,* was issued from Canterbury, New Hampshire, only in 1852, although a printed compilation of 140 hymn texts only, *Millennial Praises, Containing a Collection of Gospel Hymns, in Four Parts* [meaning sections, not voice parts] *Adapted to the Day of Christ's Second Appearing; Composed for the Use of His People,* had been published from Hancock, Massachusetts, in 1813.

However, almost eight hundred manuscript sources remain. While the bulk of these were produced in the eastern communities, twenty-six can definitely be associated with Union Village, eleven with White Water, and four with North Union. Those figures suggest the importance of Union Village as the parent settlement in the West, with supervisory authority over its offspring. The music circulated freely among the communities and can often be found in multiple sources, usually unattributed. Shakers felt that their songs were "received" by divine inspiration, "that the Spirit flowed forth in songs as in other impulses of the regenerate Believer and that new songs were unceasingly provided."[6]

It therefore remains difficult to quantify how much of the larger repertory was actually generated in the Ohio communities. It is known that the first Shaker song from Ohio to be notated (by Benjamin Youngs, one of the trio of pioneering missionaries to the West) was sung on May 23, 1805, during the first service held at Turtle Creek (later Union Village): "With him in praises we'll advance / And join the virgins in the dance."[7]

We can also identify several of the principal creators, Isaachar Bates (1758–1837), for instance, one of the original missionaries, reputed to have traveled 38,000 miles and received the confessions of 1,100 converts between 1801 and 1811; Richard McNemar (1770–1839), a schismatic Presbyterian minister active in the great Kentucky religious revivals, whose "New Light" Turtle Creek church became the center of the Union Village community after his conversion; and James McNemar (1796–1875), Richard's son, nine years old at the time of his father's transformation in 1805.

However, chronology and provenance become more than a little murky. Perhaps a few examples will suffice: "Mount Zion," an anthem composed by Elder Bates while he was living in Watervliet, was sung by Shakers of the Enfield, Connecticut, community in 1819, was preserved in a manuscript collection there, and was eventually printed in the *Sacred Repository* of 1852.[8] Or, a hymn called "Christ and Herod," whose six verses begin "The name of Herod signifies / *The glory of the skin*; / But Christ th'annointed purifies / The living soul from sin," was supposedly penned by Richard McNemar on August 26, 1810, perhaps presaging events of the following day, when an armed mob of five hundred, incited by apostate members of the community, stormed Union Village, demanding the release of children the offending Shakers had supposedly imprisoned and insisting that members of the community renounce their faith and leave the area, only one of several such incidents.[9] The words were printed in *Millennial Praises* but the tune exists only in a Lebanon, New York, manuscript. Son James compiled his own manuscript collection, *James M'nemar's Book of Anthems, December 27, 1846*. Its 291 pages contain 258 pieces, probably none of them by the compiler, who apparently copied them between 1848 and 1854 as he encountered and then wished to preserve them, a typical procedure. Fifteen of the works are dated, some even with the specific day on which they were copied. Only seven are attributed to a specific composer.[10] James, however, about 1845 apparently wrote at least the words to a hymn beginning "I did set out while in my youth and prime / The way of everlasting life to learn," which is included in the 124 manuscript pages of *A Selection of hymns Composed After the year ending 42 / Written mostly by Vincy McNemar / Sketches from 1842 till 1856.*

However, not everything was perpetuated in handwritten form. In 1833, using the pseudonym, Richard McNemar, then in Watervliet, published *A Selection of Hymns and Poems; For the Use of Believers. Collected from Sundry Authors, by Philos Harmonae.* Many of the volume's more than 150 items were written by western Shakers, including the compiler and Bates, although there are only sporadic attributions (for example, some of the hymns are by "E. W.," and the first poem is, "By Elder I. B. W. U. Feb. 1817"). The hymns are named: "Birth of Christ," or "Spiritual Marriage"; there are Christmas hymns dated 1825 and 1828 and one for New Year, 1832. Part 2 consists of twenty hymns dealing with death, many of them memorializing specific individuals: No. 4, "To the memory of Father Dwight Darrow who deceased, on monday June 27th 1825: aged 75 years and 6 days," or No. 6, "Memorial of Eldress Ruth Darrow, who deceased at West Union, Sep. 18th, 1814, aged 34 lacking 11 days." Part 3 begins with poems dealing with death, but also includes (as 21) "*A Covenant-Hymn, dated U. V., sep. 18, 1813[.] This hymn was publicly used in the Church, both at Union Village and Pleasant Hill, so that no room was left for any to say that the covenant was not well understood.*" There is also "*A beautiful little anthem*" of two paragraphs, dated April 1, 1834, at Watervliet; an extended "Christmas Colloquy" between the sisters and brothers; poems on a diversity of subjects, including (as 43) "Intemperance abdicated. R. M. 1817" and a following poem in which "The subject [is] continued. 1820."

McNemar's preface asserted,

The object of this Selection is, in the first place, to preserve a variety of Hymns & Poems which have been composed by the Believers of different places and which, at the time, were considered more or less edifying and useful, and may be so in [the] future, on similar occasions. With this view they are submitted to the several orders, to be read or sung as Wisdom may direct, whether in worship, or on other occasions of mutual edification.

Another object is—To promote general union among Believers, and perpetuate the various impressions attending those gifts in their first operations: For in singing a lively hymn, or perusing any striking piece of poetry, it is not uncommon to imbibe a degree of the spirit that dictated it. But we think it improper to attach such a degree of importance to any composition whatever, as would bind or embarrass the free exercise of genius, or limit the living effusions of the Divine Spirit. Yet we fondly hope that so great a taste for novelty will never be indulged as to see at nought those simple gifts, which from the earliest date of our social existence have been mighty through God to the support and increase of the gospel.[11]

The Musical Messenger. A Compilation of Hymns, Slow and Quick Marches, Etc., Used in Worship by Believers, the last Shaker hymnal to use letteral notation, was published at Union Village in 1881. Its ninety-six pieces in two volumes included many written by members of the community, especially the compiler, Oliver C. Hampton (1817–1901), the settlement's most prominent musician at the time and a member of the community since 1822.

Roger L. Hall has provided the most immediate access to the Shaker musical legacy in Ohio through *A Western Shaker Music Sampler* and *Love Is Little: A Sampling of Shaker Spirituals.*[12] The former includes transcriptions of twelve pieces, ranging from Bates's "Mount Zion" of 1815 to Ephraim Frost's "Slow March" from White Water about 1872, as well as works by Richard McNemar, Hampton, and Hervey L. Eades (1807–92) of Union Village. Three of these are duplicated among the five Ohio spirituals in the later anthology.

The nature of this remarkable musical legacy is perhaps summarized in a song sent by one Polly Champlain of the North Union community to New Lebanon, where it was preserved. Its first verse:

O the simple gifts of God, They're flowing like an ocean,
And I will strive with all my might To gather in my portion.
I love, I love the gifts of God, I love to be partaker,
And I will labor day and night To be an honest Shaker.[13]

CHAPTER 24

White Gospel Song

White gospel song arose from the revival movements that flourished after the middle of the nineteenth century, particularly the urban revivalism of Dwight L. Moody (1837–99) and after 1879 his musical associate, Ira D. Sankey (1840–1908). The gospel song is related to music designed for use in the Sunday schools of the era, literature meant both to teach and to proselytize. All of this had its origins in the urban hymnody that had emerged in the pre–Civil War period under the aegis of Lowell Mason and his camp, particularly Thomas Hastings, George F. Root, and William Bradbury.

The idiom that evolved is described in *The New Grove Dictionary of American Music:*

> The texts of gospel hymns are generally subjective or hortatory, are often addressed to one's fellow man, and center upon a single theme which is emphasized through repetitions of individual phrases and a refrain following each stanza. The poems deal with such subjects as conversion, atonement through Christ, the assurance of salvation, and the joys of heaven; their character ranges from the militant and didactic to the meditative and devotional. The music is generally composed for a specific text, and there are few instances of the exchange of tunes between different texts.[1]

Those texts often emphasized a personal relationship with one's God and sought in Christ an intimate friend and protector. Their musical settings smacked of the secular popular song of the era, strophic in structure (primarily in the verse and refrain format), with tunes and harmonizations intended to be immediately approachable and appealing.

The transition from Sunday school song to gospel hymn or gospel song was gradual. Most students of the phenomenon agree that it was Moody and Sankey, through their campaigns across both Great Britain and this country, who firmly established it, but there is little agreement as to the specific point of transition or who was responsible for the new terminology. One scholar asserts that the term was coined by another of the pioneers in the field, Philip Phillips, "The Singing Pilgrim,"[2] while yet another attributes the label to the title of a collection of *Gospel Hymns* published in 1874 by Philip P. Bliss (1838–76), soon to become an associate of Sankey.[3]

Several Ohioans played significant roles in the tradition. Augustus Dameron Fillmore (1823–70) settled in Cincinnati during the 1840s after working as a frontier preacher in Illinois. He composed revival hymns and compiled several tunebooks, using conventional shape-notes, a "Mathematically Constructed Plan of Notation" perhaps created by his brother, Comfort Lavius Fillmore, and the arcane system of numerical notation devised by Thomas Harrison, which departs completely from convention. His collections included *The Christian Psalmist* (1847), *The Universal Musician* (1850), *The Temperance Musician* (1854), *The Nightingale* (1856) and *Fillmore's New Nightingale* (1859), *Fillmore's Christian Choralist* (1864), and the *Harp of Zion* (1865).[4] Three of Fillmore's seven children followed him into the trade, jointly founding the publishing firm of Fillmore Brothers in 1874. James Henry Fillmore (1849–1936) issued his *Songs of Glory* in 1874, *Songs of Gratitude* in 1878, *Songs for the Wee Ones* in 1883, *Grateful Praise* in 1884, and *Hymns for Today* in 1920. Brothers Fred A. Fillmore (1850–1925) and Charles M. Fillmore (1860–1952) joined him in contributing to these and other collections, such as *Songs of Rejoicing* (1888), *Fillmore's Gospel Songs* (1898), *Fillmore's Sunday School Songs* (No. 1 in 1898, No. 2 in 1900, and No. 3 in 1905), *Fillmore's Missionary Songs* (1898), *Fillmore's Gospel Songs No. 2* (1902), and *Fillmore's Prohibition Songs* (1903). Charles, also an ordained minister, compiled *A White Flower for Mother: A Service for Mothers' Day* (1917) and edited *Hymns for Today* (1920), as well as the firm's monthly periodicals, the *Musical Messenger*, published with two interruptions from 1891 until 1924, and its companion, *Choir: a Monthly Journal of Church Music*, issued from 1899 until 1922.

The prolific William Howard Doane (1832–1915) was born in eastern Connecticut. He apparently imbibed some initial musical education from a regional singing master as a youngster, at age fourteen became director of the Woodstock (Connecticut) Academy Choir, and eventually received more formal instruction from several pedagogues, including Benjamin F[ranklin] Baker (1811–89), who succeeded Lowell Mason as superintendent of music in the Boston public schools and also founded the Boston Music School. Doane became a financial officer of the J. A. Fay and Company of Norwich, makers of woodmaking machinery. In 1858 he moved to Chicago as the firm's representative and four years later relocated to Cincinnati, where he was to purchase the interests of the founding partners and become the corporation's president. He applied for numerous patents and raised the quality of the company's products to the point that it won awards at various international expositions, including the 1889 gathering in Paris where the firm was awarded the *Grand Prix,* and Doane was made a *Chevalier* of the Legion of Honor. Immensely wealthy and a collector of musical instruments, rare books, and manuscripts (the remnants of which are owed by the Cincinnati Museum of Art), he was also a generous philanthropist.

While Doane wrote solo songs and a series of Christmas cantatas between 1870 and 1894 (most of them having to do with Santa Claus and built on words by the noted blind poet, Fanny J. Crosby [1820–1915]), this longtime superintendent of the Mount Auburn Baptist Church Sunday School concentrated on the creation of Sunday school music. As a compiler he published at least twenty-eight immensely popular volumes (the bulk of them jointly with Robert Lowry [1826–99] and issued by Biglow and Main of Chicago and New York) between 1867 and 1909. Sales of *The Silver Spray* of 1868 supposedly reached 300,000 copies. His reputation was such that 50,000 prepublication copies of *Pure Gold* (1871) were sold and perhaps as many as twenty times more later on. Sales of *Royal Diadem* (1873) supposedly reached 700,000 copies, while both *Brightest and Best* (1875) and *Good as Gold* (1880) purportedly sold more than a half million copies each.

Doane's profit from these literally millions of volumes was "given back to the Lord." Many of his hundreds of original hymns were built on words by Crosby, a personal friend, their authorship often camouflaged by her extensive use of pseudonyms. Only a few have survived in modern mainline hymnals, particularly "Rescue the Perishing" and "Tell Me the Old, Old Story," although Doane creations were appropriated by performers in the black gospel tradition during the 1940s and 1950s and still have currency today in certain theological and musical circles.[5]

Philip Phillips (1834–95), born in upstate New York, began to teach singing schools while still a teenager. After meeting his wife-to-be in Marion, Ohio, and marrying her in 1859, he settled in Cincinnati and established a firm that retailed musical instruments and published Sunday school songbooks. One of his collections, *Musical Leaves for Sabbath Schools* (1865), supposedly sold about 750,000 copies. The entire stock of Philip Phillips and Company was destroyed when Pike's Opera House burned in 1866, and Phillips relocated to New York, from where he issued *The Singing Pilgrim* (1866) and at least eleven other volumes; he also edited the *New Hymn and Tune Book: An Offering of Praise for the Methodist Episcopal Church* (1867). Beginning in 1868 he embarked on a career of presenting solo gospel song services; one commentator estimated that he mounted about four thousand of these, "for benevolent purposes," around the planet. A three-year tour initiated in 1875 took him across this country from New York to San Francisco and then to Australia, Japan, Ceylon, India, Palestine, Egypt, continental Europe, and England before returning to New York.[6] "His voice was the magnet that drew the masses, and his sweet moral nature the tendrils that bound them to him." He died in Delaware, Ohio, only miles from where he had met his wife thirty-seven years earlier.[7]

Tullius C[linton] O'Kane (1830–1912) was born in rural Fairfield County and attended Ohio Wesleyan University, where he received both a B.A. in 1852 and an M.A. three years later. During several years of postgraduate study and beyond he served on the Ohio Wesleyan faculty as a tutor in mathematics. He also functioned as the "musical precentor" at daily chapel services, became the first instructor of music in the school's female college, and organized a choral society. In 1857 he was appointed a principal in the Cincinnati public school system but left that position in 1864 to join the Philip Phillips establishment. When Phillips moved to New York, O'Kane chose instead a return to Delaware, site of his alma mater, where he apparently spent the rest of his life, traveling the region as a freelancer and promoting his publications at conferences and conventions. J. H. Hall pictured him as

> an excellent leader of choirs, but his forte seems to be in leading large congregations, Sunday-schools and social religious meetings in sacred song. He sings "with the spirit and the understanding also"—with a due appreciation of both words and music—and very naturally infuses his enthusiasm into his audiences so that they cannot "keep from singing."[8]

O'Kane first published as a contributor to Phillips's *Musical Leaves* in 1865. His initial solo collection was *Fresh Leaves: For the Use of Sunday Schools* (1868). This was followed by a sequence of other volumes (many published in Cincinnati by Hitchcock and Walden), including *Dew Drops of Sacred Song* (1870), *Songs for Worship* (1873), *Every Sabbath* (1874), *Jasper and Gold* (1877), *Joy to the World* (with C. C. McCabe and John R. Sweney, 1878), *Redeemer's Praise* (1881), *Glorious Things in Sacred Song* (1886), *Morning Stars* (1890), *Songs of Praises, for General Use in Revival Meetings* (self-published from Delaware in 1892), and *Both Young Men and Maidens. Sunday School, Social Meetings, and Family Songs for Worship* (Cincinnati, n. d.).

William A[ugustine] Ogden (1841–97) was born in Franklin County, but his family moved to Indiana when he was only six. Having learned music as a singing-school student and church chorister, he organized a male choir while serving in the 30th Indiana Volunteer Infantry during the Civil War, a regiment that saw service in many of the bloodiest battles of the conflict, ranging from Shiloh to Chattanooga and Atlanta. After returning to civilian life in 1865 he studied in Boston with notables like Lowell Mason, Thomas Hastings, and Benjamin Baker and became a teacher, first in Bellefontaine in 1869 and then in Iowa, where he served as director of music at the Iowa State Normal College for six years. In 1881 he moved to Toledo and spent the rest of his career there, serving as superintendent of music in that city's public schools, beginning in 1887; one notable accomplishment of his tenure was a chorus of three thousand children he organized for a Sängerfest held in the city during August 1894.

His first collection (with substantial but not exclusive contributions by the compiler as composer and arranger), *The Silver Song, a Choice Collection of New Sabbath School Music*, was published in 1870 in Toledo by W. W. Whitney, as was virtually all of his subsequent output, and supposedly sold more than 500,000 copies. Other similar collections followed: *New Silver Song, Consisting of Beautiful Songs for the Sunday School* in 1872, *Silver Carols* in 1874 (jointly with J. H. Leslie and a subtitle suggesting that they intended to cover every possible base: *A Collection of New Music for District Schools, Seminaries, Academies, Colleges, Juvenile Conventions and The Home Circle*), *Crown of Life* in 1875, *Joy Bells for the Sunday School* in 1878 (with a sequel two years later), *New Silver Carols* in 1884, and *Gathered Jewels* in 1886 (and its sequel three years later). He also issued volumes of anthems (*The Anthem Choir* in 1872, *Royal Anthems* in 1880, and *Crown Anthems* in 1890), at least one oratorio (*Josiah, King of Judah* in 1879), a cantata (*Birth of Christ* in 1880), a comic opera (*Three Old Maids* of 1885), and various didactic works. He also self-published an edited volume of *Infant Songs*, done jointly with Mrs. Emma Pitt from Bellefontaine in 1881.

Odgen became such a beloved public figure that his death of a stroke became front-page news in the *Blade* on October 14, 1897, and the paper reported extensively in two subsequent issues about preparations for the funeral and the event itself, replete with copious and effusive encomiums. The city's public schools were closed and their flags hung at half-mast, his body lay in state in Memorial Hall, and the service was graced by a phalanx of Civil War veterans (since he had retained his links with the military and held the rank of Major General in the Union Veterans' Union of Ohio, Indiana, and Kentucky). A solo quartet, a chorus of schoolchildren, and the local German singing societies performed some of his best-known works.

Will L[amartine] Thompson (1847–1909), son of a prosperous merchant, banker, and state legislator who had moved to East Liverpool from Beaver County, Pennsylvania, when Will was a child, attended Mount Union College before three years of study, beginning in 1870, at the Boston School of Music and New England Conservatory of Music. He returned to East Liverpool and established a retail store and publishing house in 1875 (and then went off to the Leipzig Conservatory of Music in 1876 for four months of polishing as a composer), a firm successful enough that by 1891 it had a branch in Chicago. As was typical of such enterprises, Thompson offered for sale sheet music in his imposing headquarters building (that still exists), housing as well "warerooms" for pianos and reed organs. For example, one undated list of "Confidential Prices to Music Dealers" announced that Thompson had become general agent for the Ohio Valley Piano Company, founded downriver in Ripley in 1869 with the grandiose intention of establishing agencies "in every suitable place in the United States." Thompson offered to deliver "to your Railroad Station" three styles of square pianos and two varieties of uprights, ranging in price from $550 to $675. However, he stipulated, "Our terms are invariably cash with order. Please do not write asking us to break this rule. Our prices are too low to send an instrument without first receiving the cash."[9]

Thompson primarily published his own work, much of it under a variety of pseudonyms. He established a reputation as a writer of secular popular songs (beginning with "Gathering Shells from the Seashore" in 1873),[10] but he also wrote ephemeral piano pieces (for example, *Lamartine Waltzes* of 1874) and a considerable number of hymns, including "Softly and Tenderly Jesus Is Calling" of 1880, which became a favorite of Dwight Moody and still has currency. He also edited and issued volumes such as *Thompson's Popular Anthems* (1894), *The New Century Hymnal* (1904), and *Enduring Hymns* (1908).

R. E. Hudson from Alliance, about whom little is known, self-published at least three collections. *Salvation Echoes: For Sabbath School, Gospel, Prayer and Praise Meetings* (1882); *Songs of Peace, Love, and Joy: For Sabbath Schools and Gospel Meetings* (1885); and *Purest Gems: For Sabbath Schools and Gospel Meetings* (1891) all contain heavy doses of material from other major figures in the field but also include Hudson's own songs (some with his own words), many with dedications such as "to my esteemed friends, Rev. C. G. Hudson and wife," or "to my Pastor, Dr. G. B. Smith."

Finally, two native Buckeyes found fame only after migrating to Chicago. E[dwin] O[thello] Excell (1851–1921) was born in Stark County and began teaching rural singing schools in 1871.[11] Marriage that same year to a Pennsylvanian led to Excell's departure to that state. Between 1877 and 1883 he participated as a student in George Frederick Root's Normal Musical Institutes and also studied voice with Root's son, Frederick W., one of the country's most prominent vocal pedagogues. Although Excell had established himself as a church musician in Oil City, Pennsylvania, in 1881, two years later he moved to Chicago, home base for both the Roots. In consort with several prominent evangelists, he toured the country, providing music for their revival meetings, and also led the music at Sunday school conventions in virtually every state and Canadian province as well. As a composer, he created what one commentator suggested might total in excess of two thousand gospel songs. Many of these appeared in the nearly eighty collections he edited singly or jointly between 1880 and 1918, with titles such as *Sing the Gospel* (1882), *The Gospel in Song* (twenty-third edition, 1885), *Triumphant Songs* (five parts between 1887 and 1896), *The Gospel Hymnal* (1899), and *Flying Squadron Temperance Songs* (1914?). Most were issued in Chicago, where he eventually established his own publishing house, but at least one appeared in Cincinnati, and his edition of *The Anti-Saloon League Song Book* (American Issue Publishing Company, date unknown, likely between 1910 and 1920) emanated from Westerville, a prohibitionist hotbed. By 1914 he had supposedly sold nearly 10 million copies of his various publications, with more than 1.25 million volumes being purchased every year.[12] A volume that appeared in 1915, *Joy to the World* (its title derived from the Handel-Watts Christmas carol, no. 1 in the collection), was issued by the Hope Publishing Company in Chicago, "Printed in Round and Shaped Notes with Orchestration," for use by a fourteen-member ensemble of strings, flute, clarinets, cornets, trombones, and horns. It included such Excell standards as "Let Him In" (no. 13), "Since I Have Been Redeemed" (no. 38, with words by the composer), "God Is Calling Yet" (no. 56), "Scatter Sunshine" (no. 87), "Count Your Blessings" (no. 110), and "I Am Happy in Him" (no. 192, again with words by the composer and part of the second section of the volume, "Children's Songs").

Although he was raised in Tennessee, Homer A. Rodeheaver (1880–1955) was born near Union Furnace in Hocking County and attended Ohio Wesleyan University before establishing his reputation as evangelist Billy Sunday's musical director from 1910 until 1931. Rodeheaver created his own publishing firm in Chicago in 1910 and eventually issued about eighty collections of gospel music, including *Great Revival Hymns* (1911) and *Rodeheaver Spirituals* (1923). In 1916 he also established one of the earliest recording companies devoted to gospel song. Thus, although not a composer of note, he became a significant merchandiser and popularizer of the genre. He also established in 1920 the Rodeheaver Sacred Music Conference at Winona Lake, Indiana, where he retired in 1945. "The World's Greatest Song Leader," a self-imposed title, with his trademark trombone traveled across the country and eventually to the Belgian Congo, Egypt, Palestine, China, Japan, and other exotic locales, relentlessly proselytizing through the medium of the gospel song. A photo on the back page of the *Musical America* of April 21, 1917, was titled "Billy Sunday's Musical Director, 'Rody,' Helps Convert New York." A caption explains that the nickname was one applied by Sunday to "The Human Dynamo Who Makes Gigantic Audiences or Congregations Stand Up and Sing for Dear Life."[13]

CHAPTER 25

The Moravians

Of the Germanic religious groups that settled in Ohio, the Old Order Amish attract the most attention because of their rejection of modern technology, their idiosyncratic dress, and their numbers (Ohio has become home to the country's largest Amish population, estimated to total as many as 35,000). However, their music-making consists purely of singing from a hymnal dating from 1564 as a principal feature of four-hour-long services conducted in the homes of members of congregations constituted of perhaps twenty-five families each.[1] The Amish are often confused with the Mennonites, since both dress in a similar fashion. Not averse to contact with the "English" world, Mennonites gather in formal churches and sing from hymnals containing both words and music. Although no evidence of their work remains in the current Mennonite hymnal, several Ohioans earlier contributed to the repertory. Among them: Henry B. Benneman (born in 1831 in Fairfield County), Bishop John Brenneman of Elida, Henry Harbaugh (1817–67), and Abram Metzler (1854–1918) of Columbiana.

Of the emigrant German groups, the Moravians loom largest in this study because of the strength and breadth of their musical heritage. The *Unitas Fratrum* (Unity of the Brethren), followers of the Czech reformer Jan Hus, was organized in Bohemia in 1457. Following a precarious existence in Bohemia, Moravia, and Poland, the sect was virtually obliterated in the chaos of the Thirty Years War (1618–48). During the 1720s, under the leadership and patronage of Count Nikolaus Ludwig von Zinzendorf, remnants of the Brethren regrouped on the count's estate in Saxony and established the village of Herrnhut (A Place the Lord Watches Over) as their headquarters. With reinvigorated zeal, the Moravians (a nickname apparently applied by Zinzendorf himself) soon sent missionaries abroad, preaching a form of pietism that emphasized a personal relationship to the savior. Two arrived in the Danish West Indies during 1732, a larger group in Savannah, Georgia, four years later. Health concerns and border skirmishes with the Spanish in Florida, which conflicted with the Moravians' pacifism, led them to Pennsylvania in 1741, where, supervised by Zinzendorf himself, they established their New World headquarters in Bethlehem. Other communities were settled later, including Nazareth (1748), Lititz (1756), and Bethabara, North Carolina (1766).

Music was important in the Moravians' services, particularly the Singstunde (Song Hour) and Lovefeast (centered around a nonsacramental communal meal).[2] At first only hymns were employed, accompanied by whatever instruments were available, but eventually Moravian churches were furnished with organs, and each community of substance mounted a collegium musicum, or orchestra, whose proficiency certainly surpassed that of ensembles elsewhere in the young country until well into the nineteenth century. The Moravian ensembles performed choral, chamber, and orchestral music by the leading composers of their day. More importantly, as early as the 1760s Moravian composers (most of them of European birth and training) in Pennsylvania and later North Carolina began to create an immense repertory of congregational hymns, anthems for solo and choral voices with orchestra, and some chamber music, works often of high quality that reflected their European parentage.

During his two-year stay in the New World, Count Zinzendorf began missionary work among the Delaware Indians in northeastern Pennsylvania, and that same missionary zeal led Christian Frederick Post to the Tuscarawas Valley in 1761, where the Delawares had established a new capital at the site of present-day Newcomerstown. Post was joined the following year by Johann Heckewelder (1743–1823), but their work soon faltered, in part because of the political tensions that led to the French and Indian War. By the beginning of the following decade David Zeisberger (1721–1808) had become the principal missionary to the Delawares, based in western Pennsylvania. Consequently, the Ohio Delawares invited Zeisberger to establish a mission in their territory, and on May 3, 1772, he arrived in the Tuscarawas Valley with five Indian families and founded Schönbrunn (Beautiful Spring), near present-day New Philadelphia, the first European settlement in present-day Ohio. Soon joined by other missionaries and as many as two hundred Indian converts, Zeisberger supervised the construction of a village laid out in the form of a "T," with a chapel at the intersection of its two broad streets. A schoolhouse was built across from the chapel, and individual houses sat on fenced lots with gardens designed to provide the basic needs of the residents.[3]

Two daily services were held, with as many as six services and instructional meetings on Sundays. Hymn singing was the focus of these ceremonies, particularly the *Singstunden*, and the hymns were taught to the Indians in singing schools. The first of these of which evidence remains was held at Schönbrunn on September 2, 1774, surely the initial example of music instruction in what became Ohio. It is assumed that at first the singing was in unison and unaccompanied, with a leader establishing pitch and tempo, joined by the congregation once they recognized tune and text, although by July 1775 there is reference to the use of a spinet at the nearby Gnadenhütten mission.[4] Nicholas Cresswell, an English traveler, left a colorful description of a service he witnessed on Sunday, August 27, 1775:

> In the evening went to the meeting. But never was I more astonished in my life. I expected to have seen nothing but anarchy and confusion, as I have been taught to look upon these beings with contempt. Instead of that, here is the greatest regularity, order, and decorum, I ever saw in any place of Worship, in my life. With that solemnity of behavior and modest, religious deportment would do honour to the first religious society on earth, and put bigot or enthusiast out of countenance. The parson was a Dutchman, but preached in English. He had an Indian Interpreter, who explained it to the Indians by sentences. They sung in the Indian language. The men sit on one row of forms and the women on the other with the children in the front. Each sex comes in and goes out of their own side of the house. The old men sit on each side of the parson. Treated with Tea, Coffee, and Boiled Bacon at supper. The Sugar they make themselves out of the sap of a certain tree.[5]

Gnadenhütten (Tents of Grace) had been established in October 1772, only six months after Schönbrunn and was followed by other settlements at Salem (1778), near present-day Port Washington, Lichtenau (1778), near the second Delaware capital in Coshocton, and New Schönbrunn (1780), across the river from its parent. However, the missionaries and their followers became pawns in the frontier struggles between the British, headquartered in Detroit, and American revolutionaries, operating from Fort Pitt. In September 1782 they were forcibly removed to a spot near present-day Upper Sandusky called Captive's Town. The winter proved particularly harsh, so the prisoners were allowed to send a group to harvest crops at Salem and Gnadenhütten. The ninety Christian Indians at the latter settlement were arrested by American militiamen, falsely accused of murdering white settlers, and then brutally massacred, a tragedy depicted each summer through the outdoor drama, *Trumpet in the Land,* presented in an amphitheater east of New Philadelphia.

The Society of the United Brethren for Propagating the Gospel among the Heathen demanded indemnification from Congress, resulting in a land grant of twelve thousand acres in 1784. However, it was not until 1797 that John Heckewelder arrived to survey the three tracts, and permanent resettlement began only in May 1799. Gnadenhütten was reestablished by German-speakers, while Beersheba (or, Yankee Town) housed English-speaking immigrants on the west bank of the river. Zeisberger, who had been ministering to Chippewa Indians in Ontario, returned in 1798 to found the mission settlement of Goshen, about two miles south of the original Schönbrunn settlement. Other Moravian congregations were established at Sharon (1815), Dover (1842), Fry's Valley (1857), Uhrichsville (1874), and Port Washington (1881).

Zeisberger's final labor was his completion of the *Delaware Hymnal*, over which he toiled from 1772 until 1802.[6] The Moravians believed that singing at their missions ought to be in the Indians' own tongue, and they came to prefer the Delawares' Lenape, since they had achieved their greatest successes among that nation. Bernhard Adam Grube's *Dellawärishes Gesang-Büchlein* (*Little Songbook of the Delawares*) had appeared in 1763, but in 1772 a missionary conference determined that it required revision, a task assigned to Zeisberger, who was to be assisted by another missionary and a committee of Delawares. The result was published in Bethlehem and employed for the first time at a *Singstunde* in Goshen on October 9, 1803, held as part of a missionary conference.

Other than hymn singing, only slight evidence remains of music making in the mission settlements of the 1770s. On September 4, 1775, in Newcomerstown Mr. Cresswell "[h]eard an Indian play upon a Tin Violin and make tolerable music."[7] Johann Jakob Schmick, probably the most proficient musician among the first wave of missionaries (he played the spinet, zither, guitar, and violin, and sang as well) moved from Friedensstadt in western Pennsylvania during August 1773, probably bringing with him the spinet built for that community in 1767 referred to earlier. Among the Indian converts who accompanied him was one Joshua Jr., who had received training under Schmick and then was further educated in Bethlehem. That Joshua Jr. served the Gnadenhütten community as chapel keyboardist is suggested by two bits of evidence. During the summer of 1775, his dying father (the elder of the Delawares whose request for a mission station had initiated the Moravians' activities in Ohio) was visited by friends from the area, and a surviving diary tells of Joshua Jr. playing for a Shawnee chief on July 3, surely the first keyboard "concert" in what was to become Ohio.[8] That same summer a visiting Virginian attended services on August 6 and noted in his diary "a very indifferent spinet on which an Indian played"[9]; on September 5 Nicholas Cresswell also commented on "a spinet made by Mr. Smith [*sic*] the parson, and played by an Indian."[10]

One traditional musical element of the services on the first Sunday in Advent and Palm Sunday was and is an antiphonal "Hosanna" written by Christian Gregor (1723–1801) in 1765. Although we can hardly know how elaborate the performance might have been under the circumstances, Schmick recorded in his diary on November 27, 1774, that the children had sung "Hosanna."[11]

While the music made in the Ohio Moravian communities established after 1799 never rivaled that of the more mature centers in Pennsylvania and North Carolina, the Ohio Moravians attempted to emulate their eastern brethren and even contributed a bit to the larger tradition.

Several individuals might represent the capacities of the musicians who settled in Ohio. David Peter (1766–1840), a stepbrother of Simon (1743–1819) and Johann Friedrich Peter (1746–1813), the latter perhaps the finest of the American Moravian composers, was born in Nazareth and educated there. He apparently played both the guitar and organ and used his bass voice after arriving in Gnadenhütten in 1799 as manager of the society's general store to lead the congregation at Lovefeasts and *Singstunden*.[12]

Peter Wolle (1792–1871), credited with about sixteen anthems and songs, also edited the first Moravian hymnbook published in this country—*Hymn Tunes Used in the Church of the United Brethren* (Boston: Shepley and Wright, 1836)—and also contributed to the *Liturgy and Hymns for the Use of the Protestant Church of the United Brethren or Unitas Fratrum* (Bethlehem: Julius W. Held, 1851). He served as interim pastor in Dover from 1853 until 1855 and in the same capacity in Sharon for a year, beginning in 1861. He also apparently directed the Dover choir during his tenure there and wrote an anthem employed at an ordination service in Gnadenhütten in 1854. Its manuscript, now in the Bethlehem archives, tells us that it was "composed by P. W. at Canal Dover, March 1854," and an entry in the diary of the Gnadenhütten church for April 2 of that year recorded that "At 2 o'clock the ordination of Br. Myers as a Deacon of the U. B. Church took place, Bishop Wolle officiating. Our meeting house was filled with attentive hearers. The choir from Dover was present and added to the solemnity of the meeting with good singing."[13]

The most important of the Ohio Moravian musicians was Georg Gottfried Müller (1762–1821), who served as pastor to the Beersheba congregation from 1805 until 1814. Müller had been educated in Saxony and went first to Nazareth, where he taught writing, arithmetic, and drawing, as well as music. Apparently a fine bass singer, he also played the organ, violin, and double bass. Of the eleven pieces ascribed to him, at least two, both with English texts, were written during his Ohio sojourn. *Lamb of God, Thou Shalt Remain Forever*, for chorus, flutes, strings, and organ, was noted as having been written at "Beersheba, Ohio State, April 1, 1814," while *O Sing All Ye Redeem'd from Adam's Fall* was also probably written that same year. In addition, on May 23, 1812, several branches of the Blickensderfer family arrived from Lititz, where Müller had served before coming to Ohio. On July 5 a Lovefeast was held to honor the new arrivals. The Gnadenhütten diary of that day noted, "In order to obtain more room, a wagon cover was spread before the church and seats were erected under it but there was still not room enough. The love feast was celebrated with suitable song and two musical selections."[14] It is tempting to assume that those "selections" might have come from the pen of Pastor Müller.

While documentary evidence only suggests that Müller was able to mount performances of music for trained voices and instruments during his Ohio tenure, the appearance of more and more skilled musicians allowed at least a semblance of the musical culture of the eastern settlements soon thereafter. A choir participated in the dedication of the Sharon church on Christmas Eve 1817. The several services dedicating a new church in Gnadenhütten on August 13 and 14, 1820, contained five anthems, their titles suggesting works by Johannes Herbst (1735–1812), John Gambold (1760–95), and Johann Christian Bechler (1784–1857). All were intended for voices and instruments, but it is not known whether an orchestral ensemble was assembled for the occasion. The church diary does record, "We went out with the sound of trombones."[15]

The Moravians' use of trombone choirs reflects the German *Stadtpfeiffer* (town piper) tradition, in which the players of brass instruments who had earlier sounded the hours and alarms from the tops of civic towers eventually provided "tower music" for major events of all sorts. The use of trombones in Gnadenhütten dates back to at least 1818, and the church there displays the four original instruments, a soprano made by Johann Simon Schmidt in 1804, and alto, tenor, and bass trombones signed by Johann Joseph Schmied, also of Pfaffendorf, Germany, in 1789, both regular suppliers of such instruments to the eastern communities. The Gnadenhütten collection also includes David Peter's guitar and a cello of uncertain provenance.[16] It is tempting to imagine that it might be the instrument mentioned in the Sharon diary of August 5, 1838, which recorded that "for the first time in the preaching service some of the Sharon brethren accompanied the singing with clarinets, violins, and violoncello. The last of which had been bought for the church music by means of subscription."[17]

This event occurred during the 1837–41 Gnadenhütten pastorate of Herman Julius Tietze. Just before moving to Ohio Tietze had married Susanne Elisabeth Stotz, a soprano who had taught music at the Female Seminary in Bethlehem and served as soloist several times with the Bethlehem Philharmonic. Tietze immediately established singing schools at both Gnadenhütten and Sharon with the purpose of training literate musicians who could sing the church hymns in parts and provide more elaborate anthems at the major festivals. The Tietzes were soon joined by Israel Ricksecker and his new bride, Lizette Bleck, further depleting Bethlehem's stock of musicians, since Bleck had been a fellow soloist with Stotz, and Ricksecker had served as the Philharmonic's principal flutist, although in Ohio he became Dover's first jeweler and clockmaker.

Later in the century, these Moravian communities ceased to be closed societies and succumbed to outside influences. The inherited musical traditions were abandoned, only to be reclaimed during the latter half of the twentieth century, marked by the creation of a series of American Moravian Music Festivals beginning in 1950 (directed for many years by Thor Johnson, son of a Moravian bishop and conductor of the Cincinnati Symphony from 1947 until 1958) and by the founding of the

Moravian Music Foundation in 1956. The 1961 festival was held in Tuscarawas County, in part to mark discovery of what was called the Cracker Box Collection.

Only recently has Moravian music been circulated in printed editions. Earlier, congregations assembled manuscript collections that were put aside as their own literature was abandoned in favor of printed mainline fare borrowed from other religious traditions. Tietze, for example, assembled a personal library of nearly eight hundred handwritten items, now part of the archives in Bethlehem. A modest manuscript collection remains in Gnadenhütten, but a workman involved in the remodeling of the Dover First Church between 1948 and 1950 stumbled on a cracker box made by the Akron Baking Company that had become the repository of 189 different pieces, including previously unknown anthems by John Antes (1740–1811) and Georg Gottfried Müller. The collection consists mostly of anthems by a variety of Moravian composers and surely represents the repertory of the Ohio Moravian choirs during the mid–nineteenth century, a rich legacy indeed.

CHAPTER 26

Zoar

The Tietzes, Rickseckers, and Blickensderfers must have enjoyed making music apart from their church responsibilities. For example, the Cracker Box Collection includes soprano arias and associated flute parts from Haydn's *The Seasons*, a work that the Rickseckers had performed in Bethlehem. Furthermore, the Gnadenhütten diary records that on June 15, 1840, the three couples visited the German separatist community at Zoar,[1] in the northern part of the county.

What became the Society of Separatists at Zoar (a biblical name from Genesis 19, suggesting the sanctuary Lot found following the destruction of Sodom) had been established early in the nineteenth century by pietistic religious dissenters from the area of Württemberg near Stuttgart. Mystic chiliasts who believed in the imminent second coming of Christ (originally calculated to occur in 1836), their theology precluded the sacraments of baptism, confirmation, and marriage; they also abhorred public education and any form of military service. The community of some three hundred immigrated to Philadelphia via Antwerp in 1817, having sold virtually all their possessions and, in some cases, even indentured themselves as servants. After a difficult three-month crossing, they arrived on August 14 and were immediately befriended by Quakers in the City of Brotherly Love. One offered them a 5,500-acre tract along the Tuscarawas River for the sum of $16,500, to be paid over a period of fifteen years. With a loan from their Quaker benefactors and personal notes from Joseph Bäumeler, chosen as their leader, the purchase was consummated and a handful of the group immediately left for Ohio, where they plotted the town of Zoar and on December 1 finished its first log cabin.

The community gradually assembled, although some were forced to remain in Philadelphia until they worked off their indentures. The winter of 1818–19 proved particularly harsh, forcing some to work on neighboring farms in order to survive. This dependence on outsiders conflicted with the desire to create a closed, totally self-sufficient community, leading to the Articles of Association of the Society of Separatists, signed by all members (53 males and 104 females) on April 15, 1819. All individual property and wealth was pooled, and in return for their work in the fields and shops members were to be provided with the necessities of daily life. Women and men had equal political rights, although no woman was ever elected to an office. A constitution of 1833 formalized a governing structure that included a board of trustees, a standing committee, which functioned as a kind of court of appeal from decisions of the trustees, a cashier (or treasurer), and an agent general who acted as liaison with the outside world, buying and selling goods for the society. Bäumeler held the latter two positions until his death in 1853.

The economic system of this complex communal society was based on agriculture (grains, as well as fruits and vegetables, dairy products, a herd of beef cattle, and a flock of more than one thousand sheep), although blacksmith, wagon, tin, and cooperage shops were developed, as were flour, woolen, saw and planing mills, tile works and a pottery, a bakery and brewery, a stove foundry, and two blast furnaces to smelt the ore found on the society's lands. As the Ohio and Erie Canal linking Portsmouth with Cleveland was built between 1825 and 1833, the society earned $21,000 in 1828 by constructing the portion that crossed their territory and eventually operated at least four of the boats that carried their surplus goods to outside markets. Hard work, thrift, and Bäumeler's business skills allowed retirement of the society's debt and virtual self-sufficiency by 1830. By 1852 the Zoar property was valued at a million dollars.

The canal allowed a thriving commerce with the outside world, and completion of a railroad line to Cleveland in 1882 and to Pittsburgh two years later increased the number of summer visitors who thronged the imposing hotel (the core of which dates to 1833), making it a destination resort that was considerably extended in 1892.

Early visitors, however, encountered a community that defied societal norms. Joseph Bimeler (the anglicized form of his name) established principles banishing all ceremonies, declaring them "useless and injurious," meaning that marriages were "contracted by mutual consent, and before witnesses. They are then notified to the political authority; and we reject all intervention of priests or preachers." Funerals likewise were anonymous affairs, with the body conveyed in an open wagon to the cemetery from which tombstones were proscribed, the only public recognition a funeral sermon the following Sunday. Bimeler also asserted, "All intercourse of the sexes, except what is necessary to the perpetuation of the species, we hold to be sinful and contrary to the order and command of God. Complete virginity or entire cessation of sexual commerce is more commendable than marriage."[2]

Given the preponderance of women in the early years, they were required to work in the fields and shops; childbearing was considered a nuisance, leading to the adoption of celibacy about 1822, a policy maintained until 1830. During that period the members were divided into numbered households, each responsible for an assigned task. Nurseries were created to which all children were consigned at age three and returned to their parents only at age fourteen, a system that began to disintegrate in 1840 and was finally abolished twenty years later.

The community gathered on Sundays in a meetinghouse constructed during 1853 for morning and evening services, bracketing an afternoon gathering of the children that involved singing and reading from the Bible. Having separated themselves "from all ecclesiastical connections and constitutions, because true Christian life requires no sectarians, while set forms and ceremonies cause sectarian divisions,"[3] these services even avoided any sort of audible or public prayer, consisting entirely of the singing of hymns and a spontaneous discourse by Bimeler about morality, temperance, cleanliness, domestic housekeeping, personal health, and the like. The Zoarites' spiritual leader definitely did not consider himself a preacher, reproving those "who enter the pulpit only for the wages and for the comfort of life it affords, and who promote the hypocritical worship and ceremonies." His "meeting speeches," or "Sunday Discourses," were later published in three large volumes and after his death were read to the community by the leaders who succeeded him.[4]

This posthumous deference suggests that Bimeler proved the catalyst who galvanized his followers from 1817 until 1853. Perhaps not even he could have withstood the social forces that led to the disintegration of the idealism that had motivated the original Zoarites. The resulting loss of community was to some degree occasioned by an economic decline fostered by the community's refusal to countenance modern methods of production. However, not even that can explain the bitter dissension that led to a decision of March 10, 1898, to dissolve the society, including a complicated formula through which most of its assets were distributed to the remaining members. Today seven buildings survive under the management of the Ohio Historical Society, while others remain in private hands.

Hymns were evidently sung to accompany the daily toil, for even the public practice of folksong was banned until 1850. At first the Zoarites apparently sang from the *Psalterspiel* (*Performance of the Psalter*), originally gathered for the Community of True Inspiration, another separatist group that first settled in Ebenezer, New York, and then Amana, Iowa. However, in 1854 they turned to a hymnal that bears an uncanny resemblance to one of the same title published in Reutlingen, Württemberg, in 1850: *Sammlung auserlesener geistlicher Lieder, zum gemeinschaftlichen Gesang und eigenen Gebrauch in Christlichen Familien* (*A Collection of Choice Spiritual Songs, for Communal Singing and Individual Use in Christian Families*). In fact, the volume was self-described as a *Neu Ausgabe* or "New Edition," seemingly admitting its parentage. It contained the words for thirty-five hymns (one with twenty-six verses), their melodies suggested by titles. For example, no. 8 was to be sung to "Lobe den Herrn," no. 16 to "Alle Menschen müssen sterben." However, several were

The Zoar Band, probably during the 1880s. Ohio Historical Society.

associated only with the generic cue, "To the familiar melody" (*In bekannten Melodie*), while no. 23 was to be sung "To its own melody" (*In eigenen Melodie*). In 1867 a second "expanded and improved" (*vermehrte und verbesserte*) edition contained forty-nine hymns. No attributions were made, but at least a few must have been written for Zoar; as an example, no. 37 contains these lines:

> *Führ mich aus Gefahr und Pein*
> *In dein stilles Zoar ein,*
> *Ist's Dein Wille!—*

> Lead me out of danger and pain
> To thy peaceful Zoar,
> For it is Thy will!—[5]

The hymns were led by a choir consisting of the more adept singers, who occupied the front pews.

A modest organ built by the Gottlieb Ferdinand Votteler Company of Cleveland was installed in the meeting house in 1873,[6] but commentary suggests the presence at the meetings of some sort of orchestra, eventually led by Louis Zimmerman, who became assistant secretary and treasurer in 1882, and secretary and treasurer seven years later. Perhaps orchestra is too imposing a label, for during the 1880s one roster contained two violinists, one cornetist, a clarinetist, one bass viol player, a trombonist, and two pianists.

A brass band was organized as early as 1840 and flourished until dissolution of the society in 1898. Comprised of as many as thirty men, all self-taught, the ensemble attracted considerable attention by giving summer concerts in Zoar and surrounding communities. The group was not allowed to use drums since such instruments smacked of the military, and, although later photographs show them in smart uniforms, they were supposedly denied the first prize at a state contest in Columbus only because they appeared in their own motley, "homespun home-tailored suits."[7] The band also participated in local celebrations, presenting performances on Christmas afternoon and New Year's Eve toward the end of their history. Also, at the conclusion of the wheat harvest the members took their instruments to the fields and then rode home atop the final load, playing from their repertory.

Surviving manuscript partbooks and shreds of other evidence suggest that the ensemble performed the same literature as any similar ensemble of the period: transcriptions of popular orchestral and operatic literature (the *Carnival of Venice, Tannhäuser March,* and the Chopin "Military" Polonaise), as well as marches (particularly those of Sousa), but also works by unknowns such as R. B. Hall, George D. Sherman, Jean M. Missud, William G. Votteler (the *C. V. G. March,* perhaps designed for the Cleveland Grays), Yingling (the *Cycle Club March*), John S. Duss (1860–1951, bandmaster of the Harmony Society; *Liberty-Chimes March*), Jacob Rohr (1827–1906, another bandmaster of the Harmony Society; *Erinnerung an Zoar (In Memory of Zoar),* labeled a "trombone march"),[8] an unattributed *Zoar Quickstep,* quadrilles, waltzes, galops, polkas, and so forth.

The Zoar repository also includes handwritten partbooks for the orchestra (those for violin II, viola, bass, and clarionet survive) containing schottisches (Ripley's *Cleveland Belle*), quadrilles, polkas, galops (*Schneeflocken,* or *Snow Flakes,* as well as *Der Luftballon,* or *The Air Balloon*), waltzes, mazurkas, and redowas (similar to the mazurka, but of Bohemian origin) attributed to Ripley, Pettee, T. H. Rollinson, Kiesler, and others. The anomaly is a set of variations for solo clarinet and accompanying ensemble on "Comin' Thro' the Rye," by E. S. Thornton. The Zoar archive also includes a copy of the clarinet and piano version of the piece from which the arrangement was made, published in Boston in 1882 by W. H. Cundy.[9]

Since that score was part of a considerable cache of diverse clarinet music from the library of William Bimeler (1876–1928), a great grandson of the founding patriarch, it is tempting to infer that such an orchestration was made for him. Active in Zoar musical circles, he married Lillian Knof (1876–1942), a pianist of some accomplishment if we are to believe the evidence found in her library of piano works. Her parents operated the Zoar Hotel, and after dissolution of the society in 1898 the family became its owners. Bimeler and his wife presided over the enterprise after the deaths of her parents until his demise.

However, the printed program of the New Year's Concert of 1892, its location unspecified (although Peter Bimeler as organist played a "Sonata" by Beethoven and a "Pastorale" by Batiste, suggesting either the meeting house or the flour mill), presents David Harr as the clarionetist in a "3rd Air, Variation" by Thornton. The event had opened with the Zoar Band playing Albert Beuter's *National Union March* and W. S. Ripley's *Serenade: Soldier's Dream* and was to conclude with Janvertino Roses's *Sobre Las Olas Waltzes* and G. Southwell's *Overture: Northwestern Band Carnival*. The Männerchor presented partsongs by R. S. Taylor, Mendelssohn, Robert Musiol, and Friedrich Silcher. Violinist Joseph M. Bimeler played two works by H. Haessner (the *Thüringer Volkslied*, opus 41, and *Carnival von Venedig [Carnival of Venice]* Variations, opus 44) and joined three other string players for the *Danube Waltzes* of Matthias Keller (1813–75).

Jacob Albert Beuter, son of the community's gardener, had demonstrated an aptitude for music as a child. In 1862, at age eighteen, he was sent to the Harmony Society in Pennsylvania for the sort of advanced training not available in Zoar. Father Simon wrote rather plaintively, requesting his Albert's admission to that community:

> If you can make a good Harmonite out of him, I shall bless you forever; bitter would it be for me if he should fall among the world. He has had experience with garden, greenhouse and nursery work, binding of books, and has substituted for me, at times, in teaching school. He is talented particularly in music. Since his thirteenth year has played first violin in church and the first alto in the band. He has spent his evenings during three years at the piano, and thus becoming the butt of ridicule on the part of the boys and girls, so that already last winter, he complained about this, and has asked me to permit him to go to Economy, where he would be free from the like, and where there would be greater opportunity. . . . And so far as I know, he has always conducted himself in a proper and moral manner. He has no vices, and as to love affairs with the other sex, which is a troublesome cancer, his piano has been his all.[10]

Beuter became a teacher in the Harmony schools, was later a member of the faculties of Beaver College and the Pennsylvania College for Women, and eventually directed the Bloomington Conservatory of Music in Illinois. Of his marches, schottisches, and waltzes little trace remains,[11] although they were apparently popular with the Zoar Band, especially one entitled *Tuscarawas*. On June 26, 1892, a local observer made this entry in his diary:

> Now the band plays the "Tannhäuser March," and memories of old days come home. I have heard it in London and New York, in the midst of luxury and blazing jewels. Now in this remote village, its stately rhythm, like the tread of invisible hosts, lifts up my soul. . . . They now play the march Albert Beuter wrote before he died.[12]

The displays in the Number One House (an imposing Georgian-style mansion of 1835 that stands at the center of the community, originally intended as a home for the aged and infirm of the society but eventually the residence of Bimeler and two other families and now a museum) include several brass instruments, a bassoon, a ceramic horn (in the coiled shape of the traditional hunting horn) that was supposedly used during the first decades to rouse and assemble the workers to receive their assignments for the day, as well as several keyboard instruments, since the community produced at least two amateur builders. One, cabinetmaker Jacob Fritz, constructed the two spinets on display (small, rectangular pianos with short keyboards) and perhaps two grand pianos, probably during the 1840s, since an extant bill for pianoforte wire is dated 1845 and the 1847 tax duplicate contained no fewer than seven pianofortes, although that number had dwindled to five the following year and four by 1854.[13]

Peter Bimeler, a grandson of the founding patriarch and manager of the larger of the community's two flour mills during the last quarter of the century, who also played bass violin in the orchestra and cornet in the band, decided to build a pipe organ using as a model the 1873 Votteler instrument in the meeting house. The façade and some of the pipes of his seven-stop, two-manual instrument, finished in 1892, remain. It was originally located in a room adjacent to his office in the mill, the two spaces connected by double doors that could be opened to create a modest concert hall. It was winded by the same water turbine that powered the grist mill. This autodidact apparently taught himself to play his creation with some skill, and a vintage photograph shows him presiding proudly at its keydesk, a symbol of the musical culture of this unusual society.

CHAPTER 27

The German Singing Societies

During the 1880s the men of Zoar organized the Männerchor Eintracht (Men's Choral Harmony) of fifteen singers, later known as the Zoar Männerchor.[1] The group rehearsed weekly under the direction of Levi Bimeler and specialized in the singing of familiar German folksongs; Mrs. Bimeler directed an associated singing school.[2] This male chorus might symbolize the gradual intertwining of the society with the larger, pervasive German culture of the state. In fact, the Zoarites hosted at least one Sängerfest (Festival of Singers), a gathering of similar organizations from the Pittsburgh area, Canton, Cleveland, and Toledo held outdoors in a grove near the village to mark the eightieth anniversary of the community. A report in the *Tuscarawas Advocate* of June 3, 1887, tells of the "feasting and feting" that attracted as many as two thousand spectators on Sunday and Monday, May 30 and 31. The two groups from Pennsylvania brought with them the Economy Band; the three Cleveland societies and their hangers-on filled eleven railroad coaches.

Although a unified German nation did not exist until 1871, those who considered themselves German emigrated in great numbers beginning in the 1830s, fleeing the Vaterland for political, economic, and religious reasons. More than 4,850,000 arrived before 1900, the bulk during the 1840s and 1850s and then again during the 1880s. By 1900 Ohio's population included more than 200,000 German-born residents. Cincinnati and Columbus attracted large numbers (as residual witness, today's Over-the-Rhine district in the former and German Village in the latter). More than 44 percent of Cincinnati's population in 1900 was German-born, although that proportion would decline to about 16 percent by 1920; at the turn of the century the city could boast of four German-language newspapers; thirty-nine Protestant churches of various persuasions, and thirty-four Catholic parishes that still held services entirely or partially in German; the public elementary and intermediate schools offered classes with instruction in German, and a small galaxy of social, cultural, and charitable societies, rifle clubs, and mutual-aid associations ministered to the needs of immigrant Germans.[3] In addition, many smaller towns had substantial German communities, marked by names denoting the origins of their settlers (including Bremen, Dresden, and Leipsic). German Lutherans founded what has become Wittenberg University in Springfield in 1845 and Capital University in Bexley in 1850, the same year that members of the Reformed Church established Heidelberg College in Tiffin.

Whatever their origins, new immigrants usually attempt at first to reincarnate their native culture. A prominent example of this impulse was the male singing society. Frédéric Louis Ritter, in his *Music in America* of 1883, asserted that the Germans "brought with them their love for poetry and music, and established singing societies; for, wherever at least four Germans gather together, one may be sure to find a Männerchor."[4]

A few years later, critic Henry Krehbiel waxed poetic about the transplanted German, who did not neglect the custom of social singing "in the new life opened to him here. In the midst of the bustling noises of the city he manages to hear the song of the Loreley and the murmur of the Rhine, and on the treeless western prairie he can yet find the shadows of the Schwarzwald. It is because of this that every American community containing a few hundred Germans boasts its singing society."[5]

The tradition's model was the Berlin Liedertafel (Song Feast), founded by Carl Friedrich Zelter (1758–1832) in 1809; Zelter aspired to emulate the spirit of the Meistersinger guilds, which dated back to at least the fourteenth century. The first similar American society, the Philadelphia Männerchor, was organized in 1835. The Liederkranz (Wreath of Songs) was founded in Baltimore, followed soon thereafter by the Cincinnati Deutscher Gesangverein (German Singing Union) in 1838 or 1839, and the Cincinnati Deutsche Liedertafel in 1844 (or perhaps a year earlier). The movement spread so rapidly that in 1849 three Cincinnati societies were joined by groups from Louisville and Madison, Indiana, for the first Sängerfest of what became known as the North American Sängerbund (Singers' Federation). The three-day festival in late June culminated in a concert during which the individual ensembles strutted their stuff following a welcoming song from the local societies, while the massed group of 118 singers presented four of the program's thirteen items. The literature was totally German, from the pens of Mozart and Franz Abt (1819–85), as well as some whose names evoke no general recognition today: Gustav Reichardt, Conradin Kreutzer (1780–1849), Friedrich Silcher (1789–1860), Heinrich Proch (1809–78), and others.

At first festivals were held annually, later two or three years apart as they became evermore elaborate. Many were hosted by Ohio cities: Cincinnati again in 1851 (eighteen societies with a total of 247 singers), Columbus the following year (twelve societies and 200 singers), Dayton in 1853 (eight societies and 131 singers), Canton the next year (twelve societies and 146 singers), Cleveland in 1855 (eighteen societies and 300 singers), Cincinnati the following year (eighteen societies and 300 singers), Cleveland in 1859 (twenty-four societies and 400 singers), Columbus in 1865, following a hiatus caused by the Civil War (seventeen societies and 300 singers), Cincinnati in 1870 (sixty-one societies and 1,800 singers), Cleveland in 1874 (fifty-six societies and 1,600 singers), Cincinnati five years later (thirty-nine societies and 1,100 singers), Cleveland in 1893 (eighty-five societies and 2,200 singers), Cincinnati six years later (120 societies and 2,757 singers), Cleveland in 1927 (104 societies and 3,000 singers), Cincinnati in 1952 (sixty-nine societies and 2,146 singers), Columbus in 1970 (sixty-eight societies and 2,100 singers) and again in 1983 (sixty-nine societies and 2,300 singers), Cleveland three years later (sixty societies and 1,600 singers), Canton in 1995 (sixty-two societies and 1,800 singers), and Columbus in 1998 (sixty-four societies and 1,500 singers).

But what about the individual societies? They were in large part social organisms whose purpose was to maintain a connection with the cultural heritage of their members, primarily through singing. Membership was divided into active and passive classes. The actives were selected through audition by the music director, a professional nonmember who served at the pleasure of those under his jurisdiction. The passives were nonperformers who joined to take advantage of an extensive calendar of dances, excursions, picnics, festive dinners, and the like, as well as of the facilities of the society's hall, which might offer a library, billiard room, ballroom, restaurant, Bierstube, and so forth. In most cases the passives far outnumbered the actives and provided not only the financial underpinning of the organization, but also the bulk of the auditors at concerts, which were often not open to the public and were usually followed by a social event, such as a ball.

Variants on this model were the Turner Societies (Turnvereine), based on parent organizations in Germany (*turnen* means gymnastics or other forms of physical training). The movement was founded by Friedrich Ludwig Jahn (1778–1852), who not only wrote about the importance of preserving German culture and national identity, but also about the benefits of physical training. He invented some of the equipment employed by modern gymnasts and advocated what became the motto of the American Turner Societies: "Building a sound mind in a sound body." With a different primary focus, these Turnvereine did, however, offer their members other opportunities, usually including a male Gesangsektion (Singing Section). The first American Turner Society was founded in Cincinnati in 1848. Its imposing Turnhalle contained a gymnasium on the ground floor, to the rear of street-level spaces rented to retail businesses; the second floor contained a theater seating eighteen hundred, while the top floor housed facilities for the society's drill team, band, and chorus, as well as concert rooms and offices for the directors.

The repertory performed by all these societies ranged from strophic partsongs or arrangements of folksongs by specialists in this literature to major oratorios with orchestra and even fully staged operettas and operas. At first the partsong repertory was entirely Germanic and published in Germany, much of it by conductors of their own choruses. The programs were often graced with interpolations by guest soloists, some of them instrumentalists, often women. When orchestras were available, either in-house or hired, they accompanied some of the singing and provided an overture to preface the evening, as well as instrumental interludes. Later in the century the repertory became more eclectic, with excerpts from opera composers like Rossini and Verdi the norm. Obviously, those societies that aspired to literature beyond the male partsong required the active involvement of female voices, which often led to the creation of associated Damenchoren, as happened with the Cleveland Gesangverein during the 1880s. In rare instances singing schools were established for the children of members, who received basic instruction and then put it to use learning German folksongs, with the expectation that graduates of the resulting Kinderchoren would eventually join their parents in the adult choruses; one example of this practice was the Knaben Musikverein (Children's Musical Association), organized in Cleveland during the 1860s.

It is impossible to postulate an exact number of Ohio's German singing societies. An 1885 history of the Philadelphia Männerchor, whose author proudly listed the cities hosting offspring of that parent organization, contains a daunting number of Ohio societies: Cincinnati, Columbus, Cleveland, Dayton, Hamilton, Canton, Chillicothe, Massillon, Sandusky, Akron, Mount Eaton, Tiffin, and Toledo.[6] Obviously, some of the larger cities sported more than a single society. A more recent attempt at listing every German American singing society of which there exists any evidence found one in Akron (a Liedertafel, founded in 1855), one in Chillicothe (the Eintracht, from 1852), thirty in Cincinnati (many of them founded in 1867, the youngest in 1911), sixteen in Cleveland (also dating from 1867 to 1911), four in Columbus (the eldest founded in 1848), five in Dayton (1867 to 1908), and single clubs in East Liverpool, Hamilton, Lima, Mansfield, Martin's Ferry, Newark, Piqua, Pomeroy, Sandusky, Sidney, Tiffin, and Toledo.[7]

Attempts at accuracy are further skewed by amalgamations and changes of name, but the *Cincinnati Musical Directory, 1886–87* named twenty-seven singing societies, all but two apparently German: Arbeiter Sängerbund, Arctic Glee Club, Aurora Männerchor, Badischer Liederkranz, Cincinnati Liedertafel, Bäkker Gesang Verein, Cincinnati Musik Verein, Concordia Männerchor, Corryville Sängerbund, Deutscher Pioneer Gesang Verein, Druiden Sängerchor, Frohsinn Singing Society, Garfield Liederkranz, Goodfellow Sängerchor, Goodwill Socials, Harmonia Männerchor, Harugari Männerchor, Herwegh Männerchor, Oddfellows Sängerchor, Pioneer

Sängerchor, Rheinpfälzer Männerchor, Schwäbische Sänger, and the Walnut Hills Liederkranz.[8]

While somewhat diminished, the tradition still flourishes. For example, the Central Ohio Singers' district as of this writing comprises choruses in Canton (the Arion Gesang Verein), Cleveland (Banater Chor, Bayerischer Männerchor, Cleveland Männerchor, Eintracht-Saxonia Sachsenchor, Heights Damenchor, and the Ost-Seite Liedertafel), Columbus (the Männerchor, Germania Damenchor, Germania Gesang und Sport Verein, and the Harmony Glee Club), Newark (both a Damenchor and Männerchor), Toledo (separate women's and men's Teutonia choruses), and Youngstown (the Youngstown Männerchor Mixed Chorus, a seeming oxymoron). In addition, the southern Ohio-Kentucky-Indiana district includes the Kolping Sängerchor from Cincinnati, the Liederkranz and Eintracht from Dayton, and the Springfield Liedertafel.

The most venerable of these extant societies is the Columbus Männerchor, still flourishing in its "Haus" on South High Street after an unbroken history of more than 150 years. Twelve "Forty-Eighters," refugees from the political upheavals of that year who had made their way to Columbus, then a town of about 12,800 inhabitants, met on October 24, 1848, and organized what was first known as the Deutscher Männerchor. They elected officers and selected as their music director Karl Schneider (1808–92). Schneider had been born in Saxony and settled in Lancaster in 1839. He later headed the music department of a female seminary in Granville but had left that position and moved to Columbus in 1848; his tenure with the Männerchor was brief, since he returned to Lancaster in 1850.[9] In fact, many of his successors enjoyed equally transient careers. For example, Otto Engwerson (who was in 1893 to organize the Conservatory of Music at the Shepardson College for Women in Granville, later amalgamated with Denison University) served in 1863 and then again in 1892; Herman Eckhardt was first elected *Dirigent* in 1872 and served for two seasons, after which he reappeared in 1876, from 1883 to 1887, and in 1893; however, Professor I[sadore] A. Leinhauser held the baton in 1920 and then returned to lead the group from 1930 until 1959.

Little is known about the dozen founding members. President William Siebert was a bookbinder; treasurer Jonas Kissel, a schoolteacher; Heinrich Tryens, a shoemaker; Philip Conrad, a carpenter; John P. Bruck (1807–83), a justice of the peace and notary public; Martin Krumm (1812–69), a machinist whose firm made wagon parts, farm implements, fire escapes, stairways, and ornamental iron fences, among other items. A cholera epidemic the following year precluded their participation in the founding of the North American Sängerbund and its first Sängerfest in Cincinnati, although the Columbus ensemble was involved with the 1850 Fest in Louisville. In fact, the infant organization had matured to the point where it offered a concert in the Mechanics-Halle on February 12 of that year, which included a handful of partsongs intermingled with works for horn and trombone, initiated with the overture to Auber's *Die Stumme von Portici* (originally *La Muette de Portici*, first heard in 1828), and concluded with an unidentified polka, presumably played by the same no-name orchestra.

The group met and rehearsed in private homes and rented quarters until December 1872, when they took possession of space in the Germania Hall, on the southeast corner of Main and Fourth Streets. After a decade they again became transients until 1921, when they purchased the former Independent Protestant (earlier, the First German Protestant) Church parsonage, which remains their home; a concert hall and Ratskeller were constructed a decade later in anticipation of the sixteenth Sängerfest of the Central Ohio Singers Union (that had been founded in 1878), and further modifications were completed in anticipation of the centennial celebrations of 1948.

Like other societies in the larger cities, the Columbus Männerchor mounted fully staged operas such as Lortzing's *Zar und Zimmermann* in 1869 and again several years later (with other reprises); Weber's *Der Freischütz* in 1872 and 1873; Flotow's *Martha* in 1885; and Lortzing's *Der Waffenschmied (The Armorer)* in 1889. This musical theater tradition had been initiated during December 1857 with a performance of *Die deutsche Hausfrau*, a play by August von Kotzebue (1761–1819), with incidental music, presented in collaboration with the Thalia Verein, a local theatrical club founded in 1855. Its success was followed in May 1858 by the first of several presentations of Pius Alexander Wolff's *Preciosa*, a work of 1820 with incidental music by Weber. The Männerchor even maintained its own Dramatic Section, which presented both spoken plays and operettas from 1873 into the 1930s (*Der schwarze Peter*, a one-act farce by Karl August Goerner [1806–64] and a burlesque, *Eine Nacht mit dem Olentangy Club oder der Traum eines Candidaten,* by Columbusite Charles G. Schenk, both in 1895; *Die grosse Glocke [The Big Bell]*, a comedy by Oskar Blumenthal [1852–1917] the following year; a five-act evening called *Lorle vom Schwarzwald oder Stadt und Land* by Charlotte Birch-Pfeiffer in 1901; and Richard Thiele's *Die Räuber [The Robbers]* in 1935).[10] A Damen Sektion was organized in 1903 to foster the social life of the organization, but a formal Damenchor was not founded until 1931; a Kinderchor-Jugendchor for children from four to sixteen years of age was added to the mix in 1968.

The Männerchor's golden anniversary celebrations were initiated with an elaborate banquet on September 24, 1898, marked by an 1848 vintage wine from Nierstein as well as partsongs by the Chillicothe Eintracht, Indianapolis Männerchor, and the host chorus. The evening also included eight toasts, including ones to "The German Singers," "The German Drinker," and "The Ladies," and the centerpiece, "German Song in America," apparently delivered in English by Judge Tod B. Galloway, an ac-

Members of the Columbus Männerchor, perhaps from the 1880s. The photo was found in the effects of Charles F. Gerhold, a member of the group from 1872 until 1926, one of the five generations of his family to participate. The original caption reads, "'A good time was had by all' as M'chor singers do what they do best." Courtesy Columbus Männerchor.

tive member who was also the composer of numerous published solo songs. Four days later the Dramatic Section presented *Hans Huckebein* by Oskar Blumenthal in the Southern Theater (that had opened two years earlier), and the "Principal Concert" was presented in that same space on October 23. Fred L. Neddermeyer's Festival Orchestra played the March from Wagner's *Tannhäuser* and the last movement of the Beethoven Fifth Symphony; violin soloist Franc Ziegler (billed as "the favorite pupil" of virtuoso Joseph Joachim) played Henryk Wieniawaski's Second Violin Concerto and several slighter works; soprano Hedwig Theobald presented an aria from Ambroise Thomas's *Mignon* and solo songs by Schumann and Karl Bohm (1844–1920); tenor soloist Heinrich Lippert sang an aria from Flotow's *Stradella* and joined the massed choirs in a work by Baldamus; several of the visiting choruses sang, and the hosts presented Abt's "Schiffers Traum" ("The Sailor's Dream," noted as a prize song of the 1866 Sängerfest in Louisville, when the Columbus chorus won a silver cup donated by the New York Liederkranz); the combined choruses also opened the second part of the evening with a German folk song and concluded the festivity with Ferdinand Möhring's "Schlachtgebet" ("Battle Prayer"). Because of the length of the program, da capos were not permitted.

The group's sixtieth anniversary was marked with several notable events. Famed contralto Ernestine Schumann-Heink had been presented in recital in the new Memorial Hall during October 1907. The following year Gustav Braun's *Der Rattenfänger von Hameln (The Pied Piper of Hamelin)*, described as a "historical folk drama with songs in six scenes," was presented in the Great Southern Theater on October 12. Its companion was the Festival Concert in Memorial Hall on October 26, involving ten visiting choruses, imported soprano and piano soloists, and Neddermeyer's Orchestra, all under the direction of Professor Hermann Ebeling. Auditors heard Ebeling as organist present a transcription of the prelude to Wagner's *Lohengrin*, pianist Hans von Schiller's paraphrase on Wagner's *Meistersinger* and shorter works by Schubert and Liszt, Jeanne Jomelli in arias by Beethoven and Verdi as well as solo songs by Schubert, Brahms, and Herman Bemberg (1859–1931), partsongs by Köllner, Voigt, Dudley Buck, and Rheinberger (the latter two apparently sung in English by the Orpheus Club of Indianapolis), as well as several works for the massed choruses and orchestra, concluding with Mohr's *Dem Genius der Töne (To the Genius of Sounds)*. The audience was again informed, in German, that encores would not be permitted because of the length of the program.

A toast to "The Ladies" was one element in the banquet and concert celebrating the group's seventy-fifth anniversary on November 4, 1923. The meal followed an opening "Willkommen" ("Welcome") by Tschirch, sung under the direction of Professor Karl Hoenig. Speeches by the national and district presidents, several other toasts, plus piano and vocal solos were interspersed with partsongs by Baldamus, Simon Breu, and Karl Zöllner. The formal program concluded with "The Heavens Are Telling" from Haydn's *The Creation*, apparently sung in English. Tafelmusik (table music) was provided during the meal by John Purger's Konzert-Orchester.

A centennial history of the Männerchor asserted that by the end of the nineteenth century Columbus was home to as many as fifteen German singing societies, including the Germania Gesangverein, which was founded in 1888 and merged with the Columbus Turnverein (dating from 1866) in 1920 to form the Germania Turn und Gesang Verein (later, the Germania Singing and Sport Society), with its own clubhouse on South Front Street from 1926 to the present. Yet it was the Männerchor legacy that was celebrated in 1948 as "One Century of German Song," with proclamations from Mayor James A. Rhodes and Governor Thomas J. Herbert designating October 30 to November 7 as "Columbus Maennerchor Week." Professor Leinhauser presided over the October 30 centerpiece concert, which opened with a hired orchestra's performance of the overture to Weber's *Oberon*. The orchestra then joined the Männerchor in works by R. Weber (the "Singers Greeting," written for the occasion), Ruland Aysslinger, Julius Achenbach, Franz Abt, and Herman Wenzel. After some speeches, the orchestra presented Weber's *Invitation to the Dance* and then joined the Damenchor in pieces by Léhar, Tchaikovsky, and Schubert, after which the women and men joined the orchestra for the "March and Chorus" from Wagner's *Tannhäuser*. Guest tenor Albert Bauer sang works by Gustav Pressel and Wagner, the orchestra played the Strauss *Tales from the Vienna Woods*, and guest pianist Augusta Frank presented unidentified literature. Bauer then joined the men and orchestra for pieces by Schubert, Abt, Doering, Stephen Foster ("Old Folks at Home"), and Baldamus before the combined forces brought the evening to what presumably was a rousing conclusion with J. Festenek's "Festival Song."

The 125th anniversary was celebrated in October 1973 as "A Return to Yesteryear." A Grand Konzert at the Ohio Theatre on the fourteenth opened with the singing of the appropriate national anthems and *Tales from the Vienna Woods*. Director Jack Stierwalt (at the helm since 1970) then led the Männerchor in a group of German folksongs and the Damenchor in partsongs by Nico Dostal, Toni Ortella, and Ludwig Baumann. Metropolitan Opera star Mildred Miller joined the orchestra for works by Mozart, Rossini, Richard Strauss, and Mendelssohn, interrupted by an orchestral excerpt from *Der Rosenkavalier*, concluding with a "Viennese Medley." The men then took the stage for partsongs by Johann Wenzel Kalliwoda, Maria Reible, and Schubert, after which they were joined by the women for Schubert's "Die Allmacht" ("The Almighty"). That evening all adjourned to the Männerchorhalle for the Festival Ball. A series of other events, concluding with the Grand Banquet on the twenty-eighth, included a "Guest Chorus Night," with singing by companion clubs from Dayton, Cleveland, and Newark, as well as several from the Chicago area. All of this was undoubtedly intended to manifest the club's motto:

Im Frieden und im Streit
Ein Lied ist gut Geleit.

In peace and in strife
A song is a good companion.

The Männerchor initiated a celebration of its sesquicentennial by hosting the Fifty-sixth National Sängerfest of the North American Singers' Association, May 22–24, 1998. Clubs from Canton, Cincinnati, Cleveland, Newark, Springfield, Toledo, Youngstown, St. Louis, Chicago, Milwaukee, Detroit, Pittsburgh, New Orleans, Dallas, Houston, Washington, and elsewhere gathered to sing a pair of concerts as regional ensembles and then as the massed Festival Chorus. The literature came from the pens of familiar names, such as Handel, Mozart, Schubert, and Humper-dinck, as well as from those inside the tradition, like Robert Edler, Viktor Keldorfer, Heinz Buchold, Conradin Kreutzer, Gustav Klauer, Wilhelm Berger, Arnold Kemp-kens, and others. One hundred years after celebrating its golden anniversary in the same space, the Columbus Männerchor then returned to the newly renovated South-ern Theater on October 1, 1998, in a concert shared with a visiting chorus from Dresden, a sister city of Columbus, to conclude the celebration of its first 150 years of singing and socializing.

Grand potpourris like that of 1898 and later can be viewed as nostalgic antholo-gies designed to evoke a sense of the Vaterland in the hearts of performers and audi-tors, most of them surely assimilated, for whom German was at best a cultivated language. This pattern was, however, not unique to Columbus. For example, a con-cert of September 17, 1950, celebrating the diamond jubilee of the Goodfellow Sing-ing Society at the Steuben Social Park in the North College Hill neighborhood of Cincinnati. The group had joined the North American Sängerbund in 1876 and en-joyed music directors of long tenure, since Albert Geyer held the position from 1883 until his death in 1931, and was succeeded by Professor William Kappelhoff, who still wielded the baton twenty-nine years later. The Goodfellows had marked their golden jubilee with a performance in Emery Auditorium in 1925, presumably a more formal event than this concert, which was to be followed by refreshments, a plate lunch, and dancing. The last was probably provoked by Klaber's Orchestra (whose ad in the printed program promised "Modern Music and German Style"), since that ensemble opened the afternoon with a march. The program does not clarify what other Cincinnati societies participated, but the "Combined Singers" then presented what was apparently a motto song: "Grüss Gott mit hellem Klang: Heil deutschem Wort und Gesang" ("Greet God with Bright Sounds: Praise to German Word and Song"). The Goodfellow Singers (all twelve of them, their ranks surely thinned in part by the anti-German sentiments spawned by World War II) then sang partsongs by Pracht, Mozart, and Quirin. A solo Lied of Hugo Wolf by a guest baritone intro-duced the Social Male Chorus of Louisville, performing "Der Studenten Nachtge-sang" ("Night Song of the Students") of Fischer. The "Combined Singers" then con-cluded the concert with partsongs by Wengert and Kistler.

That same format prevailed on November 7, 1954, when the Clifton Heights Gesangverein (also anglicized in the program as a "Singing Society") gathered in the same Steuben Hall to mark its sixtieth anniversary. The group had almost im-mediately joined the North American Sängerbund after its first meeting on June 18, 1894. The Ladies Society was organized four years later and a clubhouse built in 1907. This group also enjoyed music directors of long tenure: founding conductor Max Weiss served until his death in 1913. He was succeeded by Edward Strubel, who was then followed by the ubiquitous William Kappelhoff in 1929. The printed program acknowledged the assistance of the Bäcker Gesang-Verein (Bakers' Singing Association) "for their participation in all the songs of today's Concert, which was so necessary to present the songs more effectively." A minihistory admitted that the active ranks had first been thinned by the aftermath of World War I, and that a similar pattern of attrition was apparent in 1954, since

> many of those who have done so much to perpetuate a tradition of which we all can be proud, are no longer among us and so we look again towards those who have come to the U. S. recently to help us in this task of maintaining a little of German Culture which can contribute so much to the spiritual life of so many.[11]

The concert opened with the singing of "America" by the "Whole Assembly," after which the men sang partsongs by Voigt, Moeller, and Bastyr, as well as a folksong arrangement by Rebbert, and an undifferentiated "Lieder-Potpourri." The "Combined Singers" of Cincinnati then joined in a pair of partsongs by Uthmann, another of those many composers within the tradition whose names hardly resonate today.

Most of the activities of these societies were closed affairs, with passive members furnishing an audience. Extraordinary events were sometimes offered to the general public, as were the Song Festivals of the North American Singers' Union. That organization was subdivided into districts, so that the Southern Ohio, Kentucky, and Indiana District gathered at the Steuben Hall on June 6 and 7, 1959, for their twenty-fourth Song Festival, marking what was billed as the fiftieth jubilee of the district. It had been founded in 1907 in Hamilton and by May 1908 included fourteen ensembles, the majority from Cincinnati. Its members had convened with regularity, excepting a war-induced hiatus between 1916 and 1923 and again between 1940 and 1950; virtually all these conclaves had been held in Ohio cities.

This gathering was directed by none other than William Kappelhoff, who also seems to have been the conductor of at least three of the eight ensembles involved—what was now called the Cincinnati Bakers Singing Society, plus the Goodfellows and Clifton Heights Societies—which included the Dayton Liederkranz Turner and the Springfield Liedertafel, as well as the Harmony Singing Society (its location not noted) and groups from Evansville and Louisville. The repertory was predictable for the most part, with partsongs by Franz Wagner, Schumann, Richard Arnold, Emil Krämer, Silcher, and Attenhofer. However, the program began with John Philip Sousa's "Stars and Stripes Forever," either played by an unidentified ensemble or sung with an imposed lyric, as well as two entries by Stephen Foster and a pair of solo songs by a guest soprano with the distinctly non-Teutonic name of Militza Kosanchich. The chair of the event spoke, as did district president, Carl L. Schultheis, a first bass from Dayton, who also furnished a printed quatrain neatly summarizing the event's goals:

Was in uns jubelt, drängt, und klingt,
Zur Andacht alle Herzen zwingt,
Von Not and Kummer uns befreit,
Ist deutscher Lieder Seligkeit.

Whatever rejoices, presses and resounds in us,
Compels all hearts to prayer,
Frees us from need and sorrow,
Is the bliss of German song.

Earlier district conclaves had been considerably more elaborate. For example, the Eighth Sängerfest of the Central Ohio Sängerbund was held in Chillicothe July 20–23, 1896. Hosted by the local Eintracht, fifteen choruses from Akron, Canton, Columbus, Dayton, Lima, Massillon, Newark, Springfield, Tiffin, and Toledo were joined by eight vocal soloists and the Festival Orchestra (perhaps the Cincinnati Grand Orchestra, since its conductor, Michael Brand, served as cello soloist at the final event) in a series of four concerts. Each was a potpourri of solo pieces and partsongs presented either by the individual societies or by the massed Sängerbund. The orchestra provided a preface to each event, such as Ambroise Thomas's Overture to *Raymond* or Rossini's to *Semiramide,* and also concluded two of the concerts, for example, the Matinee Concert of July 22 with the Strauss "Artist's Life" Waltzes. However, the initial Reception Concert of July 20 featured the Festival Mixed Chorus, which concluded that evening with "The Heavens Are Telling" from *The Creation,* presumably sung in English. The final performance concluded with "Die Wacht am Rhein" ("The Watch on the Rhine") and "The Star-Spangled Banner" performed by the "Mass Chorus, Bands, Orchestra and Audience."

As imposing as this may seem, the program contained a history of all its predecessors in parallel columns of English and German. The writer waxed ecstatically nostalgic over the fifth such Sängerfest, held in Columbus in late July 1887, to his mind the grandest in the history of the district. Twenty-nine societies totaling five hundred singers joined the sixty musicians of the Cincinnati Orchestra. Following the Grand Concert (one of three) all processed by torch light to Hessenauer's Garden for a reception offered by the host Männerchor and Liederkranz. The festivities concluded with a grand parade and party in a city park: "Notwithstanding the oppressive heat 10,000 people participated. The festival was crowned with perfect success, both in musical as in social respect, but it still resulted in a deficit of $5,000, if we are not mistaken. The guarantee fund amounted to $100,000."[12] Of course, these district gatherings paled in comparison to the Song Festivals of the North American Singers' Association.

An editorial in the *Ohio State Journal* of June 8, 1852, rejoiced in what the writer termed the fourth "German music festival," since it tended

> to unite, in one common Brotherhood, the many honest hearted, noble Germans, who have made the land of freedom their home; and while cultivating this most beautiful of all arts—music—it serves to give them a still higher appreciation of the principles of liberty, and builds up a love, not to be broken, for the perpetuity of free, liberal institutions, and to make despotism abroad feel and understand they claim no love or sympathy with it while it has tyranny for its motto. Germany is a land of songs and music, and to its sons, who have made free America their home, do we owe much for the improvement of this art in this county.

On May 6 a clarion call had been issued in the *Westbote (Messenger of the West)*, the most prominent local German-language newspaper:

> Friends and Singing Brothers, near and far! Get ready to leave your stale places of work, renounce the dull every-day life and follow your heart's desire to enjoy the freedom of care-free life here in the sanctuary of the down-trodden and the oppressed, here under the wings of the American Eagle and the stars of freedom, where the oppressed of the world unite to defy tyranny, here in the Scioto Valley bordering on the expanse of the virgin forest; here awaits you a cheerful welcome and a true German greeting.
>
> > Among trusting brothers
> > Songs of poetic harmony
> > Give comfort after work
> > And relief from labor's sweat.

The *Journal* gave rather complete coverage of the gathering, starting with an article on Monday, May 31, including not only the agenda but also a listing of the twelve participating ensembles. These included the Liedertafel and Sängerbund of Cincinnati, the Social Sängerbund and Liedertafel of Dayton, the Liederkranz of Canton, groups from Galena, Mount Eaton, Sandusky, Wooster, and Chillicothe, as well as ensembles from Louisville and Detroit.

On Friday evening, June 4, the Festival Committee, with an accompanying band, met the visitors at the railroad station and escorted them to City Hall for an appropriate welcome. The following morning the visitors assembled at the

> headquarters, for conversation and [to] secure tickets for the Festival, which, for those taking part in it, are fixed at 15 cents (children accompanied by their parents have free admission): whence the participating Unions, together with the Gymnasts of Cincinnati and this city, and the Grenadier company will march in procession through the city.

The itinerary included a stop at the new court house, "where a banner will be presented to the Maenner-chor, by the German ladies of Columbus." The order of march included several bands, named in a Tuesday *Journal* editorial:

> The Cincinnati Band discoursed most eloquently: MACHOLD'S SAXHORN Band, though it has had an experience of only three or four months acquitted itself in a manner and style that a Dodworth[13] might feel proud of, and that Columbus should boast of. It is destined to be one of the first Bands in the country. GOODMAN's Band, its familiar notes, always pleasant and pleasing, rung sweeter than ever on the ear.

At 2:00 P.M. the singers rehearsed for their concert that evening in "Neil's New Hall," with its "large, new and elegant stage, capable of holding a large company of performers, [that was] erected expressly for the occasion." The event was to feature five works, "selected from the latest and best German music," "lithographed in beautiful style, at Cincinnati." This volume of *Festgesänge (Festival Songs)* included three works by Julius Otto (1804–77) and two each by Zöllner and Valentin Eduard Becker (1814–90), plus individual partsongs by Speier, Weber, Neithardt, and François-Adrien Boieldieu. The performance also included "several new and popular pieces of instrumental music" by the bands:

> The concert will be the musical gem of the Festival, and we doubt not the house will be filled to overflowing. The Germans are essentially a musical people, and those among us, we are glad to say, did not leave their musical taste in the distant Fatherland, but have brought it with them, and now cultivate it with success in this land of their adoption.

The public, admitted for one dollar, must have been treated to quite a spectacle, since the singers first gathered at the festival headquarters and then proceeded, "attended by music," to Neil's.

Sunday offered a day of rest involving only informal singing and Gemütlichkeit at Schneider's Garden, perhaps to prepare the participants for a strenuous Monday, which began at daybreak with a "salute of several cannon shots." Assembly was set for 7:30 A.M., with the procession to Stewart's Garden (the present site of Schiller Park) underway a half hour later. One band was followed by the Grenadiers, the visiting singers; the Columbus Männerchor; another band; the gymnasts; and the festival committee. Two hours were allotted for "rest and refreshment," including a "wholesome collation," after which three more cannon shots announced an address from the organization's president and welcoming responses from local dignitaries. Singing bracketed the "gymnasium exercises," which "astonished all who witnessed them. The skill, dexterity and strength exhibited showed they were familiar with a science that tends so much to promote health and strength." Toasts then preceded a "Feast." Another cannonade announced the second part of the program, "and after the conclusion of this, the regular formula of the Festival will be regarded as ended, and every one will be at liberty to amuse himself according to his own discretion."

A local historian limned a portrait of this grand finale:

> At six o'clock in the evening, a large procession was formed, preceded by Captain Schneider's company, with bands of music, gymnasts, song societies, together with citizens formed on the left of the military. It marched in fine order into the city and up High to Town Street, and thence to the city hall. The hall was filled to overflowing. Here a farewell was sung in a style seldom if ever equaled. The festival was closed by a grand ball, in the evening at the Odeon.[14]

It almost seems as though the singing was little more than a catalyst for a grand party, celebrated in full view of and with the cooperation of the local citizenry. The economic impact of these gatherings must have been substantial, which probably fueled the civic boosterism they provoked.

The eleven hundred singers who gathered in Cincinnati in 1879 were offered, with the "Compliments of the John Church Company," a bound volume of the *Festgesänge für das 21st Gesangfest des ersten Deutschen* Sängerbunde*s von Nord Amerika (Festival Songs for the 21st Song Festival of the First German Federation of Singers in North America)*. While each of the thirty-nine societies performed its own repertory, as a massed chorus they presented Schumann's *The Charm of Eden-Hall* (*Das Glück von Eden-Hall*), opus 143/8; Ferdinand Hiller's *Easter Morning* (*Ostermorgen*), opus 143; Ferdinand Möhring's *German Warrior's Oath and Prayer* (*Deutscher Kriegers Schwur und Gebet*); and William Tschirch's *God, Fatherland, Love* (*Gott, Vaterland, Liebe*), opus 42.

Assuming that German was still the communal speaking and singing language of the participants, it thus seems curious that English assumed precedence in the titles. The translations were furnished by H[einrich] A[rmin] Ratterman (1832–1923). Ratterman had emigrated in 1846 and eventually established the German Mutual Fire Insurance Company of Cincinnati and Hamilton County, which was housed in the Germania Building at Walnut and 12th Streets (and was later known as the Hamilton Life Insurance Company). Astoundingly prolix, he published forty-four books (many on German American history), countless articles, perhaps six hundred poems, and innumerable translations for vocal pieces (including as many as ten opera libretti), while concurrently editing *Der Deutsche Pionier* and the *Deutsch-Amerikanisches Magazin*, two prominent Cincinnati periodicals.[15]

The literature was sung under the direction of another prominent Cincinnatian, Carl Barus (1823–1908), a church and temple organist who also conducted the Cincinnati Sängerverein and his own Barus Symphony Orchestra. He had led Sängerfests in Canton (1854), Columbus (1865), Indianapolis (1867), and Louisville (1877). For this event he organized a festival chorus of four hundred mixed voices that, supported by an orchestra of one hundred and eminent soloists, presented Verdi's new *Requiem* (1874) and Anton Rubinstein's *Paradise Lost*, opus 54, a "sacred opera" written in 1856 but first performed only in 1875. Whatever the musical triumphs, the festival apparently lost money, and the public eventually learned that Barus had received no compensation for his labors. Consequently, a "Grand Testimonial Concert" was mounted in Music Hall on November 29, 1880. The German singing societies of the city, the soloists, and many members of the orchestra volunteered their services gratis, uniting under the direction of Theodore Thomas to replicate much of the 1879 literature, including the Verdi, Hiller, and Möhring. The *Cincinnati Enquirer* of November 30 applauded this "tardy effort" at recognizing Barus's accomplishments, but took Thomas to task, since he "did not seem to take great interest in his work, but he always conducts skillfully."

The festivals held in Cleveland equaled those of its sister cities. For the 1874 event a temporary hall was erected at the corner of Euclid and Sterling avenues, which could contain fifteen hundred performers and nine thousand spectators; the Philharmonic Society Orchestra of New York and conductor Carl Bergmann (1821–76)[16] were imported to provide the orchestral portions of the program.

Clevelanders in 1893 raised funds for another temporary festival hall to house the twenty-seventh Sängerfest:

> The large sum which was needed for the expenses of the festival was raised almost entirely from the middle class—from those citizens who are indeed citizens of this glorious country in heart and soul, but who have kept up the old love for the German language, German manners, German customs, and

German song. These are the ones who, with the fully appreciated help of American business men, built the Festival Hall at last, who will receive the singers with open arms, and who will make their stay here one never to be forgotten.[17]

But for pure magnitude, perhaps none can rival the Sängerfest held in Cleveland June 22–24, 1927. Twenty-seven special trains had been chartered to transport some of the almost ten thousand participants and their families from places like St. Louis (three trains carrying fourteen societies) and Chicago (thirty societies, the number of their conveyances not specified). The 3,000 members of the 104 visiting ensembles were joined by the 1,000 United Singers of Cleveland (consisting of twelve local societies), cameo appearances by an ensemble of 2,000 Cleveland public school children, and the Glenville High School Choral Club, plus solo appearances by the Orpheus Male Chorus and the Singers Club, both local single-gender "American" groups. The array of soloists included two members of the Metropolitan Opera Company: mezzo-soprano Julia Claussen (1879–1941) and baritone Lawrence Tibbett (1896–1960). The Festival Orchestra of one hundred, drawn mostly from the Cleveland Orchestra, was conducted by Bruno Walter (1876–1962), then music director of the State Opera in Berlin. Ceremonial visits by the German ambassador and governor were promised, although the latter had to cancel because of the illness of his wife. The breadth of the project is perhaps suggested by a cartoon in the Thursday edition of the *Plain Dealer*, featuring founder Moses Cleaveland in period dress singing a hearty welcome. City manager W. R. Hopkins served as general chair of the festival committee and Edwin Arthur Kraft, organist and choirmaster of Trinity Episcopal Cathedral, as chair of the music committee.

Five concerts were presented in the Public Auditorium, three in the evening, two in the afternoon; Beethoven was given special prominence, to mark the centenary of his death. The content and format of the Thursday evening concert was typical. It included the massed male chorus led by Karl Reckzeh and Hugo Anschuetz (who had earlier circulated across the land, drilling the individual societies in advance of their arrival in Cleveland), soprano Elsa Alsen (1880–1975) of the Manhattan and Chicago Civic Opera Companies, and the Festival Orchestra, under Walter's baton. The program opened with Weber's overture to *Oberon*, followed by Franz Wagner's "Weihegesang" ("Dedication Song"), an unaccompanied partsong. Miss Alsen then sang an aria from Beethoven's *Fidelio*, and the men responded with Beethoven's *Hymn to the Night*, probably an arrangement of the slow movement of his Piano Sonata in F Minor (*Appassionata*) with imposed words in English. Walter then led the orchestra in the "Prelude" and "Love Death" from Wagner's *Tristan und Isolde*. The chorus and orchestra presented Reckzeh's *Das Schloss am Meer* (*The Castle on the Lake*), after which Miss Alsen sang the final scene of Wagner's *Götterdämmerung*. The men offered partsongs by Kirchner ("Beim Holderstrauch" ["By the Elderwood Bush"]) and August von Othegraven (1846–1946) ("Der Jäger aus Kurpflaz" ["The Hunter from the Palatinate"]). The orchestra played Beethoven's Overture to Leonore No. 3, and the event concluded with Miss Alsen joining the men and orchestra for the *Frühlingsnacht* (*Spring Night*) of Max Filke (1855–1911).

Although his math may have been a bit slippery, critic James H. Rogers of the *Plain Dealer* captured the essence of the undertaking in a column of June 19:

> For sheer numbers, the massed ensemble of men's choruses that will be heard in the Saengerfest concerts in Public Hall beginning Wednesday of this week surpasses any previous array of singers in local history. Four thousand trained voices! An incredible total. One hundred and twenty-five choruses from a hundred different cities, with Cleveland represented by ten or twelve. The magnitude of the enterprise is breath-taking.

As was and is the magnitude of this long-lived tradition in which German Buckeyes have played so significant a role.

CHAPTER 28

The Welsh

Permanent Welsh settlement in what became Ohio began during 1801 at Paddy's Run (now Shandon), northwest of Cincinnati in Butler County. Other immigrants came overland from Pennsylvania into Licking County in 1802 to colonize an area between Granville and Newark, still known as the Welsh Hills, joined the following year by a group that established Radnor in neighboring Delaware County. In 1818 settlers originally intent on joining their countrymen at Paddy's Run instead settled near the village of Centerville, joined beginning about 1835 by others, leading to a sizable Welsh presence in Jackson and Gallia counties, swelled two decades later by an influx of miners who worked the area's iron ore deposits. In 1833 some families from Paddy's Run migrated north to the more fertile farmland of Allen County and established Gomer, followed during the 1840s by other predominantly Welsh communities like Venedocia and Delphos. During that same decade, what became Mahoning and Trumbull counties attracted Welsh miners from Pennsylvania to the region's coal deposits, leading to a major Welsh presence in Youngstown.[1] The pattern of immigration was rather constant throughout the nineteenth century, with peaks in 1860 and again during the 1890s, so that the census of 1900 reported a total of about 267,000 immigrants of Welsh origin, of which almost 36,000 lived in Ohio, far behind Pennsylvania's slightly more than 100,000. The bulk of this population was concentrated in the northeast quadrant, with more than 8,600 resident in Mahoning and Trumbull Counties but only about 1,350 in Allen and Van Wert counties.

Whether farmers or miners, the Welsh sang as an avocation. The two principal outlets for this impulse were the Eisteddfod (Eisteddfodau in the plural), a competition involving both choral and solo singers (often with a literary component as well), and the Gymanfa Ganu (Gymanfaoedd Ganu), an elaborate communal hymn festival. Hybrid musical ceremonies on March 1 were also organized to honor the Welsh patron saint, David, on his name day.[2]

The Eisteddfod tradition is by many of its practitioners assumed to have ancient roots, although scholars are quite circumspect in determining what these might have been. As witness, some excerpts from a fanciful minihistory printed by the Southern Ohio Eisteddfod Association on page 15 of the printed program of their tenth annual gathering, held in Jackson on November 5–6, 1931 (reprinted there from the program of the fourth such gathering).

The anonymous author suggested that the word means, in its broadest sense, a "session of bards and songsters in friendly contests for excellence under adjudication of the chief bards, harpists and musicians." Implicitly recognizing that choral singing did not become part of the tradition until 1825, these earlier Eisteddfodau were the province of poet-singer bards who accompanied themselves on the harp:

> The first Eisteddfod of which there is a detailed record was held on the banks of the Conway in the sixth century. Maelgwyn Gwynedd, Prince of North Wales, was the moving spirit of this event and in order to prove the superiority of song over stringed music he offered a prize to those who would swim the Conway before the contest. When the competitors arrived on the opposite shore the harpists were unable to play, owing to the damage to their harpstrings by the water, while the bards were in as good a tune as ever.

> One of the most noted places for holding Eisteddfods was the ancient town of Caerwys, in Flintshire; here Gruffydd ab Cynan is supposed to have held a great Eisteddfod in 1100. And during the reign of the Tudors we read of an Eisteddfod being held there during the fifteenth year of the reign of Henry VIII. In the year 1568 Queen Elizabeth ordered that an Eisteddfod be held at Caerwys. This was the last Eisteddfod that was held at this time, for, Queen Elizabeth herself appointed a commission to check the "bad habits of a crowd of lazy illiterate bards who went about the country begging."

Colorful speculation at best, for the first Eisteddfod of which there is tangible record occurred in 1176. Others followed, even after Wales was annexed to England by Edward I in 1282 (for instance, one held at Carmarthen in 1450 and another at Caerwys in 1523), but the Act of Unification of 1536 certainly had a major impact, since it signified an attempt on the part of the English to dilute Welsh culture to the point of extermination.

An interest in hymn singing began to surface during the eighteenth century, and the Eisteddfod tradition was revived during its waning decades. In 1789 competitions for nonprofessional poets and singers were held in Corwen and Llangollen and perpetuated regularly after that. The first National Welsh Eisteddfod was held at Llangollen in 1858, and a National Eisteddfod Association was organized twenty-two years later. Amateur choral societies in an increasingly urbanized population became the focus of these gatherings, their repertory gradually expanding from hymns to cantatas and oratorios, and, beginning in the 1860s, anthems by composers like Joseph Parry (1841–1903) and David Evans (1843–1913). The first Welsh hymnal was published in 1744, to be followed by many others, and hymns became the principal path to musical literacy for most Welsh choral singers. John Roberts issued his *Llyfr Tonau (Book of Tunes)* in 1859 and was one of several who then introduced the tradition of the Gymanfa Ganu, often held on religious holidays.

The Welsh who first settled in Ohio left their homeland during the reestablishment of the Eisteddfod tradition. Although it is assumed that they did not leave their singing voices in Wales, little documentation remains from those early decades beyond mention of a choir organized at the log church in Gomer during 1843. Common sense dictates that the slight size of the original communities and the challenges involved in providing the basic necessities of life probably precluded most organized music making.

However, both Gymanfaoedd Ganu and Eisteddfodau can be documented during the 1860s. The former were being developed in Ohio concurrently with the advent of the practice in Wales. A Gymanfa supposedly occurred in Gomer during 1860, and a four-day session was held in Moriah near Oak Hill the following year. This event was more likely a "preaching meeting," since the Welsh words can possess that connotation, but it seems that the singing of hymns figured prominently in the proceedings. And while the Welsh label was not applied, a "song festival" was held in the church at Soar near Oak Hill in March 1863 in which the locals were joined by Welsh hymn singers from churches in Oak Hill, Bethel, and Horab.

The first Ohio Eisteddfod of record was held in Youngstown in 1860, lagging behind those in Pennsylvania by a decade. Others were then held there in July 1863 and on Christmas Day, 1865. Similar gatherings followed in Cincinnati in 1872, 1874, and 1875; Delphos, Oak Hill, and Columbus during 1875; and Jackson and Gomer in 1877. Regional associations were organized, such as the Eisteddfod of the Western Reserve about 1865, the Central Ohio Eisteddfod Association in 1886, the Southern Ohio Eisteddfod Association in 1922, and the Trumbull County Eisteddfod Association in 1930. The First Annual Ohio State Eisteddfod was held in Youngstown in 1885, and the first Ohio musical celebration of St. David's Day was mounted in 1866, sponsored by the Welsh Congregational Church of Cincinnati.[3] Historically, these gatherings seem to have celebrated the Welsh cultural legacy but with spectators more passive than active. For example, the one held in Youngstown in 1891 involved several addresses (including "60 Years of the Welsh in Youngstown"), four vocal solos (such as something called "St. David's Day"), a vocal quartet, and a final hymn, sung by the full assemblage.

The principal focus of the Eisteddfodau was competition among the participating singers, the adjudicators awarding prizes donated by local sponsors or drawn from funds accumulated through admission fees, from which the participants were often not exempt. Separate categories were established for solo singers, small and large ensembles, and mixed and single-gender choruses; the test pieces were prescribed in advance. In addition, the competing singers often combined under a guest conductor to present works of varying complexity. There were also often contests in musical and literary composition, spelling bees, and even competition in such categories as the raising and display of house plants, thus generating a bit of the flavor of a county fair.

For example, the 1931 gathering of the Southern Ohio Eisteddfod Association in Jackson included contests in public recitation for children twelve to eighteen, under twelve (Edgar A. Guest's "Dirty Hands" or "Practicing Time"), and over eighteen (Amy Lowell's "Patterns"); recitation in Welsh of Beriah G. Evans's "Anerchiad Glyndwr"; orations on the subject of "Peace"; penmanship for elementary and high school students; sketches of "Ohio's First Three State Houses," done by those younger than eighteen; a drawing in pen or pencil of the late Moses Morgan of Jackson (the prize of $25 donated by Daniel F. and James W. Morgan); short stories written by those of that same age; original poetry; essays on "Experiences and Prospects of Interdenominational Churches"; translations of William Davies's "Arglwydd Y Lluoedd" into English and the Gettysburg Address into Welsh; and book reviews of Elizabeth Madox Roberts's *The Great Meadow*.

In addition, the almost bewildering array of categories included contests for solo pianists of various ages, vocal solos for girls and boys of various ages, adult solo singers by vocal range, female and male duets, mixed and male quartets, school bands, grade school choruses, high school girls' choruses, and church choirs (with the stipulation that their singers had to be "bona fide members of [the] choir or regular attendants of the church represented." For this last category, the test piece was John Henry Maunder's "Praise the Lord, O Jerusalem," and the prize was $150; for ladies' choruses the prize of $300 was donated by the *Columbus Dispatch*. Male choruses competed for a prize of four hundred dollars, and for mixed choruses the designated competition piece was an arrangement of Sir Arthur Sullivan's "The Lost Chord," the $500 prize surely signifying the organizers' priorities.

Each of the four sessions was initiated with hymn-singing by the assembled audience. That repertory included Joseph Parry's familiar "Aberystwyth," its words by Charles Wesley translated into Welsh, drawn from a publication of 1796, and Alaw Gymreig's "Y Delyn Aur," its Welsh words by William Williams (1717–91),[4] translated by Edward Roberts. Assuming musical literacy on the part of its performers, the printed program not only contained the texts in both languages, but also specific performance suggestions, especially as to quite varied dynamics.

Thus the spirit of the Gymanfa Ganu was melded with that of the Eisteddfod, and it is the former form of expression that has persisted in Ohio. Such freestanding celebrations are sponsored by various local, regional, and national Welsh associations but are sometimes interwoven with events of wider scope. As example, a Gymanfa Ganu was associated with the dedication of a newly endowed professorial chair at the University of Rio Grande on August 3, 1990. Interpolated among the speeches and other bits of ceremony (including the singing of the national anthems of both the United States and Canada) were a solo song, a choral arrangement of a Welsh folksong, the traditional offering, and fifteen Welsh hymns, conducted by Lloyd Savage of Chillicothe, a veteran of such events. Of these, a few would have been familiar to any Protestant hymn-singer, such as "Aberystwyth" or "Cwm Rhondda." All were bundled into a "Notebook," complete with bilingual texts, copious notes in English on composers, authors, and translators, a minihistory of each item, and a pronunciation guide to Welsh.

Such compilations were common in the Gamanfa tradition, but the Ohio Welsh also issued at least a handful of conventional hymnals intended for quotidian use. For example, *A Collection of Welsh and English Hymns* was published for the Welsh Presbyterian Church of Columbus by the F. J. Heer Company in 1915. It contains words only, some entirely in Welsh, others in English, the remainder in Welsh with English translations. However, John D. Lodwick's *Canaidau Moliant (Songs of Praise for Sunday School and Revival Meetings)*, self-published in Youngstown in 1898 and entirely in Welsh, contains ten hymns composed by Lodwick, as well as an even healthier representation of works by T. J. Davies of Pittsburgh.

Eisteddfodau were sponsored by individual choruses and churches, regional associations, and finally the National Eisteddfod Association of America, which was established in 1923, with national gatherings in Jackson in 1930 and Warren in 1938 and 1940.[5] Prior to these events there were other claimants to such a label. For example, the Cincinnati Eisteddfod Association was incorporated in June 1899, and on December 31 of that year, and the following day, it celebrated by mounting in Music Hall what was proclaimed as a National Eisteddfod,[6] with adjudicators from Montréal, Pittsburgh, and Marysville; a conductor from Scranton, Pennsylvania; and choruses from Cincinnati (two), Columbus (two), Cleveland, Lima, Newburgh, Venedocia, Painesville, and Youngstown, plus two from Pennsylvania. The mixed groups competed for $600, employing Eaton Faning's popular "Song of the Vikings" and a movement from Mendelssohn's *Elijah*; the all-male choirs quested for $400 with Gwilym Ghent's "Sleep, My Lady Love" and "The Pilgrims' Chorus" of Joseph Parry; the top ladies' group took home $200, having sung Alfred R. Gaul's "At Eventide It Shall be Light" and Henry Smart's "Oh, Skylark, for Thy Wing."

However, Jackson has always been a hotbed of Welsh musical activity. Eisteddfodau were held there in 1877, 1880, and 1897. During 1913 a male chorus was drawn from Jackson, Oak Hill, Wellston, and other surrounding communities to compete in the International Eisteddfod held in Pittsburgh during early July;

afterward its members returned home and divided themselves into four choruses that then competed against one another in Jackson during late October. Eisteddfodau were held in the auditorium of Rio Grande College beginning in 1915, events that drew from a surrounding five-county area and continued until 1924. However, creation of the Southern Ohio Eisteddfod Association in 1922 led to an October Eisteddfod in Jackson with the eminent Daniel Protheroe as adjudicator.[7] That year competition was restricted to groups from eleven southern counties, but success expanded the restriction to include the whole state the following year, the world the year after that. By 1927 five thousand people attended, and the prize money for the various categories of choirs ran from $100 for church choirs to $500 for mixed choruses.

The early gatherings were held in a rented tent, since the town lacked a hall large enough to house the assembled multitude. The expense of the tent, coupled to its inadequate acoustics and problems engendered by inclement weather, led to construction of the Eisteddfod Auditorium in 1928, unique in this country. The building attracted the national gathering in 1930 (overlaid on the ninth Southern Ohio Eisteddfod) and progressively larger regional assemblages, such as that of 1931 described earlier, with prizes eventually as substantial as $1,500 in the male and mixed voice categories. However, the Great Depression led to smaller crowds, which in turn generated slighter pots of prize money, precluding the participation of larger choruses that had to travel any consequential distance. Thus, the auditorium outlived its usefulness, was sold to the local farmers' co-op in 1939, and has since been razed. A modest Eisteddfod was held in the local high school auditorium in 1940, the end of that proud tradition, although a Central Ohio Eisteddfod was held in Memorial Hall in Columbus in late February 1941, and the Trumbull County Eisteddfod Association organized a Hugh and Haydn Owens Memorial Eisteddfod in Warren's Harding High School on July 3, 1943. A plaintive lament that appeared on the first page of the program for the gathering in Jackson during late October 1940 suggests a reluctant resignation to the changing culture:

> The Southern Ohio Eisteddfod is one of the few educational institutions remaining in this section of the state. The debating societies, literary schools, spelling bees, rural singing schools, and the chautauquas have all one by one passed away. We regret to say that their places have been taken by entertainments very shallow and empty. The radio, boxing and wrestling matches, athletic events, picture shows, and the like have forced out the traditional educational institutions.

However, all was not lost, since the core of the legacy persists in annual Eisteddfodau held in the Jackson City Schools. In 1913 Professor R. R. Thomas organized a program paralleling that of the community's Eisteddfod. When D. Merrill Davis succeeded Thomas as supervisor of music in 1938, he decided to decrease the competitive emphasis. Rather than designating only winners and losers, all students were categorized as having achieved a superior, excellent, or good status as solo singers or pianists or, particularly at the high school level, as members of small ensembles. Participation was universal in the first four and final three grades, less so with the intervening levels. Davis recalls handing out between 2,000 and 2,500 ribbons during his era. His successors since 1974 have maintained a tradition that involves hundreds of students in a festival spanning more than three weeks, including not only musical performances but also handwriting contests. Elementary school students present a song selected from a group of five chosen by the music staff, while their elders perform pieces drawn from the annual Ohio Music Education Association contest lists. The names of those who receive ribbons and medals for their participation are recorded in the Eisteddfod Book.[8]

While John Stanley Morgan, president of the 1928 Jackson Eisteddfod, could hardly have anticipated the longevity and durability of the legacy, he surely enunciated its goals in his foreword to that year's program:

> The Eisteddfod offers to young people the incentive to take an interest in music, literature, and art, and to excel in them. It offers to all the opportunity to have their talents observed by competent adjudicators and to receive commendation or constructive criticism which will encourage them to press on to higher attainments. It is a place where both the victor and the vanquished may profit, and defeat be made a stepping stone to future success. The sessions of the Eisteddfod can be described in the words of the poet as being "The feast of reason and the flow of soul."[9]

What is known of the origins of Welsh singing in the northeastern corner of the state arises from a retrospective article in the *Youngstown Vindicator* of June 15, 1924, based on the musings of eighty-seven-year-old Joseph Aubrey. Mr. Aubrey suggested that the 1860 Eisteddfod, Ohio's first, was conducted by "J. W. Jones, editor of 'Ydrych,' a Welsh publication," while the "Rev. John Morgan Thomas, a musician and composer of ability, was chosen as literary and musical adjudicator." If Mr. Aubrey's memory served him correctly, Thomas's responsibilities could not have proved terribly onerous, since the single choir involved came from the village of Crab Creek. The same was apparently true at a gathering of July 4, 1863, while that of Christmas Day 1865 was marked by creation of a $7,000 fund to support the further education of Joseph Parry,[10] who served as adjudicator. The Eisteddfod committee and other Youngstown citizens contributed, and about twenty local singers, including Mr. Aubrey, gave concerts in the area with Parry. "We piled an organ onto a sled and drove around the country. It was zero weather—but what was that to us?"

Annual Eisteddfodau during the Christmas season were organized until 1894, when the high cost of renting the local opera house led to a hiatus that lasted until 1922, when the tradition was revived for a period of five years under the aegis of the local St. David's Society. A full array of competitive events in music, literature, and declamation was judged by distinguished panels of experts, and substantial prizes ($1,000 in both the male and mixed voice categories in 1924, the event that provoked that *Vindicator* article) led to participation by ensembles from a wide area. The contest pieces were performed by the competing choirs en masse before they submitted to individual adjudication.

Despite the lack of a formal association in the northwestern quadrant of the state (although a local organization in Lima labeled itself the Northwestern Ohio Eisteddfod Association), an abundant history of gatherings developed. Gomer and Lima were the principal venues, with periodic visits to Delphos (where the activities were sometimes held in the Mammoth Rink), Ada, Van Wert, and Findlay. Later the geographical perspective widened with an Eisteddfod in Kenton's Hardin County Armory in 1929 (3,600 auditors and participants, including choruses from Lima, Findlay, Fostoria, Van Wert, Ada, and the host city) and assemblies in Marion in 1932, 1935, and 1936 and Mount Vernon in 1934.

Lima, however, remained the principal venue. Assemblages in 1906 and 1907 had proved so popular that hundreds of would-be spectators were turned away from sessions held in the Faurot Opera House.[11] This dilemma provoked a campaign that led to the building of Memorial Hall, where a grand Eisteddfod was held on the first day of 1909. Groups and individuals from more than thirty cities and towns in five states competed. For example, women's choruses from Newark-Mount Vernon, Gomer, and Cincinnati vied for a $200 prize. The YMCA Singers Club of Lorain, the Seneca Indians of Fostoria and Tiffin, the Venedocia Male Chorus, and the Gomer-Lima Male Chorus were finalists for the $300 male chorus prize; the contest piece was Protheroe's "Nun of Nidaros." The Cincinnati Choral Club, Seneca County Choral Union, Venedocia-Van Wert Chorus, Newark-Mount Vernon Chorus, and Lima Choral Society competed for the $500 mixed chorus prize, employing works by Sir Edward German (1862–1936) and Handel. Again, following the competition the individual groups combined as a massed chorus to perform the contest pieces before the results were announced.

While considerable cachet was derived by importing Welsh conductors, soloists, and adjudicators, at least one Ohio native of Welsh lineage achieved considerable renown. [Henry] Evan Williams (1867–1918) was born in the Trumbull County village of Mineral Ridge and raised in Thomastown, a community of Welsh coal miners now assimilated into Akron. Trained as a machinist, he attracted attention at age seventeen during an Eisteddfod in Akron, which led to formal study in Akron, Cleveland, and New York, where he became a professional church soloist. He traveled with the Primrose and West Minstrels for a season and then established an active career as a recitalist and oratorio soloist. He made a first tour of the British Isles in 1903 and later lived in London for three years. He made about eighty recordings for the Victor Red Seal label between 1907 and his premature death in 1918, which some attribute to a rigorous schedule entertaining American troops during World War I. He sang his final recital in Akron and in 1908 had drilled its Tuesday Musical Club Chorus in preparation for their prize-winning performances at an Eisteddfod in Canton.

Thus, while the Welsh musical tradition in the state is both rich and venerable, only the hymn festivals persisted into the latter half of the twentieth century. For example, annual Gymanfaoedd Ganau have been held on Labor Day weekend in Venedocia's Salem Presbyterian Church for more than ninety years and also in nearby Gomer, with its legacy of such gatherings there dating back to 1860 and annual celebrations since 1917. The present-day descendants of the original homesteaders of these tiny communities still subscribe to the maxim asserting that "To be born Welsh is to be born privileged, not with a silver spoon in your mouth, but with music in your blood and poetry in your soul." Local churches and Welsh societies sponsor numerous such gatherings (the Welsh Society of Central Ohio organized a "State of Ohio Gymanfa Ganu" at Capital University on July 16, 1994, complete with both a soloist and conductor from Wales), and the Welsh National Gymanfa Ganu Association met in Cleveland in 1934 and 1956, Youngstown in 1935, Akron in 1946 and 1947, Canton in 1950, Columbus in 1952, 1986, and 1998, and Cincinnati in 1991.

While, with the single exception of the Jackson school competitions, the Eisteddfod tradition lies dormant in Ohio at the moment, let us recall its impact through the period language of those who propagated it. First, from Dan W. Williams's "History of the Eisteddfod" in the *Preliminary Program of the National Eisteddfod*, that gathering held in Cincinnati on the first day of 1900:

> Aside from its purpose to instruct, interest and please, the eisteddfod has a definite mission. It is to foster worthy ambition in music, in the arts, and in literature; to fan the enduring flame, the faint spark of embryonic genius; to encourage struggling mediocrity in its pathetic and apparently hopeless buffeting of the waves of adverse circumstances and conditions—in a word, to uplift, to promote, to cherish. . . . [I]n our own land the beneficence of this nestor of music and literature has been attested in numerous instances.

J. W. Mathews was even more grandiloquent in his "Eisteddfod Greetings" in the *Official Program of the Fourth Annual Eisteddfod*, held in Jackson on October 2, 1925:

No institution, apart from religion, has been of such inspirational power, in the history of the Welsh nation as the Eisteddfod. It has inspired our young people with high ideals in art, science, literature, poetry and music. Competitors have been stimulated to devote their time and talents in preparation for the prizes offered. Choirs have been formed and drilled for these contests. Music of a very high order has been cultivated. The Eisteddfod has been the means of producing, especially in recent years, some of the finest scholars, professors, lawyers, musicians and preachers. Eminent men in all walks of life acknowledge their indebtedness to this great institution for the inspiration it has given them, to carve their way to fame and honor.

I am pleased to think of the powerful moral force the Eisteddfod has been in the past. We have only to glance at its motto ["Y Gwir yn erbyn y Byd," or, "The Truth against the World"] to be convinced of this fact.[12]

Part Five

From Folk through Minstrelsy
to Pop, Jazz, and Rock

CHAPTER 29

Indigenous Folk Song

A folk song may be broadly defined as any song of whatever origin which achieves wide currency independently of print, and is remembered and sung over a considerable period of time.[1]

James H. Hanford's opening thrust from his introduction to Mary O. Eddy's *Ballads and Songs from Ohio* can serve to remind us of the true nature of folk music in an era when so much of what Mrs. Eddy and her contemporaries would have considered valid has been commercialized and transformed into a facet of the entertainment industry.

True folk music remains an organic part of the everyday life of everyday people, unstable and elusive in that it is perpetuated in oral form and thus subject to constant metamorphosis by intuitive performers who, in the process of claiming each song as their own, unwittingly or self-consciously put their own spin on words and music. They sing unaccompanied or perhaps with the support of a dulcimer, guitar, or fiddle. Most of their repertory is inherited, learned by ear and rote, often from an older family member. A new creation is more often than not fitted to an existing tune.

We will look principally at the vast repertory of Anglo-Celtic folk song practiced in Ohio. The first Ohioans imported the wealth of English, Scottish, and Irish songs that had traversed the Atlantic with them or their ancestors: ballads narrating specific historical events or describing social situations, lullabies, nursery songs, sea chanteys, and other kinds of work songs. To that literature were added topical songs about the Revolutionary and Civil Wars, Ohio River and canal songs, abolitionist and underground railroad songs, temperance and political campaign songs, as well as narrative ballads that told, among other topics, of wars, murders, railroad accidents, or the travails of miners or other laborers.

Of course, Ohioans sang those songs that came to have universal currency. Mrs. Eddy's anthology includes four variants on "Lord Randal" (no. 5) that translate the Scottish original into Lord Ronald, Henry, and Jimmy Randal; similar variants infect her three collected versions of the sad tale of "Barbara Allen" (no. 16), who in some instances became Barbara Ellen, with the story set in both Storytown and Scarlet Town, and in one version of "Frankie and Johnny" (no. 108) "Frankie pulled back her kimono, / Took out her little forty-four, shot three times / Right through the hardwood door," while in another Frankie Lee has been wronged by Alfred and goes "up to the president's house / For to get a glass of beer."

Mrs. Eddy was one of several collectors of Ohio folk song who circulated widely, patiently seeking out every possible source, and then notating the results as accurately as possible, a process considerably facilitated with the advent of audio recording. Other noted collectors include Anne Grimes (1912–2004), a longtime resident of Granville who claimed to have collected more than three thousand songs over the span of her career, and Harry Lee Ridenour (1884–1966), a member of the faculty of Baldwin-Wallace College, whose massive collection of 131 notebooks and more than four thousand file folders has been edited and made available for public scrutiny by his former student and colleague in the Baldwin-Wallace Department of English, William Alwyn Ashburn. In addition, nationally noted folklorists Alan, Elizabeth, and John Lomax made 171 field recordings in Ohio between 1937 and 1940 under the aegis of the Library of Congress.

All such collectors face daunting challenges of various sorts. The words of popular folk songs were often printed in broadside form (that is, single sheets of paper printed on only one side, thus resembling a handbill) or in bound collections of the popular songs of the day, confusingly called songsters, since they normally contain only the words. The lyrics of folk songs were also preserved in handwritten form, perhaps on single sheets tucked inside family books such as the Bible, in scrapbooks, or account books. Mrs. Eddy also discovered that in country schools children sometimes created communal scrapbooks by writing out the words of their favorite songs on individual pieces of paper that were then sewn together. Unfortunately, the melodies to which these words were sung were usually not written down by their musically illiterate scribes; at times they were simply suggested by a tune name that may or may not be meaningful today. Even when collectors have transcribed tunes, either directly from their field experiences or from audio recordings made on site, the subtleties of pitch and rhythm, the fluidity and spontaneity of unschooled and instinctive performers, can rarely be notated accurately. However, collectors of folk songs seem akin to those of stamps or antique automobiles—constantly in quest of the rare and the exotic, elated by the novel and unique.

Let us embark on a kind of Ohio history lesson through a sampler that touches on events of import, at least to the anonymous makers of their songs.

The historical ballad called "Sinclair's Defeat," commemorating a bloody, disastrous defeat at the hands of a seemingly invincible Indian confederation, one of whose leaders was Blue Jacket, the Shawnee war chief, was sung to a tune known as "Bonaparte's Retreat" or "Napoleon Crossing the Rhine." A raid in January 1791 on the settlement of Big Bottom, about thirty miles above Marietta on the Muskingum River, led to the death of more than a dozen settlers, and that spring President Washington and Congress authorized Arthur St. Clair, governor of the Northwest Territory and a major general in the army, to raise by midsummer a punitive force numbering three thousand. His second in command was Maj. Gen. Richard Butler, also a veteran of the Revolutionary War, as was the unknown writer of this ballad, who was certainly a close observer of the debacle. A motley army was finally assembled and moved north from Fort Washington at Cincinnati on October 4. Hobbled by his decision to create and provision a chain of forts, as well as massive desertions, a force of only fourteen hundred encamped a month later on the banks of a branch of the Wabash River (confused by the songwriter with the St. Mary's) near the present-day Indiana border. On the morning of November 4, led by Little Turtle and Blue Jacket, the Indians inflicted on St. Clair's army the largest defeat American troops ever suffered at the hands of American Indians. St. Clair survived but lost 630 soldiers and uncounted numbers of civilians; Butler, who had offended his foes during earlier negotiations, was tomahawked and his heart cut up, its pieces dispersed among the Indian tribes.

The words were widely published, including in *The American Songster* (Baltimore: John Kennedy, 1836) and *The United States Songster* (Cincinnati: U. P. James, 1836):

'Twas November the fourth in the year of ninety-one,
We had a sore engagement near t' Fort Jefferson:
Sinclair was our commander, which may remembered be,
For there we left nine hundred men in the Western Territory.

At Bunker's Hill and Quebeck, where many a hero fell,
Likewise at Long Island (it is I the truth can tell),
but such a dreadful carnage may I never see again
As happ'ned near Saint Mary's upon the river plain.

Our army was attackéd just as the day did dawn,
And was soon overpoweréd, and driven from the lawn.
They killed Major Oldham, Levin, and Briggs likewise,
While horrid yells of sav'ges resounded through the skies.

Yet three hours more we fought them, 'til then we had to yield,
When nine-hundred bloody warriors lay stretched upon the field.

Says Colonel Gibson to his men, "My boys, be not dismayed,
I am sure that true Virginians were never yet afraid.

"Ten thousand deaths I'd rather die than they should gain the field."
With that, he got a fatal shot, which causéd him to yield.
Says Major Clark, "My heroes, we can here no longer stand.
We'll strive to form in order and retreat the best we can."

The word "Retreat!" being passed around, there was a dismal cry.
Then helter-skelter through the woods, like wolves and sheep they fly!
This well-appointed army, which but a day before
Had braved, defied all danger, was like a cloud passed o'er.

Alas, the dying and wounded (how dreadful was the thought!),
To the tomahawk and scalping-knife in mis'ry are brought,
Some had a thigh and some an arm broke on the field that day,
Who writhed in torment at the stake to close the dire affray.

To mention our brave officers, is what I wish t' do.
No sons of Mars e'er fought more brave or with more courage true.
To Captain Bradford I belonged; to his artillery.
He fell that day amongst the slain, a valiant man was he.

Mrs. Grimes collected an added couplet in Ross County that improbably links Butler with General Anthony Wayne, whose decisive victory over the Indians under Blue Jacket at the Battle of Fallen Timbers in August 1794 brought an end to the Indian wars:

Oh, sweet Dicky Butler, Wayne'll nae see ye more.
A Miami did scalp you, and the ground ran with gore.

A song collected by Mrs. Eddy (no. 117) reflects the eventual aftermath of Wayne's triumph: the enforced exodus of the American Indians from their homelands. Eddy received it from Eunice Lea Kettering (1906–2000), then a member of the faculty of Ashland College. Miss Kettering wrote, "The song has been transcribed by Rev. Earl L. Lea. He learned it in childhood from his father, Rev. James Lea (1851–1909), a Methodist minister, who was born near Osceola, Ohio, a village near the streams mentioned in the song. The words of the song were printed in an Upper Sandusky paper, Oct. 24, 1845."[2] The seven verses of "The Wyandotte's Farewell Song" were sung by the Leas to a tune resembling one found in Patrick Weston Joyce's *Old Irish Folk Music and Songs* called "The Enniskillen Dragoon" (no. 399):

Adieu to the graves where my fathers now rest!
For I must be going afar to the West;
I've sold my possessions, my heart's filled with woe
To think I must lose them. Alas! I must go.

Farewell, ye tall oaks, in whose pleasant green shade
In childhood I rambled, in innocence played:
My dog and my hatchet, my arrows and bow,
Are still in remembrance. Alas! I must go.

Sandusky, Tymocktee, and Brockensword streams
Nevermore shall I see you except in my dreams;
Adieu to the marshes where the cranberries grow,
O'er the great Mississippi. Alas! I must go.

Farewell, my white friends, who first taught me to pray
And worship my Maker and Saviour each day;
Pray for the poor native whose eyes overflow
With tears at our parting. Alas! I must go.[3]

Pure doggerel again, but obviously a heartfelt elegy from a sympathetic observer of
the Indians' plight.

Another song, "Pleasant Ohio," widely printed in nineteenth-century songsters,
where it was usually suggested as sung to an "air" called "The Belle Quaker," limns
the feverish expectations of the white settlers who displaced the defeated Indians:

Come all ye fine young fellows
Who have got a mind to range
To some far off countree
Your fortune for t' change.
We'll settle in the land
Of the pleasant Ohio;
Through the wildwoods we will wander
And hunt the buffalo.
    Sweet and shady groves!
    Through the wildwoods we will wander
    And hunt the buffalo.

Come all ye fine young women
Who have got a mind to go,

That you may make us clothing:
You may knit and you may sew.
We'll build y' fine log cabins
In the pleasant Ohio.
Through the wildwoods we will wander
And chase the buffalo.
    Sweet and shady . . .

There are fishes in the river
Just suited to our use.
Beside there's lofty sugar trees
That yield to us some juice.
There is all kinds of game, m' boys
Beside the buck and doe,
When we settle down
In the blessed Ohio.
    Sweet and shady . . .

'Tis you can sow and reap, m' love,
And I can spin and sew,
And we'll settle in the land
Of the pleasant Ohio.
For the sun shines bright
From morn 'til night,
And down the stream we go.
And good and great will be our state:
The mighty Ohio!
    Sweet and shady . . .[4]

This is almost a paean from a chamber of commerce brochure, and there were even local variants. New Englanders immigrating to the Western Reserve sang:

All ye girls of New England
Who are unmarried yet,
Come along with us
And rewarded you shall get.
Now, just be brisk and cook and spin.
The boys will make things grow.
And we'll raise a great big fam'ly
In the land of Ohio.[5]

Those who migrated during 1805 from Granville, Massachusetts, to Granville, Ohio, in what became Licking County sang:

> In these long and tedious winters
> Our cattle they must starve.
> We work and tug from month to month
> To dig through drifts of snow.
> Sez I, "My boys, we'll leave this place
> And yonder we will go.
> And we'll settle Licking Crick
> In the pleasant Ohio." [6]

Since Ohioans played such a major role in constructing and managing what became known as the Underground Railroad, it seems a bit odd that there remains virtually no home-grown musical repertory celebrating or documenting the process. John E. Fleming writes, "The Underground Railroad was neither 'underground' nor a 'railroad' but a system of human connections, both formal and informal, which aided enslaved blacks in escaping slavery by traveling from the south to the north, west and other areas where there was the promise of freedom."[7] Ohio was laced with routes on which escaped slaves made their precarious way north from the Ohio River and into Canada following passage of the Fugitive Slave Act of 1850. Prior to that the former slaves had found sanctuary, particularly in Oberlin and Wilberforce (named for the British abolitionist, William Wilberforce), although the cities and towns that served as stations along the various "tracks" were legion.[8]

While the network that aided and abetted the escaping slaves was manned principally by Quakers and other like-minded whites serving as "conductors" and "agents," only recently has there been recognition that both liberated blacks and those born free in a state where slavery had been outlawed through the Northwest Ordinance of 1787 played crucial roles in this venture.

One reflection of that heritage is the unique work of Joshua McCarty Simpson, who in 1854 published *The Emancipation Car, Being an Original Composition of Anti-Slavery Ballads Composed Exclusively for the Underground Railroad* and then twenty years later offered an expanded edition with several additional essays and a handful of new songs.[9]

Simpson, who wrote in the first person, felt compelled to inform readers in his 1874 "Note to the Public," "Those who have read my composition, who have no history of my life, support that I have been a "Slave"; but this is not the case. I am a MAN, free-born—educated (superficially) in the Oberlin Collegiate Institute, Lorain County, Ohio."[10]

In an 1874 essay, "How I Got My Education," he wrote about having been born into poverty and being made the foster child of an "English stonemason" after his birth father's death. After the foster father died, his widow remarried, and Simpson became the ward of two of her nephews, who evidently treated him harshly. When he was ten, they both married; Simpson was removed from their care and bonded to a farmer under whose supervision he managed a bit of rudimentary education, which had become a passion with him. After being refused admission to several schools in the district, he finally found a refuge at what he called the "Abolition" School in Big Bottom on the Muskingum River, after which he matriculated at Oberlin, where he studied for two and a half years.

> I spent no time in the public square, playing foot-ball, running races, jump- ing and other gymnastics, with the students for exercise, or recreation of mind. Neither did I stand in the grounds of loungers, around the hall doors, nor on the corners, nor sit in fellow-students' rooms, cracking jokes for so- cial amusements. Swinging the axe and maul, scythe and cradle, and other implements common to farming, from three to nine hours a day, was gym- nastics enough for a poor man as I was. As for recreation of mind, I sought frequent opportunities for this during my labouring hours, when in the fields and forests, where I could contemplate the great works of creation, and adore the great Creator. I did my own washing and mending also.
>
> I spent no money foolishly to gratify my carnal appetite, bought no broad- cloth nor satin vests, smoked no cigars, chewed no tobacco, drank no liquor. I slept on straw summer and winter while at College.[11]

What little is known about Simpson as an adult was gleaned by local historian Norris F. Schneider for a pair of articles in the *Zanesville News* for January 19 and 26, 1941. Schneider discovered that Simpson had been an elder of the Zion Baptist Church, and a bit of sleuthing led him to a woman who recalled that her great-uncle had owned a drugstore and practiced herbal medicine before his death in 1876. She recalled Simpson as having lived in pro-slavery Zanesville, while other sources placed him in Putnam, an abolitionist community across the Muskingum River. Whatever the truth, Simpson reflected the violent tensions between these opposing attitudes in his admission:

> I was educated to believe that it was all right for us to be slaves, though a native of Morgan County, Ohio, I pretended to believe it too, and when quite a boy, would ridicule the Abolitionists as fools, devils, mischief-makers, etc., whenever I was in the presence of my old Boss or the Anti-Abolitionists. Per- secutions in 1836 against Abolitionists became quite prevalent, and the man that dared to say "colored men," "colored ladies and gentlemen," "Mr." or

"Mrs." to colored people, did it at the risk of a coat of rotten eggs, or a fancy ride on an ugly rail, or to be dressed up with a shirt of tar and feathers for Sunday, even in Morgan Country, but my heart secretly moaned all the time and said "Lord what can be done for my people[?]" As soon as I could write, which was not until I was past twenty-one years old, a spirit of poetry, (which was always in me) became revived, and seemed to waft before my mind horrid pictures of the condition of my people, and something seemed to say, "Write and sing about it—you can sing what would be death to speak." [12]

His assertive apology to his readers:

I have often thought, that, if I had been well disciplined under the lash, that this experience would have so assisted my natural poetical endowments, that my style, taste, and spirit of writing would have been much more interesting. But when the Public understands, that I was bound out when quite young, served under a hard master until twenty one years old; after which, I got all the education that I now enjoy, (which is no more than a common English education,) the considerate portion of the community will excuse my simple figures and plain undressed mode, remembering that I do not profess to be a Byron, Milton, Pollock, nor Young.

In my selection of "AIR's," I have gathered such as are popular, and extensively known. Many superstitious persons, and perhaps, many good conscientious, well-meaning Christians, will denounce and reject the work on account of the "TUNES"; but my object has been to change the flow of those sweet melodies (so often disgraced by those Comic Negro Songs, and sung by our own people,) into a more appropriate and useful channel; and I hope that my motives may be duly appreciated; and that this little work, (the *first* of the kind in the United States) may find a resting place, and a hearty welcome in every State, community and family in the Union, and as far as a friend to the Slave may be found.

This work is *all original*, though several of the songs have been republished, several times, under other names, and by other persons, *they are my own Composition*.[13]

Simpson's "compositions" were entirely literary, usually with the suggestion of a well-known tune to which his poems were to be sung; in a few instances he allowed the performer to appropriate any melody whose meter matched that of the lyric. Unfortunately, the title song of the collection, "Emancipation Car," is one of those lacking even a hint of the intended "Air." The first of its five verses is:

Here comes Emancipation's Car,
    I hear the bell resound;
Her head's toward the Northern States,
    For Canada she's bound;
And I am bound to leave the land
    Of slavery tonight.
        So hie me away to Canada,
        That cold and dreary shore—
        Oh! carry me back to Alabama,
        To Alabama no more—
        To Alabama no more.[14]

Regardless of its unnamed melody, the poem obviously borrows imagery from "Get Off the Track," a signature song of the Hutchinson Family, written in 1844 and sung to the tune of "Old Dan Tucker." Certainly among the most popular musical entertainers of the era, various configurations of the Hutchinsons toured this country and the British Isles from 1840 into the 1880s. They adopted both abolition and temperance as causes; "Get Off the Track" pictures the newfangled steam engine as a potent symbol of emancipation, mighty and inexorable, noisily warning the opposition to clear out of its way.

Simpson's obvious parody of and tribute to the Hutchinsons, "The Car of Education, In Honor to the Present School Laws," was even sung to the same melody. However, it also incorporates the author's belief that education offered one means of escaping oppression. Six of its eight verses:

Ho! the car of Education
Loudly thunders through the nation.
Come ye little lads and lasses[,]
Jump on board before she passes.
    Jump on the cars[,] all are singing[,]
    Jump on the cars, all are singing.
    Jump on the cars, all are singing,
    Education's bell is ringing.

Some folks say we have no knowledge
Though we go to school and college;
We intend to prove them liars
Though we travel through the fires.
    Jump on the cars . . .

We intend while young and ruddy
Never to forsake our study;
For when'er we look around us
Ignorance does quite confound us.
    Jump on the cars . . .

Lo! a brilliant light is rising
Which to some is quite surprising:
People once despised—rejected,
Now enlightened, are respected.
    Jump on the cars . . .

We are making preparations
Now to fill some useful stations;
Same for doctors, teachers, lawyers:
None for "*boot-blackers*" & *wood-sawyers*.
    Jump on the cars . . .

Prejudice will not retard us,
Neither poverty discard us;
We are bound for "Art and Science"
At our enemies' defiance.
    Jump on the cars . . .[15]

However, Simpson was preoccupied with the Underground Railroad as a conduit across an Ohio that, following passage of the Fugitive Slave Act, no longer guaranteed a safe haven. Queen Victoria, John Bull, and the town of Chatham in southwestern Ontario offered sanctuary. Thus, a song called "Queen Victoria Conversing with Her Slave Children," or "Albert Moris," sung to "We're traveling home to Heaven above." Five of its seven verses:

I'm going to see the old North Star,
    Will you go, will you go[?]
They tell me "*freedom*" reigns up there[;]
    Will you go, will you go?
I've long resolved with all my heart,
This very night to make a start,
From chains, forever to depart;
    Will you go, will you go?

I'm going to see Victoria's face;
    Will you go, will you go?
At her right hand I'll find a place;
    Will you go, will you go?
Her arms of love extend to me,
She says, "my son, I'll set you free,"
"A slave, no more, you e'er shall be;"
    Come away, come away!

I'm going to see Old Johnny Bull;
    Will you go, will you go?
And drink a draught at freedom's pool,
    Will you go, will you go?
Old Johnny, long has been our friend,
And will be until time shall end;
To black men, aid he'll always lend,
    Will you go, will you go?

I'm going to hear the cannon roar,
    Will you go, will you go?
Upon Lake Erie's Northern Shore,
    Will you go, will you go?
I cannot stay—I must be gone;
I hear the rolling fife and drum,
And Queen Victoria bids me *come*;
    Let me go, let me go!

I hope the time will not be long,
    I must go, I must go.
When I shall join that happy throng,
    I must go, I must go.
I've many friends to Chatham gone,
And many more will follow on—
To Master, lash and "Negro Gong,"
Fare-you-well, Fare-you-well.[16]

At times Simpson's message must have been seemed terribly unsubtle to those asked to impose his poetry on the displaced lyric of the borrowed melody. For example, "To the Whites of America," sung to "Massa's in the Cold, Cold Ground." The middle pair of its four verses:

Lo! ten thousand steeples shining
    Through this mighty Christian land,
While four millions slaves all pining
    And dying 'neath the Tyrant's hand.
See the "*blood-stained*" christian banner
    Followed by a host of Saints
While they loudly sing Hosannah,
    We hear the dying slaves['] complaints.
        Hear ye that mourning?
        Anglo-sons of God,
        O! ye Hypocrites take warning,
        And show your sable brothers['] blood.

In our Legislative members,
    Few there are with human souls,
Though they speak in tones of thunder
    'Gainst sins which they cannot control[.]
Women's rights and annexation,
    Is the topic by the way,
While poor Africa's sable nation
    For mercy, cry both by night and day.
        Hear ye, that mourning[?]
        'Tis a solemn sound,
        O! ye wicked men take warning,
        For God will send his judgment down.[17]

The "Song of the 'Aliened American,'" sung to "America," seems even more uncompromising:

My country, 'tis in thee,
Dark land of Slavery,
    In thee we groan.
Long have our chains been worn—
Long has our grief been borne—
Our flesh has long been torn,
E'en from our bones.

The white man rules the day—
He bears despotic sway,
    O'er all the land[.]

He wields the Tyrant's rod,
Fearless of man or God,
And at his impious nod,
    We *fall* or *stand*.

O! shall we longer bleed?
Is there no one to plead
    The black man's cause?
Does justice thus demand,
That we shall wear the brand,
And raise not voice or hand
    Against such laws?

No! no! the time has come,
When we must not be dumb,
    We must awake.
We now *"Eight Millions Strong,"*
Must strike sweet freedom's wrong—
    Our chains must break.[18]

Simpson even evoked ancient Greece in language and revolutionary France in music by mating "The Voice of Six Hundred Thousand, Nominally Free" with the "Marseilles Hymn." Its first and last verses:

Come friends, awake! The day is dawning,
'Tis time that we were in the field;
Shake off your fears and cease your yawning,
And buckle on your sword and shield;
And buckle on your sword and shield.
The enemy is now advancing,
    The Tyrant-host is great and strong;
    But ah, their reign will not be long,
We shrink not at their war-steeds prancing.
    Stand up, stand up my boys,
    The battle field is ours:
Fight on, Fight on, all hearts resolved,
    To break the Tyrant's power.

'Tis true, that we are few in number,
And yet, those few are *brave* and *strong,*

Like Athen's mighty sons of thunder,
Upon the plains of Marathon;
Upon the plains of Marathon.
With courage bold, we'll take our station,
   Against the mighty host of whites,
   And plead like *men* for equal rights,
And thus exalt our fallen Nation.
   "To arms! to arms! my braves,"
   The sword of truth unsheath.
March on, March on, all hearts resolved,
On Liberty or death.[19]

Another of Simpson's songs (sung to "Come to the Old Gum Tree") dealt with the allure of Liberia, the republic on the west coast of Africa created in 1822 as a sanctuary for freed American slaves. Simpson commented in a footnote that one Moses Walker had reported back "that all a man need do to live in Liberia is to lay down and roll, and eat." The song's initial verses:

Come all ye Colonizationists,
   My muse is off to-day
Come listen while she's singing
   Her soft and gentle lay.
Before she's done you'll understand,
   Whoever you may be,
That Old Liberia
   Is not the place for me.

Although I'm trodden under foot,
   Here in America—
And the right to life and liberty,
   From me you take away.
Until my brethren in the South
   From chains are all set free—
The Old Liberia
   is not the place for me.

Although (as Moses Walker says,)
   There, children never cry:
And he who can well act the hog,
   For food will never die;

For there the yams and cocoa-nuts,
    And oranges are free—
Yet Old Liberia
    Is not the place for me.[20]

Bypassing other curious musical borrowings, such as a "Temperance Song" ("In Honor of the Ohio Liquor Law, Passed 1854") attached to the *Marseilles Hymn;* or "No Master, Never," a narrative of escape to Canada via Cleveland and across Lake Erie sung to "Pop Goes the Weasel"; one final category seems especially puzzling: Simpson's use of hit tunes from the blackface minstrel repertory. Recall that his object in doing so was "to kill the degrading influence of those comic Negro Songs, which are too common among our people and change the flow of those sweet melodies into more appropriate and useful channels."[21] Simpson appropriated the "Air" of Ohio-born Daniel Decatur Emmett's "Dandy Jim from Caroline" (published circa 1844) to support his "The Fugitive in Montréal"; it is difficult to comprehend how a mid-nineteenth-century listener could have reconciled the tension between Emmett's second (of ten) verses—

I've often heard it sed ob late,
Dat sout Carolina am de state
Whar hansome niggs are boun to shine,
I'm Dandy Jim from Caroline.
Den my old Massa told me, O,
I'm de best lookin nigg in de county O;
I looked in de glass an foun it so,
Jis what massa told me O.[22]

—with Simpson's superimposed message:

Come all my brethren, now draw near;
I have a tale to tell you;
I have escaped the Auctioneers,
Though hard the blood-hounds did pursue.
Far in the south I was a slave
Where Sugar-cane, and cotton grows;
My Master was a cruel knave,
As every body may suppose.
    My old master don't like me;
    I begged him so to set me free—

He swore before he let me go
He'd feed me to the carrion crow.[23]

In an explanatory note Simpson informed his audience that one horrifying punishment was to bind the slave and leave him hanging or lying until the crows ate his flesh away: "They commence their dissection at the eyes, which many times are both plucked out before the sufferer is dead."

Simpson also plundered Stephen Foster liberally. For example, "The Son's Reflections" was an obvious parody of "Old Folks at Home," which had been issued in 1851. The first of its six verses:

'Way down upon the Mobile river,
　　Close to Mobile bay,
There's where my thoughts are running ever,
　　All through the live-long day.
There I've a good and kind old mother,
　　Though she is a slave,
There I've a sister and a brother
　　　Lying in their peaceful graves.
　　　　Oh! could I some how or other,
　　　　Drive these tears away;
　　　　When I think about my *poor old mother*,
　　　　Down upon the Mobile bay.[24]

"The Final Adieu" was performed to "I'm Bound to Run All Night," (the tune of "Oh, Susanna," published in 1848). Simpson even suggested a bit of musical dialogue:

Come all my brethren now draw near—
　　Good-bye, Good-bye.
My resolution you shall hear,
　　I'll soon be on my way.
Last night I heard some spirit say,
　　Good-bye, Good-bye.
"Tis time to go to Canada,"
　　I'll soon be on my way.
First Voice
I'm bound to run all night—
Second Voice
I'm bound to sleep all day;

Let the wind blow high,
  Come wet or dry,
I'm bound for Canada.[25]

"The Fugitive[']s Dream," attached to a brand-new "My Old Kentucky Home" (1853), even creates a bit of puzzling suspense for the first-time auditor:

I dreamt last night of my Old Kentucky Home,
Of my Old Kentucky Home, far away;
I thought old Master and I were all alone
In the Parlor about the break of day.
I thought old Master was weeping like a child,
Said I, Old Master, what is wrong?
He heard my voice, and he then began to smile;
"Why," said he, "what made you stay so long?"
  Weep no more, Old Master—
  Weep no more I pray;
I will sing one song at my Old Kentucky Home,
And return again to "Old Canada."[26]

The narrator then relives his life as a slave, including a bolt for freedom pursued by hounds, but abruptly awakes from what has become a nightmare to sing a final refrain about his "Old Kentucky Home, far away."

Although Anne Grimes sang "The Underground Railroad" to a tune she collected in the 1950s from Reuben Allen, a descendant of free blacks who had been a vaudeville entertainer, by then working as a houseman for a wealthy Zanesville family, she surmised that Simpson must have had Foster in mind, since one chorus reads:

O Susannah, don't you cry for me.
I'm going up to Canada
Where colored men are free.[27]

However, what Mrs. Grimes collected manifests the fundamental nature of folk song, since that language was a later accretion. The song was one of the handful added to the 1874 edition and was to be sung to a tune named "Nancy Till." Despite Simpson's use of the present tense almost a decade following Appomattax, the Underground Railroad had obviously become obsolete and fallen into disuse. A few of the original verses:

The Underground Railroad
  Is a strange machine,

It carries many passengers
And never has been seen.
Old Master goes to Baltimore
    And Mistress goes away.
And when they see their slaves again
    They're all in Canada!
        Come boys, come, and go along with me,
        And I'll take you up where colored men are free.
        Come, boys, come—make no delay,
        And I'll take you up to Canada.

Ohio's not the place for me;
    For I am much surprised,
So many of her sons to see
    In garments of disguise.
Her name has gone throughout the world,
    Free labor,—soil,—and men;—
But slaves had better far be hurled—
    In the lion's den.
        Come boys, come, . . .

Uncle Sam has tried hard
    To find the mystic route;
But well do our engineers
    Know what they are about.
While he is sleeping soundly,
    They are wide awake,
And firing up the engine,
    That runs across the Lake.
        Come boys, come, . . .

The Underground Railroad
    Is doing mighty well;
The number of her passengers
    Is very hard to tell.
When once they ship for Canada,
    It's hard to bring them back,
For "Johnny" runs a strong race,
    And never jumps the track.
        Come boys, come, . . . [28]

During the post–Civil War decades, pioneering ethnomusicologists traveled in the South, collecting and notating as best they could black folk songs, both sacred and secular. One Ohio-born outcome of that effort is *A Collection of Revival Hymns and Plantation Melodies* by Marshall W. Taylor (who from his portrait appears to have been African American). Taylor began his preface by asserting that "If you would know the colored people, learn their songs." Of the collection that follows:

> These melodies have sweetened the bitter pang of cruel mockings and lash-ings, and turned the gall into honey for the praying, singing slave. . . . In slave-pen, barn, jungle or palace, these melodies have done good wherever they were sung or heard. Slaves have leaped, freedmen shouted, kings and queens have wept, and Presidents have been moved to tears of joy, when these songs, ringing in their ears, burned into their hearts, and left the fires of phi-lanthropy, if not of religion, aglow, to burn on forever there. They have might-ily lifted and strengthened the hands of the Negro's friends in the North, while for their success they have pierced the ears of the Lord of Sabaoth.[29]

Taylor was undoubtedly alluding to the impact of the Fisk Jubilee Singers, orga-nized in late 1871 to make a fundraising tour in support of the newly established Fisk University in Nashville. They relied primarily on choral versions of black spiri-tuals made by director George L[eonard] White (1838–95), sanitized so as not to offend northern white sensitivities. After initial difficulties in Ohio, their first six-month journey became so successful that the financially troubled institution found itself debt-free; successive tours of the British Isles in 1873 and 1874 (during which Queen Victoria commissioned a life-size portrait of the ensemble) and of Europe from 1875 to 1878 led to international acclaim and even more extended travel.

Although he had been born in upstate New York, White taught school in Ohio and was a member of the 73d Ohio Volunteer Infantry from 1862 until his medical dis-charge in July 1864. The following year this fervent abolitionist left Chillicothe for Nashville, where he worked in the Freedman's Bureau and also taught music and pen-manship at what was initially called the Fisk Free Colored School. Given his Ohio connections and his goal of leading his singers along the route of the Underground Railway, Ohio became their proving ground.[30] They followed a zigzag course across the state during the last three months of 1871, with appearances in Cincinnati, Chillicothe, Cincinnati again, Springfield, Yellow Springs, Xenia (where they were welcomed by faculty and students from the newly reestablished Wilberforce Univer-sity), London, Columbus, Worthington, Delaware, Wellington, Oberlin (where they appeared before the National Congregational Council), Cleveland, Columbus again (after which the Fisk Singers became the Fisk Jubilee Singers, named for the Old Tes-tament "year of Jubilee"), Zanesville, Mount Vernon, Mansfield, and Akron.[31]

They faced indifference and even hostility, small crowds, and income meager to the point that it often failed to cover their expenses despite moments of genuine success. White and his charges had difficulty finding proper accommodation, being refused admission to two hotels in Chillicothe and at the third being allowed "to sit at table before it was time for others to come in."[32] It was only in Delaware, where they enjoyed their greatest success, offering them "fresh courage," that they "were entertained at a hotel, the proprietor of which, though a Democrat, gave them the pleasure of enjoying 'equal rights' for the first time at a hotel. They were allowed to sit at the same table with the white people, occupy the parlor, and exercise perfect freedom."[33] The local paper declared, "The concert is no negro minstrel affair, but an elevating, a refining, and remarkably delightful entertainment."[34]

Taylor may have been aware of such indignities a decade later. He was bold to assert the efficacy of his project, rescuing these melodies from oblivion, since they "have many a mighty task to perform, in lifting up bowed hearts to Jesus and overturning the prejudices against color, which are so ruinously widespread. Whoever will learn and sing these melodies, drinking from the same spring whence they flow, will of necessity grow warmer in feeling for those whose fathers sang them first."[35] Unfortunately, a flamboyant addendum by Bishop Gilbert Haven confused Taylor's "plantation melodies" with those of Stephen Foster and other contributors to the blackface minstrel tradition. Although finding the newly freed slaves "[n]aturally gifted in imaginative and musical ability," nonetheless, "while retaining much of the old, we have also laid hands upon the new order of things, accompanying each song or melody with music originally prepared for it."[36] The resulting musical crudities conflict with the assertion of F. S. Huyt, editor of the *Western Christian Advocate*, in his laudatory introduction, applauding especially the timeliness of the collection at a point when the "material was obtainable in matured form, but as yet unspoiled by the people who gave it birth and growth, or by the hands of ruthless innovators of the white race who would soon 'adapt' it into conformity with the 'high-art' tastes."[37]

Of course, the Civil War provoked responses in song, as had the War of 1812.[38] "How Are You, John Morgan," sung to a tune called "Here's Your Mule," recounts the outcome of the only action fought on Ohio soil. Confederate general John Hunt "Morgan's Raiders" had crossed the Ohio River into Indiana during June 1863 and then plundered their way across southern Ohio, intending to sow confusion and demonstrate Union vulnerability. They attempted to recross the river near Bluffington Island in Meigs County on July 19 but were thwarted, with half the force taken prisoner. Morgan and the rest of his troops continued northward until they were captured in Columbiana County on July 26. Morgan was jailed in the state penitentiary in Columbus, but he and six officers tunneled under that structure's formidable walls on November 27 and made their way south, where he continued to lead Confederate troops until he was killed during a battle in Tennessee the following year:

A famous rebel once was caught,
With saber bright in hand,
Upon a mule he never bought,
But pressed in Abram's land.
The Yankees caught his whole command,
In great Ohio state;
And kept the leader of the band,
To change for Colonel Streight.
    Then raise the shout, the glorious shout,
    John Morgan's caught at last,
    Proclaim it loud, the land throughout,
    He's into prison cast.

A felon's cell was then prepared,
At David Tod's request,
And in Columbus prison shared
The convict's shaven crest.
And thus the Rebel chieftain's pride,
They sought to humble low.
But Southern valor won't subside
Nor less in prisons grow.
    Then raise . . .

But prison fare he did not like,
And sought the time to leave,
And with greenbacks and pocket knife,
The keepers did deceive.
They say he dug a tunnel 'neath
Its gated walls so grand,
And from the North he took "French leave"
Away for Dixie's land.
    Then raise . . .

John Morgan's gone like lightning flies,
  Through every state and town;
  Keep watch, and for the famous prize,
  Five thousand dollars down.
  But he is gone, too late, too late,
  His whereabouts to find.
  He's gone to call on Master Jeff,

Way down in Richmond town.
    Upon his mule, he's gone, they say,
    To Dixie's promised land,
    And at no very distant day
    To lead a new command.[39]

Ohioans also sang about the loss of loved ones in that most bloody of wars. One of
the most widely circulated songs was variously titled "Ohio," "Stone River," or "The
Dying Volunteer."[40] It marked the death of an unnamed Ohio boy during the Battle
of Stones River near Murfreesboro, Tennessee, from December 31, 1862, through
January 2, 1863, during which Ohioans under the command of Gen. Phil Sheridan
of Somerset suffered heavy casualties. Anne Grimes discovered that its melody
seems to have numerous ancestors, including "Young Charlotte" (that tells of a young
girl's death by freezing on the streets of New York in the 1840s), "The Drunkard's
Dream" (a temperance song), a hymn tune named "Walbridge," and "James Harris
(The Daemon Lover),"[41] whose several variants tell of a sailor apparently lost at sea
whose spirit returns home seven years later to haunt his wife, who was by then
happily remarried. Grimes also collected variants, including one sung by a ninety-
plus-year-old Lawrence County woman in 1955. A sampling of these various sources:

    Among the pines that overlook
    Stone River's rocky bed,
    Ohio mourns for many a son
    That's numbered with the dead.

    That day, when all along our lines
    Rained showers of shot and shell,
    Thus many a brave young soldier died,
    Thus many a hero fell.

    As night closed down the bloody scenes,
    Returning o'er the dead,
    I heard the pitiful moans of one
    Laid low by mortal wounds.

The narrator builds a fire and fills the dying man's canteen before inquiring about
any parting words for family and friends. These include:

    "Tell them I died a soldier's death
    Upon the battlefield,

But lived to know the field was ours
And see the rebels yield.

"I'm very tired of talking now,
Please raise me up some high,
And fold my blankets close round,
And build a larger fire."

But, ah, he died that stormy night,
No friends nor kin drew near
To wipe death's damp from off his brow,
Or shed affectionate tear.

Considerable tension gripped Ohio throughout the war years because of the strength of the antiwar Peace Democrats, designated "Copperheads" by their opponents, who considered them as dangerous as snakes. One of their principal leaders was Clement Laird Vallandigham, born in Columbiana County but of southern ancestry. A congressman representing Dayton in the House of Representatives when the war broke out, he vigorously proclaimed constitutional protection for slavery and the right of states to secede from the Union. Defeated in his bid for reelection in the fall of 1862, he continued with vehement protests during the lame-duck session of Congress that followed. The federal Conscription Act went into effect the following year, sparking resistance and even desertion. On April 13, 1863, Maj. Gen. Ambrose Burnside, commander of the Department of Ohio, with headquarters in Cincinnati, issued a general order defining several classes of "enemies of our country." On May 1 Vallandigham was one of several who addressed a Democratic rally in Mount Vernon, with language deemed seditious by Burnside. Vallandigham was arrested and exiled to the South by order of President Lincoln. However, the Confederates were uncomfortable with his presence, and by early summer he had managed to reach Canada on a blockade-runner via Bermuda. He was then nominated by acclamation as the gubernatorial candidate of the Democratic Party by those intent on rebuking Lincoln's conduct of the war, but was defeated in October by Unionist John Brough, who then died after only a year in office. Vallandigham was later allowed to return from exile and exerted some influence in his party until 1871, when he killed himself demonstrating how a client charged with shooting another man could have discharged his pistol accidentally.

In 1953 Mrs. Grimes collected from a retired professor in Mount Vernon a song that he had learned from an uncle who had served in the Union Army, a song whose two verses encapsulate the sentiments that Vallandigham must have provoked almost a century earlier:

O ho! The Copperheads they cried,
"O'er Uncle Sam we're bound to ride."
And loud they blustered and they lied,
And all for Jefferson D., Sir.
Vallandigham said "Uncle Sam
Should never have another man,"
When to Mount Vernon off he ran,
And there proclaimed his tory plan.
And what was that kicked up the row?
'Twas just to let J. D. and Co.
Have what they wanted or let them go!
And this is what the Copperheads
Meant, when Vallandigham he said,
"Oh, let us stop this carnage red,
And treat with Jefferson D., Sir."

The people on the other side
Will never let the Union slide,
But wish to keep the thing they've tried,
And hang your Jefferson D., Sir!
And when they found this tory pack
Were trying to keep our armies back
From following the traitors' track,
Said they, "These Copperheads we'll crack!"
And that's the cause of all the row,
For treason we won't allow;
And Uncle Sam shall never bow
To Jefferson Davis anyhow!
And that is what the Copperheads
All wanted, when to Abe they said,
"Oh, let our armies backward tread,
And treat with Jefferson D., Sir."[42]

Various modes of transportation also provoked an outpouring of song. As noted earlier, the Ohio River furnished the principal conduit during those early decades, and remains an important artery today. One of the European tourists who employed it was an English judge, James Hall, who floated downriver in April 1820 and then published letters describing the experience eight years later. He recorded extracts of what he called "River Melodies," although, of course, without any reference to the tunes to which they were sung. Most were of a general nature. For example,

To the admirers of the simplicity of Wordsworth, to those who prefer the naked effusions of the heart to the meretricious ornaments of fancy, I present the following beautiful specimen, *verbatim*, as it flowed from the lips of an Ohio boatman:—

> It's oh! as I was a walking out,
>   One morning in July,
> I met a maid, who ax'd my trade—
>   Says I, I'll tell you presently,
> Miss, I'll tell you presently."

In the meantime I bid you good night, in the words which the rowers are even now sounding in my ears, as they tug at the oar, timing their strokes to the cadence:

> Some rows up, but we rows down,
> All the way to Shawnee town,
> Pull away—pull away![43]

The young state faced the challenge of forging viable transportation links with the outside world, as well as within its own confines. Ground was broken in St. Clairsville on July 4, 1825, marking a determination to extend the National Road westward from Wheeling. Constructed across Ohio in increments between 1825 and 1840 (later designated as U.S. Route 40), it was memorialized in *The National Road in Song and Story*, compiled by members of the Writers' Program of the Work Projects Administration and published by the Ohio Historical Society in 1940 to mark the centenary of completion of the project within the state. However, whatever "songs" the collection was meant to include are not graced with even a hint of music.

However, water still seemed to offer the most obvious means of transport, given Ohio's natural boundaries to the north and south and substantial internal river systems, already navigable to some degree. With New York's Erie Canal, built between 1817 and 1825, offering water transport from Ohio's northern ports directly to the Atlantic Coast, planning for a system of canals in Ohio began in 1822, although construction was initiated only in early 1825 after a Canal Fund Commission had successfully marketed bonds in eastern money markets. The ceremonial spade marking the beginnings of Ohio's extensive system of canals was wielded by New York governor DeWitt Clinton, responsible for the building of the Erie Canal, at the Licking Summit, south of Newark, on July 4, the same day as the St. Clairsville festivity. What resulted was an extensive network of canals; the principal arteries were the 309-mile-long Ohio and Erie linking Cleveland and Portsmouth (completed in 1832) and the 250-mile-long Miami and Erie, connecting Cincinnati and Toledo (completed only in 1845). A major means of commerce and passenger traffic until perhaps 1861, after which more efficient and omnipresent railroads led to the loss of economic viability, the canal system gradually fell into disrepair (although a new boat was launched in Akron as late as 1907). However, the devastating floods of March 1913 led to abandonment, a process that had begun as early as 1876. Remnants can be visited at many locations, and the flavor of canal life can still be captured aboard seasonal boats operating on restored portions of the original waterways near Piqua, Grand Rapids, Coshocton, and Canal Fulton.

Flavor of equal potency can be sensed in an extensive series of recordings made of Capt. Pearl R. Nye (1872–1950) by Alan and Elizabeth Lomax in 1936 (sixty-nine songs were captured for the Library of Congress Archive of Folk Song); another series of Nye songs was recorded at Ohio State University, transcribed by Cloea Thomas of Ohio State, and issued in pamphlet form by the Ohio Historical Society in 1952 (and reprinted in 1971) as *Scenes and Songs of the Ohio-Erie Canal*.[44]

Although Nye obviously could not have experienced canal life during its heyday, he was born on the *Reform*, one of the family boats that operated as a pair in tandem to accommodate the Nyes' eighteen children, then docked at Chillicothe.[45] Although he postured as "the last of the canal captains," that title was not quite legitimate since it was normally reserved for owners, and "Captain" Nye merely supervised the operation of the boat owned by his widowed mother. He eventually built himself a retirement home in the shape of a canal boat atop an abandoned lock near Coshocton and made it his life's work to collect and perpetuate canal lore, becoming a folk singer of considerable repute. John Lomax described Nye as a "big, breezy, wholesome, smiling man" who "brought with him an armful of manuscripts rolled into scrolls, each scroll made up of twenty or thirty long yellow sheets pasted end to end together. Before he had finished his recordings, he was almost covered in a pile of manuscript." Over a period of two days Lomax not only recorded canal-related songs but standard ballads as well, remarking, "The Library of Congress has eighty-three versions of *Barbara Allen*, but none more beautiful than the tune Captain Nye sang for us." Nye's nostalgic passion was summarized in his parting statement: "These songs are sacred to me. They bring back memories of the silver ribbon, the Ohio canal. That was the best life a man ever had."[46]

A selection of verses from "A Canal Dance" (with seven verses and sung to a slightly altered version of "Little Brown Jug") perhaps best captures the active social life of those who worked the canal boats:

One night in Cleveland we had a dance,
On the weightlock[47] platform we did prance,

It was ice-cream cake, O what a time;
In a little while the sun did shine.
    Ha, ha, ha, ha, O what fun
    We had that night, yes everyone.
    The mules would winnow, kick and prance,
    They tried so hard to join our dance.

And so it was all along the line,
We had our fun though it rain or shine;
Our deckboats they would serve as halls,
In a corner, music; one would call.
    Ha, ha . . .

Some would clog, others buck and wing,
But the old square dance beat anything;
Yes, it made you feel so young and gay,
And after all it was just play, play, play.
    Ha, ha . . .

At the lockhouse, how the cats would yell!
The dogs would bark, mules throw a spell;
How the chickens cackled and would crow
Was better than Mr. Barnum's show!
    Ha, ha . . .

Well, I'm up in years, yet young, young, young,
But a better life could never come;
Let others do as they choose, dear pal,
But I will stay on the old canal!
    Ha, ha . . .[48]

Of course, not all was dancing and prancing. Traffic jams on congested portions of
the canal provoked the intemperate behavior depicted in the first and last verses of
"Get That Boat":

Get that boat! my lucky little driver,
Get that boat, get that boat, I say.
We've heard them say they'd make us divers,
Get that boat, get that boat, I say.

Skin them alive, hang the carcass on the fence;
Don't stop for naught, no matter what expense;
Pound them on the back till they lay over,
Pass, pass them, get that boat, I say.

Get that boat! we will teach a lesson;
Get that boat, get that boat, I say!
We'll send her below with all our blessings;
Get that boat, get that boat, I say!
They're poking along, we're tired of it too;
And if must, will polish up the crew;
So crash her, boys, if she won't lay over!
Get that boat, get that boat, I say![49]

Furthermore, the work must have been onerous and even tedious. "Last Trip in the Fall," sung to a tune called "Between Me and the Wall," describes taking on eighty tons of coal, "At Nick Hert's mine near Trenton," after which the crew managed to make it safely to Cleveland, where they tied up at the end of the season. However,

Window-glass ice everywhere,
We handled line with gloves,
They soon were wet, our hands so cold,
And that nobody loves;
But coon we were all winter-set,
O yes, were feeling fine,
And eating nuts while cracking jokes
Of things along the line.

A third verse makes it clear that Nye's passion for life on the canal quickly obliterated any thought of adversity:

That winter was the limit, O yes,
For us Big Ditch boys;
Had everything at our command
That city folk enjoy.
No matter how the cards would run,
My heart would sing and smile;
I learned these things, yes, years ago
Upon the old canal.[50]

"Fairy Palace," sung to a borrowed melody called "On the Banks of Salee," offers a detailed travelogue of the complete trek "[o]n our little Fairy Palace" from Cleveland to Portsmouth, mentioning by name virtually every town, and taking obvious pleasure in the experience, summarized in the last two of sixteen verses:

> Katydids and locusts, crickets,
> Birds, Oh, all serenade,
> From Cleveland to our Rainbow Town,
> Then who shall be afraid?
>
> So we'll enjoy it all along,
> And what things you will behold!
> The canal is so entrancing,
> 'Tis a life that ne'er grows old.[51]

"The Old Canal," sung to variants of tunes called "Little Old Log Cabin in the Lane" or "The Little Sod Shanty on My Claim," offers an even more specific travelogue, its seventy-eight verses recounting every possible detail of the Portsmouth to Cleveland journey, an ecstatic paean to the life of the canaler.[52]

Nye also created individual songs devoted to places like Columbus and Lockbourne. The latter verses of his unpublished "Chillicothe," sung to what he called the "Canal Version" of "Shortnin' Bread," tell of persons and places of his acquaintance in that port (including unfortunate references to the "Chink" and "dago"). However, Nye's associations with Chillicothe were quite intimate:

> In Chillicothe, where I was born,
> I used to have a dear but she had no horns;
> She lived near the Canal up in Old French Town,
> I used to stop and see her going up or down.
> One day I said, "Now, with me you skip,
> For I'm going North, this is my last trip."
> She looked at me, became so sad,—
> I said, "You'll be my wife and make me Shortnin' Bread."
> Shortnin', shortnin', shortnin' bread,—
> Everybody on my boat loves shortnin' bread!
>
> So we to the parson then did go,
> He "tied us up" so gently, that all folks know.
> O, we are so happy as we run along,
> And every trip is full of music, love and song!

O, what a time we have, such a "Family Game";
Seems we know no better,—all is so glad—
And everybody on my boat loves shortnin' bread.
Shortnin', shortnin' . . .[53]

Nye's enormous delight in the lifestyle of which he represented only a residue is perhaps best manifested in "The Clever Skipper," a song he supposedly inherited from his parents. It tells of an Akron captain "[w]ho had a lovely woman, and a tailor she loved well," each verse concluding with a "Tum a rally dally, Tum a rally tally day" refrain. The captain and some of his crew surprise the wife and tailor at a rendezvous, where they had "wined, dined and danced." The tailor hides in a chest containing the husband's "coat, boots and hat." Of course, in the fifth verse the captain announces that "I didn't come to rob / Or break you of your rest; / I am going on south / And came for my chest." Two verses later, members of the crew have managed to lug the chest to the boat, although "the weight of the tailor / Made the sweat trickle down." The chest is unlocked "And there lay the tailor / Like a hog in a stall." The clever skipper announces,

Now I have got you,
'Twill be like on sea,
Not leave you here
Making trouble for me.
They took him on board,
For Portsmouth they did steer.
This is the last
Of the tailor we do hear.[54]

Nye's nostalgia for an idealized past is perhaps summarized in two songs. First, the second and fourth verses of his "That Old Towpath," sung to the tune of George Kiallmark's "The Old Oaken Bucket" and described by Nye as having been "written at Lock 6, Akron":

Upon that old towpath, oh, I was so happy;
Most free of all mortals, the world ever knew;
I'd love to go back and remain there forever;
'Twas so unexcelling, most beautiful, true;
The air was so freighted with fragrance from flowers;
The moss, honey locust, clover, new-mown hay,
And, oh, nature's song, in what glee she would greet us,
No picture so grand as she would there display.

That beautiful towpath, such splendor, so glorious,
With dear Mother Nature I'd ramble along.

The hills, valleys, creeks, rivers, yes, all were with them,
They'd smile, sing and dance, 'twas an excellent scene.
I'd give all the world, yes, and what e'er my future,
If I could live over this wonderful dream.
No place in creation can ever approach it;
The Lord set His seal on it, beautiful, grand;
'Twas God, man, and nature all working together,
A handiwork, marvelous, water and land.
That beautiful towpath . . . [55]

He sang "The Old Skipper," an even more retrospective and intimate elegy, to his
adaptation of the "Whiskey Waltz":

I'm an old canal boat skipper with black snake in hand,
So fare you well darling, my mules will not stand.
The line's on the deadeye, for Portsmouth I'm bound.
I love the old towpath, best place I have found.

I've been on the lakes and the rivers, Oh boy,
But my dear Silver Ribbon is the place I enjoy.
'Tis a place, oh so matchless, each day new things born,
And I love to boat wheat and the big yellow corn.

There's tanbark and hoop poles, wet goods, merchandise,
Clay, coal, brick and lumber, cordwood, stone and ice.
Yes, all that was needed, we boated, dear Pal,
Best time of our lives we had on the canal.

I will not be a rover, for I love my boat,
I am happy, contented, yet, work, dream and float.
My mules are not hungry; they're lively and gay.
My plank is pulled in; we are off on our way.[56]

Ohioans also sang about other forms of transportation, especially railroads and
the romance of dramatic wrecks. Bruce Buckley, as part of his repertory of *Ohio
Valley Ballads*, introduces a song about a catastrophe in the village of Rarden in
western Scioto County during the summer of 1893. Three crewmembers of a Cin-

cinnati, Portsmouth, and Western train (through poetic license the "W" becomes a "V" in the ballad) were killed because of an improperly aligned switch. Their fate (although Marion Weaver, a watchman, is not mentioned in this version of the piece) was then memorialized in a song said to have been written by the engineer's daughter, sung to a tune bearing a passing resemblance to Henry Clay Work's "The Ship that Never Return'd":[57]

It was on a summer's eve when the wind was sighin'
Through the branches of the trees,
A train rolled out for Cincinnati
On the old C. P. & V.
They'd been switching cars and sending back signals
When the engineer took flight.
For he was killed at Rarden Station,
That's why he never came back.
    Did he ever come back?
    No, he never come back,
    His fate was easy learned.
    For he was killed at Rarden Station,
    That's why he never returned.

The engineer was poor George Glasgow,
He was runnin' number four,
And little he thought when he left Portsmouth
That he'd run that train no more.
He was runnin' into Rarden Station
Eleven minutes late,
And when he saw the switch was opened,
He lept blindly to his fate.
    Did he ever . . . ?

The fireman's name was little Robert Little,
He was kindlin' up a fire,
And when he started to rush through,
He was crushed between the cars.
He'd been shov'ling coal in the fiery furnace,
His face it was all black.
And he was killed at Rarden Station,
That's why he never came back.
    Did he ever . . . ?[58]

Naturally, Ohioans were fascinated by mayhem of a different sort. For example, Gustave Ohr and George Mann were hanged in Canton in December 1879 for having murdered one John Whatmaugh by striking him on the head with a coupling pin and then stealing his clothing, a silver watch, and six dollars in cash. The crime was committed in Alliance, and the two criminals were apprehended in the nearby village of Beloit. Their stories[59] were purportedly written in jail after they had been sentenced to death and then sung by others to a tune associated with words beginning "My name is Charles Giteau." While their tales coincide in most detail, each accuses the other of the actual deed, and each arrives at a different conclusion. Ohr's:

> I am thankful to the Sheriff
> For his kindness to me,
> Likewise my noble lawyer
> Who tried to set me free;
> And also to my clergymen
> Who brought my mind to bear
> That there is a good and holy judge
> Way up in heavenly sphere.[60]

Mann's:

> Now my life is ended,
> I from this world must part,
> For of my bad misfortune
> I am sorry to my heart.
> Let each young wild and vicious youth
> A warning take by me:
> Be led by your parents
> And shun bad company.[61]

Although choosing to concentrate on folk song as the most tangible form of the traditional arts with direct Ohio roots, other kinds of expression are legion. The annual Gambier Folk Festivals and Black Swamp Dulcimer Festivals at Lima are perhaps only the most noticeable of such gatherings. Folk and dulcimer societies can be found across the state, and players of the fiddle, banjo, and guitar abound; Columbus is even home to "Harpers Bizarre," a quartet of harmonica players. (For a sampling, see *Traditional Music from Central Ohio* [Traditional Arts Program TALP–001, 1979] or *Seems Like Romance to Me: Traditional Fiddle Tunes from Ohio* [Gambier Folklore Society GFS 901, 1985], with an ample essay, "Traditional Fiddling in Ohio History.")

Singing games, more recently called play party games, were also practiced widely in Ohio during the nineteenth century. Rediscovered and collected by folklorists early in the twentieth century, they were extensively employed by recreation specialists like Lynn Rohrbough of Delaware, Ohio, who founded the Cooperative Recreation Service during the 1930s. He issued collections like the *Play Party Games*, reincarnated as the *Handy Play Party Book*, edited by Cecilia Riddell. Its ninety-three entries are arranged in order of ascending difficulty, with line dances leading to circle dances. The songs themselves often suggest the choreography, precluding the need of a caller. Many hearken back to their European roots; a sizable number were collected from Ohio practitioners. A pair of examples might suggest the tradition.

"I want to be a farmer" was collected from R. Bruce Tom of Columbus. The dancers arrange themselves in a single circle of couples with the ladies to the right of their men. The movement is then coordinated with the progress of the song:

(1) I want to be a farmer, a farmer, a farmer,
I want to be a farmer and by my lady stand,
(2) With a pitchfork on my shoulder, my shoulder, my shoulder;
With a pitchfork on my shoulder and a (3) sickle in my hand.

(4) Bow, ladies, bow; (5) Gents, you know how;
(6) Swing that left-hand lady 'round, (7) All promenade,
All promenade; All promenade;
Swing that left-hand lady 'round, All promenade.[62]

At the beginning, all join hands and circle to the left. At (2) everyone takes two steps toward the center of the circle, keeping hands joined. Somehow, each person then puts a right arm over the head, resting the hand on the shoulder. At (3) the arms return to their original position. At (4) each "balances" to his or her partner, dropping hands with a bow and curtsey, after which (5) each balances to his or her corner, with another bow and curtsey, the men turning to the left, ladies to the right. The men swing the lady on the left twice (6), and then (7) promenade with that lady counter-clockwise with hands joined in a skating position, resuming their original positions on the final phrase of the song.

Mrs. Earl Koontz of Vandalia contributed "Down the River," a line dance with couples facing one another:

The river is up, and the channel is deep,
The wind is steady and strong,
Oh, won't we have a jolly good time,
As we go sailing along[?]

Down the river, oh, down the river, oh, down the river we go-o-o;
Down the river, oh, down the river, oh, down the O-hi-o.[63]

The choreography:

> The head couple advances to the center, links arms and reels (as in the Virginia Reel): Partners link right arms in the middle; then the head girl goes to the second boy, links left arm with his left arm, turns one-half way. He steps back to his place and she goes back to the middle. At the same time the head boy has turned the second girl by the left and returns just in time to hook right arms again with his own partner in the middle. Each then turns the third by the left arm, returns to swing partner by the right, and on down the line, to the foot where the boy steps in place at the foot of the boy's line, the girl at the foot of the girls' line.
>
> Meanwhile, as soon as the first couple has reached the fourth couple, the second couple starts to reel, and others follow in turn until all have reeled entirely down the line.[64]

Thus, while Ohioans have abundantly employed the core folk repertory, often adding their own variants to songs with a universal currency, it seems evident that they have also generated a considerable body of interesting literature reflecting numerous facets of the state's history and culture.

CHAPTER 30

Blackface Minstrelsy

The immense popularity of our first homegrown form of musical entertainment, with its ugly caricatures of Southern blacks created by Northern whites, leaves us terribly uncomfortable today. Yet, since Ohio audiences devoured the product voraciously and several Ohioans played crucial roles in creating and marketing the phenomenon, there is little choice but to discuss it.[1]

While white impersonation of black music-making dates back as far as 1751, it was only during the 1820s that the blackface minstrel show began to take on a perceptible form. Performers like George Washington Dixon (1808–61) and Thomas Dartmouth Rice (1808–60) blackened their faces with burnt cork and created costumes that came to represent stereotypical Southern blacks: Jim Crow, uncouth and offhand in ridiculously tattered clothing, and Zip Coon, the pretentious urban dandy in a swallowtail coat and white gloves. These pioneers and others gradually expanded their acts into what became known as Ethiopian Operas, comprised of what they called plantation songs in crude dialect; ugly, violently racist humor; and banjo and fiddle tunes, which usually evoked elaborate dancing.

At first these acts were attached to other kinds of theatrical enterprises, particularly circuses. The classic, freestanding minstrel show is usually dated to the Virginia Minstrels' "concert" at the Bowery Amphitheatre in New York on February 6, 1843. Four performers gathered in a semicircle on the stage, playing the violin, banjo, tambourine, and bone castanets. The endmen were called Tambo and Bones; one of the group served as a master of ceremonies, later called the interlocutor. What evolved by the 1850s was a tripartite evening, with a series of hit songs followed by the olio, a potpourri involving dancing and parodies of Italian opera arias and the like, and, to conclude, the walk-around, a grand ensemble finale with lots of singing and dancing. The Virginia Minstrels' success sparked a rage for the genre, with a host of professional companies like Bryant's Minstrels, Christy's Minstrels, or the

Sable Harmonists, resident in cities like New York or on touring circuits that took them to every nook and cranny of this country and to England as well.[2]

After the Civil War, the small classic companies were driven out of business by increasingly larger troupes like W. S. Cleveland's Colossals.[3] The subject material gradually changed as well, with the satire directed at new immigrant groups like the Irish, American Indians, suffragists, and the like. Women entered the field, as did black performers. A few of the latter had taken up the profession before the war, but black companies like Haverly's Colored Minstrels, Richard's and Pringle's Georgia Minstrels, and W. S. Cleveland's Colored Minstrels, usually managed by whites, flourished during the final decades of the century. Interest in minstrelsy waned as the century drew to a close and the public turned to vaudeville, burlesque, the revue, and the infant musical comedy. At least one professional company survived until the 1920s, but amateurs continued the practice into the 1950s, when the initial phases of the civil rights movement made minstrelsy increasingly untenable.

Ohio and Ohioans played significant roles in the creation and practice of blackface minstrelsy. While none can claim Stephen Foster (1826–64) as a Buckeye, he spent a week in Cincinnati during May 1833 as part of a holiday that took part of the Foster family as far west as Louisville. He then worked in the Queen City from late 1846 until January 1850 as a bookkeeper for his brother, Dunning McNair Foster, a partner in the firm of Irwin and Foster, commission and forwarding merchants and agents for various steamboat companies.

It seems reasonable to assume that Foster imbibed much of the flavor and imagery of his sentimental, genteel parlor songs and "Plantation" or "Ethiopian" melodies" during this Cincinnati sojourn, since what he called "our city" was located on the cusp of the South.[4] While supposedly enjoying "the happiest years of his life"[5] he had ample opportunity to observe black roustabouts at work on the nearby levee, as well as the Southern culture symbolized by the packet boats from Louisville, Memphis, and New Orleans, which Irwin and Foster represented.[6] As example, "Gwine to Run All Night" ("De Camptown Races" of 1850) or "Away Down Souf" (copyrighted by W. C. Peters on December 30, 1848, with lyric by the composer suggesting, "We'll put for de souf / Ah! dat's the place, / For the steeple chase and de bully hoss race—") possibly reflect action at the Queen City Course or, especially in the latter case, excursions advertised for Cincinnatians by steamboat to races staged by the Louisville Jockey Club.

Cincinnati succumbed to the minstrelsy craze of the 1840s, so that Christy's Minstrels first played the Queen City in 1844 and then returned in November 1846 and August 1847. The Ethiopian Serenaders also appeared in 1844 and returned during the two following seasons, all of these visits involving multiples performances. The Sable Harmonists first appeared in 1845 and 1846, then enjoyed engagements lasting as long as a week in March, April, and September 1847 and again in August 1848 and

August 1849. Other troupes of lesser reputation appeared, including the Empire Minstrels, who achieved a record of fifty-nine local performances in late 1849.

Scholars have documented that young Foster gave manuscript copies of various songs to some of these itinerant performers, with one famous result. "[Oh!] Susanna" was offered to M. J. Tichenor of the Sable Harmonists, who presented it at the Melodeon Theater in March and April of 1847; the W. C. Peters edition of the following year employed Tichenor's recognizable name beside that of the unknown composer. Foster also gave a copy of the song to George N. Christy, with the result that when the earliest copyrighted edition of the piece appeared (Foster's lack of business acumen and lax copyright laws led to a host of unauthorized and pirated editions of his hit songs)[7] it was unattributed but noted as, "Sung by G. N. Christy of the Christy Minstrels." Ironically, for a composer whose best-known melodies were to achieve universality ("folksongs by destination, if not by origin," in a memorable phrase), this anonymity even extended at times to local advertisements of his work. For example, in an announcement of late March 1848:

UNCLE NED.—Just issued this
day, the favorite and popular Negro
Melody entitled "Uncle Ned" arranged
for the Piano Forte, Solo and Quartette.
MASON, COLBURN & CO.

In June of that same year, Peters, Field and Company announced a

NEW SONG—This day issued No. 3
Songs of the Sable Harmonists entitled SUSANNA

and later that year,

Songs of the Sable Harmonists—
consisting of "Susanna"
"Uncle Ned"
(the original copy)
"Lousiana [sic] Belle."[8]

Foster had entrusted "[Old] Uncle Ned" to William Roark of the Sable Harmonists; the title page of one edition noted, "Written & Composed for Wm. Roark, Of the Sable Harmonists. By S. C. Foster of Cincinnati." "Lou'siana Belle" (issued by W. C. Peters in Cincinnati, 1847) became a vehicle for Joseph Murphy of the Sable Harmonists. "Way Down in Ca-i-ro" was noted, "Written and Composed for James F.

Taunt of the Empire Minstrels by Stephen C. Foster" when it was published by Firth, Pond, and Company of New York in 1850.

Firth, Pond, and Company had become Foster's principal publisher even before he left Cincinnati for Pittsburgh and, later, New York. However, William Cumming Peters (1805–66) established a reputation as a publisher and probably earned himself a considerable amount of money by issuing several of Foster's early works, the first copyrighted in October 1846. English-born, he had arrived in Pittsburgh during the early 1820s and opened the Musical Repository, one of that city's first music stores. He also wrote and arranged music, in part occasioned by his involvement with the Harmony Society at nearby Economy and, according to some scholars, served as a music teacher in the Foster household, ministering to Stephen's younger sisters. It seems probable that he had established himself as a music publisher in Louisville and later in Cincinnati. Thus, many of the early Foster editions were copyrighted in Kentucky but issued concurrently in both Ohio River cities.

Foster published three works in 1847, five the following year, four in 1849, and fully sixteen in 1850, although it is not clear how many of these were actually written in the Queen City. Of those not already mentioned, noteworthy is "Santa Anna's Retreat from Buena Vista," a "Quick Step as Performed by the Military Bands," published in a piano version during August 1848. War with Mexico had broken out in May 1846; the Treaty of Guadalupe Hidalgo signed in February 1848 resulted in the acquisition of California as well as New Mexico, later to become the states of Arizona, Utah, and Nevada. Furthermore, Zachary Taylor's victory at Buena Vista had occurred in March 1847. While the conflict was opposed by many, the 4th Ohio Regiment of Volunteers was formed and steamed off for New Orleans on July 2, 1847, shortly after Dunning Foster traveled upriver to enlist in the Pittsburgh Blues. He returned to his post in Cincinnati only in June 1848, weakened by the rampant illness that had sapped the strength of the American forces, costing some units as many as half their numbers. Brother Stephen's single identifiable contribution to the war effort must have been performed long before it appeared in print.

Two Buckeyes, one a native, the other an immigrant, might be considered the alpha and omega of professional blackface minstrelsy, since their careers neatly bracket the history of the tradition. Daniel Decatur Emmett (1815–1904), born in Mount Vernon, was one of the original Virginia Minstrels of 1843; Al. G. Field (1848–1921), although born in Virginia, organized the Al. G. Field's Minstrels in 1886, a large touring company headquartered in Columbus whose demise in Cincinnati during the spring of 1928 marked the effective end of the tradition.

As a youth Emmett taught himself to play the fiddle and became a printer for newspapers in Norwalk and Mount Vernon. During May 1834 he enlisted in the army, where, during an abbreviated career (he was discharged in July 1835 when the authorities discovered that he had falsified his age and was still a minor), he became a skilled fifer and drummer and in 1862 was to issue the *Fife Instructor: Being a Thorough and Progressive Method, Embracing the Rudiments of Music and a Complete Collection of All the Calls and Tunes as Used in the Regular Army of the United States*; he also prepared *Emmett's Standard Drummer*, although that volume was never published. He resurfaced in Cincinnati as a circus performer and issued his first song: "This is the first negro song that I wrote—twas written in Cincinnati, Ohio, for Mr. Frank Whitaker (Equestrian and negro singer) about the year 1838 or 9. D. D. Emmett." "Bill Crowder," apparently performed by a blackface performer atop a trained horse, was sung to a borrowed tune, a standard Emmett practice. It told of a black arriving in the Queen City who almost immediately found himself engaged in a brawl. Emmett's first quatrain:

> I 'ribed at Cincinnati and I gits upon de landin
> De first place I found mysef was fotch up a standin,
> I heard a great noise like a rassle jack brayin.
> Tinks I to mysef dis is no place for stayin.[9]

During the early 1840s Emmett traveled with various circuses throughout the East and Midwest as a banjo player and singer, probably in blackface. By November 1842 he had made his way to New York and established himself as an "Ethiopian Minstrel." By January of the following year he and three associates had conceived the idea of a "minstrel band," which metamorphosed into a weeklong engagement at the Bowery Amphitheatre, opening on February 6, 1843. A newspaper announcement heralded the

> First Night of the novel, grotesque, original, and surprisingly melodious Ethiopian band, entitled the *Virginia Minstrels*, being an exclusively musical entertainment combining the banjo, violin, bone castanets, and tambourine, and entirely exempt from the vulgarities and other objectionable features which have hitherto characterized negro extravaganzas.[10]

After immediate triumphs in New York and Boston, the quartet sailed for England on April 21. Following performances in Liverpool and Manchester, they discovered popular success in mid-June at the Adelphi Theatre in London with their "Grand Ethiopian Concert," billed as "The Greatest Novelty ever brought from America." However, interest quickly slackened, and the original group disbanded. Emmett and two of his colleagues remained in Britain until September 1844, performing individually and collectively across England, Ireland, and Scotland. Emmett's stature is perhaps best represented in a series of thirteen songs from his repertory published in London either during his British sojourn or immediately thereafter as *Emmit's* [*sic*] *Celebrated Negro Melodies, or Songs of the Virginny Banjoist*, and noted, "Composed & Sung with great applause at all the Principal Theatres by D. D. Emmit." Emmett was portrayed in costume and blackface on the covers of his standards, songs like "Old Dan Tucker," "Boatman's Dance," and "Dandy Jim from Caroline."

Emmett returned home to confront a host of competitors in an entertainment medium he and his colleagues had virtually created less than two years earlier. During the following decade he appeared with various minstrel troupes and as a solo banjo act in a variety of theaters, circuses, and amusement parks; he also wrote and acted in "Ethiopian Burlettas" like *The Rappers*, *The Barber Shop in an Uproar*, and *Hard Times*, billed as a "Negro Extravaganza." By September 1855 he had become proprietor and manager of and periodic performer in Emmett's Burlesque Ethiopian Varieties in Chicago, a venture that lasted for about a year. By April 1857 he had organized a new company in St. Paul, which may have functioned until the autumn of 1858.

We do know that Emmett joined Bryant's Minstrels in New York about that time, an association that lasted until July 1866 except for an interlude from the summer of 1861 until spring of the following year, during which he returned to Chicago to organize his own shows following the outbreak of the Civil War. For the Bryants, he not only sang and played the banjo but also participated in parodies of the popular singing families of the day, burlesques of Italian operas, and satires of current political and cultural happenings. However, his principal responsibility was the creation of walkarounds, the grand finales of their shows. The best known of these was "Dixie's Land," introduced by the Bryants in New York's Mechanic's Hall on April 4, 1859, as "Mr. Dan Emmett's new and original Plantation Song and Dance." Emmett dallied for more than a year before giving the piece to a publisher, so that Firth, Pond, and Company submitted "I Wish I Was in Dixie's Land" for copyright only on June 21, 1860. Since it had in effect already entered the public domain, the country was flooded with a host of unauthorized editions and parodies, in one instance even attributing it to another composer. Incongruously, it became a marching song of the Confederate Army, an anomaly that led in 1861 to Northern antidotes with new lyrics: "Dixie for the Union" and "Dixie Unionized" (the former with lyrics by Fanny J. Crosby). Its universality is suggested by a contemporary observation that whenever Emmett's "irrepressible institution" was heard, "the pen drops from the fingers of the plodding clerk, spectacles from the nose and the paper from the hands of the merchant, the needle from the nimble digits of the maid or matron, and all hands go hobbling, bobbling in time with the magical music of '"Dixie."'[11]

But what about Emmett's authorship? His most prominent biographer analyzed in considerable detail Emmett's appropriation of imagery, language, and both melodic and rhythmic bits from earlier minstrel songs and the larger Anglo-American folk song repertory that he had first imbibed from his mother in Mount Vernon, attributing this approach to "professional custom."[12] More recent scholarship has demonstrated that Emmett probably borrowed the song from Ben and Lew Snowden, members of the "Snowden Family Band," which entertained both white and black audiences in the Mount Vernon area beginning about 1850, although the two brothers remained active with their fiddle and banjo until the early years of the following century. Bought individually out of slavery during the late 1820s, the parents had become farmers after their marriage, and, despite their race, the lives of the Snowdens and the Emmetts surely intersected in the Mount Vernon of midcentury, thus facilitating such an exchange.[13]

"De Boatman's Dance," Emmett's first published song (Boston: C. H. Keith, 1843),[14] offers another example of unacknowledged plagiarism. Presented as "An original Banjo Melody, by Old [sic] Dan. D. Emmit," at least the chorus of the song had been sung by boatmen on the Ohio River during the pre-steamboat era. Its long shelf life is represented in a version Anne Grimes collected, as well as a parody called "Girls of Ohio." "Hi! row. The boatman [sic] row. / Floating down the river, / The Ohio" became, "Hi-ho, the world may know / The very best girls are / From Ohio."[15] However, it was Emmett's version that was immediately appropriated by rival minstrel companies, parodied in numerous campaign songs and by the Forty-Niners on their way to California, and eventually borrowed by Aaron Copland as one of his *Old American Songs* in 1950, with its "accompaniment in imitation of minstrel banjo playing."[16]

Emmett lived in Chicago for much of the time between 1867 and 1888, when he retired to Mount Vernon. Despite brief engagements with Haverly's Minstrels and Leavitt's Gigantean Minstrels, his voice failed and his more rough-hewn style was deemed incompatible with the slicker, large-scale shows of the period. Word of his penury led to benefit performances in 1880 and two years later, at which he performed. His last hurrah occurred between August 21, 1895, and April 11, 1896: a "farewell tour" of twelve thousand miles across fourteen states with the Al. G. Field Minstrels, beginning in Newark and ending in Ironton, although many of the intervening engagements were in the South. Advance hype for the January 2 performance at the Valentine Theater in Toledo almost implied an act of resuscitation:

> The vast majority of patrons of minstrelsy know but little of how their favorite form of amusement originated; and fewer still are aware that the originator of the time-honored negro first part, and also the only surviving originator of this popular style of entertainment is still alive. But such is the case. Uncle Dan Emmitt [sic] is the oldest living minstrel. He is eighty years of age, enjoys excellent health, and possesses a remarkably vigorous mind. He looks fully twenty years younger than he is.[17]

Field's invitation to his friend proved shrewd, since Emmett provoked rapturous ovations, especially whenever "Dixie" was sung or played.

Emmett performed only once again, an informal appearance at the Elks Lodge in Mount Vernon in 1902:

> The hall was crowded, and when he walked on the stage he was given an ovation, the audience rising. This mark of esteem was too much for the old minstrel, and the tears coursed down his cheeks. The orchestra played the introduction and played it again, but Uncle Dan was all unmindful of the situation, and stood with tears streaming down his face. It was a pathetic spectacle. Finally a tenor caught and hummed the refrain, and then Uncle Dan picked up the verse and sang it.[18]

Two years later it was the Elks who buried Emmett under the supervision of Field.

In 1875 Field's family had moved from western Pennsylvania to Columbus, where his father opened a contract paint shop. Considerable work was done for the Sells Brothers Circus, then headquartered in Chillicothe, and Al. soon found employment with that organization as a musician and clown.

The company he founded in 1886 remained in business for a record forty-one years, and, although the troupe that opened in Marion (followed by engagements in Upper Sandusky, Bucyrus, Akron, Warren, and Youngstown) on October 6 comprised only twenty-seven performers,[19] Field eventually mounted the most elaborate touring extravaganzas of his era, with as many as one hundred performers on stage (the 1897–98 show even included an hour-long burlesque called "Utopia," involving eight Shetland ponies and two Arabian horses). The Field Minstrels carried their stage settings with them, traveled in custom-designed railroad cars that held both personnel and equipment (one of the sleeping cars was named the "Dan Emmett"), and presented noted performers of the tradition in seasons of as many as forty-six weeks. Field paid his stars handsomely (up to $475 per week, plus expenses and wardrobe costs), lavished as much as $10,000 per season on costumes, and commissioned elaborate sets from the noted scenic studio of M. Armbruster and Sons in Columbus, representing locales such as "The Paris Exposition," "The Pan-American Exposition," and "The Roof-Garden—A Night in New York."

Field directed his shows, wrote sketches and afterpieces, and for many years performed in blackface as an endman or monologist.[20] He became a prosperous and substantial citizen of Columbus as a bank director and owner of considerable real estate, including a city home on Third Avenue as well as Maple Villa, a three-hundred-acre farm on Olentangy River Road in southern Delaware County, complete with its own electric plant and an artificial lake.[21]

Another proprietor of national note was not a native Buckeye but found his career in Toledo between 1858 and 1866. A native of Pennsylvania, Col. John (Jack) H. Haverly (1837–1901), eventually known as "The Prince of Showmen," immigrated via Cleveland and Elyria. He first established himself as a fishmonger but later became the owner of the Gem Saloon and Billiards, which he eventually converted to the Gem Concert Saloon, offering variety shows that included individual minstrels. At the outset of the Civil War, Haverly enlisted in the Home Guards of the 100th Regiment Reserves and was finally dubbed a second lieutenant, later promoting himself to the rank of colonel.

During the summer of 1862 he organized a tour to county fairs in Ohio, Michigan, and Indiana with a small troupe of minstrels. He then returned to Toledo and bought another saloon, but the Haverly Minstrels toured Michigan and northern Indiana during August 1864 prior to a winter season in Toronto. Subsequent performances in Toledo were interrupted by an eight-week tour of the Haverly-Mallory Minstrels beginning on December 27, 1865. What had become the Haverly-Sands Minstrels then left Toledo in August 1866 for a tour of only a few weeks' duration, after which Haverly sold both his theater and home in Toledo and launched himself on a colorful career that lasted until 1898.

Marked by extremes of boom and bust, Haverly managed his own companies, including the 40, Count 'Em, 40 Mastodon Minstrels (later doubled in size), which were organized in 1878 and later toured the British Isles several times, including a seventeen-week engagement in London in 1880, or the Georgia Colored Minstrels, one hundred strong, and an offshoot, the Genuine Colored Minstrels, based in London. He owned a controlling interest in other minstrel companies and also managed diverse theater companies of a different ilk, including two devoted to Gilbert and Sullivan's *H.M.S. Pinafore*. He gradually assembled a chain of theaters in New York, Philadelphia, Chicago, and San Francisco to house the various components of his empire, which at one point totaled twenty-two houses with more than fifteen hundred resident employees. In retirement Haverly wrote a guidebook for the trade, *Negro Minstrel—Burnt Cork Specialties*, which was published posthumously in Chicago in 1902.[22]

These individuals were only the most prominent Buckeyes involved in the minstrel tradition. Of the literally hundreds of biographical profiles limned by Edward Le Roy Rice (himself a retired minstrel hoofer) in his copiously illustrated *Monarchs of Minstrelsy* (1910), scarcely thirty were described as Ohio natives. A considerable number of these were involved with either Haverly or Field. For example, the three brothers Frohman (Gustave, Daniel, and Charles, all born in Sandusky during the 1850s) worked as managers (particularly as advance agents) for Haverly beginning in 1874, either with the core company or with Callender's Colored Minstrels, which had been bought by Haverly. In fact, Charles served as treasurer of Haverly's Mastodon Minstrels from their inception in 1878 until 1882, when he and brother Gus bought and managed Callender's.[23]

Of those whose careers intersected with Field's, the most noted might be John W. Vogel, born in 1863. He first worked on the staff of the Sells Brothers Circus in his native Chillicothe but by 1882 had joined the staff of Thatcher, Primrose, and West's Minstrels in Cleveland. After being named manager of that troupe, he held similar positions with other companies, including seven years with Field. By 1896 he owned and managed John W. Vogel's Big City Minstrels and by 1910 Rice was able to comment, "Mr. Vogel's success is attested [to] by his elegant Summer residence at Vogel's Beach, Buckeye Lake, Ohio, and a Winter home in Columbus, Ohio."[24]

Others followed even more independent careers. One of the most successful was E. N. Slocum (1836–95), a native of Columbus who first appeared with an amateur company in Warren in 1849 and was described by Rice as "one of the best interlocutors and actors in minstrelsy."[25] Much of his professional career was spent in Philadelphia, where by 1870 he had organized Simmons and Slocum's Minstrels, which played in its own theater. That venture lasted until 1877, when Slocum joined another company in Philadelphia and a decade later became associated with Dockstader's Minstrels in New York. Billy Manning (1839–76), born in Piqua, enjoyed a career that took him across the country, including stints with Newcomb's Minstrels in Cincinnati and the Simmons and Slocum troupe in Philadelphia. Between 1868 and 1872 he was proprietor of his own company, at first with partners and by 1870 as the single owner of Manning's Minstrels, both at the Dearborn Theater in Chicago and on tour. Michael O'Connor, who was born in Cincinnati and died in Xenia in 1882, described by Rice as "one of the best neat song and dance men in minstrelsy,"[26] began his career as a jig dancer with W. W. Newcomb's Minstrels in Cincinnati during October 1868, assuming the stage moniker of "Cincinnatus." During a considerable career, he even organized his own Cincinnatus Minstrels, which toured for a period, beginning with a show in Xenia on May 5, 1873.

However, another Ohio-born minstrel had considerable influence, since he became a composer for the tradition and also eventually entered the worlds of vaudeville and mainline theater as Uncle Tom in several productions of dramatized versions of Harriet Beecher Stowe's *Uncle Tom's Cabin.*

Sam Milady (1840–1916), born in Washington Court House, is identified today as Sam Lucas, his assumed stage name. Prior to service in the Union army, he had appeared with Hamilton's Celebrated Colored Quadrille Band in Cincinnati. He studied briefly at Wilberforce University in 1869 but soon thereafter embarked on a stage career as a member of companies such as Callender's Original Georgia Minstrels, Sprague's Georgia Minstrels, and Haverly's United Genuine Colored Minstrels. He first assumed the personality of Uncle Tom in 1878 in a production mounted by the

Frohman, Stoddart, and Dillon Company (and was eventually to play the title role in a 1914 film). By the mid-1880s, he had turned primarily to vaudeville and later strutted the boards in Broadway musicals like *A Trip to Coontown* in 1897, *Shoo-Fly Regiment* from 1906 to 1908, and *The Red Moon* from 1908 to 1910, shows involving major black talent of the period, such as Bob Cole and J. Rosamond Johnson. Composer of more than one hundred songs, this versatile showbiz personality was eventually dubbed, "Dean of the Colored Theatrical Profession."[27]

Vestiges of the practice survive in several Ohio communities, including Jackson County's Wellston and the village of Millersport, at the western end of Buckeye Lake. In December 1947 the Wellston Rotary Club, according to a minihistory recorded in the March 1957 program, "needed a project to provide a source of supplemental funds for community projects and to draw the members closer together in a common interest after the stress and strains of the war years." A large cast of local amateurs was transformed into thespians by Dwight and Karl Denton and J. Lester Haberkorn of Lancaster, who as Habb and Denton were veterans of the waning years of professional minstrelsy, especially as members of Al. G. Field's company. All the trappings of traditional minstrelsy were retained: an interlocutor and four end men, who apparently appeared in blackface and traditional costuming well into the 1970s; an Act 2 Olio, described one year as a "random collection of music and news throughout the years"; and a grand singing and dancing finale. Topical themes provided coherence (for example, *Here Comes the Showboat* in 1972 and *Levy Lullabies* in 1981) to what increasingly has taken on the flavor of a revue. Nonetheless, perennial songs such as "Alabamy Bound," "Are You from Dixie?" "Rufus, Rastus, John Brown," and "Swanee" maintain at least a residual reference to the historical tradition.

The Millersport tradition originated in 1958, also as a fundraising venture, in this case for the local Athletic Booster's Club (although it later became a project of the Millersport Community Theater). Pete Mees, a retired railroader then living in Portsmouth who had been a professional entertainer and directed minstrel shows there and in other southern Ohio communities such as Corning, Pomeroy, Middleport, and Shawnee, was imported to stage *The Dixie Land Minstrel*.[28] Whatever his earlier experience, Mees structured a format with at least some tangible links to the tradition: a first part starring an interlocutor, four end men, and a pair of "Premiers," initially all in blackface, and a chorus. Offerings by the chorus in a static position bracketed a series of vocal solos, jokes, and comic repartee. Part 2, originally labeled *The Vaudeville Show* but soon thereafter *The Olio*, presented a series of as many as ten or more acts, ranging from tap dancers to banjo players, barbershop quartets, solo singers, and specialty acts (such as a "Salute to Hawaii," admitted as a state in 1959, involving both a "Heeia Stick Dance" and hula dancing to an "Hawaiian War Chant" as part of *The Freedom Minstrel* of 1961), all capped with a grand patriotic finale involving the chorus. One peculiarity was the Spiritual Choir, singing arrangements of black spirituals, a medium antithetical to the historic tradition.

While the earlier manifestations included song titles such as "Are You from Dixie?" "Dixie Volunteers," "Ah Jest Wasn't There, Dats All," and "Swanee River," the shows have been gradually infiltrated by mainstream pop music, particularly excerpts from standard Broadway musicals, often presented in semistaged versions. While many have been titled thematically in predictable ways (for example, *Minstrel Classics* of 1963, *Train Ride thru the South* in 1968, or *Showboat Minstrel* in 1966 and 1984 [the last still featuring the six endmen, two of them female, in partial blackface]), other themes, such as *The Irish Minstrel* in 1969 and 1981, the *Old West Minstrel* of 1982, or the *Hollywood Revue* of 1992, might seem almost to have betrayed the tradition.

CHAPTER 31

Popular Song

Although Benjamin Russell Hanby (1833–67) is recalled today for a handful of songs that became enormously successful during his brief life span and have maintained a certain currency even to the present (another example of composed pieces achieving the status of folksongs), he led a multifaceted career as a teacher, minister, editor of children's music for a major Chicago publishing house, and even as an endowment agent for his alma mater, Otterbein University (now College).[1]

The eldest of eight children, Hanby was born on a farm near the village of Rushville, in Fairfield County northeast of Lancaster. His father was a United Brethren of Christ minister who at one point rode a 170-mile circuit covering twenty-eight different locations in the Scioto Valley. He became financial agent and treasurer of the Printing Establishment (at first located in Circleville but later as the United Brethren Publishing House in Dayton), was elected the fifteenth bishop of the conference in 1845, and compiled one of his denomination's first hymnals, *The Church Harp*, in 1841. The initial pocket version went through five editions by 1844 and was replaced by a revision in 1852 (noted as the "Latest Compilation of Sacred Songs, Designed For all Denominations").

His son displayed musical aptitude at an early age, attended singing schools with his father, sang in church choirs, and by age fourteen had bought himself a handsome mahogany flute adorned with silver keys and ivory mountings, for which he made a walnut case.

Hanby registered at Otterbein for the first time during September 1849 and alternated study with teaching in three different rural schools over a period of nine years, finally standing as a member of Otterbein's second graduating class in June 1858, a ceremony at which he delivered both a senior oration and an address in Latin. While in Westerville, he helped found and served as the first president of the Philomathean Literary Society, Otterbein's first such organization, and also served as coeditor of the school's first student publication, *The Star of Otterbein University*. He began piano study during the fall of 1852 after Otterbein purchased its first instrument but worked at music theory only after graduating from the preparatory to the collegiate level. By 1855 he had become proficient enough to organize a "juvenile class in singing" on Saturday afternoons. Although Bishop Hanby eventually relocated his family to Westerville (he was a founding trustee of the institution, which opened for business in September 1847 as a coeducational institution with a woman on its first faculty, radical stances advocated by the bishop and pioneered by Oberlin a scant thirteen years earlier), the son at first lived in a log cabin and supported himself with "Exhibitions" of songs and recitations in the area, as a tutor, with work as a maintenance man and in the harness shop, as a scribe of legal documents, and as a surveyor, a landscaper, and a wood chopper.

Undertaking a career as a public school teacher in 1850 at age seventeen, he taught the normal academic subjects, as well as music, drawing, and drama. He began and concluded each school day with singing, penning his first song for the Infant School he founded in Westerville (an institution for children ages three to twelve and indirectly a precursor of the kindergarten concept), the "Dismission Hymn," designed to send the youngsters on their way home (the patter part of its second verse is, "When life's lessons and its labors, / All, all are o'er[,] / May we with Thy ransom'd millions, / Meet Thee on the Golden shore"). During this period he also wrote the "Excursion Song" ("Ho! ho! ho! / Out to the beautiful groves we go") and "Willie's Temptation," a didactic "Song for Children" (published only posthumously by the John Church Company in 1868) about a brother who almost stole an apple from an abundantly furnished tree, but at the last minute was challenged by his conscience:

> And he sang, "Little Willie, beware! Oh, beware!
> Your father has gone, but your Maker is there.
> How sad you would feel if you heard the Lord say,
> 'This dear little boy stole an apple today.'"

He also wrote other didactic songs meant to teach the multiplication tables and principal vowels.

Evidence suggests that what eventually became "Darling Nelly Gray" was begun during a term of teaching in Rushville during the fall of 1855, although it was only during the following year that he dedicated it to his Otterbein theory teacher and sent its five verses and refrain off to the Oliver Ditson Company in Boston. Ditson promptly copyrighted the piece on June 18, 1856, since its young creator had failed to do so, and published it without notifying Hanby. A sister heard it sung in Columbus, provoking Hanby to write the publisher requesting royalties. Their eventual response: "Your favor received. 'Nelly Gray' is sung on both sides of the Atlantic. We have made the money and you the fame, that balances the account."[2]

Hanby's lawyer finally extracted $100 from the company, half of which was retained as his fee. This modest recompense is the only pecuniary benefit Hanby received from a song that achieved universality during the Civil War. It had been inspired not only by the fervent abolitionist stance of his parents and observations of their work as "conductors" on the Underground Railroad, but more especially by his response to a slave auction he witnessed in Lexington, Kentucky, during the spring of 1856 while traveling in the company of his father.

The following year Hanby wrote "The Reveller[']s Chorus," a temperance song that achieved considerable currency after its publication by Ditson in 1857 (and later by Root and Cady in 1865); it reflected the environment in which Hanby was nourished, since Westerville was a hotbed of the temperance movement. A note from the score:

> The incident which prompted this song actually occurred a few years since in a city in California. Some nineteen abandoned inebriates had been for days and nights together carousing in a fireman's club house until delirium tremens ensued. As soon as reason began to return, one of them, stung with feelings of deep self reproach, declared his intention never to drink another drop, and urged his companions to join him. His proposition was heartily agreed to, and a league was formed which from that day rapidly increased until its membership was numbered by thousands.

After graduation and marriage Hanby spent a year of travel soliciting funds for Otterbein and was licensed to preach in January 1859. In January of the following year he was appointed principal of the Seven Mile Academy in Butler County near Hamilton, where, during a two-year tenure, he employed a daily music class as a vehicle for new exercises and songs. These included "Little Tillie's Grave," published by John Church in 1860, and "Ole Shady, the Song of the Contraband," issued by Ditson the following year.[3]

"Little Tillie" told of a young black slave whose wife was taken from him, after which he fled with their daughter to a secluded island, where the child perished of swamp fever. Its chorus:

> Weep, zephyrs, weep in the midnight deep,
> Where the cypress and vine sadly wave;
> I have taken down my banjo for I could not sleep,
> And I'm singing by my little Tillie's grave.

The chorus to the fifth and final verse concludes with "Let my fingers keep tumming [*sic*] and my fond heart weep / Till I die by my little Tillie's grave," after which the father does succumb in an appended coda.

"Old Shady," written in black dialect ("Oh! yah! yah! darkies laugh wid me, / For de white folks say Old Shady's free"), portrayed the emotions of a slave on his way to freedom ("Dis chile breaks for ole Uncle Aby") and was provoked by the decision of Maj. Gen. Benjamin F. Butler not to return escaped slaves under the provisions of the Fugitive Slave Act (that earned Butler a dedication as "Columbia's Noble Son"). The song (for which Ditson paid Hanby $300 and royalties) became an immediate hit, but it aroused the ire of a school trustee who was a Southern sympathizer and led to Hanby's forced resignation.

In 1862 he became a pastor in Lewisburg and later New Paris, both in Preble County, west of Dayton, and was retained as a house composer by publisher John Church. In both church positions Hanby generated the opposition of fundamentalist members of those congregations by employing his flute, a reed organ, dramatized stories presented in costume, and other such heresies as means of attracting and retaining the interest of his younger parishioners, this at a time when the General Conference had banned both formal choirs and the use of musical instruments. One byproduct of the period is "Terrible Tough," a comic tale of the reluctant enlistment of one Timothy Huff while Governor John Brough was desperately attempting to fill Ohio's quota of soldiers at a time when the political climate was still soured by the Vallandigham affair. The song was dedicated to the Ohio National Guard and published by Church in 1864, its comic intent manifest in the composer's performance note, "The Choruses should be sung in a chant-like style, rather slow, in a mock-pathetic manner, slightly approaching a whining tone." By the way, Hanby was inadvertently drawn into the Vallandigham brouhaha when the tune of "Darling Nelly Gray" was appropriated without his assent as a vehicle for a Vallandigham campaign song called "Hero in Exile."

In 1864 Hanby resigned from his second pastorate but remained in New Paris and established a music school, where he taught voice and singing classes, directed plays, and continued to compose. The most notable artifact of this period is "Up on the Housetop," originally titled "Santa Claus May Be Recognized." It was first heard at a Christmas dinner for needy children hosted by the Quaker Society of nearby Richmond, Indiana, and then in New Paris, where Hanby taught his young charges to snap their fingers or clap their hands in unison with the very rhythmical "click, click, click" of the refrain. After publication in 1866 it quickly assumed the status of a folksong, maintained in oral form and thus considerably altered over the years. (The original begins: "Up on the house top, no delay, no pause, / Clatter the steeds of Santa Claus.") Among the other songs written for Church during this period was "The Nameless Heroine" of 1865, inspired by the tale of a young Confederate beauty who aided Union prisoners in escaping from their captors ("Hail to the angel who goes on before, / Blessings be thine, loyal maid, evermore!").

Hanby had attracted the attention of George Frederick Root and thus spent the final two years of his life in Chicago, where he was appointed director of the juvenile field and children's editor of Root and Cady, then one of the largest publishing firms in the country. With a handsome salary of $3,000 per annum, Hanby traveled for three of every four weeks as a representative of the company, promoting the use of Root and Cady publications through singing schools and children's concerts. These included "monster" performances in Crosby's Opera House, with six hundred children on stage reading from Root and Cady songbooks; other such concerts have been documented in various Midwestern towns and cities, including one in Leavenworth, Kansas, involving almost one thousand youngsters. The schedule at times must have been rigorous. For example, on June 6, 1866, he wrote to a friend, "I have just said good night to my little family and am finishing this at the music store. I start in a few minutes and must ride all night."[4] He was about to embark on a trip to Minnesota during which he suffered a hemorrhage that manifested the tuberculosis (then designated as "consumption") that would lead to his death the following March 16 and burial in the family plot in Westerville.

However, prior to that untimely end, Hanby had created a musical quarterly for children, for which he wrote much of the material and even designed the artwork. He added to the some twenty songs he had written in New Paris for the Our Song Bird Series, each volume named after a seasonal bird. The four issues of 1866 (that were actually published by John Church in Cincinnati) included The Snow Bird in January, The Robin in April, The Red Bird in July, and The Dove in October. The last of this quartet contained the first publication of "Up On the Housetop," as well as "Who Is He in Yonder Stall," a call-and-response hymn still available in The United Methodist Hymnal, 1989 (no. 190). Of the two other issues in the series, The Blue Bird in spring 1867 included three more Hanby songs. He was also noted as coeditor with Root of Chapel Gems: For Sunday Schools; Selected from "Our Song Birds," for 1866, with subsequent, "enlarged" editions in 1868, 1872, and 1894. Of its ninety-nine songs, as many as thirty-one were by Hanby. He supposedly also contributed to The Forest Choir: A Collection of Vocal Music for Young People. Embracing "Our Song Birds Singing School," Music for Concert, School and Home and Songs, Hymns, Anthems and Chants for Worship, since the copyright was filed in January 1867, although the first edition appeared after his death announcing Root as its single editor (subsequent printings occurred in 1872 and 1895). Authorship is difficult to establish, but it appears that Hanby probably contributed many of the vocal exercises and as many as thirty-three of the songs in this volume.[5]

Despite all this concern with music for children, Hanby during these final months of his life also wrote "Now Den! Now Den!—'The Freeman's Song'" and "In a Horn—'A Song for the Times—Adapted and Arr. by B. R. H.," both published in 1865 by Root and Cady. The former became a hit on the minstrel circuit, and today both seem imponderable because of Hanby's creation of black dialect ("De darkies say dis many a day" and "Say darkies, old massa is calling to you") for songs surely intended as antislavery social commentary.

Although obviously not as gifted as other composers with whom he shared the fate of abbreviated careers, the fact that at least a handful of his works have endured to this day as virtual folksongs perhaps validates the title proclaimed by a latter-day advocate, "The Bard of Ohio."[6]

While some of Hanby's songs retain a modicum of currency, even when performers or listeners may not be able to name their composer, and Hanby remains a recognizable figure to scholars, surely even few of these are aware that Ohio can claim a native son who became vice president of the United States and also wrote a tune popular enough to become a Motown hit.

Charles Gates Dawes (1865–1951) was born in Marietta, graduated from Marietta College in 1884, and received a master of arts degree from Marietta in 1887, a year after completing law school in Cincinnati. Marietta also offered him an honorary doctorate in 1921, and he was a longtime trustee of the school. He worked as a civil engineer for the Marietta, Columbus, and Northern Railway Company while completing his law studies and was admitted to the Nebraska bar in 1887. A practice in Lincoln led him into business, so that by 1893 he was resident in Evanston, Illinois, as a utility company executive. A member of the Republican National Executive Committee, he vigorously supported William McKinley in 1896 and was rewarded for his efforts by an appointment as comptroller of the currency. He resigned that post in 1901 to wage an unsuccessful campaign for the U.S. Senate and afterward settled in Chicago as a banker. In 1917 Dawes was commissioned a major and as a member of General Pershing's staff in charge of purchasing supplies for the American Expeditionary Force reached the rank of brigadier general. He resigned his commission in 1919 to campaign for ratification of the Treaty of Versailles and our membership in the League of Nations. He was appointed the first director of a new congressional Bureau of the Budget, and in 1923 became chair of a committee established to stabilize the German currency and reorganize that country's banking system. The resulting Dawes Plan won him co-ownership of the Nobel Peace Prize in 1925. He was then nominated as Calvin Coolidge's vice president and during his four years in that office lobbied vehemently, albeit unsuccessfully, for reform of what he viewed as archaic rules allowing unlimited filibustering. He served as ambassador to Great Britain from 1929 until 1932 and then briefly as president of the Reconstruction Finance Corporation before resigning to pursue his own interests in banking and philanthropy. He authored nine books before his death in Evanston, most of them autobiographically reflective, the first an analysis of the country's banking system in 1892.

Dawes apparently had a good ear and musical memory, played the flute and piano, and involved himself with all sorts of household music-making as a child. His claim to immortality arises from a *Melody in A*, apparently his only attempt at composition. The chronology remains murky, but supposedly violinist Francis Macmillen (1885–1973), another Marietta native and a family friend who enjoyed a considerable concert career, performed the piece and also brought it to the attention of Fritz Kreisler (1875–1962), the most prominent violin virtuoso of the period. Kreisler became notorious for writing pieces under the names of earlier composers, successfully aping their idioms, a hoax he maintained until 1935. He briefly appropriated General Dawes's tune and presented it as the work of an anonymous author, but the truth was soon out, and the violin and piano arrangement published by the Gamble Hinged Music Company of Chicago in 1921 was marketed, "As played by KREISLER." The *Melody* was also issued in versions for cello and piano, piano and organ solo, orchestra, both waltz and military bands, and even saxophone and piano. Gamble published a vocal version with attached words beginning, "Let me dream," which was employed as a campaign song with words by one Zeph Fitz-Gerald, announcing, "All over Yankee land they're humming a tune." However, the gist of the message was to present "Coolidge and Dawes for the nation's cause."

But as "It's All in the Game," its lyrics by Carl Sigman, Dawes's tune has enjoyed an enormously extended shelf life and may very well be the most circulated bit of music ever conceived by a Buckeye. Issued in sheet music form, it became a vehicle for an enormous variety of entertainers. Some of the pop and rock musicians who have recorded their version are Nat King Cole in 1957, Jane Morgan the following year, Dinah Shore in 1959, Liberace in 1962, Ricky Nelson and Andy Williams in 1963, Sammy Davis the following year, Bing Crosby and Bobby Vinton in 1968, the Four Tops in 1970, George Benson in 1978, and Van Morrison the following year. It was also in the repertory of several of the big bands such as those of Carmen Cavallero during the late 1940s, Sammy Kaye in 1959, and Lawrence Welk in 1962. It even became a country song in the hands of Sandra Posey (1966), Floyd Cramer (1970), Slim Whitman (1974), and Merle Haggard (1984). Columbus-born jazz saxophonist Rahsaan Roland Kirk (1935–77) recorded his response to Dawes in 1966, and "It's All in the Game" surfaced in the sound tracks of two films in the 1980s—*Diner* and *She's Having a Baby*.

And what might General Dawes have thought of all this hoopla? Apparently aware of his own limitations, he asserted, "My business is that of a banker, and few bankers have won renown as composers of music. I know that I will be the target of punster friends. They will say that if all the notes in my bank are as bad as my musical ones, they are not worth the paper they are written on."[7]

Foster, Emmett, and Hanby were not the only names gracing the sometimes elaborate covers of sheet music during an era when the piano, rather than the television set and VCR, was the focus of at-home entertainment, a period when self-entertainment was active rather than passive, when a degree of musical literacy was a required social grace for the middle class. However, there is no way of accurately estimating how many genteel songs and one-movement character pieces for the piano were churned out by Ohio composers, lyricists, and publishers during those decades when every parlor piano was adorned with sheet music of sundry sorts, their contents often directly reflecting current events or concerns. Significant treasuries of this material in the collections of the Public Library of Cincinnati and Hamilton County, the Ohio Historical Society, the Ohioana Library, and the Cleveland Public Library furnish a distinct impression of the cultural, political, and economic history of the state and nation of their period. A generous sampling, presented chronologically, is presented in Appendix B.

Obviously, most of this material proved ephemeral, its authors garnering a well-deserved obscurity (note how much of it was self-published). However, Ohio did produce a handful of pop composers whose work achieved considerable recognition.

The most celebrated of these was Ernest R. Ball (1878–1927). Although a major part of his career was spent elsewhere, he was born and trained in Cleveland, proclaimed in a song of 1918, "I'm from Ohio," and at his request was buried in his hometown's Lakeview Cemetery.[8] Ball studied at the Cleveland Conservatory of Music and then taught privately in Cleveland before moving to New York, where he made a living as a pianist in various vaudeville theaters before being hired as a staff pianist by M. Witmark and Sons, eventually his principal publisher. Ball established himself as a composer with the ballad "Will You Love Me in December as You Do in May?" written in 1905 to lyrics by Jimmy Walker, later New York's flamboyant mayor. He became known as an Irish balladeer because of the numerous songs he wrote for the tenors John McCormack (1884–1945) and Chauncey Olcott (1860–1932; a native of Providence, Rhode Island, who had earlier enjoyed a successful career on the minstrel stage and also collaborated at times with Ball as co-author or lyricist), standards like "Mother Machree" (1910), "When Irish Eyes Are Smiling" (1913), and "A Little Bit of Heaven" (1914). When George Graff Jr., one of Ball's principal librettists (others included J. Keirn Brennan and Caro Romo), was later asked how Ball, who possessed not a drop of Irish blood, could write such convincing Irish songs, he explained, "We were professionals. If we had been required to write Scottish songs, we would have written Scottish songs."[9] But even though Ball could assert in 1915, "Ireland is Ireland to me," his songs were also employed by crooners like Rudy Vallee, and "Let the Rest of the World Go By" (1919) became a theme song of Buckeye-born Roy Rogers and wife, Dale Evans. Although Ball became a charter member of ASCAP in 1914 and wrote about four hundred songs, he eventually took to

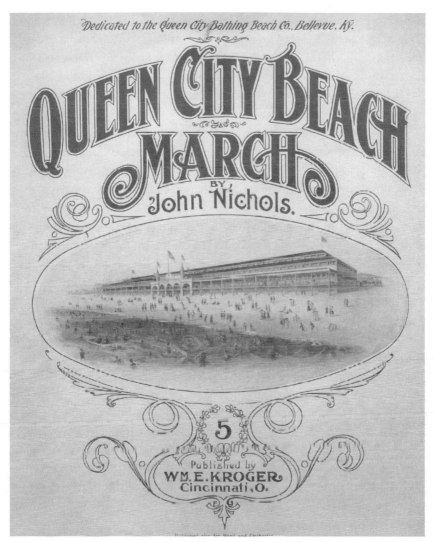

The cover of the *Queen City Beach March* by John Nichols. Public Library of Cincinnati and Hamilton County.

the vaudeville circuit with a double quartet of entertainers; he died in his dressing room following a performance in Santa Ana, California.

Few realize that "Down by the Old Mill Stream" was a commercial pop song, that the stream in question was the Blanchard River east of Findlay, and that the mill actually had a name—the Misamore. Its composer, Tell Taylor (1876–1937), was born in the nearby hamlet of Vanlue and sang in a Findlay church choir while working as a Hancock County deputy clerk. However, a chance encounter at the Pan-American Exposition in Buffalo in 1901 led to a modest musical comedy stage career in long-forgotten shows. Taylor also began to write songs, some of which were apparently published through a New York enterprise that involved Ernest Ball. Taylor migrated to Chicago, where he appeared for several seasons in musical comedies, but in 1908 he established the Tell Taylor Music Publishing House (renamed Forster Music Publishers at his death), attempting to attract attention with songs like "When the Maple Leaves Were Falling" of 1913 or "She Sold Her Soul for the Sake of Gold" the following year.

"Down by the Old Mill Stream" was popularized by a touring vaudeville quartet known as the Orpheus Comedy Four, which apparently first presented the song in Saginaw, Michigan, in 1910, although Taylor may have written it two years earlier. Taylor himself went on the road hawking the song, for example, managing to sell the one thousand copies he had in hand during a two-day stint at a Woolworth store in Kansas City. It reputedly sold more than four million copies during the composer's lifetime. Alas, Taylor seems to have been a one-mega-hit tune writer, since none of his other twenty-seven songs has survived (he cooperated with others or furnished the lyrics for perhaps another sixteen).[10] With the advent of the radio era he turned to that medium as a performer but spent the last decade of his life in Findlay in a state of semiretirement. During the spring of 1937 he wrote a song commemorating Findlay's Golden Celebration of Oil and Gas, since the well that had ushered in the gas boom of the 1880s was situated on the Taylor farm. At the time of his death he had just completed an offspring of *the* song ("On the Banks of the Old Mill Stream") and was en route to California to participate in the making of a film based on it; his body was returned to Findlay for burial.

Tod B. Galloway (1863–1935) warrants attention because of his unique career.[11] Most obviously, how did this Columbus judge become composer of "The Whiffen-poof Song"? Galloway was the son of an Ohio secretary of state who became a one-term congressman and a mother who was a talented amateur musician. He took two degrees at Amherst College, read law, and was admitted to the bar in 1888. He became chairman of the Franklin County Republican Party, was elected to the Columbus City Council, served two terms as a probate judge, and served as secretary to Governor Myron T. Herrick from 1904 until 1906. He then returned to the private practice of law, dividing his time between Columbus and New York. Galloway moved to Manhattan in 1910, where he worked as an editor for the MacMillan publishing house but in 1933 returned to Columbus, where he died.

Apparently a proficient pianist and singer, as well as a popular public speaker, he was both president of the Republican Glee Club and an important member of the Columbus Männerchor. For some thirteen months during World War I he entertained troops in Europe under the auspices of the YMCA as a speaker and performer of his own songs. In fact, fifty of those songs were published (virtually all by the Theodore Presser Company), even though Galloway was an untrained, purely instinctive musician who relied on others to transcribe his ideas into formal notation.

A charming tale suggests that one catalyst was a woman brought before the judge, who determined that she should not be committed to a hospital for the insane; in gratitude the defendant prepared for publication what became the eight *Memory Songs*, opus 30, issued in 1897 (that were followed by the seven *Friendship Songs*, opus 42, of 1907). Beginning in 1925 Galloway also wrote at least twenty-five articles for *The Etude* (also a Presser publication) on subjects as diverse as "Church Music before Palestrina," "Great Poet [Heinrich Heine] as Music Critic," "Why a Conductor?" "The Irresistible Lure of Gypsy Music," "Music in the Bible," "The Romance of Mendelssohn," "The Divine Purcell," and "Noted Women in Musical History."[12]

The fact that Galloway built his songs on poems appropriated from the likes of Shelley, Kipling, Paul Laurence Dunbar, and Sara Teasdale suggests that they aspire to the condition of art song. In fact, "The Gypsy Trail" (one of the *Memory Songs*), based on a poem by Kipling, provoked "The Whiffenpoof Song." The Yale Glee, Banjo, and Mandolin Clubs appeared in Columbus on January 1, 1908, at the Board of Trade Auditorium, during which one of the Glee Club's soloists, a senior from Cleveland, sang "The Gypsy Trail." At a postconcert smoker in the Columbus Club, Galloway entertained the undergraduates with one of his unpublished songs, built on Kipling's "Gentleman-Rankers." Its refrain:

> We're poor little lambs who've lost our way,
>> Baa! Baa! Baa!
> We're little black sheep who've gone astray,
>> Baa—aa—aa!
> Gentlemen-rankers out on the spree,
> Damned from here to Eternity,
> God ha' mercy on such as we,
>> Bah! Yah! Bah!

Five of the founding Whiffenpoof Singers of January 1909 were in that Columbus sing-along a year earlier. In their hands, Kipling's "Gentleman-rankers" became "Gentlemen songsters," and references to Mory's Temple Bar and the like were ladled into the mix, which became the Whiffenpoof anthem. A lawsuit over the patrimony of the song eventually established Galloway's role, so that a 1944 edition of "The Whiffenpoof Song: Baa! Baa! Baa!" (New York: Miller Music) is attributed to Meade Minnigerode (Yale, 1910), George S. Pomeroy (Yale, 1910), and Tod B. Galloway (as revised by pop singer Rudy Vallee, with some special lyrics by Moss Hart).

While Judge Galloway, despite his admitted abilities, by status remained an amateur, two of the Spitalny brothers achieved considerable renown as professional songwriters and leaders of theater orchestras. Phil (1890–1970) studied at the conservatory in his native Odessa and toured Russia as a prodigy on the clarinet before the family immigrated to Cleveland during 1905. He directed local theater orchestras in his adopted city but soon migrated to Boston, where he presided over a fifty-piece orchestra in one of that city's movie houses. In New York by 1930, he conducted his own orchestra in theaters, movie houses, and hotels, as well as on the radio and in recordings. He was best known for having organized an "all-girl" orchestra ("Phil Spitalny and His 32 Musical Ladies"), which made its first appearance at the Capitol Theater in New York in 1934 and then became headliners on General Electric's *Hour of Charm*, broadcast nationally over the NBC Red Network. This unusual ensemble flourished even into the television era.[13] Spitalny also wrote a number of pop songs with titles like "The Kiss I Can't Forget" (1925), "My Name Will Always be Chickie" (1925), "I Love No One But You" (1927), "Madelaine" (1941), "You, Mother Dear" (1948), and "It's You—No One But You" (1950).

Phil's younger brother Maurice (1893–1986) attended public schools in Cleveland before music study at the American Conservatory in Chicago and the Royal Conservatory in Berlin. He returned to Cleveland as an accomplished violinist and served the new Cleveland Orchestra during its first season as assistant concertmaster. However, he soon turned to his true *métier*, directing various theater orchestras during the two decades before he was appointed supervisor of music at KDKA in Pittsburgh, where one of his shows, *A Festival of Music*, was broadcast nationally by NBC. Before retiring to Florida in the late 1960s he led orchestras on other radio and television stations in Pittsburgh. Maurice was also a writer of such songs as "Parting Kiss" of 1925, "Broken Dreams" of 1927, "Since I Fell in Love with You" of 1938 (with Harold Dellon and featured by Guy Lombardo and His Royal Canadians), and "Angels with Dirty Faces" of the same year ("suggested" by a Warner Brothers film starring James Cagney).

Harry C[arleton] Eldridge (1872–1946) was a composer with much different aspirations. A public school music teacher in both Franklin and Miamisburg, during 1906 he entered into a partnership with Seymour S. Tibbals, publisher of the [Franklin] *Chronicle*; their goal was to create a mail order business marketing church and school entertainments, particularly their own. They first operated out of quarters in the newspaper's building, but what became the Eldridge Entertainment House (and after the founder's death the Eldridge Publishing Company) incorporated and moved into its own quarters in 1926; a Denver branch (that closed in 1969) was opened at least by 1921.[14]

Eldridge got his start with *The Captain of Plymouth*, a comic opera with words by Tibbals, published in 1908 by "The House That Helps." The constituency at which such a piece was aimed is perhaps indicated by the creators' prescriptions. The role of Miles Standish was to be sung by a baritone, "short and stout, if possible—with GOOD dramatic ability." The soldiers were assigned a "burlesque act, extremes in size desired," while the Indian squaws were preferably brunettes and could be double cast as the Puritan maidens of the first act. That "sextette of Plymouth Daises" sang only in unison and were supposed to be "pretty and clever." Eldridge churned out other stage pieces, including *Midsummer Eve*, a "musical fairy play" with words by Elizabeth F. Guptill (1910), as well as *In Little Folks Town*, a "Novelty Operetta for Children" with words by Willis N. Bugbee (1913), and other children's operettas, such as *Santa in Southland* and *Under the Sugar Plum Tree*.

Eldridge also wrote what may have been more than two hundred children's songs. For example, a series of *Novel Entertainment and Action Songs for Concert, Home and School-Room Use* included "The 'Champeen' Baseball Nine (For Nine Small Fellows)" of 1911, complete with a suggestion that the stage could "represent a miniature diamond, and the pitcher, catcher and other players take relative positions." "The Haymakers and the Dairymaids" (of the same year and also with words by Bugbee) was to be staged with boys (who whistled), carrying rakes and forks, and girls (who sang "tra la, la"), carrying milk pails. During the final statement of the chorus (after all had sung, "We don't care a fig for the ways of the town, / Nor for concerts and operas grand, / But when the day's over and work is all done, / Then we join in the haymakers' band.") the boys could substitute sounds on "zobos [*sic*], whistles [and] jewsharps," while the girls were supposed to bang on their pails at the end of each line while they all exited the stage. "The Youthful Politicians" (1912) suggests a didactic bent, since the five boys and one girl proclaim successively in Bugbee's chorus (all the Eldridge songs fall into the predictable format of piano introduction, multiple verses, and a repetitive chorus), "I'm a real Republican, / And I'm a Democrat, / And I'm a Prohibitionist, / Bull Moose am I, you bet, / And I'm a loyal Socialist, / And I'm a Suffragette."

A more specific political agenda surfaced in "The Little Housewives' Club" of 1916, again with words by Bugbee. The girls were "supposed to be on their way home from market. They wore long gingham dresses, large white aprons, plain hats, and carried market baskets filled with packages." Their chorus became a straightforward polemic, intended as "an invitation to the audience":

Now, don't you think you'd like to come
And join our merry throng,
And help to swell our membership
To twenty million strong?
And when the trusts see what's to pay,
'Twill make them all look sick,
For if they try to raise the price,
We'll make an awful kick.

This after complaints about eggs at sixty cents a dozen and butter at eighty cents a pound (although "the prices may be changed to suit the occasion"), plus threats of combines and boycotts, ending with, "And then you'll see the biggest strike / You've ever seen in town," during which the girls were supposed to "shake forefingers warningly to audience."

Several other series followed, including *New Juvenile Song Recitations for Either the Reader or Singer* in 1921 (with words by Margaret Fassett and music by Eldridge and his cousin Anna), including such memorable titles as "I've Been and Had the Measles" and "When Daddy Took Me Up in a 'Plane," and *Song Novelties for Young Ladies. A Group of Songs with Action for Entertainments, Etc.* of 1923 included "I Can't Do a Thing with My Hair Since It's Washed," "My Arrow Collar Man," and "Mixed Recipes." This last gem, subtitled "A Domestic Science Tragedy," its conceit a supposed culinary demonstration for the "delectation" of the inept girls' parents, required three kitchen tables and all sorts of props suggested by the lyric. These included actual sponges to be mixed with the sponge cake dough, as well as the real side-splitter: dressing of a chicken was to involve a real "dead chicken with feathers off on table. Make for it a sort of slip which will go over body and through which its legs can go."[15]

Eldridge published such things as late as 1934, but his legacy actually predates the Franklin enterprise, since two series had been issued in 1905 by March Brothers of Lebanon. *The Guptill-Eldridge Action Songs. For Public Entertainments and Social Celebrations*, their words by Elizabeth Guptill, included such titles as "The Bethlehem Babe," "Dolly, You Must Go to Bed," "The Merry Farmers," "Mud Pies," and "Wave, Old Glory." Eldridge's *Entertainment Novelties for School Celebrations and Public Entertainments* involved a considerable amount of flag-waving, with titles like "The Greatest General" and "Wrap Me in the Dear Old Flag, Boys."

Of the myriads of other Buckeye song composers, one deserves at least an acknowledgment, although attempts to learn much about him have proved frustrating. Fred D. Heltman was born in Ashland in 1887 and attended both Ashland College and the Oberlin Conservatory. He supposedly self-published his *Carrie Belle Waltzes* at age sixteen but established a reputation in 1908 with the "School Ma'am March," written for a convention of the National Education Association in Cleveland. Soon thereafter he established his own publishing house in Cleveland (at first Popular Music Publishers and then the Fred Heltman Company). He also wrote some pedagogical works for piano as well as solo piano pieces of various sorts (lots of rags ["Chewin' the Rag," 1912], marches and two-steps ["Sunflower Babe," 1909], and waltzes ["Fairy Ring Waltz," 1912]). Some of his songs were said to have sold copies that perhaps reached into the millions; some were even used in movie sound tracks, such as *State Fair*, the 1933 hit starring Will Rogers and Janet Gaynor. Virtually everything was published during the second and third decades of the century; Heltman supposedly retired to his summer home in Michigan in 1942.[16]

He seems to have acquired a considerable number of collaborators, especially A[lbert] H[arvey] Eastman (1865–1947). It isn't clear where the responsibility lies in the ballads for which they get equal billing, but Eastman issued at least one song under his own name as both composer and lyricist ("Sweet Leonore," published by the Fred Heltman Company in 1919) and during the 1920s and 1930s, often employing a pseudonym, published a slew of arrangements of familiar tunes (both composed and folk) for piano and anywhere from one to five violins. Heltman also published Eastman's *Progressive Course for Violin* in 1924.

Others fascinate, if only because of their fecundity or perseverance, even though their obscurity seems well deserved. Clevelander Edward J. Grant, obviously a patriot of considerable conviction, self-published more than twenty works between 1913 and 1927, including two-steps ("Old Uncle Sam," "Yankee Land," "The Moose," and "Knights of Columbus"), schottisches ("Dancing 'Neath the Harvest Moon"), and "concert waltzes" ("Dream of the Future" and "Love and Roses"), plus songs of various sorts, ranging from "My Old Ireland Where the Shamrock Grows" and "Under the Stars and Stripes" (a "march song"), to "Holding Hands" and "Dancing on the Old Barn Floor" (described as "song schottisches"), "Love, Sweet Love" (a "song redowa or three-step"), and "Bad A'gin Madigan."

Even more intriguing is one Sam Tuffias, who published at least four songs during 1914. "Back to Our Old Fatherland" (with a portrait of the composer and lyricist on the front cover, which is also emblazoned with the exhortation to BE A ZIONIST AND SING THIS SONG, billed as a "beautiful Zion song hit!") and "When I Lost My Dear Old Dad" (again with words by the composer) were both self-published from 2062 West 25th Street in Cleveland. However, "I'll Never Spoon Beneath the Moon" (his lyric, with music by C. M. Arthur) and "Sadie, Be a Lady and Write a Letter to Me" (in collaboration with Harry J. Edwards) were both published in New York.

Even more exotic is Jacob S. Rosenberg, creator of at least nineteen pieces, beginning in 1916 (although many were issued without a date, most apparently from a vanity press sometimes called the Evangelical Publishing House or Evangelical Press). Rosenberg was introduced in his scores via an excerpt from the *Cleveland Leader* of September 4, 1916, as president of the Cleveland Household Supply Company, for whom, until eighteen months earlier, music had been only a "means of spending spare moments. Today it means everything to him. For today he is blind, and since he was stricken sightless a year and a half ago he has turned the darkness into light by music." He was described as expressing "his ideas of melody on his violin," which were then notated on paper by an assistant. A song like "Mother and I (A Dream)" was arranged by Herman A. Hummel (who is also pictured and defined as the composer of more than five hundred "song hits," although the only piece of his encountered is "Poppies. Patriotic Waltz Ballad," dedicated to the American Legion, with words by Ida H. Morrison and published by her in 1926). Rosenberg's horizon extended from "Nation Israel, Der Yid" and "March O. K. O. J." (written for the composer's lodge, the Order of the Knights of Joseph), to "America, My Sweet Land, Americans in France," and "The True American," as well as "Der alter Millyunaire," "The Band Master's Dream," and "In Our Own Sweet Home."

All in all, a kaleidoscopic outpouring of popular song, the dimensions of which are best captured by the title of Maurice Spitalny's "Some Day You'll Know" (with words by Sam Coslow and published by Spier and Coslow in New York in 1927; Spitalny was pictured as conductor of the Stillman Theatre Orchestra in Cleveland).

CHAPTER 32

The Cleveland-Style Polka

The Spitalny brothers' origins might remind us that Cleveland became one of the country's most ethnically diverse cities, so that in its various neighborhoods during the early decades of the last century one could hear Czech, German, Italian, Hungarian, Polish, and Slovenian polkas. And while other cities might claim preeminence of a sort (Chicago for its Polish-style polkas and Milwaukee for the German idiom), Cleveland can claim not only its idiosyncratic take on the polka but also Frank Yankovic, crowned "America's Polka King" in 1948.

The polka as a social dance appeared in Bohemia during the 1830s and quickly swept across Europe during that decade and then into this country during the 1840s during a fit of universal polkamania that persisted until the end of the century. Cleveland musicians responded to the rage by adding polkas to their repertories as early as 1845. Eventually new pieces from regional composers were added to the mix, including the *Put-in-Bay Polka* of Frank M. Davis (Toledo: Whitney, 1871), Frank Hruby Jr.'s arrangement of *Na-Mariance; or The Village Tavern*, described as a polka or two-step (Cleveland: Great Western Music, 1903), or Anthony L. Maresh's *Village Maid*, presented as an all-encompassing Bohemian polka, march, and two-step (Cleveland: Clerien, 1914).

Slovenes arrived in large numbers during the 1880s so that by 1897 Cleveland boasted its first Slovenian orchestra, the Austrian Cornet Band (recall that Slovenia was not an independent political entity at the time), organized by Ivan Zorman Sr. Accordions became a principal means of presenting the polka, and "button boxes" (a label that may have originated in Cleveland, denoting the most elementary form of the instrument, capable of producing only the sounds of the major diatonic scale) were not only imported from Europe but by the early years of the twentieth century were manufactured in Cleveland by Anton Mervar (1885–1942), John Mikus, and Nick Shkorka, as were the more versatile instruments with keyboards that gradually came to predominate.

Accordions were in great demand at ethnic social gatherings like weddings, dances, and parties. With the addition of a clarinet or tenor saxophone, guitars or banjos, piano (later, electric keyboard instruments like the Solovox, employed by Frankie Yankovic as early as 1943), bass, and drums, the accordion (later in pairs) became the core of the polka bands that were organized by the 1920s. The advent of radio and commercial recordings during that decade marked the beginnings of a polka boom. The Matt Hoyer Trio became the first Slovenian American group to record, issuing some one hundred pieces on the Columbia and Victor labels between 1919 and 1930 (one of their hits was the "Jack on St. Clair Polka"). Bands led by Louis Spehek and Victor Lisjak (who was also a composer) also recorded for national labels during the same period.

During the latter part of the 1920s various Cleveland radio stations developed programs directed at specific ethnic groups, several of which survived into the 1960s and 1970s. These offered employment to polka musicians, since union regulations demanded exclusive reliance on live performance. From this exposure came bookings, recordings, and the gradual development of an idiosyncrasy associated with Cleveland. One of the crucial figures in this evolution was pianist William Lausche, a dentist (and brother of Senator Frank Lausche), who recorded for both Victor and Columbia. He wrote several classics, such as "Cleveland, the Polka Town," but also Americanized traditional Slovenian tunes by imposing on them a contemporary dance-band feel, smoother and more polished than other polka idioms, an accommodation to the mainstream musical trends reflected in Johnny Vadnal's "Jazz Time Polka."

World War II marked a lull preceding a virtual explosion of polkamania. The principal figure in the postwar development was Frankie Yankovic (1915–98). Born in West Virginia, Yankovic arrived in Cleveland at the tender age of five days and was playing Slovenian folksongs on a button accordion at age nine. By age sixteen he had graduated to the piano accordion and led his own band, playing for local dances and other social events and appearing on ethnic radio programs as early as 1932.

However, having opened his first bar in November 1941 (in 1965 he was to become proprietor of a Cleveland steak house), his career was interrupted by World War II. After suffering severe frostbite while trapped at the front during the Battle of the Bulge, he was transferred to Special Services and toured Army camps entertaining the troops. His prewar recordings on the Cleveland Recording Company label had sold well (beginning in 1938 as the Slovenian Folk Orchestra and again in 1943, this time as the Happy Slovenians), and in 1946 he was contracted by Columbia Records, under whose aegis Frankie Yankovic and His Yanks sold literally millions of albums and singles over a period of twenty-six years. For example, "Just

A vintage portrait of Frankie Yankovic and His Yanks, perhaps from the late 1940s. Frankie is surrounded (in clockwise order) by Johnny Pecon, Church Srnick, George Cook, and Al Naglitch. Courtesy Ida Yankovic.

Because" (a remake of a country-style tune by Bob and Joe Shelton), first recorded in 1948, is reputed to have sold an aggregate of at least three million copies; another standard, "Blue Skirt Waltz" (a tune called "Vaclav Blaha" with imposed lyrics by Mitchell Paris), first recorded in 1949, may well have sold more than four million copies in its various versions.

Note that *polka* became somewhat of an umbrella label, since at least to outsiders *waltz* at first blush suggests an entirely different tradition. Polka bands traditionally alternate sets of three waltzes and three polkas. The idiom eventually became vocal as well as instrumental. Yankovic recalled that the "Rendezvous Waltz" of 1947 was the first vocal item in his recorded repertory. He also created a series of fourteen songbooks with piano and accordion arrangements, which were issued by the Mills Publishing Company of New York, as well as at least one volume of the Yankovic Slovenian Polka and Waltz Series (with arrangements for both accordion and piano plus B-flat or E-flat instruments), issued by Trophy Products.

The titles of some of the Yankovic hits suggest a kind of playful, even whimsical catholicity: "Hoop Dee Doo Polka," "Accordion Man Waltz," "Play Ball Polka," "Happy Hour Waltz," "I'm Gonna Get Me a Dummy Polka," "Anniversary Waltz Prune Song," "Too Fat Polka," and the "Clinker Polka," named for the family's cocker spaniel who earlier had been named for all the wrong notes Yankovic was hitting on his accordion at the time. Regional parochialism was presumably avoided with the "Pennsylvania Polka" and "Milwaukee Polka" or Johnny Vadnal's "Chicago Town Polka." Vadnal (b. 1923) added to the eclectic mélange of subject material with a "Mountain Climber Polka," "Last Time I Saw Paris Waltz," and a "Vas Is Das Polka?"

While the brash assertiveness of his autobiography[1] might suggest total dominance of the field, Yankovic, active until the year before his death at age eighty-three (an event widely noted in the national media), proved not only durable, but also seminal in that he staffed his bands with able sidemen like Johnny Pecon (1915–75) and Joey Miskulin (b. 1949), who as Yanks alumni often founded their own successful bands. But in their heyday the Yanks toured incessantly in this country and abroad, playing as many as three hundred engagements a year. Yankovic received a Grammy Award in 1986 (for his *70 Years of Hits,* originally released on Cleveland International Records), earlier had his own weekly television programs in Cleveland, Chicago, and Buffalo, and was a guest of Arthur Godfrey, Kate Smith, Patti Page, Lawrence Welk, Johnny Carson, Phil Donahue, David Frost, and the like. In other words, he was a major showbiz personality.

Cleveland became a polka mecca during the 1950s as the local polka idiom nudged itself closer to mainstream pop music. Fans flocked to various bars and ballrooms (for instance, the Pol-kats Social Club, opened in 1957), as well to weekly dances at the Slovenian National Home, and on summer Sundays to the Slovene National Benefit Society Farm in suburban Kirtland. Radio and television programs appeared as early as 1947, when *Polka Lover's Time* débuted on WSRS, for a while a daily offering, hosted by Kenny Bass, who presided over polka broadcasts in Cleveland for some thirty-five years; *Polka Varieties* became a Sunday staple for a quarter of a century on WEWS, beginning in 1958, and was syndicated nationally, followed in the early 1960s by the *TV Polka Party,* also syndicated nationally. The Johnny Vadnal Orchestra recorded for RCA Victor and for a period broadcast nationally from a local ballroom; Vadnal had also hosted the first polka show on television, for WEWS-TV, beginning in 1948. Johnny Pecon had a contract with Capitol Records and also appeared on radio and television; his major hit, "Sweet Polka Dot," was issued in 1956.

While national interest in the polka began to wane under the onslaught of rock, the lull in Cleveland was only temporary. New polka bars appeared. Tony Petkovesk Jr. (b. 1941) began presiding over a daily polka broadcast in 1961, which is carried today by WELW (joined by others during the 1970s), began hosting an annual Thanksgiving weekend Polka Party (held for many years at the Slovenian National Hall but later housed in area hotels), and in 1971 opened Tony's Polka Village, a retail outlet for everything related to the polka (closed in 1991); Delta International, a local label, issued more than forty albums of several generations of performers between 1963 and 1978; in a kind of reverse cultural thrust, Richie Vadnal's Orchestra visited Slovenia in 1971 and made recordings there; a new interest in the diatonic button-box accordion surfaced during the early 1970s; two local polka month-lies (*Polka News and Events* and *Polkarama*) and a newspaper (*Polka Scene*) appeared; in 1988 the American-Slovenian Polka Foundation opened its National Cleveland-Style Polka Hall of Fame in suburban Euclid, complete with an illustrated history of the tradition, a retail shop, and displays honoring those who have received Crystal Awards as inductees into the Hall of Fame or as recipients of the Foundation's Annual Achievement Awards.

Today "Polkatown, U. S. A." remains home to many polka bands,[2] and the degree to which the polka culture is associated with the city can surely be inferred from the lyrics of Lausche's "The Cleveland Polka":

Up where the buckeyes tumble down
You'll find the country's grandest town.
It seems a lady's kiss means more
Out on Lake Erie's southern shore.
From water's edge to Waterloo
From Shaker Square to Brookside Zoo
You'll find the best location in the nation
If you travel to good old Cleveland town.

If you would like a million friends
Come where the Cuyahoga bends.
You'll watch the Indians and the Browns,
And cheer the Barons' hockey crowns.
There are a million dreams of bliss
In every Cleveland lady's kiss.
You'll find the best location in the nation
If you travel to good old Cleveland town.

CHAPTER 33

Bands

In a state whose land-grant university prides itself on possessing TBDBITL (for the uninitiated, "The Best Damn Band in the Land"), there needs to be a look at bands of all sorts, ensembles of wind instruments, sometimes mobile, sometimes confined to a stage, sometimes purveying functional music destined only to govern the movement of others, often presenting music intended to entertain or even edify.

Given its dominant presence and pervading influence, some might assume that band music in the Buckeye State dates from 1878, when the Ohio State University's first band was organized. Even in years when the football team's efforts have led to despair among loyal fans, members of the Ohio State University Marching Band have generated all sorts of fervor with their intricate routines (especially the "Script Ohio," with the coveted honor of dotting the "i" reserved to a designated sousaphone player or distinguished guest) and spirited renditions of favorites like "Across the Field," "Hang On, Sloopy," and the "Buckeye Battle Cry."[1]

That first Ohio State ensemble consisted of three fifes, eight snare drums, and a bass drum. By the end of the 1878–79 academic year, a military-style band of sixteen members had been organized by a student leader and offered its first public appearance at the home of the university's president during a reception he tendered members of the class of 1879. Soon thereafter the board of trustees allocated fifty dollars for the purchase of secondhand brass instruments of the style then popular, with their bells over the shoulders of their players. The band was a quasi-military organization and dressed in regulation cadet uniforms. However, after a student prank in May 1881, the military department in effect gave the ensemble a dishonorable discharge. Even so, for the next decade and a half, bands of as many as twenty-four players survived under student management and leadership, dressing in uniforms and even playing for military reviews.

In 1896 the military faculty decided to resurrect an official band and hired Gustav Bruder (1869–1941) as its director. Bruder, who played the clarinet, cornet, and violin, had enjoyed extensive experience as a member of the Marine Band under Sousa, as the leader of a circus band, as a member of various theater orchestras, and as the founding director of the Columbus Rifles Band. Although he inherited a ragtag, dispirited group of players, by 1914 the band numbered sixty-four, all freshman and sophomore men, and was to total one hundred only six years later. While they were charged by their sponsors with providing marching music for the cadets, the band also played concerts and for athletic events (their first appearance at a football game occurred in 1899). The first graphic formation (O-H-I-O) was created in 1921, to be followed only three years later by its first floating, choreographed formation.[2] The band participated in dedicating Ohio Stadium in October 1922. Earlier its members had relied on collection buckets passed at half time during games at the Ohio Field for funds allowing them to travel to out-of-town football games.

A major shift took place in 1929, when Eugene J. Weigel (1894–1973), then supervisor of instrumental music in the Cleveland Public Schools, was lured back to his alma mater, where he directed the marching band until 1938, after which he became chair of the Department of Music and from 1945 until 1959 director of what had become a school of music. By the second year of his tenure Weigel had increased the band to 120 men. In Baltimore for the Ohio State–Navy game, Weigel introduced a floating anchor that traveled the field from end zone to end zone; as part of that trip the band also performed a special concert for President Herbert Hoover at the White House. More innovations followed: In 1932 members were asked to memorize the music; in 1934 Weigel eliminated all but brass and percussion instruments, instantly creating what has remained the largest all-brass band in the world (and generating special orders for instruments that were no longer being manufactured because of the lack of demand); the trademark "Script Ohio" formation was introduced during the 1936 season.

Weigel was succeeded by his assistant, Manley R. Whitcomb (1913–87), who soon faced the challenge of keeping the organization functional during the war years. In fact, he himself entered the Army in 1942 and was replaced by William B. McBride until 1946, when Whitcomb returned to civilian status. As the links to its military origins faded, reliance on marches was replaced with material drawn from the pop and film world; tongue-in-cheek humor became more common, and a shorter step allowed lightning-fast tempi (up to 180 beats per minute).

Trombonist Jack O. Evans (1915–2001) had served as Whitcomb's assistant since 1947 and succeeded his mentor in 1952, the year in which the formal relationship with ROTC was terminated, leaving the marching band under the joint sponsorship of the athletic and music departments. The Department of Music also sponsored a symphonic band, and Evans organized the Activities Band, which not only presented concerts, but also performed at home basketball games; this group became so popular that it was eventually split into Buckeye Scarlet and Gray bands. The first three of the marching band's twenty-one commercial recordings were released between 1958 and 1963; "Hey! Buckeyes!" the latest in the series, dates from 1998.

In 1965 Evans passed the baton to Charles L. Spohn (b. 1922), a percussionist with graduate degrees from Ohio State. Spohn emphasized theme shows based on arrangements by Richard Heine, John Tatgenhorst, and others, including Tatgenhorst's "Hang On, Sloopy," a tradition that seems to have achieved immortality (it was even proclaimed "the official rock song of the State of Ohio" by the General Assembly in November 1985). Spohn also fostered the idea of an alumni band, which made its début in 1966 when about three hundred men marched. While the band had given an outdoor concert during the Whitcomb era for Ohio State alumni in Toledo while en route to Ann Arbor, Spohn spawned the seemingly oxymoronic idea of indoor concerts by a stationary marching band. Performances at Butler University in Indianapolis (the conductor's alma mater) and the Peristyle of the Toledo Art Museum were followed by concerts at Ohio State's Mershon Auditorium, the school's regional campuses, and other venues.

Paul E. Droste (b. 1936), another Ohio State alumnus (and practitioner of the euphonium), directed the band between 1970 and 1983, years of tumultuous change. In 1972 the ensemble was expanded to 250 members (although since the number has drifted down to 192), and, because of Title IX of the Higher Education Act of 1972 banning gender discrimination, five women were admitted to the ranks the next year (a first female drum major was to follow in 1981). During the Droste era the ensemble marched in the Nixon inaugural parade of 1973, traveled to numerous bowl games, entertained fans at a World Series baseball game in Cincinnati and a pro football game in Cleveland, concertized extensively en route to other engagements as well as at the Ohio Theatre in downtown Columbus, and welcomed as the dot in "Script Ohio" a host of personalities, ranging from Bob Hope and Woody Hayes, to an alumnus of the 1907 band. The Buckeye Invitational Marching Band Competition was initiated in 1983, in part intended as a recruiting tool.

Droste retired after a twenty-two-year association with the band (and then founded the Columbus Brass Band, a nonmarching professional ensemble that celebrates the British brass band tradition), and was succeeded by his assistant of a decade, trombonist Jon R. Woods (b. 1939). To the inherited traditions, Woods has added the use of computer technology to chart shows, tributes to the Cleveland Orchestra and Vietnam veterans (with colorful arrangements from Jim Swearingen, Ted McDaniel, Marcia LaReau, and others), distinctive new uniforms in 1988, and an appearance the following January at the presidential inaugural parade of George

Bush in Washington; twelve years later the band marched again on January 20, 2001, to mark the inauguration of the elder Bush's son George W. Bush as the forty-third president.

A story about TBDBITL in the *USA Today* edition of October 24, 1988, took note of a $100,000 budget that accommodated a physical trainer and Saturday morning warm-up sessions that attract as many as twelve thousand fans. But perhaps the headline above the story describing this "high-stepping tradition" tells it all: "Ohio State Marchers Strut Their Stuff with Pride."

Despite the prominence of the Ohio State Marching Band, a high school ensemble in Massillon may have had as much influence on the transformation of the marching band from an arm of the military to an adjunct of the show business industry. The catalyst was George T. "Red" Bird (1900–79), band director at Washington High School from 1938 until 1946.[3] A native of Fayette in Fulton County west of Toledo, Bird began with the cornet at age ten and played in a professional band in Detroit following graduation from high school. He then spent two years as a student at Ohio State where he played in the marching band, after which he returned to the professional world, including stints in amusement parks, theaters, radio stations, and dance bands directed by the likes of Jimmy and Tommy Dorsey. However, in 1926 he enrolled at the University of Cincinnati, graduating in 1931 with a degree in public school music. Prior to Massillon, Bird taught in Cincinnati, Trotwood, and Dayton. His challenge in the new position was to create a band that would complement the renown of the school's football program, coached by the legendary Paul Brown, later at Ohio State and then the founding coach of the eponymous Cleveland Browns and later of the Cincinnati Bengals.

Although Bird did not completely abandon the prevalent military review style and its basic block or spelling formations, led by a drum major, he achieved unparalleled precision by measuring the steps between yard lines and preplanning each routine through the use of "note cues," calibrating every move of each player with a specific musical beat. This modified the role of the drum major who, with as many as eight female majorettes, was featured in flashy baton and dance routines. Bird also introduced a tiger mascot ("Obie," for the school's orange and brown colors), more flamboyant uniforms, and structured theme shows (for example, a salute to George M. Cohan or the Navy), involving props, costuming, and even special lighting (colored flood or spot lights or even battery-powered lights on the players to outline a maneuver in an otherwise dark stadium). These shows gradually expanded to a half hour or longer, thus impinging on the momentum of the game itself, and Bird eventually pledged that the Tiger Band would hold forth for no more than fifteen minutes at half time. The band's fame led to appearances in the Cleveland Stadium and the Ohio State Stadium in Columbus, as well as recognition in national magazines such as *Life* and *Collier's*, the latter of which lauded a Bird production as "a show that might have been done by [flamboyant Broadway showman] Billy Rose."

Bird considered himself an educator, whose students after the marching season performed a full range of significant literature and were privileged to host guest conductors like Percy Grainger and Frank Simon. However, his name remains associated mostly with his accomplishments on the football field, symbolized by his *Football Band Show Chart Forms* of 1946 and *Marching with Music*, a text from 1950 directed at both students and teachers. He came to resent the public's concentration on the short pleated skirts and prancing steps of the Tiger majorettes (all of whom were required to be performing musicians in other ensembles) and threatened to create a band made up entirely of majorettes, which he in effect accomplished later when, as director of entertainment for the Cleveland Browns (whose fight song he wrote), he created the Musical Majorettes, an all-female band in majorette costumes.

The history of band music in Ohio is, however, considerably more ancient and diverse than that of the modern high school or college marching band. All-brass bands date back to the 1830s, following the introduction of keyed brass instruments—fitted with holes and keys akin to those on woodwind instruments like the clarinet and oboe—that allowed the creation of a larger variety of pitches. Valved brass instruments were introduced soon thereafter but took precedence only after the mid-1840s with the introduction of a family of such instruments of various sizes called "saxhorns" after Adolphe Sax, one of their developers, recalled today primarily for his creation of the saxophone. By 1860 the valved brass instruments had relegated those with keys to oblivion, since they were easier to play and the sounds they created were more even and accurate, but by the mid-1830s all-brass bands of as many as twenty players had been organized to play at highly structured formal balls or to offer polyglot concerts of vocal and instrumental music. The literature of these bands was mostly captured in manuscript partbooks, consisting of arrangements made by the local bandmasters reflecting the unique instrumentation of each ensemble and the capacities of its players. However, during the 1840s Elias Howe, Allen Dodworth, and others began publishing collections intended to meet the needs of the burgeoning movement. In 1859 A. C. Peters and Brothers of Cincinnati contributed *Peters' Sax-Horn Journal*, arrangements by one J. Schatzman of "New and Beautiful Marches, Waltzes, Polkas, Schottisches, etc., Intended for a Brass Band of 13 Instruments, or a Less Number if Desirable." The one anomaly was "E Pluribus Unum, National Air," which William C. Peters, patriarch of the firm, considered the ideal national anthem.[4]

Many of these bands were mobilized during the Civil War. Nominally noncombatants, bandsmen were sometimes conscripted as medics, but otherwise they boosted morale at recruitment rallies, led the troops while on the march (with the aid of those over-the-shoulder instruments whose bells projected the sound more clearly to those marching behind), provided the music for dress parades and other ceremonies while in camp, and offered evening sit-down "serenades," consisting of arrangements of the popular songs and dance tunes of the period.[5]

The return of thousands of these bandsmen to civilian status sparked an explosion of interest in the band that to some degree persists to the present, although the introduction of radio, phonograph records, and eventually television lessened the dependence of small-town America on the local band for entertainment and edification. D. S. McCosh's *Guide for Amateur Brass Bands* asserted, "The most practical way of indulging a taste for the arts, is in the organization of a brass band."[6] Professional touring bands and local amateur ensembles became omnipresent at outdoor band concerts.

In fact, one observer discovered evidence of more than forty such bands in Akron alone between 1840 and the late 1940s.[7] That history began with the Akron Brass Band in 1840, organized by jeweler Henry S. Abbey. The group made its début at ceremonies acknowledging the formation of Summit County in March, followed by a competition with the Cleveland Grays Band on July 4 and an appearance at festivities opening the Ohio-Pennsylvania Canal on August 5. The group enjoyed a life of two decades, considerably longer than many that followed it. These included bands sponsored by local industry (the American Hard Rubber Company Band, active during the 1890s and then revived as the [B. F.] Goodrich [Company] Band in 1919, a group active for about a decade; the Diamond Rubber Company Band, organized informally in 1898 and known at first as "The Cow Pasture Band" because of its alfresco rehearsals, although it became official in 1900 and lasted into the early years of the Depression; the N[orthern] O[hio] T[raction] and L[ight] Company Band; the Pennsylvania Railroad Band dating from 1915; plus bands sponsored by the Goodyear and Firestone Rubber and Tire Companies beginning in 1917), fraternal organizations (the Moose and Masons beginning in 1914, the Grotto in 1921, the Knights Templar the following year, the Shriners in 1924, and Oddfellows in 1925), and ethnic groups (Italians in 1912, Hungarians shortly thereafter, and Romanians in 1917). Other bands were built around the personalities of their founding directors (particularly those of English-born William Richard Palmer [1866–1925] in 1908 and Adam George Ranck in 1916), while others defy categorization: the Barberton Ladies Band was organized in 1914 and retained that name even after its headquarters was moved to Akron in 1924, four years before dissolution caused by internal strife; the Clan MacKenzie Band, the official pipe band of the local lodge of the Order of Scottish Clans, was formed in 1914 but dissolved when its members enlisted in the Canadian and American armed forces during World War I;[8] and the Soap Box Derby Band, created for the first Derby in 1936, was a fixture of that event until 1948, with daily concerts and a presence at the Derby itself.

Especially small-town bands became a matter of civic pride, coequal in importance with churches, schools, and libraries. These bands were usually self-supporting, although upon its incorporation in 1863 the Marysville Union Brass Band made a formal contract with the town. In return for the town's furnishing twelve instruments and a drum, the resulting ensemble would "play as a Band for the citizens who Assist in procuring the instruments, at any time & on any occasions, when and wherever they may require Band Music, within one mile of the public Square . . . for the term of three years . . . Free of Charge."[9]

Conscious of their status, these self-governing bands adopted detailed membership policies, such as a residency requirement. Most stipulated a minimum number of players, such as the Navarre Citizens Band, which required at least six, stipulating that they also had to be of "good moral standing and character, and of temperate habits."[10]

In smaller towns these civic bands became the principal purveyors of musical culture. The typical program offered a considerable diversity. As witness, the fifth annual concert of the Cornet Band and Orchestra of Tallmadge, presented in the Tallmadge Town Hall on November 9, 1859, directed by D. Marble of Boston and assisted by A. James, "The Popular English Harpist" (identified elsewhere as a resident of Cleveland and downgraded from his status at an earlier event as "The Great English Harpist"). The program was unusually specific in its attributions, perhaps because so much of it came from the pen of the guest maestro:[11]

Part First

1. Overture, Lucrezia Borgia	*Grafulla*	Band
2. Serenade, Maid of Lodi	*Beethoven*	Band
3. Quickstep, Opera of Leonora	*White*	Orchestra
4. Solo, Harp	*James*	James
5. Waltz, Know Nothing	*Streeter*	Orchestra
6. Quickstep, Gov. Hale's	*Marble*	Band
7. Gallopade, Cornet Bands [sic]		Orchestra
8. Storm March (Descriptive)	*Bilse*	Band

Part Second

9. Quickstep, Capt. Coe's	*Coates*	Band
10. Andante, Twilight Dews	*Marble*	Band
11. Quickstep, Capt. Shepherd's	*White*	Orchestra
12. Solo, Blue Bells of Scotland	*James*	James
13. Quadrille, Mountain Sylph	*Marble*	Orchestra
14. Andante & Waltz, Sleigh Ride (Descriptive)	*Marble*	Band

15. Solo, Harp	*James*	James
16. Andante, Departed Days	*Marble*	Band
17. Finale, National Airs	*Marble*	Band

The first identifiable band in Tallmadge, which had been founded in 1807, dates from 1817, with passing mention of what was called a military band although its instrumentation supposedly included only clarinets, a clarion (presumably a trumpet), a haughtboy [*sic*] (an oboe), and a violin. Little record remains of that ensemble beyond a notice that in 1821 it played at the closing exercises of the winter term at the Western Reserve College (now Academy) in nearby Hudson.

In 1834 a group variously called the Pioneer Band or Pioneer Orchestra was organized by a group of "Progressive Young Americans." Led by Charles Cook Bronson of Tallmadge (clarionetist and later a prominent local historian), the group also at one time included son William H. Bronson of Tallmadge (flute), Henry W. Bill and Horace Camp of Cuyahoga Falls (clarionets), R. H. Devin of Seville (violin), A. J. Huse of Akron (cello), and Amos Wright of Tallmadge (double bass). Hardly typical instrumentation for a band. In fact, manuscript partbooks owned by the Tallmadge Historical Society, designated as primo and second [*sic*], coordinate with random parts for instruments such as the bassoon and trombone. The two oblong volumes contain twenty-seven individual pieces, mostly marches and quicksteps, including a few familiar titles ("Hail to the Chief," "The Star-Spangled Banner," and "Auld Lang Syne"). Interlarded with "Colburn's Quickstep," the "Cossack March," the "Brunswick Waltz," and "La Fayette's Arrival," there are oddities like "Handel's Clarinett" (an instrument certainly unknown to that composer), "Serenade by the Celebrated George Frederick Handel," and "Mozart's Military Waltz." Tradition attributes most of this legacy to the elder Bronson (although a vintage photograph of the Pioneers includes an unidentified director with baton in hand surrounded by six players, including both Bronsons), and indeed a "Federal March" was designated as "C. C. Bronson's." However, a "Cincinnati Schottische" was inscribed "To H. W. Bill by J. F. Jay." Confusion as to the configuration of the ensemble is compounded by several scores for three parts designated simply as Air, 2nd, and Bass.

Although lists remain of those almost sixty subscribers who in 1854 pledged anywhere from fifty cents to twenty dollars, "for the purpose of purchasing instruments for a Brass Band," after which $200 was expended for two cornopeans, three saxhorns, an E-flat horn, a baritone, two tubas, and a drum, the literature presented in that fifth year of the group's history was clearly shared between what was presumably a brass band and another ensemble clearly specified as an orchestra. On September 4 the instruments were assigned to specific players, and E. Hull was employed "to give instruction for one or more terms, at 35$. and board for terms of twelve lessons." A week later a set of bylaws was adopted, their preamble announcing that since the band's members had determined "for our pleasure & profit to culti-vate a different style of music from that heretofore cultivated in Tallmadge (viz. music on Brass Instruments) we form ourselves into an association for the purpose . . ." The musical leader of the Cornet Band of Tallmadge was also to serve as its presi-dent. The members owned their instruments jointly with the organization, and anybody who resigned "shall leave his instrument & receive for it whatever the Band may be disposed to give." Also, "if any member, through carelessness or neglect shall damage or spoil an instrument, he shall pay whatever it costs to make it good." Also, "each member shall bear an equal proportion of the expenses incurred by the Band," and anybody absent "from the regular meetings of the Band, without suffi-cient excuse . . . shall pay a fine of 25 cents." Furthermore, after each "meeting" was called to order by the leader, "no disturbance shall be made by the members, either by loud talking, or sounding their instruments, excepting with consent & direction of the Leader."[12]

Early in 1855 the band made its first public appearance—a local benefit concert that raised $9.87. They were then invited by the junior class of Western Reserve Col-lege to play at an April exhibition and performed in Tallmadge the evening before, each event providing about $25, although tutor Hull had been asked to assist and was recompensed with $7.75 for his pains. The group then played on July 4 in Ravenna ($28) and for Western Reserve's commencement ($43, minus $3.47 for expenses). A handwritten chronicle found in the collections of the Tallmadge Historical Society records several changes of personnel, as well as concerts in Mogadore, Akron, a Republican convention in Massillon, Uniontown (for which they were promised $25, "recd but $13.62, the balance supposed not to be collectable"), Brimfield, the Sum-mit County Fair, and multiple visits to Western Reserve College. In August 1858 the ensemble furnished music on the steamer *City of Cleveland* for two trips between the ship's namesake city and Superior, Wisconsin. Prior to that, the band in 1856 had purchased from the local firm of Oviatt and Sperry a handsome "carriage" at the cost of $250, $154 of which had been raised by subscription from the local citizenry, who pledged anywhere from fifty cents to ten dollars. They apparently made a fine appearance atop their ornate wagon, so much that when the band played at the Summit County Agricultural Society's Fair that summer, they "recd a premium of five dollars on our carriage." When this first incarnation of the band disbanded in 1866, the carriage was sold to the Solon Band. But the Tallmadge Cornet Band was later resurrected under new leadership, and an extant photograph thought to date from the 1870s or even later presents seventeen players of brass and percussion in-struments in spiffy uniforms arrayed on the village green.

An undated list of expenses suggests the management of such an organization at mid-century:

Ten Music Books ($6.25)

Oil and candles (50¢)

Cleaning Town Hall (25¢)

Straps for carriage ($1)

Sweet Oil for carriage (50¢)

Horse Hire ($1)

Building Fires ($1)

A letter of March 15, 1858, from Isaac White, who during the 1840s had been a band-master in Youngstown but was then working in Toledo, suggests that music was regularly borrowed and exchanged among like ensembles.[13] White addressed him-self to "Friend Wright," presumably Clement Wright, who had been elected secre-tary-treasurer after the death of C. S. Wright, the original secretary-treasurer, on October 7, 1854, "by the accidental discharge of a gun, in his own hands":

> I re'ded your Letter & the music you returned. I have written you two other pieces and I think you will like them. You mention that you have received four new pieces from [Claudio S.] Graffula. If you want to exchange I would be glad to do so. I have some very heavy pieces for Brass Band and they are first rate for Concert. They each occupy about 4 pages. One is from the Opera of Norma, one from Opera of Sonnambula, one for the opera of Lucia DeLammermore and one From the Opera of Leonora. I have plenty of heavy Quick Steps. If you want to work I will send you some in exchange. I will mention some viz. Continentals Quick Step by Graffula, Constullation Quick Step by Graffula, Capt. Smith's Quick Step by Graffula, Ripvanwinkle Quick Step by Graffula, Wood Side Quick Step, Wood Up Quick Step, John Ander-son and dozens of others that are rather difficult to perform so if you want some work to do I can accommodate you. Please remember me to all yours.[14]

White was also active in Lima, probably one of the first directors of a series of bands there dating back to 1855, known successively as the Lima Sax Horn Band, the Lima Silver Horn Band, or the Lima Silver Band, and finally merely the Lima Band. This ensemble also owned its own wagon, as reported in the *Lima Gazette* on November 25, 1859: "The Lima Band in their splendid carriage paraded over princi-pal streets on Monday afternoon last, and discoursed sweet music. That Prince of Buglers, Professor White, of Toledo, accompanied them."

As elsewhere, the Lima Band seems to have spawned an associated ensemble that included string instruments, one purpose that of furnishing dance music. White again seems to have been the catalyst. On October 26, 1860, the *Gazette* described a

"Promenade Concert" that had taken place a week earlier dedicating a new performance space incorporated in a downtown business block:

> A large and appreciative audience assembled at Ashton's Hall on Friday evening last, at which time and place a concert by the Lima Brass and String Bands had been announced. After a few pieces by the Brass Band, which were executed with much skill, the String Band made its appearance; and for the time and labor spent by the members composing it, in preparation for this event, they were amply rewarded by the evidence of satisfaction of those present, expressed in continual rounds of applause. . . . Professor WHITE deserves much credit for the very successful efforts he has made in establishing what has long been needed in our town, a first class Cotillion Band.

As further witness to the integral role these bands played in local cultures, here is a brief history of the New Concord Cornet Band, founded in 1873: Its first leader was apparently William Rainey Harper (1856–1906), a native of New Concord and graduate of Muskingum College (at age fourteen), who later became the first president of the University of Chicago. Rainey, who played the E-flat cornet (as well as the piano) was joined by his younger brother, a cousin, and at least one other friend, plus others: "Under his inspiration the band practiced assiduously, and he soon began to lead them about the state to give concerts. They visited Cambridge, Bellaire, Zanesville, Newark, Granville [where he was later to teach at Denison University for two years beginning in 1876 at age twenty], and other places."[15]

In 1884 the group was renamed the Silver Cornet Band.[16] The *New Concord Enterprise* of January 7, 1885, included the announcement:

> The members of the New Concord Silver Cornet Band will give a concert in [Muskingum] College Hall on Thursday evening, Jan. 15th. The boys have an excellent program, which will appear in our next issue, and we predict it will be rendered to a crowded house. Proceeds will go toward paying for the elegant new uniforms purchased. Tickets will be on sale on and after Saturday, Jan. 10 at Gault's Drug Store. Persons at a distance will be supplied upon receipt of price by addressing T. F. Gault, New Concord, Ohio. Admission, 25 cents, reserved seats, 35 cents.

A week later the paper suggested, "If you want to give your money to a worthy organization, go to the concert Thursday night." The program:

Crown of Victory, Band
Harp Solo: Selection Trovatore, Prof. D. Trani

Vocal Quartette, Moonlight Dance
Piccolo Solo, Poisson d'arvil
Andante and Waltz, Band
Vocal Solo, "Who will buy roses red" from Somnabula
Baritone Obligato from Cassandra
Piccolo Solo, Medley
Tuba Solo
Prize Polka, Band
Vocal Duet, Sol Fa
Quickstep, Band.

Notice that the band provided only a skeletal framework for the evening's entertainment.

On January 21 the paper pronounced the concert "A Delightful Entertainment, but a Miserable Night." Members of the military band of Company B of the 17th Regiment of the Ohio National Guard, headquartered in Zanesville, were guests and apparently somehow involved in the proceedings. In fact, there was to have been a parade at 4:00 P.M., but the locals met the Zanesville contingent at the railroad station and merely escorted them to the McCloud House, since "it was a miserably dark, rainy and woefully muddy night." Thus, attendance "was necessarily, chiefly, confined to the people of New Concord and vicinity. The large attendance of college students was also noticeable." A "$70 house was obtained," although twice that might have been expected on a normal night. The opening march "was rendered in beautiful style and with masterly skill. The vocal and instrumental soloists were perfectly familiar with their, in most cases, difficult pieces, and they were sung or executed in such a manner as to call forth the hearty plaudits of the audience." Besides, "The Boys make a fine appearance in their dazzling uniforms."

On May 6 the paper announced that a noted comedian was to give two benefit performances at College Hall, "with the assistance of his wife and local talent." And further, "As the Band boys are endeavoring to make some money for the benefit of their organization, everybody patronize the entertainment."

A Band Festival was announced on June 10 and then "reviewed" the following week in somewhat lurid prose:

The boys in their superb uniforms paraded the streets a little before the setting of the sun and discoursed excellent music to the music-loving inhabitants of our picturesque village, situated as it is on the winding banks of the glowing Crooked Creek, amidst the lofty hills of the surrounding country with its sloping fields of green pastures and fertile soil. O, seraphic village! Happy people! Invincible band!

The predictable program included four pieces from the band, violin, cornet, and xylophone solos, a vocal quartet, and a violin duet. The review further noted, "There were a few discordant notes, but these were unavoidable. The refreshments were served after half of the program had been disposed of. At least two hundred and fifty people were royally served with ice-cream, strawberries, cake and lemonade."

In August the band made a jaunt to Springfield, where they received "very complimentary notices." However, by November 25 a notice in the *Enterprise* implored the populace to patronize an entertainment to be mounted on December 3, the proceeds of which were to be "devoted to paying a very burdensome debt." The issue of December 9 asserted,

> The Cornet Band gave a very creditable dramatic entertainment in College Hall last Thursday to a fair sized audience, the receipts amounting to $60.75. We are pleased to note that New Concord has within her borders some talented "comedians," "sophettes," etc., second only to professional actors.

A similar thespian venture was announced in the *Zanesville Courier* of April 22, 1886. "The Drummer Boy of Shiloh," labeled "a grand dramatic entertainment," was to be offered on Decoration Day. The band played a concert in early October, and on December 23 members participated in a festival mounted by the Cambridge Band. On January 18, 1887, they celebrated their third anniversary; the guests included "members of the old band and their wives."

However, only weeks later the *Enterprise* announced,

> The Cornet Band will give a concert and a box social Saturday evening, February 5 at Caldwell and Wilson's Hall. All are cordially invited. A gold pen will be given to the prettiest lady present and a pipe to the ugliest gent. These inducements we trust will bring out a good crowd. The band was recently organized and should be patronized.

The prizewinners were announced on February 9. On March 2 the paper reported in breathless prose a botched benefit offered the public on Washington's Birthday. Apparently part of the audience had already paid their admission fees and been seated when it was discovered that a committee of three had in fact never arranged for any performers. The paper inferred that the unnamed triumvirate had sabotage in mind:

> There can be no other reason for the committee doing as they did other than they were desirous of breaking up the New Concord Band, which they did most completely, as at a meeting of the band the next evening they decided to hang up their horns, uniforms, and everything belonging to the organiza-

tion and offer them for sale. Anybody wishing to purchase a good set of German silver instruments and a nice uniform would do well to confer with C. S. Johnson [the treasurer], who was appointed to sell the stock.

However, the crisis was soon resolved. The *Enterprise* of March 16 trumpeted,

New Concord is not to be without a band. It will be a cold day when our musical pride and talent freezes out. Storms may come and sweep away one organization, but the clouds are scarcely out of view when another organization "bobs up serenely" to take the place of the departed. So it is, and so it may always be, but to have no band is a misfortune we never expect to realize. Only a few weeks ago—not yet a month—our efficient band stacked their weapons and laid down their uniforms to take them up no more forever. Already another band has been organized. The boys have taken up the work of their predecessors and will from now on endeavor to learn how to "toot their horns."

New officers were announced, as were eleven players of brass instruments and snare drummer Jimmie Smith, with a bass drummer yet to be chosen: "The boys have purchased the splendid instruments of the old band, and if they take the time necessary and apply themselves they will soon be able to entertain us with some good music."

Periodic announcements over the next three decades of serenades, socials, appearances at picnics and football games, and at least one more theatrical venture (*The Scout of the Philippines*, a "military comedy in three acts," staged on February 8, 1900) suggest a continuity that lasted at least until the 1900s.

Although the tradition of the community band waned during the first half of the twentieth century, ensembles remain in towns and cities such as Bryan, Bucyrus, Lancaster, Medina, Westerville, and Worthington, as well as smaller locales like the village of New Washington in Crawford County.

The earliest New Washington Band of record was founded in 1865 and then resurrected in both 1878 and 1898 after periods of inactivity (and at times functioned concurrently with a band sponsored by the local German Lutheran Church from 1887 into the 1890s, as well as the Tabor–Cranberry Township Band, headquartered in a hamlet only three miles distant and active during the 1890s until early in the following century).[17]

The present New Washington Community Band dates from 1924 and performs a summer concert series on Saturday evenings in its own downtown gazebo, still employing a bass drum purchased for the ensemble at its founding. Their repertory consists of marches, polkas, patriotic melodies, and the like, often played from well-worn scores purchased by the band's first director, E. F. Ulmer, who had led earlier bands beginning in 1890. Ulmer was succeeded in 1937 by Kenneth Cummins

(1911–98), a trumpeter (and Kent State University professor of mathematics) who had joined the band back in 1926. Cummins presided with only a year's sabbatical until 1997, trumpet in one hand, baton in the other, over an ensemble whose forty members assemble from various towns in the region to rehearse weekly from March until June before embarking on its ten Saturday concerts (funded by the village although attendance is presumably encouraged by the $65 prizes handed out at the conclusion of each performance, courtesy of a local bank) as well as appearances at festivals and fairs in the area. This legacy is noted by the Ohio Historical Markers Program of the Ohio Bicentennial Commission's Longaberger Legacy grant program with an appropriate plaque erected adjacent to the bandstand.

However venerable the New Washington tradition, the Bryan City Band was recognized by Governor George V. Voinovich on August 1, 1991, as "the oldest continuously playing city band in the state of Ohio."[18] The resolution was presented to director John Hartman following a miniconcert in front of the Statehouse in Columbus marking the band's 140th season. The ensemble's first performance had occurred on a Saturday evening on the grounds of the Williams County courthouse during the summer of 1852; the initial instrumentation consisted of a cornet, several trombones, a cornopean, two clarinets, and some drums. The band's ranks were depleted at the outset of the Civil War when several of its members became musicians of the 38th Ohio Volunteer Infantry. With construction of the present courthouse, beginning in 1888 and continuing until 1896, the courthouse park did not include a permanent bandstand, so the group played from its own horsedrawn wagon, which on successive weeks was positioned on each of the four corners of the square. During the Spanish-American War, the Bryan ensemble served as the Ohio Naval Reserve Band and in 1900 became the Sixth Regiment Band of the Ohio National Guard. During the waning decades of the century the band had begun to travel about the region, playing at political rallies, ice cream socials, and the like, and in 1904 was one of the ensembles that participated in funeral ceremonies for President McKinley in Canton. Until World War II the group remained resolutely all-male, but for the 1943 season fourteen young women from the high school band had to be recruited as substitutes for the men who had gone off to fight, thus permanently altering a tradition. The group has been identified sequentially as the Fountain City Brass Band, the Fountain City Saxhorn Band, the Bryon Union Band, the Northwestern Silver Cornet Band, and even the Tubbs Municipal Band, after director Forrest A. Tubbs, who held that position from 1888 until 1892, and then again for thirty years beginning in 1896. He was succeeded by Dale Connin, whose tenure lasted thirty-six years. The incumbent director, John Hartman, presided over musical activities in the Bryan school system from 1943 until 1973, and, having succeeded Connin in 1962, raised his baton in the Connin-Hartman Bandstand on June 6, 2001, to initiate the 150th consecutive season of summer concerts. Since 1949 these have been held on Wednesday evenings, although earlier the performances were the focal point of Saturday evenings, when the entire community gathered not only to listen but also to shop in stores that often remained open until almost midnight.

Apart from the military, bands were sponsored by all sorts of civic groups, manufacturing companies and, eventually, colleges and universities (the first Ohio Intercollegiate Band Festival was held in 1929). However, it was not until the 1920s that the band became a fixture in the public schools, in part encouraged by the manufacturers of band instruments whose market was contracting with the disappearance of civic bands, which had played a role the school bands would gradually assume. The rapid expansion of the public school band movement can perhaps be gauged by the spread of band contests. The first national contest was held in Chicago in 1921, sponsored by several makers of band instruments, and the National Band tournament was organized by C. G. Conn Limited, two years later, again in Chicago; that event was won by the Fostoria Concert Band. This arrangement was found a bit unseemly, and the next such national contest was held in 1926 in Fostoria under the aegis of something called the National Bureau for the Advancement of Music working in consort with the Music Supervisors National Conference; 315 bands participated. The Fostoria band director, John W. Wainwright, had gathered a group of peers in February 1925 to form the Ohio High School Band Association; their purpose was to plan a state band contest. With the addition of orchestras to the mix in 1929, the organization was renamed the Ohio School Band and Orchestra Association, which in 1932 became the Ohio Music Educators Association. Its goals were to promote statewide contests in both the instrumental and vocal fields, as well as to field all-state bands, orchestras, choruses festivals, and clinics.

One of several Ohioans who became professional bandmasters was Karl L[awrence] King (1891–1971). Born the son of an amateur tuba player in the Greene County hamlet of Paintersville, his family apparently moved to Cleveland about 1901 and soon thereafter to Canton. King began to study the cornet at age eleven but soon switched to the baritone horn. In Canton he worked with the director of the Thayer Military Band and soon became a member of that ensemble. He began composing as a youngster, but the earliest works to survive appeared in 1909: the "March T. M. B." and "March 'Greater Canton'" (both dedicated to William Straussner, current director of the Thayer ensemble), the "Carrolton March" (dedicated to an area tuba player), the "Canton Aero Club" (dedicated to a local hot air balloon club), and "Moonlight on the Nile, Valse Oriental." The following year King wrote "The Gateway City" for a Canton convention of the Eagles Fraternal Order and "The Melody Shop" for a local retail music store.

King then moved to Columbus and joined the band of Fred[erick L.] Neddermeyer (1866–1924). Neddermeyer had apprenticed in Columbus theater orchestras as a string player. In 1883 he went to Leipzig for intensive study of the violin and piano and became a member of the string section of the famed Gewandhaus Orchestra for several years. He then returned home and toured with various theater orchestras for several years. In 1908 he organized a fifty-piece concert band in Columbus, a group that played several series of concerts, both in- and outdoors, presenting significant literature that had a decided impact on the musical tastes of the city. It was this group that nurtured the young Karl King and inspired his "Neddermeyer Triumphal March" of 1911. Neddermeyer also conducted various theater orchestras in both Columbus and Detroit and founded the *Columbus Dispatch* Newsboys Band.

King served a brief stint in the Soldier's Home Band of Danville, Illinois, before becoming a member of several circus bands, including that of Barnum and Bailey (for which he wrote "Barnum and Bailey's Favorite March" in 1913) and the Sells-Floto and Buffalo Bill Combined Shows, whose band he led for three seasons beginning in 1914. He returned to Canton and married but quickly was lured from this temporary retirement to lead the Barnum and Bailey band for two seasons. In 1918 he again returned to Canton, opened his own publishing house, and became conductor of a band sponsored by the Grand Army of the Republic, a period during which he issued more marches with an Ohio connection: "Ohio Division" of 1919, dedicated to the Ohio National Guard; "Tuscarawas" the following year; and "The Attorney General" of 1921, in honor of John Price, a Canton native then the state's attorney general. However, two years later he was appointed director of the Fort Dodge Municipal Band and spent the rest of his life in Iowa. He became an active member of the American Bandmasters Association and was in great demand as a guest conductor across the country. A prolific composer, he left almost three hundred marches, waltzes, galops, overtures, serenades, intermezzos, and other works, including a few other marches with Buckeye references, such as "McKinley's Own" of 1923 (dedicated "To Emil Rinkendorf and the Famous Grand Army Band, Canton, Ohio"),[19] "Nazir Grotto" of 1928 to the Canton Shrine Band, "Co-Eds on Parade" of 1942 to Oberlin's all-female band, and "The Ohio Special" of 1946.[20]

The Thayer Military Band had been founded in January 1892 by H. Clark Thayer (1860–1926). Trombonist Thayer entered Dana's Musical Institute in Warren in September 1879 and received a diploma in June 1881. He then joined the faculty of his alma mater and taught Dana students until 1890 (and then again from 1903 until 1906). He settled in Canton during January 1891, establishing himself as a teacher of brass instruments and piano; he also played in several local ensembles and directed a church choir. By January 1892 the thirty-member Thayer Military Band had been attached to a local battalion of the Ohio National Guard. A semiprofessional organization, it gave concerts, appeared at fairs, and marched in parades. It also accompanied local fraternal organizations to their conventions and its affiliated National Guard unit to encampments. The Thayer Military Band also played at campaign appearances by William McKinley in his quest for and then inaugurations as both Ohio governor and national president and then for his funeral in 1901. In September 1903 Thayer shared the podium at a farewell concert with his successor, Henry Restorff, an oboist who had played for both bandmaster Patrick Gilmore and Theodore Thomas. The Thayer Military Band retained its founder's name into the 1960s, when it merged with two other local bands to create the Canton City Band. Thayer published a handful of marches, and after his second stint at the Dana Musical Institute established the Susquehanna College of Music in Clearfield, Pennsylvania.

The two other Ohio bandmasters who achieved national prominence were both from Cincinnati. [James] Henry Fillmore [Jr.] (1881–1956) was one of an extended clan, grandson of the patriarchal Augustus D. Fillmore, son and nephew of the three offspring who had founded the Fillmore Brothers Publishing House in Cincinnati in 1874. After graduating in 1901 from the Miami Military Institute (a junior college located in Germantown), Henry studied briefly at the Cincinnati College of Music and then worked in the family business for four years (during which time the Fillmores opened a retail music shop that flourished for many decades), but conflict with his father over the propriety of band music (the pious Fillmores to that time had issued only religious music) led to a temporary rupture and a year's membership in a circus band. Reconciled with his father, Fillmore returned to Cincinnati and played in various theater orchestras through early 1912. He also rejoined the staff of the family publishing house, which as early as 1907 began to publish most of his known 250 original works and as many as 750 arrangements for band.

In 1921 Fillmore was appointed director of the Syrian Temple Band, which under his baton was reputed to be the finest such fraternal band in the country. He resigned that post in 1926 after a dispute with Shrine officials and was soon asked to created a twenty-two-piece professional studio band for station WLW, a group that began to concertize with a series of performances at the Cincinnati Zoo during the late summer of 1928, a tradition perpetuated until 1936. One notable gimmick was that Mike, the family dog, had learned to bark in time, and several of Fillmore's pieces incorporated the talents of this "radio hound" (one 1930 piece was "Giving Mike the Ha Ha"); Mike the dog became a national celebrity and provoked Fillmore's only commercial recording, a Columbia release of 1928 that invited listeners to "Hear 'Mike' Bark his Bit" in "The Whistling Farmer Boy" and "Golden Friendships."

Heart problems led to retirement in Miami in 1938, but Fillmore regained his health to an extent that confounded his doctors, and he became a father figure to Florida bandsmen over the remaining decades of his life. He nurtured countless high school bands as a guest conductor, was named Permanent Guest Conductor of the University of Miami "Band of the Hour," presided over a summer band camp at the university, served as master of ceremonies and conducted the bands at the annual Orange Bowl festivities beginning in 1943, and guest conducted across the country. The Fillmore Brothers firm had been sold to the Carl Fischer Company in 1951, but Fillmore willed future royalties from his scores to the University of Miami Band; the Henry Fillmore Band Hall and its Fillmore Museum can be found on the Coral Gables campus.

Fillmore's legacy as a composer is confusing because he wrote under various pseudonyms, including Harold Bennett (four elementary teaching volumes, the Bennett Band Books, sold millions of copies after the first was published in 1923), Al Hayes, Will Huff, Harry Hartley, Ray Hall, Gus Beans, and Henrietta Moore.[21] Collectively they wrote marches, waltzes, serenades, overtures, fox trots, and many novelty numbers. The best known of these featured Fillmore's trombone and its ability to "smear," for example, "Miss Trombone" (1908), "Lassus Trombone" (1915), "Shoutin' Liza Trombone" (1920), and "Ham Trombone" (1929). Although not among his most-played works, a handful of his marches evoke Ohio through their titles: "Men of Ohio" (1921, dedicated to President Warren G. Harding), "The Crosley March" (1928; the Crosley Broadcasting Company owned station WLW), "The Cincinnati Zoo" (1929, but published as "Americans We"), and "King Karl King" (1959). Others have covert Ohio connections: "The Victorious First" (1907, written while Fillmore was a member of the band of the 1st Regiment of the Ohio National Guard), the "136th U. S. A. Field Artillery" (1918, for what had been a unit of the Ohio National Guard), "Gifted Leadership" (1927, to Frank Simon), "The Klaxon" (1930, for a Cincinnati automobile show), "His Honor" (1934, to the incumbent mayor of Cincinnati), and "The Footlifter" (1935, "To Henry T. Garner, Secretary of the Cincinnati Automobile Dealer Association").

Although Frank Simon (1889–1967) was born in Cincinnati, his family moved to Middletown while he was still a toddler. He first studied the flute but at age eleven took up the cornet under the tutelage of the director of the Middletown Band and conducted that group at age fourteen when his mentor moved elsewhere (what had been known colloquially as "Buckles' Band" became "Simon's Band"). He also began to study with William J. Kopp, principal trumpeter of the Cincinnati Symphony, and played cornet in Kopp's professional band, as well as in the Sorg's Opera House orchestra in Middletown. In 1905 he became a student of Herman Bellstedt (1858–1926),[22] the noted cornet soloist of Sousa's band, who as composer and arranger was later to dedicate much to his prize pupil. Consequently, Simon was named a soloist with Kopp's group in 1909 (Henry Fillmore also played with the ensemble during this period). For five years he played with the Cincinnati-based Weber's Prize Band of America, including two tours of the West Coast during the 1912–14 seasons. He also served in the Cincinnati Symphony under Stokowski during the 1912–13 season.

In 1914, on Bellstedt's recommendation, Sousa hired Simon as a stand partner to the legendary Herbert L. Clarke; Simon succeeded Clarke as soloist and assistant conductor when Clarke retired three years later, a position he held until 1920. During World War I Simon served as bandmaster of the United States Aviation School in Fairfield and from 1919 until 1931 led the Antioch Temple Shrine Band in Dayton. During the summer of 1920 he played in the Mason City [Iowa] Municipal Band, which led to his meeting an eighteen-year-old flutist named Meredith Willson. Simon recommended Willson to Sousa, who immediately hired him. Some see an act of gratitude manifested in a later smash Broadway hit, discovering hints of the personality of Frank Simon in Willson's *The Music Man*.

That same year the American Rolling Mill Company of Middletown hired Simon to organize and conduct an employees' band, a venture so successful that by 1923 the Armco Band had recorded on the Gennett label and two years later was offering programs over stations WSAI and WLW in Cincinnati. The band was funded by the Armco Association, comprised of every employee of the company, each of whom paid fifty cents per month, with the company matching an equal amount. This eventually allowed an office staff of seven people, including a business manager and others involved in copying and arranging music and whatever else was required for the functioning of the organization. The association also provided $6,000 for a series of twelve summer concerts at the band shell on Armco field (with audiences averaging ten thousand per event), while the Middletown Civic Association funded another seven afternoon concerts in a local park. In addition, by 1927 the city was subsidizing a series of nine free winter concerts in the high school auditorium.[23] The band played regularly in Cincinnati, Dayton, and Hamilton, toured extensively in Pennsylvania, West Virginia, and Indiana, and appeared at both the Ohio State Fair in Columbus and the Canadian National Exhibition in Toronto.

With the onslaught of the Great Depression, the band was dissolved, but Simon persuaded the company to sponsor a new ensemble made up of professional musicians hired on a part-time basis. Weekly broadcasts over WLW were initiated, and by 1932 twenty-six weekly Sunday afternoon *Iron Master* broadcasts by the Armco Concert Band were being heard nationally over the NBC networks. Simon and his band became a national institution, rivaling Amos and Andy in popularity. He generated favorable publicity by featuring the broadcast début of a young soloist on each program. For three years he also enjoyed the capacities of the noted composer and arranger Ferde Grofé ([1892–1972] who had made his reputation as arranger for Paul Whiteman); besides arrangements, in 1935 Grofé wrote his pictorial *Rhapsody in Steel* for the band. The tradition lasted until 1939, when Armco abruptly withdrew its sponsorship, and the ensemble was disbanded, but not before Simon made a tour of Ohio and Pennsylvania with what was billed as his "Radio Band."

In 1930 Simon had received his first honorary doctorate—from the Capitol College of Oratory and Music in Columbus—and hosted the first meeting of the new American Bandmasters' Association in Middletown, an event sponsored by Armco that brought to town John Philip Sousa, Karl King, and Edwin Franko Goldman, the group's first president. The convention's finale was a concert by the Armco Band, led by a dozen different conductors (including Sousa), broadcast over a mini-network of six stations.

Simultaneously, Simon had become an influential educator, having joined the faculty of the Cincinnati Conservatory of Music in 1930 and organized that school's instrumental department, which included both a band and orchestra. In 1949 he also became a member of the faculty of the rival Cincinnati College of Music but retired from both positions in 1955, when he was diagnosed with emphysema, and moved to Arizona. The following year he was appointed a visiting professor at the University of Arizona, a position he held for a decade. He then left his enormous personal library at the Arizona school and moved back to Cincinnati, where at age seventy-six he resumed teaching on a part-time basis at what had become the College-Conservatory of the University of Cincinnati (that was to award him another honorary doctorate in 1966). During the interim he had returned to Ohio to conduct events such as a massed high school band assembled in the University of Cincinnati stadium in November 1963, as well as a concert by the College-Conservatory Symphonic Band, at which he was dubbed the group's conductor emeritus. During the following summer he conducted a retrospective Sousa concert in Dayton that attracted about eight thousand auditors, with hundreds turned away, followed almost immediately by surgery to remove polyps on his colon. He suffered a stroke while offering a lesson to one of his students and died at age seventy-seven on a day when he had been scheduled to conduct a Sousa memorial concert in Columbus.[24]

Primarily a performer, Simon did however leave a large handful of works for band, including the "*Cincinnati Post* March," published by the Fillmore Brothers in 1931.

CHAPTER 34

Jazz

Ohio certainly remained peripheral to the great arc of migration that carried jazz from its gestation and infancy in New Orleans during the early decades of the twentieth century, north to Chicago during the teens and 1920s (with a Kansas City tributary), and then on to New York and increasing universality, with a corresponding progression of styles, from big band swing during the 1930s and early 1940s, and antidotes to that craze such as bebop, cool, and modern during the 1940s and 1950s, to various kinds of experimental jazz and attempts at third stream idioms (that is, currents flowing beside those of art music and mainstream jazz), plus fusion with other styles of pop and rock.

Of course, jazz has been practiced in Ohio and with a vengeance. Beyond the club and concert scene, colleges and universities, as well as high schools across the state, field significant jazz programs, often focused on the big band style. Furthermore, Ohio can boast of at least one nationally recognized professional ensemble. What is now known as the Columbus Jazz Orchestra (christened the Jazz Arts Group) celebrated its twenty-fifth anniversary in 1998, boasting of two concert series and various appearances on the road, as well as a $1.1 million budget that has allowed the ensemble to host guest soloists ranging from Sarah Vaughan, Tony Bennett, Rosemary Clooney, and Doc Severinson, to the Ink Spots and Four Freshmen.[1]

Ohio has given birth to jazz musicians who achieved luminary status elsewhere. The best known of these was Toledo-born Art Tatum (1909–56). This partially sighted pianist was playing professionally in his hometown while still a teenager and by 1929 was hosting a fifteen-minute live radio program over station WSPD, which was also carried on the NBC Blue network. Singer Adelaide Hall hired him as her accompanist, and their road trips led to New York in 1932, where Tatum made his first recording the following year. He played clubs in Cleveland and Chicago for a few years beginning in 1934 and spent the 1936–37 season in Hollywood but then returned to New York, where he established a reputation in clubs and on radio shows, leading to dates in England the following year. Tatum assembled a trio in 1943 and toured extensively with them and as a soloist, appearing not only in clubs but also in concert venues, including an appearance on the Metropolitan Opera stage in 1944. His virtuosity inspired other jazz greats, ranging from Charlie Parker to Lennie Tristano and Herbie Hancock, although he never managed a public following approximating the admiration with which he was held by members of the jazz fraternity. His legacy lives in the more than six hundred performances he recorded, many of them committed to vinyl after 1953 in association with musicians such as Benny Carter and Lionel Hampton under the aegis of producer Norman Granz.[2]

Since his family left Dayton after the birth of [William] Billy Strayhorn (1915–67) and the composer, arranger, and pianist received his education elsewhere, protocol might suggest it improper to classify him as a Buckeye. In December 1938 he sent an original composition to Duke Ellington, initiating a professional relationship that lasted for the rest of his life and led to his influence on more than two hundred pieces in the Ellington canon. Strayhorn worked briefly as a pianist for Mercer Ellington during 1938 but joined the Duke's band in the autumn of 1939 as an associate arranger and second pianist and eventually collaborated on about two hundred items in the Ellington repertory. Although he recorded keyboard duets with Ellington in 1950 and also can be heard on recordings with Ellington sidemen ranging from Cootie Williams and Barney Bigard to Louie Bellson and Clark Terry, his major legacy remains the Ellington classics he composed, such as the immortal "Take the A Train."

Perhaps the most unusual figure in this minipantheon is Rahsaan Roland Kirk (1935–77). Blinded soon after birth, Kirk was educated at the Ohio State School for the Blind in his native Columbus. He was first attracted to the trumpet, but after a doctor suggested that playing that instrument put a strain on his eyes, Kirk turned to the tenor saxophone and clarinet. By 1951 he had established his own rhythm-and-blues band. However, his eventual notoriety arose from his ability to play three instruments simultaneously. In the back room of a local music store he had found some unusual instruments, perhaps originally used in late-nineteenth-century Spanish military bands. The manzello (he sometimes referred to it as the "Moon Zellar") resembled an alto saxophone with an outsized, flat bell, and the strich approximated a large soprano sax. He added these to his conventional tenor sax and established himself as a persona, with all three instruments hung from his neck. By modifying the tenor so that he could play it with his left hand, he was able to employ the right hand on the more exotic instruments. At first he used drones and other devices to keep the various instruments sounding, but he eventually developed a circular breathing technique that allowed uninterrupted sounds. He also played the three basic instruments separately and added others to his arsenal, such as the nose flute, harmonica, claviette, slidesophone (a miniature trombone), and trumpophone (a soprano saxophone played with a trumpet mouthpiece). A technical virtuoso, he dabbled in styles ranging from rhythm and blues to bebop and various avant-garde idioms. He recorded extensively, beginning in 1956, and toured the world with his own Vibration Society in 1970. After a stroke in November 1975 left him paralyzed on his right side, he taught himself to play left-handed and began to tour again, until a second stroke silenced him forever.

Jazz singer Nancy Wilson was born in Chillicothe in 1937 and got her start in various Columbus clubs and on local television shows like *Skyline Melodies,* which she hosted on WTVN. She made a first recording in 1956 and then toured nationally with Rusty Bryant's band for several years. By the end of the decade she had worked with George Shearing and Cannonball Adderley and signed a contract with Capitol Records. During the following decades she drifted between the worlds of jazz and pop with extended tours and more than fifty recordings; by the beginning of the 1980s she allied herself more closely with jazz musicians, touring Japan several times with Hank Jones's Great Jazz Trio in 1981 and 1982. She has continued to tour and record into the new century, including appearances at major festivals in New Orleans in 1995, San Francisco in 1997, and Los Angeles during 2001.[3]

But Wilson was not the first Buckeye-born singer to attract attention. Mamie Smith (1883–1946), a native of Cincinnati, was the first African American female to record, in this case an Okeh Records release of February 1920 that included two Perry Bradford tunes—"That Thing Called Love" and "You Can't Keep a Good Woman Down." This was followed only months later by an August release of Bradford's "Crazy Blues," an instant hit that sold more than a million copies in its first year. By 1922 she had created her own band, the Jazz Hounds, which offered a first job to the young saxophone player Coleman Hawkins. Blessed with a vibrant stage presence, amplified with lavish costuming and jewelry, Smith's career extended into the early 1940s, including several Hollywood film roles.

Ohio has also furnished a considerable number of lesser lights. One of the most prominent of these is tenor saxophonist Frank Foster, born in Cincinnati in 1928. As a music major at Wilberforce University he became a soloist and arranger for the Wilberforce Collegians jazz band, which performed at Carnegie Hall in 1947. He then played in the Detroit area before a stint in the armed forces. Foster joined the Count Basie Orchestra in 1953 as a soloist, arranger, and composer, but left after eleven years (having also worked with others, including Woody Herman) and organized his own big band, later called the Loud Minority (as well as its subsets, labeled the Living Color and the Non-electric Company), concurrently playing with other groups, both large and small. In 1986 he became leader of a reactivated Basie Orchestra on tours across this country and Europe. He taught at the State University of New York in Buffalo from 1972 until 1976 and in 1986 was awarded an honorary doctorate by Ohio's Central State University. His distinctive style can be sampled via recordings dating from 1955 into the 1990s. Among his compositions is the *Lake Placid Suite* for jazz orchestra, commissioned for the Winter Olympics of 1980.

Noted trumpeter Harry "Sweets" Edison (1915–99) became another Basie colleague. After an early childhood in Kentucky, he returned to his native Columbus, where he played in local bands before joining the Jeter-Pillars Orchestra in Cleveland during 1933. A year later that group migrated to St. Louis, but by 1937 Edison had arrived in New York, where he soon became an important soloist, composer, and arranger with the Basie Orchestra (saxophonist Lester Young, a fellow sideman, is credited with creating Edison's nickname); he also played a prominent role in the 1944 film, *Jammin' the Blues*. After the Basie ensemble disbanded in 1950, Edison led his own groups and freelanced with other bands, such as Jazz at the Philharmonic. He eventually settled in California, where he functioned as a studio musician (working with Nelson Riddle and Benny Carter, among others), fronted his own groups, and traveled extensively in this country and Europe with the likes of Frank Sinatra and Basie. He also taught at Yale University in the Duke Ellington Fellowship Program and was honored by the National Endowment for the Arts at the Kennedy Center in Washington in 1991.

Jon Hendricks, born in Newark in 1921, is a jazzman of an unusual sort. As a teenager he sang with Art Tatum after his family had moved to Toledo. Following a stint in the Army, he entered the University of Toledo, studying literature and later the law. However, he concurrently taught himself to play the drums and organized his own trio. It was no less an authority than Charlie Parker who suggested that Hendricks turn to music as a profession. After moving to New York in 1952 he formed a trio with Dave Lambert and Annie Ross, which became known for imposing Hendricks's new lyrics and scat lines on existing jazz tunes, a style of singing he labeled "vocalese." Their first big hit was *Sing a Song of Basie* (1957), followed by other releases, such as *The Swingers* (1959), *The Hottest New Group in Jazz* (also 1959), *Lambert, Hendricks, and Ross Sing Ellington* (1960), and *High Flying* (1961). Illness forced retirement on Ross in 1962, and other changes of personnel led to the trio's demise two years later. Hendricks had written and directed the *Evolution of the Blues* for the Monterey Modern Jazz Festival in 1960 and then continued with a solo career, including some five years based in London beginning in 1968, a period during which he performed across Europe and into Africa. He then settled in California, where he taught and briefly served as a jazz critic for the *San Francisco Chronicle*. Since then he has performed with the likes of Bobby McFerrin and maintained a reputation as a skilled performer of his own witty lyrics, as well as a virtuoso scat singer amazingly adept at imitating instrumental sounds. He received a Lifetime Achievement Award at the 1995 San Francisco Jazz Festival, and the opening event of the 1996–97 Jazz at Lincoln Center season became a celebration of his seventy-fifth birthday. In May 2000 it was announced that seventy-eight-year-old Hendricks would come home and join the faculty of the University of Toledo to teach jazz history and his art of vocalese.

Ohio has provided the jazz world with many sidemen who have done yeoman service for various jazz notables, too numerous to enumerate in detail. Nonetheless, a small handful:

Ripley saw the birth of the Smith brothers, both noted trumpeters, sons of a father who led a brass band in Cincinnati. Joe (Joseph C., 1902–37) had arrived in New York by the early 1920s and soon was touring and recording with the likes of Ethel Waters and Mamie Smith. He directed the band for Noble Sissle and Eubie Blake's *The Chocolate Dandies*, a revue from 1924, and was a member of Fletcher Henderson's Orchestra from 1925 until 1928, allowing him to record with blues singers of the stature of Bessie Smith. Joe then worked with other groups and later settled in Kansas City, but ill health caused by excessive drinking forced an end to his career, even before his premature death. Russell "Pops" Smith (1890–1966) had begun playing professionally about 1906 and arrived in New York four years later. After a European tour with the Joe Jordan Band in 1914 he performed in Army bands during World War I and then worked with James Reese in Europe and in the pit for various New York shows. However, in 1925 he joined Fletcher Henderson, for whom he played lead trumpet until 1941. During that period he also worked with Horace Henderson and Benny Carter, later became a member of Cab Calloway's band and, from 1945 until 1950, Noble Sissle's Orchestra. During the 1950s he drifted into semiretirement in California, dividing his time between teaching and playing occasional gigs.

An example of a Buckeye who ventured into the world beyond and then returned to his roots is William "Buddy" De Arango, a guitarist born in Cleveland in 1921. De Arango first picked up a guitar while a student at Ohio State and taught himself to play by listening to recordings of eminent contemporaries. After a two-year stint with an Army band at Fort Sill, Oklahoma, he played in various Cleveland clubs but moved to New York in 1944, where he was quickly engaged by saxophonist Ben Webster. By the following year he was recording with bopper Charlie Parker and in 1946 made with Dizzie Gillespie what historians consider one of the seminal recordings in the evolution of bebop. However, only two years later, De Arango "retired" to Cleveland, although in 1954 he returned to New York to make yet another recording, an album titled *Alone Together*. Back home, he opened a retail music store in University Heights, taught, and played club dates with his own trio. In 1983 De Arango recorded again with fellow Clevelanders Jamey Haddad and Joe Lovano, and, well into his seventies, he returned to the studio with those two colleagues in 1993 to record an album of "free jazz" titled *Anything Went*, which was released in late 1996.[4]

So, even though Ohio is considered by most a "go through" rather than a "go to" place by the jazz world (borrowing from scholar Ted McDaniel), I trust that I have been able to suggest that the state has nurtured a vibrant jazz culture worthy of note.

CHAPTER 35

Cleveland Rocks

So, why a museum dedicated to the history of rock and roll, born in the 1950s and brought to a first maturity during the chaotic 1960s, and in Cleveland, rather than Memphis, home of Graceland, or Detroit, home of Motown, or other cities more organically connected to this preponderant idiom? Why do locals claim that, indeed, "Cleveland Rocks?"[1]

This assertion was actually the title of a song on British-born Ian Hunter's album *You're Never Alone with a Schizophrenic*, released in 1979, also issued as sheet music. Hunter was managed by Steven Popovich (b. 1942), who had founded Cleveland International Records during April 1977. Five months later the company's first release, *Bat Out of Hell* by Meat Loaf, was to sell more than twelve million copies.[2]

WMMS-FM, "The Radio Station That Storms the Nation," was named the best rock-and-roll station in the country for nine straight years by *Rolling Stone* magazine, beginning in 1979.[3] *The Big 5 Show*, renamed *Upbeat* in 1965, first appeared on WEWS-TV in August 1964 and was eventually syndicated on more than one hundred stations across the country, providing a launching pad for performers like Simon and Garfunkel and Stevie Wonder. Then there was the renowned Leo's Casino,[4] 7500 Euclid Avenue, one of several local venues for black artists like James Brown, the Four Tops, the Supremes, and Otis Redding, who performed there several times between 1963 and 1972. His last appearance was on December 9, 1967—the following day Redding died in a crash of his private plane. These and other insights could be gleaned from an exhibit at the Rock and Roll Hall of Fame and Museum from January to September 1997 that showcased the rock history of "My Town," the title of a song by the Michael Stanley Band.

Michael Stanley (b. 1948), a Rocky River High School graduate, had recorded with a group called the Tree Stumps beginning in 1969 and then issued two solo albums. He organized his self-named band in 1974; they generated eleven albums on national labels over the next thirteen years and performed extensively in northern Ohio. Since then Stanley has remained active as a solo performer and a deejay at WNCX.[5]

But why has Cleveland been home since September 1, 1995, to a dramatic I. M. Pei–designed building, its massive glass pyramid an obvious evocation of the architect's controversial entrance to the Louvre in Paris? Why do visitors flock to this $92 million monument, with its kaleidoscopic array of informative exhibits, memorabilia, and artifacts; multiple video theaters; interactive computer stations; and library, its 150,000 square feet housing the largest public collection of rock and roll-related material in the world, a veritable orgy of sight and sound?

Persistence and money certainly helped. The Rock and Roll Hall of Fame Foundation actually dates back to 1983.[6] The idea of its founders was to honor annual inductees in some sort of modest space. That remains a function of the present structure, although the first Hall of Fame, initially sequestered atop the structure, its funereal atmosphere the antithesis of a rock event, has since been moved to a spacious cylindrical room originally intended as an auditorium. Frankly, although Cleveland figures in the seminal development of rock as the temporary home of deejay Alan Freed, the pioneer who organized what many consider the first true rock concert, Clevelanders won the prize simply because they managed to raise the money to build what quickly became a major tourist attraction.[7]

The crucial figure was a son of Latvian immigrants named Leo Mintz, originally a pawnbroker, who opened a record store in 1939 at 214 Prospect Avenue. By 1945 the shop was known as Record Rendezvous, the base of a chain of stores in northeastern Ohio that Mintz forged before his death in 1976. He was a retail pioneer who created the idea of the open browsing bin, as well as the listening booth where patrons could sample a product before purchasing it. He advertised, "You'll Enjoy Our Pick and Play. 20 Private Booths to Listen and Choose Your Favorites from Thousands of Records." During the late 1940s Mintz decided to specialize in jazz ("Classical and Hot Jazz Our Specialties") and then moved into rhythm and blues in an attempt to capture a white audience, thus suggesting the fusion of black and white styles that was to metamorphose into rock and the social revolution it fomented.

Pennsylvania-born Aldon (Alan) James Freed (1921–65) was raised in Salem, where he played trombone in the high school marching band and orchestra and helped organize a dance band dubbed the Sultans of Swing.[8] After graduation in 1940 Freed enrolled at Ohio State, intending at first to major in journalism and then mechanical engineering, although he abandoned his studies after less than a full year. Following months of military service, terminated with a medical discharge, he worked at radio stations in New Castle, Pennsylvania, and Youngstown before establishing himself at Akron's WAKR in 1945 as a news and sports announcer. By the following year he had become host of the *Request Review*, a top-rated listener call-in show with a studio audience of teenagers that concentrated on jazz, swing,

The Moondog Coronation Ball, March 21, 1952. Photo Peter Hastings. Courtesy Gloria Hastings.

and the pop music of the day. By early 1950 he was living in Cleveland, hosting an afternoon movie program on WXEL-TV, where he attempted to adapt his radio format to television in its infancy, billing himself as a "teejay."

However, in February 1951 Freed became host of a classical music program on WJW. With Mintz as his mentor and sponsor, Freed then originated a rhythm-and-blues program on July 11, 1951, soon adopting the moniker, "Moondog." His show, *The Moondog House,* was heard nightly from 11:15 P.M. until 1:00 A.M.; its motto: "He spins em Keed—He's HEP, that Freed." He opened each show by screaming into the microphone and pumped up the beat by ringing a cowbell and pounding percussively on a hefty telephone directory.[9]

Freed and his patron booked Varetta Dillard, the Dominos, Tiny Grimes and His Rockin' Highlanders, and Paul Williams and His Hucklebuckers for the Moondog Coronation Ball at the Cleveland Arena on March 21, 1952, but only Williams had performed when the police closed the event because of dangerous overcrowding and unruly behavior.[10] It would be perilous to postulate that evening as representing the birth of the era of what he called rock 'n' roll, but Freed can at least be given credit for popularizing the label (although the basic terminology had been available for some decades; as witness, "My Daddy Rocks Me [With One Steady Roll]," recorded by Harold Ortli and His Ohio State Collegians in Cleveland in 1925 on the Okeh label). However, only three days later, Lakewood native Jane Scott (b. 1919) was hired as an assistant society reporter by the *Cleveland Plain Dealer*. Scott later became a pioneering and much-celebrated critic of the rock idiom after the paper's "Young Ohio" section became her responsibility in 1958, a vocation she pursued for many fruitful decades.[11] Freed remained in Cleveland until 1954, when he was hired by WINS in New York City. However, his career was then sullied by his involvement in a major payola scandal, which led to a guilty plea to two counts of commercial bribery in 1962 and an indictment for income tax evasion two years later.

Cleveland's other claim on history during the 1950s was then-unknown Elvis Presley's first appearance outside the South, at Brooklyn High School on March 20, 1955, an event arranged by another important local deejay, Bill Randle (1923–2004), an evening that also included pop singer Pat Boone, Bill Haley and the Comets, and the Four Lads.

In fact, a local group achieved some national prominence during that same decade. A teenaged vocal trio from suburban Brush High School that became known as the Poni-Tails reached no. 2 on the national charts in 1958 with their version of "Born Too Late," a song with a lyric by Fred Tobias and music by Broadway composer Charles Strouse.[12] This short-lived fame allowed extensive touring, but their "Seven Minutes to Heaven" failed to attract notice and the ensemble disbanded in 1960.

However, chronological precedence must be given to the Isley Brothers, a Cincinnati family group formed during the early 1950s. The original foursome included Rudolph (b. 1939), Ronald (b. 1941), O'Kelly (soon known only as Kelly, 1937–86), and Vernon (who died in 1955). Encouraged by their musical parents, the remaining threesome went to New York in 1957 but had no commercial success until two years later when a representative of RCA contracted them and produced their first hit single, "Shout," a call-and-response song in gospel style. The piece quickly became an R&B standard and sold more than a million copies, the sales of which allowed the whole family to relocate to Teaneck, New Jersey. The Isleys began to tour extensively with a back-up band that included Jimi Hendrix and recorded for various labels but only occasionally achieved commercial hits, including "Twist and Shout" in 1962 and "This Old Heart of Mine" four years later. They based their career in England from 1966 until 1969 but returned to create their own T-Neck label, named for their adopted hometown. "It's Your Thing," their first self-produced release, became their biggest hit, since it sold more than two million copies and was awarded a Grammy in 1969 for the best R&B vocal performance. A new generation of the family was added to the ensemble in the same year, prefacing a series of major R&B hits that persisted throughout the 1980s (a period when the Isleys also entered the disco market), despite significant changes in personnel. The Isley Brothers were inducted into the Rock and Roll Hall of Fame in 1992.

Another black vocal group, the O'Jays, had its origins at Canton's McKinley High School after Eddie Levert (b. 1942) and Walter Williams (b. 1942), who had been singing as a duo called the Triumphs, became the Mascots in 1959 with the addition of Bobby Massey, Bill Isles, and William Powell. Their new name was imposed by Syd Nathan of King Records, who offered them a contract that year and issued two discs, in 1960 and 1961. After receiving professional advice from a Cleveland deejay named Eddie O'Jay, the group renamed itself in his honor and began to establish a stage persona in part through their elaborate "vocal choreography." In 1965 Isles departed, transforming the quintet into a quartet, this during a period when the group produced only a few minor successes.

However, in 1968 a Philadelphia-based pair named Kenny Gamble and Leon Huff became their producers, leading to a series of hits during the following decade, including three albums that reached gold status, while three others became platinum. Massey departed in 1971, and cancer wreaked sufficient vengeance on Powell that by 1975 he was forced into retirement and died two years later in Canton. However, the group soldiered on with 1979's *Identify Yourself*, a platinum release. During the first half of the 1980s, founders Levert and Williams began to rely less on Gamble and Huff (who had actually created many of the group's popular social commentary songs); their last cooperative venture was the album *Love Fever*, released in 1985. However, the ensemble's later history has included *Emotionally Yours*, a gold album of 1991, *Heartbreaker* in 1993, *Smooth Love* in 1999, and *For the Love* in 2001, benchmarks of a longevity quite amazing in their business. An offspring of the parent group are Levert's sons, Gerald and Sean, joined by Marc Gordon, forming the R&B trio Levert in 1982; Eddie and Gerald allied in 1995 for a hit album simply labeled *Father and Son*.

Some pioneering Ohio-born or based groups are today recalled mainly by historians and aficionados; for example, Bocky and the Visions (a Cleveland group formed in 1961 heard on the Philips label in 1964 before the group's demise in 1965), or Tom King and the Starfires, later known as the Outsiders (another Cleveland group, one that issued four albums on the Capitol label between 1966 and 1968).[13]

Others achieved and have even retained widespread currency. The James Gang was organized by Cleveland drummer Jim Fox in 1966 and, despite several changes of personnel, became one of the favorite hard-rock bands before disbanding in 1976. A major force on the concert circuit (one memorable performance filled the seventy-thousand-seat Akron Rubber Bowl on June 16, 1972; they even attracted the attention of Pete Townshend and opened the Who's concerts in Europe during 1971), some of their hits are still available on CD, including their second album, *James Gang Rides Again* of 1970. The best-known configuration of the group (Fox plus bassist Dale

Peters and guitarist Joe Walsh [b. 1947]) was revived by presidential candidate and fan Bill Clinton at a 1996 campaign event in the Cleveland State University Convocation Center and then at one of his Inaugural Balls in Washington the following January. The trio then appeared on *The Drew Carey Show* in 1999 and reunited again on February 22, 2001, for an appearance in the theater of the Rock and Roll Hall of Fame and Museum, which included a performance of "Funk #49," a hit from *James Gang Rides Again*, supported by eight percussionists from the Beachwood High School marching band. Questioned about the rationale for such a reunion, Walsh replied, "I thought it was appropriate to . . . celebrate the old days here in Cleveland."[14]

The Raspberries were formed in 1970 around the personality of singer Eric Carmen (b. 1949) and the remnants of two earlier groups. Drummer Jim Bonfanti (b. 1948) had become a member of the Mods (a group organized at Mentor High School in 1964), who as the Choir achieved at least regional fame with "It's Cold Outside" in 1967, a year after their renaming. Carmen and Bonfanti then allied themselves with two other alums of the Choir to create a group that some critics deemed immediately antiquated, with their mod suits and "power pop" style, perhaps too obviously reminiscent of the Beatles. However, during the first half of the decade, they achieved considerable success, initiated with a self-titled album of 1972, sporting a raspberry-scented scratch-and-sniff sticker on the cover. The song "Go All the Way" of 1972 (marketed via a "foxiest Raspberry" contest, won by Bonfanti, who then presented to the winner of a drawing a custom-made "Raspberry Rollswagon"), which sold more than 1.3 million copies, was followed by "Let's Pretend" (a cut on their second album, *Fresh*) the following year, and "Overnight Sensation" in 1974, all of them by Carmen. Tours took them across the country (including a standing-room-only crowd at the Los Angeles Coliseum in 1973) and to Europe. However, internal dissension had already led to major changes of personnel, and even though "Overnight Sensation" reached no. 12 on the charts in 1974, the title proved prophetic, and the group disbanded the following year.[15] Carmen then embarked on a solo career that sporadically produced hits into the first half of the next decade, most notably his performance of John DeNicola and Frank Previte's "Hungry Eyes," which became part of the soundtrack of the film *Dirty Dancing* in 1988. He also collaborated with his brother Fred (a lawyer who had become mayor of suburban Mayfield Heights) to write and record "The Rock Stops Here," a song that in early 1986 became part of the campaign to locate the Rock and Roll Hall of Fame and Museum in Cleveland.

Other cities in northeastern Ohio participated in the rock revolution. For example, Devo was organized in Akron during 1972. This New Wave band was supposedly based on the philosophical principle of devolution, postulating a humankind embarked on a negative course, culturally and genetically. Highly electronic, their music was meant to evoke the mechanical and robotic and was presented and marketed in a similar satirical manner, with futuristic uniforms that made them resemble nuclear reactor workers but adorned with inverted red flower pots as hats and protective gear meant to evoke roller derbies. Add to these in-your-face anomalies potato masks and quasi-military stage groupings as a means of social commentary. Their first release, in the summer of 1977, was issued on their own label, Booji Boy Records, and the robot Booji became the group's corporate mascot. This was followed by *Q: Are We Not Men? A: We Are Devo!* in 1978, *Duty Now for the Future* the following year, and *Freedom of Choice* in 1980, which contained "Whip It," their first single hit that sold more than a million copies. However, as the decade progressed, the critics increasingly felt that the group had lost its momentum and passed its innovative edge to other groups modeled on it, although *Total Devo* of 1988 garnered some tributes. The group never attracted the MTV crowd but did perform the theme song of the movie *Doctor Detroit* and also was involved with television shows like *Pee Wee's Playhouse*. Its more recent activities have been intermittent: A re-formed Devo made a thirty-city tour of Europe in 1991 and four years later created a new song for the movie *Mighty Morphin Power Rangers*.

Pere Ubu was formed in Cleveland in 1975 from the remnants of several experimental groups, such as Rocket from the Tombs and Foggy and the Shrimps, and, despite sequential changes of personnel (for much of their history singer David Thomas [b. 1953)] was the primary catalyst), has managed to survive for more than a quarter of a century (with a hiatus between 1982 and 1987), virtual eternity in the field. This New Wave band was named after a character created by surrealist playwright Alfred Jarry in his *Ubu Roi* because "(1) It seemed like a good idea at the time; (2) The name looked good, sounded good, had 3 syllables, and wasn't likely to mean anything to anyone."[16] The Pirate's Cove, a bar in the Flats (a riverfront entertainment section in downtown Cleveland), was the quintet's first home, and several singles (for example, "30 Seconds Over Tokyo") prefaced their initial collection, *The Modern Dance* (released in February 1978), which was followed by *Dub Housing* (also 1978, its title a reference to the terraced housing patterns of Baltimore), *Datapanik in the Year Zero* (1979), *New Picnic Time* (also 1979), and *The Art of Walking* (1980). Their propulsive "art-rock" sounds, which at moments veered toward the realm of anarchy, received critical acclaim and provoked extensive tours of this country, the United Kingdom, and continental Europe. However, even by 1980 some were finding their idiom "obtuse," consequently consigning them to the margins. The following year Thomas embarked on a solo recording career, leading to the group's virtual implosion, despite the albums *390 Degrees of Simulated Stereo* (1981) and *Song of the Bailing Man* (1982), both deemed lightweight. Pere Ubu had temporarily disintegrated several times before, and their apparent obituary was symbolized by the archival release, *Terminal Tower*, in 1985. However, at least the name was resurrected in Cleveland in 1987, albeit largely with new personnel (but including Allen Ravenstine, the original synthesizer player, until he departed in 1989 to pilot jets for Northwest Airlines). A series of five releases followed, from *The Tenement Year* in 1988 to *The Story of My Life* in 1993, their style tangibly reminiscent of the group's early work, but to the critics' ears considerably less opaque.

While the various categories that differentiate the diverse species of American popular music are often lumped under the generic category of rock, many of the resulting pigeonholes seem to be based on marketing categories rather than clearly discernible and definable idioms. However, a style known as funk, while not of Buckeye provenance, enjoyed a substantial infusion of influence from groups born in Dayton during the late 1960s and slightly beyond.

Historians date the origins of the style to James Brown and others during the mid-1960s. An offshoot of rhythm and blues, with a vocal delivery derived from gospel, a heavy backbeat from the drums above a syncopated bass line, and countermelodies from guitar and keyboard, music meant for dancing, the style eventually prefaced the disco idiom and even the more recent hip-hop style.

In 1970 Brown, the patriarch of funk, hired wholesale a Cincinnati band named the Pacemakers, which included bassist Bootsy Collins and his older brother, guitarist Phelps "Catfish" Collins. The resulting band, the JBs, was said during the following two years to have perfected the funk style created by the James Brown Revue.[17]

However, the Ohio connections to funk probably had their origins a decade earlier, when the Reid Brothers Band migrated from Georgia to Dayton in 1959. Almost immediately, its blues guitarist, Robert Ward, organized the Ohio Untouchables, a seminal ensemble from which the Ohio Players evolved. During that decade, several west Dayton high schools with substantial music programs generated as many as twenty different teenaged bands, which at first predictably aped established artists like Brown, the Four Tops, the Temptations, and the Untouchables. As extracurricular activities, these groups honed their skills at in-house talent shows mounted as fundraisers, as well as by playing for school and community dances, private parties, and at local nightclubs and commercial dance halls. Primarily instrumental, the bands in part established their public personae not only by searching for unique musical personalities but also by sporting flashy stage outfits; in fact, a group called the Imperials changed costumes as many as two or even three times at each performance. As summarized by funk historian and curator Rickey Vincent in commentary greeting visitors to *Something in the Water: The Sweet Sounds of Dayton Street Funk*, a comprehensive show at the National Afro-American Museum and Cultural Center in Wilberforce during the summer of 1998:

By 1974, the series of talent shows, nightclub gigs and afternoon "Battle of the Bands" had developed a string of strong bands that would not quit. These young outfits were well trained, enjoying the support of stable families, public school musical training, and a thriving party life in Dayton.[18]

An important local catalyst in the evolution of this style was "Turk" Logan, program director and principal deejay at WDAO-FM, which, with its fifty thousand watts of power, became Dayton's first black-oriented station in 1967. Logan was crucial in generating local exposure for these groups through airtime and interviews.

Of the professional groups that evolved from this culture, Lakeside dates back to 1969 as the Ohio Lakeside Express, named for the amusement park on the west side of Dayton in whose palladium they frequently played, although its members had earlier staffed groups called the Bad Bunch and the Young Underground. After a regional career, they moved to Los Angeles in 1972 and began recording on the Solar label six years later, having in the interim played club dates and issued one release on the Motown label. Their first album of note, *Shot of Love*, contained "It's All the Way Live," described by one critic as "a multilayered, stomping hurricane of a funk jam."[19] The two drummers, two keyboardists, guitarist, bassist, and four singers were costumed on their album covers in a thematic manner. *Shot of Love* presented them as members of Robin Hood's band with cocked bows and arrows "of love," *Rough Riders* (1979) as mounted cowboys, *Fantastic Voyage* (1980) as pirates hoisting sail aboard their own ship, *Your Wish Is My Command* (1981) as Arabian potentates, and *Untouchables* (1983) as gangland cops from the 1920s. Their 1984 release, *Outrageous*, pictured them as valiant rescuers of Indiana Jones, capitalizing on the current hit movie. Their last formal project was *Party Patrol* of 1990, but the group was already plagued by changes of membership and soon thereafter was making only intermittent appearances.

Sun was formed in 1976 as an offshoot of the Over Night Low Show band, itself an outgrowth of the Majestics. The group signed a contract with Capitol Records (later, with American International) and issued a series of albums into the mid-1980s, many with obvious thematic connections: *Sun Power* (1977), *Sunburn* (1978), and *Destination Sun* (1979). All of this provoked a reliance on visual imagery drawn from *Star Wars* and *Close Encounters of the Third Kind*. Their live shows included three mechanical robots and some seventeen thousand dollars worth of glittering, sun-gold costumes.

Zapp was a family band from Hamilton that during the 1970s had played traditional blues overlaid with digitized, high-tech rhythms. Guitarist and singer Roger "Zapp" Troutman (b. 1951) was the guiding force (and simply as "Roger" was to lead a parallel solo career), joined by three brothers: drummer Lester (b. 1956), bassist Terry (b. 1961), and conga player Larry (b. 1944). In 1975, as Roger and the Human Body, they made a recording featuring as its hook the vocoder, an electronic device that filtered the singing voice, making it sound otherworldly and robotic. The result came to the attention of George Clinton, who facilitated a recording contract with Warner Brothers. Assisted by Bootsy Collins and renamed, the band produced *Zapp* in 1980; its hits propelled this début album to gold status. The group quickly established an idiosyncratic public persona with Roger's "talk box," buttressed by glittering, sometimes-zany costumes and high-kicking dance steps, what one critic called a blend of "outer space slick meets country funk twang."[20] Success followed success with *Zapp II* (1982), *Zapp III* (1983), and *The New Zapp IV U* (1985). However, by the end of the decade, the group seemed to have been dislodged from its niche so that *Zapp V* (1989) hardly made the charts. In 1993, by then known as Zapp and Roger (thus allying the leader's ensemble and solo trajectories), the Troutmans almost announced their obsolescence with an archival *All the Greatest Hits*.

The most prominent and longest-lived of these southwestern Ohio bands is the Ohio Players, a group that defined funk for a time in the mid-1970s and eventually garnered a total of seven gold and three platinum albums. As the Untouchables the group labored during the early 1960s as a backup band for the Falcons. After a name change in 1965, the Ohio Players made their initial recording, *First Impressions*, three years later. In 1970 they signed a contract with Detroit's Westbound label and two years later issued *Pain*, to be followed by *Pleasure* in 1973 and *Ecstasy* and *Climax* in 1974. Their almost outrageously aggressive style, coupled to the sexually suggestive lyrics implicit in their album titles, was further buttressed by their album covers, which for their Westbound releases featured a completely bald black female model dressed in leather and chains, posing in various unsubtle positions.

Their increasing notoriety, fueled by "Funky Worm," no. 1 on the R&B charts in early 1973, led to a contract with Mercury Records the following year and a string of immensely successful albums, including *Skintight* (1974), *Fire* (1974), *Honey* (1975), *Gold* (1977), and *Mr. Mean* (1978). Fans doted on their versatility, an often quirky, unpredictable idiom, increasingly rowdy and sexy: "The nasty, sassy Players kept music fans interested, misogynists interested, feminists interested, white rock fans interested, black teenagers *obsessed*, and Mercury Records in the black."[21] At least part of this fascination was engendered by those controversial album covers, for some as eagerly anticipated as their musical contents. Attempting to capitalize on the Westbound legacy, Mercury hired a prominent *Playboy* photographer to create a series of sexually explicit and enormously provocative images of nude black women, shattering previous standards of the acceptable. The most memorable of the series was *Honey*, whose external cover featured a model drizzling honey into her mouth, while inside the same model appears rearing back on her haunches, virtually covered with the sweet stuff. Both poses contain insets of the band, obviously observant. The marketing ploy, as summarized by drummer James "Diamond" Williams: "As a male group, we knew we were not going to appeal to too many guys. So the covers were a way to get the opposite side of the sex spectrum. If the guys were looking at the covers, the girls might be looking at us. You don't have too long to catch the eye of the buyer."[22]

The octet left the Mercury fold in 1978; their last big hit of that era was "O-H-I-O" from *Angel* of 1977, its entire lyric encompassed in the song's title. The previous year the mayor of Dayton had proclaimed May 16 as Ohio Players Day, presenting each member of the band with a key to the city. Since that heyday the band has recorded for several other labels and has also issued archival collections like *Orgasm: The Best of the Westbound Years* in 1994 and *Funk on Fire: The Mercury Anthology* the following year. These, coupled to concerts that never proved quite as wild as the image they developed offstage, have served to maintain the group's currency. An enduring influence on younger groups, their credo was perhaps pronounced most cogently in 1995 by drummer Williams: "There's not enough light-hearted in the music world today. Nothing serious or heavy, just good dance records that everybody relates to. Silly, even! People can relate to silly all day long!"[23]

Several individual Buckeye rockers have achieved prominence. As noted earlier, Bootsy Collins (born William Collins in Cincinnati in 1951), a bassist and composer in an idiom identified as "Parliament-Funkadelic" (after the bands of its chief proponent, George Clinton), had organized the group known as the Pacemakers. Collins was working as a session musician for King Records in Cincinnati when the eighteen-year-old was recruited by James Brown, with whom he played for two years. He then worked with Clinton, creating many of that star's most-noted songs and personally contributed through his consciously bizarre clothing and manner to Clinton's avowed aura of "silly seriousness." However, concurrently Collins organized his own Bootsy's Rubber Band, which included several of the Pacemakers, as well as some of the Complete Strangers, another Cincinnati band that Collins had sponsored. He aimed his product at kids twelve and younger, "geepies," who took a fancy to his various alter egos, such as Bootzilla and Caspar the Friendly Ghost. Collins had ten R&B hits between 1976 and 1982, and his second and third albums achieved gold status; the third, *Bootsy? Player of the Year*, also became no. 1 in the R&B category in 1978. During a six-year hiatus, Collins worked with a variety of other musicians but resurfaced in 1988 with a collection that asked, *What's Bootsy Doin'?* Another stage of his career was reached in 1994 with a retrospective issue that proclaimed that he was *Back in the Day: The Best of Bootsy*.

Another Cleveland native, Tracy Chapman (b. 1964), achieved instant recognition with a self-titled début album released in the spring of 1988, which was followed that summer with a solo performance at a celebrity-rich tribute to Nelson Mandela in Wembley Stadium outside of London and a six-week international tour raising funds for Amnesty International in the company of Bruce Springsteen and other notables. The product of a black working-class neighborhood, Chapman studied the guitar and clarinet at the Cleveland Music School Settlement and began writing songs interweaving folk and rock idioms while in secondary school. At Tufts University she majored in anthropology and African studies and made the demo recordings that catapulted her to instant stardom. She was awarded several Grammies in 1988, including that for best new artist. Her releases since then include *Crossroads* in 1989, *Matters of the Heart* in 1992, both of which deal with topics ranging from racism to spiritualism and neither of which reaped the same sort of commercial and critical acclaim, and *New Beginning* in 1995, nominated as pop album of the year. She was inducted into the Ohio Women's Hall of Fame in 1989.

Although born in Mercer, Pennsylvania (in 1965), Trent Reznor, the creator of the industrial rock band known as Nine Inch Nails, dropped out of Allegheny College and moved to Cleveland, where he played with various local groups and made the demo recording that led to his first commercial release, *Pretty Hate Machine*, in 1989. That title suggests the leitmotifs of Reznor's idiom: rage and alienation, expressed at an unusually noisy level. He assembled a band and spent three years on tour in this country and abroad promoting the recording. A pair of 1992 releases (*Broken EP* and *Fixed EP*) led to controversial video versions of some of the individual songs, which showed a man being sexually tortured and ground into pulp by a machine, as well as examples of genital piercing and gay men smearing blood over one another. As if those hadn't produced sufficient outrage, Reznor then moved to Los Angeles and took up residence in the house in which the disciples of Charles Manson had murdered Sharon Tate in 1969 (although he denied previous knowledge of the building's history). This led to *The Downward Spiral* in 1994 and its sequel, *Further Down the Spiral*, the following year. The group's latest release, in 1999, is titled *The Fragile*. In 1994 Reznor created the soundtrack for Oliver Stone's *Natural Born Killers*.[34]

While Ohio can hardly be considered the New Orleans of rock, enough activity and history has been generated in the state, particularly in the northeastern quadrant, to justify pilgrimages by fans to I. M. Pei's theatrical pyramid on the shores of Lake Erie.

Part Six

The Music Industry

CHAPTER 36

Instrument Makers

Pianos

Although considerably humbled in recent decades, the Ohio-born musical brand name with the widest recognition is surely that of Baldwin.[1] The company's founder, D[wight] H[amilton] Baldwin (1821–99), was born in northwestern Pennsylvania and attended the preparatory department of Oberlin College during the 1840–41 academic year, intending to enter the ministry. However, because of poor health he was advised not to pursue that career, and consequently established himself as a singing teacher in Maysville, Kentucky. Sometime early in the next decade he moved north across the Ohio River to Ripley and by 1857 had become a teacher in the Cincinnati school system. As superintendent of various Presbyterian Sunday Schools in the city and a prominent figure in local musical circles, he was often asked advice by those purchasing pianos and reed organs; by the latter part of 1862 he apparently decided to act as an agent in the sale of the Decker Brothers instruments he was recommending, gradually abandoning his teaching career. The first formal advertisements of Baldwin as an instrument dealer date from 1865, when he offered Chickering pianos for sale from 92 West Fourth Street. By 1866 he had taken up quarters on the second floor of Pike's Opera House but lost all but one of the twenty-two pianos in stock when the building burned on March 22. By 1871 Baldwin had relocated to his own building, at 142 West Fourth Street, where the firm was to conduct retail operations until 1955. In 1873 Lucien Wulsin, who had been employed by Baldwin as a bookkeeper since March 1866, became a one-sixth partner in the firm of D. H. Baldwin and Company, "Wholesale and Retail Dealers in Pianos and Organs," capitalized at $50,000.

Wulsin became the driving force behind a firm that experienced rapid growth—within two decades becoming the largest dealer of pianos and reed organs in the "western" states. Retailers in surrounding towns took instruments on consignment, and by 1877 Baldwin had opened a company-owned retail store in Louisville followed by another in Indianapolis two years later. Much of this aggressive expansion was based on the use of the installment sales contract, an innovative leasing arrangement that became profitable in its own right and led to the establishment of hundreds of new dealerships.

While Baldwin acted as an agent for firms like Steinway and Sons and the Estey Organ Company, sales restrictions meant that Baldwin could not market certain brands in certain areas, and thus eventually contracted for pianos manufactured in Ripley by the Ohio Valley Piano Company, labeled as, "Expressly Made for D. H. Baldwin & Co."[2] In 1887 Steinway terminated its agreement with Baldwin, provoking discussion about the possibility of Baldwin making its own instruments. Ironically, the first such venture involved the manufacture of Hamilton and Monarch reed organs in 1888 by what was incorporated as the Hamilton Organ Company, located in Chicago. Two years later a decision was made to produce pianos according to the design of John Warren Macy, who since 1883 had made a considerable reputation in Troy and Dayton tuning and maintaining instruments for the company. The first Macy-designed instrument, an upright, was produced in what had been a planing mill on Gilbert Avenue opposite the entrance to Eden Park and shipped to the retail store downtown in late February 1891. Macy became factory superintendent of the Baldwin Piano Company and soon designed a Baldwin grand piano as well as a moderately priced upright, produced beginning in 1893 by a new corporation called the Ellington Piano Company (named for a longtime friend of Mr. Baldwin) in a factory on the north side of the city. Baldwin also purchased the Ohio Valley Piano Company and renamed it the Valley Gem Piano Company; it then turned out the company's Valley Gem and Howard brands. A business begun with an investment of $2,000 was by 1898 capitalized at $537,000. The facility on Gilbert Avenue was expanded in 1895, and four years later operations were consolidated at that location, the expanded plant dedicated only weeks before the founder's death. According to Baldwin's will, the bulk of his estate went to the Board of Home and Foreign Missions of the Presbyterian Church, creating a considerable crisis for the three surviving partners since the estate controlled 80 percent of the company. However, they managed to raise the requisite $400,000 and consolidated the various arms of the business into the Baldwin Company in 1901, capitalized at $1.25 million.

Baldwin established itself as a power in its field by winning a Grand Prix at the Paris Exposition of 1900, as well as considerable mention and awards of various sorts for its elaborate exhibition of Ellington pianos and Hamilton reed organs, a display of the materials involved in the creation of a piano, and a factory model, arranged so that the public could trace the entire manufacturing process. Lucien

Wulsin was also made a *Chevalier* of the Legion of Honor. Business boomed. Two additional buildings and a powerhouse were added to the Gilbert Avenue complex in 1902, while the Chicago organ operation moved to a new and larger space the following year. At the Louisiana Purchase Exposition of 1904 in St. Louis the company was awarded Grand Prizes both for the Baldwin piano and a corollary exhibit, and a decade later another Grand Prize was won at the Anglo-American Exposition in London.

In 1904 the firm remodeled its retail store on West Fourth Street to include a concert hall seating 400 and a recital hall accommodating 150. Apparently cost was no object, since contemporaneous accounts described the larger hall as defined by Corinthian columns and pilasters on three walls (two of which displayed gold-and-ivory framed Watteau tapestries), a fourth wall covered in frosted-glass panels whose focus was defined by a stained-glass representation of a harp, and a circular ceiling decoration eighteen feet in diameter painted with some sort of a metallic luster whose circumference was illuminated by seventy-two ground-glass electric bulbs. Baldwin presented its own stable of artists in recital, and the concert hall was also borrowed by the Cincinnati Symphony for some of its lighter programs.

An imposing new building was added to the Gilbert Avenue complex in 1924, an eight-story structure that still looms prominently over Interstate 71, its most prominent feature a central tower with a clock whose numbers were displayed in Rookwood pottery designs.

The company also prospered through the first half of the century because of a strong sales department, a chain of company-owned stores (eleven by the early 1950s), and a unique sales approach of consigning instruments to independent dealers and then requiring them to finance their customers' installment contracts with the company itself, clever in that customers sent their payments directly to Baldwin, meaning that the dealer was not paid until the sale was complete.

With its various brand names Baldwin offered instruments to every facet of the socioeconomic spectrum, and it also capitalized on the player-piano fad of the first quarter of the century with its Manualo, touted as "The Instrument You Were Born to Play," and later, " . . . He was Born to Play," complete with a grinning Uncle Sam pumping away. A 1921 poster titled "Make the Home Ties Stronger with Music" asserted,

> Music is the greatest contribution to universal enjoyment. It is ever a source of wholesome pleasure. With the advent of the Manualo, The Player Piano that is all but human, every family can now have access to the entire world of music. If you would have your home all that it should be, tie the circle closer together with music—with a Manualo.

The ABC of the Manualo, a pamphlet surely from the same period, employed pages of elaborate prose and several diagrams to explain the superiority of the Baldwin mechanism because of a device called the air finger, coupled to the patented accent block, all of this controlled by the "performer's" feet, since,

> It is a scientific fact that musical impulses travel naturally to the feet. We beat time with the feet. We dance to music. A lively jig puts action into our feet— not our hands. We walk in rhythmic time.
>
> Therefore, when you sit down to player-piano you instinctively try to express your feeling through the pedaling.

This "scientific" deduction led Baldwin engineers to create "an instrument that would play in sympathy with the musical feeling as expressed through the pedaling." And further,

> We decided that the Manualo should be so responsive that when you naturally increased the force of your pedaling, the volume would increase instantly just as you imagined it should. That when you exerted a sudden, powerful pressure on the pedals there would be a crashing chord. That your efforts to secure diminuendos and crescendos through the pedals should have a complete and ready response.
>
> *In other words, we had in mind a player-piano that would be just as much a musical instrument in the way it would respond to the instinctive movements of the performer and in the kind of music it would give, as the piano is the musical instrument of the pianist; the violin, of the violinist; the voice, of the vocalist.*

Designed to accommodate paper rolls from any source, the firm produced six different styles of upright Manualos, as well one for the Baldwin grand. It also offered an electrified version, which still allowed the operator to control some of the expression by the use of various buttons. Thus,

> No matter what the roll may be, a simple ragtime song or a Wagnerian music drama, you feel the music spring from you. It is colored with your thoughts, your ideas, your feelings—not by mechanically controlled devices. It is human, full of life, contrast, individuality because it is yours just as much as the pianist's music is his . . .
>
> In nine words—
>
> You PLAY the Manualo;
>
> You Do Not Operate It. [3]

The company depended on the endorsements of noted pianists and campaigned actively to keep them in the fold. Major Baldwin artists prior to World War II included Wilhelm Backhaus, Béla Bartók, Harold Bauer, Walter Gieseking, Joseph Lhévinne, and José Iturbi, later joined by Claudio Arrau, Jorge Bolet, Sidney Foster, Abby Simon, André Watts, Beveridge Webster, Earl Wild, and others, including Liberace. An undated company brochure from the early 1940s describing *The Incomparable Baldwin Grand Piano, Standard of Piano Excellence* listed fifty ensembles and festivals employing Baldwins (ranging from the Albuquerque Civic Symphony to the Virginia Orchestra but also more prestigious groups such as the orchestras of Berlin, Boston, and Chicago), as well as the names of 156 celebrities who purportedly relied on their Baldwins, ranging from conductor Ernest Ansermet to violinist Efrem Zimbalist (including conductors Sir Thomas Beecham, Leonard Bernstein, Arthur Fiedler, Charles Munch, Pierre Monteux, and André Previn; composers Benjamin Britten, Aaron Copland, Lukas Foss, Roy Harris, Darius Milhaud, and Igor Stravinsky; singers Pierre Bernac, Lily Pons, Helen Traubel, and Margaret Truman; violinist Zino Francescatti and cellist Gregor Piatigorsky), many of whose epigrammatic, somewhat stilted endorsements were included (Stravinsky: "I am sincerely happy to use the Baldwin in my varied activities"; Pons: "The Baldwin's tonal qualities make it a noble instrument with which to sing in genuine satisfaction"; Gieseking: "Baldwin . . . the most beautiful tone I have ever found in a piano").

The Artist Department was devoted to nurturing these relationships and warding off the blandishments of archcompetitor Steinway. Each month a house organ, *The Baldwin Keynote*, flourished not only the names of individual performers who depended on Baldwins but also important events at which Baldwins starred, such as the April 1927 Carnegie Hall presentation of George Antheil's *Ballet Mécanique*, with its sixteen pianos, or the four Baldwins on the stage of Aeolian Hall in New York for a performance of Stravinsky's *Les Noces* conducted by Leopold Stokowski. The Baldwin publicity machine also delighted in Will Rogers's declaration, "The Baldwin is the best piano I ever leaned on," evangelist Billy Sunday's exclusive reliance on Baldwins, the Baldwins that resided in the White House for the private use of first ladies Taft, Harding, and Coolidge, and the designation of Baldwin as the official piano of Vitaphone productions, thus allowing Al Jolson to assert in *The Jazz Singer*, "Boy, you ain't heard nothin' yet until you hear the Baldwin—the perfect piano." Vitaphone's engineers had decided that the Baldwin recorded the most accurately of any of the five pianos they tested, and many of the nation's motion-picture houses installed Baldwin grands, as did radio stations, beginning with WLW in 1922, so that by 1929, 222 operations across the country housed Baldwins, allowing *The Keynote* to assert, "The Air Is Full of Baldwin Every Night." By 1948 a company brochure celebrating *Baldwin: Today's Great Piano* claimed, "Over 350 Radio

Stations have chosen Baldwins for broadcasting to millions of listeners." Baldwin stores sold radios (and later, phonographs), and for a time the company even manufactured its own house brand, the Hamilton. In addition to its aggressive print advertising, Baldwin turned to the new medium of radio to broadcast its message that a piano was essential to any well furnished home. *At the Baldwin*, an immensely popular Sunday evening series initiated in February 1929 over WJZ and the NBC network, each week featured a distinguished performer in what was supposed approximate the nature of "an informal home musicale."

With America's entry into World War II, the company shipped its inventory to dealers, stored both machinery and materials, and turned to fabricating instruments of an entirely different sort: the outer wing panels of the C-76 cargo plane, wings and other parts for what became known as the PT-19 training plane, aluminum wing tips for the B-29 bomber, aileron enclosures for the B-24 bomber, disposable fuel tanks for the P-39 and other fighters, wing panels for the AT-21 (another trainer), proximity fuses for bombs and artillery shells and, late in the game, 105 millimeter shells themselves. The capacity to manufacture the fuses was retained at war's end (and into the Korean conflict) and, with other electronics work, was moved to Little Rock, Arkansas, under the umbrella of a new subsidiary, Baldwin Electronics.

A concern for the scientific underpinnings of Baldwin products dates back to 1927, when the company's engineers undertook collaborative research with the physics faculty of the University of Cincinnati into the nature of piano sounds. Early in the following decade the Baldwin staff became interested in the new field of electronics, assuming the possibility of synthesizing an artificial piano sound through electronic means, although the first outcome of this project was the Baldwin Electronic Organ. Baldwin engineers had developed what they called a tone spectrograph, which allowed analysis of the sounds they were attempting to imitate electronically, and actually produced a prototype church model electronic instrument in late 1940 or 1941, although the project then had to be mothballed for the duration of the war.

When piano production resumed, Baldwin turned first to its prewar best seller, the Acrosonic Spinet, which had been developed during the 1930s (the coined name supposedly an amalgam of the Greek *akros* and the Latin *sonus*, the result loosely translated as "supreme tone"). The Acrosonic gradually became the company's workhorse, touted for its patented "full blow" action. It was eventually produced in a range of cabinet styles—eighteenth-century English or French, modern, Victorian, colonial, French empire or provincial, and contemporary—obviously intended to mate with almost any conceivable pattern of interior design. An undated catalog even mentioned,

> Acrosonic styling is the creation of the nationally noted stylist and designer
> of furniture, William Millington, who has been on Baldwin's staff for many

years. Mr. Millington's many outstanding furniture designs as Chief Designer for the Baker Furniture Company have brought him world-wide respect and acclaim as one of the deans of contemporary American designers . . . [,] a recognized authority on distinctive style and good taste.

Production of a full line of pianos soon resumed after World War II, and company engineers continued their research efforts, culminating in a series of SD grands, the most prominent of them the SD-10, designed during the 1960s for the concert hall and employed prominently by pianist Lorin Hollander as soloist with the Cincinnati Symphony on its world-girdling tour of 1966.

Baldwin waded into the production of electronic organs for home and church, although without overwhelming success in an increasingly competitive field, despite their patented "gradual key contact" switches, which supposedly allowed smoother contact and release, "assembled [according to an undated brochure] in a special room where the air is electrically filtered to eliminate dust and dirt." The company later produced custom-designed "Photoelectric" organs,[4] including an instrument installed in Cincinnati's Music Hall and first played there by conductor Thomas Schippers in 1974. Baldwin also attempted to penetrate the home market with its "Orgasonic," an instrument with solo and accompaniment keyboards of differing sizes intended to rival the Hammond, and, later, a partially automated synthesizer called "The Baldwin Fun Machine."

The guitar rage of the 1960s led to Baldwin's unsuccessful pursuit of the prominent Fender company. Unrequited by Fender, Baldwin bought a solid-body electric guitar company in England that had been established by Jimmy Burns, but that venture foundered because of the impracticality of importing the finished products. An assembly operation was established on Gilbert Avenue in cooperation with the Cincinnati Association for the Blind, but that too failed. Baldwin also purchased Gretsch, a highly esteemed maker of guitars, but soon sold that venture. Other sidelines were a short-lived electronic harpsichord, a brief excursion with several partners into the silicon chip business (Siliconix Incorporated), and a powerful amplifier for the electric guitar nicknamed "The Exterminator," complete with an attached warning that Baldwin accepted no liability for the impaired hearing that might result from the use of or exposure to the product. Although it was also sold during the 1980s, Baldwin did make one other purchase at least logically related to its tradition, the venerable Bechstein firm, founded in 1853, whose Berlin facilities had been almost completely destroyed during World War II but that had resumed production of grand pianos in 1951.

During the 1950s the work force on Gilbert Avenue, then the company's only production facility, was unionized, and management began to look south as a means of lowering labor costs. During the following decade Baldwin first started to assemble vertical pianos at a facility in Conway, Arkansas, followed by construction of an electronics plant in Fayetteville, Arkansas (in part for the production of organs), a woodworking plant in Greenwood, Mississippi, and two other Arkansas facilities for the production of organ tone cabinets, guitars, and related equipment. Eventually even the building of grand pianos was moved to Conway and later Trumann, Arkansas, their actions and other parts actually fabricated in Juarez, Mexico. Thus, by the late 1970s, little was left on Gilbert Avenue except the corporate offices, and even those were eventually relocated to suburban Loveland in 1986. A major fire destroyed the original factory buildings, but what is now identified as "The Grand Baldwin" remains as an office condominium complex.

Beginning in 1964 new leadership abandoned reliance on the manufacture and sale of musical instruments and moved aggressively toward the acquisition of financial services companies, first the Central Bank and Trust Company in 1968 and the Empire Savings Building and Loan Association the following year. Both companies were located in Denver. Various insurance companies and mortgage banks were also purchased, and what became the Baldwin-United Corporation in 1977, after purchase of a closed-end investment company, created leasing subsidiaries and a data processing division. The company began selling single premium deferred annuities, a wildly successful venture that earned Baldwin-United $1.8 billion in 1981. The firm even ventured into the world of trading stamps with the purchase of T[op] V[alue] Trading Stamps and then of Sperry and Hutcheson Green Stamps in 1981. More than 150 companies were eventually acquired, including the MGIC Investment Corporation, parent of the nation's largest private mortgage insurer, the Mortgage Guaranty Insurance Corporation, this in 1982. Musical instruments became a peripheral concern.

In December 1982 *Forbes* magazine characterized Baldwin-United as a financial house of cards, provoking a violent drop in the company's stock price and several shareholder suits charging company officers with having artificially inflated the stock's value.[5] On March 29, 1983, *Fortune* asked, "Where Have Baldwin's Millions Gone?" and only weeks later President Morley P[unshon] Thompson, mastermind behind Baldwin's madcap expansion into a financial conglomerate, asked for a leave of absence following a reported 23 percent decline in earnings during 1982. The company announced a first quarter loss of $617 million, and on July 1, 1983 trading in Baldwin-United stock was suspended for ten days following reports of an accumulated debt of $900 million. Two weeks later regulators in Indiana and Arkansas seized insolvent Baldwin-United annuity insurance companies representing more than 50 percent of the firm's assets. On September 18 a story in the *Enquirer* proclaimed, "Baldwin's Old-Boy Network Unravels," provoking a $111 million libel suit; the company filed for bankruptcy on September 28, after its accumulated debt ballooned to more than $1 billion. In June of the following year, the Baldwin Piano and Organ Company was sold to its executives for $53 million. The following month the much-vilified Thompson was sued for $1 billion by the Arkansas insurance commissioner and ordered by the bankruptcy court to pay Baldwin $1.04 million owed on promissory notes that had been issued to him by the company (although the company later settled for a mere $300,000).

The mess became even more convoluted: In September 1984 Baldwin-United sold the MGIC Investment Corporation for $720 million, having paid $1.2 billion for its acquisition in 1981. May 1985 saw a $140 million settlement ending class-action lawsuits against firms that had sold Baldwin-United annuities, and in September Baldwin filed a $1.3 billion lawsuit against Merrill Lynch and Company, claiming that the brokerage firm had given it wrongheaded advice leading to the purchase of MGIC, although that suit was later dropped. In November 1986 Baldwin-United emerged from bankruptcy, but as PHILCORP, based in Philadelphia. Assets that at their apogee had totaled $9 billion had been reduced to $498 million.

Thus the Baldwin Piano and Organ Company survived this debacle and still makes pianos (although not in Ohio), but recent years have not offered much serenity, and what remains is obviously only the shell of a once proud giant. For example, when Karen L. Hendricks, a former vice president of Procter and Gamble, was named Baldwin's CEO in 1994, the company employed 1,600 and enjoyed net sales of $122.6 million. However, by November 1996 income had declined considerably, and Hendricks announced the release of about 15 percent of the current work force, not only in the Loveland headquarters but also at the manufacturing plants in Mississippi and Arkansas. The company was no longer to make furniture under contract but would concentrate on building pianos (including digital electronic instruments), electronic parts like printed circuit boards, and the venerable practice of financing customer purchases of Baldwin products. However, many of the pianos made by Baldwin were produced under contract and retailed under other brand names (such as Chickering and Wurlitzer), and Baldwin had suffered a further setback when Kimball International, for which Baldwin had made pianos, exited the business entirely earlier that year. In March 1997 the church organ systems unit, which had actually been importing electronic instruments from Italy and selling them under the Baldwin brand name, was sold to a Baldwin vice president, who relocated the business to Baldwin, Wisconsin. A month later another seventy-eight jobs were eliminated, bringing the hourly work force to about 975, and a decision was made to eliminate the consignment sales system. All this restructuring, coupled to increased piano sales, led to a 75 percent surge in earnings during fiscal 1997.

The company continued to innovate, not only creating a leasing program for its instruments but also introducing a new digital ConcertMaster piano in the spring of 1997 and in late 1998 a new high-gloss, durable polyester finish for its grand pianos, costing about $1,000 more per instrument than the traditional lacquer. The ConcertMaster, a reproducing and player piano born of the computer age, attracted considerable attention. Complete with an Internet connection and Worldwide Web browser, plus an internal hard drive that accepts music from both floppy and compact discs, the piano to which this machinery was connected could thus "play" music derived from a variety of sources. Furthermore, active pianists could "record" on the instrument and then immediately ask it to repeat their performance, an invaluable tool for students and performing artists alike. At the time of its introduction the ConcertMaster imposed on a top-of-the-line SC-10 concert grand cost around $70,000.

An apparent equilibrium in the company's fortunes was disturbed in early 1999 when the Asian financial crisis led to an upsurge in low-cost imports from Japan and Korea, with a severe impact on Baldwin's sales and profits. A decision was made to consolidate the assembly of all pianos in Trumann, leading to the dismissal of 180 workers, fully three-quarters of the employees in Conway, leaving the company with a workforce of only six hundred. In November 1998 its headquarters had been relocated a bit further north in suburbia, abandoning the location in Loveland it had occupied since 1986 in favor of an office park in Deerfield Township. Hendricks, under relentless criticism from some stockholders and dealers, stepped down in February 2001 as the firm found itself again in federal bankruptcy court, having sustained net losses of $18 million over a period of two years, leading to an accumulated debt of $40 million by the end of 2000. Her successor, Robert Jones, hired away from a Korean competitor named the Samick Music Corporation, undertook yet another reorganization program that cut another $3.3 million from the payroll during his first several months on the job.

Given its earlier flirtation with the world of the guitar, it may seem a bit ironic that the Baldwin Piano and Organ Company is now owned by the Gibson Guitar Corporation. On May 30, 2001, Jones announced that the firm would file for Chapter 11 bankruptcy protection. Baldwin's assets were consequently acquired by GE Capital in an auction held in mid-October and then sold to Gibson the following month. In its newest incarnation the company continues to market a wide variety of pianos, including Chickering and Wurlitzer, all of them produced in the firm's two remaining Arkansas plants.

While Baldwin became dominant in its field, other Ohio firms manufactured pianos in the state.[6] Charles Cist, in his *Sketches and Statistics of Cincinnati in 1851*, portrayed two firms employing a grand total of four, this at a time when the city was also home to a pipe organ factory employing twelve, and three firms manufacturing reed organs, with a total of between forty and fifty workers. One of the these companies produced a melodeon piano, some sort of hybrid

that will supply the place of the piano-forte, better than any instrument ever made; better, for anything slow and plaintive, than the piano. It is intended for parlor, lodge-rooms, churches, and singing societies, and is the cheapest

and best parlor instrument extant. Murch & White are the only manufacturers of these instruments west of the mountains.[7]

In a similar report of 1859 Cist reported a modest increase in the Queen City's piano industry to four factories, but still "on quite a small scale, as the aggregate of
the whole is ten hands, and nine thousand dollars of product value."[8]

Extant evidence makes it virtually impossible to create an exact census of piano
makers in Ohio. However, although what follows is probably only a sampling, the
state certainly furnished its fair share of companies organized in response to the
piano craze of the waning three decades of the nineteenth century, when every respectable middle-class home was adorned with a parlor piano, the "entertainment
center" of its day, through the pre–World War II period, after which home entertainment became increasingly passive, dominated by the radio and later television
and the computer, with a precipitous decline in piano sales. Furthermore, as demonstrated in the Baldwin narrative, brand names become confusing, especially when
pianos may not have actually been made by the firm whose nameplate is attached to
the instruments. For example, the John Church Company, a major retailer and publisher, sold Harvard pianos, produced in Dayton, Kentucky, from 1889 until at least
1925 and also owned the Everett brand, produced in Boston from 1883 until long
after the parent company had disappeared.[9]

Smith and Nixon was another venerable Cincinnati retailer. In 1852, nine years
after its founding, the firm constructed a substantial auditorium as part of its store
on Fourth between Main and Walnut Streets. The concerts and lectures it housed
proved unprofitable, so in 1855 the space was leased to the Chamber of Commerce
and Merchant's Exchange as an office and conference center. However, in 1872 the
firm repossessed the room and expanded it with a seating capacity of more than
two thousand. A decade later a third version of the Smith and Nixon Hall, reduced
to seven hundred seats, was inaugurated on October 5, 1882, with a star-studded
cast of performers, including Leopold Damrosch, Julie Rivé-King, and Clara Louise
Kellogg. Although the *Enquirer* the following day praised the event as "heralding a
reawakening of [the firm's] public-mindedness" and the *Post* described the room
as "nonpareil in the west," it was sold only seventeen months later and after March
1884 devoted to nonmusical purposes.

An ad in the Cincinnati City Directory for 1883 presented Smith and Nixon as
dealers in pianos by Chickering and a large handful of other brands, with branches
in Lexington, Louisville, and Indianapolis. However, from at least 1890 until its demise in 1909, the firm made pianos under its own name as well as that of Ebersole,
the latter surely to mark the 1889 entry of Joseph G. Ebersole into the firm as a partner; after graduation from Cornell University, Ebersole had worked in the wholesale

grocery business, but his "training and practical knowledge of commercial methods aid[ed] largely in the success of the concern."[10] Although the brand name hardly is recognized today, William H. Sherwood, perhaps the best-known American concert pianist of his era, was touted in ads from the spring of 1905 as employing a Smith and Nixon grand on tour with the Theodore Thomas Orchestra in Canton on May 15, Oberlin on May 16 and 17, Mount Vernon, Iowa, on the twentieth, Buffalo on the twenty-sixth, and South Bend on June 2 and 3. Their slogan: "If it's not a SMITH & NIXON it's not a GRAND in the UPRIGHT CASE." James H. Butler became superintendent of the Smith and Nixon works in 1893 and patented several improvements to the soundboards of the company's instruments as well as an unusual device for achieving especially soft sounds. After Smith and Nixon expired in 1909 the Butler Brothers Piano Manufacturing Company made pianos in its predecessor's facilities until 1924.

In 1911 another former Smith and Nixon factory in suburban Norwood was purchased by siblings Ernest J. Knabe Jr. and William Knabe III, offspring of the venerable family owned W[illiam] Knabe and Company of Baltimore, founded in 1837. Knabe became part of the conglomerate American Piano Company in 1908, with the brothers as senior officers of the corporation. However, they must have felt confined by the new arrangement, since they withdrew the following year to create Knabe Brothers, producing both upright and grand pianos that purported to retain the family traditions, rebuilding their facilities completely after a disastrous fire in 1912. Potential confusion must have resulted for the would-be customer attempting to distinguish the relative merits of Baltimore and Cincinnati Knabes.

Another Cincinnati firm concentrated on the production of player pianos. Albert Krell emigrated from Germany during the great exodus of 1848 and settled in the Queen City the following year. An instrument-maker by trade, he established himself as a builder and repairer of violins but also eventually began selling Steck pianos and Mason and Hamlin reed organs. In 1889, in consort with sons Albert Jr. and Alexander, he established the Krell Piano Company. Alexander had earlier apprenticed himself since 1857 to George Steck, the New York City–based builder, and had also carefully studied the instruments of other American and European builders but died in 1895, the father five years later. The remaining sibling became a pioneer in the development of the player instrument, eventually the holder of as many as twenty-eight patents in his field. He even experimented as early as 1899 with a sort of electric piano, its keys activated by battery-powered magnets under the keys. Apparently Krell's "Royal" pianos, whether or not graced with the Auto-Player mechanism, sold well. However, in 1927 the company was renamed the Auto-Grand Piano Company, and its operations were moved to Connorville, Indiana; in 1949 it fell under the control of the Starr Piano Company of Richmond, Indiana.

Other Ohio firms enjoyed relatively short life cycles. For example, the Columbus Piano Company produced Boudoir, Convertola, Lindenberg, and Wondertone pianos from 1905 until about 1928. The Compton-Price Piano Company of Coshocton, according to one of their brochures, "Scientific Builders of Artistic Piano-Fortes," remained in business for only eight years, beginning in 1910.

However, A[llen] B. Chase and Company of Norwalk not only achieved longevity but also a considerable national presence. The company was incorporated in 1875 and, although it too became a division of the American Piano Company in 1908, continued to manufacture instruments until at least 1938. The firm produced a variety of uprights, as well as a parlor grand and a player mechanism called the Artistano, and took enormous pride in the quality of materials and workmanship manifested in its instruments. An undated catalog overflows with the supposed advantages of Chase products: "Improved patent frictionless, non-squeakable pedal action," as well as other patented features like the "*Octavo attachment*, which doubles the power of the piano, producing at will, echoes, harmonics, and other desirable musical effects," or "A *Pedal Manual attachment*, with twenty-seven notes, for pipe organ pedal practice." All were touted as justifying the company's virtually limitless warranty. Chase offered prizes of several hundred dollars annually to employees who suggested possible improvements to its instruments, as well as a personal interest in any patent that resulted from such suggestions. The catalog also included an ominous statement about a policy described as "enforced watchfulness":

> Every man through whose hands any part of the piano passes is obliged to report on its condition while in his hands. If he fails to make a correct report, or allows any defective workmanship or material to enter into the construction of any A. B. CHASE piano, he is subject to summary discharge from the service of the Company.

One period business method that warrants notice is that customers were advised when ordering pianos by telegraph to employ code words to avoid any mistakes. Thus, the "cipher" for upright Style A in mahogany was "Artistic," in walnut, "Attractive," and in oak, "Artless." Strangely, the upright Style M, with elaborate external decoration, was coded "Monumental," while the parlor grand was denoted as "Sensible."

The endorsements contained in this particular pamphlet included no musicians of note, but former President William McKinley asserted that the family's Chase instrument was "much admired by our musical friends, and gives entire satisfaction to us in every particular." In fact the McKinleys seem to have been major Chase patrons, since Governor McKinley had bought a Chase for the family home in Canton, and then a custom-designed instrument was ordered for the White House parlor in 1897, where, Chase ads informed the public, it became the first lady's "most constant companion."[11]

While "The Mighty Wurlitzer," that most widely distributed theater organ, was never actually manufactured in Ohio, the company had its origins in Cincinnati about 1855 and maintained its headquarters there until 1941.[12]

Rudolph Wurlitzer (1831–1914) was born in Saxony of a family of instrument makers and merchants. He emigrated in 1854 and arrived in Cincinnati a year later. First employed as a porter in a dry goods establishment, he soon doubled his salary of four dollars a week at the banking firm of Heidelbach and Seasongood, with the additional perk of sleeping in a loft above the company's offices. He noticed the high prices being charged for musical instruments by retailers who were forced to deal with various middlemen and was soon importing flageolets, flutes, oboes, clarinets, and bassoons directly from Saxony and retailing them at more reasonable prices. For three years he sold such instruments part-time from three rooms in the Masonic Building at Fourth and Sycamore Streets, while continuing to work as a cashier at the bank. In 1858 the Rudolph Wurlitzer Company was relocated to 123 Main Street, and two years later full-time commercial retailing was undertaken with the creation of the necessary display rooms as well as offices and stockrooms.

The Civil War created a demand for band instruments, and Wurlitzer responded with a factory from which issued many of the bugles and drums employed by the Union bands. By 1865 Wurlitzer had become the largest manufacturer and wholesaler of band instruments in the country and had also opened a retail store in Chicago. By 1879 the firm was also selling music boxes and mechanical organs with either reeds or pipes, as well as the Automatic Pianista, all activated by a hand crank. Wurlitzer had for some time marketed various brands of conventional pianos, but during the following year the first upright piano bearing the Wurlitzer nameplate was made under contract. Wurlitzer had brought his brother Anton into a partnership in 1872, but in 1890 Rudolph Wurlitzer and Brother was incorporated as the Rudolph Wurlitzer Company, with an initial capitalization of $200,000.

Eugene DeKleist of North Tonawanda, New York, manufactured a variety of automatic musical instruments, ranging from barrel organs to Orchestrions and an extremely elaborate military band organ, many of them distributed by Wurlitzer. At the turn of the century, DeKleist was commissioned by Wurlitzer to create the Tonophone, a sort of piano–barrel organ hybrid. The coin-operated instrument became a fixture in hotels and restaurants. This precursor of the jukebox accepted nickels and contained a repertory of ten tunes; it also won a gold medal at the Pan-American Exposition of 1901.

Momentarily distracted by the manufacture of drums for our troops engaged in the Spanish-American War, by 1904 the company occupied eleven floors in two adjacent buildings. However, in December of that year, a disastrous fire completely razed both structures. Within three weeks Wurlitzer restocked temporary quarters nearby. Two years later, at age fifty, the firm occupied a new six-story building at 121 East Fourth Street, faced with glass-covered brick (its first use in this country) and sporting the company name worked in mosaic glass imported from Venice; a bronze marquee extended across the sidewalk. The retail areas contained invisible-edge plate glass display counters, soundproofed demonstration rooms, an immense Player Roll Library to serve the appetite of its own player pianos (which were among those available for inspection in the spacious Piano Display Rooms), and eventually individual phonograph listening rooms. The company offices remained at this location until 1941, when new executive offices were opened in Chicago.

The company's wholesale operations had burgeoned, with retail merchants across the country purchasing their stock from increasingly larger Wurlitzer catalogs. In 1908 Wurlitzer opened its first retail store in New York City. It also bought the DeKleist plant in North Tonawanda and added to its output of automatic instruments the manufacture of its own pianos, both conventional and reproducing. Two years later Wurlitzer purchased the assets and patents of the Hope-Jones Organ Company, launching platform for "The Mighty Wurlitzers" that were to grace so many of the luxurious movie palaces springing up across the country. British-born Robert Hope-Jones (1859–1914), trained as an electrical engineer, invented much of the innovative gadgetry that marks the theater organ, with its distinct sounds (many of them imitative of orchestral timbres but also including real percussion instruments, ranging from drums to glockenspiels and pianos) and double-touch (one sound at the first level, another generated by a bit more pressure). In fact, Hope-Jones called the outcome of his innovations the Unit Orchestra. He had immigrated in 1903 and established his own firm in Elmira, New York, in 1907. However, after building only about forty instruments, financial difficulties forced its sale; Hope-Jones became the nominal head of the new operation until he committed suicide in 1914. Hundreds of Wurlitzer pipe organs, with their distinctive horseshoe-shaped consoles, were installed not only in movie theaters but also in churches and concert halls across the land and abroad. If the conventional instrument was beyond the financial means of the buyer or performers of competence were not available, the company also produced the Wurlitzer Motion Picture Orchestra, a more modest machine, which could be played by rolls.

In 1910 the company also began to manufacture harps in Chicago and won a medal for these instruments at the Panama-Pacific Exposition in San Francisco in 1915. It was during this same period that Wurlitzer extended its outreach with Student-Lesson and Pay-As-You-Play Lesson Plans, promising quick results for the novice musician. In 1914 it became a distributor of Melville Clark pianos and five years later bought the company and its DeKalb, Illinois, plant. Wurlitzer grand pianos of all sorts (including a Butterfly Grand, with a top hinged at its center, so that it could be opened from either or both sides) were then manufactured in DeKalb, and all piano production was consolidated there in 1935. In that same year Wurlitzer introduced a compact version of its upright piano, the Spinette, only thirty-nine inches high, and the following year created a stylish form of the instrument framed in plastic and fabric.

Wurlitzer had also begun building accordions in DeKalb in 1932, and the following year acquired manufacturing rights for an automatic record-changing machine that allowed patrons with coins to spare a chance to select the music of their choice, the device commonly known as the jukebox. The Wurlitzer Model P10, or Simplex, provided the would-be listener with ten tunes whose order could be programmed. The number of available selections was quickly expanded to a dozen and then sixteen, twenty-four by 1940, double that a decade later, and then to two hundred during the 1950s. The original sober walnut cabinets were supplanted by fanciful designs built of various plastics and metals, featuring interior, indirect lighting.

The war years were spent developing and making radar indicators, photoelectric proximity fuses, and the like, but by 1947 the firm had introduced its first electronic organ and in 1954 an electronic piano designed particularly for classroom use, since the instrument was both portable and self-contained and could be monitored through earphones, an instrument so successful that a new plant for its production was erected in Corinth, Mississippi, in 1956.

Wurlitzer had become so omnipresent that its slogan by its centennial year had become "The Name That Means Music to Millions." Indeed, Wurlitzer and a few other firms dominated the heady market for theater organs during the first decades of the century, but at least one firm actually built such instruments in Ohio. In 1918, Dode Lamson and Harry Page Maus constructed an organ for the Quilna Theatre in Lima and, based on its success, established the Page Organ Company in 1923. They eventually sold about one hundred instruments, perhaps half of them to theaters, many in Ohio, but one as far away as California's Catalina Island (where it still serenades patrons of the resort's one-thousand-seat Art Deco movie palace) and others to radio stations in Chicago and Fort Wayne. Introduction of the talkies led to a downturn in business, and destruction of the factory by fire in 1931 sealed the fate of the enterprise.

Pipe Organs

Ohio has been home to a fair number of builders of conventional pipe organs, although many enjoyed only short shelf lives. For example, Hillgreen, Lane, and Company of Alliance left a considerable legacy between 1898 and 1973. By contrast, the Stevens and Klock Company, founded in Marietta in 1892 to build the Stevens Combination Reed-Pipe Organ, was reorganized as the Stevens Organ and Piano Com-

pany. Under the leadership of Collins R. Stevens (1848–1921), the firm was soon building about six hundred of these novel instruments a year. Allan Gordon Sparling (1870–
1950) left the Lyon and Healy firm of Chicago in late 1908 when that company abandoned its pipe organ business and joined Stevens in Marietta. Under his leadership
the firm apparently prospered for a few years, although only five Stevens instruments
survive. Sparling departed for Cleveland in 1911, and the company was forced to sus-
pend operations following the devastating Ohio River flood of 1913. However, in 1919
Stevens was advertised as "Manufacturers of Pianos, Organs and Builders of Pipe
Organs and Talking Machines," the last a reference to a phonograph that Collins
Stevens named the "Alethetone." The firm survived its founder by three years.[13]

Carl Barckhoff (1849–1919) relocated the Carl Barckhoff Church Organ Company to the village of Salem in 1882.[14] His organ-builder father had immigrated in
1865 and established himself in Philadelphia. The son succeeded his father as head
of the firm at the latter's death in 1878 and promptly moved the operation to Pittsburgh. He built an instrument for the Presbyterian Church of Salem and served as
organist at its dedication during 1880. The soprano soloist that evening became his
wife the following year, and by 1882 Barckhoff had constructed in Salem a plant
with "an organ hall 35 feet high, which made it possible to construct the largest
organs built at that time."[15] "Prof." Barckhoff also became director of a new Salem
Choral Union, which met for the first time in the hall on April 27, 1882, and by the
following year had managed to present Haydn's *The Creation*. Business prospered
to the point that an 1889 directory contained the names of fifty-four employees. By
1891 Barckhoff claimed in ads that he presided over "The Largest Pipe Organ Works
in the World," a dubious proposition but one certainly closer to the truth than his
assertion that the company had been "Established 1850," the year after its proprietor's birth. By the following year Barckhoff had agents in New York, Washington,
Atlanta, Pittsburgh, and Minneapolis and was contracted to build a major organ
for the Music Hall of the 1893 World's Columbian Exposition in Chicago. However,
the instrument was never installed because of objections from music director
Theodore Thomas that the acoustical properties of the building might be impaired;
the company received $10,000 as a forfeit.

A major financial panic in 1893 led to reverses, and two years later Barckhoff
withdrew from what became the Salem Church Organ Company. He reestablished
himself with a sizable work force (supposedly all German natives) in appropriately
named Mendelssohn (now Clairton), Pennsylvania, on the Monongahela River
south of Pittsburgh. After fire destroyed that factory, Barckhoff set up shop in nearby
Latrobe but by 1900 was back in Ohio. The Barckhoff Church Organ Company of
Pomeroy was joined the following year by the American Organ Supply Company,
of which Barckhoff became manager. The latter firm apparently not only made
and supplied pipes, actions, leather, and glue to its sister firm but also to the organ

trade in general. Business boomed again, since Barckhoff concentrated on stock models that were reasonably priced and were often sold through catalogs. In 1902 a branch office was established in St. Louis, and the company boasted of shipping an instrument every three or four days, accelerated two years later to a reported average of three instruments per week. The disastrous 1913 Ohio River flood not only did severe damage to the factory but also destroyed accounts and records. Soon thereafter Barckhoff abandoned Ohio yet again and established himself in Basic (now Waynesboro), Virginia, where he was reputed to have widened his vision to include theater-style and player organs, although none of these is known to exist. Bankruptcy was declared again in 1916, and the final incarnation of the Barckhoff Organ Company was sold in 1917, not long before the declining health of its founder led to his death. His legacy survives in the numerous extant instruments (dating from 1882 to 1915) of the 2,500 to 3,000 he installed literally across the country, ranging from Santa Barbara, California, to Bath, Maine.

Tiny Salem for a bit became a true organ building center, since Philipp Wirsching (1858–1926), another German immigrant, established the Wirsching Organ Company there in 1888, having gone to Salem directly upon his arrival in this country, perhaps at the invitation of Carl Barckhoff.[16] After considerable success, Wirsching was laid low by that major economic panic of 1893, after which he worked for firms in Detroit and Chicago for four years beginning in 1894. He then reestablished himself in Salem by purchasing the facilities of the Salem Church Organ Company, that reorganized form of the Barckhoff enterprise. During the following decades he patented several technical innovations, rebuilt his factory after it was destroyed by fire in 1904, built Orgues de Salon (complete with a self-playing mechanism called the Organola) for the Art Organ Company of New York City, and completed several acclaimed church organs, particularly in the New York area, as well as more modest instruments subsidized by grants from Andrew Carnegie, many of them located in Pennsylvania.[17] In 1917 he sold the firm to his son, Clarence Eddy Wirsching (named for the most noted American concert organist of the era), and Eugene Martin Binder, although they retained the elder Wirsching as superintendent of the works. The resulting Wirsching-Binder Organ Company acquired another partner's name in 1919, but was sold that same year to the M. P. Möller Company of Hagerstown, Maryland. Wirsching then built a few instruments on his own and during the last four years of his life designed and supervised the voicing of instruments by the Wangerin Organ Company of Milwaukee before returning to Salem, where he died.

However, the history of pipe organ building in Ohio predates these developments by decades since an instrument was completed in the village of Cincinnati as early as 1808 by English-born Adam Hurdus (1763–1843).[18] Hurdus had settled in Cincinnati in 1806 and evidently amassed considerable wealth as a merchant, farmer, and manufacturer of cotton goods. He apparently began his organ-building career as an avocation.

Hurdus was a Swedenborgean and founded the first New Jerusalem Society west of the Alleghenies in 1808. Services were initially held in his home, and it was for those activities that Hurdus completed his first organ, unusual in a sect that generally frowned on instrumental music in support of public worship, considering the organ "a blasphemous engine for the destruction of souls." The Hurdus instrument proved somewhat of a marvel:

> One very curious and singular circumstance about Mr. Hurdus' worship at his own house was that he frequently had the presence and attention of Indians. These Indians, in those days, used frequently to be in the town of Cincinnati, and sometimes passing on Sabbath day the residence of Mr. Hurdus, they would be attracted by the music of the organ, and thus drawn they would enter the house, and soberly and politely remain silent and serious spectators of what was going on. They would always stay, when once in the house, until the services were through—a fact characteristic of the Indian.[19]

After he constructed an instrument for the first New Jerusalem Temple in 1819 and was then ordained, Hurdus established a shop on Sycamore Street and built instruments (including one for Christ [Catholic] Church in 1822) in tandem with his ministerial responsibilities.

Hurdus was soon joined by Connecticut-born Luman Watson (1790–1834), who had first established himself as a clockmaker in 1809. By 1818 the firm of Reed and Watson employed fourteen (expanded to twenty-five by 1829) and was producing clocks with an annual value of some $30,000. By 1825 Watson advertised himself both as "Clock-Maker and Organ Builder." The instruments he built may have been in large part mechanical clock-organs, but there is record of at least two traditional pipe organs. Watson was one of the founders of Christ Church Episcopal in 1817 (and a year later became president of its Episcopal Singing Society) and by 1823 was also president of the Haydn Society. By 1819 the Christ Church Episcopal Society had a five year lease on an existing church building but had already purchased a site on Sixth Street for its own home. By October 1820 Watson had received partial payment for a new organ, although he did not receive the final installment until August 1823. That instrument was deemed inadequate, and the Haydn Society set out to raise funds for a larger replacement, which they would share with the Episcopalians. This second instrument (supposedly containing seven stops—diapason, principal, flute, twelfth, fifteenth, trumpet, and harp) was placed in the church during October 1822 and its unsatisfactory predecessor put in storage. It elicited at least one bit of local chauvinism in the *Independent Press and Freedom Advocate* of December 19:

We take much pleasure in mentioning that the elegant and fine-toned organ recently purchased by the "Haydn Society" and put up in the Episcopal Meeting House, has been manufactured entirely in Cincinnati. It is probably altogether the best piece of workmanship of the kind ever produced in the Western Country. It was made by our fellow citizen Luman Watson, except the carved work which (including the splendid Frontispiece) was designed and executed by C. W. Green, also of this city. (Footnote: The Boston folks send to England for their organs [an insupportable bit of hyperbole]).

While the scope of his activity remains unclear, Watson employed at least one assistant for a period of six years, beginning in 1822. Although he was later to become one of the most noted sculptors of his day, Vermont-born Hiram Powers (1805–73) was involved in the design of at least one unusual instrument, a mechanical clock-organ built for Joseph Dofeuille's Western Museum. This "Pan-Regal" was fronted by thirteen life-sized waxen figures, the men playing trumpets, the women chimes, all of which moved about in formation. The instrument was programmed to sound forth with popular tunes like "Hail, Columbia" and "Hail to the Chief."

The first Cincinnati builder of more than local note was German-born Matthias Schwab (1808–62), who arrived in 1831. The following years were ones of rapid expansion in these western lands, and Schwab may have built as many as thirty-seven instruments during his first decade in business. By 1851 he employed twelve and was generating an annual gross of $20,000.[20] Not only did he pretty much monopolize the local market, he also placed instruments north in Detroit, east in Baltimore, west in St. Louis, and in many other river communities as far south as New Orleans. The vast majority of his sales were to Catholic churches, and at least some of his prominent instruments were substantial. For example, in 1838 he built for the Catholic Cathedral of St. Louis a two-manual instrument of twenty-seven stops at a cost of $4,000, certainly one of the largest pipe organs in the West at that time. He built at least two large instruments for Baltimore—thirty-three stops for St. Alphonsus in 1843 and thirty-eight stops for the Church of the Immaculate Conception in 1845—but in 1846 placed his magnum opus of as many as forty-four stops and around 2,700 pipes in Cincinnati's Cathedral of St. Peter in Chains. Unfortunately, almost no trace of his work remains extant.

Schwab apparently relinquished ownership of his factory at Sycamore and Schiller streets in 1860 to several partners, principally Johann Heinrich Koehnken (1819–97) and Gallus Grimm (1827–97). Saxon-born Koehnken had arrived in Cincinnati in 1839, having served as an apprentice cabinetmaker in Wheeling for almost two years. Adept at his new trade, Koehnken was elevated quickly from apprentice to principal assistant to successor in 1860, when he established Koehnken and Company. In fact, records suggest that he dominated the company for perhaps a decade before assuming control. Grimm had served his apprenticeship to a German organ builder before moving to Cincinnati in 1853, where he went directly to work for Schwab. The partners enjoyed considerable success, manufacturing sixteen new organs between March 1860 and September 1864, the largest of them costing $3,200.

Although the company was soon identified informally as Koehnken and Grimm, the official name change occurred only in 1876. It prospered for two more decades until shortly before the death of the two partners, Koehnken on February 23, 1897, Grimm on August 1 of that same year. Most of their instruments were destined for the Cincinnati area. One of the largest of their extant instruments (built in 1866, with thirty-eight stops on three manuals) still exists in the Isaac M. Wise Temple; it is to be restored by the Noack Organ Company of Georgetown, Massachusetts, a process that will be completed during September 2005. Perhaps their most unusual instrument was one of nine stops and 665 pipes commissioned by Theodore Thomas for the first May Festival in 1873. This "chorus organ" was designed to compete with 1,082 choral singers and an orchestra of 108. Consequently, despite its modest size, its pipes were wider than normal and the wind pressure doubled, so that it required four men to blow its bellows properly. About this same time the firm was commissioned to build an instrument for the Central Christian Church on Ninth Street, one of their few non-Catholic installations. The instrument may have had as many as thirty-five stops on three manuals and cost five thousand dollars. A notice in the *Cincinnati Daily Gazette* of March 1, 1872, surely betrays the taste of the period:

> The organ concert at the Christian Church last night, for the benefit of the Ladies' furnishing committee, was well attended. The program consisted of selections from Aubei, Batiste, Handel, Wely, and Schubert. The performers were church organists of this city—Messrs. M. Dell, C. M. Currier, W. F. Gale and Henry J. Smith. The Serenade by Schubert, played by Mr. Gale, was a beautiful piece, and the improvisation of home melodies by Mr. Currier delighted the audience. The program was one suited to test the capabilities of the organ and the instrument, we believe stood the test to the entire satisfaction of its friends.

Although apparently none of his instruments has survived and almost no biographical remnant remains, mention should be made of Johann Heinrich Koehnken's elder brother, Johann (1812–ca. 1863). Also German-born, he appears to have been active in Cincinnati during the mid-1840s, although the possibility is that contemporaneous observers confused the two. Charles Cist, proprietor of the *Western General Advertiser*, touted the work of his "friend" frequently, although consistently referring to him as "Koehnke." For example, on January 1, 1845, Cist asserted that Koehnke was "extending his business and customers, as his operations are becoming known." He was at work on four instruments, one for a parlor, the others for churches; his instruments were claimed to "compare advantageously wherever taken, with those in use, being not only superior in richness and sweetness of tone, but vastly cheaper in price." The organist and vestry of the St. Luke Episcopal Church of Marietta were noted as having certified approval of their Koehnke[n] instrument which, according to parish records, had been installed during 1843. However, as noted previously, the instrument was deemed inferior by its purchasers, soon became inoperable, and was replaced after only a few years.

The following month Cist marveled at the parlor organ just completed for Thomas J. Strait of Mount Auburn, a "splendid specimen of the art," and recounted a conversation of a year earlier:

> "I was on a visit to Vermont, a few weeks since," said [Strait], "and intended to buy a parlor Organ, which I was told were made in the Eastern cities, first rate articles. I called at the shops in Boston and New York, to see what they could show me. They all fell short of what I supposed a first rate article of parlor Organs ought to be, and I concluded not to buy one; and for the rest of my visit Eastward, and for some time after my return to Cincinnati dismissed the subject from my thoughts. One day, however, while calling on business, just beyond the corporation line, I heard the sound of an Organ, which I followed to a shanty from which it proceeded, and there I found a German playing on an Organ which he had just finished. I fell into conversation with him and examined his work, and from what I saw and heard, was satisfied that he could build me the organ I wanted."

On April 1, 1845, Cist mentioned new contracts for Koehnke instruments in Lancaster, Ohio ($500), Memphis ($800 and $2,000), New Orleans ($875), and St. Louis ($800 and $3,500). Reference was also made to a parlor organ with an extended compass, "an experiment for which the community is indebted to the ingenuity of Mr. K." On June 1 Cist exclaimed over an instrument made for Cincinnati's Zion Church by "Mr. John Koehnke." "It is wonderful that organs made by *Erben* and others are brought from the East, when at less expense a far superior article can be obtained of Cincinnati manufacture." Cist's last reference to Koehnke appeared in August 1847, when, having "lost sight for some months of Koehnke and his organ operations," he found the builder "finishing a parlor organ for Walker, the brewer, an instrument well worth a visit from those have either a taste or talent for music. It will cost five hundred and fifty dollars and is well worth the cost." Koehnke was concurrently installing an instrument in Cincinnati's German Reformed Church and completing one for the Presbyterian Church of Yazoo City, Mississippi, after which he was to build a church instrument for Newark, Ohio. Cist concluded by confirming that the two Koehnken brothers were separate phenomena: "All the organs now built for the west and south west, are made in Cincinnati, either by Koehnke or Schwab."[21]

Of the builders who have survived to the present, the most prominent names are those of Schantz and Holtkamp.

The former firm was created by Abraham J. Tschantz, who was born in the Wayne County hamlet of Kidron in 1849, the grandson of Swiss Mennonite immigrants of 1821.[22] He began by building reed instruments and then pipe organs, but demand for the former (some were even shipped overseas) caused Tschantz to relocate to nearby Orrville in 1873, where a new facility was constructed during 1891. The financial panic of 1893 led to a suspension of activity, during which Tschantz concentrated on the creation of devices such as a disk harrow, a pneumatic oil can, and the Zephyr Electric Organ Blower, which is still used in all Schantz organs and also by other firms. In 1901 Schantz dropped the initial consonant from his name, discontinued the manufacture of reed organs, and built a new factory, the core of today's facility. In 1913 Schantz conveyed what had become known as A. J. Schantz, Sons, and Company to his three sons and turned his interests elsewhere before his death in 1921.

The company grew slowly during the next decades, constructing modest instruments for destinations in Ohio and adjacent states with a staff numbering fewer than fifteen. Schantz produced tool benches, munitions boxes, and other war-related products during World War II, after which three grandsons of the founding patriarch made the company into a major player, with a staff of more than one hundred building as many as thirty organs per year by the early 1960s. Still a family operation, leadership has now passed to a fourth generation, and the company has installed more than 2,100 instruments across the country, including high profile locations such as the Sacred Heart Cathedral in Newark, New Jersey. During the late 1990s Schantz was also entrusted with the rebuilding of instruments in Cleveland's Severance Hall and the Town Hall of Melbourne, Australia.

What is now known as the Holtkamp Organ Company has also been a family enterprise, but with a considerably more complex lineage. Gottlieb F. Votteler (1817–94) emigrated from Germany in 1847 and by 1855 had established the Votteler Brothers Music Store in Cleveland, the brother being Henry J., who continued the retail operation after Gottlieb devoted himself exclusively to the building of organs. This apparently occurred about 1870 in partnership with his son, Henry B. Votteler. G. F. Votteler and Company became Votteler-Hettche in 1903 with the infusion of capital by John Hettche, a local brewer, although that arrangement was to last only two years, when Henry retired (and was to die in 1922) and Hettche lost interest in the business.

However, another crucial figure had joined the mix in 1903. Herman Heinrich Holtkamp (1858–1931; he preferred to be called Henry) was born in the Auglaize County village of New Knoxville, the son of a German immigrant. He attended Calvin College and by the early 1890s had established a thriving retail music business in nearby St. Mary's, selling pianos, reed organs, and the occasional Votteler pipe organ. Votteler was impressed by Holtkamp's capacity as a salesman, so he was invited to Cleveland in 1903. He then served in the Army during World War I and briefly represented the company in Minnesota during the early 1920s. Allan Gordon Sparling, who had worked for several builders in his native Canada and had become superintendent of the Stevens Organ and Piano Company of Marietta in late 1908, moved to Cleveland in a similar capacity three years later at what in 1914 became the Votteler-Holtkamp-Sparling Organ Company, a cumbersome label employed until 1951.

While little evidence of the pre-Holtkamp era survives (the organ in Zoar is probably the only extant example), the firm prospered during the 1920s, delivering as many as twenty-three instruments a year. These were conservative even by the standards of the day, with no hint of the innovations pioneered by Walter B. Holtkamp Sr. (1894–1962). Born in St. Mary's, he moved to Cleveland with the family in 1903 and worked intermittently in the business, although he dropped out of high school to become a crewmember on various Great Lakes ore carriers. He enlisted in the Army in 1917, a stint that included almost a year of duty in France. After discharge in 1919 he joined the family firm as an apprentice, although he spent much time on the road as a salesman. With the death of his father in 1931, he assumed control of the company, with Allan Sparling as the only other major player. That first decade proved difficult, with the Great Depression in full force, but it was during those years that Holtkamp evolved his ideas of an instrument reflecting its classical heritage, one better able to project the nature of the organ's core literature. In the process, he became one of the leading figures in a renaissance of the instrument that evolved during the three decades leading into the 1960s, one that had its origins in Germany during the 1920s, and is often referred to as the organ reform movement. In fact, Holtkamp created a unique profile as a builder, one perpetuated to the present day by two succeeding generations, often dated from the landmark instrument in the Cleveland Museum of Art, a symbol of the then-radical instruments produced by Holtkamp beginning in 1933.[23]

After World War II, he gravitated toward a mature, even predictable idiom, so that Holtkamp instruments are immediately recognizable by their appearance and sound. While the firm's nameplates can be found across the country, the Holtkamp tradition is manifested most prominently through installations at Syracuse and Yale Universities, the Massachusetts Institute of Technology, and earlier at Oberlin College's Warner Concert Hall, an instrument since replaced. Walter ("Chick") Holtkamp Jr. joined the family enterprise in 1956 and succeeded his father as president at the latter's death in 1962; grandson F. Christian Holtkamp came aboard in 1987 and has since succeeded his father at the helm of this proud tradition.

One other prominent organ builder deserves mention, although he has since emigrated. John Brombaugh was born in Dayton in 1937. After graduating as an electrical engineer from the University of Cincinnati, he first worked for the Baldwin electronic organ division, during which time he applied for seven patents on behalf of the company. He then apprenticed himself to several major pipe organ builders, both in this country and Germany. An advocate of a return to design principles and tuning systems derived from northern European instruments of the late-sixteenth and seventeenth centuries (mated, however, with modern engineering), he established a firm in partnership with George Taylor and John Boody near Middletown in 1968, and among his sixty some organs are notable instruments in Lorain, Toledo, and Oberlin. In 1977 he went solo and relocated his shop to Eugene, Oregon, having finished a large instrument there the preceding year, in the process becoming enamored of the Pacific Northwest. Taylor and Boody inherited the Middletown facility and produced some important organs there before relocating to Staunton, Virginia, in 1979.

Bells, Brass Instruments, and the MacArthur Harp

Ohio is also home to the world's largest supplier of cast bells, carillons, tower clocks, glockenspiels, and electronic "Singing Tower" instruments, the latter based on digital sampling. While the bells it supplies today are actually cast in the Netherlands, the Verdin Company of Cincinnati earlier assimilated what was known as the E. W. Vanduzen Bell Company, or the Buckeye Bell and Brass Foundry. One of a number of American foundries eventually forced out of business during the war years of the twentieth century due to shortages of bronze, that indispensable raw material, Vanduzen made history in January 1896 with the installation of "Big Joe," at 29,390 pounds and nine feet in diameter the largest swinging bell ever cast in this country; the behemoth still hangs in Cincinnati's St. Frances de Sales Church, although in a stationary position.[24]

The Verdins emigrated from Alsace-Lorraine to Yorkville, Indiana about 1835, where they manufactured and repaired tower clocks. However, François de Sales Verdin and Michael Verdin soon moved to Cincinnati and by 1842 had placed one of their devices in Old St. Mary's Church.[25] While continuing to concentrate on clocks, later in the century the firm began to fabricate the hardware necessary for the hanging of tower bells, and in 1926 Innes Theophilus, the third generation of Verdins to head the company, invented an electric ringing device, which precluded the need for human contact with the bells (for the purist surely a heretical approach). After World War II, the fourth generation of Verdins created an agreement with Petit and Fritsen, the Royal Dutch Bell Foundry, for the casting of bronze bells whose supporting mechanisms are made in Cincinnati. During the early 1950s the company entered the electronic carillon field. The firm documents more than thirty thousand installations of various sorts across this country, Canada, and even as far afield as Chile and Indonesia.

However, the Verdins found themselves again casting bells as they assumed a role in celebrating the bicentennial of Ohio's statehood in 2003. The Ohio Bicentennial Commission asked the firm to create a bell for each of Ohio's eighty-eight counties; in addition, both the Ohio House of Representatives and Senate possess a bell. A unique mobile foundry was created to produce the 250-pound, two-feet-tall bells on site. The two-day process involved allowing the molten bronze to cool overnight, after which the mold was broken by a local dignitary. After cleaning and polishing, the result was dedicated and presented to the county commissioners, after which it was rung for the first time. Each bell is emblazoned with the state and bicentennial logos, the forging date, and the name of the county. Remnants of each casting were retained and included in the raw material of each succeeding bell in the series, concluding with the one designed for Ross County, site of the first state capital.

In 1981 the fifth generation of Verdins purchased St. Paul Church, a building in the Pendelton area opened in 1850 but inactive since 1974 and slated for demolition. Meticulously restored, its imposing nave has since 1988 housed not only Verdin's corporate headquarters, but also its Bell and Clock Museum, which contains all sorts of oddities, including the first clock made by the Verdin ancestors in the Alsace-Lorraine village of Marlenheim and the first bell cast in this country early in the nineteenth century for the Barnum and Bailey Circus.

Accordions to service the polka craze, as well as tamburitzas and mandolins, were produced for the Slovenian and Croatian communities of Cleveland early in the twentieth century. During the 1950s Cleveland was also home to Oahu Instruments, which produced Hawaiian and steel guitars.

However, the Cleveland instrument maker with the most impact was surely Henderson N. White, who in 1893 custom-made a trombone for Thomas King, a soloist with the Lyceum Theater Orchestra. The H. N. White Company was established soon thereafter on Superior Avenue and created a reputation for its King Band Instruments, trumpeting the improvements and advantages of its "Master" trumpets, cornets, trombones (both slide and valved), horns of all sizes, euphoniums (including a double-bell version), and tubas. Advertisements usually proclaimed the advantages of White-King products in sweeping generalities, but White got specific in a recurrent illustrated ad in Fillmore's *The Musical Messenger* during the 1910s proclaiming, "Again White Blazes the Trail! This Time in Perfecting a Method of Making Superior Valves." After a discussion of the disadvantages of using copper as an alloy, White asserted that he had overcome the problem, in part by employing a "high percentage of German silver, harder than that used in making high-explosive guns." And further,

> The new valve is one piece, head and all, without seams and with hardness almost unbelievable, as each operation increases the density of the metal.

The spring barrel is threaded into the head of the valve, and not into a separate piece soldered into position as is the usual practice. . . .

Nothing manufactured will compare with these valves in lightness, in strength, in smoothness of ground surface, in quick, positive and responsive action or in wearing qualities. They will outwear ordinary valves many times.

White has again hit the target square on the bull's eye.[26]

In 1964 the White factory was moved to suburban Eastlake. Typical of the times, the White-King legacy has been gradually diluted through a merger that later led to a mere slot in a conglomerate known as United Musical Instruments.

Many singers accompany themselves on traditional instruments, particularly the dulcimer and its several manifestations, and skilled Ohio craftspeople continue to supply these performers what they need to practice their art (including at least two who have created reproductions of the instrument about to be discussed). However, in the early years of the century, the Harp-O-Chord Company of Columbus turned out a type of harp-zither, today generally known as the MacArthur Harp after Margaret MacArthur, a Vermont-based folksinger who in 1961 stumbled across an example of the instrument, had it restored to playing condition, and then popularized the hybrid. Various such mongrels were being constructed at the time, but the only one to survive beyond the 1920s was the autoharp. The Harp-O Chord Company's instrument possessed twenty-three strings, a dozen of them designed to articulate the three basic chords, the rest designed to carry a melody. Although played in various positions, it traditionally is held horizontally in front of the player, the left hand playing the chords, the right the tune.

The instrument was apparently distributed at least in part by door-to-door salesmen. An advertisement of 1908 asserted,

All of our patent articles are SOLD THROUGH SALESMEN who are given EXCLUSIVE CONTROL of their choice of territory and PROTECTED against other salesmen.

MANY COLLEGE MEN pay their entire expenses THROUGH COLLEGE by working for us through vacation.

There is NO better selling article now ON THE MARKET than the HARP and we give LIBERAL COMMISSIONS.[27]

Ohioans over the past two centuries have churned out an amazing variety of musical instruments, ranging from the exotic to the quotidian: concert grand pianos and "fun machines," staid church and concert pipe organs, as well as colorful theater organs destined for the lavish movie palaces of the day, bells of bronze and brass, and a unique folk instrument akin to the zither. The sum total represents a considerable heritage.

CHAPTER 37

Music Publishers

It should be apparent by now that Ohio became home to a small galaxy of music publishers, dating from the publication of *Patterson's Church Music* in Cincinnati in 1813.

One of those whose name has appeared several times earlier in this narrative is W[illard] W. Whitney of Toledo, who opened a one-room retail store selling pianos, reed organs, and other musical instruments in 1860. Eight years later competition appeared in the person of William H. Currier (1840–1911). Currier, who had been born in upstate New York, learned to play the cornet, violin, and flute and in 1859 became a member of a family band of six brothers who toured Michigan, Indiana, and Illinois. Currier settled in Coldwater, Michigan, where he sold pianos and reed organs. The two gentlemen became partners in 1870, although Whitney and Currier was not incorporated until 1888. Success led to increasingly more commodious quarters and even a six-story Currier Hall in 1896, although by that time Whitney had sold his interest in the company and retired to San Diego where he died on New Year's Day, 1923. While representing firms like Steinway, in 1875 the two partners bought the Loring and Blake Organ Company of Worcester, Massachusetts, and manufactured the Palace [Reed] Organ there for thirteen years. In 1885 they also became half-owners of Boardman and Gray, piano builders in Albany, New York. Whitney and Currier was subsumed by Grinnell Brothers of Detroit following Currier's death.[1]

No documentation remains about Whitney's publishing activities, which date from at least 1863 and continued at least until 1890. He issued sacred music of various sorts (for instance, he was W. A. Ogden's principal publisher), as well as popular parlor songs and piano pieces in sheet music form (W. Phelps Dale's "Death of Our Darling" of 1867, with words by Lizzie Lincoln and a dedication to Mrs. John H. Klippart of Columbus, or Dale's "I Would I Were a Child Again," of the same year, on his own lyric and dedicated to Mrs. Wm. B. McLung of Troy). Whitney's establishment was self-described as the "Palace of Music" on several of these publications.

He also published *Whitney's Musical Guest* in fourteen volumes between 1867 and 1881, a typical trade periodical of the era. For example, the issue of November 1870 (vol. 4, no. 1) contains snippets of "Musical Notes"; ads for everything new from the publisher as well as complementary flattering "Opinions of the Press"; specimen pages from a new W. A. Ogden collection, *The Silver Song*; four pieces of sheet music, which, of course, were also available independently ("Birdie Tell Winnie I'm Waiting," a song and chorus with words and music by Frank Howard; "I Will Remember Thee," a song and chorus by C. F. Shattuck, with words by A. A. Weed; the *Pacific Grand March* for piano by Frank M. Davis; and "Room among the Angels," a song and chorus by W. A. Ogden); several frothy articles, including "Origin of the Ox Minuet," a real musicological gem supposedly resurrecting a conversation between Haydn and a Hungarian cattle dealer, and "The Popular Taste of America," excerpts from an address delivered by Bostonian S. A. Emery to the National Musical Congress; the first installment of some serialized fiction, *The Organist's Love*; and several examples of what apparently passed for humor at the time:

> SENATOR NYE put his new silk tile carelessly upon the sofa. A few minutes after, the veteran philosopher Greeley, sat down upon and crushed the hat fearfully.—"Blast it," roared Nye," I could have told you it wouldn't fit you before you tried it on."
>
> "The greatest old organ in the world," said a wicked old bachelor, "is the organ of speech in a woman, because it is an organ without stops" [this on a page immediately adjacent to listings of the several reed organs for sale by Whitney, with varying numbers of stops].[2]

Of the first phase of Cincinnati publishers, William Cumming Peters (1805–66) certainly deserves the most attention. His family emigrated from Devonshire about 1820, and Peters worked as a music teacher and retailer in Pittsburgh, perhaps as early as 1823, but at least for three years beginning in 1825. Extremely peripatetic, he abandoned Pittsburgh for Louisville in 1832, where he was noted in the directories of 1832 and 1836 as a "Professor of Music" (in partnership with brothers Henry J. and John in a venture that included instruction in music, English composition, reading, and geography, plus ancillary services, including the tuning of pianos and the binding of books, and eventually even a circulating library), and two years later was listed as proprietor of a "Piano and Music Store." While W. C. was to become organist of the St. Louis Catholic Church, Henry J. held the same position at Christ Church Episcopal Cathedral. W. C. was also active during these years as William

Cumming, composer of songs and piano pieces destined for performance in the middle-class parlors of the day, but also of a two-movement symphony and other works written or arranged for the Harmony Society at Economy, northwest of Pittsburgh, with which he had considerable involvement, beginning in 1827.[3]

It remains unclear exactly when Peters established himself as a music publisher. Imprints from perhaps as early as 1842 were issued simply by W. C. Peters, later Peters and Company, and from about 1846 Peters and Webster, in partnership with Frederick J. Webster, a local songwriter and "Teacher of Music." Although Peters opened a Cincinnati retail branch in 1839, the first Cincinnati imprints perhaps date from 1845, the year in which he moved up river to the Queen City; the 1846 city directory lists Peters and Company, which was quickly to become Peters and Field, a configuration that seems to have involved Joel D. Field and William M. Peters, a son. Peters moved to Baltimore in 1849 but in 1851 returned to Cincinnati, when the firm became known as W. C. Peters and Sons, the new family addition being Alfred C. That year a local historian sketched the Peters operation:

> W. C. Peters and Sons, Melodeon Building, are publishers of various approved works of instruction for the piano, guitar, violin, etc., of which they are the authors or hold the copyrights. They also issue the newest and most popular musics of which their catalogue presents a variety of solos, duetts, trios, and glees, adapted to vocal and instrumental use, marches, quicksteps, etc., to the extent of one thousand six hundred pieces, sixty of which have been published during the last six months. Of these the paper is of Cincinnati manufacture, and the engraving, printing, etc., is all executed here. The firm supplies eastern publishers, and the business exchange is largely in favor of Cincinnati. Their stock of engraved copper and zinc plates, cost upward of thirty thousand dollars, and they have paid out during the past year, three thousand dollars for copyrights; also manufacture rule music paper for copyists. They employ thirty hands; value of product, fifty thousand dollars; raw material 25 per cent.
>
> This establishment is largely in the piano-forte line of business, having since its first establishment as W. C. Peters, sold one thousand of A. H. Gale and Co.'s pianos and upward of two thousand of those of Nunns and Clark of New York.[4]

Later in the decade, John L. replaced his brother in the firm so that the Cincinnati directories of 1858 through 1860 list William M. as a music retailer and publisher at 50 West Fourth, not far from the father's enterprise at 76 West Fourth. By 1862 W. C. Peters and Sons had published more than three thousand items, and four years later the composite plate numbers of the various Peters enterprises exceeded four thousand (A[lfred] C. Peters and Brother and J. L. Peters and Brother gradually replaced the earlier designation and the firm relocated to Pike's Opera House, probably late in 1864). During this period the company continued to issue popular music of all sorts, as well as pedagogical volumes (for example, *Sofge's Piano-Forte School* in 1856 or *Peter's Melodeon School* the following year, as well as *The Eclectic Piano Forte School* [of 1855, which enjoyed a one hundredth edition in 1883], the *New Accordeon* [sic] *Instructor*, *Elements of Thorough Bass* [1856], *Peters' Eclectic Vocal Instructor*, and *The Flutist's Parlor Companion*). However, Peters (who directed the choir of St. Peter Cathedral in Cincinnati) also turned to a new market: liturgical music for the Roman Catholic Church, including *Peter's Catholic Harmonist* of 1850; settings of the Mass, including a *Collection of Popular Masses: Selected and Arranged by W. C. Peters* (mostly composite pieces assembled and adapted from the work of other composers, primarily from 1860 and 1861); or *Peters' Catholic Harp* of 1863.

On March 22, 1866, the entire Peters legacy burned in the fire that engulfed Pike's Opera House, consuming not only existing stocks of musical scores, but the plates as well. W. C. Peters died of heart failure the following month, ending the Peters presence in Cincinnati, although members of the family remained active in Louisville, New York, and St. Louis into the 1890s.

The patriarch's legacy was captured in an obituary in the *Cincinnati Commercial* of April 21, 1866:

William C. Peters, the music publisher, and one of the most enterprising business men of Cincinnati, died yesterday at his residence on East Walnut Hills. Mr. Peters was one of the greatest musical amateurs, and the most indefatigable composers in America, and may fairly be considered the father of that business in the West. After laboring zealously in his profession in Pennsylvania, at Baltimore and Louisville, he commenced a store in this city in 1839 and gradually built up the largest catalogue of music in the West. His chief pride was in church music, and some of his masses have been favorably received even in Europe. He was a hard worker to the last, having on the very day before his death completed the music to the beautiful song Jerusalem the Golden, which recently appeared in the Commercial. The destruction, by the late fire, of the immense collections of plates, which was his creation and on which he doted, may have hastened the sad event we have announced, though he apparently bore the loss philosophically, There will be a solemn requiem mass celebrated at the Cathedral on Monday, and several music societies, who owe so much to his kindly protection, will assist in the musical part of it.

In 1874 the three sons of Augustus D. Fillmore founded Fillmore Brothers, a Cincinnati firm that at first specialized in religious and educational music but by 1912 concentrated almost exclusively on works for band. The firm even issued its own house organs, particularly *The Musical Messenger*, which appeared with several interruptions from 1891 until 1924. It contained news of the trade, inspirational messages from recognized composers and performers, reviews of new music and books on the subject, Charles Fillmore's witty "Fillmore Filsosofics," poetry, instructional courses, question-and-answer columns (since this was a practical rather than a scholarly publication), "business cards," and examples of Fillmore publications. By 1890, flourishing business suggested the need for larger printing facilities, leading to the [George A.] Armstong and Fillmore Printing House; a year later the firm opened a retail store in New York City, this in addition to their shop at 528 Elm Street where they marketed instruments and accessories as well as scores published by the Fillmores. The retail operation came to be identified as the Fillmore Music House. The company was bought by Carl Fischer of New York in 1951.

However, the Cincinnati publisher with the widest influence was John Church, whose firm dates from 1859. David Truax had established himself as a music publisher in 1851, an enterprise known as Curtis and Truax by 1855, and Baldwin and Truax two years later. In 1859 Oliver Ditson of Boston, one of the country's preeminent music publishers, bought the firm, concurrently establishing a partnership with John Church Jr. (1834–90), who had apparently entered the music trade as a youngster of fourteen with Ditson in Boston and had perhaps been dispatched to the Queen City to establish this new venture.[5]

Church first appeared in the city directory of 1860, described as a "Dealer in Sheet Music and Importer of Musical Instruments." In 1869 he bought Ditson's interest and with John B. Trevor as a partner established John Church and Company, which became an astoundingly prolific publisher of religious music, educational materials (George F. Root's *The New Musical Curriculum*, son Frederick W. Root's *The School of Singing*, H[oratio] R[ichmond] Palmer's influential *Palmer's Theory of Music*, and the various series of Cincinnati Music Readers), art songs, piano music, and later many of the marches of John Philip Sousa (*King Cotton* [1895], *El Capitan* [1896], *The Stars and Stripes Forever!* [1896], and *Hands Across the Sea* [1899]). A major expansion occurred in 1873 when Church purchased the catalog of Root and Cady of Chicago, as well as the stock of musical instruments in the inventory of Root and Sons Music Company, a subsidiary. George Root remained a major contributor to *Church's Musical Visitor*, a monthly magazine with a national circulation that was issued between 1871 and 1897.

From 1859 until 1885 the firm was located in modest quarters at 66 West Fourth Street, but in the latter year (when the John Church Company was incorporated, with a capital stock of $1,250,000 and a total of 840 employees in the publishing, retail, and two associated piano manufacturing factories) moved into an "elegant five-story stone-front building erected especially for their purpose" at 72–74 West Fourth Street:

The new building is one of the handsomest in the city, having a frontage of 50 feet and a depth of 110 feet, and is supplied with every possible convenience. It is heated throughout by steam, and lighted by incandescent electric lights and gas. The passenger and freight elevators are of the most approved type, and are run by hydraulic power. The basement is used for storage purposes, and in it are built the large fire-proof vaults containing thousands of engraved music plates from which their sheet music is printed.

The first floor is devoted to the Retail Department and the general offices of the company. In the retail department are displayed small musical instruments, such as violins, guitars, flutes, banjos, mandolins, accordions, etc., in seemingly endless variety, while along the walls and running from floor to ceiling is shelving holding over 5,000 large folio boxes, which contain upwards of 300,000 different pieces of American and foreign sheet music, all ingeniously arranged by a system of alphabetical division, in such a manner that it is but a moment's work to find any piece of music that may be wanted. The retail business of the Piano and Organ Department occupies the entire second floor, and this superb room, 50 by 100 feet, constitutes one of the most magnificent and best-appointed piano warerooms in the United States. An elegant line of instruments, finished in various woods, is displayed, including the matchless Knabe Piano, the world renowned Everett Piano [owned by Church], and the Hazelton and Harvard Pianos [the latter also owned by Church]; also the Clough & Warren and the John Church Co. organs. . . .

Sales are made not only for cash, but also on easy monthly payments, so that the luxury of a piano or organ is brought within the reach of those of moderate means. On the third floor is the wholesale stock of small instruments and general musical merchandise, also the surplus organ stock and the repairing rooms of the Piano and Organ Department. The fourth floor contains the wholesale stock of books and sheet music, of which there are tens of thousands of copies stored away to meet the ever-increasing daily demand. Of the 10,000 square feet of floor and wall space in this department, along which are ranged, tier after tier of shelving, fully two-thirds of which is required for the stock of sheet music and book publications issued by the company. On the fifth floor are located the editorial rooms of the *Musical Visitor*, a monthly musical paper of national reputation, edited by James R. Murray, the plate engraving department, and the engraved plate and lithograph printing departments. . . . Many of the sheet music publications of the company, and by far the larger number of their books, are printed from electrotype plates, but this branch of the business has grown to such large proportions that a vast amount of work is supplied the year round to one of the largest and most complete printing and binding establishments in the city, the capacity of which is frequently taxed to its utmost to supply the demand for the company's publications.[6]

The company continued to prosper after its founder's death in 1890 under the leadership of Frank A. Lee, who had worked in insurance before associating himself with the Wilstach-Baldwin Publishing Company. He then became a lumber merchant before joining the Church empire through his presidency of the Everett Piano Company of Boston, beginning in 1883. Two years later he was also named president of the Harvard Piano Company, originally located in Cambridgeport, Massachusetts, but in Dayton, Kentucky, after 1889. Both firms were controlled by Church. Lee presided over a move in 1893 to even grander quarters at Fourth and Elm Streets, a seven-story structure identified as the Hooper building, configured in a manner similar to that of its predecessor and housing a firm that defined itself as "Manufacturers and Dealers in Pianos and Publishers of High-Grade Music."

After the turn into a new century, with branches in New York, Chicago, London, and Leipzig, Church proclaimed itself, "The House Devoted to the Progress of American Music," but the firm disappeared in 1930 when its remaining catalog was bought by Theodore Presser of Philadelphia.

Silas Brainard (1814–71) moved from New Hampshire to Cleveland in 1834 and soon established himself as a leader of the young community's burgeoning musical culture. Brainard's father was a grocer, and the son apparently worked in that business until 1836, when in partnership with Henry J. Mould he opened a retail music store identified as Brainard and Mould and later as Brainard's Bazaar. In a familiar pattern, what became known as S. Brainard and Company also began to publish music in 1845, the same year in which its proprietor bought Watson Hall and renamed it Melodeon Hall (and then Brainard's Hall from 1860 until 1872), which soon became a favorite venue for music making.

While the firm published didactic works, songs, piano pieces, and various kinds of religious music (one observer estimated that almost twenty-thousand individual titles had been issued by 1886), its reach and influence were considerably extended with the appearance of the *Western Musical World: A Journal of Music, Art and Literature* in January 1864. This monthly magazine was retitled *Brainard's Musical World* five years later. Karl Merz became its associate editor in 1871 and then editor from 1873 until 1890; it appeared until 1895 when it was merged with Theodore Presser's *Etude*. During its heyday it swelled to as many as forty-eight pages per issue, nearly half of them filled with what eventually totaled 1,580 pieces of music, much of it for the piano, designed for use in the home by amateurs and about to be published separately by Brainard. The prose pages contained national reporting on musical events from a network of correspondents, articles on a vast range of musical subjects, lists of recent publications of music (starting, naturally, with Brainard but including most of the major houses of the country as well as some regional names little recognized today), lots of advertising (some of it merely implicit, such as a February 1866 puff piece on Mason and Hamlin's cabinet organs and an August 1866 article by Henry Ward Beecher on the virtues of Chickering pianos), "comical cadences," editor Merz's "Musical Hints for the Millions" from 1868 until 1871 (published in book form in 1875), and a series of 144 "Biographies of American Musicians," which appeared from 1877 through 1889.[7]

In 1864 Brainard took his two sons, Charles Silas and Henry Mould, into a firm renamed S. Brainard's Sons; they assumed control of the business when the founding father died seven years later. In that same year the company bought the plates of the Root and Company of Chicago, which had suffered considerable damage in the great Chicago fire. While they maintained an electrotype foundry and bindery in a separate structure, in February 1876 the sons inaugurated a new headquarters building on Euclid Avenue, self-described as "A Musical Palace." The basement contained the furnace, printing presses, wholesale order department, and a vault housing some 75,000 plates encompassing about 15,000 pieces of music. The retail sales room, mailroom, and company offices were found on the ground floor, while the second floor housed the piano warerooms, which doubled as a concert space. The third floor contained imported goods, books, secondhand pianos, and reed organs, while the top floor was devoted to the actual engraving and printing of musical scores. The firm indulged in lavish descriptions of what it depicted as "The Model Music House of America" in the *Musical World* issues of March, May, and June 1876. The second installment featured an engraving of the first-floor retail department, a space 130 feet long, 30 feet wide and 17 feet high, its side walls lined to the ceiling with drawers holding sheet music, split midway, with balconies allowing access to the upper tiers. A grand staircase at the rear of the room led to the piano parlors above, with two "elegant bronze figures, 'Faust' and 'Valentine,' each supporting a cluster of gas jets" on the newel posts. The May issue pictured those piano parlors, housing "a complete assortment of the unrivaled Chickering Pianos," the house specialty, as well "other reliable" brands. The article commented on the series of subscription concerts offered during the previous winter months, as well as the "perfect" acoustical properties of the space, plus "woodwork and fixtures [which were] neat and substantial without being gaudy." The engraving also pictured the steam-driven elevator, which allowed easy transport of pianos either upwards for exhibition, or downwards for shipment.

The firm had established a Chicago branch in 1879, and its headquarters were transferred there a decade later where it existed until 1931, concurrently surviving somewhat into the twentieth century in Cleveland as the H. M. Brainard Company.

Cleveland was also the home of Sam Fox (1882–1971), who apparently became a proficient violinist and conducted the Central High School Orchestra. However, he soon was hired as a traveling salesman of musical instruments by and publications from the H. N. White Company and in 1906 borrowed $300 to establish the Sam Fox Publishing Company. He issued popular songs, novelty pieces for the piano, and didactic works, many of them by Cleveland composers, but is recalled today as a pioneer in the printing of movie music, at first fragments to be fitted against the silent films and later complete scores for companies like Warner Brothers and Paramount. Much of this material was at first written by Cleveland native John S. Zamecnik (1872–1953). Fox later supplied scores for Movietone News and March of Time newsreels. He became John Philip Sousa's exclusive publisher in 1917 and maintained that relationship until Sousa's death in 1934. A major player, with branches in New York, Chicago, Los Angeles, London, Paris, Berlin, and Melbourne, around 1935 the company's headquarters were moved to New York, although offices were later opened in Fort Lauderdale and Santa Barbara. Fox also entered the world of the Broadway musical as publisher of hits like *Brigadoon* of 1947 and *Man of La Mancha* of 1965. In his waning years Sam Fox made his home in Miami Beach but was visiting San Francisco when he died at age eighty-nine.

Although now a part of the Augsburg Fortress catalog, Ohio's Chantry Music Press for half a century achieved accolades for its concentration on church music of high quality and editions virtually unique in their attention to arresting graphic design.[8]

Founder Frederick Martin Otto (1905–99) was the son of a German Lutheran pastor sent from the homeland as a missionary to cowboys in the wild west of Kansas, although the rationale for this venture remains unclear. Soon thereafter he was assigned a German congregation in upstate Michigan, and later in Detroit, where he ministered to his flock for fifty years. The son became completely bilingual due to a family regimen: each morning consensus was reached as to which language was to be employed that day. Otto matriculated at Wittenberg University and spent his junior year in Leipzig as a Gustavus Adolphus Fellow, studying both at the university and conservatory. During that sojourn he not only sang in the choir of Bach's St. Thomas Church but also was introduced to the repertory of Bach's Lutheran musical forbears, including Otto's discovery of some previously unknown music in manuscript by Georg Böhm (1661–1733). Following graduation, Otto immediately entered Wittenberg's Hamma School of Theology and, after ordination in 1930, assumed his first pastorate, a small church in Toledo.

After five years the Ottos moved to Fremont, where the young pastor supplemented his modest salary by printing church bulletins, wedding announcements, and the like on a press in his garage. He had become fascinated with and informed about the printing process as a member of the student newspaper staff during his undergraduate days. Several other factors propelled him toward a parallel career as a music publisher. For his marriage to coworker Georgia in 1934, Otto had imposed the language of Ruth 1:16 on a secular work by Heinrich Schütz (1585–1672), and the result (later to become a Chantry best-seller) enchanted many guests at the ceremony who requested copies of this "new" work. Also, beginning in 1935, he organized a weeklong Institute for Lutheran Church Music, first held at the Lakeside conference facilities near Port Clinton and later in Fremont. During its twenty-year run, the institute offered nourishment to Lutheran church musicians from the region, often under the tutelage of recognized figures such as Healey Willan (1880–1968), the eminent English-born Canadian church musician and composer. Otto at first furnished his own mimeographed editions of music for the institute's Choir Laboratories but later relied on commercial editions, including his own, introducing to his constituency works by composers ranging from Michael Praetorius (1571–1621), Schütz, and Dietrich Buxtehude (1637–1707), to Max Reger (1873–1916), Hugo Distler (1908–42), and Ernst Pepping (1901–81).

In 1942 Otto entered the realm of commercial music publishing as the chief editor of two cycles of Bach's "Chorales for the Church Year" (Advent–Christmas and Lent–Easter), issued by the Neil A. Kjos Music Company, then in Park Ridge, Illinois. Three years later, informed by Kjos that the *Christmas Cantata* by Vincent Lübeck (1654–1740) would be unmarketable, Otto, in league with several financial partners, established Chantry. The name was selected as the loose English equivalent of *Kantorei*, to the Ottos signifying those groups of singers who joyfully propagated the Reformation during the sixteenth century.

Some continuity was maintained during the period 1956 to 1965 while Otto served as a representative of the Lutheran World Federation in Berlin, responsible for maintaining the viability of Lutheran churches marooned behind the Iron Curtain. At the request of the U.S. Army, he also organized church music institutes for musicians serving military chapels throughout Europe, held for six summers in Berchtesgaden in the Bavarian Alps. Forced home after the admittedly subversive nature of his position was revealed, Otto accepted appointments as a lecturer in both the seminary and school of music of his alma mater, positions from which he retired in 1970. He was also asked to establish Chantry Music Press, Incorporated, "at Wittenberg University." For the next three decades Chantry manifested in abundance its implicit credo: "We practice a Trade in the spirit of an Art." The artwork, engraving, and calligraphy that often characterized its elegant editions, whether borrowed or new, was usually acknowledged; the firm won some thirty prizes and several citations from the Music Publishers Association.

As the etymology might suggest, Chantry concentrated on vocal music, although its catalog contained a handful of organ pieces. Another practice, increasingly unique in the trade was that Chantry never allowed any of its editions to go out of print, a tradition violated by Augsburg Fortress after it purchased the company in

1994, although in 2000 the company issued a *Chantry Choirbook*, an attractive anthology of "Sacred Music for All Seasons" containing fifty of Otto's more than two
hundred editions.

Much of Chantry's anthems, cantatas, hymn settings, and liturgical music was
by American composers. The most frequently represented composer and editor of
earlier music (including a reconstruction of Bach's *The Passion According to Saint
Mark*) was Richard T. Gore (1908–94), longtime chair of the Department of Music
at the College of Wooster, a friend of the publisher from the time Gore first served as
a headliner at one of the summer institutes. Another frequent name was that of Jan
Bender (1909–94), the Dutch-born organist and composer, who was trained in Leipzig
after his family moved to Germany in 1922 and who served various churches in his
adopted country from 1930 until 1960. Otto first made his acquaintance during 1954,
while Bender was working in Lübeck. Otto had been sent to Germany as a member
of a commission whose task was that of assisting in the preparation of dossiers for
Germans who considered themselves refugees desiring emigration to this country.
After several visiting professorships in this country Bender became a member of the
faculty of what was then called Concordia Teachers College in Seward, Nebraska, in
1960 but five years later joined the Ottos in Springfield as a professor at Wittenberg,
a position he occupied until mandatory retirement in 1975. He continued to teach
part-time in Springfield in addition to short-term stints at other Lutheran institutions, such as Valparaiso University in Indiana and Gustavus Adolphus College in
Minnesota, before returning "home" to Germany.

As noted earlier, William C. Peters published a considerable amount of Roman
Catholic liturgical music from Cincinnati during the mid-nineteenth century. A
century later both Cincinnati and Toledo became home to firms active in the creation and publication of Catholic music, especially in response to the upheavals
promulgated by the major church council that concluded its deliberations in 1964,
usually referred to as Vatican II.

The Gregorian Institute of America was founded at Sacred Heart Church in Pittsburgh during December 1941 by its music director, Clifford A. Bennett. Bennett,
who transferred the institute to Toledo the following year, wishing to provide adequate training for Catholic church musicians, created a home-study course of 110
lessons. This Catholic Choirmasters Correspondence Course was followed by mandatory attendance at the National Summer School staffed by some of the principal
Catholic musicians of the day, after which the students were provided a certificate
of accomplishment. The program thrived until the 1960s and graduated literally
thousands of participants, but its curriculum was not revised in the aftermath of
Vatican II, leading to its demise. In 1948 the institute was authorized to offer a bachelor of music degree in collaboration with the University of Montréal as an exten-

sion of the original program. Between 1945 and 1977 it also offered five-day summer workshops across the country, ventures independent of the home-study course.

During the late 1940s the newly established Gregorian Institute Press (GIA) began issuing the materials employed in its educational programs, followed soon thereafter by editions of music for use in parish churches, with a stable of composers eventually to number in the hundreds. Much of that music is still in print; men like Joseph Roff and Carroll Thomas Andrews remained active for many decades. Publication of the Masses, motets, and collections of organ music, as well as volumes of Gregorian chant (supplemented by recordings), gradually altered GIA's focus, as did the success of the firm's Holy Week participation cards for congregational use, introduced in 1955 after a revision of the Holy Week rites. After the conciliar reforms mandated liturgies celebrated in the vernacular with extensive congregational participation, they were reissued in English (and have since sold millions of copies), and another generation of composers like C. Alexander Peloquin and Gerhard Track provided Roman Catholic choirs with a new repertory; composers like Dom Gregory Murray created "People's Masses" with unison singing by the congregation; GIA introduced Americans to the Psalm settings of Joseph Gelineau (b. 1920); and Bennett coedited with Paul Hume a *Hymnal of Christian Unity*.

During the 1960s Carl Fischer, Incorporated, became the distributor of GIA Editions, and in late 1967 Edward J. Harris, manager of the company's Chicago store, bought GIA from Bennett, hired Chicago church musician Robert J. Bastastini as his vice president, and the following year moved the entire operation, including its extensive printing plant, to Chicago, where it still thrives as GIA Publications, Incorporated.[9]

One of GIA's principal competitors, the World Library of Sacred Music, was located in Cincinnati. Founder Omer Westendorf (1916–97) studied at the College of Music, obtaining an undergraduate degree in organ and a master's degree in Gregorian Chant, after which he was appointed organist and choirmaster of St. Bonaventure Church, only a block from his birthplace. As a GI in Holland during World War II, he encountered the sacred music of composers like Hendrik Andriessen (1892–1981) and resumed his work in Cincinnati in 1946, intent on introducing this progressive repertory to his choirs. Requests for catalogs and on-approval copies from various European publishers led to a trip in 1950, during which Westendorf made contacts establishing him as the American agent for various Dutch, German, French, and Italian publishers of Roman Catholic liturgical music; soon thereafter the World Library of Sacred Music was established in a former barber shop next door to the Westendorf family home.

During its first decade the World Library functioned primarily as an importer and distributor, although it did publish a handful of Masses. In 1955 Westendorf issued *The People's Hymnal*, a collection of eighty-five hymns with English words that resulted from collaboration with a group of seminarians at the Theological College of Catholic University in Washington, D.C. The volume contained hymns adopted from the Protestant tradition and then theologically purified, as well as borrowed tunes with new words by several of the seminarians. Despite the reality that the Mass was still being celebrated in Latin, offering little opportunity for congregational participation in the vernacular, Westendorf kept collecting hymns, and issued a series of revised and expanded hymnals between 1955 and 1964. Many of the hymn texts were of his own creation (including standards like "Where Charity and Love Prevail"), their authorship often masked by his use of pseudonyms.

The firm remained unprofitable, subsidized by its owner's position at St. Bonaventure and as choral director at the Summit Country Day School. However, Westendorf's pioneering efforts placed him in the vanguard when, after November 1964, the Mass was to be said and sung in English, since his *People's Mass Book* was the single publication available at the time. It sold two million copies within two years and eventually reached more than a dozen editions, erasing the firm's debt and allowing a move to more spacious quarters on Central Parkway.

The following years proved remarkably productive. What became known as World Library Publications issued hundreds of Mass settings, as well as other sacred choral and organ music, hymn collections, recordings (including some by Westendorf's Bonaventure Choir), choral arrangements of folksongs, and other secular choral music, and even some music education methods (including an English translation of the Montessori method). However, financial exigency caused by this riot of activity led to a takeover of the firm by the J. S. Paluch Company in 1971. Paluch discontinued all the secular issues, while continuing to publish contemporary liturgical music in print and recordings, as well as the missalettes for congregational use on which they had earlier built their reputation. In 1983 the firm was moved physically to Schiller Park, Illinois. Westendorf continued to work as a consultant to the new owners until 1976, when he again began publishing on his own, issuing under the Sing a New Song imprint about fifty sacred choral works by various composers, employing his own words.[10]

Two widely recognized Ohio music publishers have survived to the present as independent entities: The Willis Music Company, now headquartered in Florence, Kentucky, almost within sight of downtown Cincinnati, and the Lorenz Corporation of Dayton.

On April 1, 1899, Charles H. Willis opened a retail music shop at 41 East Fourth Street in Cincinnati, so successful that he moved to larger quarters at Fourth and Elm two years later. During the first decade of the new century he began publishing, concentrating on method books and teaching pieces for young students of the piano, a niche the company has maintained to the present (although a noticeable amount of choral music was issued in earlier years). During 1910 Willis purchased the assets of George B. Jennings and Company, another Cincinnati publisher, and incorporated as the W. H. Willis and Company. Two years later Willis bought the local retail branch of the Cable Piano Company, thus assuming control of the entire seven-story building that had been its home since 1901.

However, in 1919 Willis was sold to Gustave Schirmer and became a subsidiary of the Boston Music Company, which was already owned by G. Schirmer, the dominant music publisher of the day. Four years later, John J. Cranley, who had started working as a stock boy with the Boston Music Company, was named general manager of the Willis operation and began the process of gradually acquiring total control of the entity. Cranley continued emphasis on teaching methods and pieces, adding to the catalog in 1936 John Thompson's *Modern Course for the Piano*, surely the most widely employed piano method in the world.[11] Several generations of Cranleys have presided over the company, at this point entirely owned by the family. In 1969 Willis headquarters were moved to suburban Florence. At the time of its centenary Willis claimed a catalog of twelve thousand titles and a chain of eight retail stores in shopping malls across Ohio, Kentucky, and Tennessee.

The founding patriarch of the more prominent surviving house, Edmund S[imon] Lorenz (1854–1942), was born in Stark County. After graduating from high school in Toledo he taught for a while before receiving a degree at Otterbein University. He then attended the Union Biblical Seminary in Dayton before graduating from the Yale Divinity School with a bachelor of divinity degree in 1883. After two years of advanced study in philosophy and church history at the University of Leipzig, he served as a United Brethren pastor in Dayton before becoming president of Lebanon Valley College in Annville, Pennsylvania. The pressures of that position led to his physical collapse. After recuperating, he returned to Dayton in 1890 to found the publishing company that still bears the family name. He issued at least fifty volumes of Sunday school and gospel music, anthems, hymns, service music, cantatas, and the like, as well as a series of handbooks for those working in the revival trade: *The Coming Revival* (1887), *The Gospel Worker's Treasury of Hymns and Revival Anecdotes*, and *Getting Ready for a Revival* (1888). The firm also published monthly periodicals: *The Choir Herald*, bought in 1899 (it had been in existence for two years), *The Choir Leader*, from 1898 (both containing a new anthem for every Sunday of the year), *Der Kinderchor* (1898), *The Volunteer Choir* (1913), as well as *The Organist* (1897). Of these, *The Volunteer Choir* and *The Organist* have survived to the present, joined by *The Organ Portfolio* (1937), *The SAB Choir* (1970), *The Sacred Organ Journal* (1971), and *The Church Pianist* (1975).

Karl Kumler Lorenz (1879–1965), born in Westerville, became business and advertising manager of his father's firm in 1901, the year he graduated from Columbia University, where he had studied with composer Edward MacDowell. He further extended the reach of an enterprise originally conceived as unofficial publisher for the United Brethren Church. His daughter, Ellen Jane Lorenz (1907–96), graduated from Wellesley College with a major in music and then taught for two years in the Akron public schools, concurrently doing graduate work at the University of Akron. She then spent a year in Paris working with Nadia Boulanger, the legendary teacher of composers, before returning to Dayton in 1932 where she became an associate editor (and later, editor-in-chief) of the family firm. After retirement from that position in 1967 she earned a master's degree from Wittenberg University and at age seventy-one was awarded a doctorate in Sacred Music from the United Graduate School. She also wrote articles about church music and hymnology, as well as literally hundreds of cantatas, anthems, sacred solo songs, works for organ, children's operettas, and, late in her career, music for handbells.

The fourth and fifth generations of the family have managed the firm in recent years. The Lorenz Corporation maintains branch offices in New York, Chicago, and Nashville and controls a group of subsidiaries, among them Sacred Music Press, Heritage Music Press, Roger Dean Publishing Company, Laurel Music Press, and Unity Music Press.

CHAPTER 38

Recorded Sound

A Cleveland suburb served as incubator for the "elevator music" now transmitted to millions of "listeners" across the planet by the Muzak Corporation and its imitators. Michigan-born General George Owen Squier (1865–1934), a West Point graduate who also received a Ph.D. in electrical science from Johns Hopkins University, constantly experimented with various aspects of telegraphy and telephony (including his 1910 invention of multiplexing, allowing for the first time transmission of multiple conversations over the same pair of telephone lines) and eventually became the Army's chief signal officer. On his retirement to civilian life in 1922 Squier presented to the New York offices of the North American Company, a Cleveland utilities combine, his patented idea of wired transmission into homes and businesses of music, unaccompanied by advertisements and public service announcements. The firm established a subsidiary, Wired Radio, Incorporated, and undertook experiments in the New York area. In 1930 the Cleveland Electric Illuminating Company began to pipe music into homes in one area of the city over its own power lines, offering three channels for only $1.50 per month. Technical difficulties doomed that venture, but three years later Wired Radio, with headquarters in suburban Lakewood, began transmitting as many as six channels of varied fare over leased telephone lines to homes, businesses, and hotel dining rooms. The firm relocated to New York City in 1936 and became Wired Music. However, Squier, before his death, had created the sales moniker Muzak by scrambling "Music" with "Kodak," and with that marketing tool the company began its pervasive conquest of the world.[1]

Of the several Ohio-based recording companies specializing in commercial popular music, only King Records of Cincinnati has achieved a national profile. The others suffered from limitations of product or distribution. Syd[ney] Nathan (1904–68) opened a record store in Cincinnati in 1938 and six years later issued his first two recordings, hillbilly songs actually recorded in his shop and then committed to vinyl at a facility in Dayton. The company was incorporated in August 1944 and opened a recording studio in a converted factory. While Nathan initially created a subsidiary label, Queen Records, as a conduit for black artists, he abandoned the production of "race" records in 1947 and became noted for his progressive color- and race-blind policies. During the late 1940s King flourished and became the sixth-largest recording company in the country in the mid-1950s. In fact, some argue that Nathan was an important catalyst in fostering the evolution of rock with his almost five hundred hit records over the course of a quarter of a century, since he contracted performers from across an immense span of genres, ranging from the blues and R&B, country, bluegrass, and hillbilly, to jazz, and finally rock and roll; Wynonie Harris and James Brown were among the most noted of King's large stable of artists.[2] Nathan was posthumously inducted into the Rock and Roll Hall in 1997.

Another Ohio-born firm has achieved international renown, primarily with its issues of performances by the Cleveland Orchestra, Cincinnati Pops and Symphony, Atlanta Symphony, Robert Shaw Festival Singers, Cleveland Quartet, Empire Brass Quartet, Ohio-based organist Michael Murray, Peter Schickele in his alias as P. D. Q. Bach, and numerous others, including most of the major orchestras of this country and Europe. Telarc International Corporation of Cleveland, one of the largest independently owned labels in the world, with a catalog of more than five hundred titles, was officially formed in 1977 when it issued a direct-to-disc recording of the Cleveland Orchestra.

Cofounder and chair Jack Renner's career had begun in 1962 as an engineer with a firm making vanity recordings for a variety of nonprofessional ensembles. Eight years later he formed his own company, Advent Recording Corporation, intending to make artist-subsidized recordings for professional musicians; he was later joined by Robert Woods, who began as a tape editor but now serves the resulting firm as president. They christened their new label with an amalgam of the Greek prefix *tel,* meaning termination point, and the acronym for the parent Advent label. Renner and Woods continued to innovate, in 1978 making the first commercial digital recording of an orchestra—complete with a warning not to play the Tchaikovsky *1812 Overture* at too high a volume to avoid damaging the owner's speakers—five years before the advent of commercial compact discs, a realm Telarc entered in 1983, one of the first to do so. In 1989 Telarc embraced the world of jazz (Dave Brubeck, Count Basie, Garry Mulligan, Oscar Peterson, George Shearing, Bobby Short, and others of lesser renown), in 1993 added the blues to its product mix, and more recently has introduced a Telarc Jazz Zone label meant to carry the more audacious and experimental kinds of contemporary jazz as well as world musics. In 1998 this Ohio-born-and-bred company earned its thirty-first Grammy award.

Biographies of Prominent Ohioans in Music

In 1942 Mary Hubbell Osburn published her *Ohio Composers and Musical Authors* (Columbus: F. J. Heer), a dictionary that categorized these individuals as "Native and Adopted," "Resident for a Time," and "Concert Artists (Ohio-born)."[1] Despite its numerous inconsistencies and errors, this slender volume remains valuable, if only because of her attempt to become all-encompassing, profiling virtually anybody of whom she had the slightest knowledge. Consequently, she described many who have otherwise disappeared without a trace, and suggested copious outputs from composers who apparently never published a thing, making it impossible to evaluate their importance. She also included many whose extremely brief sojourns in the state would seem to classify them as mere transients.

What I have attempted in updating her work is to concentrate on those who have had a significant impact in their fields, either regionally or nationally, and whose biographies are treated fleetingly in the preceding narrative.

The list of composers of art music concentrates on the past, wittingly bypassing contemporaries of recognizable merit, many of them associated with the state's colleges and universities. However, the Cleveland Composers' Guild, the most prominent and active of several such associations in the state, certainly warrants mention. One of the most venerable such organizations in the country with a continuous history, the guild had its origins in the Manuscript Section of the Fortnightly Music Club, which was organized in 1928, although works by Cleveland composers had been sponsored by the club as early as 1912. Spun off as the guild in 1957, the organization has sponsored public performances of its members' works, two publishing projects (*Piano Music for the Young: Early Grade Contemporary Repertoire*, with contributions by six different composers, issued by Galaxy in 1968, and Klaus George Roy's *Serenade for Cello Solo*, written for Lynn Harrell and published by Ludwig in 1975), as well as seven recordings on the CRI, Crystal, and Advent labels (the earliest dating from 1964), presenting a variety of work by Rudolf Bubalo (b. 1927), Marcel Dick (1898–1991), Donald Erb (b. 1927), Cleveland-born Frederick Koch (b. 1924), Bain Murray (1926–93), Roy (b. 1924; articulate program annotator for the Cleveland Orchestra from 1958 to 1988, whose catalog as a composer runs to more than 140 opus numbers), Lakewood native Howard Whittaker (b. 1922), and many others.

JOSEPH W[ADDELL] CLOKEY (1890 [New Albany, Ind.]–1960 [Covina, Calif.]). Purists may discount Clokey as a Buckeye, but his advanced training was undertaken in Ohio, and he spent significant parts of his career in the state. Clokey received a B.A. from Miami University in 1912 and then studied at the Cincinnati Conservatory of Music until 1915; his principal instructor was Edgar Stillman Kelley. He then taught theory at Miami until 1926, when he was named organist of Pomona College in California. However, he returned as the dean of Miami's School of Fine Arts in 1939, a position from which he retired to California in 1946, although he was then lured back into service as professor of church music at the Claremont Graduate School. He left a daunting amount of small-scale choral music of various sorts, cantatas, church and programmatic recital music for the organ (including several substantial pieces for organ and piano and a trio for violin, cello, and organ), chamber music, two symphonies, three short operas (including two first performed at Miami—*The Pied Piper of Hamelin* in 1920 and *The Nightingale* in 1925), and quite a few solo songs. He also issued two pedagogical manuals: *Plainsong: Interpretation, Notation, with Examples in Modern Notation* (1934) and *In Every Corner Sing, An Outline of Church Music for the Layman* (1945).[2]

MARTIN G. DUMLER (1868 [Cincinnati]–1958 [Cincinnati]). Dumler graduated from the College of Music in 1901 following European study. Although he apparently never taught at his alma mater, the college awarded him an honorary master of music degree in 1924 and an honorary doctorate a decade later. Xavier University conferred an honorary doctorate of laws in 1927. He made his living as president of the Chatfield and Woods Sack Company and served on several boards, including that of the College of Music. A prolific and widely published composer, he issued an enormous amount of Latin liturgical music (both Masses and motets), as well as larger works for chorus and orchestra (*Stabat Mater*, opus 40 [1935] and *Te Deum*, opus 45 [1940]), orchestra (a suite, opus 23, *Easter Prelude*, opus 29/1, and *Four Ballet Scenes* [1943]), chamber music (a *Reverie Pastorale* for violin and piano [1929], a *Meditation* for violin, cello, and piano, opus 28/1 [1930], a String Quartet, opus 47 [1948], *Berceuse* and *Petite Valse* for string quintet [both 1952]), and *Piano School* (1890).

SIDNEY C. DURST (1879 [Hamilton]–1957 [Hamilton]). Durst received a diploma in 1890 from the College of Music in Cincinnati and taught there for five years before further study with Joseph Rheinberger in Munich. A theorist and organist, he rejoined the college faculty in 1923 and was named acting director in July 1930 before serving as director from 1931 to 1934. After relinquishing that role, he later served as director of studies and for seven years before his retirement in 1951 as dean, when he was named dean emeritus, and his Concert Piece for Organ and Orchestra was performed to mark the occasion. He was an active composer of works for piano, both sacred and secular solo songs, and church music, as well as a cantata for male chorus (*Indian Love Song*, 1897) and a children's operetta (*Snow White*, 1911). His interest in Iberian music resulted in *Modern Spanish Organ Music: Edited and Prepared for the American Church and Concert Organ* (1920). He was also active as an organ recitalist, served several Cincinnati churches and one synagogue as organist, became a Fellow of the American Guild of Organists in 1916, and served as dean of the Southern Ohio Chapter of the AGO for a decade. Miami University conferred an honorary doctorate on him in 1925. His charming memoir,

"My Student Days at the College of Music," found in a commemorative booklet issued by the college to celebrate its diamond jubilee in 1953, details not only his life as a college student but also the lavish musical culture available to residents of the Queen City from 1887 until 1890.

NICHOLAS J. ELSENHEIMER (1866 [Wiesbaden, Germany]–1935 [Cincinnati]). Elsenheimer studied both music and the law in Munich, received the doctor of laws degree from the University of Heidelberg, and after further work in Strasbourg, emigrated during October 1890. He taught piano, voice, and theory at the Cincinnati College of Music and also lectured on music history and aesthetics. Apparently Elsenheimer concurrently maintained his own Academy of Music in the Pike Building, as evidenced by a catalog issued for the 1897–98 academic year. According to his entry in *The Musical Personnel of Cincinnati and Vicinity for 1896* (Cincinnati: Universal Publishing, 1896), he wrote songs, teaching pieces for the piano, at least one German partsong for male voices (he had been appointed conductor of Cincinnati Orpheus, a German singing society, in 1895), *Valerian* (a cantata for male voices and orchestra, 1893), *Eventide* (for women's voices, strings, harp, and organ), *Belshazzar* (for solo soprano and tenor with orchestra), and other works in various media. He also produced a prize cantata for the Golden Jubilee gathering of the North American Sängerbund in Cincinnati in June 1899, *Weihe der Künste* (translated as *Consecration of Arts* when it was published in 1902), a *Scherz und Ernst, Humoresque for Strings* (1894), and at least one pedagogical work for piano: *Scale Climbing. A Set of Exercises for the Development of Scales* (1917).

HERBERT ELWELL (1898 [Minneapolis]–1974 [Cleveland]). A degree from the University of Minnesota was followed by study with Ernest Bloch and Nadia Boulanger, plus a three-year stint in the City of Light after winning the Rome Prize. In 1928 he was appointed head of the theory and composition department of the Cleveland Institute of Music, where he taught and served as assistant director until an early, self-imposed retirement in 1945. He also taught at Oberlin College and the Eastman School of Music and headed the composition department of the Cleveland Music School Settlement. He served as program annotator for the Cleveland Orchestra from 1930 until 1936 and wrote criticism for the *Cleveland Plain Dealer* from 1932 until 1964. He left a large handful of orchestral pieces (particularly *The Happy Hypocrite*, a ballet score), chamber music (including a piano quintet and violin sonata), solo piano pieces (including a sonata of 1930), large-scale choral works (especially *Lincoln: Requiem Aeternam* for solo baritone, chorus, and orchestra on words by John Gould Fletcher published in 1916 and beneficiary of the Paderewski Prize the following year), as well as more modest pieces, some of them created for Cleveland ensembles (such as "A Midnight Farewell" for the Singers Club or "Toward This House," for the choir of the Fairmont Temple), and a large number of solo songs, including some supported by orchestra.

DONALD ERB (b. 1927 [Youngstown]). After military service in World War II, Erb received his undergraduate degree from Kent State University in 1950 and a master's degree from the Cleveland Institute of Music three years later. Following work with Nadia Boulanger in Paris he enrolled at Indiana University for study with Bernard Heiden and received a doctorate in composition in 1964. He then returned to Cleveland, where he was appointed composer-in-residence and Kulas Professor in a program supported jointly by the Cleveland Institute of Music and Case Western Reserve University. An expatriate from 1981 until 1987, he first served as Meadows Professor of Composition at Southern Methodist University and then on the faculty of Indiana University, after which he returned to the Cleveland Institute of Music, a position from which he retired in 1996 as Distinguished Professor of Composition. Recipient of manifold awards and grants (including one from the Rockefeller Foundation, 1968–69, during which he functioned as composer-in-residence for the Dallas Symphony), he has also been widely commissioned, published, and recorded. His idiom evolved from interests in jazz, neoclassicism, the serialism of the Second Viennese School, electronically synthesized sounds, the unorthodox use of traditional instruments, and fusions of both idioms and media. His compositional corpus includes works for orchestra (particularly *The Symphony of Overtures* of 1964 and *The Seventh Trumpet* of 1969, as well as a handful of concerti for various instruments), band, a variety of chamber ensembles, some of them quite unorthodox, and chorus (for instance, *Kyrie* of 1965 for chorus, piano, percussion, and taped sounds).

SAMUEL RICHARD GAINES (1869 [Detroit]–1945 [Boston]). Although Gaines achieved his larger reputation as a resident of the Boston area, we can claim him as a Buckeye since he spent 1893 to 1900 in Toledo as a church organist and conductor of the Apollo Club (which in February 1899 gave the first performance in this country of Sir Hubert Parry's *Judith*, an oratorio written in 1888) and from 1912 to 1924 in Columbus as organist of Temple Israel and cofounding director (with Oley Speaks) of the Musical Art Society, a choral organization patterned on a similar ensemble in New York City. Many of Gaines's choral works were written for the Musical Art Society or other Ohio ensembles (see, for example, "The Autumn Woods" of 1910 for the Singers Club of Cleveland or "Sweetheart" of 1917 for the Bell Telephone Male Chorus, also of Cleveland). His copious corpus for chorus ranges from partsongs and folksong arrangements to cantatas such as *The Village Blacksmith* of 1925 or *Out Where the West Begins*, published the following year. He also wrote numerous solo songs (issued between 1890 and, posthumously, 1946, many of them to his own words), a children's opera, *Lady-Bug-Lady-Bug*, in 1924, and *Daniel Boone*, a light opera published in 1931.

ARNOLD J[OHAN] GANTVOORT (1857 [Amsterdam]–1937 [Los Angeles]). Gantvoort emigrated in 1876 and eventually studied at the College of Music in Cincinnati. He taught piano in Lebanon and Harrison, Ohio, before joining the faculty of the State Teachers College in Bowling Green, Kentucky, and then Miami University. After teaching public school music in Norwood, Ohio, he was appointed to the college faculty, teaching piano and theory, lecturing on the both music history and aesthetics, and training teachers in the public school music department. Active in both the National Education Association and Music Teachers National Association, he served a three-year term as president of the Ohio Music Teachers Association beginning in 1891. He resigned as manager of the college in 1920 and two years later left to become dean of the Cornish School in Seattle, Washington. Four years later he joined the faculty of the University of California in Los Angeles and in 1932 became dean of the Zoellner Conservatory, also in Los Angeles. A noted lecturer, he composed a bit (a cantata, *Paul Revere's Ride* of 1921) and proved a prolific author: *The Model Music Course: A Natural System of Instruction specially prepared for the Study of Music in Public Schools* (with J. A. Broekhoven, 1895), *Gantvoort's Music Reader: A Complete Music Course for Public and Private Schools, Singing Classes and Teachers' Institutes* (1895, later subtitled as appropriate for "Rural and Village Schools"), *Gantvoort's Progressive Course in Harmony* (1915), *Familiar Talks on the History of Music* (1913), as well as several music readers, including *Model Popular Class Book for the Study of Sight Reading and Vocal Music in Classes* (1897), *The High School Ideal; A Collection of Songs* (1898), and other didactic works, such as *Studies for the Acquiring of Sight Singing* (1908).

ALBINO GORNO (1859 [Cremona, Italy]–1944 [Cincinnati]). Gorno studied at the conservatory in Milan where he received gold medals in recognition of his proficiency as pianist, organist, and composer. After winning a prize in composition at an exposition in Milan in 1881 for a pair of *Ave Maria*s, he was engaged as pianist by Adelina Patti for her extended American tour and, after a considerable triumph in Cincinnati, joined the faculty of the College of Music in 1882. While primarily noted as a pianist and piano pedagogue, he at various times taught organ and composition and took charge of both the ensemble and opera departments. Soon after it was awarded the authority to do so, the college conferred on Gorno an honorary doctorate in 1924. The long list of his compositions, many of them inferred from secondary sources, includes an opera (*Cuor e Patria*), works for chorus and orchestra (*Elegie, Gondoliera, Fantasie, after Dante's Divine Comedy,* and *The Feast of the Mountaineers*), piano and orchestra (*Marinnesca*), solo piano and piano duet (*Burlesca, or Concert Study,* for two pianos, opus 9, 1899), pedagogical studies for the piano, and more modest works for choral and solo voices, including an *Elegia Funebre* for four solo voices, chorus, piano, and organ or harmonium (1899). After sixty-two years of teaching and having been struck by an auto, his death at age eighty-five was treated as front-page news in the local papers. The library of the University of Cincinnati's College-Conservatory of Music is named in his honor.

CARL HUGO GRIMM (1890 [Zanesville]–1978 [Cincinnati]). Grimm was a prolific musician whose name hardly resonates today but who enjoyed considerable success during his lifetime. Grimm studied with his father and then, after 1905 in Cincinnati, including some work with Frank Van der Stucken. He held organ positions at both the Reading Road and Isaac M. Wise Temples, as well as at several churches, and taught at the Conservatory of Music after 1930. The Conservatory eventually anointed him with an honorary doctorate. He served as president of the Ohio Music Teachers Association during the 1927–28 academic year. He was considered important enough to be noted briefly by John Tasker Howard in *Our American Music.*[3] He left a considerable corpus, much of it both published and performed. It includes a handful of programmatic works for orchestra (an *Erotic Poem,* opus 24 [after Poe's *Eleanora,* which was awarded a prize by the National Federation of Music Clubs (NFMC) in 1927 and then played by both the Chicago and Cincinnati Symphonies], *Thanatopsis,* opus 25 [after William Cullen Bryant], *Abraham Lincoln,* opus 26 [also a winner of a NFMC prize in 1931 and was then performed both in Cincinnati and Rochester], an orchestral tone poem, *The 116th Psalm,* opus 32, *Five Pictures for "Peter and Wendy," A Children's Suite after James M. Barrie,* opus 38 [published by the Cincinnati Conservatory Composers' League in 1941 and performed as far afield as Los Angeles], and *Montana, Two Impressions for Orchestra,* opus 45 [first performed by the Cincinnati Symphony under Eugene Goossens in March 1943]); several chamber works (including *A Byzantine Suite,* opus 31, for flute, oboe, clarinet, bassoon, horn, trumpet, and strings, each of its short movements "featuring the Byzantine scale"; a String Quartet in A minor, opus 35, heard by the Ohio Music Teachers Association (OMTA) in 1939; and *Four Stencils,* opus 39, for piano, flute, and cello, played at the OMTA convention in 1938); *The Feast of the Kol Folk, An Exotic Scene,* opus 22, for mixed or women's voices, solo soprano, and orchestra on words by John Greenleaf Whittier (1925), the music supposedly based on Hindu scale systems; *A Phrygian Rhapsody*, for solo contralto, women's voices, flute, and harp, opus 21 (1928), written to words by Alberta Kumler Grimm for the Mothersingers of Cincinnati; *The Song of Songs*, opus 23 for soloists, chorus, and orchestra (awarded a thousand dollar prize by the MacDowell Club of New York in 1930); several church cantatas; at least four Sabbath morning services and a Friday evening service, as well as other Jewish service music; solo and partsongs; and various instructional manuals for the piano, including five volumes of *Grimm's Inspiration Studies* (1915).[4]

EDGAR STILLMAN KELLEY (1847 [Sparta, Wis.]–1944 [New York]). After study in New York and Stuttgart, Kelley settled in San Francisco, where he worked for six years as a freelance composer and teacher. The next six years were spent in New York, after which he returned to the Bay Area to become music critic of the *San Francisco Examiner*. His peripatetic career took him back to New York in 1896, to New Haven during the 1901–02 academic year for a temporary position on the Yale University faculty, and then to Berlin, where he lived until 1910, teaching piano and composition. He then relocated to Ohio when he was appointed to the faculty of the Western College for Women (later incorporated into Miami University) and in 1911 to the faculty of the Cincinnati Conservatory of Music, where he taught until 1944. Both Miami and the University of Cincinnati conferred honorary doctorates on him in 1916, the same year in which members of the class of 1916 of Western College, assisted by the college trustees and other friends and admirers, had built on campus a "composition studio" that provided a new home for the Kelleys. He wrote incidental music to both Shakespeare's *Macbeth* (opus 7, 1882–84) and Lew Wallace's *Ben Hur* (opus 17, 1902), as well as two operettas (*Pompeiian Picnic*, opus 9, 1887, and *Puritania, of the Earl and the Maid of Salem*, opus 11, 1892). His orchestral music was primarily programmatic: *Aladdin, a Chinese Suite for Orchestra* (opus 10, 1887–93); *Symphony No. 1, Gulliver, His Voyage to Lilliput* (opus 15, 1900) and *New England, Symphony No. 2 in B-flat Minor* (opus 33, 1913); plus *Alice in Wonderland: A Series of Pantomime Pictures for Grand Orchestra* (1919) and *The Pit and the Pendulum: A Symphonic Poem after the Narrative of Edgar Allen Poe* (1930). In 1930 he also wrote the score for *Corianton*, a film that was never produced. In addition, he issued a small amount of chamber music (including both a quintet and quartet for strings [opera 20 and 25]), solo songs (most notably, *Phases of Love*, opus 6, 1882), and quite a bit of choral music, including those major works mentioned earlier, as well as pieces of more modest dimensions. He also wrote a considerable number of articles, as well as *Chopin the Composer* (1913) and *Musical Instruments* (1925).

EDWIN ARTHUR KRAFT (1883 [New Haven, Conn.]–1962 [Cleveland]). After undergraduate work at Yale University, Kraft spent 1903 to 1905 in Europe studying with Guilmant, Widor, and others. On returning to this country he labored for two years at St. Matthew Episcopal Church in Wheeling, West Virginia, before being appointed the first organist of Cleveland's Trinity Episcopal Cathedral in 1907. Except for eighteen months during 1914 and 1915 (during which he served as Atlanta's Municipal Organist), he remained in that position until 1959. A noted and widely traveled recitalist, he was also director of the Singers Club for three years beginning in 1921, director of music at Lake Erie College in Painesville from 1933 until 1951, head of the organ department of the Cleveland Institute of Music, and choral director at the Laurel School. He published an impressive number of transcriptions of piano and orchestral music for the organ, including works that became his signature pieces. His papers at the Western Reserve Historical Society contain a journal book listing his stable of students and their contemporaneous places of residence.[5] Most were from the region and many of their names provoke no response today, but at least a handful went on to achieve some reputation: Ralph Clewell (Canton), Richard Ellsasser (Los Angeles), Harold Einecke (Los Angeles), Frank Jordan (Des Moines), Paul Manz (Minneapolis), Edward Gould Mead (Oxford, Ohio), Arthur Poister (Syracuse), and Homer Wickline (Pittsburgh). Kenyon and Lake Erie Colleges conferred honorary doctorates on Kraft in 1954 and 1957 respectively. Marie Simmelink Kraft, the organist's second wife, also cut a wide swath through Cleveland's musical life. A Cleveland native, she received a bachelor of arts degree from Western Reserve University in 1922. From 1920 until 1934 she was a soloist at the First Baptist Church, later at the Euclid Avenue Temple. She taught at the Cleveland Institute of Music from 1937 until 1963 (she died in 1967) and headed its voice department after 1949. A popular recitalist, she also made many appearances with the Cleveland Orchestra, especially in works by Arthur Shepherd and Herbert Elwell, who wrote his *Pastorale* for her.

FRANCESCO BARTHOLOMEW DE LEONE (1887 [Ravenna]–1938 [Akron]). After teenage study at Dana's Musical Institute in nearby Warren, de Leone spent 1907 to 1910 at the Naples Conservatory before making his home in Akron (he was later to work with Ernest Bloch in Cleveland). In 1920 he became the founding director of a department of music at the University of Akron, a position he left in 1935 to create his own school of music. He conducted opera in both Akron and Cleveland and was organist and choir director of the First Baptist Church of Akron. His major opus was an opera, *Alglala*,[6] on a libretto by Cecil Fanning (who was also a member of the initial cast), which was performed in Akron and Cleveland in May and November 1924 and then in New York in December by the English Grand Opera Company, with the composer conducting. He also left several other stage works—*The Millionaire's Caprice* (its libretto in Italian, since it was performed in Naples and other Italian cities in 1919), *Cave Man Stuff: A Prehistoric Operetta in Three Acts* (with words by Frederick A. Martens, published in 1928), *Princess Tin Ah Ling* (an operetta published in 1930), and *New York: A Lyric Drama in Three Acts and Four Scenes* (1942). He also wrote a considerable amount of choral music (including *Pocahontas*, a children's cantata on words by Martens, and anthems), quite a few solo songs, and a large handful of piano pieces.

ARTHUR LOESSER (1894 [New York]–1969 [Cleveland]). A half brother of Broadway composer Frank Loesser, Arthur studied in New York and then toured extensively in this country and abroad before joining the faculty of the Cleveland Institute of Music in 1926. He headed the institute's piano department from 1953 until his death. He was also the Cleveland Orchestra's program annotator from 1937 until 1942 and wrote criticism for the *Cleveland Press* from 1938 until 1956. While he continued to concertize throughout his career, he is recalled today primarily for his authorship of *Humor in American Song* (1943) and *Men, Women and Pianos* (1954).

EDWIN LONDON (b. 1929 [Philadelphia]). London received his undergraduate education at the Oberlin Conservatory and a doctorate from the University of Iowa in 1961. His composition teachers include Gunther Schuller, Luigi Dallapiccola, and Darius Milhaud. He joined the faculty of Smith College in 1960 and then taught at the University of Illinois for a decade beginning in 1968, interrupted by a year at the University of California at San Diego. In 1978 he became chair of Cleveland State University's Department of Music and in 1980 founded the Cleveland Chamber Symphony, a professional ensemble whose mission has been to present the work of living composers. More than 110 first performances have been intermingled with lesser-known examples of conventional literature. London himself has produced a considerable corpus, much of it theatrical or involving voices. He has also received numerous awards and grants.

ARTHUR MEES (1850 [Columbus]–1923 [New York]). Mees began teaching at the Cincinnati Female Wesleyan College in 1870 and assisted Theodore Thomas as organist for the first May Festival in 1873. After several years of study abroad he returned to Cincinnati, where he joined the faculty of the College of Music when it was organized. Mees was appointed May Festival organist in 1880 and director of the festival chorus in 1882, conducting the off-year *Messiah* performances. He also succeeded Carl Barus as conductor of Orpheus and wrote music criticism. After Thomas's departure as director of the college, Mees also resigned and joined with others to create the Cincinnati Music School. Despite inferred hostility between the pair, Mees was later involved with Thomas, both in New York and Chicago. He conducted at the Worcester (Mass.) and Norfolk (Conn.) Festivals, as well as choral societies in Albany, Boston, Bridgeport, and New York, where he succeeded Edward MacDowell as director of the Mendelssohn Glee Club in 1898, a position he held until 1904. He wrote program notes for the New York Philharmonic from 1887 until 1896 and in 1901 published *Choirs and Choral Music*, still available in reprint. He also left chamber and orchestral music, partsongs, and a volume of piano studies.

KARL MERZ (1834 [Bensheim, Germany]–1890 [Wooster]). After early training as an organist and violinist, Merz emigrated in 1854. Following stints in Philadelphia, Lancaster, and several towns in western Virginia, he joined the faculty of what was then called the Oxford Female College in 1861, where he taught for twenty-one years. He then was asked to organize the Department of Music at the College of Wooster, where he remained from 1882 until his death. The school conferred an honorary doctorate on Merz the year of his arrival on campus. In 1868 he initiated a parallel career as a writer by contributing his "Musical Hints" to *Brainard's Musical World*. He was made assistant editor in 1871 and was promoted to sole editor of the periodical two years later. His collected 434 *Musical Hints for the Million* were issued by Brainard in 1875.[7] Granville L. Howe and William S. B. Mathews considered Merz in their *A Hundred Years of Music in America* (Chicago: G. L. Howe, 1889) "A facile and graceful writer [who] unites literary polish with profound musical skill to a degree that leaves him without a superior in musical journalism." Brainard also published his *Modern Method for the Reed Organ* in 1878, *Elements of Harmony and Composition* the same year, and *Karl Merz' Piano Method* in 1885. Theodore Presser issued *Music and Culture,* a volume of collected essays and lectures edited by his son, in 1890. Merz was an enormously prolific composer of solo and partsongs, character pieces and a sonata for piano, chamber music (including a piano trio), and at least three operettas: *The Runaway Flirt* (published by Brainard in 1868), *The Last Will and Testament* (1877, then issued by John Church in 1905), and *Katie Dean* (1882).[8]

ZENOBIA POWELL PERRY (1908 [Boley, Oklahoma]–2004 [Xenia]) is little noted today, since virtually nothing of her work has been published to this point. Born to an African American physician and a mother with both African American and Creek Indian blood, Perry did not begin composing with any diligence until she was in her forties. She assisted the legendary William Dawson at the Tuskegee Institute in Alabama, studied with the black pianist-composer R. Nathaniel Dett at the Hampton Institute and Eastman School of Music, and studied later with composers Darius Milhaud and Charles Jones. From 1947 until 1955 she taught at what is now the University of Arkansas, Pine Bluff, and then served as a faculty member and composer-in-residence at Central State University in Wilberforce until her retirement in 1982. A prolific composer of songs, atmospheric works for the piano, and instrumental chamber music of various sorts, she also wrote *Tawawa House*, an opera based on the history of Wilberforce, written under a commission by the Ohio Arts and Humanities Councils and first heard in 1987. Her works are now being published posthumously in print and sound by Jaygale Music of La Crescenta, California.[9]

JAMES H[OTCHKISS] ROGERS (1857 [Fair Haven, Conn.]–1940 [Pasadena, Calif.]). After study with organ virtuoso Clarence Eddy in Chicago, Rogers tutored in both Berlin and Paris from 1875 until 1882 prior to a year working in Burlington, Iowa, after which he settled in Cleveland, where he prospered as organist (of the Euclid Avenue Temple, which he served for fifty years, as well as of various churches), composer, teacher at the Cleveland School of Music, critic (of the *Cleveland Plain Dealer* from 1915 to 1932), and publisher (both of his own works and those of others) before retirement to California. He apparently wrote as many as 550 pieces, and his more than 130 songs (published between 1878 and 1933), organ, and church music enjoyed wide currency in their time. His extensive corpus for organ includes three sonatas, two sonatinas, three suites, and many one-movement genre pieces. His sizable choral repertory includes secular partsongs, cantatas for both Christmas and Easter, several settings of the Latin Mass, and both a *Sabbath Morning Service for the Synagogue* and a *Temple Service for the Evening of the New Year*. He also issued a substantial number of pedagogical volumes for the piano, including *Ten Etudes for the Piano: For the Promotion of a Facile and Brilliant Technic* [sic] *and the Development of Bravoura-Playing* [sic] (1895), *Daily Trill Studies* (1898), *Special Studies in Staccato* (1898), *Double Note Velocity* (1913), and *Fifteen Exercises and Studies on Broken Chords* (1919). He also edited several volumes of organ pieces drawn from a variety of sources.

BERYL RUBINSTEIN (1898 [Athens, Ga.]–1952 [Cleveland]). After study in this country and Berlin and widespread concertizing, both as a soloist and in collaboration with violinist Eugène Ysaÿe, Rubinstein joined the faculty of the Cleveland Institute of Music in 1921 and served as its director from 1932 until his death. During that period he joined with colleague Arthur Loesser in an admired two-piano team. Western Reserve University conferred an honorary doctorate on him in 1931. In addition to a piano concerto and an opera, *Sleeping Beauty*, Rubinstein issued a variety of programmatic music for solo piano (including a set of *Scenes from Carroll's* Alice in Wonderland, as well as a handful of transcriptions of Gershwin hits), a suite for two pianos, a rhapsody for piano and orchestra, orchestral pieces (including a scherzo, presented by the Cleveland Orchestra in its ninth season), two violin sonatas, "Scherzo Serenade" for violin and piano, two string quartets, songs, and a partsong for male voices ("Prayer of Praise," written for the Singers Club, which he directed until 1935). He also published an *Outline of Piano Pedagogy* (1929) and *The Pianist's Approach to Sight-Reading and Memorizing* (1950).

CHARLES V. RYCHLIK (1875 [Cleveland]–1962 [Cleveland]). After early violin study with Johann Beck and composition with James H. Rogers, Rychlik matriculated at the Prague Conservatory in 1894, where he spent five years playing viola in the conservatory quartet and touring with the Bohemian String Quartet. All this activity allowed him the privilege of meeting Brahms, Bruckner, and Dvořák; he even played the last quartets of the Bohemian from manuscript in their composer's home. Rychlik returned to this country to become a member of the Theodore Thomas Orchestra but settled in Cleveland after the death of his father. He established himself as a teacher, as well as a member of various orchestras (including the first several seasons of the infant Cleveland Orchestra under Sokoloff) and the Philharmonic String Quartet until its demise in 1928. He left several substantial works for orchestra, most of them performed in Cleveland: a *Soliloquy*, opus 1; *Caprice*, opus 2; *Elegy*, opus 7; Dramatic Overture, opus 9; Spring Overture, opus 16; and Prelude and Fugue, opus 22. He also wrote an imposing number of works for violin and piano, published in Prague during the late 1920s and early 1930s. Most are single-movement character pieces—*Album Leaf, Caprice Bohème, Dumka, Lullaby, Novelette, Perpetuum Mobile, Romance, Slavonic Dance, Valse Caprice*, and others—but he also wrote sonatas for violin and viola. Among his other accomplishments were cadenzas for the violin concerti of Mozart, Beethoven, and Brahms, and a projected twenty-five-volume *Encyclopedia of Violin Technique*, left in manuscript form to the Cleveland Public Library.

ARTHUR SHEPHERD (1880 [Paris, Idaho]–1958 [Cleveland]). After training at the New England Conservatory of Music, Shepherd worked as a teacher and orchestral conductor in Salt Lake City from 1898 until 1909. He then returned to Boston and joined the faculty of his alma mater, where he stayed (interrupted by wartime service in France) until a move to Cleveland in 1920. He served the Cleveland Orchestra as Nikolai Sokoloff's assistant conductor until 1926 (and also annotated the orchestra's programs from 1920 until 1930), after which he joined the faculty of Western Reserve University, where he taught until 1950 and chaired the department of music from 1933 until 1948. He wrote criticism for the *Cleveland Press* from 1928 until 1931, lectured extensively and authored many articles, as well as numerous contributions to *Cobbett's Cyclopedic Survey of Chamber Music* (1929) and *The String Quartets of Ludwig van Beethoven: Historic and Analytic Commentaries* (1935). His rather prodigious output included major works for orchestra (including two symphonies and a violin concerto), chamber music (including five string quartets), forty-three piano pieces (including two sonatas), forty-two songs, and other solo vocal pieces involving stringed instruments.[10]

WILSON G[EORGE] SMITH (1855 [Elyria]–1929 [Cleveland]). After preliminary study with Otto Singer in Cincinnati, Smith spent two years in Berlin with a variety of mentors, including Xaver Scharwenka and Moritz Moszkowski. He returned to Cleveland in 1882 and established himself as a freelance teacher. He became active in the Music Teachers National Association and served as its president during 1888. In 1902 he was appointed music critic of the *Cleveland Press* and during the 1920s became founding president of the Cleveland Musical Association, organized as a forum for local performers. Smith also edited the association's *Cleveland Musical Review*. His reputation was established by an enormous corpus for the piano and more than one hundred songs (for a grand total of perhaps a thousand pieces). The piano works range from a *Valse Caprice* (opus 5, issued by Edward Schuberth and Company of New York in 1879) to *Hommage à Edvard Grieg* (opus 18, published in 1884 by A. P. Schmidt of Boston), a *Love Sonnet* (opus 59, published by the Boston Music Company in 1894 and dedicated to Edward MacDowell), and *At the Bal-Masqué, Épisode d'Amour* (opus 112, published by Sam Fox in Cleveland in 1912 in an ornate edition with graphic illustrations of its four movements: *Melodie Érotique, Promenade, Danse Exotique*, and *Pierrot's Sadness*), as well as *Two Impressions* (opus 113, published by Theodore Presser in 1918 and 1919 and dedicated to Mr. Presser). All are one-movement character pieces, either retrospective and generic (*Echoes of Ye Olden Time*, opus 21, issued by Schmidt in 1885) or frankly illustrative (*Five Nature Sketches*, opus 105, published by Sam Fox in 1912). His *Bal Masqué* and *Autumn Sketches; A Book of Autumnal Impressions for the Piano* were later orchestrated. He also edited several volumes of standard piano literature and issued at least four volumes of technical studies, including *Five-Minute Studies Designed for Daily Practice* (1895), *Thematic Octave Studies; In the Form of Variations on an Original Theme* (opus 68, 1902), and *Transposition Studies for Daily Practice* (opus 70, 1902). *Heart to Heart* (Cleveland: Eastman, 1902), for an "orchestra" consisting of three mandolins, mandola, guitar, violin, flute, cello, two banjos, and piano, may be the most exotic item in his legacy.

OLEY SPEAKS (1874 [Canal Winchester]–1948 [New York]). Although several of his more than 250 songs achieved an almost universal popularity, they certainly aspired to artsong status, and even though Speaks lived in New York City for most of his career, he seems to have left his heart in central Ohio. After the death of his father in 1884 the family moved to nearby Columbus where Speaks worked as a railroad clerk and sang in various churches, particularly First Congregational, whose pulpit was then occupied by the acclaimed Washington Gladden (to whom Speaks was later to dedicate a sacred solo song and an anthem). During 1898 he arrived in New York for study with Will C. Macfarlane and Max Spicker, supporting himself as a soloist at Macfarlane's St. Thomas Episcopal Church and elsewhere. In 1906 he returned to Columbus, where he again served First Congregational, but he eventually returned to Manhattan, buoyed by his success as a composer following his first publication in 1900. Several of his hit songs sold well over a million copies (most were published by G. Schirmer and the John Church Company), and Speaks assisted in their propagation through frequent recital tours. Beautifully crafted for both voice and keyboard, middle-class audiences reveled in works like "On the Road to Mandalay" (1907), "Morning" (1910), "When the Boys Come Home" (1911), and "Sylvia" (1914). Speaks also left partsongs and quite a few anthems.[11]

PATTY STAIR (1869–1926 [Cleveland]). Stair was trained entirely at the Cleveland Conservatory of Music; she joined its faculty in 1889 and four years later that of the University School. She progressively served six different Cleveland churches as organist and became Ohio's first female Fellow of the American Guild of Organists. She was elected president of the Women's Music Teachers Club and conducted the choruses of the Cleveland Women's Club. She wrote several solo and partsongs, perhaps twenty anthems, a three-act light opera, an orchestral intermezzo, and a *Woodland Scene* for an orchestra of toy instruments. Her unpublished works were deposited in the Library of Congress.

BETTY ALLEN (b. 1930 [Campbell]). A noted mezzo-soprano who enjoyed an illustrious international career in opera and on the concert stage during the 1950s, 1960s, and 1970s. In 1979 she was appointed executive director of the Harlem School of the Arts.

JULIUS BAKER (1915 [Cleveland]–2003 [Danbury, Conn.]). A student of the legendary William Kincaid at the Curtis Institute in Philadelphia, Baker embarked on a noted career as principal flutist with the Pittsburgh Symphony, CBS Symphony, Chicago Symphony and, from 1964 until 1983, the New York Philharmonic. He also performed with the Bach Aria Group and presented the American premières of concerti by Jacques Ibert and Andrew Imbrie. He taught at both the Juilliard School of Music and his alma mater.

EDWARD BALLANTINE (1886 [Oberlin]–1971 [Oak Bluffs, Mass.]). After obtaining a Harvard bachelor of arts degree, Ballantine studied in Berlin from 1907 to 1909. He joined the faculty of his alma mater in 1912 and taught there until retirement in 1947. He is recalled mostly for his two sets of piano variations on "Mary Had a Little Lamb," each variation couched in the style of a different composer, although he wrote other music for the piano, illustrative orchestral music, a violin sonata, choral music, and solo songs.

ROSE BAMPTON (b. 1909 [Lakewood]). An operatic mezzo-soprano who metamorphosed into a soprano, Bampton studied at the Curtis Institute in Philadelphia and then appeared on the major stages of the world, including the Metropolitan Opera (1932–50), the San Francisco Opera (1942–45), and the Teatro Colón in Buenos Aires (1945–50). She married Canadian conductor Wilfred Pelletier in 1937 and after her retirement from the stage taught at the Manhattan School of Music from 1963 until 1979, the North Carolina School of the Arts for five years beginning in 1964, and at the Conservatoire in Montréal from 1972 to 1974, after which she joined the faculty of the Juilliard School in New York. She received honorary doctorates from Drake University in 1940 and Hobart and William Smith Colleges a decade later.

HOWARD BARLOW (1892 [Plain City]–1972 [Bethel, Conn.]). Barlow organized an American National Orchestra in 1923, after which he joined the CBS staff as a conductor in 1927 and served as the network's general music director from 1932 through 1943. During the last three years of that tenure he concurrently conducted the Baltimore Symphony. From 1943 until 1961 he directed *The Voice of Firestone* series on NBC, at first over the radio, after 1949 on television. An active advocate of American music, he commissioned works from composers such as Aaron Copland, Roy Harris, and Randall Thompson.

WAYNE BARLOW (b. 1912 [Elyria]). This Barlow studied at the Eastman School of Music between 1930 and 1937 with Bernard Rogers and Howard Hanson (also briefly with Arnold Schoenberg in California). After receiving two graduate degrees he joined the faculty of his alma mater, where he taught until retirement in 1978. He has left a considerable and diverse corpus of orchestral, chamber, and choral music, some of it involving the use of taped sounds. He also issued *Foundations of Music*, a music appreciation text, in 1953.

KATHLEEN BATTLE (b. 1948 [Portsmouth]). After study at the University of Cincinnati College-Conservatory of Music (which awarded her a bachelor of music degree in 1970, a master of music degree a year later), Battle was noticed by both Thomas Schippers and James Levine. The former launched her career at the Spoleto Festival of 1972, the latter became her patron at the Metropolitan Opera. Notorious for her volatile temperament, she was declared persona non grata at the Met but continues to enjoy an active career on the principal opera, concert, and recital stages of both this country and Europe.

THOMAS BINKLEY (1931 [Cleveland]–1995 [Bloomington, Ind.]). After graduating from the University of Illinois in 1954, Binkley studied musicology in Munich, where he founded the Studio für alte Musik, a group with which he toured and issued more than forty recordings, thereby becoming one of the most influential individuals in the burgeoning early music movement. Binkley returned home in 1978 as a visiting professor at Stanford University and a year later was appointed director of the Early Music Institute at Indiana University. While in Bloomington he initiated a Focus Recording Series and a "Scholarship and Performance" publication series.

RUTH CRAWFORD [SEEGER] (1901 [East Liverpool]–1953 [Chevy Chase, Md.]). Barely a Buckeye, since she spent only her first year in East Liverpool followed by two more in Akron, Crawford was educated in Jacksonville, Florida, and Chicago, and then in New York by ethnomusicologist and composer Charles Seeger, whom she married in 1931, thereby becoming the stepmother of singer and songwriter Pete Seeger and mother of folk singers Mike and Peggy Seeger. She wrote a considerable amount of challenging chamber and vocal music and also became active in teaching young children. She also engaged in the Seeger family pursuit of collecting, transcribing, and editing American folksongs. While contributing to the publications of others, like Carl Sandburg and the John and Alan Lomax team, she also issued three of her own: *American Folk Songs for Children* in 1948, *Animal Folk Songs for Children* in 1950, and *American Folk Songs for Christmas* three years later.

DENNIS RUSSELL DAVIES (b. 1944 [Toledo]). A conductor who has come to specialize in the newest of music, Davies made his debut as a pianist with the Toledo Symphony in 1961. After receiving three degrees from the Juilliard School between 1966 and 1972, Davies achieved initial renown as music director of the St. Paul Chamber Orchestra beginning in 1972 and then of the Württemberg State Opera in Stuttgart after 1980. In 1976 he became musical advisor to the American Composers Orchestra in New York and more recently conductor of the Brooklyn Philharmonic.

JAN DEGAETANI (1933 [Massillon]–1989 [Rochester, N.Y.]). Her multitudes of admirers mourned the death of mezzo-soprano Jan DeGaetani of leukemia at age fifty-six. A graduate of the Juilliard School, she established a reputation as a specialist in contemporary music with the first performance of George Crumb's *Ancient Voices of Children* in 1970. However, her repertory, which encompassed every form of expression except opera, was one of enormous breadth, ranging from John Dowland and Stephen Foster to Arnold Schoenberg's *Pierrot lunaire*, Cole Porter, and far beyond. In 1973 she joined the faculty of the Eastman School of Music and also was named an artist-in-residence at the Aspen Music Festival.

BILL FONTANA (b. 1947 [Cleveland]). Fontana studied philosophy at John Carroll University and composition with conductor Louis Lane before taking a bachelor of arts degree from the New School for Social Research in 1970. Since then he has specialized in the creation of "soundscapes" or "sound sculptures." Ambient sounds are recorded and then manipulated and organized using advanced electronic techniques. Among his works: *Oscillating Steel Grids along the Cincinnati-Covington Suspension Bridge* (1980).

HENRY LAWRENCE FREEMAN (1869 [Cleveland]–1954 [New York]). Freeman studied theory and composition with Johann Beck and served as a church organist in Cleveland before a move to Denver in the early 1890s, where the first of his fourteen operas, *The Martyr,* was produced in 1893 (and then revived at Carnegie Hall in 1947). Freeman taught at Wilberforce University from 1902 to 1904 but was otherwise active as a musical theater conductor, principally in Chicago and New York. Mentor Beck performed excerpts from *Nada* (of 1898 and later retitled *Zuluki*) with the Cleveland Symphony about 1900. *Valdo* was then presented in Cleveland in 1906, *The Tryst* in New York in 1911, *Vendetta* at the Lafayette Theater in Harlem in 1923, and *Voodoo* at New York's 52nd Street Theatre in 1928. Freeman also left *The Slave,* a symphonic poem for chorus and orchestra (1925); *The Zulu King,* a ballet score of 1934; several cantatas, songs, and period pieces for the piano.

HAROLD GLEASON (1892 [Jefferson]–1980 [La Jolla, Calif.]). After studying civil engineering at the California Institute of Technology, Gleason turned to the organ and was serving New York's Fifth Avenue Presbyterian Church when he was hired as personal organist to George Eastman in Rochester in 1919. Two years later he joined the faculty of Eastman's School of Music and headed its organ department until 1953. He was also appointed a professor of musicology in 1932 and of music literature in 1939. His *Method of Organ Playing* first appeared in 1937 and has gone through multiple editions since then. He also issued *Examples of Music before 1400* in 1942 and coauthored several *Music Literature Outlines* (1949–55), as well as an anthology, *Music in America* (1964).

SIDNEY HARTH (b. 1929 [Cleveland]). After study at the Cleveland Institute of Music and elsewhere, Harth won several major prizes and awards. He served as concertmaster of the orchestras of Louisville, Chicago, and Los Angeles, and for several years as music director of the San Juan Symphony. He also taught in Louisville, Chicago, and, for a decade beginning in 1963, at Carnegie Mellon University in Pittsburgh. In 1981 he was named orchestral director at the Mannes College in New York City and a member of the faculty at the State University of New York at Stony Brook. He has been widely esteemed as a recitalist and chamber music player and while in Louisville enjoyed the fruits of that orchestra's notable history of commissioning new works by performing the solo lines of several pieces, including Herbert Elwell's Concert Suite of 1957.

DONAL HENAHAN (b. 1921 [Cleveland]). For more than a decade Henahan's opinions as chief music critic of the *New York Times* gained a national audience. After attending Ohio University he graduated from Northwestern University in 1948. He joined the staff of the *Chicago Daily News* in 1947 and served as that paper's music critic for a decade beginning in 1957. He then moved to New York and succeeded Harold Schonberg at the *Times* in 1980.

CHARLES HAUBIEL (1892 [Delta]–1978 [New York]). Haubil left a considerable corpus, including operas and operettas (including one for children), mostly programmatic orchestra works, chamber music for diverse ensembles, piano pieces (including pedagogical works intended for children), choral works ranging from cantatas to partsongs and a motet, and solo songs, as well as a symphonic song cycle for solo voice and orchestra. He studied with distinguished pedagogues in Europe and this country and taught in various places, including piano at the Institute for Musical Art for a decade beginning in 1920 and theory and composition at New York University from 1923 until 1947. He concertized to some extent, for a time concentrating on lecture recitals dealing with subjects like "The Path of Music" and "Musical Architecture." He founded the Composer's Press in 1935 and served as its president until it was subsumed by Southern Music in 1966.

ARTHUR L. JUDSON (1881 [Dayton]–1978 [Rye, N.Y.]). After studying the violin in New York City, Judson joined the faculty of Denison University's Conservatory of Music in 1900 and became its director in 1903. In addition to playing the American première of the Richard Strauss Violin Sonata in 1903, he organized major spring festivals in Granville involving the Cincinnati Symphony and soloists of major stature. He moved to New York in 1907 to become advertising manager of *Musical America* and then turned to artist management, becoming for a period the most powerful such figure in the country. He managed the Philadelphia Orchestra from 1915 until 1936 and the New York Philharmonic from 1922 to 1956. He also dealt with individual performers and in 1926, as a means of gaining radio bookings for his clients, organized a network that eventually became CBS. In 1932 he gathered a coalition of independent managers ultimately known as Columbia Artist Management, Inc. After stepping down as Columbia Artist Management's president in 1962 he created his own independent agency, from which he finally retired in 1972.

JAMES LEVINE (b. 1943 [Cincinnati]). Levine received his early training in Cincinnati. A piano prodigy, he gave his first recital at six and performed the Mendelssohn Second Concerto with the Cincinnati Symphony at age ten. After further study at the Marlboro Festival and the Juilliard School he became George Szell's assistant conductor with the Cleveland Orchestra from 1964 until 1970. During that period he taught at the Cleveland Institute of Music and organized the University Circle Orchestra. He was also involved with the Aspen Music School and Festival at Meadow Brook, summer home of the Detroit Symphony. He made his début at the Metropolitan Opera in 1971 and was named the company's principal conductor two years later. His title has varied (music director in 1975, artistic director in 1986), governed in part by reconfigurations in the Met's administrative structure, but his tastes clearly govern who sings what at the country's most important opera house. He has also served as director of the Cincinnati May Festival and the Ravinia Festival (summer home of the Chicago Symphony) and has appeared as guest conductor at all the major opera houses of the world and with most of its leading orchestras, concurrently turning the Met's orchestra into a world-class ensemble that offers acclaimed symphonic concerts in New York and elsewhere. In fall 1999 he succeeded the late Sergiu Celibidache as music director of the Munich Philharmonic Orchestra and in 2004 succeeds Seiji Ozawa at the helm of the Boston Symphony. He also continues to perform as a pianist, principally in song recitals.[12]

ROBERT C. MARSH (b. 1924 [Columbus]). After receiving degrees in journalism and philosophy from Northwestern University in 1945 and 1946, Marsh became a college teacher, a career that lasted until 1968. In 1956 he was appointed music critic of the *Chicago Sun-Times* and won awards for the quality of his work in that position. He has also written articles for philosophy journals and published *Toscanini and the Art of Orchestral Performance* (1956), a history, *The Cleveland Orchestra* (1967), a study of the repertory produced by resident opera companies in Chicago between 1910 and 1984, and a 1998 biography of James Levine.

SYLVIA McNAIR (b. 1956 [Mansfield]). McNair studied piano and violin as a child and entered Wheaton College in suburban Chicago as a violin major. However, one of her teachers suggested that she take voice lessons, asserting that members of a string quartet had to be able to breathe together on their way to mastery, since she originally intended a career as an ensemble player. While pursuing a graduate degree at Indiana University she was discovered by Robert Shaw, who became one of her principal advocates. In addition to oratorio and other appearances with most of our major orchestras, she has been an active recitalist and, since winning the National Metropolitan Opera Auditions in 1982, has appeared in most of the noted opera houses of Europe, as well as the Met, Lyric Opera of Chicago, and the Opera Theater of St. Louis. A crossover artist whose role models include the late Ella Fitzgerald, soprano McNair has with pianist André Previn issued a Jerome Kern disc, *Sure Thing*, and *Come Rain or Shine: The Harold Arlen Songbook*. On February 11, 1999, McNair was honored with a Governor's Award, bestowed by Governor Bob Taft during a program jointly sponsored by the Ohio Newspaper Association.

MILDRED MILLER (b. 1924 [Cleveland]). Operatic soprano Miller graduated from the Cleveland Institute of Music in 1946, having worked with Marie Semmelink Kraft. After further study in Boston she initiated her career in Germany, where she met and married Col. Wesley W. Posvar. She made a successful Metropolitan Opera début during 1951 in Mozart's *Marriage of Figaro* and became a mainstay of that company. Posvar's subsequent career as an academic finally led to the University of Pittsburgh, where he was named chancellor. Miller's second career became that of gracious first lady and an active force in the cultural affairs of her adopted city.

WILLIAM S. NEWMAN (1912 [Cleveland]–2000 [Chapel Hill, N.C.]). After receiving three degrees from Western Reserve University (in 1933, 1935, and 1939), Newman undertook postdoctoral work at Columbia University before appointment to the University of North Carolina faculty in 1945, where he influenced generations of pianists and musicologists before retirement in 1977. He performed widely as a pianist and published many journal articles and several important tomes, including a trilogy encompassing "the history of the sonata idea": *The Sonata in the Baroque Era* (1966), *The Sonata in the Classic Era* (1963), and *The Sonata Since Beethoven* (1969). He also produced a music appreciation text (*Understanding Music*, [1953]) and dealt with more practical matters for the keyboardist—*The Pianist's Problems: A Modern Approach to Efficient Practice and Musicianly Performance* (1950, with a preface by Arthur Loesser), as well as three pamphlets in a series issued by the Summy Publishing Company, in his case dealing with "styles and touches" in the keyboard music of Bach, Mozart, and Chopin (1956 and 1957), and *Performance Practices in Beethoven's Piano*

Sonatas (1971). His last major work appeared in 1988: *Beethoven on Beethoven—Playing His Piano Music His Way*.

LIONEL NOWAK (1911 [Cleveland]–1995 [Bennington, Vt.]). Nowak studied piano with Beryl Rubinstein and composition with Herbert Elwell, Roger Sessions, and Quincy Porter at the Cleveland Institute of Music, from which he received an undergraduate degree in 1933 and a master's degree three years later (plus an honorary doctorate in 1988). After a brief stint on the faculty of Fenn College in Cleveland, he joined the Doris Humphrey–Charles Weidman Modern Dance Company in 1938 as composer and music director. He then was appointed to the faculties of Converse College in 1942, Syracuse University in 1946, and Bennington College two years later. In addition to his dance scores for Humphrey, Weidman, and José Limón, Nowak wrote chamber music of various sorts, plus orchestral and choral works.

JULIE RIVÉ-KING (1854 [Cincinnati]–1937 [Indianapolis, Ind.]). A student of William Mason in New York and Franz Liszt in Weimar after childhood training with her mother in Cincinnati, Rivé-King (Frank King was her tour manager) enjoyed an enormously successful career as a touring piano virtuoso after débuts in Leipzig in 1874 and New York the following year. For example, she supposedly made more than two hundred appearances with the Theodore Thomas Orchestra. She also wrote for the piano, several examples of which she employed in recitals, and later taught at the Bush Conservatory in Chicago.

DAVID STANLEY SMITH (1877 [Toledo]–1949 [New Haven, Conn.]). Childhood training led to appointment as organist of Toledo's Trinity Episcopal Church at age fifteen. In 1895 he matriculated at Yale and became a protégé of Horatio Parker, who conducted his young charge's *Ode for Commencement Day*, opus 4, at Smith's graduation ceremony in 1900. Smith then studied in Europe for three years, after which he returned to his alma mater as a theory instructor. He remained on the Yale faculty until retirement in 1946, succeeding Parker as dean of the School of Music in 1920. Smith also followed Parker as conductor of the New Haven Symphony Orchestra and Oratorio Society in 1912 and conducted many of his own works with major orchestras across the country. He received honorary doctorates from Northwestern University in 1917 and the Cincinnati Conservatory in 1927. He left four symphonies and a substantial number of programmatic works for orchestra, ten string quartets, and a string sextet, as well as a variety of other chamber music, choral works of various dimensions, and solo songs.

HALE SMITH (b. 1925 [Cleveland]). Some still consider this Smith a Clevelander, although he migrated in 1958. After early piano study, nurture as one of a group of young black artists at Cleveland's noted Karamu House, and army service, Smith received his bachelor of music and master of music degrees from the Cleveland Institute of Music in 1950 and 1952, where he worked with Marcel Dick. In New York City he labored as an editor, arranger for jazz groups, and college teacher before joining the faculty of the University of Connecticut in 1970, retiring from that position in 1984. He has written a wide variety of instrumental and vocal music, some of which manifests his ethnic background and jazz upbringing: *Comes Tomorrow*, a jazz cantata from 1972, or *Symphonic Spirituals* of 1979, for soprano and orchestra. Two pieces from 1953 manifest the hometown connection: a chamber opera, *Blood Wedding*, first performed in Cleveland, and *In Memoriam—Beryl Rubinstein* for chorus and chamber orchestra, written after the death of the institute's longtime director to words by Cleveland poet Russell Atkins.

ROBERT WARD (b. 1917 [Cleveland]). After study at the Eastman School of Music, where several of his initial ventures for orchestra were conducted by Howard Hanson, he continued at the Juilliard School for two years beginning in 1939. After service as an army band leader he taught at Juilliard for a decade beginning in 1946, followed by ten years as managing editor of Galaxy Music. He was then named chancellor of the North Carolina School for the Arts, a position he held until 1972; he later served on the Duke University faculty. Although he has written a considerable corpus of music for orchestra, band and chamber ensembles, as well as choral pieces of various sorts, he is noticed today mainly for his operas, particularly *The Crucible* of 1961, which has enjoyed a wide currency.

EMERSON WHITHORNE (1884 [Cleveland]–1958 [Lyme, Conn.]). Whithorne studied with James H. Rogers and toured Ohio for several years as a teenaged concert pianist. In 1904 he went to Europe for work with Theodor Leschetizky and Artur Schnabel. He then lived in London from 1907 until 1915, teaching, writing criticism, and studying oriental musical systems at the British Museum (which later gave rise to works such as an orchestral suite, *Adventures of a Samurai*, of 1919). He served as executive editor of the Art Publication Society in St. Louis from 1915 to 1920 and then settled in New York, devoting most of the rest of his life to composition. While his music has since disappeared almost without a trace, it was widely noticed and performed during his lifetime. In addition to several works played by the Cleveland Orchestra, he momentarily flirted with "machine music" in *Aeroplane* of 1920 and wrote *Saturday's Child*, opus 42, of 1926 on words by Countee Cullen for two soloists and chamber orchestra, as well as a symphonic poem, *Fata Morgana*, opus 44, of 1927. He also left numerous other programmatic orchestra pieces, two string quartets, a piano quintet, and a violin sonata, in addition to a bounty of other vocal and piano music.

JOHN FINLEY WILLIAMSON (1887 [Canton]–1964 [Toledo]). After graduating from Otterbein College in 1911 and further voice study in New York, Williamson became minister of music at the Westminster Presbyterian Church in Dayton, where in 1920 he organized the Westminster Choir, "composed of young men and women taken from various walks of life in Dayton and vicinity."[13] A Dayton Westminster Choir Association was soon incorporated, and from that ensemble's immediate success, both in Dayton and on tour under professional management as early as 1922, arose the Westminster Choir School, created in 1926 with the express purpose of training church musicians. Williamson transferred the school to Ithaca, New York, in 1929 and then in 1932 to Princeton, New Jersey, where it still flourishes on its own campus, although financial exigency has led to a loss of independence and assimilation into Rider University. Williamson remained his school's president until retirement in 1958, conducting his choir across this country and abroad, in the process becoming one of the most influential choral musicians of his era. Both the College of Wooster and his alma mater dignified his accomplishments with honorary doctorates.[14]

LEE ADAMS (b. 1924 [Mansfield]). Adams first studied at Ohio State before work at Columbia University's Pulitzer School of Journalism. However, a meeting with Broadway composer Charles Strouse in 1949 transformed Adams into a lyricist and librettist. They achieved their first smash hit with *Bye Bye Birdie* in 1960. *Golden Boy*, a 1964 vehicle for Sammy Davis Jr. proved a commercial success, *It's a Bird, It's a Plane, It's Superman* of 1966 less so, but *Applause*, a 1970 showcase for Lauren Bacall, played on Broadway for two years. Adams and Strouse as a team failed to produce another hit show and drifted apart. Adams later teamed with composer Mitch Leigh, of *Man of La Mancha* fame, but their partnership on shows in 1988 and 1993 did not yield triumphs. Adams was inducted into the Songwriters Hall of Fame in 1989.

KAYE BALLARD (b. Catherine Gloria Balotta, 1926 [Cleveland]). Teenaged Ballard first trod the boards as the straight woman in a comedy act at a Cleveland burlesque house. She toured the burlesque circuit in the South and in 1943 was performing at a Detroit club when she was hired by wacky bandleader Spike Jones, with whom she toured for two years. She appeared in a New York revue as early as 1946 but established herself as a stage performer only in 1954 with her portrayal of Helen of Troy in *The Golden Apple*. This led to other Broadway successes, such as a replacement for Beatrice Lillie in the *Ziegfeld Follies* of 1957 and in *Carnival* four years later. She first mounted her one-woman show, *Hey Ma . . . Kaye Ballard*, off-Broadway in 1984. She made her television début on *The Mel Tormé Show* in 1952 and later became a regular on *The Perry Como Show* and *The Steve Allen Show*. She also played with Eve Arden in the TV series *The Mothers-in-Law* (1967–70), followed by a single season as the star's neighbor on *The Doris Day Show*. She was hired for guest spots on other TV series and became a regular guest of Merv Griffin and Johnny Carson. This versatile entertainer also enjoyed a modest film career and has played clubs and cabarets across the country.

WILLIAM BOYD (1898 [Hendrysburg in Belmont County]–1972 [South Laguna Beach, Calif.]). Boyd's family moved to Cambridge soon after his birth and then to Oklahoma when he was thirteen. By age twenty he had reached Hollywood, where in 1919 he made his début as an extra in a film directed by the legendary Cecil B. De Mille. Boyd achieved considerable notice in De Mille releases like *The Volga Boatman* of 1926 and *King of Kings* the following year. His attractive voice then allowed a seamless transition to the new era of talkies, and by 1932 he was certified as a star by the Pathé people. However, immortality arrived in 1934 when Boyd became Hopalong Cassidy, the western Robin Hood in black astride his all-white horse, Topper. The original six pictures, based on Clarence E. Mulford's stories, became the basis of six-a-year releases (for a total of 106 shows before Boyd's retirement in 1953). Hopalong became even more universal in 1949 when NBC began its weekly television presentation of the character, and the following year the Mutual Radio Network initiated a Sunday afternoon radio series. Boyd added to that exposure a comic strip syndicated by the *Los Angeles Mirror*, as well as comic books, recordings, personal appearances (for instance, twenty-six cities during the 1959–60 season), and the aggressive marketing of themed regalia to create a financial empire that allowed his notable philanthropy to children's hospitals and homes. Although Cambridge was only briefly Hopalong's residence, in 1991 that city's downtown merchants renamed their annual street festival in his honor; the Hopalong Cassidy Festival in early May includes a parade, a little Buckaroo contest, and gratis showing of vintage Cassidy films. Cambridge is also home to a national fan club of some five hundred members and a museum containing more than a thousand artifacts, acknowledging Boyd's many visits to Ohio and his purchase of $10,000 worth of World War II bonds, which he credited to Guernsey County.[15]

TERESA BREWER (b. Theresa Breuer, 1931 [Toledo]). Brewer made her first appearance on the radio at age two and was a regular fixture on the *Major Bowes Amateur Hour* from 1938 until 1943. She signed her first recording contract in 1949 and a year later hit the top of the charts with "Music Music Music," backed by the Dixieland All Stars. Other hits followed (six recordings between 1950 and 1956 reached gold status), as did club, radio, and television appearances, and a first film in 1953. She remained active into the 1980s as a recording artist on various labels.

DORIS DAY (b. Doris Von Kappelhoff, 1922 [Cincinnati]). Trained as a dancer, Day turned to a singing career at age sixteen, working with the Bob Crosby and Les Brown Bands, achieving her first success with a recording on the Columbia label of "Sentimental Journey," which sold more that a million copies. Her film career was initiated with *Romance on the High Sea* in 1948 and involved almost forty films over the next two decades, including *Tea for Two* (1950), *West Point Story* (1950), *Lullaby of Broadway* (1951), *April in Paris* (1952), *Calamity Jane* (1953), and *Pillow Talk* (1959).

MICHAEL FEINSTEIN (b. 1956 [Bexley]). Even as a child Feinstein was able intuitively to play songs by the legendary Broadway tunesmiths. In California as a piano salesman, he soon became archivist and personal assistant to both Ira Gershwin and Harry Warren. During the 1970s and into the following decade Feinstein not only cataloged their work but also discovered some previously unknown alternate lyrics by Ira Gershwin. Through Gershwin he met the lyricist's goddaughter and soon became her accompanist. While he also played for other singers like Rosemary Clooney, he rapidly became the leading advocate and purveyor of the standard popular song, with recorded anthologies of songs by George Gershwin (1987), Irving Berlin (1987), Burton Lane (1990 and 1992), Jule Styne (1991), and Jerry Herman (1994). He established himself as a cabaret singer both in this country and England and then made his Broadway début in 1988 with *Michael Feinstein in Concert*. He has also toured extensively and has hosted his own television specials. His retrospection includes an autobiography, *Nice Work If You Can Get It: My Life in Rhythm and Rhyme* (1995).

JOEL GREY (b. 1932 [Cleveland]). Actor, singer, and dancer Grey entered the showbiz world via an appearance in 1951 on a network television program hosted by Eddie Cantor. This led to nightclub performances and various roles on Broadway and in films and television before he achieved stardom in 1966 as the Master of Ceremonies in *Cabaret* (reprising that role in the 1972 film version of the show). He met with equal success in the title role of *George M!* a musical stage biography of George M. Cohan, which he played on Broadway in 1968 and on television two years later. He has continued to work in the various media and to record, although with less visibility.

CLARE GRUNDMAN (b. 1913 [Cleveland]). Grundman received a bachelor of science degree in education from Ohio State in 1934 and then taught public school in Lexington, Kentucky, for three years before returning to Columbus. A clarinetist by training, he taught the instrument and orchestration and disciplined the Ohio State bands while working toward the master of arts degree he received in 1940. In 1941 he moved to New York as an arranger for the *Hit Parade* show on CBS after a performance of his First Suite for Symphonic Band in Columbus's Memorial Hall in February of that year had led to a summer's study with Paul Hindemith at the Berkshire Music Center in Massachusetts. That sort of bifurcated personality characterized his subsequent career, since, while he has written for films, radio, and television and orchestrated and conducted Broadway musicals, he also composed eighty-five instrumental works between 1947 and 1988, more than fifty of them for symphonic band, some now standards of that literature.[16] Grundman has also served as coeditor of the New York Times *Crossword Puzzle Dictionary*.

PEE WEE [WALTER] HUNT (1907 [Mount Healthy]–1979 [Plymouth, Mass.]). The teenaged banjo player studied at the Cincinnati Conservatory of Music and Ohio State University, after which he played both banjo and trombone with various regional bands before joining what became known as the Casa Loma Orchestra, this in Detroit. He became a Hollywood disc jockey in 1943 and, after a few years in the Merchant Marine, formed his own Dixieland band, which played the Hollywood Palladium with great success and appeared in the film *Make Believe Ballroom* of 1949. He first appeared on the Capitol label in 1948 and left a considerable recorded legacy, including *Pee Wee Hunt Plays and Sings Dixie* (1958), *Blues à la Dixie* (1959), and *Dixieland Kickoff!* (1959).

SAMMY KAYE (1910 [Lakewood]–1987 [Ridgewood, N.J.]). As a student at Ohio University, clarinetist Kaye operated the Varsity Inn and headed its resident collegiate band. In 1933 he organized his own professional band, which first appeared at the Statler Hotel in Cleveland, but by the end of the decade he was playing New York hotels like the Astor and New Yorker, having migrated east via Pittsburgh. Inviting listeners to "Swing and Sway with Sammy Kaye," the band also was featured on various radio and later television shows, its popularity assured by gimmicks such as a "So You Want to Lead a Band" stunt, in which members of the audience became instant conductors in a contest whose outcome was determined by applause from the listeners. The band (of which Kaye relinquished direct control only in 1986) recorded several anthologies, including in its repertory Kaye songs like "Hawaiian Sunset" and "Until Tomorrow."

TED LEWIS (b. Theodore Leopold Friedman, 1892 [Circleville]–1971 [New York]). As a child, clarinetist Lewis learned to play his instrument in the traditional klezmer style but was sent off to a business school in Columbus by a family wary of a show business career. However, he joined the vaudeville circuit in 1906 and had his own band by 1918, the year after he adopted a battered top hat as his trademark. By the following year the group was recording for Columbia (and left an extraordinary legacy on disc), appearing on the radio and in several musical revues, including the *Greenwich Village Follies* of 1919 and 1921, *Ziegfeld's Midnight Frolics* of 1919, the *Ted Lewis Frolics* of 1923, and *Artists and Models* of 1927. His sidemen included major jazz artists like Frank Teschemacher, Jack Teagarden, Jimmy Dorsey, Benny

Goodman, and Fats Waller. He remained active into the 1960s, playing hotels, resorts, and nightclubs, as well as on radio and television, reprising his venerable vaudeville routines and perpetually inquiring of his loyal audiences, "Is everybody happy?" Lewis surely received an affirmative response to that question from residents of his hometown, since he endowed Circleville with several generous acts of philanthropy.

RUTH LYONS (1907–1988 [Cincinnati]). Cincinnati's "First Lady of Broadcasting" virtually invented the TV daytime talk show with her ninety-minute, five-days-a-week-at-noon *Fifty-Fifty Club*, broadcast on WLW beginning in 1948 and WLW-TV a year later, a tenure that lasted until ill health forced her retirement in 1967. Tens of thousands watched her via Crosley-AVCO stations in Columbus, Dayton, and Indianapolis (she frequently broadcast from those cities), and as many as seven million were mesmerized by her spontaneous banter when NBC began airing the show in 1952. The original fifty who constituted her studio audience were doubled in number when the waiting list for tickets led to a seven-year backlog; commercial sponsors waited as long as three years for the opportunity to have Lyons endorse their products. Lyons began her career on WKRD in 1929, accompanying singers on both piano and organ, and when the Crosley Broadcasting people brought her to WLW and WSAI a decade later her songs were an important part of the personality she developed. In fact, not only did she write several signature songs involving audience participation (for example, "The Waving Song" and "The Marching Song," some of which were published: "Let's Light the Christmas Tree" in 1943 and "The Birthday Song" and "The Nu-Maid Song" in 1946, the last issued by the Miami Margarine Company of Cincinnati), but she even improvised jingles touting sponsors' products. Little wonder that every celebrity of the day joined her, and she became a model for those who followed in her stead.[17]

HENRY MANCINI (1924 [Cleveland]–1994 [Los Angeles]). Composer, arranger, and pianist Mancini had already made some arrangements and sent them off to Benny Goodman when he enrolled at the Juilliard School in 1942. His student days were interrupted by military service, after which he worked as pianist and arranger for Tex Beneke, who was then leading the Glenn Miller Orchestra. Mancini became a staff composer at Universal Pictures in 1952 and eventually wrote about seventy film scores, contributing to perhaps another thirty. He first made his mark with two musical biographies, *The Glenn Miller Story* of 1954 and *The Benny Goodman Story* of 1956, although immortality was assured with the score to *Breakfast at Tiffany's* of 1961, which included "Moon River." His jazz-influenced style was also applied to the sound tracks of the *Peter Gunn* television series and the Pink Panther film series. Much of this material was rewritten for recordings, and Mancini appeared widely as a piano soloist and as an orchestral conductor of pops concerts.

DEAN MARTIN (b. Dino Paul Crocetti, 1917 [Steubenville]–1995 [Beverly Hills, Calif.]). Martin left school after the tenth grade and worked as a shoeshine boy, gas station attendant, welterweight boxer, and casino croupier before turning to a singing career in 1941, followed by recordings on several labels. He first worked with comedian Jerry Lewis in 1946 in Atlantic City, gradually developing a song-and-comedy act for radio and television; they made the first of their sixteen films in 1949. The partnership dissolved in 1956, after which Martin embarked on a new career as a dramatic actor, although he appeared in a few comedies and musicals, most notably *Bells Are Ringing* of 1960 with Judy Holliday. He had recorded for Capitol Records beginning in 1948 and achieved further success with hits on Frank Sinatra's Reprise Records, beginning in 1961. Martin also had his own variety show on NBC-TV, which ran for nine seasons and was eventually syndicated for international distribution. He remained a headliner in clubs, especially those of Las Vegas, and as late as 1987 embarked on an extended tour of forty performances in twenty-nine cities with his former Rat Packers Sinatra and Sammy Davis Jr. although a kidney ailment forced him to withdraw from the project.[18]

MAUREEN MCGOVERN (b. 1949 [Youngstown]). Blessed with a four-octave range and a dazzling coloratura technique, McGovern nonetheless worked as a typist and toured for six years as a singer with a rock band before making her first recording in 1972. "The Morning After" became the love song in *The Poseidon Adventure*, the first of several such successes. Besides appearances in regional productions of standard Broadway musicals, she attracted attention as Mabel in Joseph Papp's updated Broadway version of Gilbert and Sullivan's *The Pirates of Penzance* in 1981 and eight years later as Polly Peachum opposite Sting's Macheath in a modernized *Threepenny Opera*. She also made a solo appearance in Carnegie Hall in 1989, having played the singing nun, Sister Angelina, in *Airplane* back in 1980. She has recorded extensively, has appeared in concerts across the planet, and has sung in both nightclubs and cabarets, employing a literature ranging from George Gershwin to John Lennon and beyond.

THE MCGUIRE SISTERS (Christine/Chris, b. 1929; Dorothy/Dotty, b. 1930; and Phyllis, b. 1931 [Middletown]). This close-harmony vocal trio reached the peak of their popularity during the 1950s and into the next decade. As youngsters they sang with local church choirs and won an amateur talent contest, which led to a three-week engagement at a Middletown movie house and appearances over the local radio station. In 1950 and 1951 they made a nine-month tour of army camps and hospitals and then worked in Cincinnati clubs and radio stations before moving to New York in 1952. They soon became regulars on *The Arthur Godfrey Show* and also appeared on Kate Smith's radio show. Hit recordings led to appearances on *The Phil Silvers Show* and *The Red Skelton Show*, plus hotel and club dates across the country and in England. When their sweet style went out of fashion the group disbanded, only to be resuscitated in 1985, leading to a national tour the following year and a currency that lasted into the following decade.

THE MILLS BROTHERS (Herbert, 1912–89; Harry, 1913–82; John Jr., 1911–36; and Donald, 1915–99 [Piqua]). All sons of barber John Sr. (1882–1967), while still in their teens the four brothers (John played the guitar and imitated the string bass, while the others generated a signature style by imitating instruments like the saxophone, trumpet, and trombone, an idiom that evolved from their earlier reliance on the kazoo) had created a close-harmony group that performed in regional vaudeville and tent shows and had its own radio program on WLW in Cincinnati. They moved to New York in 1930, signed a record contract, and released their first of many hit records the following year (they eventually recorded about 1,200 individual titles); their imitations of instrumental sounds became so notorious that the labels of their discs often assured listeners that no actual instruments were involved. They also appeared with Bing Crosby in *The Big Broadcast*, the first of several such films over the next two decades. John Jr. died suddenly and was replaced by his father, who had been a sometime singer himself. They toured extensively during the late 1930s, here and abroad, their success perhaps symbolized by the 1943 release of "Paper Doll," which sold more than six million copies. Although they gradually abandoned reliance on simulating instrumental sounds, this long-lived ensemble survived the retirement of John Sr. in 1956 and Harry's death in 1982. The trio became a duo, and even after Herbert's demise, Donald teamed with his son John in a nightclub act that prolonged the family legacy.

HELEN MORGAN (1900 [Danville]–1941 [Chicago]). Morgan's career as a singer began in small Chicago clubs and then in New York revues like *George White's Scandals of 1925*. She attracted the notice of impresario Florenz Ziegfeld and achieved instant fame as Julie La Verne in his 1927 production of Jerome Kern's *Show Boat*, a role she reprised in its 1932 revival, as well as in both the 1929 and 1936 film versions of the work. She appeared in other Broadway shows and Hollywood films and made several hit records, including a legendary version of the Gershwins' "The Man I Love." Her career disintegrated under the influence of alcohol, leading to a premature death from cirrhosis of the liver. Her life was memorialized in a film biography of 1957.

ROY ROGERS (b. Leonard Slye, 1911 [Cincinnati]–1998 [Apple Valley, Calif.]). The Slyes moved upriver to Scioto County when Leonard was just a child and settled on a farm at Duck Run, twelve miles northwest of Portsmouth. Although Slye left the area before graduating from high school, he visited many times, as recently as the early 1990s, and at one point was given an honorary diploma. Portsmouth is the home of the Roy Rogers–Dale Evans Collectors Association, which sponsors an annual Roy Rogers Festival in early June, including a flea market specializing in western movie memorabilia and tours to the boyhood home. Slye migrated to California as a young man and picked fruit before establishing himself as another Ohio-born singing cowboy. In 1933 he organized the Sons of the Pioneers, a group known in an earlier incarnation as the O-Bar-O Cowboys, who appeared in several western films, sang over various Los Angeles-area radio stations, and released several albums, beginning in 1934. Rogers played his first prominent role as a singing congressman in *Under Western Skies*, released in 1938. After the death of his first wife, he married a fellow actor, Dale Evans, in 1947. His other constant companion, the palomino Trigger, was a co-star in many of Rogers's eighty-seven films before 1952 and the offshoot television series (one hundred of *The Roy Rogers Shows* between 1951 and 1957, followed by *The Roy Rogers and Dale Evans Show* in the 1962–63 season), although Rogers also appeared on the screen with figures like Jane Russell and Bob Hope. Trigger died in 1965 at age thirty-three, but Rogers had already turned from film to the fast-food business, with a successful chain of restaurants that were sold in 1990, although he returned to the screen in 1975 and to the recording studio as late as 1991.

J[OHN] S[TEPAN] ZAMECNIK (1872 [Cleveland]–1953 [Los Angeles]). Zamecnik was born in Cleveland of parents who had immigrated from Bohemia. He may have studied with Dvořák in New York during that composer's tenure as director of the National Conservatory of Music from 1892 to 1895. It is certain that he worked with Dvořák in Prague during 1896 and 1897. We also know that Johann Heinrich Beck conducted his *Slavonic Dances* with the Cleveland Symphony in the Grays' Armory in February 1900. Beginning in 1901 he played violin for three seasons in the Pittsburgh Symphony under Victor Herbert. He then returned to Cleveland and in 1907 was named music director of the new 3,548-seat Hippodrome Theater. He wrote the music for its opening spectacle, *Coaching Days*, which involved horses diving into the theater's enormous water tank, and was reputed to have created music for other Hippodrome spectaculars, as well as six operettas. Little evidence of that activity remains other than a score for *The Hermits in Africa*, "A Musical Comedy in Two Acts," with words by five members of the Hermit Club and music by Zamecnik and H. L. Sanford, a work produced by the club members between May 31 and June 6, 1909. Although Zamecnik published *The Cleveland News March* in 1906, it was only in 1911 that he began to issue through Sam Fox various kinds of commercial dance music and songs (for instance, a release of 1919, "My Cairo Love: An Egyptian Serenade," with words by Harry D. Kerr, described as an "Operastyle Song Success"). He became prolific enough that Fox encouraged his house composer to assume as many as twenty-one pseudonyms to avoid the appearance of being too dependent on Zamecnik. In 1923 he moved to Los Angeles as a film composer, having earlier won a $2,500 prize from the Los Angeles Booster Club for his song "California" (it was published by the *Los Angeles Examiner* in 1915). His departure was probably prompted by his earlier success in writing silent film cues, generic tidbits not intended for any particular film that could be stocked by movie house music directors and patched together to create silent film scores. This activity apparently dates from as early as 1913 with what became the four volumes of the *Sam Fox Moving Picture Music*, popular enough that they were still in print a decade later. The *Sam Fox Photoplay Edition, A Loose Leaf Collection of High Class Dramatic and Descriptive Motion Picture Music* was issued in four volumes between 1920 and 1927 (the individual titles ranging from "Dramatic Tension" and "Storm Scene" to "The Furious Mob," "Queer Antics," and "Air Flight"). This was followed by a series of ten *Sam Fox Motion Picture Themes*, published in 1921. Fox also issued for the Paramount Famous Lasky Corporation Zamecnik's score for *Wings* of 1927, consisting of 180 separate cues plus exit music (most of it by Zamecnik but with acknowledged borrowings from Bach, Mendelssohn, Gounod, Verdi, and others), with specific instructions both to the conductor and the projectionist. Two years later Fox issued a volume of thirty-two cues for *Redskin* ("Navajo Jim," "The Medicine Man," "Tensive Agitato," and "Speeding Auto"), five of them by one L. De Francesco.[19] Zamecnik seems to have enjoyed a considerable success with "Neapolitan Nights (Oh, Nights of Splendor)," the theme song of *Fazil*, which starred Charles Farrell and Greta Nissen, since it was issued by Fox beginning in 1925 in a wide variety of arrangements for various instruments and combinations thereof, ranging from orchestra and band to ukulele, the Hammond organ (in Ethel Smith's series), mixed chorus, and accordion band. Lucien Cailliet even made a band paraphrase in 1948. Zamecnik also wrote the march *World Events* in 1935, which achieved universality as the title music for Movietone newsreels, and some non-film music (*Gypsy Wildflower*, "An Orchestral Fantasia with Mixed Chorus Arrangement" [sic] in 1930, or *Southern Miniatures* for band in 1951). But he also became a workhorse arranger for Fox, including a series of Concertized Grand Operas (*Faust* in 1929, followed in successive years by *Carmen* and *Martha*), *Fox Old Masters Folio for Band or Orchestra* (1932), *Fox Famous Composer String Ensemble Folio* (1933), *Fox Repertoire of Classics for Four Horns* (1934), and a *Fox Collection of Treasure Songs* (1934), plus a *Fox Symphonic Band Folio* in 1936 and the *Fox Classicana Band Folio* the following year.

Although headquartered in New York City since 1982, BILLBOARD was founded during November 1894 in Cincinnati by William H. Donaldson and James H. Hennegan.[20] A monthly, dubbed *Billboard Advertising*, its original intent was devotion to "the interests of advertisers, poster printers, bill posters, advertising agents and secretaries of fairs." At first, little more than an organ for the Associated Bill Posters' Association, its horizons began to expand as early as June 1896 with the addition of the "Fair Department" devoted to news about these outdoor, seasonal events. Renamed *The Billboard* in February 1897, by May 1900 it had become a weekly proclaiming itself "The Official Organ of the Great Out-Door Amusement World." As witness, John N. Klohr's *The Billboard March* (Cincinnati: John Church, 1902), "Dedicated to the 'Greatest General Amusement Paper–The Billboard, Cincinnati, O.'"[21] By 1906 "America's Leading Theatrical Weekly" had expanded its horizons to include "Theatres, Circuses, Fairs, Musicians," and although still published in Cincinnati (by 1912 with its own building at 25–27 Opera Place), it boasted of bureaus in New York, Chicago, San Francisco, and London, soon expanded to include Cleveland, St. Louis, Kansas City, Baltimore, and Paris. While emphasizing departments like "New Theatrical Productions," the journal gradually introduced "Motion Picture News," plus a growing concern for commercial popular song. This was manifested in 1911 with a column called "A Boon to Members of the Profession," reprinting refrains from "the latest productions of the various music publishers." "Song Reviews," "from the performer's angle," was added the following year, as was a listing of "Popular Songs Heard in Vaudevil [*sic*] Theaters Last Week" in 1914, an intimation of the charts rating the consumption of their products so important to the industry today, a feature by the end of 1912 named "The Billboard's Song Chart." During the following decade the publication profiled both songwriters and music publishers in the columns "Land O' Melody" and "Who's Who in Songland," which led during the 1940s to substantial studies of major songwriters, as well as "The Billboard Music Popularity Charts: The Honor Role of Popular Songwriters," still focused on print rather than recordings. Today, proclaiming itself "The International Newsweekly of Music, Video and Home Entertainment," its principal motivation is those charts that track sales and thus trends in a small horde of thirty-one music categories, ranging from the venerable (Hot 100, Hot R&B Singles, Hot Country [all dating from 1958], Top Classical [1964], Hot Adult, Most Popular Albums [both from 1965] and Top Jazz [1967]), to the middle-aged (Top Gospel [1973], Top Christian Contemporary [1980], Album Rock, Latin, Top Music Videos [all 1985], Classical Crossover [1986] and Top New Age [1988]), to newer idioms (Hot Rap [1989], Hot World Music [1990], and Top Reggae [1994]).

A Sampling of Sheet Music Published in Ohio, 1847–1943 (By Year)

J. E. Jungmann, *Cincinnati American Republican March* (Cincinnati: J. C. Groene, 1847). "Respectfully Dedicated to General Winfield Scott."

E. K. Thatcher, "May, Dewy May: A New Song of May Day" (Cincinnati: W. C. Peters, 1847). "The words written and the music partly composed on an Alpine melody and inscribed to her pupils in the public schools of Cincinnati by Mrs. E. K. Thatcher."

Dr. Wosencraft, *Rio Grande March* (Cincinnati: W. C. Peters, 1847). "Most Respectfully Dedicated to General [Zachary] Taylor."

Frederick Werner, *The Floral Waltz* (Cincinnati: Peters, Field, and Co., 1848). "Composed for and Performed at the Cincinnati Orphan Asylum Floral Festival."

William Cumming [Peters], "Gentle Eva" and "Uncle Tom's Grave," *Uncle Tom's Cabin Songs*, with words by Mrs. R. S. Nichols (Cincinnati. W. C. Peters, 1852).

D. Albert, *First Rate Schottisch* (Cincinnati: Colburn and Field, 1854)."à Mlle. Kate Collins, son aimable élève."

Mrs. L. L. Deming, *Cleveland Plain Dealer Mazourka* [sic] (Cleveland: S. Brainard, 1857).

Solon Nourse, "I've Been Gathering Flowers, Mother," with words by H. B. Wildman (Cincinnati: Truax and Baldwin, 1858). "Dedicated to the Young Ladies of the Wesleyan Female College. Cincinnati O." [1]

Alf-Squire, arr., *Masonic Quick Step* (Cincinnati: John Church Jr., 1859). "As Performed by Menter's Band." "Dedicated to the Masonic Fraternity by the Publisher," and adorned with an engraving of the "New Masonic Building."

Mary E. Adams, *The Vacation Polka* (Cincinnati: John Church Jr., 1860?). "Composed and Dedicated to the Class of 1860, Western Female Seminary, Oxford, Ohio."

Mrs. M. A. Schultz, *Ohio White Sulphur Springs Schottisch* (Cincinnati: A. C. Peters, 1860).

C. M. Currier, *Sheridan's Ride, a Descriptive Fantasie* (Cincinnati: John Church Jr., n.d.).

L. H. Johnson, *Artillery Waltz* (Cleveland: S. Brainard, 1862?). "Composed and Respectfully Dedicated to the Officers and Members of Company D, Light Artillery of Cleveland."

Jessie Brinley, *Squirrel Hunter's March* (Cincinnati: John Church Jr., 1863). "Dedicated to Those Brave and Loyal Men Who Hastened to the Defence of Cincinnati in Her Hour of Danger."

L. Mathias, *Street Rail-Road Galop* (Toledo: L. Doebele; Cleveland: S. Brainard, 1863).

George W. Work, "How Are You, Telegraph?" with words by William A. Collins (Cleveland: S. Brainard, 1863).

T. Brigham Bishop, "Abraham the Great and Genl. Grant His Mate" (Cincinnati; J. Church Jr., 1864).

H. E. Habenbach, *Sherman's Advance on Savannah, Gallop for the Piano* (Cincinnati: G. Sutterer, 1864).

James S. Porter, "His Life, It Was Given, Columbia for Thee! Dedicated to the Memory of 1st Lieut. Jas. W. Burbidge, Co. H., O. V. I.," with words by Mary Madeira (Cincinnati: John Church Jr., 1864).

Jules Schulhoff, *Galop di Bravura (Gold Fever Galop)* (Cincinnati: A. C. Peters, 1864).

C. Jos. Fischer, *Lincoln's Funeral March* (Dayton: Ch. J. and A. Fischer, 1865).

anon., "Have You Struck Ile?" with words by Joseph B. Quinby, arranged by a speculator (Cleveland: S. Brainard, 1865).[2]

O. I. L. Wells, "Petroleum, Petroleum, or Oil Upon the Brain," with words by the composer (Cincinnati: John Church Jr., 1865).

Oily Gammon, esq., or O. I. L. Wells, *Petroleum Gallop* (Cincinnati: J. Church Jr., 1865?).

Henry Mayer, *Suspension Bridge* (Cincinnati: C. Y. Fonda, 1867).

W. Phelps Dale, "Death of Our Darling," with words by Lizzie Lincoln (Toledo: W. W. Whitney, 1867). "Dedicated to Mrs. John H. Klippart, Columbus, O."[3]

Henry Atkins, *Velocipede Galop* (Cincinnati: John Church Jr., 1868). "To the members of the Queen City Velocipede Club."

Frank Howard, "We'll Show You When We Come to Vote. The Great Woman's Suffrage" (Toledo: W. W. Whitney, 1869).

H. D. Sofege, arr., *Exposition March* (Cincinnati: John Church, 1870). "Respectfully Dedicated to the Patrons of the Cincinnati Industrial Exposition, 1871."

Charlie Baker, *The Gibson House Waltz* (Cincinnati: F. W. Helmick, 1874).

Sidney Ryan, *Governor Hayes Grand March* (Cincinnati: John Church, 1876).

Thos. P. Westendorf, "Vote as You Shot Boys: Hayes and Wheeler Campaign Song," with words by the composer (Cleveland: S. Brainard's Sons, 1876).

Chas. Ed. Prior, "We'll Blow Our Horn for Hayes," with words by Samuel N. Mitchell (Cincinnati: F. W. Helmick, 1876).

Prof. Thos. N. Cauldfield, *Governor Thomas Young's Grand March* (Cincinnati: F. W. Helmick, 1877).

John T. Rutledge, "Tally One for Me, Base Ball Song and Chorus," with words by the composer (Cincinnati: F. W. Helmick, 1877).

Jack Sparrow, *Who Killed Cock Robin? Funeral March, Solos and Quartette,* opus 1st and last (Cincinnati: Geo. D. Newhall, 1880). "To the 5 and 40 Blackbirds; Cincinnati, O."

Gabriel Miesse, *Sounds From the Hock-Hocking, Valse Elegante for the Piano or Organ* (Lancaster: Gabriel Miesse and Son, 1881).

J. V. Ghio, *Governor Foraker's Grand March* (Cincinnati: Newhall and Evans, 1887).

D. W. Crist, *Ohio Centennial March,* for the piano or cabinet organ (Moultrie: D. W. Crist, 1888).

Stephen. S. Bonbright, *Moerlein's Cincinnati Centennial Waltzes*, opus 115 (Cincinnati: Queen City, 1888). "Composed Expressly for The Christian Moerlein Brewing Co."[4]

Ross Mansfield Eversole, *Centennial March* (Cincinnati: Newhall and Evans, 1888). "Dedicated to the Commissioners of the Centennial Exposition of the Ohio Valley and Central States."

Wm. E. Van Curt, *O-Y-O, Valse de Concert* (Cincinnati: Smith and Nixon, 1888). "As played by the Cincinnati Orchestra at the Exposition Grand Concerts in Music Hall"[5]

W. T. Porter, "McKinley's the Man: A Campaign Song and Chorus" (Cincinnati: Fillmore Bros., 1891). "As sung by the Glee Club of the Young Men's Blaine Club, of Cincinnati."

Carl Wilhelm Kern, *Governor Bushnell March* (Springfield: D. A. Syman, 1895).

Max Faetkenheuer, *Cleveland Centennial March*, opus 153 (Cleveland: Weil, 1895).

Will S. Ashbrook, "The Cleveland Exposition, March and Song," with words by J. Edmund Cooke (Cleveland: Cleveland Press, 1897).

W. W. McCallip, "'Tell Mother I'll Be There,' President McKinley's Message to His Dying Mother," with words by the composer (Columbus: n.p., 1897).

Gus. W. Bernard, *Big Four Two-Step* (Cincinnati: J. C. Groene, 1897). "Respectfully Dedicated by Permission to the Big Four Route."[6]

A[rnold] J. Gantvoort, "Hurrah for the Schools of Ohio. Rallying Song Dedicated to the School teachers of Ohio," with words by W. H. Venable (Cincinnati: John Church, 1898).

Dan Ress, "He Sleeps upon Havana's Shore," with words by Thomas Killen (Youngstown: D. O. Evans, 1898).

Louis Lambert, "William McKinley Is the Man," with words by B. S. Driggs (Cleveland: B. S. Driggs and A. F. Wands, 1900).

C. S. Stanage, *The Skyscraper, March and Two Step* (Cincinnati: W. H. Willis, 1900).[7]

Gus. W. Bernard, *Ganymede "76" March* (Cincinnati: Sig. and Sol. H. Freiberg, 1903).[8]

T. Mayo Geary, "Your Dad Gave His Life for His Country: Decoration Day," with words by Harry J. Breen (Columbus: Columbus Press Post/Advance, 1903).

Domenico DeLuisi, *McAlpin March* (Cincinnati: McAlpin Store, 1906).

Effie Louise Koogle, *Col. Zoozoo's Zobo Band, A Patriotic Medley* (Lebanon: March Bros., 1906).

Nancy Bierbaum, *Zinzinnati, German Rag* (Cincinnati: N. Bierbaum, 1907).

Ian Van Wordragen, "Taft and Oherman, March Song," with words by F. A. Kaiser (Cincinnati: Groene, 1908).

Edna Furry and Bertha Kern, *Cigarettes: The Smoking Waltz* (Lancaster: Furry and Kern, 1910).

Louis Rich, *The Ideal Home Exposition March* (Cleveland: Louis Rich, 1911). Dedicated to the Hiland B. Wright Realty Co.'s Crown Pointe Subdivision.

E[d] C. Cannon, "That Red Cross Girl of Mine" (Columbus: Buckeye, 1912).

Ross C. Coffman, "Ohio, My Ohio! The Greatest Patriotic Ohio Song Ever Written," with words by Raymond Zirkel (Columbus: Rialto, 1912).[9]

E. C. Deibel, "Where the Grossvater Flows Everywhere, A Waltz Song," with words by Lee Sprankle (Akron: George J. Renner Brewing, 1915).

Louis Rich, "Chugging Along" (Cleveland: Louis Rich, 1915). To the Cleveland Automobile Show.

Roy H. Pitzen, "I'm Going Down to Chillicothe, Respectfully Dedicated to Selective Service Soldiers Located at Camp Sherman" (Toledo: Jacobs and Pitzen, 1917).

Harriet Carter, *War Song Cycle*: "The Boy's Departure," "Our Country's Flag," "The Boy's Return," "The Soldiers and Sailors Welcome Songs," with words by Jane Gibson (Cleveland: Carter and Gibson, 1918).

Jacob Dettling and Charles Roy Cox, "The U. S. A. Will Lay the Kaiser Away" (Columbus: Buckeye, 1918).

George H. Klay, "Why We Want to Lick Germany," with words by Raymond Leroy Blymyer (Lima: Klaymyer, 1918).

George Allenbaugh, "Mansfield, Ohio: The Trunk Line City, A Booster Song" (Mansfield: George Gail Allenbaugh, 1922).

George Hunt, "He's an Odd Fellow," words by the composer (Cincinnati: Circle, 1923). "Dedicated to the Sovereign Grand Lodge I. O. O. F. of Cincinnati."

Joe S. Newman and Don Knowlton (arranged by Romo Falk), "Listen to My Radio. Dedicated to Station WJAX on the occasion of CLEVELAND'S FIRST RADIO SHOW" (Cleveland: Newman-Stern, 1924).[10]

Marion Campbell, "My Hygrade Sweetie" (Cleveland: Baker-Evans Ice Cream, 1924).

Marion Campbell (arranged by H. A. Hummel), "The [Belle Vernon] Cream Top Bottle," with words by the composer (Cleveland: Telling-Belle Vernon, 1925).

H. A. Hummel, "Yes We Got, It, No Hot Dogs," with words by D. K. Coukoulas (Cleveland: D. K. Coukoulas, 1925).

Glenhall Taylor, "Dream of Love and You," with words by the composer (Cleveland: Sam Fox, 1925). "Featured by the Silver Masked Tenor [who is pictured]: Soloist with the B. F. Goodrich Silvertown Cord Orchestra."

Arthur Johnston, "Her Waltz," words by the composer (Akron: B. F. Goodrich Rubber, 1927). Sung at the "opening of [the] Goodrich Silvertown Broadcasting Program."[11]

Stanley Drewes and Clarence Berger, "Hills of Cincinnati. An Appreciation to the Dearest Spot in All the World—Cincinnati, and Particularly to the Gentle Hills which Rise around the Downtown District and upon which Are Built Those Beautiful and Magnificent Residential Suburbs for which Cincinnati Is Justly Renowned" (Cincinnati: Awanda Cincinnati Studio, 1928).[12]

Tommie Milet, "Onward Cincinnati: I'm Mighty Proud of My Home Town," with lyrics by the composer (Cincinnati: Kroger Grocery and Baking in the Interest of Greater Cincinnati, 1928).[13]

Harry Ainsworth Dawson [identified as No. 54763 at the Ohio Penitentiary], "I'm Just a Black Sheep (A Real Prisoner's Song)," with words by the composer (Chicago and New York: Joe McDaniel, 1929).[14]

Deana Eberle, "Old Depression's Knock Out" (Lakewood: Deana Eberle, 1932).

Earl Black, "I'll Meet Her By the Parking Meter" (Mansfield: Earl P. Black, 1941).

Roy Cameron, "The Jahco Victory Song," with words by the composer. (Cleveland: Jack and Heintz, 1943).[15]

Notes

1. The Pre-Urban Wilderness

1. The protracted process of subjugation and exile can be studied in any of the general histories of the state. For a succinct summation see Laura Pienkny Zakin, "The Passing of a People," *Columbus Monthly* (July 1993): 87–91. The growing number of American Indians who have settled in Ohio were described by Randall Edwards and Dean Narciso in "Returning to Their Roots: Indians Find Purpose in Ohio Homeland," *Columbus Dispatch*, November 26, 1995.

2. Christopher Gist, *Christopher Gist's Journals* (Pittsburgh, Pa.: J. R. Weldin, 1893), 46.

3. Qtd. in Emily Foster, ed., *The Ohio Frontier: An Anthology of Early Writings* (Lexington: Univ. Press of Kentucky, 1996), 14.

4. James Smith, *An Account of the Remarkable Occurrences in the Life and Travels of Col. James Smith, during his Captivity with the Indians in the Years 1755, '56, '57, '58, & '59* (Cincinnati: Robert Clarke, 1870), 18. The original was printed in Lexington, Kentucky, by John Bradford in 1799. Excerpts can be found in Foster, *The Ohio Frontier*.

5. James Smith, *An Account*, 19–20.

6. Ibid., 46.

7. John May, *Journal and Letters of Col. John May, of Boston Relative to Two Journeys to the Ohio Country in 1788 and '89* (Cincinnati: Robert Clarke, 1873), 92–95.

8. F. Cuming, *Sketches of a Tour to the Western Country, through the States of Ohio and Kentucky* (Pittsburgh, Pa.: Cramer, Spear, and Eichbaum, 1810), repr. as vol. 4 of Reuben Gold Thwaites, *Early Western Travels, 1748–1846* (Cleveland: Arthur H. Clark, 1904), 208.

9. Thwaites, *Early Western Travels*, 210.

10. Ibid., 223.

11. John Melish, *Travels through the United States of America, in the Years 1806 & 1807, and 1809, 1810, & 1811* (Philadelphia, Pa.: printed for the author, 1815; repr. 1818; New York: Johnson Reprint, 1970), 353.

12. Ibid., 360. A strathsprey is a slow Scottish dance, its name derived from the strath or valley of the river Spey. The first published collection of strathspeys dates from 1780.

13. Ibid., 466–67. Melish suggests in an extended footnote that the version of the song he encountered was taken from George Thomson's *A Selected Collection of Original Scottish Airs for the Voice*, prepared with the collaboration of Robert Burns and published in London between 1793 and 1797. He printed the poetry in full, since "the circumstance of meeting with it on the banks of lake Erie, was to me so novel and unexpected."

14. James Hall, "Letter 11: Scenery, Sciences, and Fiddling," *Letters from the West; Containing Sketches of Scenery, Manners, and Customs; and Anecdotes Connected with the First Settlements of the Western Sections of the United States* (London: Henry Colburn, 1828), 181–83.

15. Unfortunately, due to the lack of evidence our chronicle cannot include the music that was practiced by the misled French émigrés who fled premonitions of revolution to Gallipolis (i.e., "City of the Gauls") in 1790, only to discover that the Scioto Company agent had misrepresented a supposed paradise in the midst of primitive wilderness and that they actually didn't own the land they thought they had purchased. See also Reginald Horsman, "A French Village in Frontier Ohio," *Timeline* 20, no. 5 (Sept.–Oct. 2003): 18–31.

2. MARIETTA

1. Joseph Barker, *Recollections of the First Settlement of Ohio*, ed. George Jordan Blazier (Marietta: Marietta College, 1958), 6–7.

2. *The Journal of Colonel Ichabod Nye*, vol. 2 (typescript, Dawes Memorial Library of Marietta College, Marietta, Ohio, 1937), 89–90. The original can be found at the Western History Research Center of the University of Wyoming in Laramie.

3. John May, *Journal and Letters of Col. John May, of Boston Relative to Two Journeys to the Ohio Country in 1788 and '89* (Cincinnati: Robert Clarke, 1873), 87.

4. Barker, *Recollections of the First Settlement of Ohio*, 31.

5. Ibid., 61.

6. Samuel S. Forman, *Narrative of a Journey Down the Ohio and Mississippi in 1789–90* (1888; repr. New York: Arno, 1971), 27.

7. See Ray Zwick, *An Island Called Eden: An Historical Sketch of Blennerhassett Island near Parkersburg, West Virginia, 1798–1806* (Parkersburg, W.Va.: for Blennerhassett Island Historical State Park by Parkersburg Printing, 1996), for an extensive description of the original house (16–22), descriptions of the couple (24–30), and other details. Zwick is the official historian of the West Virginia State Parks system.

8. William H. Safford, *The Life of Harman Blennerhasset* (Cincinnati: Ely, Allen, and Locker, 1850), 41–43.

9. S[amuel] P[rescott] Hildreth, *Biographical and Historical Memoirs of the Early Pioneer Settlers of Ohio* (Cincinnati: H. W. Derby, 1852), 497.

10. For a facsimile of the score and more detail, see Richard D. Wetzel, *"Oh! Sing No More That Gentle Song": The Musical Life and Times of William Cumming Peters (1805–66)* (Warren, Mich.: Harmonie Park, 2000), 208–12. I have maintained the variant spellings of the family name.

11. Safford, *The Life of Harman Blennerhasset*, 44–47.

12. Hildreth, *Biographical and Historical Memoirs of the Early Pioneer Settlers of Ohio*, 503.

13. Nellie Best Speary, *Music and Life in Marietta, Ohio* (Marietta: MacDonald, 1939), 10.

14. Reuben Gold Thwaites, *Early Western Travels, 1748–1846* (Cleveland: Arthur H. Clark, 1904), 130.

15. The reconstruction has been accomplished in a meticulous manner based on the available evidence. The building is handsomely populated with period furnishings, a substantial number of the pieces original to the household, donated in many cases by area families whose forbears had taken possession of them in 1807. After a disastrous attempt at cotton farming in Mississippi, Harman Blennerhassett retreated to Canada and then to Europe, where he died. The mother and surviving children died in New York City. In 1996 their remains were disinterred and reburied in a plot just to the northwest of the house.

16. Wilson Waters, *The History of Saint Luke's Church, Marietta, Ohio* (Marietta: J. Mueller and Son, 1884), 39.

17. Ibid., 204.

18. Speary, *Music and Life in Marietta, Ohio*, 25.

19. Other evidence of music making at the college: In 1833 the trustees had purchased a melodeon for their chapel, and by 1840 the school hosted a Mozart Society.

20. Speary, *Music and Life in Marietta, Ohio*, 25.

21. Dennis P. Adams, "Journal, September 1845–November 1846, of a Trip from Marietta, Ohio, to Boston, Massachusetts, on a Sailing Vessel Built at Harmar, Ohio, and Return Overland." The original was apparently transcribed by an unknown hand at Marietta College in 1937. A carbon copy of what is identified as vol. 2 is at the Ohio Historical Society, VFM 3. The bibliographic record states that vols. 3–5 are missing, leaving the incongruity that vol. 2 begins with a September 3, 1845, entry.

22. Ibid.

3. CINCINNATI

1. Charles Theodore Greve, *Centennial History of Cincinnati and Representative Citizens*, vol. 1 (Chicago: Biographical, 1904), 209–20.

2. Qtd. in F. E. Tunison, in *Presto! From the Singing School to the May Musical Festival* (Cincinnati: Criterion, 1888), 4.

3. Qtd. in Greve, *Centennial History of Cincinnati and Representative Citizens*, 410.

4. Leonie C. Frank, *Musical Life in Early Cincinnati and the Origin of the May Festival* (Cincinnati: Ruter, 1932), 4; Charles Frederic Goss, *Cincinnati: The Queen City, 1788–1912*, vol. 1 (Chicago: S. J. Clarke, 1912), 82.

5. Greve, *Centennial History of Cincinnati and Representative Citizens*, 365.

6. H. A. Ratterman, *Early Music in Cincinnati: An Essay Read before the Literary Club, November 9, 1879* (Cincinnati: s.n., 1879), 2. This eight-page pamphlet can be found in the collections of both the Public Library of Cincinnati and Hamilton County and the Ohio Historical Society.

7. Harry R. Stevens, "Adventure in Refinement: Early Concert Life in Cincinnati. 1810–1826," *Bulletin of the Historical and Philosophical Society of Ohio* 5, no. 3 (Sept. 1947): 8–9.

8. Don Heinrich Tolzmann, ed., *The First Mayor of Cincinnati: George A. Katzenberger's Biography of Major David Ziegler* (Lanham, Md.: Univ. Press of America, 1990), 44.

9. Stevens, "Adventure in Refinement," 9–10.

10. Ibid., 10.

11. Tunison, *Presto!* 11.

12. Stevens, "Adventure in Refinement," 12–13.

13. Walter Sutton, "Cincinnati As a General Publishing Center: The Middle Years, 1830–1860," *Historical and Philosophical Society of Ohio Bulletin* 16 (1958): 311.

14. Stevens, "The Haydn Society of Cincinnati, 1819–1824," *Ohio State Archeological and Historical Quarterly* 52, no. 3 (Apr.–June 1943): 104. Meinecke was supposedly from Baltimore. [John] Husband was from Lancaster, Pennsylvania.

15. Greve, *Centennial History of Cincinnati and Representative Citizens*, 917.

16. Stevens, "The Haydn Society," 104–5.

17. Ibid., 107.

18. Ibid., 108.

19. Ibid., 112.

20. Stevens, "Adventure in Refinement," 20, 22.

21. Stevens, "The Haydn Society," 115.

22. Stevens, "Adventure in Refinement," 24.

23. Tunison, *Presto!* 21.

24. Stevens, "Adventure in Refinement," 26.

25. Tunison, *Presto!* 20.

26. Ophia D. Smith, "Joseph Tosso, the Arkansaw Traveler," *Ohio Archeological and Historical Quarterly* 56 (Jan. 1947): 16–45.

27. According to B[enjamin] Drake and E. D. Mansfield in their *Cincinnati in 1826* (Cincinnati: Morgan, Lodge, and Fisher, 1827), 30, the theater was situated on Columbia between Main and Sycamore. It had been built in 1819 but at the time of their writing had recently been sold and was being remodeled to seat eight hundred, with "a pit, two tiers of boxes, and a spacious gallery, with commodious lobbies, punch room &c."

28. *Cincinnati Gazette*, September 27, 1830.

29. According to Charles Cist, *Cincinnati in 1841: Its Early Annals and Future Prospects* (Cincinnati: published for the author, 1841), this society had been organized on April 29, 1835, had gone into suspension, "but has recently been revived, and promises much for the cultivation of musical taste and science in our city." One of its original goals had been the establishment of a musical academy, another "the relief of distressed musicians, and, in case of death, of their widows; and providing for their orphan children['s] education and employment."

30. *Cincinnati Gazette*, January 27, 1840.

31. Charles Cist, *Sketches and Statistics of Cincinnati in 1859* (Cincinnati: published for the author, 1859), 179.

32. Charles B. Wyrick, *Concert and Criticism in Cincinnati, 1840–50* (master's thesis presented to the College-Conservatory of Music of the University of Cincinnati, 1965). Wyrick analyzes Tosso's "classical" repertory on pages 49–52.

33. Printed in its entirety in Smith, "Joseph Tosso, the Arkansaw Traveler," 44–45.

34. Ibid., 16–17.

35. From a reprint of the 5th edition of Francis Trollope, *Domestic Manners of the Americans* (London: George Routledge and Sons, 1839), 41.

36. Ibid., 36–37.

37. Ibid., 59–60.

38. Tunison, *Presto!* 22. One definition of allopathy: The treatment of disease by remedies that produce effects different from or opposite to those produced by the disease.

39. Harriet Martineau, *Retrospect of Western Travel* (London: Saunders and Otley, 1838). Cincinnati furnished a single chapter in the three volumes detailing a journey that took her from New England to New Orleans. For a generously illustrated study of the two women, see Lenora Hobbs's "Sizing Up the Queen City: Frances Trollope and Harriet Martineau," *Timeline* 21, no. 3 (May–June 2004): 14–27.

40. Martineau, *Retrospect of Western Travel*, 249–50.

41. August Jean-Jacques Hervieu is recalled by historians mainly for his painting of *General Lafayette's Landing and Reception at Cincinnati*, a work that has disappeared but supposedly contained copious depictions of prominent local citizens, whether or not they were actually present at the ceremony in May 1825.

42. Smith, "Joseph Tosso, the Arkansaw Traveler," 25.

43. Trollope, *Domestic Manners of the Americans*, 73–74, 76.

44. Mrs. Trollope considered it "excellent; a little wild and romantic, but containing scenes of first-rate interest and pathos" (147).

45. The most recent, accessible and objective of these is James K. Folsom, *Timothy Flint* (New York: Twayne, 1965).

46. *Cincinnati Daily Gazette*, April 16, 1834. Qtd. in Charles Gary, "A History of Music Education in the Cincinnati Public Schools" (Ph.D. diss., University of Cincinnati, 1951), 9. For more information on Mason and his career, see Christina Chenevert Mennel, "Change in Early Cincinnati's Musical Identity: Shape-Note Tunebooks from Timothy Flint's *Columbian Harmonist* (1816) to Timothy and Lowell Mason's *Sacred Harp* (1834)" (Ph.D. diss., Ohio State University, 1997), 48–66.

47. Charles Cist, *Cincinnati in 1841* (Cincinnati: published for the author, 1841), 136.

48. In 1839 Nixon published *A Guide to Instruction on the Piano-Forte; Designed for Use of Both Parents and Pupils: In a Series of [Twenty] Short Essays, Dedicated to the Young Ladies of the Musical Seminary*. The Public Library of Cincinnati and Hamilton County also owns *A Compendium of the Theory of Musicke as Taught in the Musical Seminary of Mr. and Mrs. Nixon, and Miss Nixon*, a manuscript notebook belonging to Sibella Winston, dated 1839. It contains scales, chords and their inversions, a series of waltzes, a "Quick March," "Miss Winston's Favorite Gallopade," a poetic epilogue, and fragments of a "Newport Polka." By the summer of 1835 Nixon was also selling pianos, advertising that "[t]he stock of Eastern Piano Fortes, at the Saloon, and Musical Seminary, has again been completed by an arrival from Portsmouth." The assortment included "horizontal, plain, square, and the elegant tablet, with grand action, harp pedal, & c." Used pianos from the seminary were offered on "reduced terms."

49. Robert C. Vitz, *The Queen and the Arts: Cultural Life in Nineteenth-Century Cincinnati* (Kent: Kent State Univ. Press, 1989), 14.

50. *Chronicle*, January 18, 1840, qtd. in Wyrick, *Concert and Criticism in Cincinnati*, 10.

51. Noted in Mennel, "Change in Early Cincinnati's Musical Identity," 340–41.

52. *Chronicle*, November 16, 1842, qtd. in Wyrick, *Concert and Criticism in Cincinnati*, 10–11.

53. Tunison, *Presto!* 35.

54. Lowell Mason Jr. was listed in the city directory in both 1843 and 1846 and then as "Professor of Music" in 1860, although we know nothing about him or any professional relationship to his uncle.

55. Wyrick, *Concert and Criticism in Cincinnati,* 67–68.

56. For the known details, see ibid., 12–15.

57. *Chronicle,* May 2, 1842.

58. Greve offers the full menu of the December 22, 1843, venture in *Centennial History of Cincinnati and Representative Citizens,* 920. See also Tunison, *Presto!* 31–32.

59. Tunison, *Presto!* 32.

60. Greve, *Centennial History of Cincinnati and Representative Citizens,* 921.

61. Cist, *Sketches and Statistics of Cincinnati in 1859,* 176–77.

62. Greve, *Centennial History of Cincinnati and Representative Citizens,* 921.

63. Tunison, *Presto!* 43.

64. Ophia D. Smith, *The Life and Times of Giles Richards (1820–1860)* (Columbus: Ohio State Archaeological and Historical Society, 1936), 90. Chapter 6, "Social Life in Cincinnati, 1838–1848," consists of letters written to and by Elizabeth Richards, which periodically offer revealing reflections on music making of the period. For example, one from Martha Holmes dated November 19, 1842, speaks of a party at which "Mr Tosso was engaged to play" (94). One from Mary Hinman written on November 8 of that same year speaks of another party at which, "Old Davy fiddled, and sang two songs, the worst of it was though that we did not know whether he was singing or tuning his violin. Poor Mary Conclin in the first of the evening sat down to the piano to sing, and you know she is always very timid about singing, and her voice trembled very much; when she had sung about a verse and a half Old Davy struck up a delightfully provoking accompaniment on his old violin that set every one to laughing" (92–93). Hapless Mary Conclin then wrote on August 17, 1845, about a concert in Dayton given by twin sisters, one of whom "played on the 'base viol' and the other on the 'violin[,]' quite a novel sight, and the only thing at all passable about them, they sang songs without sentiment, anything but ennobling in their tenor though not decidedly disgusting, but still, the idea of two great girls going before a crowd of people and singing 'Dan Tucker' and the like, appeared to me, to speak for itself, as to the refinement and general character of them, and as for the man who accompanied them, he was insupportable, sickening beyond everything. The 'elite' of Dayton were there; in so small a city it is difficult to discriminate, and there not being any too much musical talent in it; they will be like to be taken in, for some time yet" (106).

65. See Wyrick, *Concert and Criticism,* 117–27.

4. CLEVELAND

1. See Douglas Reece Breitmayer, "Seventy-Five Years of Sacred Music in Cleveland, Ohio, 1800–1875" (master's thesis, Union Theological Seminary, 1951); F. Karl Grossman, *A History of Music in Cleveland* (Cleveland: Case Western Reserve University, 1972); Francis Hawthorne Grant, "The Emergence of Cultural Patterns in a Great American City: Cleveland," *Fine Arts* 19, no. 893 (July 26, 1971): 2, 4–5, 13; no. 895 (Aug. 2, 1971): 3–5, 16–17; no. 900 (Sept. 6, 1971): 4–5, 7, 11–13; no. 901 (Sept. 13, 1971): 6–7, 10–13; no. 909 (Nov. 8, 1971): 4–8; and J. Heywood Alexander, *It Must Be Heard: A Survey of the Musical Life of Cleveland, 1836–1918* (Cleveland: Western Reserve Historical Society, 1981).

2. Much qtd., for example, in Grant, "The Emergence of Cultural Patterns," *Fine Arts* 19, no. 893 (July 19, 1971): 3.

3. See John J. Horton, *The Jonathan Hale Farm: A Chronicle of the Cuyahoga Valley* (Cleveland: Western Reserve Historical Society, 1990). Observations about Hale as a musician occur on pages 48–49, 125–130, and 175.

4. Qtd. in Grant, "The Emergence of Cultural Patterns," *Fine Arts* 19, no. 893 (July 19, 1971): 3.

5. Grant, "The Emergence of Cultural Patterns," *Fine Arts* 19, no. 894 (July 26, 1971): 4.

6. The program was published in the *Daily Advertiser*, June 27, 1837. Qtd. in Alexander, *It Must Be Heard*, 5–6.

7. Programs of the period, especially when available only via newspaper announcements, are maddening in their elusiveness, and often laden with errors. In this instance, we should probably presume that one of the composers was James Kent (1700–76), organist of Trinity College, Cambridge, and then of Winchester Cathedral, who issued two volumes of *Kent's Anthems*. Webb must have been Samuel Webbe (1740–1816), recalled today mostly for his mastery of the glee, but also the writer of a substantial corpus of sacred music.

8. See Grant, "The Emergence of Cultural Patterns," *Fine Arts* 19, no. 909 (Nov. 8, 1971): 7.

9. Breitmayer, *Seventy-Five Years of Sacred Music*, 27; Grant, *Fine Arts* 19, no. 894 (July 26, 1971): 11, 13; and Alexander, *It Must Be Heard*, 10, all printed the modest instrument's disposition.

10. *Herald and Gazette*, January 15, 1839.

11. Balthasar fathered Orlando V. Schubert, one of the city's first native-born visual artists. An amateur musician, he studied painting in Europe and then returned home, where he became a charter member of the Brush and Palette Club. Recalled today mainly for his *The Battle of Lake Erie*, he died in 1927. For more detail (and extended comment on the history and state of the arts in Cleveland), see Steven Litt, "A Longtime Love Affair with Culture," *Plain Dealer*, December 31, 1995.

12. Breitmayer printed the programs and response to them in *Seventy-Five Years of Sacred Music*, 40–43.

13. Qtd. in Alexander, *It Must Be Heard*, 6.

14. Qtd. in Grant, "The Emergence of Cultural Patterns," *Fine Arts* 19, no. 895 (Aug. 2, 1971): 3–4.

15. *Cleveland Herald*, July 1, 1842.

16. This an event of 1853 noticed by Grant in "The Emergence of Cultural Patterns," *Fine Arts* 19, no. 895 (Aug. 2, 1971): 5.

17. Noted in Holly Rarick Witchey, with John Vacha, *Fine Arts in Cleveland: An Illustrated History* (Bloomington: Indiana Univ. Press, 1994), 13. The entire piece, "Little Patti," can be found in *The Complete Works of Artemus Ward* (London: Chatto and Windus, 1922), 90–92. The humor inherent in the tale of Ward's visit to Oberlin (59–61), where he has gone to exhibit his "wax works and beests of Pray," during which "Perfesser Finney" is bitten by a kangaroo, is much mitigated by the ugly racism expressed in the piece, whether intended as satire or not. The least offensive bit: "It is a very good college, too, & a grate many wurthy yung men go there annooally to git intelleck into 'em. But its my onbiassed 'pinion that they go it rather too strong on Ethiopians at Oberlin."

18. See Francis Hawthorne Grant, "Foundations of Music Education in the Cleveland Public Schools" (Ph.D. diss., Western Reserve University, 1963), 340–45.

1. See J. F. Everhart, *History of Muskingum County, Ohio, with Illustrations and Biographical Sketches of Prominent Men and Pioneers* ([Columbus]: J. F. Everhart, 1882), 246–50; J. Hope Sutor, *Past and Present of the City of Zanesville and Muskingum County, Ohio; Together with Biographical Sketches of Many of Its Leading and Prominent Citizens and Illustrious Dead* (Chicago: S. J. Clarke, 1905); Thomas W. Lewis, *Zanesville and Muskingum County, Ohio* (Chicago: S. J. Clarke, 1927); Norris F. Schneider, *Y Bridge City: The Story of Zanesville and Muskingum County, Ohio* (Cleveland: World, 1950); plus a small host of articles by Schneider from several Zanesville newspapers that appeared between 1940 and 1975 and have been collected in scrapbook form at the Muskingum County Library.

2. For more detail see Schneider and Clair C. Stebbins, *Zanes' Trace* (Zanesville: Mathes, 1973). Stephen Ostrander, "Tracing Zane," *Ohio* (April 1996): 34–42, 90–91, explores present-day remnants of Zane's Trace.

3. This fluvial intersection was later spanned with the famed "Y Bridge," with its midstream intersection and two wings reaching the west bank of the Muskingum just above and below the mouth of the Licking.

4. Rhea Mansfield Knittle: "Early Ohio Taverns," (Ashland: published for the author, 1937), 18. The booklet was reissued in the Ohio Frontier Series, no. 1, 1976.

5. Everhart, *History of Muskingum County*, 247.

6. Schneider, "Zanesville's Music," *Zanesville Times Signal*, January 9, 1955.

7. Bauer (1830–1912) was apparently a protégé of Atwood. In addition to the Bauer Band, which he led until his retirement in 1910, he prospered as a grocer, and was named director of the Muskingum Cornet Band in 1871.

8. Everhart, *History of Muskingum County*, 247.

9. Ibid., 248.

10. Schneider, "Zanesville's Music," *Zanesville Times Signal*, January 16, 1955.

11. Lewis, *Zanesville and Muskingum County*, 239. Frank P. Bailey, the druggist son of the builder, is quoted as believing the organ dated from 1835 or even 1838.

12. Everhart, *History of Muskingum County*, 248.

13. Schneider, "Zanesville's Music," *Zanesville Times Signal*, January 23, 1955.

14. Everhart, *History of Muskingum County*, 248. Apparently in Zanesville at this time the venerable practice of placing the tune in the tenor part was still viewed as *au courant*, although in the outside world it had migrated to the sopranos in the fashionable idiom of Lowell Mason and his colleagues.

15. Schneider, "Zanesville's Music," *Zanesville Times Signal*, January 9, 1955.

16. Schneider, "Zanesville Heard First Important Musicians From 1850 to 1860," *Zanesville News*, March 14, 1943.

17. Schneider, "Zanesville's Music," *Zanesville Times Signal*, January 16, 1955.

18. Ibid.

19. Everhart, *History of Muskingum County*, 249.

20. The saga is described in Lewis, *Zanesville*, 257–62. Some local boosters claimed that Ross was the first in the country to capitalize on Daguerre's process, discovered in 1829 and described in print for the first time only in August 1839. A translation was soon printed in the New York papers, and Ross undertook his experiment in November of that year.

21. Ibid., 264.

22. Ibid., 266.

6. The Singing School

1. Timothy Flint, *Recollections of the Last Ten Years Passed in Occasional Residences and Journeyings in the Valley of the Mississippi* (Boston, Mass.: Cummings, Hilliard, and Co., 1826; repr. New York and London: Johnson Reprint, 1968), 44.

2. A facsimile of the 5th edition, with a preface by Irving Lowens, was issued in Philadelphia, Pa., in 1954 by Albert Saifer for Harry Dichter's *Musical Americana*.

3. Thomas Symmes, *The Reasonableness of Regular Singing; or, Singing by Note* (Boston, Mass.: B. Green, 1720), 20.

4. Qtd. in Henry Wilder Foote, *Three Centuries of American Hymnody* (Cambridge, Mass.: Harvard Univ. Press, 1940), 100.

5. See Irving Lowens, *Music and Musicians in Early America* (New York: Norton, 1964).

6. See Edward C. Wolf, "The Convivial Side of Scottish Psalm Tunes," *American Music* 14, no. 2 (Summer 1996): 141–60, a study of several similar handwritten tunebooks from southeastern Pennsylvania. For more on Johnston and his publications, see Allen Britton, Irving Lowens, and Richard Crawford, *American Sacred Music Imprints 1698–1810: A Bibliography* (Worcester, Mass.: American Antiquarian Society, 1990), 374–79.

7. See Lloyd C. Savage, "A Bicentennial Celebration from the Music Archives!" Ross County Historical Society, *First Capitol Chronicle* 1, no. 1 (Dec. 1990): 3–9.

8. William Cooper Howells, *Recollections of Life in Ohio, from 1813 to 1840* (Cincinnati: Robert Clarke, 1895), 143–44. The volume contains an introduction by the author's son, the illustrious Ohio-born novelist, essayist, critic, and journalist William Dean Howells (1837–1920).

9. Frank W. Grayson, in the second of a series of colorful articles about "Singing in Cincinnati," published in the *Times Star* between January 6 and March 5, 1937, indulged on January 9 in a memorable, albeit fanciful description of these frontier singing masters:

> The singing master was a man of more educational endowment than the homespun folk to whom he had ventured far to teach the marvels of song. His "book l'arning" transcended the limitations imposed by the simple "Three R's" and he was a person of charm and polish. As the singing master, he was on an equal footing with the heroic circuit rider or the itinerant herb doctor in sharing the plain but wholesome hospitality extended by the settlers. No cabin door, no matter how humble or isolated, was shut against him. Its latchstring was always out for him to pull.
>
> A master woodcraftsman, he traversed afoot the dimly-lit corridors of the wilderness from settlement to settlement, many miles apart, with a knapsack filled with singing books slung over his shoulders and with his trusty flintlock constantly in his hand.
>
> He slept under the stars when night overtook him on his lonely and precarious pilgrimages and in a hundred ways he absorbed the wood-sense of the Indian and improved upon that knowledge tenfold. He was attired in homespun of a dingy gray. He wore his hair long, and the hirsute arrangement was emphasized by the coonskin cap with the tail intact which he favored as headgear. On his feet were square-toed

shoes with huge iron buckles at the instep. Perhaps he would wear a buckskin shirt, tastily embroidered, if his purse was sufficiently plethoric to permit its acquisition.

On tour he was not a prepossessing individual at best, but before entering a settlement he would make his simple toilet and be spick and span. He was industrious, energetic and filled with guile. His propaganda was simple and understandable and it carried an undeviating appeal to the plain folk of the woods.

In less time than it takes to tell it he was domiciled in some friendly home and was succeeding in interesting the community in singing at so much a lesson. As the scene of his operations in preaching the gospel of music, he would select the crude schoolhouse, if any. Usually these schools were held on Monday nights and it was not long before a passion for singing was born in the rough environment.

While much of the series hews more closely to fact, this sportswriter-turned-music historian signed off his final column with the admission that "we are compelled by the approach of spring to turn from song to baseball which, we must frankly confess, is much more suitable to this kind of cluck."

10. J. Merton England, ed., *Buckeye Schoolmaster: A Chronicle of Midwestern Rural Life, 1853–1865* (Bowling Green: Bowling Green State Univ. Popular Press, 1996), 79.

11. Ibid., 182

12. Ibid., 198

13. Ibid., 196, 227, 230

14. See David Warren Steel's edition of *Stephen Jenks: Collected Works*, Recent Researches in American Music Series, vol. 18 (Madison, Wis.: A-R Editions, 1995). One other implicit Buckeye connection: *The Harmony of Zion* (1818) contains a tune titled "Ohio."

15. See James William Scholten, "The Chapins: A Study of Men and Sacred Music West of the Alleghenies, 1795–1842" (Ph.D. diss., University of Michigan, 1972).

16. See John Lawrence Brasher's introduction to his facsimile edition of *Warren's Minstrel* (Athens: Ohio Univ. Press, 1984).

17. See Terry E. Miller, "Alexander Auld and American Shape-Note Music" (master's thesis, Indiana University, 1971); also Miller, "Alexander Auld 1816–1898: Early Ohio Musician," *Bulletin of the Cincinnati Historical Society* 33 (1975): 244–60.

18. Part 3 contained a selection of "Choice Temperance Songs." Temperance societies found many apt subjects of concern in Ohio; Auld, probably a teetotaler, sympathized with their goals. The sentiment of these songs might be inferred from a couple of titles: "Oh! Father, Leave Me Not" and "The Drunkard Lamenting His Wife." The later collections contained similar material. For example, the title page of *The Farmers' and Mechanics' Minstrel* promised "a few Appropriate Moral Songs, for the use of Temperance Societies, Schools, Academies, Orchestras, etc."

19. Seth Ely (1790–1857) figures so prominently in Auld's collections that it might be tempting to infer that he was an Ohioan, especially since Ely's single collection, *Sacred Music*, had been published in Cincinnati in 1822 (a second collection was planned, but its manuscript was destroyed when a Cincinnati printing house burned in 1836), and many of its tunes bear Ohio place names: "Cadiz," "Cambridge," "Columbus," "Dayton," "Mansfield," "Portsmouth," "Steubenville," "Urbanna," and "Zanesville." However, Ely had been born in Connecticut and later made his home in Germantown, Pennsylvania. He circulated widely as an

itinerant singing master and must somehow have known Auld, since the latter published 116 of Ely's works (18 in the 1852 edition of *The Ohio Harmonist*, 3d ed. [Columbus: J. H. Riley, 1852], many defined by dates of composition ranging from 1828 to 1843, and 98 more in *The Key of the West*). A cordial relationship between the two is perhaps reflected in Auld's printing in its entirety an anthem that Ely had presented only in part in his own collection. On page 177 of *The Ohio Harmonist*, Auld claimed that, "the public will be pleased to find several pieces in this book from the pen of this eminent writer, who is superior to any other writer of music in the *United States*."

20. Auld, "Advertisement," *The Ohio Harmonist* (Washington: A. Auld and Joshua Martin, 1847), 3. Auld's, however, was only one of many seven-shape systems to appear during the nineteenth century, and had been preceded by Jesse B. Aiken's approach, first employed in his *Christian Minstrel*, published in Philadelphia in 1846. Auld's notice in *The Ohio Harmonist* that, "all persons are hereby warned not to use the Notes *Doe, Ray*, and *See*, without my permission," surely betrays his ignorance of Aiken's publication. Aiken's system proved predominant (the volume was also printed in Cincinnati and went through 171 editions by 1873) and forced the others, including Auld's, into obscurity. Among those who appropriated the Aiken system was Amos Sutton Hayden (1813–80). Hayden was a Disciples minister who from 1850 until 1856 served as the first principal of the Western Reserve Eclectic Institute, which in 1867 became Hiram College. His *The Sacred Melodeon* was first issued by Oliver Ditson in Boston in 1849 with a preface dated November 1848 from Euclid. It contained "a great variety of the most approved church music, selected chiefly from the old standard authors, with many original compositions [none apparently by Hayden] on a new system of notation, designed for the use of churches, singing societies and academies," and was popular enough that it was issued by Moore, Wilstach, Keys, and Company in Cincinnati in 1856 and again the following year. Part 2 of *The Ohio Harmonist* was presented in the traditional four-shape system (and Auld acknowledged its existence in his Rudiments section), perhaps to increase the volume's appeal or to convince its readers of the superiority of his system. For examples of other seven-shape systems, see W. Thomas Marrocco, "The Notation in American Sacred Music Collections," *Acta Musicologica* 36 (1964): 136–42. For an exhaustive study of the whole tradition, see Earl Oliver Loessel, "The Use of Character Notes and Other Unorthodox Notations in Teaching the Reading of Music in Northern United States During the Nineteenth Century" (Ph.D. diss., University of Michigan, 1959).

21. Auld, *The Ohio Harmonist: Enlarged and Revised* (Pittsburgh, Pa.: W. S. Haven, 1850), 235.

22. Auld, *The Key of the West or, The Ohio Collection of Sacred Music* (Columbus: J. H. Riley, 1856), 361.

23. Henry Howe, *Historical Collections of Ohio*, vol. 1, Ohio Centennial Edition (Norwalk: Laning, 1896), 297.

24. Details from Rebecca R. Ogden, "Glory Light Shines for Me: The Black Tradition of Shape Note Singing in Ohio" (photocopy, School of Music, Ohio State University, 1991).

25. James D. Vaughan (1864–1941) created a firm based in Lawrenceburg, Tennessee, which issued 105 collections between 1900 and 1964 as well as a series of four instructional manuals, initiated with B[enjamin] C. Unseld, *Unseld's Popular Rudiments of Music* in 1912. Unseld served as chief editor from 1913 until 1923 and was succeeded by Pace, his assistant, who occupied the position until 1959. The company kept no figures after November 1, 1940, but estimated that total sales of their fifty-two available collections had then reached 6.1 million. See Jo Lee Fleming,

"James D. Vaughan, Music Publisher, Lawrenceburg, Tennessee, 1912–1964" (Ph.D. diss., Union Theological Seminary, 1972).

26. Ogden, "Glory Light Shines for Me," 4.

27. My knowledge of the recent state of the tradition was derived from an Aug. 1999 conversation with Boyd Holliman, a semiretired Columbus barber who leads the Christian Joyful Singers. Brother Boyd succeeded his father, Prince Holliman, born in Georgia in 1898, who migrated to Columbus early in the 1920s. From that legacy arose an extended link to comparable groups in Rome, Georgia, with gatherings held in alternate years in Rome and Columbus.

28. Thomas Harrison, *Music Simplified: or A New System of Music, Founded on Natural Principles; Designed Either for Separate Use, or as an Introduction to the Old System, and Intended Chiefly for Educational and Religious Purposes: To Which Is Added a Collection of Christian Melodies* (Springfield: printed at the office of "The Republic," 1839), iii, Ohio Historical Society: 781.24/H248m.

29. Harrison, *The Juvenile Numeral Singer* (Cincinnati: published for the author, 1852), no pagination.

30. Harrison, *Music Simplified*, iv.

31. Ibid., 19. For further explication, see Thomas J. Elward, "Thomas Harrison's Patented Numeral Notation System," *Journal of Research in Music Education* 28, no. 4 (Winter 1980): 218–24.

32. Although seen and studied at the Ohio Historical Society, the broadside cannot presently be located.

33. Qtd. in Charles Hamm in "Patent Notes in Cincinnati," *Historical and Philosophical Society of Ohio Bulletin* 16 (1958): 293–310. See in the biography in Appendix A that Harrison at some point served on the staff of *The Advocate*.

34. Harrison, *Music Simplified*.

35. Augustus Dameron Fillmore, *The Universal Musician*, 12th ed. (Cincinnati: Applegete, 1859), 3–4.

36. Timothy Flint, *The Columbian Harmonist: In Two Parts. To Which Is Prefixed a Dissertation upon the True Taste in Church Music* (Cincinnati: Coleman and Phillips, 1816), iii.

37. Ibid., x–xi.

38. Ibid., xii.

39. Ibid., iii–iv.

40. Qtd. in George Pullen Jackson, *White Spirituals in the Southern Uplands* (Chapel Hill: Univ. of North Carolina Press, 1933), 19–20.

41. Lowell Mason and Timothy B. Mason, *The Sacred Harp, or Eclectic Harmony*, new ed. (Cincinnati: Triuman and Smith, 1843), 4.

42. Ibid., 2.

43. Timothy B. Mason, "Elements of Vocal Music," *The Sacred Harp, or Beauties of Church Music*, new ed., vol. 2 (Boston, Mass.: Kidder and Wright, 1845), 1.

44. J. J. Fast, *The Cantica Sacra; A Collection of Church Music, Embracing, Besides Some New Pieces, a Choice Selection of German and English Chorals, Set Pieces, Chants, etc.* (Hudson: Hudson Book, 1854), 6.

45. Ibid., 5.

46. Ibid., 6.

1. Arthur Lowndes Rich, *Lowell Mason. "The Father of Singing Among the Children"* (Chapel Hill: Univ. of North Carolina Press, 1946); or Carol A. Pemberton, *Lowell Mason: His Life and Work* (Ann Arbor, Mich.: UMI, 1985).

2. Qtd. in Rich, *Lowell Mason*, 18.

3. See Michael L. Mark and Charles L. Gary, *History of American Music Education* (New York: Schirmer, 1992). See also the seminal and now dated volume by Edward Bailey Birge (1868–1952), *History of Public School Music in the United States* (Boston, Mass.: Oliver Ditson, 1928; rev. 1937; repr. 1966).

4. Gary, "A History of Music Education in the Cincinnati Public Schools" (Ph.D. diss., University of Cincinnati, 1951).

5. "Eclectic Academy of Music in Cincinnati," *American Annals of Education and Instruction for the Year 1834*, vol. 4 (Boston, Mass.: Ticknor, 1834), 289.

6. For more about the seminary, including its inception in 1829 and its momentary intersection with Oberlin College, see Donald L. Huber, "The Rise and Fall of Lane Seminary: An Antislavery Episode," *Timeline* 12, no. 3 (May–June 1995): 2–19.

7. Nathaniel D. Gould, *History of Church Music in America* (Boston, Mass.: Gould and Lincoln, 1853), 139–40.

8. Qtd in Gary, "A History of Music Education in the Cincinnati Public Schools," 12.

9. Stowe had married Harriet Beecher, daughter of the preacher and eventual author of *Uncle Tom's Cabin*. While the Harriet Beecher Stowe House in Ohio has become a museum devoted to the Beecher family and the abolitionist movement, Stowe accepted an appointment at Bowdoin College in Brunswick, Maine, in 1850, so that while Mrs. Stowe obviously had ample opportunity to observe the nature of and passengers on the Underground Railroad during her years in Cincinnati, she left before the volume was written. It was issued in serial form in *The National Era* beginning in June 1851 and in book form the following March.

10. C. E. Stowe, "Report on the Course of Instruction in the Common Schools of Prussia and Wirtemberg," *Western Academician and Journal of Education and Science* (Cincinnati: James R. Allbach, 1837–38), 689.

11. See Charles G. Miller, "The Background of Calvin E. Stowe's 'Report on Elementary Instruction in Europe' (1837)," *Ohio State Archeological and Historical Quarterly* 49 (Jan.–Mar. 1940): 185–90.

12. Paul D. Sanders, "Caleb Atwater's Contribution to Music Education in Ohio," *Contributions to Music Education* 24, no. 2 (Dec. 1997).

13. On page 292 Atwater described the Institute as "the most popular and useful institution in the western country, if not, in the Union, and which has already accomplished wonders in the advancement of the cause of general education in the West."

14. Caleb Atwater, *An Essay on Education* (Cincinnati: Kendall and Henry, 1841), 60.

15. Ibid., 22.

16. Ibid., 22–23.

17. Ibid., 23.

18. Ibid., 22.

19. Ibid., 20–21.

20. Timothy Mason and Charles Beecher, "Report on Vocal Music, as a Branch of Common School Education," *Western Academician and Journal of Education and Science* 1, no. 11 (1837–38): 631–50. The presentation was edited by John W. Picket and published in Cincinnati. "Report on Vocal Music" was also printed in *Common School Advocate* 2, no. 8 (1838): 89–95. Paul D. Sanders wrote a study of the nine music-related articles that appeared in this journal, published in Cincinnati between 1837 and 1841, in a paper, "The *Common School Advocate* (1837–41): Propaganda Sheet for Music Education in Ohio," *Bulletin of Historical Research in Music Education* 28, no. 3 (May 1997): 173–87.

21. Mason and Beecher, "Report on Vocal Music," 635.

22. Ibid., 637.

23. Ibid., 640.

24. Ibid., 642.

25. Ibid., 643.

26. Ibid.

27. Ibid., 644.

28. Ibid., 649

29. Ibid., 648.

30. Qtd. in Gary, "A History of Music Education in the Cincinnati Public Schools," 17.

31. *Cincinnati Daily Gazette*, October 3, 1838.

32. *Fifteenth Annual Report of the Trustees and Visitors of Common Schools for the School Year Ending June 30, 1844* (Cincinnati: Daily Gazette, 1844), 10. Qtd. in Gary, "A History of Music Education in the Cincinnati Public Schools," 19.

33. "Report of the Committee on Music to the Board of Trustees and Visitors of Common Schools," found in "Minutes of the Board of Trustees and Visitors of Common Schools, Cincinnati, June 3, 1844." Qtd. in Gary, "A History of Music Education in the Cincinnati Public Schools," 39.

34. Gary, "A History of Music Education in the Cincinnati Public Schools," 104. Appendix A contains the prescribed course of study of 1858 (281–82), 1862 (282–83), and 1887 (283–84), as well as examination questions from 1861 (285–86), 1872 (286), 1873 (287–89), and 1874 (290–91).

35. Ibid. Gary summarizes the literature sung by school children in the May Festivals between 1873 and 1950 in Table 1, 221–24.

36. Walter H. Aiken, "Music in the Cincinnati Schools," *Journal of the Proceedings of the Annual Meeting of the Music Supervisor's National Conference* (Apr. 7–11, 1924): 52.

37. Noble K. Royse, *Charles Aiken: An Address Delivered in Music Hall, Cincinnati, November 15, 1884, at the Unveiling of the Aiken Memorial* (Cincinnati: Robert Clarke, 1885), 13.

38. As evidence, see Constantine F. Soriano, "Cincinnati Music Readers" (master's thesis, College-Conservatory of Music of Cincinnati, 1957). She quotes critic Henry Krehbiel's laudatory description of the Philadelphia display, complete with copious examples (pages 77–79) and three appendixes that present questions employed in 1861, 1868, 1872, and beyond (154–66).

39. Common Schools of Cincinnati, *Forty-Third Annual Report for the School Year Ending June 30, 1872* (Cincinnati: Wilstach, Baldwin, and Co., 1873), 101. Qtd. in Gary, "A History of Music Education in the Cincinnati Public Schools," 53.

40. Common Schools of Cincinnati, *Forty-Fourth Annual Report for the School Year Ending June 30, 1873* (Cincinnati: Wilstach, Baldwin, and Co., 1874), 61. Qtd. in Gary, "A History of Music Education in the Cincinnati Public Schools," 53.

41. Luther Whiting Mason, D. H. Baldwin, Elisha Locke, and Charles Aiken, *The Young Singer: A Collection of Juvenile Music, Compiled (at the Request of the Board of Trustees) for the Cincinnati Public Schools, by Messrs. Mason, Baldwin, Locke and Aiken, Teachers of Music in Those Schools* (Cincinnati: Sargent, Wilson, and Hinkle, 1860), 7.

42. Charles Aiken, Alfred Squire, J. P. Powell, and Victor Williams, *The Young Singer's Manual* (Cincinnati: Van Antwerp, Bragg, 1866), 3.

43. Probably included among these accomplishments is Aiken's appointment in 1874 as the first music instructor at Cincinnati's segregated Colored Schools, a fact noted in Soriano's "Cincinnati Music Readers," 24.

44. Vermont-born Hiram Powers (1805–73) had moved to Cincinnati in 1822 and served for six years as assistant to organ builder Luman Watson. Apparently he became interested in sculpting during that period and initiated a new career by creating figures from Dante's *Inferno* for a Cincinnati wax museum. With Nicolas Longworth as his patron, Powers spent several years in Washington doing portrait busts before moving to Florence, where he lived the rest of his life. He portrayed in marble many notable figures of his day, ranging from President Jackson to Chief Justice Marshall, Senators Calhoun and Webster, General Sheridan, poet Longfellow, and Robert Hamilton Bishop, first president of Miami University. While in Italy he also turned to ideal figures, such as *The Greek Slave* of 1843 and *The Fisher Boy* of 1848. His works reside in major museums across the country. Stephen May, "Marble Man: Hiram Powers," *Timeline* 18, no. 5 (Sept.–Oct. 2001): 2–17, contains copious illustrations, as well as a list of Powers's works extant in Ohio. It thus seems natural that those wishing to honor Aiken should turn to Hiram's son, Preston, with their commission. Unfortunately, Mantle Fielding, *Dictionary of American Painters, Sculptors, and Engravers*, ed. Glenn B. Opitz (Poughkeepsie, N.Y.: Apollo, 1986), 740, offers little information about Preston other than that he was born in Florence in 1843 and practiced both as a sculptor and portrait painter there and in Portland, Maine, Boston, and Washington.

45. Royse, *Charles Aiken*, 21.

46. Members of the Board of Trustees and Visitors of Common School, Cincinnati, April 25, 1859, 98. Qtd. in Soriano, "Cincinnati Music Readers," 67–68.

47. Perhaps better understood as F, D, and E, since the terminology of the period labeled the grades in reverse alphabetical order, ranging from H to A, so that what would today be called first grade was actually H, and so forth.

48. For more on this Mason, see Sondra Wieland Howe, *Luther Whiting Mason: International Music Educator* (Warren, Mich.: Harmonie Park, 1997), 13–21.

49. Homeopathy was a fairly new system of medical treatment based on the idea that certain diseases could be cured by administering small doses of drugs that in larger quantities would produce symptoms of the disease in question.

50. *The Musical Personnel of Cincinnati and Vicinity for 1896* (Cincinnati: Universal, 1896), 43.

51. Walter H. Aiken, "Music in the Cincinnati Schools," *Musician* 11, no. 5 (May 1906): 252–53.

52. See Soriano, "Cincinnati Music Readers," 88–102.

53. Ibid., 102–27.

54. G. F. Junkermann and J. L. Zeinz, "Notice to Teachers," *The Cincinnati Music Reader,* part 3 (Cincinnati: John Church, 1875), 2.

55. Zeinz taught from 1868 until 1905, mostly at the Third Intermediate School and Sixth District School.

56. See Soriano, "Cincinnati Music Readers," 127–49.

57. Junkermann and Zeinz, *The Cincinnati Music Reader,* part 1 (Cincinnati: John Church, 1875), 2.

58. Junkermann and Zeinz, *The Cincinnati Music Reader,* part 4 (Cincinnati: John Church, 1875),2.

59. Junkermann and Zeinz, *The Cincinnati Music Reader,* part 5 (Cincinnati: John Church, 1875), 2.

60. He was also a composer of original works, including *The Pied Piper of Hamelin*, an operetta for treble voices, with words by C. J. Brooks (1917).

61. Walter H. Aiken, "Music in the Cincinnati Public Schools," 51.

62. Ibid., 50.

63. In a June 14, 1927, letter from R. W. Shafter, clerk of the Cincinnati Board of Education, qtd. in Gary, "A History of Music Education in the Cincinnati Public Schools," 77. Aiken's affection for the city he served was manifested in a "Cincinnati Civic Song," with words by Callie King Walls, published in 1929, and "Dedicated to the Civic Work of the Cincinnati Public Schools."

64. Gary, "A History of Music Education in the Cincinnati Public Schools," 98.

65. Randall J. Condon, "A Supervisor as Seen by a Superintendent," *Journal of Proceedings of the Fifteenth Annual Meeting of the Music Supervisors National Conference* (1922): 37.

66. For example, "Go to Sleep, My Baby Dear," opus 6, with words by Blanche Estelle Kahler (Cincinnati: John Church, 1891). The piece also contains a cornet obligato and a dedication, "To Little Elaine Carew."

8. THE FOUNDATIONS OF PUBLIC SCHOOL MUSIC IN OBERLIN,
ZANESVILLE, CLEVELAND, AND COLUMBUS

1. "Historical Sketch of the Public Schools of Zanesville," *Historical Sketches of Public Schools in Cities, Villages, and Townships of the State of Ohio* (Columbus: State Centennial Educational Committee, 1876). Qtd. in Paul D. Sanders, "Early Public School Music Education in Zanesville, Ohio." *Bulletin of Historical Research in Music Education* 19 (May 1998): 187–96.

2. Qtd. in Sanders in "Early Public School Music Education in Zanesville, Ohio." I have relied on both this paper and *Historical Sketches of Public Schools in Cities, Villages, and Townships of the State of Ohio.* The tentative nature of such instruction can be inferred from several entries in that volume. For example, the Dayton report admits,

> After much discussion it was determined in 1849 to introduce music as a branch of study in the public schools. An effort was made to pay the salary of the teacher by subscription, but that failing, it was ordered to be paid out of the contingent fund.

Only a few hours of each week were devoted to music, and instruction was given in the upper grades only. This arrangement was continued until 1870, when the board employed a superintendent of music, and an assistant, both of whom were to devote their whole time to the schools, and give instruction in all the grades.

When Steubenville introduced music study in 1855, "Mr. McLain was permitted to teach vocal music in the schools, the pupils paying for his services." In 1870 the Circleville school board "employed a special teacher of Music, who, each week, gave a lesson of one hour to each room of the departments above the Primary. Thus Music continued to be taught in each white school. It was considered an optional study, and but one text book was used from the Intermediate through the 9th year." However, in 1879 *Jepson's Graded Music Readers* were introduced and music study "was made obligatory in all except the Grammar grades, and lessons of 15 to 20 minutes each were given daily by the special and regular teachers alternately. The same plan was carried out in the colored as in the white schools." As late as 1876 students in Ripley were offered music only in their final high school year: "Vocal Music, Composition and Declamation throughout the whole course. Instrumental Music, optional, with extra charge."

3. Francis Hawthorne Grant, "Foundations of Music Education in the Cleveland Public Schools" (Ph.D. diss., Western Reserve University, 1963), 43.

4. William Joseph Akers, *Cleveland Schools in the Nineteenth Century* (Cleveland: W. M. Bayne, 1901), 9.

5. Grant, "Foundations of Music Education in the Cleveland Public Schools," 50.

6. *Cleveland Herald and Gazette*, January 10, 1838.

7. *Cleveland Herald and Gazette*, May 16, 1838.

8. The public letter, signed by three members of the group's committee, appeared in the *Cleveland Herald and Gazette*, March 20, 1839.

9. Qtd. in a letter to the editor of the *Cleveland Herald and Gazette*, March 30, 1839.

10. *Cleveland Herald and Gazette*, January 4, 1839.

11. Ibid. January 10, 1839.

12. Ibid. September 18, 1839.

13. Grant presents others in "Foundations of Music Education," 321–24.

14. Andrew Freese, *Early History of the Cleveland Public Schools* (Cleveland: Robison, Savage, and Co., 1876), 101.

15. Cleveland School Board, "Annual Report of the Managers, 1849" (Cleveland: Mayward, 1849), 13.

16. Cleveland School Board, "Annual Report of the Managers, 1852" (Cleveland: Harris, Fairbanks, and Co., 1852), 11.

17. George N. Heller, "N. Coe Stewart (1838–1921): Cleveland Composer, Author, Compiler, Music Educator, and Administrator" (unpublished paper delivered to members of the College Music Society meeting in Cleveland, November 1997).

18. Russell V. Morgan, "Music in the Cleveland Public Schools," *The Fine Arts Guide of Ohio: Season 1929–1930* (Cleveland and Cincinnati: Fine Arts Service of Ohio, 1929), 29, 31.

19. Ibid., 31.

20. See George Sidney Marshall, *The History of Music in Columbus, Ohio: February 14, 1812–July 1, 1953* (Columbus: F. J. Heer, 1953).

21. See Miriam B. Kapfer, "Music Instruction and Supervision in the Public Schools of Columbus, Ohio, from 1845 to 1900" (Ph.D. diss., Ohio State University, 1964), 75–78.

22. Ibid., 76.

23. See also Kapfer, "Early Public School Music in Columbus, Ohio, 1845–54," *Journal of Research in Music Education* 15 (Fall 1967): 191–200, a compressed version of her dissertation.

24. Kapfer, "Music Instruction in the Public Schools of Columbus, Ohio, from 1845 to 1900," 143.

25. Ibid., 131.

26. Peletiah W. Huntington, "Old-Time Music of Columbus," *The "Old Northwest" Genealogical Quarterly* 8 (Apr. 1905): 136–40.

27. Osman Castle Hooper, *History of the City of Columbus, Ohio* (Columbus: Memorial, 1921), 171.

28. Ibid., 159–66.

29. Kapfer, "Music Instruction in the Public Schools of Columbus, Ohio, from 1845 to 1900," 164–65.

30. Kapfer's Appendix 3 includes this plan on pages 345–52, preceding its even more daunting successor of 1887 (353–71). For more on Eckhardt, see pages 166–72.

31. Alfred E. Lee, *History of the City of Columbus: Capital of Ohio* (New York and Chicago: Munsell, 1892), 567. For more about Scarritt, see Kapfer, "Music Instruction in the Public Schools of Columbus, Ohio, from 1845 to 1900," 224–30.

32. Kapfer, "Music Instruction in the Public Schools of Columbus, Ohio, from 1845 to 1900," 207.

9. The Cleveland Music School Settlement

1. See Silvia Zverina, *And They Shall Have Music: The History of the Cleveland Music School Settlement* (Cleveland: Cobham and Hatherton, 1988); despite its publication date, the study covers only the period through 1974.

2. Ibid., 14

3. Ibid., 45–46. This program can be seen as a premonition of the music therapy program to be developed during the 1960s.

4. Russian-born Goldovsky had originally aspired to the career of concert pianist, having studied with Artur Schnabel in Berlin and soloed with the Berlin Philharmonic at age thirteen. He later worked with Ernst von Dohnányi at the Franz Liszt Academy in Budapest and with Josef Hoffman at the Curtis Institute in Philadelphia.

5. Zverina, *And They Shall Have Music*, 66.

6. Ibid., 76.

7. The release was called *Masters of Music and Gifted Young People Play Great Music of the Past and Present*. The disc also contained works by Corelli, Mozart, Bloch, Beethoven, and Alexander Tscherepnine performed by students. A public relations effort, it was not released commercially.

8. Among Whittaker's other works: *In Memoriam: Beryl Rubinstein*, a choral work of 1952, *Two Murals for Orchestra*, first performed by the Cleveland Orchestra under George Szell on March 31 and April 2, 1960, and a *Sonatine* for cello and piano of 1977.

9. Zverina, *And They Shall Have Music*, 163–64.

10. The Lane Conservatory of Music

1. The "Announcement of the Lane Conservatory of Music, 1899–1900," Ohio Historical Society: PA Box 281/2.

2. Ibid.

3. Ibid.

4. Other works include "The Story of the Country Dance, or, Turkey in the Straw," a song with new words attached to the familiar tune, supposedly written especially "for dancers in flowery Park Hall, which was built by Mr. Lane in 1909, on the west bank of the Muskingum River, six miles north" of Zanesville. Also *Filtered Thoughts*, supposedly a set of three volumes containing his, "Philosophical observations of nature, human nature, men and women, their general trend, [whose] actions, voice and power are shown in these books." He claimed that they contained, "true and new precepts that benefit teachers of any matter, also christian [*sic*] ministers, honest lawyers, wise doctors, and intelligent musicians."

5. Leasure Porter Lane, "Loved Though It Be," sheet music (Zanesville: published for the author, 1910).

6. Lane, *Tone, Silence, and Time* (Zanesville: published for the author, 1907), preface.

7. Ibid., 96.

8. Ibid., 20.

9. Ibid., 115.

10. Ibid., 154.

11. Ibid.

12. Ibid., 155.

13. Ibid., 160.

11. The Dana School of Music

1. See Michael D. Martin, "The Band School of Dana's Musical Institute, Warren, Ohio, 1869–1941," (Ph.D. diss., Kent State University, 1996), available in microform from UMI (No. 9708714); also John R. Turk, *The Musical Danas of Warren, Ohio. The History of the Dana School of Music* (Youngstown: Dana Press of Youngstown State University, 1999).

2. Martin, "The Band School of Dana's Musical Institute," 175.

3. *Second Annual Catalogue of Dana's Musical Institute 1870–1871*, preface. Qtd. in Turk, *The Musical Danas*, 38.

4. Dana's approach was obviously modeled on what he had experienced in Friendship at what for most of its 1853–83 run was known as the [James] Baxter University of Music; for details see Martin, "The Band School of Dana's Musical Institute," 123–25.

5. Martin, "The Band School of Dana's Musical Institute," 242.

6. *Fifty-Seventh Annual Catalogue of Dana's Musical Institute*, 1926, 36.

7. Ibid., 10.

8. Martin, "The Band School of Dana's Musical Institute," 227–28.

1. See Richard Dean Skrym, "Oberlin Conservatory: A Century of Musical Growth and Influence" (Ph.D. diss., University of Southern California, 1962); and Willard Warch, *Our First 100 Years: A Brief History of the Oberlin College Conservatory of Music* (Oberlin: Oberlin College Press, 1967).

2. James Fairchlid, *Oberlin the Colony and the College (1883)*, qtd. in Skrym, "Oberlin Conservatory," 21.

3. Skrym, "Oberlin Conservatory," 24.

4. Ibid., 24–25.

5. Ibid., 28.

6. Ibid., 43–44.

7. Ibid., 49.

8. Ibid., 55.

9. Ibid., 54.

10. Warch, *Our First 100 Years*, 20.

11. Finney's migration to the frontier and his role in the building of the Oberlin Meeting House, still extant, are described in Geoffrey Blodgett, "Father Finney's Church," *Timeline* 14, no. 1 (Jan.–Feb. 1997): 20–33.

12. For a profile of the instrument, see the cover feature of the *American Organist* of July 2001, 36–38.

13. Skrym, "Oberlin Conservatory," 61.

14. Andrews also conducted choruses in Akron and elsewhere in the region. He was a founding member of the American Guild of Organists and was later named honorary president of the organization. He authored many published articles and also composed, including a considerable corpus for the organ (most of it unpublished and apparently lost), as well as chamber music, an orchestral Suite in C played by the Chicago Symphony under Frederick Stock at the 1910 May Festival, and *Lincoln, Song of Democracy* for chorus and orchestra.

15. Qtd. in an unpaginated pamphlet drawn from the *Oberlin Review* of October 31, 1901, containing a biographical sketch, a description of his October 29 funeral, and its various addresses, including a heartfelt eulogy by Lucien C. Warner.

16. Skrym, "Oberlin Conservatory," 130.

17. Ibid., 138.

18. Ibid., 148.

19. For a larger view of concert life in Oberlin prior to 1961, see Skrym, "Oberlin Conservatory," 358–85.

20. For an elegant endorsement of the decision (as well as a period view of the Conservatory), see Edward Dickinson, "The Conservatory of Music," *Oberlin Alumni Magazine* 19, no. 8 (May 1923), also issued as a fifteen-page supplement.

21. For detail on the history of public school music education at Oberlin, see Skrym, "Oberlin Conservatory," 288–357.

22. Qtd. in Warch, *Our First 100 Years*, 58.

1. See John Lewis Jr., "An Historical Study of the Origin and Development of the Cincinnati Conservatory of Music" (Ph.D. diss., University of Cincinnati, 1943), as well as B. J. Foreman, *CCM 125*, a heavily illustrated unpaginated booklet issued by the University of Cincinnati in 1992 commemorating its College-Conservatory of Music on its 125th birthday.

2. *Cincinnati Post*, March 27, 1906, described a visit paid by the young, dashing Artur Rubinstein after a concert at the Grand Opera House. Besieged by four hundred young women, he favored his youthful admirers with an impromptu recital.

3. Bohlmann arrived in 1890 and resigned in 1919 to establish his own school in Tennessee. Tirindelli had emigrated in 1895 and settled first in Boston. The following year he was invited by Frank Van der Stucken to join the Cincinnati Symphony; he also headed the violin department of the new Auditorium School of Music. After joining the conservatory faculty in 1898 he took several brief leaves to serve as concertmaster of the Covent Garden Opera Orchestra and was offered the podium of the Seattle Symphony following Henry Hadley's departure. For reasons of health, he returned to Europe on leave in 1919 and formally resigned from the conservatory faculty in 1922.

4. Described by Lewis, "An Historical Study," 151–55.

5. Ibid., 156–57.

6. Ibid., 158.

7. Ibid., 88.

8. Leighton was also a composer and the author of *Harmony, Analytical and Applied, a Practical Text-Book for Teachers, Schools and Conservatories* (Boston, Mass.: Boston Music, 1927), for many years an official text at the conservatory.

9. In that same year Tuthill, in consultation with Fritz Reiner, conductor of the Cincinnati Symphony, instigated a program which allowed seventy young men from the city's high schools to be taught free of charge at the conservatory by members of the orchestra. The program was funded for several years by Rainur, Mrs. Charles Taft and other patrons of the conservatory.

10. Brooklyn-born Evans had studied at the Leipzig Conservatory, graduating in 1886. He returned to this country and concertized for several years after an 1887 début at Steinway Hall in New York with the Metropolitan Opera Orchestra, directed by Walter Damrosch. He first came to Cincinnati in 1889 as a summer substitute for his friend, George Magrath. In addition to his success as a teacher of piano and active recitalist, he conducted the conservatory chorus for a period and was appointed dean of the faculty in 1919.

11. A Cincinnati native, Hoffman began study at the conservatory in 1901, and after several years as an instructor in piano sailed for Berlin in 1908 as a lyric tenor, encouraged to develop that instrument further by Clara Baur. He then joined the conservatory voice faculty in 1910, managed a considerable career as a performer of oratorio and lieder, and also conducted the conservatory chorus and madrigal singers.

12. Qtd. in Vincent A. Orlando, "An Historical Study of the Origin and Development of the College of Music of Cincinnati" (Ph.D. diss., University of Cincinnati, 1946), 48b.

13. Ibid., 50.

14. Ibid., 51.

15. Rose Fay Thomas, *Memoirs of Theodore Thomas* (New York: Moffat, Yeard, and Co., 1911), 145.

16. Ibid., 146.

17. Ibid., 147.

18. Ibid., 151. His daughter observed, "This contract was drawn up by business men on the simple business principle of getting the maximum of service at the minimum of compensation." His compensation as director was ten thousand dollars.

19. Thomas, *Memoirs of Theodore Thomas*, 166. For a listing of the thirty faculty, fees, etc. for the 1878–80 season, see Joseph E. Holliday, "The Musical Legacy of Theodore Thomas," *Bulletin of the Cincinnati Historical Society* 27, no. 3 (Fall 1969): 201.

20. Rose Fay Thomas, *Memoirs of Theodore Thomas*, 169, quoted her father as saying of himself, "I can be led by a silk thread, but I cannot be hauled by a ship's cable. In all matters but one—art—I am willing to give up my way, but there I am a tyrant."

21. Orlando, "An Historical Study," 57.

22. Longworth (1869–1931), after graduation from Harvard and then law school in Cincinnati, became a state representative in 1899, a state senator in 1901, and was elected to Congress two years later. He became Republican floor leader in 1923 and speaker of the house in 1925. In addition to this distinguished political career, he was evidently an amateur violinist of some accomplishment, having studied at the college.

23. Thuman's persuasive eloquence can be sampled in the pamphlet, *The College of Music of Cincinnati: An Address Delivered before the Optimists Club at the Queen City Club, Cincinnati, Ohio, Saturday, November 13, 1920*. In what was actually an assessment of the state of music in this country during that post–World War I period, Thuman asserted, "We must not forget that the people will not want American music just because it is American. Nor will they want to engage American musicians just because they are Americans. They will desire American music only if it is good music and however we may sound the tocsin for the recognition of the American musicians there will be, and there can be, no permanent response unless the American musician is the equal of the European. It is, therefore, the first task of the American musician to train himself in his art. And this training must be comprehensive, must be honest, must be thorough, and must be correct" (4). Thuman told the Optimists that Theodore Thomas had understood this principle more than a half century earlier, although he was "ahead of his time and, as is so frequently the case, his remarkable pioneer work was not recognized by the majority." However, Thuman assured his listeners that the college still adhered to Thomas's principles and that the institution was prepared to train "our young men and young women of musical gifts and talents so thoroughly and so finely, so completely and so genuinely that the European institutions can add nothing more of importance" (7).

24. Hahn was born in Indianapolis in 1872 and had studied at the college under Henry Schradieck, receiving a diploma in violin in 1890. After further work in London and Milan, he returned to Cincinnati, where he taught violin independently, concertized, played in the Cincinnati Symphony for four years, and conducted the Orpheus Singing Society. He joined the college faculty in 1921 and taught violin, directed the orchestra, and organized a faculty string quartet.

25. Picchi (1876–1937) was born in Brescia and had appeared there, as well as at La Scala in Milan and for several seasons in South American houses, before he joined the Metropolitan, where he sang for nine seasons. He had also appeared with the Cincinnati Zoo Opera, beginning in 1925.

26. Qtd. in Foreman, *CCM 125.*

27. The company had used CCM facilities for rehearsals since 1963, and soon CCM functioned as its school. Classical ballet had been part of the conservatory curriculum since 1927.

14. THE CLEVELAND INSTITUTE OF MUSIC

1. See a history of the institute, "A Conservatory of Excellence," written by Rory Meshenberg Sanders, director of publications, that first appeared in the bimonthly newsletter *Notes* during the school's seventy-fifth anniversary celebrations in 1995. Available online at www.cim.edu/cimHistory.

2. Sessions (1896–1985) had taught at Smith College beginning in 1917 and studied with Bloch in New York during 1919. He offered courses in theory, music history, and solfeggio and accompanied the institute chorus. He resigned from the institute in tandem with his mentor in 1925. He completed only three works during his four years in Cleveland, most importantly his incidental music for Leonid Andreyev's *The Black Maskers*, dedicated to Bloch, but actually written for the 1923 senior play at Smith and conducted by the composer at its performances in Northampton in June of that year. The familiar orchestral suite was derived from the larger score by the composer and first performed by the Cincinnati Symphony under Fritz Reiner on December 5, 1930. Sessions also wrote incidental music for Karl Volkmüller's *Turandot, Princess of China,* performed at the Cleveland Playhouse May 8–10, 1925, a work that remains unpublished. Sessions's relationship to his mentor can be studied through Andrea Olmstead, *Roger Sessions and His Music* (Ann Arbor, Mich.: UMI, 1985), 17–21, including some insights gained by interviews with daughter and biographer, Suzanne Bloch; and Olmstead, *The Correspondence of Roger Sessions* (Boston, Mass.: Northeastern Univ. Press, 1992), which contains several letters to, from, or about Bloch (specifically those beginning on pages 35, 36, 39, 48, 63, 80, 109). Bloch's feelings about Cleveland are evident in a letter of May 31, 1928, to Sessions about Suzanne's impending marriage. "Then the poor girl will have to settle in Cleveland" (111). Sessions's contemporary, Quincy Porter (1897–1966), also had studied with Bloch in New York and joined the Cleveland Institute of Music faculty in 1923, where he taught until 1928, when he left for three years in Paris, aided by a fellowship from the Guggenheim Foundation. Other composers of note studied with Bloch during his Cleveland sojourn: Theodore Chanler (1902–61), Douglas Moore (1893–1969), and Bernard Rogers (1893–1968).

3. Qtd. in Rory Meshenberg Sanders, "A Conservatory of Excellence."

4. Roger Sessions, "Ernest Bloch," *Modern Music* 5, no. 1 (Nov.–Dec. 1927): 9–10.

5. Other Cleveland works that have retained some currency are the Sonata No. 1 for violin and piano (1920); the *Baal Shem Suite,* also for violin and piano (1920); the Piano Quintet No. 1 (1923–24), and the *Poème Mystique,* for violin and piano (1924). For more information see Robert Strassburg, *Ernest Bloch: Voice in the Wilderness* (Los Angeles: Trident Shop, California State University, 1977).

6. José-Flore Tappy, ed., *Ernest Bloch: Romaine Lettres 1911–1933* (Lausanne, Switz.: Editions Payot Lausanne, 1984), 148.

7. David Kushner, "Ernest Bloch in Cleveland (1920–1925)," (unpublished paper presented to members of the College Music Society in Cleveland, November 1997).

8. Goldovsky described his hiring and early Cleveland Institute of Music performances on pages 239–41, 276–69, and 279–80 of *My Road to Opera: The Recollections of Boris Goldovsky as Told to Curtis Cate* (Boston, Mass.: Houghton Mifflin, 1979).

15. Art Museums and a Hall of Fame

1. See Carl Wittke, "Music in the Museum," *The First Fifty Years: The Cleveland Museum of Art 1916–1966* (Cleveland: Cleveland Museum of Art, 1966), chap. 7.

2. See Donald Rosenberg, "Putting Music in the Picture," *Cleveland Plain Dealer*, June 16, 1996.

16. The Cincinnati Symphony Orchestra

1. See Louis R. Thomas, "A History of the Cincinnati Symphony Orchestra to 1931" (Ph.D. diss., University of Cincinnati, 1972); *Cincinnati Symphony Orchestra: Centennial Portraits* (Cincinnati: Cincinnati Symphony Orchestra, 1994), a lavishly illustrated volume with text by Robert C. Vitz, which includes a discography and extensive bibliography; and *Cincinnati Symphony Orchestra: A Tribute to Max Rudolf and Highlights of Its History* (Cincinnati: Cincinnati Symphony Orchestra Association, 1967). Nancy Malitz, formerly music critic of the *Cincinnati Enquirer*, wrote "A Hardy Survivor Rides the Wave of the Future," *New York Times*, Mar. 19, 1995, tracing the orchestra's history and assessing its condition prior to a Carnegie Hall concert celebrating its centenary.

2. See Charles W. Wyrick, "Concert and Criticism in Cincinnati, 1840–1850" (master's thesis, University of Cincinnati College-Conservatory of Music, 1965), 45–56; also Ophia D. Smith, "Joseph Tosso, the Arkansaw Traveler," *Ohio State Archaeological and Historical Quarterly* 56 (Jan. 1947): 16–45.

3. Wyrick, "Concert and Criticism in Cincinnati," 72–81.

4. See Leonie C. Frank, *Musical Life in Early Cincinnati and the Origin of the May Festival* (Cincinnati: Ruter, 1932), 18–19. The literature was fully delineated by Ritter himself in his *Music in America* (New York: Scribner, 1895, a "New Edition, with Additions") as part of chapter 21, "Musical Development in the West," 410–12. Without ever identifying himself by name, Ritter describes, "a very young and very enthusiastic musician, fresh from his studies, and lately arrived in America. The young artist possessed, besides his youthful energy, a valuable musical library that he had brought with him from Europe. It was then the second best in this country, and, of course, of invaluable importance and help to the advancement of true musical culture among the members of the new society. The establishment of the Cecilia Society truly marked an era in Cincinnati's musical life." After mentioning the creation of the orchestra as "an annex to the choral society" and listing the repertory the two ensembles essayed, Ritter lavished further encomiums on his accomplishments: "These artistic labors were highly beneficial to the awakening of musical taste and progress among the inhabitants of the rising city, and also won recognition for its musical spirit abroad."

5. Joseph E. Holliday, "The Cincinnati Philharmonic and Hopkins Hall Orchestras 1856–1868," *Bulletin of the Cincinnati Historical Society* (Apr. 26, 1968): 165.

6. F. E. Tunison, *Presto! From the Singing School to the May Musical Festival* (Cincinnati: E. H. Beasley, 1888), 43.

7. Ibid., 45–46.

8. See Joseph E. Holliday, "The Cincinnati Philharmonic and Hopkins Hall Orchestras 1856–1868," *Bulletin of the Cincinnati Historical Society* 26 (Apr. 1968): 158–73.

9. George P. Upton, *Theodore Thomas: A Musical Autobiography* (Chicago: McClurg, 1905), 78.

10. Tunison, *Presto!* 33.

11. See Vernon D. Schroeder, "Cincinnati's Musical Growth, 1870–1875" (master's thesis, University of Cincinnati College-Conservatory of Music, 1971), 25–33.

12. See Joseph E. Holliday, "The Musical Legacy of Theodore Thomas," *Bulletin of the Cincinnati Historical Society* 27, no. 3 (Fall 1969): 190–205.

13. *Cincinnati Musical Directory, 1886–87* (Cincinnati: Cincinnati Wesleyan College for Young Women, 1886), 14.

14. Vitz, *Cincinnati Symphony Orchestra*, 8.

15. Thomas, "A History of the Cincinnati Symphony Orchestra to 1931," 139–41.

16. The room still exists, although it has lapsed into a state of considerable disrepair. Several attempts at restoration during the 1980s came to naught, but in the late 1990s the non-profit Emery Center Corporation, organized by advocates of the arts, preservation, and downtown development, embarked on a plan to renovate the auditorium, which is owned by the University of Cincinnati. For details, see Janelle Gelfand, "Emery Fix-up in the Wings" *Cincinnati Enquirer*, August 31, 1999; and Kathleen Doane, "Money for Nothing," *Cincinnati* (July 2003): 42, 44–45.

17. Thomas, "A History of the Cincinnati Symphony Orchestra to 1931," 366.

18. See *Discographies of Commercial Recordings of the Cleveland Orchestra (1924–1977) and the Cincinnati Symphony Orchestra (1917–1977)*, compiled by Frederick P. Fellers and Betty Meyers (Westport, Conn.: Greenwood, 1978), 165–66 and throughout.

19. *Cincinnati Symphony Orchestra Concerts; Fritz Reiner, Music Director, 1922–1931* (Chicago; Fritz Reiner Society, 1989). This eighty-four page booklet was issued by the Fritz Reiner Society in Chicago as its final publication before suspending operations. It is held by a number of libraries, including the Public Library of Cincinnati and Hamilton County and the library of the College-Conservatory of Music of the University of Cincinnati, where it is cataloged as ML1211.8/C52/C54/1989.

20. Where for the second consecutive year the orchestra collaborated with the Toronto Mendelssohn Choir in that group's annual music festival, a tradition that was to be continued. In late March 1926 the Canadian Mendelssohnians had journeyed to Cincinnati to collaborate in three concerts, including two performances of the Beethoven Ninth Symphony.

21. See Carole Rosen, *The Goossens: A Musical Century* (Boston, Mass.: Northeastern Univ. Press, 1993), esp. chapter 10 ("Welcome to Cincinnati," 142–59), chapter 14 ("Inspirational and Talented Guidance," 205–26), and chapter 15 ("A Rather Nice Person in Many Ways," 227–47).

22. Among the other contributions: Felix Borowski, *Fanfare for American Soldiers;* Henry Cowell, *Fanfare to the Forces of the Latin-American Allies;* Paul Creston, *Fanfare for Paratroopers;* Anis Fuleihan, *Fanfare for the Medical Corps;* Goossens's own *Fanfare for the Merchant Marine;* Darius Milhaud, *Fanfare de la Liberté;* Walter Piston, *Fanfare for the Fighting French;* Bernard Rogers, *Fanfare for Commandos;* Leo Sowerby, *Untitled Fanfare;* William Grant Still,

Fanfare for American Heroes; Deems Taylor, *Fanfare for Russia;* Virgil Thomson, *Fanfare for France;* and Bernard Wagenaar, *Fanfare for Airmen.* Jorge Mester recorded a full dozen of these works with members of the London Philharmonic Orchestra (*Fanfares* on Varese Sarabande VCDM 1000–240).

23. Qtd. in Rosen, *The Goossens,* 148.

24. Qtd. ibid., 213

25. See the unpaginated booklet published by the Cincinnati Symphony Orchestra, *A Half Century of Golden Music GOLDEN JUBILEE YEAR: The Story of the Cincinnati Symphony Orchestra* (Cincinnati: Cincinnati Symphony Orchestra Association, [1945?]). Still is described as, "one of the country's most promising modern composers" and a Mississippi native with "African, Indian and white blood in his veins." His new work was portrayed as having been "written and scored in the space of a few weeks, [and] has a definite American flavor. It bespeaks the pride of the composer in his native land, the warmth of the American people, the grandeur of scenic America."

26. Qtd. in Rosen, *The Goossens,* 245.

27. Ibid.

28. Those educational and outreach programs have continued to the present. In the spring of 1999 the Cincinnati Symphony Orchestra announced the multifaceted "Sound Discoveries" program, funded by a five million dollar grant from Patricia A. Corbett and the Corbett Foundation. "Music for Life" extends the concept of the orchestra's Young People's Concerts by sending orchestra musicians and volunteer docents into the schools in an attempt to integrate music into a cross-curricular approach to teaching and learning. Pilot programs began in the first and second grades with the 1999–2000 school year and were to gradually expand over the following five years. "Music for the Community" sends the orchestra and components thereof throughout the tri-state region, fosters the use of orchestra players as soloists with community orchestras, and offers orchestra musicians as mentors to aspiring musicians or speakers at school career days. "Music for a Career" attempts to facilitate the desires of those members of the Cincinnati Symphony Youth Orchestra who are considering a career in music with special coaching, scholarships, and funds for the purchase of instruments.

29. See Louis Nicholas, *Thor Johnson: American Conductor* (Fish Creek, Wis.: Music Festival Committee of the Peninsula Arts Association, 1982). Its appendix includes a comprehensive list of works premièred by Johnson, with asterisks denoting Johnson commissions.

30. See Fellers and Meyers, *Discographies of Commercial Recordings,* 183–93, for details of the recorded repertory of both Rudolf and Kunzel from 1964 to 1971.

31. Indirectly echoing the history of predecessor Reiner who, following his forced resignation, had moved to Philadelphia as principal conductor of the Philadelphia Grand Opera Company, associate guest conductor of the Philadelphia Orchestra, and head of the orchestra department of the Curtis Institute. Add Stokowski to the tale, and the Quaker City seems to have offered considerable refuge to erstwhile orchestra conductors from Cincinnati.

For a summary of the orchestra's accomplishments, see *Ohio* 25, no. 13 (Feb. 2003): 47. Of the ensemble's seventy-two releases on the Telarc label, fully fifty-two have appeared on *Billboard* charts of best-sellers. In 1998 *Copland: Music of America* won a Grammy award, while six other albums have been nominated for Grammies. Kunzel is quoted as asserting, "Our aim is to reach out and have our audience be as wide and as big as possible all around the world."

32. Vitz, *Cincinnati Symphony Orchestra,* 8.

1. See Donald Rosenberg, *The Cleveland Orchestra Story: "Second to None"* (Cleveland: Gray, 2000), which includes in its appendices a listing of personnel by instrument, a discography by composer, and lists of both world and American premières by year. Earlier studies include Robert C. Marsh, *The Cleveland Orchestra* (Cleveland: World, 1967); F. Karl Grossman, *A History of Music in Cleveland* (Cleveland: Case Western Reserve University, 1972); an essay written by David G. Tovey for *Symphony Orchestras of the United States: Selected Profiles*, edited by Robert R. Craven (Westport, Conn.: Greenwood, 1986), which was revised and updated in 1993 by Sue Sackman and Eric Sellen for the orchestra's seventy-fifth anniversary celebration program; *Fanfare: Portraits of the Cleveland Orchestra*, ed. Susan Sackman (Cleveland: Junior Committee of the Cleveland Orchestra, 1974, 1984); ed. Marilyn Eppich (1995) (all three volumes are at the Cleveland Public Library; the most recent contains not only portraits and biographies of staff and players, but mini-histories of the orchestra and its concert venues, many historical photos, alphabetical listings of the more than nine hundred members and conductors to that point, and a compilation of principal players by section through 1995); and Hope M. Klassen, "Maestros and Management: The Cleveland Orchestra, 1918–1994" (master's thesis, University of Akron, 1995).

2. Grossman, *A History of Music in Cleveland*, 20.

3. Puehringer, a student of Franz von Suppé, emigrated from Austria in 1863 and taught at Wittenberg University before settling in Cleveland in 1872. He wrote a couple of light operas and *The Hero of Erie, An Opera in Two Acts*, a musical biography of Commodore Perry, the manuscript of which is held by the Cleveland Public Library.

4. Ring also conducted a church choir and other choral societies and taught at the Cleveland Conservatory of Music, which had been organized in 1871. He is reputed to have composed for various media, including three operas. However, the only work I have seen is his *An die Tonkunst (Apostrophe to Music), Ein Hymnus für Soli* (soprano and bass), *gemischten Chor und grosses Orchester, written for the Gesangverein and published in 1900.* Its score and orchestra parts are owned by the Cleveland Public Library.

5. This philharmonic should not be confused with the Cleveland Philharmonic Orchestra organized during the summer of 1938 by F. Karl Grossman as a training orchestra for young, aspiring professionals.

6. Presumably not the same ensemble that cooperated with the Cleveland Vocal Society, conducted by Alfred Arthur, in a performance of the Verdi *Requiem* on December 12, 1895. J. Heywood Alexander, *It Must Be Heard: A Survey of the Musical Life of Cleveland, 1836–1918* (Cleveland: Western Reserve Historical Society, 1981), 21, assumes that this fifty-five member Cleveland Symphony Orchestra, Henry Miller, conductor, consisted mainly of former Philharmonic players.

7. See Mary Cleveland Wagner, "Early Orchestras in Cleveland (1900–1915)" (master's thesis, Kent State University, 1998).

8. His bust presides over the corridor leading to the Music and Art Division of the Cleveland Public Library. His manuscript and papers are held by the library—a massive trove of about nine hundred items, including clippings, letters, lecture notes, batons, etc. While he edited Beethoven symphonies for the Peters firm of Leipzig, it appears that, while many were performed, only one of his compositions was ever published and many remain

unfinished. He did complete several orchestral overtures and illustrative tone poems, two orchestral scherzos, a string quartet and string sextet, the cantata *Deukalion* (a poem by Bayard Taylor set for solo quartet, chorus, and orchestra), several pieces for solo voices and orchestra, song cycles built on the work of poets such as Shakespeare, Thackeray, and Browning, lieder (including some based on his own poems), a four-voice "Madrigal" on words from Milton, and various pieces for violin and cello. In addition to his work as a conductor, Beck had organized an active Schubert String Quartet in 1877, a group that metamorphosed into the Beck String Quartet during the 1890–91 season. For more information on Beck and his works, see Alexander, *It Must Be Heard*, 27–28.

9. Alexander, *It Must Be Heard*, 23, includes a summary of the orchestra's repertory during its first season. Wagner, "Early Orchestras in Cleveland (1900–1915)," presents a chronological listing of concerts by these orchestras, including conductor, featured soloist, and location in Appendix A. Appendix B includes sample concert programs between January 16, 1900, and January 31, 1915. Appendix C reprints several sample programs as well as the People's Symphony Concerts prospectuses for 1910 and 1911.

10. For details, see Wagner, "Early Orchestras in Cleveland (1900–1915)," 42–48.

11. For details on the naming and funding of this ensemble, see ibid., 58–66.

12. The concerts also included nonorchestral interpolations. Mrs. Marcossen accompanied her violinist husband Sol (the orchestra's Concert Meister) on several occasions, as did Adella Prentiss Hughes her husband, Felix, designated either as a baritone or bass.

13. See Wagner, "Early Orchestras in Cleveland (1900–1915)," 86–93.

14. See Adella Prentiss Hughes, *Music Is My Life* (Cleveland: World, 1947), a charming, self-serving, rambling autobiographical narrative that gives scant attention to much of anything beyond about 1920 other than the dedication of Severance Hall.

15. Qtd. in Mary Reeb, "Adella Prentiss Hughes and the Founding, Fostering, and Financing of the Cleveland Orchestra," *Gamut* 15 (Spring–Summer 1985): 66.

16. Hughes, *Music Is My Life*, 97, recalled Andrews as "a tall man, long of arm—a fine musician beloved by all. In his absorption in his task, his beat got wider and wider, with the result that his baton came down on the head of the contralto. In those days we were wearing high combs, and Marguerite [Halls]'s beautiful tortoise shell was widely distributed about the stage."

17. Ibid., 159–60.

18. Ibid., 211.

19. Alexander, *It Must Be Heard*, 22, includes a summary of the ensembles that participated in the seventeen seasons of orchestra concerts between 1901 and 1918. Mrs. Hughes often mounted parallel, complementary series. Her success at presenting individual recitals (for instance, soprano Lillian Nordica on April 7, 1902, and a dream trio of pianist Josef Hofmann, violinist Fritz Kreisler, and cellist Jean Gérardy only ten days later) led to a series of twenty-eight events in the Assembly Hall of the new Hollenden Hotel during the 1903–04 season (including the Kneisel Quartet and soprano Lillian Blauvelt). In November 1912 she inaugurated a tradition of Friday Musicales in the ballroom of the new Statler Hotel, eventually presenting more than one hundred artists; the 1914–15 series alone encompassed pianist Harold Bauer, violinist Efrem Zimbalist, and cellist Pablo Casals in his first Cleveland appearance. She also got involved in the business of managing concerts by touring college glee clubs for their local alumni, and during the 1916–17 season mounted the blockbuster

Great Artist Series in the Armory: Hofmann, Paderewski, Alma Gluck, Kreisler, Mischa Elman, and Schumann-Heink (who canceled her tour because of injuries incurred in a car accident), with duo-pianists Harold Bauer and Ossip Gabrilowitsch as a postscript.

20. Hughes, *Music Is My Life*, 249.

21. Rosenberg, *Cleveland Orchestra Story*, 55.

22. Although the orchestra remained a tenant in this new environment, the atmosphere must have been an improvement over the armory. Mrs. Hughes recalled several critical, yet comical, crises in *Music Is My Life*, 173–74. The first was purely olfactory: the Boston Symphony was booked for January 31, 1911, only twenty-four hours after the conclusion of a poultry show, but a local chemical company was able to supply a deodorizing agent that, applied liberally, made the hall habitable. Three years later the armory management booked the same show concurrently with her presentation of the New York Symphony under Walter Damrosch, with pianist Josef Hofmann as soloist, forcing a move to a smaller theater. Platforms were hastily constructed in the pit to support the podium and one leg of the piano, and some patrons were forced to sit in the pit, almost literally under the piano.

23. Hughes, *Music Is My Life*, 283.

24. Qtd. in Marsh, *The Cleveland Orchestra*, 24.

25. In 1948 her pamphlets were gathered into *A Listener's Anthology of Music*, the two volumes of which were published under the aegis of the Kulas Foundation, which distributed two thousand sets to schools throughout the hemisphere. The Silver Burdett Company of Boston then assumed responsibility for the anthology's promotion and distribution. In 1951 Silver Burdett also issued the three volumes of Baldwin's *Music for Young Listeners*, as well as *Music to Remember*.

26. See Richard Lee Massman, *Lillian Baldwin and the Cleveland Plan for Education Concerts* (Ann Arbor, Mich.: UMI, 1972). See also Rosenberg, *Cleveland Orchestra Story*, 118–20.

27. For Sokoloff's recorded legacy, see Fellers and Meyers, *Discographies of Commercial Recordings*, 6–11.

28. Rosenberg, *Cleveland Orchestra Story*, 96.

29. Mrs. Hughes had dreamed of a new concert hall as early as 1905, when she vainly approached Andrew Carnegie as a potential donor: "A Music Hall of about 2000 seating capacity, with a small recital hall, ample foyers, dressing rooms, etc., would cost around $5,000,000. If you feel we merit your beneficence to such an extent, I would ask you to give us such a building." Rather than providing Cleveland with its own Carnegie Music Hall, the philanthropist suggested, "by installing new elevators," the vacant fourth floor of the City Hall could be employed to that purpose. She also approached John D. Rockefeller Sr three times between 1911 and 1918; he eventually replied, "When the time comes that you will undertake the building of a music hall definitely, regardless of whether we make a contribution or not, you may write me again." It was also Mrs. Hughes who determined that the majority of the orchestra's patrons lived on the East Side of the city, suggesting a location there rather than downtown near the Public Square. See Reeb, "Adella Prentiss Hughes and the Founding, Fostering, and Financing of the Cleveland Orchestra," 67–68; Wagner, "Early Orchestras in Cleveland (1900–1915)," 16–17; and Rosenberg, *Cleveland Orchestra Story*, 100–106.

30. Mrs. Hughes believed that for John Long Severance the building became a sort of Taj Mahal for his wife, Elisabeth DeWitt Severance. Hughes, *Music Is My Life*, 80. Plaques facing each other in the entryway proclaim her memorial and announce these words of Plato: "Music

is a moral law. It gives a soul to the universe, wings to the mind, flight to the imagination, a charm to gaiety, and life to everything. It is the essence of order and leads to all that is good, just and beautiful."

31. Klaus G. Roy, the orchestra's program annotator from 1958 until 1988, described in lavish detail "The Acoustical Renovation of Severance Hall" in "The Gilt-Edged Second," an article that appeared originally in the March 1960 issue of *Stereo Review*. Roy included the essay in his *Not Responsible for Lost Articles: Thoughts and Second Thoughts from Severance Hall, 1958–1988* (Cleveland: Musical Arts Association, 1993), 91–97. The volume was published as part of the orchestra's celebration of its seventy-fifth birthday. The anniversary also led to a self-produced set of ten compact discs containing performances by all of the orchestra's music directors, as well as musical advisor Pierre Boulez.

32. The history and reinstallation of the instrument by the Schantz Organ Company are described and documented by several of the Schantz staff in the cover feature of the *American Organist* 35, no. 1 (Jan. 2001): 52–55. See also articles about the Norton Memorial Organ in the Cleveland Orchestra's program books from that same period (for example, Concert Week No. 13, Jan. 18–20, 2001, 79–83).

33. "Cleveland's Orchestra," *Fortune* (Nov. 1931): 56. The unattributed article is subtitled, "Its origin and organization . . . by what stratagems music love was wheedled into (and money out of) honest citizens . . . and how Adella Prentiss Hughes became the most remarkable impresario of orchestra [*sic*]."

34. For detail, see Rosenberg, *Cleveland Orchestra Story*, 149–53.

35. For Goldovsky's recollection of his first year in Cleveland, see *My Road to Opera: The Recollections of Boris Goldovsky as told to Curtis Cate* (Boston, Mass.: Houghton Mifflin, 1979), 219–21, 226–39. Goldovsky had recruited members of the Singers Club for his opera choruses and consequently was named the all-male group's conductor in 1936; for a description of his first outing that the organization, see ibid., 258–67. After the collapse of the Cleveland Orchestra's opera productions, Goldovsky, with set designer Richard Rychtarik, cofounded the short-lived Civic Opera Company of Cleveland. See ibid., 283–84.

36. John E. Vacha, "BIGGEST BASH: Cleveland's Great Lakes Exposition," *Timeline* 13, no. 2 (Mar.–Apr. 1996): 12–13.

37. See Halina Rodzinski, *Our Two Lives* (New York: Scribner's, 1976), 89–224, including numerous relevant photographs.

38. The work was performed in a version created by and in memory of Ossip Gabrilowitsch, founder of the Detroit Symphony, and its conductor from 1919 until his death in 1936. A photo reproduced in Marsh, *The Cleveland Orchestra*, 68–69, shows Rodzinski leading his densely packed forces from the piano. Boris Goldovsky, *My Road to Opera*, 282–87, describes his role in negotiating rights to present the edition from the conductor's widow, as well as his subconductor's position in the actual performance.

39. For Rodzinski's recorded legacy, see Fellers and Meyers, *Discographies of Commercial Recordings*, 12–22. Rosenberg, *Cleveland Orchestra Story*, provides a narrative in chapter 12, "Recording with Rodzinski," 177–84.

40. Qtd. in Marsh, *The Cleveland Orchestra*, 64–65.

41. One bit of evidence remains that Blossom dabbled as a composer: *My Expo Rose*, opus 2, "Dedicated and Donated to the Great Lakes Exposition" and published by Evan Georgeoff in 1937.

42. Qtd. in Rosenberg, *Cleveland Orchestra Story*, 194–95.

43. For details, see Fellers and Meyers *Discographies of Commercial Recordings*, 23–27.

44. Marsh, *The Cleveland Orchestra*, 80.

45. Leinsdorf's acerbic and brutally candid comments on his brief Cleveland residency, as well as its aftermath, can be found in *Cadenza: A Musical Career* (Boston, Mass.: Houghton Mifflin, 1976), 116–29.

46. See Vacha, "The Selling of Szell: The Cleveland Orchestra Meets Its Maestro," *Timeline* 15, no. 6 (Nov.–Dec. 1998): 2–13.

47. Rosenberg, *Cleveland Orchestra Story*, 221.

48. Controversy erupted when Szell replaced his inherited concertmaster, Joseph Knitzer, with Samuel Thaviu, whom he had lured from the same position in Fritz Reiner's Pittsburgh Symphony. However, midway through Thaviu's one-year tenure Szell surreptitiously contracted Joseph Gingold, then serving as concertmaster in Detroit. Szell seemed unperturbed by public charges of piracy and the like. Gingold remained in his position until 1960, when he joined the faculty of Indiana University. He was quoted then as telling a colleague that "[f]or the first time in fourteen years, I sleep well every night." See Rosenberg, *Cleveland Orchestra Story*, 246–49 and 314.

49. Harold C. Schonberg, *The Great Conductors* (New York: Simon and Schuster, 1967), 337.

50. Marsh, *The Cleveland Orchestra*, 105.

51. See Joseph A. Mussulman, *Dear People . . . Robert Shaw: A Biography* (Bloomington: Indiana Univ. Press, 1979), 132–48.

52. For details see Fellers and Meyers, *Discographies of Commercial Recordings*, 27–130.

53. The American and Canadian cities visited from 1946 to 1967 are represented graphically in Marsh, *The Cleveland Orchestra*, 101; the European jaunts are presented in detail, 108–9.

54. See Rosenberg, *Cleveland Orchestra Story*, 347–60, for detail. Especially fascinating is Szell's almost maniacal insistence that the stage of this alfresco facility could be air-conditioned for the comfort of the performers.

55. See Dennis Dooley, "The Orchestra Nobody Knows," *Cleveland* (Jan. 1978): 58–64, 137–47. Through interviews with many of the players, as well as Maazel and General Manager Kenneth Haas, Dooley documented THE CLEVELAND ORCHESTRA IN TURMOIL (front-cover headline). Dooley recounts on page 143 the story still making the backstage rounds of Severance Hall, sometimes attributed to Maazel himself: "In the unofficial poll taken among the orchestra in August 1971 Maazel received only two votes. When he was hired that fall a joke went around among the musicians that Maazel could unify the orchestra overnight—by firing the two people who had voted for him." Maazel's recorded 1971–77 legacy is chronicled in Fellers and Meyers, *Discographies of Commercial Recordings*, 131–42. Their volume was superceded by Denise Horstman, *The Cleveland Orchestra Discography* (Cleveland: The Cleveland Orchestra, 1985).

56. During the spring of 1935 Artur Rodzinski had vainly contacted George Gershwin about the possibility of presenting *Porgy* in Cleveland, followed by a transfer to the Metropolitan Opera. See Rosenberg, *Cleveland Orchestra Story*, 154–55.

57. He did mount *The Magic Flute* (which he also staged) in 1985 and *The Merry Widow* (in a joint production with the National Opera of Belgium) in 1986 at the Blossom Center, but finances then confined operatic ventures to concert versions of Hans Werner Henze's *The Bassarids*, Beethoven's *Fidelio*, and sequential presentation of all four parts of Wagner's *Ring* cycle.

58. An outdated discography, minibiography, and conversation in which Dohnányi betrays some of his musical philosophy can be found in Jeannine Wagar, *Conductors in Conversation* (Boston, Mass.: G. K. Hall, 1991), 51–63.

59. Foreword to Marsh, *The Cleveland Orchestra*.

18. OPERA IN CINCINNATI

1. A history of the piece can be found in the preface of John O'Keeffe and William Shield, *The Poor Soldier*, ed. William Brasmer and William Osborne (Madison, Wis.: A–R Editions, 1978).

2. See Larry Robert Wolz, "Opera in Cincinnati: The Years before the Zoo, 1801–1920" (Ph.D. diss., University of Cincinnati College-Conservatory of Music, 1983).

3. *Daily Cincinnati Gazette*, March 22, 1836.

4. See Katherine K. Preston, *Opera on the Road: Traveling Opera Troupes in the United States, 1825–60* (Urbana: Univ. of Illinois Press, 1993), 269–71, 275–76.

5. See Charles Frederic Goss, *Cincinnati: The Queen City* (Chicago: S. J. Clarke, 1912), 456–52. Also Joseph E. Holliday, "Notes on Samuel N. Pike and his Opera Houses," *Bulletin of the Cincinnati Historical Society* 25, no. 3 (July 1967): 165–83.

6. The *Cincinnati Enquirer*, April 23 and 24, 1862, praised the "orchestral arrangement of this Opera [as] entirely faultless, while the grand chorus of one hundred voices is superior to any ever heard in the Opera House" but took extreme umbrage at "the howling, shrieks, &c., added to the music during the casting of the balls." For more information on opera production by these and other German singing societies, see Suzanne Gail Snyder, "The Männerchor Tradition in the United States: A Historical Analysis of Its Contribution to American Musical Culture" (Ph.D. diss., University of Iowa, 1991): 82–93.

7. Pike rebuilt almost immediately, but the structure which opened in fall 1867 was considerably more modest, in effect a concert hall seating sixteen hundred. It was expanded in 1871 and as a theater served as one center of the city's cultural life until it burned again on February 26, 1903.

8. The *Enquirer* opined on February 5, 1879, that hers was "a magical piece of acting, full of intelligence, power, and wicked grace."

9. Henry E[ugene] Abbey (1846–96), was born in Akron, the son of a prosperous jeweler, who had organized the Akron Brass Band in 1840, an ensemble active for two decades. However, according to his extensive obituary in the *New York Times* of October 18, 1896, he "was not bent on ordinary mercantile pursuits" and initiated his managerial career by selling tickets at the Akron Opera House, which he then leased in 1869 and in which he successfully produced spoken plays. His father died in 1871, and Henry briefly took charge of the inherited business, which was soon "reduced to a very ordinary condition," once Abbey realized that "he was not fitted to pursue a calling of trade." He sold the shop and briefly managed Akron's new Academy of Music before moves to Cleveland, Pittsburgh, and Buffalo on his way to New York, where he acquired experience managing the likes of Sarah Bernhardt, Edwin Booth, Henry Irving, and Adelina Patti. In partnership with John B. Schoeffel and, later, Maruice Grau, he owned and managed theaters in Boston and Philadelphia as well as in New York; it was the firm Abbey, Schoeffel, and Grau that was granted the lease of the new Metropolitan Opera House when it opened on October 22, 1883. See also

Michael J. Pisoni, "Operatic War in New York City, 1883–84: Colonel James H. Mapelson at the Academy of Music vs. Henry E. Abbey at the Metropolitan Opera House" (Ph.D. diss., Indiana University, 1975), 56–70.

10. Oscar Wilde, in town to lecture at the Grand Opera House, was among her listeners. For Cincinnati, one important outcome of her visit was the suggestion that her accompanist, Albino Gorno, join the faculty of the College of Music, which he did, with a tenure lasting until 1943.

11. This ugly incident was provoked by public indignation over a manslaughter verdict for a man who had confessed guilt to an especially brutal murder. A mob forced itself into the local jail only to find that the criminal had been moved to Columbus. Militiamen and eventually troops were called out to restore public order, but only after the courthouse had been damaged by fire; fifty-eight people were killed and more than two hundred injured.

12. Joseph E. Holliday studies these events, as well as an 1886 festival presented by the American Opera Company of New York, in "Cincinnati Opera Festivals During the Gilded Age," *Bulletin of the Cincinnati Historical Society* 24, no. 2 (Apr. 1966): 131–49.

13 The Highland House was a resort situated at the top of the Mount Adams incline. Completed in 1876, it included a concert hall, theater, bowling facilities, restaurants, a beer garden, and picnic grounds. The pavilion, or belvedere, seated fourteen hundred, while an adjacent esplanade could accommodate another four thousand. Thomas returned in 1879 and 1881, but the place went into decline during the 1890s and was closed in 1895, to be replaced by the Sterling Glass Company in 1902.

14. Holliday, "Three World Premières of Grand Opera," *Bulletin of the Cincinnati Historical Society* 36, no. 2 (Summer 1978): 117–20.

15. See Eldred A. Thierstein, *Cincinnati Opera: From the Zoo to Music Hall* (Hillsdale, Mich.: Deerstone, 1995). The volume contains a prose history, illustrations, and a detailed statistical history of the organization's first seventy-five seasons, 1920 to 1995, with complete rosters of repertory and performers.

16 Lyford's opera, *Castle Agrarrot*, completed in 1922, had its first performances in Music Hall on April 29, 1926. The work was set in France at the time of the Crusades and had to do with the perils of the wife of a knight who was off doing battle in the Holy Land. Lyford conducted soloists mostly imported from Chicago, a chorus of sixty-five, and sixty members of the Cincinnati Symphony. For more detail, see Holliday, "Three World Premières of Grand Opera," 119–21.

17. Thierstein, *Cincinnati Opera*, 16, describes the piece as a two-act work on a libretto of Richard L. Stone, set in Vienna and having something to do with an incident in the life of Mozart. It was noted in the *Times-Star* on July 3 as the first opera to employ "the distinctly American rhythms of syncopation or jazz in the development of a musical theme." The composer supposedly justified his use of the newfangled jazz by pointing out that Mozart was prone to use the current musical practices of his day.

18. Fellers and Meyers, *Discographies of Commercial Recordings*, 162–63, 175–79.

19. That summer also saw passing reference to a local supernumerary who has since achieved international stature in opera pits and elsewhere around the globe when the *Times-Star* in its July 12 review of the previous evening's *La Bohème* noted that the head waiter of the Café Momus "was kept busy Sunday night shooing Jimmy Levine and several other street-arabs away from the tables."

20. He had been awarded an honorary doctorate by the College of Music of Cincinnati in 1944.

21. The work was sung in English, as became increasingly common. In earlier decades the company generally sang in the original languages, although not with absolute consistency. There are even humorous examples of multilingual evenings with singers unable or unwilling to relearn their roles in a tongue unfamiliar to them.

22. Saturday evening performances were being broadcast locally on WGUC-FM.

23. Janelle Gelfand, "De Blasis Led with Business Head, Artistic Soul," *Cincinnati Enquirer*, June 30, 1996, describes that career, based on an interview with de Blasis. The article includes as a sidebar, "James de Blasis' Memorable Moments."

19. MAY FESTIVAL

1. For additional information, see a history in the 1995 May Festival program book and Cecilia Scearce Chewning's "Timeline" in the 2000 program book, which also includes a list of May Festival premières, a list of repertoire by composer, including the year(s) in which each work was performed, and a list of soloists, conductors, and chorus masters, including their years of participation; Sylvia Kleve Sheblessy's chatty and unreliable *100 Years of the Cincinnati May Festival* (Cincinnati, 1973); *Cincinnati Sings: A Choral History, 1788 to 1988* (Cincinnati: Saengerfest '88, 1988); and Louis R. Thomas, "A History of the Cincinnati Symphony Orchestra to 1931" (Ph.D. diss., University of Cincinnati, 1972).

2. Theodore Thomas, *Theodore Thomas: A Musical Autobiography*, vol. 1, ed. George P. Upton (Chicago: A. C. McClurg, 1905), 78–79.

3. Granville L. Howe, ed., *A Hundred Years of Music in America*, W. S. B. Mathews, assoc. ed. (Chicago: G. L. Howe, 1889), 446.

4. Ezra Schabas, *Theodore Thomas: America's Conductor and Builder of Orchestras, 1835–1905* (Urbana: Univ. of Illinois Press, 1989), 56.

5. Rose Fay Thomas, *Memoirs of Theodore Thomas* (New York: Moffat, Yeard, and Co., 1911), 93. The 1873 festival programs are given in their entirety on pages 89–93.

6. Schabas, *Theodore Thomas*, 57–58.

7. Ibid., 64.

8. Rose Fay Thomas, *Memoirs of Theodore Thomas*, 99.

9. The saga is complex, its outcome jeopardized several times by bickering among competing constituencies. For details see Zane Miller, *Cincinnati's Music Hall* (Virginia Beach, Va.: Jordan, 1978), Section One, "Music Hall: Its Neighborhood, The City and the Metropolis," 24–32. For a more current history, see Ashley L, Ford, comp., *Cincinnati's Music Hall: A Brief History of the Grand Old Lady of Elm Street, in Timeline Form* (Cincinnati: Society for the Preservation of Music Hall, 1998).

10. For a complete chronicle, from Hannford's appointment through various stages of gentrification, see George F. Roth, "The Building of Music Hall," in Ford, *Cincinnati's Music Hall*, 60–87.

11. See Robert C. Vitz, *The Queen and the Arts: Cultural Life in Nineteenth-Century Cincinnati* (Kent: Kent State Univ. Press, 1989), 190–94. Vitz also evokes the flavor of the early May Festivals in his prologue and chapter 4, "Of Musical Matters, 1867–1878."

12. See Parvin Titus, "Famous Cincinnati Music Hall Organ Has Interesting History," *Tracker* 9, no. 3 (Spring 1965): 9–13.

13. According to a remarkably detailed description of the 1880 festival in the *Cincinnati Daily Gazette* of May 15 (including biographies of all the principal performers, a description and complete rosters of both orchestra and chorus, a history of the festivals to that point, and "In the Beginning: A Glimpse at Early Music in Cincinnati"), Singer had also written a cantata, *The Landing of the Pilgrim Fathers* ("a setting in the ultra modern style of the familiar poem by Mrs. Hemans"), as well as a symphony, two piano concerti (both of which he had played with the Cincinnati Orchestra), a rhapsodie for piano and orchestra, a fantasia for solo piano, and other more modest pieces for piano, as well as early works for piano and violin which had been published in Germany.

14. According to Rose Fay Thomas, *Memoirs of Theodore Thomas*, 142, this marked his first go at the piece in its entirety.

15. Of the twenty-four entries, apparently only the Buck and a work by Whiting remained in final contention. Whiting accused Thomas of having unduly influenced Otto Singer and even of having asked Buck, a friend and earlier colleague, to alter details of his offering. After the scandal had percolated across the country it was revealed that Whiting had not followed the regulations of the competition and should have been disqualified. For details, see Schabas, *Theodore Thomas*, 95–96.

16. Louis R. Thomas, "A History of the Cincinnati Orchestra to 1931," 84.

17. William Leonard Blumenschein (1849–1916), a German emigrant, served as an organist and choral conductor in the Ohio River towns of Portsmouth and Ironton before settling in Dayton, where he became organist of the Third Street Presbyterian Church and conductor of the Dayton Philharmonic Society as of 1881. He supposedly wrote about 150 pieces, although the highest opus number encountered is 127, attached to a *Polonaise* for piano published in 1908. His legacy includes anthems (for example, *The Blessings*, opus 21, for tenor solo, choir, and organ [1893]), liturgical music, songs, and character pieces for the piano (for instance, a *Coquette Gavotte*, opus 41 [1891] or *Napolitana, Danse Charactéristique*, opus 112 [1906]).

18. Saar (1868–1937) was to head the theory department of the College of Music from 1906 to 1917.

19. Jerrold Northrop Moore, *Edward Elgar: A Creative Life* (Oxford, U.K.: Oxford Univ. Press, 1984), 463.

20. Ibid., 498.

21. Kunwald, who returned to his homeland following the war, was later forced to flee Hitler's Germany. He was reputed to have lamented that, "I got into trouble in Cincinnati for being too German, and I got into trouble in Berlin for not being German enough." Sheblessy, *100 Years of the Cincinnati May Festival*, 55.

22. Ibid., 57.

23. Heller (1892–1971) was associated with the Isaac M. Wise Temple. In 1942 he published a history of the temple to commemorate the centenary of the founding of the congregation, and in 1965 issued a biography of Wise. He also annotated programs for the Cincinnati Symphony from 1926 until 1938 and lectured on musicology at the Conservatory of Music. Born in New Orleans, he did his undergraduate work at Tulane University, took a master's degree from the University of Cincinnati in 1914, and completed work at Cincinnati's Hebrew Union College two years later. In addition to this oratorio, he wrote three aquatints

for string quartet, opus 1 (1929), four sketches for orchestra (played for the first time by the Cincinnati Symphony under Goossens on February 8, 1939), an elegy and pastorale for voice and orchestra, a violin sonata, anthems, hymns for the *New Union Hymnal* (1932), and, in consort with C. Hugo Grimm and Sidney Durst, *Six Friday Evening Services for Solo Voice and Organ According to the Union Prayer Book* (1936).

24. Sheblessy, *100 Years of the Cincinnati May Festival*, 90.

25. Ibid.

20. BALDWIN WALLACE COLLEGE BACH FESTIVAL

1. See Elinore Barber, "Dr. Albert Riemenschneider: A Centenary Tribute," *Diapason*, September 1978, 1, 8–9.

2. See Don[ald] Rosenberg, "Bringing Bach and His Buddies to Berea," *Beacon: The Sunday Magazine of the Akron Beacon Journal*, March 18, 1979, 4–7, 22–23.

3. *A History of the Baldwin-Wallace College Bach Festival* (Berea: Riemenschneider Bach Institute, 1982) contains two essays: Selma Marting Riemenschneider, "A History of the Baldwin-Wallace College Bach Festival (1933–1964)" and Elinore Barber, "The Baldwin-Wallace College Bach Festival, 1965–1982."

4. Another considerably more modest celebration has taken place in Marietta since 1923. Thomas H. Cisler founded the Marietta Bach Society and presided over its annual gatherings on July 30, commemorating what Cisler mandated as the anniversary of the composer's death (scholars insist that it actually occurred two days earlier). After Cisler's death in 1950, the mantle passed to daughter Lillian, who presided over the seventieth gathering at Cisler Terrace before her death in February 1993. The celebration was resumed in 1994, coordinated by Barbara Beittel. During the Cislers' era, membership in the society was by invitation only, as was attendance at the annual performances. Each of these was intended to trace the progress of the liturgical year, beginning not with the First Sunday in Advent but with Reformation Sunday, employing bits and pieces drawn from the vast repertory available for that purpose. Rehearsals were held monthly until May, thereafter weekly until the commemorative day. One parallel with the Berea festival is that starting in 1928 each performance was prefaced with chorale harmonizations played by a brass choir from Marietta High School.

21. PROTESTANT AND JEWISH HYMNALS

1. Thomas S. Hinde, *The Pilgrim's Songster, or, A Choice Collection of Spiritual Songs, from the Best Authors, with Original Pieces, Never before in Print* (Chillicothe: Fredonian, 1815).

2. Joseph Muenschner, *The Church Choir: A Collection of Sacred Music* (Columbus: Isaac N. Whiting, 1839), vi.

3. A most intriguing volume once part of the Ohio Historical Society's collection but now missing is *Hymns for the Ohio Lunatic Asylum, Alphabetically Arranged*, published in Columbus in 1848.

4. The full title: *Die Kleine Lieder-Sammlung, oder Auszug aus dem Psalterspiel, der Kinder Zion's zum Dienst inninger heilzuchender Seelen, Insonderheit aber der Brüderschaft der Täufer*

zum Dienst und Gebrauch zusammengetragen in gegenwärtige kleine Form, und mit einen dreyfachen Register versehen. Translated as . . . *of Zion, for the service of those souls seeking salvation, especially, however, for the service and use of the brotherhood of the baptized, bound together in a small form and furnished with a threefold index.* The "register" includes alphabetical listings by title, tune, and appropriate liturgical use. Later editions, such as the 8th edition of 1844, referred to the *Gemeinden der Brüder* or *Congregations of the Brothers.*

5. See Donald F. Durnbaugh, "Henry Kurtz: Man of the Book," *Ohio History* (Summer 1967): 114–31, 173–76; or Harry A. Brandt, *Meet Henry Kurtz* (Elgin, Ill.: Brethren, 1941).

6. For an analysis of its history and contents, as well as that of *The Brethren Hymn Book,* its English language successor of 1867, see Nevin W. Fisher, *The History of Brethren Hymnbooks* (Bridgewater, Va.: Beacon, 1950), 35–52. Fisher also did a study of Kurtz, *A Choice Selection of Hymns,* but worked from an edition of 1852, which he assumed was the volume's first and only appearance.

7. See Ron Rarick, "The Baroque Organ at Elgin: A Saga," *Diapason* (Sept. 1998): 14–16. The instrument has been reconstructed and now stands in the Church of the Brethren in Elgin, Illinois. The description of Kurtz at the keyboard was taken by Rarick from Henry R. Holsinger, *Holsinger's History of the Tunkers and the Brethren Church* (Lathrop, Calif.: Pacific, 1901; repr. North Manchester, Ind.: L. W. Schultz, 1962), 353–54.

8. See Allan Peskin, *The Tempting Freedom: The Early Years of Cleveland Judaism and Anshe Chesed Congregation,* pamphlet, Western Reserve Historical Society: PAM. P143.

9. It would be nice to claim yet another Buckeye first (as Cohen wished us to believe), but that honor belongs to Gustavus Poznanski (1805–79), cantor of the Congregation Beth Elohim in Charleston, South Carolina, who had by 1832 assembled *Hymns Written for the Service of the Hebrew Congregation Beth Elohim,* its format resembling that of contemporaneous Protestant hymnals. Revised and enlarged editions were issued in 1843 and 1856, incorporating the work of poet Penina Moise (1797–1880). See Irene Heske, *Passport to Jewish Music* (Westport, Conn.: Greenwood, 1994), 180–85.

10. G[ustave] M. Cohen, *The Sacred Harp of Judah. A Choice Collection of Music for the use of Synagogues, Schools, and Home* (Cleveland: S. Brainard, 1864), 2.

11. Ibid., 3.

12. Ibid.

13. Cohen, *The Orpheus, or Musical Recreations, for the Family Circle and Public Worship* (Cleveland: S. Brainard, 1878), preface.

14. As noted elsewhere, later Ohio temple musicians contributed to the repertory of service music. A few of them, somewhat in chronological order, are James H. Rogers (*Service for Sabbath Evening* [1912], *Sabbath Morning Service for the Synagogue; According to the Union Prayer Book* [1913], *Temple Service for the Evening of the New Year* [1916], and *Music for the Sabbath Evening Service of the Temple According to the Union Prayer-Book* [1925]); C. Hugo Grimm (*Sabbath Morning Service for the Synagogue According to the Union Prayer Book* [1916] and, with James G. Heller and Sidney C. Durst, *Friday Evening Service: Six Services for Solo Voice and Organ According to the Union Prayer Book* [1936]); Charles De Harrack (*Sabbath Eve Service for the Synagogue* [1940?] and *Synagogue Music for the Sabbath and High Holidays* [n.d.]).

1. See Roger D. Launius, *The Kirtland Temple: A Historical Narrative* (Independence, Mo.: Herald House, 1986). The architectural gem is now a National Historic Landmark, owned and managed by the Reorganized Church of Jesus Christ of Latter Day Saints but open to the public. Also see Donald L. Huber, "The Prophet Joseph in Ohio," *Timeline* 16, no. 6 (Nov.–Dec. 1999): 2–17.

2. Emma Smith, *A Collection of Sacred Hymns, for the Church of the Latter Day Saints*, (Kirtland: F. G. Williams., 1835; repr. n.p.: Herald Heritage, 1973).

3. The service is described in Launius, *The Kirtland Temple*, 65–69, and in detail as appendix 2, pages 173–79.

23. THE SHAKERS

1. See Martha Boice, Dale Covington, and Richard Spence, *Maps of the Shaker West: A Journey of Discovery* (Dayton: Knot Garden, 1997).

2. Copland discovered "Simple Gifts" in Edward Deming Andrews, *The Gift to be Simple* (J. J. Augustin, 1940; repr. New York: Dover, 1962). See also Roger L. Hall, *The Story of "Simple Gifts,"* rev. 3d ed. (Holland, Mich.: World of Shaker, 1992).

3. See Daniel W. Patterson, *The Shaker Spiritual* (Princeton, N.J.: Princeton Univ. Press, 1979).

4. Amos Taylor, *A Narrative of the Strange Principles, Conduct, and Character Of the People known by the Name of Shakers* (Worcester, Mass., 1782), qtd. in Andrews, *The Gift to be Simple*, 143. Andrews discusses Shaker dancing in detail, 143–57; Patterson, *The Shaker Spiritual*, discusses Shaker dancing, 245–315 and 377–96.

5. Patterson, *The Shaker Spiritual*, 40–56, describes the system in detail. Donald E. Christensen in "A Transcription to Modern Notation of a Shaker Hymnal by Issac Youngs Based on His Theory Book" (master's thesis, Indiana University of Pennsylvania, 1976) analyzed and transcribed a manuscript collection of Young's found in the collection of the Ohio Historical Society, *A Collection of Anthems and Spiritual Songs; Improved in our General worship. From the year 1813 to 1837. Transcribed and Written in this Book, by INY* [New Lebanon, December], *1854*.

6. Patterson, *The Shaker Spiritual*, 32.

7. Qtd. in Andrews, *The Gift to Be Simple*, 12, from Young's manuscript *Journal of One Year, Jan. 1, 1805, to Dec. 31, 1805*.

8. Patterson, *The Shaker Spiritual*, 240–41.

9. See J. P. MacLean, *Shakers of Ohio: Fugitive Papers Concerning the Shakers of Ohio, With Unpublished Manuscripts* (Columbus: F. J. Heer, 1907), 367–79.

10. This and other Union Village collections were thoroughly studied and analyzed by Donald E. Christensen, "Music of the Shakers from Union Village, Ohio: A Repertory Study and Tune Index of the Manuscripts Originating in the 1840's" (Ph.D. diss., Ohio State University, 1988). Available through UMI.

11. Richard McNemar, *A Selection of Hymns and Poems; For the Use of Believers. Collected from Sundry Authors, by Philos Harmonae* (Watervliet, Ohio, 1833), 4.

12. Roger L. Hall, *A Western Shaker Music Sampler* (Cleveland: Western Reserve Historical Society, 1976) and *Love Is Little: A Sampling of Shaker Spirituals* (Holland, Mich.: World of Shaker, 1992), with a companion CD, Sampler Records 9222.

13. Andrews, *The Gift to Be Simple*, 106.

24. White Gospel Song

1. *The New Grove Dictionary of American Music*, vol. 2, ed. H. Wiley Hitchcock and Stanley Sadie (London: Macmillan, 1986), 249.

2. Donald P. Hustad, *Jubilate! Church Music in the Evangelical Tradition.* (Carol Stream, Ill.: Hope, 1981), 130.

3. Bernard Ruffin, *Fanny Crosby* (Philadelphia, Pa.: United Church Press, 1976), 112.

4. Three of Augustus Dameron Fillmore's works can be heard on *Where Home Is: Life in Nineteenth-Century Cincinnati*, 1977, 1995, New World Records 80251-2.

5. See William Osborne, "The echoes of his songs go from lip to lip the world 'round': William Howard Doane: Industrialist, Composer, and Philanthropist," *Queen City Heritage* 56, no. 2 (Summer 1998): 2–28.

6. His adventures are charmingly described in *Song Pilgrimage around the World. Illustrated by Pen and Pencil, Including Experiences, Sights, Anecdotes, Incidents, Impressions of Men and Things, throughout Twenty Different Countries* (New York: Phillips and Hunt, 1882). He proves an adept and captivating travel writer, and the 162 illustrations offer period views of everything from American railroad cars to the Clarendon vineyard near Adelaide, Australia, a devil dance in Ceylon, and a street scene in Cairo.

7. J. H. Hall, *Biography of Gospel Song and Hymn Writers* (New York: Fleming H. Revel, 1914; repr. New York: AMS Edition, 1971), 119–23.

8. Ibid., 61.

9. The "Thompson & Co. Confidential Price List," 1880s, Ohio Historical Society. PA Box 517/14.

10. See C. B. Galbreath, "Will Lamartine Thompson," *Ohio Archeological and Historical Quarterly* 14, no. 3 (1905): 291–312. This article is one of a Song Writers of Ohio series.

11. Excell's father deserves at least passing recognition because of the *Cantionibus Spiritualibus. A Collection of Sacred Hymns and Poems for Meditation, Thanksgiving and Praise!*, self-published in Wooster in 1901 by J. J. Excell. Besides a portrait of Reverend Excell and his wife, the poems, and a prose description of the Excells' trip to England during September and October of 1900, the volume contains sixteen hymns with both words and music by the author. He also published *The Lily. A Collection of Sacred Hymns for the Sabbath School, Sanctuary and Social Worship* (Cleveland, 1885).

12. Hall, *Biography of Gospel Song and Hymn Writers*, 298–302.

13. See Carl M. Becker's lavishly illustrated "Brighten the Corner Where You Are: Homer Rodeheaver," *Timeline* 17, no. 3 (May–June 2000): 38–53.

1. See John A. Hostetler, "Ritual Integration of the Community," *Amish Society*, 4th ed. (Baltimore, Md.: Johns Hopkins Univ. Press, 1993), 209–33 (chap. 10).

2. See Lois Zimmer Craig, "Moravian Lovefeast," *Wonderful World of Ohio* (Dec. 1967): 17–19.

3. A handsome reconstruction of the village with seventeen replicas of the original sixty log buildings is maintained as a state memorial, operated by the Ohio Historical Society. Area Moravians hold Love Feasts in the Chapel every December. See Susan Goehring, *Schoenbrunn: A Meeting of Cultures* (Columbus: Ohio Historical Society, 1997), which has also been published separately as one of a series issued by the Ohio Historical Society profiling Ohio's state memorials.

4. See Lawrence W. Hartzell's contributions to Stanley A. Kaufman, *Moravians in Ohio* (Walnut Creek: German Culture Museum, 1987). Hartzell assembled his findings in *Ohio Moravian Music* (Winston-Salem, N.C.: Moravian Music Foundation, 1988).

5. *The Journal of Nicholas Cresswell 1774–1777*, 2d ed. (New York: Dial, 1928), 106–7. Cresswell's "Dutchman" was surely a German, the common corruption of *deutsch*, still prevalent in references to the Pennsylvania Dutch.

6. See Earl P. Olmstead, *Blackcoats among the Delaware: David Zeisberger on the Ohio Frontier* (Kent: Kent State Univ. Press, 1991), as well as Olmstead, *David Zeisberger: A Life among the Indians* (Kent: Kent State Univ. Press, 1997).

7. Cresswell, *The Journal of Nicholas Cresswell*, 111.

8. Schmick returned to Lititz in 1777 and died there early the following year ministering as a chaplain to wounded Revolutionary War soldiers. See Hartzell, "Musical Moravian Missionaries: Part Three, Johann Jakob Schmick," *Moravian Music Journal* 30, no. 2 (Fall 1985): 36–37.

9. Hartzell, *Ohio Moravian Music*, 36.

10. Cresswell, *The Journal of Nicholas Cresswell*, 112. Obviously a phonetic orthographer, Cresswell heard Gnadenhütten as "Kanaughtonhead."

11. Hartzell, *Ohio Moravian Music*, 35–36. For congregational versions of the "Hosanna," see nos. 115 and 116 in *Hymnal and Liturgies of the Moravian Church* (1969).

12. Several articles sold from that store are displayed at the John Heckewelder Memorial Moravian Church in Gnadenhütten.

13. Hartzell, *Ohio Moravian Music*, 133.

14. Ibid., 47.

15. Ibid., 50.

16. Folklore attributes it to the hand of John Antes, a composer born in Bethlehem, who during early 1760s made at least seven stringed instruments, probably the first to be crafted in the colonies. Several remain in Pennsylvania museums, leading to the wishful conjecture that his single cello may have made its way to the frontier.

17. Hartzell, *Ohio Moravian Music*, 51–52.

1. See Edgar Burkhardt Nixon, "The Society of Separatists at Zoar" (Ph.D. diss., Ohio State University, 1933), and *Zoar: An Ohio Experiment in Communalism* (Columbus: Ohio State Archaeological and Historical Society, 1952; repr. Ohio Historical Society, 1996), a lavishly illustrated pamphlet with no attributed author but that obviously relies heavily on Nixon. Two other sources present charming, contemporaneous views of the community: Charles Nordhoff, "The Society of Separatists, at Zoar, Ohio," in *The Communistic Societies of the United States from Personal Visit and Observation* (New York: Harper and Brothers, 1874; repr. New York: Dover, 1966), and E[milius] O. Randall, *The Separatist Society of Zoar: An Experiment in Communism from Its Commencement to Its Conclusion* (Columbus: Ohio State Archaeological and History Society, 1900; repr. [s.i.]: Arthur W. McGraw, 1990).

2. This and similar Bimeler pronouncements were surely derived from a pre-1816 statement of "Separatist Principle." Qtd. in Nixon, "The Society of Separatists at Zoar," 14.

3. No. 7 of the "Principles of the Separatists," originally found in the works of Joseph Bimeler. Qtd. in Randall, *The Separatist Society of Zoar,* 14.

4. Randall, *The Separatist Society of Zoar,* 18.

5. These lines conclude the first of twelve verses of "Demüthige Unterwesung unter der Führung Gottes" ("Humble Instruction under the Leadership of God") and was to be sung to the tune "Stille Schaar, dein schooner Gang" ("Silent, Group, Your Beautiful Procession"). Both volumes of *Sammlung auserlesener geistlicher Lieder, zum gemeinschäftlichen Gesang und eigenen Gebrauch in Christlichen Familien* are at the Ohio Historical Society. The 1854 edition is cataloged as V245.30491/Sa45/1855, despite a clear "1854" on its title page. The 1867 version is V245.30491/Sa45/1867.

6. See Hilda Dischinger Morhart, *The Zoar Story,* 3d ed. (Strasburg: Gordon, 1981), 99. The instrument still exists in what is now the Zoar United Church of Christ, a building planned by Joseph Bimeler and completed in 1853, the year of his death. It originally had separate entrances for men and women, who then sat apart from one another but facing the doors so as to embarrass latecomers. The Votteler Company, founded in 1855, was the antecedent of today's Holtkamp Organ Company. Hints of an organ in the log structure that served as meetinghouse prior to 1853 remain undocumented.

7. Ibid., 101.

8. See Richard D. Wetzel, *Frontier Musicians on the Connoquenessing, Wabash, and Ohio: A History of the Music and Musicians of George Rapp's Harmony Society (1805–1906)* (Athens: Ohio Univ. Press, 1976), 98–101 (for information about Rohr), 102–37 (for information about Duss). Rohr's authorship can only be inferred, since the composer's name is incomplete on the part.

9. One other inference of the orchestra's repertoire during the waning years of the society is a folder bearing the imprint, "H. J. Votteler's Popular Music for Orchestra, Reed and Brass Bands. Importer of and Dealer in Musical Instruments and Merchandise. Italian, German and French Strings for All Instruments. Sheet Music and Music Books, Music Paper, Blank Music Books and Folios. No. 179 Ontario St., Cleveland, O." Assigned to Frank Kapper (1867–1937), it contains parts for the bass, some handwritten. Among them are Weber's *Invitation to the Dance,* excerpts from Verdi's *Il Trovatore,* M. Carl's *Das Hirten Klagelied,* Josef Rixner's *Aus schöner Zeit, Walzer,* opus 362, L. Franke's *Ein Frühlings Idyll,* a waltz by Emil Waldteufel, A. Parlow's *The Anvil,* and an unattributed *Amusement Quadrille.*

10. Nixon, "The Society of Separatists at Zoar," 90–91.

11. The only Beuter works with which I have had contact are *Sounds from the Ohio, A March* (New York: William A. Pond, 1869), and *Chase of the Butterflies*, opus 18, a "Polka Rondo" for piano (Cleveland: S. Brainard's Sons, 1884).

12. Nixon, "The Society of Separatists at Zoar, " 92.

13. A further sense of music making in Zoar can be inferred from 1858 bills for brass band music, a violin bow and strings, and the repair of a flute.

27. THE GERMAN SINGING SOCIETIES

1. See Suzanne Gail Snyder, "The Männerchor Tradition in the United States: A Historical Analysis of Its Contribution to American Musical Culture" (Ph.D. diss., University of Iowa, 1991). Also, Orlo Omer Sprunger, "The North American Saengers Union" (master's thesis, Ohio State University, 1951).

2. Another piece of evidence of singing schools in Zoar is a copy, in the Zoar archives, of William B. Bradbury, *The Jubilee: An Extensive Collection of Choral Music* (New York: Mason Brothers, 1858), a "new edition," one of several such publications by this prominent member of the Lowell Mason crowd, its didactic section called "The New Singing Class." The inside of the front cover is inscribed with the name of Solomon Ackermann (1853–1928), a shoemaker and tenor, "At the Zoar Singing School, Tuscarawas County Ohio: John Doershuck Teacher." Of Doershuck we know nothing, except that he was not a formal member of the Society.

3. See G. A. Dobbert, "The 'Zinzinnati' in Cincinnati," *Bulletin of the Cincinnati Historical Society* 22, no. 4 (Oct. 1964): 209–20.

4. Frédéric Louis Ritter, *Music in America* (New York: Scribner, 1883; rev. 1895), 403–4.

5. Henry Krehbiel, *Review of the New York Musical Scene, 1887–88* (New York: Novello, Ewer, and Co., 1888), 7.

6. Oswald Seidensticker, *Geschicte des Männerchors in Philadelphia, 1835–1885* (Philadelphia, Pa.: Verlag des Männerchors, 1885), 53. Seidensticker's census of other "western" states found only two societies in Kentucky and Indiana, one in Michigan.

7. Snyder, "The Männerchor Tradition in the United States," 499–507.

8. Only ten of these can be definitely linked to those listed by Snyder. *Frohsinn* means cheerfulness or gaiety; the United Ancient Order of Druids was a secret society that had been imported from England to this country in 1830 and to Germany in 1872 but is now defunct; the German order of Harugari, which by 1907 had about thirty thousand members in some three hundred lodges, honored an ancient German hero; Georg Herwegh (1817–75) was a nationalistic poet and commentator. Many of these societies were named for the area from which the majority of their members had emigrated, for instance, the Rheinpfalz or Swabia.

9. Schneider's papers were deposited at the Ohio Historical Society (MSS 643) by his son. The earliest document dates from 1858, thus reflecting his subsequent career in Lancaster. One example is "Chas. F. Hoffman's Notebook. Lancaster, Fairfield Country. Ohio 1881. Violin—Prof. Schneider." Other items refer to the career of daughter Caroline, a concert pianist.

10. See La Vern J. Rippley, "German Theater in Columbus, Ohio," *German-American Studies* 1, no. 2 (1970): 78–101.

11. Both these pamphlets are found in the University of Cincinnati Archives and Rare Books Department, Blegen Library. Don Heinrich Tolzmann, the curator, has created a two-volume *Catalog of the German-American Collection* (Munich, New York, Paris, and London: K. G. Saur, 1990); the catalog is also available on-line at www.archives.uc.edu/german.

12. *Official Souvenir of the Eighth Saengerfest of the Central Ohio Saengerbund, Chillicothe, Ohio, July, 20, 21, 22, and 23, 1896*, 8. The Ohio Historical Society owns a photographic portrait of the massed forces involved (OVS 3195) on the verso of which someone has inscribed by hand the orchestra roster, as well as the complete repertory of each concert, including the names of soloists (SC 1135).

13. High praise indeed, since the Dodworth clan, particularly Allen T. (1817–92), created what became known as the Dodworth Band, certainly the finest ensemble of its sort during this period.

14. Jacob H. Studer, *Columbus, Ohio, Its History, Resources and Progress* (Columbus: J. H. Studer, 1873), 56–57.

15. See Tolzmann, "Musenklänge aus Cincinnati," *Bulletin of the Cincinnati Historical Society* 35, no. 2 (Summer 1977): 115–29. The Heinrich A. Ratterman Collection of German American Manuscripts is housed in the Illinois Historical Survey section of the University of Illinois Library. A guide to the collection by Donna-Christine Sell and Dennis Francis Walle was published in 1979.

16. Bergmann served as the first music director of the Arion Society of New York, a prominent German singing society founded in 1854.

17. *Official Souvenir of the Twenty-Seventh Saengerfest of the North American Saengerbund, held at Cleveland, Ohio, July 11, 12, 13, and 14, 1893* (Cleveland: Williams, 1893), 38.

28. THE WELSH

1. For a sense of life in these early Welsh settlements, see B. W. Chidlaw, *The American, Which Contains Notes on a Journey from the Ohio Valley to Wales, A Look at the State of Ohio; History of Welsh Settlements in America, Instructions for Inquirers Before the Journey, On the Journey, and After Its Completion*, trans. R. Gwilym Williams (Bala, Wales: County Press, 1978). Originally published in Welsh in 1840, its intent is explicit in its title. For general information, see Edward George Hartmann, *Americans from Wales* (Boston, Mass.: Christopher, 1967), particularly chapter 4, "The Story of Nineteenth Century Welsh Immigration to America," 61–100. For a more intimate sense of the earliest Welsh influxes, see William Harvey Jones, "Welsh Settlements in Ohio," *Ohio Archaeological and Historical Society Quarterly* 16 (Apr. 1907): 194–227.

2. See Hamer Mitchell, "The Eisteddfod in Ohio" (master's thesis, Ohio State University, 1943), and Linda Louise Pohly, "Welsh Choral Music in America in the Nineteenth Century" (Ph.D. diss., Ohio State University, 1989).

3. Pohly, "Welsh Choral Music in America in the Nineteenth Century," 149–59, creates a graphic presentation of all the known Welsh musical events prior to 1900 in appendix A.

4. In this program, as was common, he was identified only as Pantycelyn, the town where he died. His best-known hymn is "Cwm Rhondda," translated from the original Welsh in 1771, beginning with the words "Guide me, O thou great Jehovah" and usually sung to music from 1907 by John Hughes (1873–1932).

5. Competitions were even held under the auspices of the Philharmonic Club of Columbus (on New Year's Day, 1898) or the Centerville Lodge, No. 371, of the Free and Accepted Masons of Thurman (a series in Rio Grande initiated during 1937).

6. Those who sponsored a similar gathering exactly a year later in Columbus highlighted the unusual chronology by naming theirs the Nineteenth and Twentieth Century Eisteddfod.

7. Protheroe (1866–1934) was a ubiquitous figure in American Welsh musical circles after his immigration from Wales in 1886, having achieved some renown there as a winner of the solo competitions at the National Eisteddfodau in 1880 and 1881 and as conductor of the Choral Society of his native Ystradgynlais for two years. He worked as a choral conductor in Scranton, Pennsylvania, until 1894, after which he settled in Milwaukee until 1909 and Chicago thereafter. He wrote a symphonic poem, two string quartets, a Mass, partsongs for male chorus, solo songs, hymn tunes (including "Wilkes-Barre" and "Milwaukee"), and a *Course in Harmony and Choral Conducting*.

8. For more information, see Raymond L. Boothe, "Unique Singing Tradition in the Jackson City Schools Celebrates 69th Anniversary," *Triad* 59 (Apr. 1992): 52–53. I gained further insights from a telephone conversation with Mr. Davis.

9. This and similar program books are in the collections of the Welsh-American Heritage Museum, Oak Hill, Ohio.

10. Parry, composer of oratorios, cantatas, anthems, and about four hundred hymn tunes, arrived in Danville, Pennsylvania, with his family in 1854. After some initial musical training by his fellow ironworkers he won his first Eisteddfod prize in composition in 1860, and the local Welsh colony raised money to send him to the normal college at Geneseo, New York. After winning other prizes in this country and a special award at the Aberystwyth Eisteddfod in the summer of 1865, he accumulated funds for advanced study in part by giving concerts of his own works. In 1868 he returned to Great Britain for three years of study at the Royal Academy and degrees from Cambridge University. After several years directing a music school in Danville, he returned "home," permanently, to a career that included professorships at the new Welsh University College at Aberystwyth and University College in Cardiff.

11. Susan Porter, in an unpublished essay, "Music in 19th-Century Lima," described the business block completed in 1882 for Benjamin C. Faurot, who had established in Lima the nation's first street railway and then made an enormous amount of money after drilling the first well in what became a major oil field. The building contained both the Music Hall, with seating for 1,000 and ancillary spaces, such as a dining room and kitchen, club room, and cloak rooms, as well as the lavishly decorated and equipped Opera House, seating fourteen hundred. During its heyday the Opera House hosted everything from high school graduations and touring minstrel and vaudeville shows to the Sousa Band and Boston Grand Opera Company. It eventually became a movie theater before being condemned in 1934; the entire Faurot block was razed in 1953.

12. This and the previous extract have been taken from programs in the collections of the Welsh-American Heritage Museum.

1. Mary O. Eddy, *Ballads and Songs from Ohio* (New York: J. J. Augustin, 1939; repr. Hatboro, Pa.: Folklore Associates, 1964), xv.

2. See also Elizabeth Anne Salt, *Buckeye Heritage: Ohio's History in Song* (Columbus: Enthea, 1992), 29–32. Anne Grime's version of the ballad (*Ohio State Ballads: History through Folksongs*, 1958, Folkways FH 5217) is based on a modern performance tradition dating back to 1935 in Darke County (side 1, band 5). A version titled "Sainclaire's Defeat" was published in Rufus King, *Ohio: First Fruits of the Ordinance of 1787* (New York: Houghton, Mifflin, and Co., 1891), as appendix 3, pages 409–12. As a preface to its thirteen verses King noted, "The following ballad is not poetry, but in the time of the pioneers was sung with sad emotion, and was so popular that it is worth reproducing as a relic." In chapter 9, "St. Clair's Administration and the Indian War," he referred to the song as "a specimen of the primitive literature of the West" (247). See also Eddy, *Ballads and Songs from Ohio*, 264–65.

3. Patrick Weston Joyce, *Old Irish Folk Music and Songs: A Collection of 842 Irish Airs and Songs Hitherto Unpublished* (London: Longmans, Green, and Co., 1909; repr. New York: Cooper Square, 1965), 208–9. See also Salt, *Buckeye Heritage*, 73–75.

4. See Salt, *Buckeye Heritage*, 33–36, and Grimes, *Ohio State Ballads*, side 1, band 1.

5. Grimes, *Ohio State Ballads*, notes, 3.

6. Ibid., 3.

7. From John E. Fleming, *The Underground Railroad: Resources and Sites to Visit* (Columbus: Ohio Historical Society, 1995), intro. Fleming is the director of the National Afro-American Museum and Cultural Center in Wilberforce. See also Wilbur Henry Siebert, *The Mysteries of Ohio's Underground Railroads* (Columbus: Long's College Book, 1951), and Ann Hagendorn, *Beyond the River: The Untold Story of the Heroes of the Underground Railroad* (New York: Simon and Schuster, 2002).

8. Ohio's crucial position in this venture is surely mirrored in the decision to locate the National Underground Railroad Freedom Center on Cincinnati's riverfront. Ground was broken for the facility on June 17, 2002, in a ceremony whose participants included Laura Bush, boxing legend Muhammad Ali (whose function was to light a symbolic flame), and the seven-hundred-member Freedom Chorus, which made its way symbolically across the famed Suspension Bridge from Kentucky to Ohio. When dedicated in August 2004, the 158,00-square-foot, $110 million facility will include a welcome hall, exhibition space, a theater, and a cafe in its three pavilions.

9. Joshua McCarty Simpson, *The Emancipation Car, Being an Original Composition of Anti-Slavery Ballads Composed Exclusively for the Underground Railroad* (Zanesville: Edwin C. Church, 1854; rev. 1874). See also Carol Bishop Myers, "The Musical Expression of Anti-Slavery Sentiment in Ohio," *Sonneck Society Bulletin* 18, no. 1 (Spring 1992): 8–11.

10. Simpson, *The Emancipation Car*, v.

11. Ibid., 131–32.

12. Ibid., iii–iv.

13. Ibid., v.

14. Ibid., 5–7.

15. Ibid., 82–83.

16. Ibid., 22–24.

17. Ibid., 11–12.

18. Ibid., 14–15.

19. Ibid., 24–26.

20. Ibid., 63–66.

21. Ibid., v.

22. For the complete song, see Hans Nathan, *Dan Emmett and the Rise of Early Negro Minstrelsy* (Norman: Univ. of Oklahoma Press, 1962), 324–37.

23. Simpson, *The Emancipation Car*, 43–45.

24. Ibid., 72.

25. Ibid., 45–47.

26. Ibid., 50–52.

27. Grimes, *Ohio State Ballads*, side 2, band 5.

28. Simpson, *The Emancipation Car*, 147–49.

29. Marshall W. Taylor, *A Collection of Revival Hymns and Plantation Melodies* (Cincinnati: Marshall W. Taylor and W. C. Echols, 1882), 6.

30. See Andrew Ward, *Dark Midnight When I Rise: The Story of the Jubilee Singers Who Introduced the World to the Music of Black America* (New York: Farrar, Straus, and Giroux, 2000). White is discussed sporadically between pages 13 and 84; the Ohio experience is described in chapter 2, "Inching Along," 127–42.

31. The tale of their journey across the Buckeye State was told by Gustavus D. Pike in *The Jubilee Singers, and Their Campaign for Twenty Thousand Dollars* (Boston, Mass.: Lee and Shepard; New York: Lee, Shepard and Dillingham, 1873), 78–100.

32. Ibid., 79.

33. Ibid., 91.

34. Qtd. in Ward, *Dark Midnight When I Rise*, 133.

35. Taylor, *A Collection of Revival Hymns*, 6–7.

36. Ibid., 6.

37. Ibid., vi.

38. For example, see "Perry's Victory" in Salt, *Buckeye Heritage*, 43–45, or "James Bird" in Eddy, *Ballads and Songs from Ohio*, no. 18.

39. Salt, *Buckeye Heritage*, 88–91. David Tod was then governor of Ohio. French leave is defined as, "an unauthorized, unnoticed, or unceremonious departure," derived from a custom prevalent in nineteenth-century France of departing from receptions without taking leave of the host.

40. Eddy, "Ohio," *Ballads and Songs from Ohio*, no. 127; Salt, "Stone River," *Buckeye Heritage*, 85–87; Grimes, "The Dying Volunteer," *Ohio State Ballads*, side 2, band 8.

41. Francis James Child, "James Harris (The Daemon Lover)," *The English and Scottish Popular Ballads*, vol. 4 (New York: Houghton Mifflin, 1890), no. 243.

42. See also Grimes, *Ohio State Ballads*, side 2, band 7.

43. James Hall, *Letters from the West; Containing Sketches of Scenery, Manners, and Customs; and Anecdotes Connected with the First Settlements of the Western Sections of the United States* (London: Henry Colburn, 1828), 90–94.

44. While Nye's recorded performances are not available commercially, Gloria Martin Houk recorded seven of the Nye songs (as well as three found in the Ridenour Collection) on her *Songs of the Ohio Country*, 1975[?], Mark Records MC 1035.

45. For photos of Mother Nye with son Pearl and the pair of Nye boats at Lockbourne in 1884, with the family atop them posed for a portrait, see Jack Gierk, *A Photo Album of Ohio's Canal Era* (Kent: Kent State Univ. Press, 1988), 236–38. A photographic portrait of the mature Nye can be found on page 261. Chapter 9, "The Canalers and Their Families," describes the sort of life the Nye clan must have led.

46. John A. Lomax, *Adventures of a Ballad Hunter* (New York: Macmillan, 1947), 242–44.

47. A device employed to determine the loaded weight of a freighter, which became the basis of the tolls levied on each trip. For explication of this and other terms, see *The Ohio and Erie Canal: A Glossary of Terms*, comp. Terry K. Woods (Kent: Kent State Univ. Press, 1995).

48. Pearl R. Nye, *Scenes and Songs of the Ohio-Erie Canal*, ed. Cloea Thomas (Columbus: Ohio Historical Society, 1952; repr. 1971), no. 9. Nye borrowed the same tune for his "Buckeye Family," in whose nineteen rhyming quatrains he managed to catalog every county and county seat in the state.

49. Ibid., no. 10.

50. The whole song can be found in Salt, *Buckeye Heritage*, 67–68.

51. Ibid., 59–61.

52. Nye, *Scenes and Songs of the Ohio-Erie Canal*, no. 2. Thomas included only six verses. Thirty-one were printed by Richard H. Swain in his "Captain Pearl R. Nye's Ohio Canal Songs," *Gamut* (Fall 1983): 28–34, an article that also includes illustrations such as that of Nye's "Camp Charming," his retirement home.

53. Unpaginated typescript of Nye lyrics, Ohio Historical Society, Pearl R. Nye Collection, 1851–1962, MSS 60.

54. Nye, *Scenes and Songs of the Ohio Erie Canal*, no. 4.

55. The complete song can be found in Salt, *Buckeye Heritage*, 64–66. Her anthology also includes Nye's "The Mules Ran Off," as well as two songs depicting life on Ohio River keelboats: "Shawneetown" and "Working on a Pushboat." Bob Gibson recorded the latter for his anthology, *Folksongs of Ohio*, 1963, Stinson SLP 76.

56. See Swain, "Captain Pearl R. Nye's Ohio Canal Songs," 26–27, for all twenty-five verses. "Black snake" denotes the whip used by the mule drivers. Nye states in his manuscript copy of the lyric that he had sung the piece five times in Washington's Constitution Hall, once in Philadelphia, and eight times at New York's Madison Square Garden. Swain also included in his anthology the song "We're Going to Pump Out Lake Erie," reflecting on the challenge of keeping the canal filled with water during times of drought; "Take a Trip on the Canal if You Want to Have Fun," claimed by Nye as totally his own creation; and "Down the River," which describes the difficulties encountered when the canal boats were forced to maneuver through heavy traffic in the Cuyahoga River.

57. Henry Clay Work (1832–84) was one of the best-known song composers of the era, remembered today principally for "Marching through Georgia." "The Ship that Never Return'd" was copyrighted in 1865 and published by S. Brainard's Sons in Cleveland.

58. Bruce Buckley, *Ohio Valley Ballads*, 1955, Folkways FA 2025, side 2, band 2.

59. Eddy, *Ballads and Songs from Ohio*, nos. 121 and 122.

60. Ibid., 276.

61. Ibid., 277.

62. Cecilia Riddell, ed., *Handy Play Party Book* (Burnsville, N.C.: World Around Songs, 1981), 92–93.

63. Ibid., 19.

64. Ibid.

30. BLACKFACE MINSTRELSY

1. Carl Frederick Witte, *Tambo and Bones: A History of the American Minstrel Stage* (Durham, N.C.: Duke Univ. Press, 1930; repr. New York: Greenwood, 1968), 86–92, traces the various companies that played Cincinnati and Cleveland during the 1870s.

2. See Dale Cockrell, *Demons of Disorder: Early Blackface Minstrels and Their World* (Cambridge, U.K.: Cambridge Univ. Press, 1997), and W. T. Lhamon Jr., *Raising Cain: Blackface Performance from Jim Crow to Hip Hop* (Cambridge, Mass.: Harvard Univ. Press, 1998).

3. Cleveland was born in Chillicothe about 1861 and was still alive in 1911 when his career was summarized in Edward Le Roy Rice, *Monarchs of Minstrelsy, from "Daddy" Rice to Date* (New York: Kenny, 1911), 306.

4. From a letter to William E. Millet in the Foster Hall Collection, qtd. in Raymond Walters, *Stephen Foster: Youth's Golden Gleam: A Sketch of His Life and Background in Cincinnati, 1846–1850* (Princeton, N.J.: Princeton Univ. Press, 1936), 49.

5. Information supplied by Foster's daughter to E. Jay Wohlgemuth and quoted by Wohlgemuth in *Within Three Chords: The Place of Cincinnati in the Life of Stephen Collins Foster: [A] Paper Read before the Literary Club of Cincinnati* (Indianapolis, Ind.: Rough Notes, 1928), 15.

6. Although his observations date from the mid-1870s, Lafcadio Hearn (1850–1904) penned an informative report of life on the Cincinnati waterfront in his "Levee Life," published in the *Commercial* of March 17, 1876 (and reprinted in a collection of pieces by Hearn in *An American Miscellany*, vol. 1, ed. Albert Mordell [New York: Dodd, Mead, and Co., 1924], 147–70). Not only did Hearn describe the rough-and-tumble life of the black roustabout in colorful detail, but he also included a copious number of the songs he heard them sing (although without their tunes). A single example, which Hearn described as enormously popular at the time:

> The air is low, and melancholy, and when sung in unison by the colored crew of a vessel leaving or approaching port, has a strange, sad sweetness about it which is very pleasing:
>
> Molly was a good gal and a bad gal, too.
>   Oh Molly, row, gal. [two times]
> I'll row dis boat and I'll row no more,
>   Row, Molly, row, gal. [two times]
> Captain on the biler deck a-heaving of the lead,
>   Oh Molly, row, gal.
> Calling to the pilot to give her, "Turn ahead,"
>   Row, Molly, row, gal.

Hearn, born in Greece of Irish and Greek parentage, emigrated to this country in 1869 and by late 1873 was writing for the *Enquirer* and later the *Commercial*, a career that lasted until early 1877, when he relocated to New Orleans, and later to New York (where he resumed acquaintance with Henry Krehbiel, a fellow Cincinnati journalist who had become the influential music critic of the *Tribune*). He moved to Japan in 1890, married, and assumed a Japanese name, under which he lectured for the last decade of his life as the first professor of English literature at the Imperial University of Tokyo.

7. For example, see a listing of twenty different editions of "Oh! Susanna" issued between February 25, 1848, and February 14, 1851, in John Tasker Howard, *Stephen Foster, America's Troubadour* (New York: Thomas Y. Crowell, 1934, 1953), 141–44.

8 For a facsimile of the ad, published 122 times between July 13 and December 1, see Walters, *Stephen Foster: Youth's Golden Gleam*, 92. Ironically, "Stay Summer Breath," "written & composed for & inscribed to Miss Sophie B. Marshall" of Cincinnati (and copyrighted on December 30, 1848) was attributed to S. C. Foster in this same announcement. See ibid., 32–35, for a description of Foster's relationship to the Marshall family and the song's genesis. This second sentimental ballad with both words and music by the composer had been preceded by "What Must a Fairy's Dream Be," copyrighted by Peters on October 18, 1847. Peters's first Foster issue was "There's a Good Time Coming" (copyrighted on October 9, 1846, with words by Charles Mackay, taken from the *London Daily News* and noted as, "Composed for & respectfully dedicated to Miss Mary D. Keller, of Pittsburgh"); he also offered a corrected reprint of Foster's first published song, "Open Thy Lattice, Love" (1844, with words by George Pope Morris), whose Philadelphia publisher had attributed it to L. C. Foster. Peters later published one Foster song in Baltimore: "Summer Longings," on a poem by Denis Florence MacCarthy that he had found in the *Home Journal*, its copyright dated November 21, 1849.

9. Hans Nathan, *Dan Emmett and the Rise of Early Negro Minstrelsy* (Norman: Univ. of Oklahoma Press, 1962), 109.

10. Ibid., 118.

11. Ibid., 271.

12. Ibid., 241–42. For an analysis of influences, textual parodies, pirated editions, etc., see chapter 16, "Dixie," pages 243–75.

13. See Howard L. and Judith Rose Sacks, *Way Up North in Dixie: A Black Family's Claim to the Confederate Anthem* (Washington, D.C.: Smithsonian Institution Press, 1993).

14. Emmett published about thirty pieces between 1843 and 1865; perhaps another twenty-five in manuscript can safely be attributed to him.

15. Grimes, *Ohio State Ballads: History through Folksongs*, 1958, Folkways FH 5217, side 2, bands 1 and 2.

16. Aaron Copland and Vivian Perlis, *Copland Since 1943* (New York: St. Martin's, 1989), 166. Emmett's original can be found in Nathan, *Dan Emmett and the Rise of Early Negro Minstrelsy*, 320–23, in a section containing a copious anthology of songs, banjo tunes, walkarounds, and sketches, including *Hard Times*. Two versions of "Dixie" are on pages 359–65.

17. Valentine [Theater, Toledo, Ohio]: "Thursday, Jan. 2, One Night Only, The Al. G. Field Minstrels and Utopia" (Toledo: Blade Printing and Paper, [1895]), a flyer found in the collections of the Ohio Historical Society: PA Box 248/7.

18. From the *Knox County Republican* of July 1, 1904, qtd. in C[harles] B. Galbreath, "Daniel Decatur Emmett, Author of 'Dixie,'" *Ohio State Archaeological and Historical Quarterly* 13 (Oct. 1904): 523. Although obviously superseded by later scholarship, Galbreath had actually met

his subject in September 1903 and demonstrated considerable sympathy for the octogenarian. The article includes an extended description of the disputes over the authorship of "Dixie," as well as generous samplings from Emmett's manuscript papers.

19. The perils of that first season are charmingly recounted in Al. G. Field, *Watch Yourself Go By* (Columbus, 1912), 500–519. Field's self-published autobiography is a bit bizarre in that he employed the third person case to spin his colorful yarns.

20. One published example of Field's field work is "Lish Murn's Pledge," *Ohio* 1, no. 3 (Sept. 1906): 241–43. Its editorial preface stated, "Mr. Al G. Field, the noted minstrel, is an enthusiastic sportsman and while on his various Southern hunting expeditions has not failed to pursue his life-long study of the negro character, notwithstanding the counter charm of camping life. The present story Mr. Field brings fresh from its native environment and he has utilized the 'reformation' of old Lish Murn to make it a scenic spectacle called 'Dreamland,' as a part of his 'Greater Minstrels' during the present season." In his prefatory observations Field proposed that "the superstitions of the negro race have ever been a theme for those who have written of the happy-go-lucky people. 'Uncle Remus' has embalmed this trait of the character of the negro in everlasting remembrance." He asserted that this tale had been recounted to him in northern Louisiana as a dream recounted by his guide and cook, "an old darky whose superstitions guided him in every move of life."

21. Another Columbus connection to the minstrel tradition is the *Minstrel Service Guide*, issued by the Jack Clifford Show Company, which a curator of the Ohio Historical Society thought might date from about 1920. (PA Box 360/13). Its preface asserts, "The Jack Clifford Show Co. has produced Minstrel shows throughout the Country for the past twenty years, and has gained a vast amount of Minstrel knowledge from this experience. This places the firm in a position to know and render exactly real Minstrel service." Obviously catering to the amateur trade, the catalog offered instruments (including a dog bark, a cyclone wind whistle, and cow and calf bawls); Steins's burnt cork; black wax ("for blacking out teeth"); wigs; costumes; sketches, skits, and afterpieces; song programs, complete with orchestrations; resource books, such as Mr. Newton's *Minstrel Crossfire* and *Laughland, A Merry Minstrel Book*; individual songs in sheet music form; scenic settings, such as a "Garden of Roses" or "Palace Interior"; electrical effects, including moon boxes and a water ripple; and posters, advertising cuts, and window cards, complete with samples.

22. For a summary of his career, see Rice, *Monarchs of Minstrelsy*, 120, 122. A considerably more romantic account can be found in Marion S. Revett, *A Minstrel Town* (New York: Pageant, 1955), 8–36.

23. The Frohmans enjoyed careers in the world of theater that far transcended the realm of minstrelsy. For example, *Daniel Frohman Presents: An Autobiography* (New York: Claude Kendall, and Willougby Sharp, 1935) mentions the author's relationship to Haverly only in the brief chapter 5, with passing references elsewhere. See also Diana Preston, "Why Fear Death? Charles Frohman aboard the *Lusitana*," *Timeline* 19, no. 6 (Nov.–Dec. 2002): 36–51.

24. Rice, *Monarchs of Minstrelsy*, 314.

25. Ibid., 111.

26. Ibid., 221–22.

27. See Ellistine Perkins Holly, "Sam Lucas, 1840–1916: A Bibliographic Study," in *Feel the Spirit: Studies in Nineteenth-Century Afro-American Music*, ed. George R. Keck and Sherrill V. Martin (Westport, Conn.: Greenwood, 1988), 82–103.

28. The tradition's historian is Bert Severance, a retired school administrator who first met Mees as a high school student in Shawnee when Mees was hired by the Shawnee Epworth League to stage the *Dixie Land Minstrel* in early February 1940. Severance performed in, scripted, and directed the early Millersport shows, and continued to sit in the pit as pianist for performances directed by his son.

31. POPULAR SONG

1. See Dacia Custer Shoemaker, *Choose You This Day: The Legacy of the Hanbys* (Westerville: Westerville Historical Society, 1983), and Jeanne Bilger Gross, "Benjamin Russell Hanby, Ohio Composer-Educator, 1833–1867: His Contributions to Early Music Education" (Ph.D. diss., Ohio State University, 1987). An early tribute by Charles B. Galbreath, "Benjamin Russell Hanby: Author of 'Darling Nelly Gray,'" appeared in *Ohio Illustrated Magazine* 1, no. 2 (1906): 182–88. Galbreath claimed that Stephen Foster "never wrote verses more sweetly simple, more beautifully and touchingly suggestive, more sadly pathetic, than *Darling Nelly Gray*. Perfect in rhyme and almost faultless in rhythm, the words flow on, bearing their message directly to the heart."

In 1937 Shoemaker became the first curator of the Hanby House, saved from demolition and moved to its present site at 160 West Main Street in Westerville, adjacent to the Otterbein College campus. An Ohio Historical Society State Memorial operated by the Westerville Historical Society, the building contains furniture and musical instruments associated with Hanby, as well as the original plates for the first edition of "Darling Nelly Gray" and a substantial collection of Hanby publications. Other Hanby materials can be found nearby in the Otterbein Room archives in the Courtright Memorial Library of Otterbein College.

2. Qtd. in Shoemaker, *Choose You This Day*, 74.

3. Gross, "Benjamin Russell Hanby," 62, deals with the seeming incongruity of Hanby's continuing to deal with Ditson after their first encounter, quoting Hanby's widow, who opined that her late husband was "lacking in combatting business sharks and weak in financial management."

4. Gross, "Benjamin Russel Hanby," 72.

5. Ibid., 181–245 Appendix B documents and thoroughly analyzes as many as seventy-seven songs that can be attributed to Hanby. Gross also profiles each of the collections in appendix C (247–303), as well as the eleven songs published individually as sheet music. The complexity of her search is explained on 98–114.

6. By Earl R. Hoover in his "Our Bard—Benjamin R. Hanby, the Stephen Foster of Ohio," included in the *Report* 5 (Dec. 6, 1965) to the Ohio Genealogical Society. Hoover also had addressed the Sunday Evening Club of the National Presbyterian Church in Washington, D.C., on August 8, 1965, with "Benjamin R. Hanby—'The Stephen Foster of Ohio,'" containing remarks read into the Congressional Record of the following day by Rep. Clarence J. Brown.

7. Roger Lax and Frederick Smith, *The Great Song Thesaurus*, 2d ed. (New York: Oxford Univ. Press, 1989), 286.

8. In 1966 the site of his birthplace at what had been 163 Sterling Street, now 1541 E. 30th Street, was designated with a marker erected by the Cleveland Kiwanis Club and the Ohio Historical Society.

9. Qtd. in the *Cleveland Press*, March 17, 1970.

10. An entry in Lax and Smith, *The Great Song Thesaurus*, 226, asserts that in 1940 Earl K. Smith claimed credit for both the title and chorus of "Down By the Old Mill Stream," obviously the most valuable parts of the property, suggesting that Taylor had contributed only the verses. Smith was coauthor of "Lonesome"(1925) and composer to Taylor's lyric of "Flowers of Love" (n.d.).

11. See Richard Theodore Boehm, "Tod B. Galloway: Buckeye Jongleur, Composer of 'The Whiffenpoof Song,'" *Ohio History* 83 (1974): 256–82, including a list of his published songs.

12. He wrote extensively on other subjects, including a lengthy diagnosis of "The Ohio-Michigan Boundary Line Dispute," *Ohio State Archaeological Historical Quarterly* 4 (1895): 199–230, a volume that also contains Washington Gladden's tribute to Tod's father, Samuel Galloway (263–78), a reprint of an address delivered to Gladden's flock at the First Congregational Church in Columbus on January 6, 1895.

13. For a period sense of the man, see *Current Biography 1940* (New York: H. W. Wilson, 1940), 751–53. In his profile Spitalny asserted that he would rather work with women since, "'They're more cooperative and they don't waste their emotions on much but their music.' His girls follow a strict and rigid routine, rehearsing five days a week for five or six hours each day. Their ages range from seventeen to thirty, and as part of their contract they pledge not to marry while members of the unit without giving six months notice. And they manage to get along together without evidence of feminine temperament. They themselves choose a governing board which has the last say about all problems of costumes, hotel rooms, the assignment of upper and lower berths, dressing rooms and general behavior."

14. See Mabel Eldridge, et al., *The History of Franklin in the Great Miami Valley*, ed. Harriet E. Foley (Franklin: Franklin Area Historical Society, 1982), although some of the information seems self-contradictory and unreliable.

15. Given his fertility, it may seem surprising that little of this material seems to exist in major Ohio collections. One must journey to the Music Division of the Library of Congress to view the copyright deposit examples of most of Eldridge's output. However, the Ohioana Library does contain some random material, including *The Captain of Plymouth* and a volume of *Song Novelties for Young Ladies* (1912).

16. See Mary Hubbell Osburn, *Ohio Composers and Musical Authors* (Columbus: F. J. Heer, 1942), 99–100.

32. THE CLEVELAND-STYLE POLKA

1. Frankie Yankovic, *The Polka King: The Life of Frankie Yankovic as Told to Robert Dolgan* (Cleveland: Dillon-Liederbach, 1977). A minibiography by Frank Smodic Jr. became the centerpiece of "The Legendary Frankie Yankovic 'Through the Years': The Life and Times of America's Polka King," a pamphlet published in 1991 to mark Yankovic's seventy-fifth birthday, replete with numerous photographs. For facts, read Joseph Valencic, "Polkas" in *The Dictionary of Cleveland Biography* (Bloomington: Indiana Univ. Press, 1996), 777–79. For the flavor of the heritage, see Derek VanPelt, "Polka: The Dance That Refuses to Die," *Cleveland Magazine*, April 1975, 82–90, and Anastasia Pantsios, "Polka Is King," *Cleveland Free Times*, May 15, 1996, 11–15.

2. I have seen claims of as many as two hundred, but only twenty-four are described in Kathleen L. Jozwiak, *Cleveland-Style Polka Directory* (Willoughby: St. Monica Publications, 1998), which includes not only profiles of each of those organizations but also indexes of the individual musicians and their instruments, as well as their recordings and song titles, and even "Places to Polka" and "Polka Organizations."

33. Bands

1. See *Script Ohio: 110 Years of the Ohio State University Marching Band* (published by the band in 1989 to celebrate its centenary). In that same year WOSU created a video documentary, *tbdbitl: The Ohio State University Marching Band*. It includes generous excerpts from shows in Ohio Stadium, mostly from the 1989 season, but including one from 1988 and a historic rendering of the Script Ohio formation in 1983 when Coach Woody Hayes dotted the "i." In one excerpt, the active band is joined on the field by five hundred alumni, for a total of around 750 players. There are also brief clips of the rigorous audition process, passing reference to Eugene Weigel, and cameo interviews with Paul Droste and current director Jon Woods (who boasts of the band's then fourteen recordings). See also Eric Lyttle, "The Real Story of 'Hang On Sloopy,'" *Columbus Monthly* 29, no. 9 (Sept. 2003): 40–46.

2. The apparent pioneer in transforming the marching band from an ensemble that simply marched and counter-marched up and down the gridiron was Paul Emrick of Purdue University. The Purdue band's first spelling feat dates from 1907, its first fluid formation from about 1919. Also, the Indiana University band pioneered the outlining of familiar objects, probably in the years immediately preceding World War I. See Arthur Charles Bartner, "The Evolution and Development of the University and College Marching Band" (master's thesis, University of Michigan, 1963).

3. See Gene F. Milford, "George T. 'Red' Bird: Innovations and Developments of Marching Band Techniques at Massillon, Ohio (1938–1946)" *Contributions to Music Education*, 1999 26, no. 1 (1999): 86–98.

4. For more detail and a partial facsimile, see Richard D. Wetzel, "*Oh Sing No More That Gentle Song*": The Musical Life and Times of William Cumming Peters (1805–66)* (Warren, Mich.: Harmonie Park, 2000), 339–41.

5. See Jon Newson, "The American Brass Band Movement in the Mid-Nineteenth Century" in *The Wind Ensemble and Its Repertoire*, ed. Frank J. Cipolla and Donald Hunsberger (Rochester, N.Y.: Univ. of Rochester Press, 1994), 77–91.

6. D. S. McCosh, *Guide for Amateur Brass Bands* (Chicago: Lyon and Healey, 1880), 3.

7. Alexander S. McCormick, "The History of the Military Bands of Akron" (n.d., typescript). McCormick (b. 1876) presented himself as "Director of the Doctor's Orchestra." His typescript (found in the Akron-Summit County Public Library) is undated but must have been completed sometime during the late 1940s. He actually listed fifty-four bands, but those include various military and school bands, outside our purview of the moment. The Hazen Collection of the Smithsonian Institution in Washington, D.C., includes pictorial evidence of bands of various sorts from the early decades of the twentieth century not only from Akron but also Basil, Benton Ridge, Bowling Green, Caldwell, Carrollton, Celina, Chillicothe, Cortland, Creston, Crystal Spring, East Liberty, Eden, Elmore, Fremont, Geneva, Hicksville,

Iberia, Kent, Lakeside, Lancaster, Mansfield, Massillon, Maynard, Mineral City, Newcomers-town, New London, New Philadelphia, New Plymouth, North Industry, Painesville, Parkman, Pioneer, Ravenna, Richville, Shawnee, Shelby, Sherwood, Springfield, Stockport, Sycamore, Tarkio, Wadsworth, Warren, Westerville, and Wilksville, as well as more substantial places like Cincinnati, Columbus, Toledo, and Youngstown.

8. Perhaps this is an appropriate place in which to introduce a unique collegiate ensemble, the Scot Symphonic Band of the College of Wooster. Reflecting the Scottish Presbyterian heritage of the school, the group has long sported an ancillary group of bagpipers, pipe drummers, and Highland dancers, but even when presenting standard literature the entire ensemble is costumed in dress MacLeod kilts, that particular tartan chosen because of Wooster's school colors: black and gold. The idea of employing Scottish dress dates back to the late 1930s. The first shipment of imported kilts was sunk by a German submarine in 1939, but a subsequent batch made it safely across the Atlantic and were first worn at a concert in 1940.

9. Qtd. in Margaret Hindle Hazen and Robert M. Hazen, *The Music Men: An Illustrated History of Brass Bands in American, 1800–1920* (Washington, D.C.: Smithsonian Institution Press, 1987), 45. The original document is supposedly owned by the Ohio Historical Society but could not be located.

10. Ibid., 46.

11. What follows is based on materials found in the collections of the Tallmadge Historical Society, as well Mrs. Fred S. Pitkin, "Music in Tallmadge," in *A History of Tallmadge, Ohio* (Tallmadge: published under the auspices of the Tallmadge Historical Society, 1957), 53–56, issued to celebrate the town's sesquicentennial.

12. From an unpaginated manuscript owned by the Talmadge Historical Society.

13. The Toledo Directory of 1858, the first to survive, presented White as leader of the Union Band, its competitors listed as Canneff's Band, the Germania Band, and the Independent Brass Band. White's transient status is perhaps suggested by the fact that he resided in the Kingsbury House, a hotel at Summit and Walnut Streets. The impermanence of these ensembles might be inferred from the fact that by 1860 (the next available directory) the Union Band had disappeared, and White was noted as the manager rather than the leader of the Aeolian Silver Band. Both that ensemble and White are absent in subsequent directories.

14. Graffula directed the Seventh Regiment Band of New York City and was one of the most prolific arrangers of his era. The quick-step march was distinguished from the older, processional-like march. The Tallmadge band was to essay one of his opera arrangements in their concert of November 1859. Also, White was represented twice that evening. White had probably moved to Toledo prior to 1846, since in December of that year Benjamin H. Grierson (1826–1911) organized a Youngstown band that flourished until Grierson moved to Illinois in 1851. Grierson was later to achieve fame as a cavalry officer during the Civil War, but before abandoning his musical vocation he created a repository of band arrangements which allow insights into the nature of his and comparable brass bands of the era. See Lavern J. Wagner, ed. *Band Music from the Benjamin H. Grierson Collection* (Madison, Wis.: A-R Editions, 1998), which includes extensive commentary about Grierson and his years in Youngstown. White's letter was found in the collections of the Talmadge Historical Society.

15. Thomas Wakefield Goodspeed, *William Rainey Harper: First President of the University of Chicago* (Chicago: Univ. of Chicago Press, 1928), 19.

16. See Jim Allen, "The Norwich Area Cornet Bands" typescript, Ohio Historical Society: 977.191 A53ta4.

17. See Kenneth Cummins, *Dutchtown, Your Days in History: A Complete History of New Washington and Cranberry Township* (New Washington: New Washington Centennial Committee, 1974), 157–63, and Jill Riepenhoff, "The Band Plays On," *Columbus Dispatch*, August 21, 1994. Further insight was gained from a telephone conversation of July 2000 with Scott Hiler, who joined the band's alto horn section in 1984 and succeeded Dr. Cummins as its director.

18. John Connin, "The Beginning of the Bryan Band," *Stories of the Fountain City 1840–1900*, ed. Paul Van Gundy (Bryan: Bryan Area Foundation, 1975), 21–23, and "Bryan City Band: History and Highlights," a lavishly illustrated twenty-page supplement in the *Bryan Times*, June 5, 2001, marking the group's 150th birthday.

19. The Grand Army of the Republic (GAR) Band was founded in 1866 by Canton veterans of the Union Army. German-born Emil Reinkendorff (the original spelling) emigrated in 1874 at age twelve, continued to study the violin, and arrived in Canton by 1885. In addition to teaching privately, he founded a choral society, led the orchestra of the local opera house, and from about 1887 until 1906 directed the GAR Band, suggesting that *McKinley's Own* may have been written long before it reached publication. For details about this and other Canton bands (particularly that of Thayer), see Michael D. Martin, "The Band School of Dana's Musical Institute, Warren, Ohio, 1869–1941" (Ann Arbor, Mich.: UMI, 1996), 94–103, 258–67.

20. See Gene F. Milford, "The Ohio March Connection," *Triad* 64 (Dec.–Jan. 1996): 41–44.

21. Paul E. Bierley has dealt with this maze in *The Music of Henry Fillmore and Will Huff* (Columbus: Integrity, 1982), including a checklist of the music of the real Will[iam L.] Huff (1875–1942) of Chillicothe. Also see Bierley, *Hallelujah Trombone! The Story of Henry Fillmore* (Columbus: Integrity, 1982).

22. German-born Bellstedt's family immigrated in 1867 and settled in Cincinnati five years later. Acclaimed a prodigy at age fifteen, he joined the Cincinnati Reed Band (there is no extant information as to how a cornet was reconciled with an ensemble of reed instruments) and played with them until 1879 and then again from 1883 to 1889. After a stint as soloist with the Gilmore Band he returned to Cincinnati and in 1892 founded the Bellstedt-Ballenger Band, which he led until 1904, when he joined Sousa. In 1913 he returned to Cincinnati and became a member of the Conservatory of Music faculty.

23. See Kenneth S. Clark, *Music in Industry*, "A presentation of Facts Brought Forth by a Survey, Made by the National Bureau for the Advancement of Music [headquartered in New York City], of Musical Activities Among Industrial and Commercial Workers," (1929). The Armco Band is profiled on pages 96–98 and pictured opposite page 104. The vested chorus sponsored by the William Taylor Son and Company of Cleveland is pictured opposite page 72 and described on page 325. Directed by Arthur Quimby, the group's principal function was to sing at least one morning a week when the department store opened for business. Two other Ohio groups are profiled in the prose section of the volume—a male chorus sponsored by the Ohio Bell Telephone Company in Cleveland (126–27) and the chorus of the Central Life Insurance Company of Cincinnati (132–33)—while many others are included in a summary of the reports (321–32), including a band at the American Fork and Hoe Company in Ashtabula; choruses in Cincinnati sponsored by the Baltimore and Ohio Railroad (conducted by Joseph Surdo) and the Mabley and Carew Company; in Cleveland

an all-male orchestra and a Girls Ukulele Club at the American Multigraph Company, an orchestra and oratorio chorus at the Cleveland Railway Company, a Bagpipe Band at the Fisher Body Corporation, an orchestra at the General Electric Company, an orchestra at the Joseph and Feiss Company ("Makers of Men's Clothing"), and bands sponsored by the Pennsylvania Railroad and the White Motor Company; a Conneaut Harbor Band at the Pittsburgh and Conneaut Dock Company; plus bands at Dennison (Pennsylvania Railroad Company), Findlay (Buckey Tr. Dichter Company and Giant Tire and Rubber Company), Hamilton (the *Hamilton Daily News* Newsboys' Band), Mansfield (the Ohio Brass Company), Massillon (Central Alloy Steel Corporation), Portsmouth (Norfolk and Western Railway), St. Mary's (St. Marys Wheel and Spoke Company), and Zanesville (the Columbia Band, sponsored by the Columbia Division of the Pittsburgh Plate Glass Company).

24. See Michael Freedland, *Music Man: The Story of Frank Simon* (Portland, Ore.: Vallentine Mitchell, 1994). Also Henry Fillmore, "Frank Simon" in *Musical Messenger* 13, no. 7 (July 1917): 2–3; the *Messenger* was subtitled "A Monthly Band and Orchestra Journal," its Motto: "More Fraternity"). Fillmore's enthusiasm immediately preceded chapter 13, Herbert L. Clarke, "How I Became a Cornet Player." See also a "Salute to the Armco Band," a thirty-minute video issued in 1993 by Globe Productions with commentary by Dr. David Simon.

34. JAZZ

1. See T. C. Bown, "A Goodbye at the Columbus Jazz Orchestra," *Columbus Monthly*, June 2002, 111–13.

2. See Joe Lasky, "The Art Tatum," *Ohio*, February 1996, 29–31, 72–74.

3. For more on Kirk, Wilson, and Harry "Sweets" Edison, see *Listen for the Jazz : Key Notes in Columbus History*, 2d ed. (Columbus: Arts Foundation of Olde Town, 1992). The volume also presents biographies of jazz musicians primarily celebrated in Columbus, such as saxophonist Rusty Bryant and keyboardist Hank Marr, as well numerous others of lesser reputation. My understanding was considerably amplified by "JazzOhio," an exhibit housed at the Ohio History Center in Columbus from May 1 until September 25, 1999, guest curated by Candice Watkins and Arnett Howard. Among the fifty musicians of note profiled who deserve the attention not possible in a study of this sort are Isham Jones (1894–1956), born in Coalton; [Myron] Tiny Bradshaw (1905–58), born in Youngstown; [William Edward] Wild Bill Davidson (1906–89), born in Defiance; [Hezekiah Leroy Gordon] Stuff Smith (1909–67), born in Portsmouth; Una Mae Carlisle (1915–56), born in Xenia; [Tadley Ewing Peake] Tad Dameron (1917–65), born in Cleveland; [John Dillard] Johnny Lytle (1932–96), born in Springfield; and [Archie] Stomp Gordon (1932–58), born in Columbus and enshrined in *Ripley's Believe It Or Not* because of his ability to play the piano with his feet. For more information on these and other Ohio-born jazz musicians, see *The New Grove Dictionary of Jazz*, 2d ed., ed. Barry Kernfeld (New York: Grove's Dictionaries, 2002).

4. De Arango was the subject of a piece by David C. Barnett on NPR's *Morning Edition* show of September 13, 1997. See also Joe Mosbrook, *Cleveland Jazz History* (Cleveland Heights: Northeast Ohio Jazz Society, 1993), 64–66.

1. See Deanna R. Adams, *Rock 'n' Roll and the Cleveland Connection* (Kent: Kent State Univ. Press, 2002).

2. Ibid., 230–35. After a hiatus from 1986 until 1995, during which Popovich served as a senior vice president of Polygram in Nashville, he reactivated Cleveland International and quickly achieved local renown with a release responding to owner Art Modell's decision to move the Cleveland Browns to Baltimore. Profits from the sale of *Dawg Gone* (which included "Go to Hell, Modell") were donated to the Save the Browns Foundation.

3. For details as to how the station dominated its market see Adams, *Rock 'n' Roll and the Cleveland Connection*, 116–33.

4. Another crucial venue was the Agora, which dates from February 1966, when Hank LoConti opened his first club near Case Western University. Relocated at East 24th Street and Chester Avenue near Cleveland State University the following year, the club's success led three years later to a companion across from the Ohio State campus in Columbus and eventually to eleven other clones across Ohio and in Texas, Florida, and Connecticut, as well as the Buckeye Music Center, an outdoor concert site in Licking County east of Columbus. For details see Adams, *Rock 'n' Roll and the Cleveland Connection*, 181–91.

5. Ibid., 261–28.

6. See Nick Talevski, *The Unofficial Encyclopedia of the Rock and Roll Hall of Fame* (Westport, Conn.: Greenwood, 1998). The volume contains a cogent biography of Alan Freed, a narrative recounting the various steps leading to the building of the Rock Hall, descriptions of the induction ceremonies from 1986 through 1997 (the first time the event was actually held in Cleveland), and biographies of all the inductees to that point.

7. For a chronology of the saga, see Adams, *Rock 'n' Roll and the Cleveland Connection*, 505–89. One notable tidbit is that as one of many promotional events, a local group calling itself Cleveland offered a marathon concert beginning at 2:00 P.M. on Monday, April 7, 1986, concluding at 6:30 P.M. on Friday the eleventh. Their one hundred hours and thirty minutes of live performance allowed their entry into the *Guinness Book of World Records*.

8. See John A. Jackson, *Big Beat Heat: Alan Freed and the Early Years of Rock and Roll* (New York: Schirmer, 1991), particularly chapters 1–4.

9. Freed became a sponsor of a male vocal quartet originally called the Crazy Sounds and renamed them the Moonglows before issuing their first recording on his Champagne label. Supposedly Freed was in the studio when "I Just Can't Tell No Lie" was committed to tape during February 1953 and was recruited as a drummer, using a telephone directory as his instrument. Founding members Harvey Fuqua and Bobby Lester were joined by Marvin Gaye when the group was reconstituted in 1959; the Moonglows were inducted into the Rock and Roll Hall of Fame in 2000.

Freed also became a sponsor of Cleveland native Screamin' Jay [Jalacy] Hawkins (1929–2000). After a career as a boxer and an entertainer at Army and Air Force service clubs, he established himself as a solo R&B performer in 1955, the moniker suggesting a flamboyant stage idiom that included costuming in a black satin suit with matching cape and being carried onstage in a coffin. As an exemplar of what became known as shock rock, he recorded on various labels, appeared in several rock films, toured extensively in Europe, played clubs in Hawaii and across the continental United States, and made frequent performances at the Apollo Theater in Harlem.

10. Built in 1937 at 3717 Euclid Avenue, the structure housed hockey and basketball games as well as rock concerts. Supplanted by the suburban Richfield Coliseum in 1974 (also now only part of history), the Arena was razed in 1977.

11. For details, see Adams, *Rock 'n' Roll and the Cleveland Connection*, 192–98.

12. The tale of their origins and a first recording made in 1956 when they were still high school seniors is told in Tom O'Connell, "Something to Sing About" in the *Pictorial Magazine* of the *Cleveland Plain Dealer*, February 24, 1957, 4–6.

13. Home-grown rock has continued to flourish. As evidence, a handful of recordings from northeastern Ohio: *From Akron*, 1977 (Clone CL–001), featuring the Bizarros and Rubber City Rebels; *The Akron Compilation*, 1978 (Stiff, no catalog information), presenting those groups, plus others, like Jane Aire and the Belvederes, the Waitresses, Sniper, the Idiots Convention, and Terraplane; *Pride of Cleveland*, 1980 (Buzzard Record and Filmworks BR–101–3), with songs by groups like the Rockers, the Generators, Rapscallion, and Flatbush; *They Pelted Us With Rocks and Garbage*, "A Compilation of Cleveland Bands," 1985 (After Hours ARCK-105), with performances by Death of Samantha, New Small Appliances, Faith Academy, the Dark, Children's Crusade, and others; and *Goodrock 107: Rock of Northeast Ohio*, 1985 (Starstream SSTS–028), the title referring to the signal of WOOS in Canton and presenting groups from Cleveland, Akron, Canton, Kent, Youngstown, and Massillon.

14. See "James Gang Rides Again" in the Rock and Roll Hall of Fame and Museum magazine, *Liner Notes* 8, no. 2 (Summer 2001), 3.

15. See Adams, *Rock 'n' Roll and the Cleveland Connection*, 252–61.

16. From the "Story of Ubu," as quoted in liner notes for the digital re-release of *Datapanik in the Year Zero*, 1996 (Geffen Records DGCD5–24969), an extensive archival retrospective of that year.

17. Rickey Vincent, *Funk: The Music, the People, and the Rhythm of the One* (New York: St. Martin's Griffin, 1996), 81.

18. This is taken from a large signboard that greeted visitors to the event. Other such commentary was posted on signboards accompanying the copious display of photos and artifacts in the show.

19. Vincent, *Funk*, 228.

20. Ibid., 280.

21. Ibid., 198.

22. Qtd. in the liner notes for *Ohio Players: Funk on Fire, the Mercury Anthology*, 1995 (Polygram: 440 063 041-2).

23. Ibid.

24. Reznor served as a guest performer and executive producer of the 1994 début album of an even more outrageous performer, Marilyn Manson, part of which was also mixed in the notorious Sharon Tate house. While Manson's band had been organized in Florida, its leader was born as Brian Warner in Canton in 1969, where he lived until graduation from high school.

36. INSTRUMENT MAKERS

1. The Baldwin narrative is based on Lucien Wulsin, *Dwight Hamilton Baldwin (1821–1899) and the Baldwin Piano* (pamphlet of an address delivered to the Newcomen Society in North

America, 1953); Morley P. Thompson, *D. H. Baldwin: The Multibank Music Company* (also a pamphlet of an address delivered to the Newcomen Society in North America, 1974); William Diehl Jr., "A Cool New Image for a Staid Old Firm," *Cincinnati Magazine*, January 1968, 46–65; James Murchie Eaton Mixter, *Music Was My Business: My Life and Times with Baldwin* (Cincinnati: published for the author, 1996) (Mixter was a prominent executive with the firm from 1940 until 1979); David Eugene Campbell, "The Purveyor as Patron: The Contribution of American Piano Manufacturers and Merchants to Musical Culture in the United States 1851–1914," (Ph.D. diss., City University of New York, 1984); and Craig H. Roell, *The Piano in America, 1890–1940* (Chapel Hill: Univ. of North Carolina Press, 1989).

2. Ripley had earlier been home to the Trayser Piano Company, founded in 1865. Trayser apparently relocated to Richmond, Indiana, in 1869 and became the Starr Piano Company three years later. Ohio Valley, which dates from 1869, probably occupied facilities vacated by the earlier firm.

3. The Public Library of Cincinnati and Hamilton County owns several original Baldwin publications. An elaborate booklet simply called *Baldwin* (Cincinnati: McDonald, 1900) contains a section, "Illustrations Showing Special Features of the Interior Construction of The Baldwin Grand Piano," as well as illustrations of specifications for various Upright Grands (including those with cases in Colonial, Empire, and Renaissance styles), parlor grands in La Fayette and Louis XVI styles, and the company's concert grand. Others include *Baldwin: The Incomparable Baldwin Grand Piano, Baldwin: Today's Great Piano* (from perhaps the late 1940s), *The Exquisite Acrosonic by Baldwin*, and *Electronic Organs by Baldwin*, which includes illustrations of and specifications for several models, especially Model 10, touted as "A complete and comprehensive organ," with thirty-one stops and "adhering to standards established by the American Guild of Organists." The company also offered the Orgasonic Spinet Organ with solo and accompaniment keyboards and a stubby thirteen-note pedal board.

4. The technology was derived from an analog to digital encoder that Baldwin had developed during World War II as a guidance device, which was later adapted to space flight.

5. This collapse was chronicled in numerous articles in both the *Enquirer* and *Post*. Particularly useful is an article in the *Cincinnati Post*, March 26, 1987, by Rich Boehne, headlined "Baldwin Ashes at Stake," with an accompanying sidebar summarizing events to that point. See also Dale Keiger, "What You Didn't Learn About Baldwin . . . Until It Was Too Late," *Cincinnati* (Dec. 1993): 74–79.

6. Information for what follows has been derived from Alfred Dolge, *Pianos and Their Makers: A Comprehensive History of the Development of the Piano from the Monochord to the Concert Grand Player Piano*, vol. 1 (Covina, Calif.: Covina Publishing, 1911; repr. New York: Dover, 1972); *Development of the Piano Industry in America Since the Centennial Exhibition at Philadelphia, 1876*, vol. 2 (Covina, Calif.: Covina Publishing, 1913); N. E. Michel, *Michel's Piano Atlas* (Rivera, Calif., 1953), and its successor, Bob Pierce, *Pierce Piano Atlas* (Long Beach, Calif.: published for the author, 1965); and Craig E. Roell, *The Piano in America, 1890–1940* (Chapel Hill: Univ. of North Carolina Press, 1989).

7. Charles Cist, *Sketches and Statistics of Cincinnati in 1851* (Cincinnati: Wm. H. Moore, 1851), 221.

8. Cist, *Sketches and Statistics of Cincinnati in 1859* (Cincinnati: for the author, 1859), 307–8.

9. In 1894 Church published "The Everett Piano March" by Herman Bellstedt Jr., described as "America's Greatest Cornet Soloist." The Church retail outlets in Cincinnati, Chicago, and New York were pictured in engravings, as were the Everett factory in Boston and two other subsidiary facilities. Other such self-promotional tools of the period include Charles W. Wright, "The Baldwin March" of 1899 and E. K. Bennett, "The Hamilton Waltz" of 1902, both published by D. H. Baldwin and Company.

10. *The City of Cincinnati and Its Resources* (Cincinnati: Cincinnati Times-Star, 1891), 130.

11. *Descriptive Catalogue of Upright and Grand Pianos* (Norwalk: A. B. Chase, [1901?]). Found in the collections of the Ohio Historical Society: PA Box 489/21.

12. What follows was derived largely from a booklet issued by the company in 1956: *Wurlitzer World of Music, 1856–1956: 100 Years of Musical Achievement*. Found in the collections of the Ohio Historical Society: PA Box 498/16.

13. See R. E. Coleberd, "Stevens of Marietta: A Forgotten Builder in a Bygone Era," *Diapason* (June 2002): 18–21.

14. See Vernon Brown, "Carl Barckhoff and the Barckhoff Church Organ Company," *Tracker* 22, no. 4 (Summer 1978); repr. *Tracker* 39, no. 4 (Summer 1995): 1, 7–11. The *Tracker* is the journal of the Organ Historical Society. See also various entries in David H. Fox, *A Guide to North American Builders* (Richmond, Va.: Organ Historical Society, 1991).

15. Brown, "Carl Barckhoff and the Barckhoff Church Organ Company," 1.

16. See Robert E. Coleberd Jr., "Philipp Wirsching: The Consummate Builder," *American Organist* (Oct. 1968): 13–15, 24–29.

17. James M. Stark, "The Wirsching, at the First Unitarian Church, Pittsburgh," *Tracker* 47, no. 1 (Jan. 2003): 25–29.

18. See Kenneth Wayne Hart, "Cincinnati Organ Builders of the Nineteenth Century" (Ph.D. diss., University of Cincinnati, June 1972), published in the *Tracker* in five segments: 20, no. 3 (Spring 1976): 8–12; 20, no. 4 (Summer 1976): 5–8, 12; 21, no. 1 (Fall 1976): 4–10; and 21, no. 2 (Winter 1977): 7–9.

19. A. G. W. Carter, *Address on the Life, Services, and Character of the Rev. Adam Hurdus. the First Minister of the New Church West of the Allegheny Mountains* (New York: New Jerusalem Society, 1865), 25.

20. Schwab was certainly one of the six Music Instrument Makers that Charles Cist enumerated in a listing of "Occupations, Trades, and Pursuits" in *Sketches and Statistics of Cincinnati in 1851* (Cincinnati: Wm. H. Moore, 1851), 49–51. He also claimed two music dealers, but fully 2,318 carpenters, 189 barkeepers, 153 druggists, 82 musicians, 42 theatrical performers, 14 undertakers, 11 soap and candle makers, 2 nine-pin alley keepers, 1 gold hunter, and a single *loafer*. Of a total population of 115,438, he asserted (in an enumeration of "nativities") that 55,468 had been born in the United States, but fully 30,628 were from Germany and 13,616 from Ireland.

21. The initial observations can be found in Cist, *The Cincinnati Miscellany, or Antiquities of the West: And Pioneer History and General and Local Statistics Compiled from the Western General Advertiser* (Cincinnati: C. Clark, 1845–46). Vol. 1 contains material from October 1, 1844, to April 1, 1845; vol. 2 encompasses April 1, 1845, to April 1, 1846. The final quotation was found in Hans Martin Heinrich Kares, "Das Deutsche Element im amerikanischen Orgelbau" ("The German Element in American Organbuilding") (Ph.D. diss., Philipps-Universität at Marburg-Lahn, 1990), 55.

22. Most of what follows is based on information supplied by John A. Schantz, who recounts a family anecdote that bears repeating. Abraham J. Tschantz was reputed to possess a maverick streak, and the young rebel in a community where musical instruments were not allowed in church would open the windows of his shop on Sunday mornings and loudly serenade the pious on their way to worship with the sounds of one of his reed organs. See also Mike Verespej, "Pipe Dreams," *Ohio* (May 2002): 78–80.

23. See John Allen Ferguson, *Walter Holtkamp: American Organ Builder* (Kent: Kent State Univ. Press, 1979). Also, Ferguson, "A Conversation with Walter Holtkamp Jr.," *American Organist* (Feb. 2001): 56–58.

24. The bell was the subject of an illustration for a brief article, "Church Bell Foundry in Cincinnati," *Scientific American* (Sept. 7, 1895): 154.

25. The device was rescued and has become the centerpiece of the firm's museum. My information has been derived almost exclusively from Verdin publications of various sorts, available only at the company's headquarters.

26. *The Musical Messenger* 13, no. 9 (Sept. 1917): 10.

27. Clipped from an unidentified source, this ad was furnished to the author by Dr Martha Maas, then a member of the Ohio State University faculty and a scholar of the subject.

37. MUSIC PUBLISHERS

1. At least to earlier historians, Currier seems to have been by far the more prominent of the duo. He warranted an individual entry in *Men of Northwestern Ohio: A Collection of Portraits and Biographies* (Bowling Green: C. S. Van Tassel, 1898), 56–57. The description of their business enterprise in Harvey Scribner, ed., *Memoirs of Lucas County and the City of Toledo*, vol. 1 (Madison, Wis.: Western Historical Association, 1910), 613–14, emphasizes Currier. In neither instance is Whitney portrayed as a publisher.

2. *Whitney's Musical Guest* 4, no. 1 (Nov. 1870): 710.

3. See Richard D. Wetzel, *"Oh! Sing No More That Gentle Song": The Musical Life and Times of William Cumming Peters (1805–66)* (Warren, Mich.: Harmonie Park, 2000), as well as his *Frontier Musicians on the Connoquenessing, Wabash, and Ohio* (Athens: Ohio Univ. Press, 1976). Also, Wetzel, "The Search for William Cumming Peters," *American Music* 1, no. 4 (Winter 1983), 27–41, and "Catholic Church Music in the Midwest before the Civil War: The Firm of W. C. Peters & Sons" in *American Musical Life in Context and Practice to 1865*, edited by James R. Heintze (New York: Garland, 1994), 203–30. More generally, Ernst C. Krohn, *Music Publishing in the Middle Western States before the Civil War* (Detroit, Mich.: Information Coordinators, 1972).

4. Charles Cist, *Cincinnati in 1851* (Cincinnati: Wm. H. Moore, 1851), 222–23. On page 308 of his similar overview of 1859, Cist stated that the firm by then employed seventy-five, imported "musical instruments of every description from headquarters in France, Germany and Italy," and were "the largest music publishers in the west."

5. This seems the most likely scenario, although George Mortimer Roe, *Cincinnati: The Queen City of the West* (Cincinnati: Cincinnati Times-Star, 1895), 137, claimed that the Church firm evolved from an enterprise founded by Abel Denison Breed and Timothy B. Mason in 1852.

6. J. W. Leonard, *The Centennial Review of Cincinnati: One Hundred Years* (Cincinnati: J. M. Elstner, 1888), 35.

7. See J. Heywood Alexander, "Brainard's (Western) Musical World," *Notes: The Quarterly Journal of the Music Library Association* 36, no. 3 (Mar. 1980): 601–14.

8. What follows is based on the forward to the last Chantry catalog, as well as an extended conversation with Georgia and Fred Otto in their Springfield home on August 3, 1999, shortly before the latter's death.

9. See Robert J. Bastastini, "From Correspondence Course to Worship III: The Story of G. I. A," *Pastoral Music* 10, no. 4 (Apr.–May 1986): 46–48.

10. This narrative has been crafted from various materials furnished to the author by Betty Zins Reiber, editor for the firm for forty years, including a typescript by Westendorf dating from 1990: "World Library–How It Began."

11. The Thompson offerings now include *Teaching Little Fingers To Play* in five books, the *Easiest Piano Course* in eight parts, and an *Adult Piano Course* in three books, as well as a full catalog page of other Thompson items.

38. RECORDED SOUND

1. See Joseph Lanza, *Elevator Music: A Surreal History of Muzak, Easy-Listening, and Other Moodsong* (New York: St. Martin's, 1994); Stephen H. Barnes, *Muzak: The Hidden Messages in Music* (Lewiston, N.Y.: Edwin Mellen, 1988); and for a rather quaint period view (with Squier misspelled as Squires), "Syndicated Syncopation," *C[leveland] A[thletic] C[lub] Journal*) (July 1943): 8–10.

2. For an extensive catalog of King artists, see Steven C. Tracy, *Going to Cincinnati: A History of the Blues in the Queen City* (Urbana: Univ. of Illinois Press, 1993), 114–53 (chapter 7).

APPENDIX A: BIOGRAPHIES OF PROMINENT OHIOANS

1. She also included a brief overview of the "Development of Music in Ohio" plus chapters on Ohio Songs, the Ohioana Library, and the Ohio Federation of Music Clubs.

2. A sense of the man can be gleaned from William G. Blanchard, "Remembering Joseph Clokey," *Diapason* (Nov. 1, 1960): 4.

3. John Tasker Howard, *Our American Music* (New York: Thomas Y. Crowell, 1930), 530–31. Howard wrote that, "Grimm is sometimes modernistic, but not unlicensed. He generally has a definite melodic line, occasionally exotic through the influence of the underlying harmonic scheme. He has what might be termed a modern conception of modal harmony, a system of exotic cadence forms through which he obtains unity of color and effect." Howard also mentioned the paternal Grimm, Carl William, who composed a bit and issued a number of pedagogical volumes, including *Modern Harmony* and *Harmony Study at the Piano*, both of which went through multiple editions.

4. Complete catalogs of his grandfather's legacy are available from Eric C. Grimm, 23 Providence Lane, Springfield, Illinois 62707.

5. The collection contains a *Gavotte pour le Piano*, unsigned but supposedly written by Kraft, and a "Music Book" filled with exercises and vocalises for the choral singer, as well as a long list of principles of singing.

6. The Cleveland Opera Company was formed sometime in the early 1920s and was funded as part of the Federal Music Project during the following decade until its dissolution in 1937. *Algala* was conducted by F. Karl Grossman with an ensemble of forty drawn from the Cleveland Orchestra.

7. Karl Merz, *Musical Hints for the Millions* (Cleveland: S. Brainard's Sons, 1875), no pagination. In his preface Merz stated, "We attach no literary value to these aphorisms, and disclaim any desire to appear as an author," asserting that he was motivated only by, "a strong desire to do all we can for the cause of music, and a willingness to be of service to our fellow-teachers." The scope of his concerns was immense, ranging from piano tuning (1 and 215) to the danger inherent in over-reliance on the metronome (425). They surely offer some insight into the musical cultural of the era. He seems preoccupied with the common practice of pressing young students at an unnatural pace: "Do you think that by forcing the rose to opens its leaves, you will obtain the flower in its full beauty?" (See esp. nos. 3, 4, 39, and 426, as well as 17, in which he fusses about musical dyspeptics who "learn too much music; do it too fast; do not masticate their musical food sufficiently, use improper music, and as a consequence will not be musically healthy"), as well as the necessity of allowing them to develop healthy bodies (9) and minds (12). He chastised those who embellished the works of others ("This is bad taste, young ladies, and is taking liberty with other people's property. Though you may have bought your own copy, nevertheless the composition itself is still the mental property of the composer, and you should respect it as such" [43]). He ridiculed the universal employment of the self-imposed title of "Professor" among his fellow teachers, likening it to a barber who proclaimed himself a "Professor of Hair-cutting" (56). At times he appears wonderfully *au courant* ("Music is too often injudiciously banished from the sick-room. There are circumstances when proper music could be more effectually applied than medicine" [11]), at other times hobbled by a ponderous cultural bias. Concluding a diatribe on church choirs led by the musically uneducated, he opined, "Musical talent among the negroes is not as decided as many believe, mistaking as they do the rhythmical feelings of the negro for a talent for music" (80), while he later commented, "The music of the savages and half-civilized nations is a mere rhythmical noise. The term music implies the higher ideas of that art, which we search for in vain among barbarous nations" (257).

He insisted on the incongruity of singers performing in foreign languages only dimly understood ("Does it denote a higher musical or literary culture? Can our fair singer express more in a language almost unknown to her, than in her mother tongue? Or does it appear more romantic, more operatic? Does her imagination supply the Italian sky, the lazzaroni, and stiletto? Or does it enable her to escape that horrible critic, who wishes to hear the words, and she may thus omit or add with impunity?" [122]); questioned the competency of music critics (156, 157, and 159); advocated the study of fugues ("There is more in them than mere form. Some persons can see no beauty in the graceful forms of the arabesque. Unless they can see trees or flowers, animals or men, in pictures, they consider them void of interest" [189]); noticed the fad of altos attempting "to force nature" by turning themselves into sopranos ("Good altos are scarce; and it is a great treat to us to listen to that richness and mellowness which characterize them. Teachers should not attempt *to make*, but simply *to cultivate* voices" [196]); and chastised those who considered the use of paid singers in church choirs un-Christian ("It is simply ungenerous to expect that musicians should be willing to give their services gratuitously, be it in the concert-room, parlor, or church" [201]) as well as those who leave concerts before their conclusion ("You may pay for attending the concert, but cannot pay for the privilege of being rude towards others." [205]) and hosts who demanded of their guests post-prandial entertainment, often on defective pianos ("If people would urge less, we would have perhaps fewer, but undoubtedly better performances. Musicians would play when ready, and hence in a manner more acceptable to themselves and the company." [277]).

Merz still makes for good reading, especially as a cheerleader: "Music deserves our closest attention, as a means of government, recreation and education in public schools. Would that our authorities could see the importance of the introduction of music" (260); "A singing child is to us the embodiment of pure happiness. Would that we could sing like children, that is, with hearts as pure and free from care as theirs" (263); or, "Music being a means to strengthen the good within us, is a powerful agent in the hands of the educator. Not until we use the art for this purpose, will it do us all the good of which it is capable" (318).

8. The life and works of Karl Merz were delineated in considerable detail by William I. Schreiber, "Karl Merz: German-American Musician" *American-German Review* (Feb. 1941): 4–7, 33; (June 1941): 24–27.

9. For more information, see Jeannie Gayle Pool, "The Life and Music of Zenobia Powell Perry: An American Composer" (Ph.D. diss., Claremont Graduate University 2002), or the same author's "Zenobia Powell Perry: An American Composer," *Journal of the International Alliance for Women in Music* 9, no. 1 (2003): 13–16.

10. The most complete and intimate overview of the man and his work is Richard Loucks, *Arthur Shepherd: American Composer* (Provo, Utah: Brigham Young Univ. Press, 1980), which also includes reproductions of the manuscript scores of fourteen piano works and twenty songs.

11. Unfortunately, I am forced to relegate to a footnote a composer who worked in a similar idiom, since I have been able to learn almost nothing about Charles S[anford] Burnham, other than that he died in 1921, having served as a member of the faculty of the Cleveland Conservatory of Music from 1888 to 1895 when it was affiliated with Western Reserve University; Burnham was listed in the 1892–93 Western Reserve catalog as a teacher of voice culture. He did leave a legacy of at least forty-five songs and three solo piano pieces published between 1900 and 1914, not only in Cleveland, but also elsewhere by companies of national import: Clayton F. Summy, Oliver Ditson, White-Smith, and G. Schirmer.

12. Identified almost universally as "Jimmy," insights into the man's philosophy (including tart comments about mentor Szell), as well as a minibiography can be found in Philip Hart, *Conductors: A New Generation* (New York: Scribner, 1979), 220–66. Fellow Buckeye Robert C. Marsh has more recently written a substantial biography, *Dialogues and Discoveries: James Levine: His Life and His Music* (New York: Scribner, 1998), complete with a discography and a listing of the repertory he has conducted at the Met.

13. From an interview with Williamson in the *Musical Courier*, November 29, 1923. Williamson's credo is already evident in this bit of self-promotion: "The Westminster Choir has proven that a chorus can be made as expressive as a symphony orchestra in its powers of artistic and spiritual revelation. The wide range of tone color possible in the human voice, in addition to the harmonic effects and the soul of the singer, give a most exalted form of the expression akin to that of a wonderful pipe-organ or a great symphony orchestra. More and better singing by the people in our churches, in our schools, in our social organizations, in our industrial plants, will react with tremendous force upon the general tonal quality of our community life."

14. The American Boychoir, another Ohio-born ensemble, is also resident in Princeton. Founded as the Columbus Boychoir by Herbert Huffman in 1938, the Columbus Boychoir School was first housed in the Parish House of the Broad Street Presbyterian Church and later moved to independent quarters in order to provide residential space for boarding students. The country's only nonsectarian boarding choir school relocated in 1950 to Albermarle, a Princeton estate that provided a larger site and better facilities. Renamed the American Boychoir early in the 1980s, the group returned to Columbus on November 23, 1997, for a sixtieth-anniversary celebration that included the participation of the Alumni Choir, many of them members of the group during its residence in Columbus.

15. Klohr (1869–1956), a Cincinnati native, was an editor and head of the instrumental department of the John Church Company. He also issued the *Cincinnati Post* march.

16. See Jeff Louderback, "The Heritage of Hopalong," *Ohio* (May 1999): 46–47.

17. See Ronald R. McVicker, *A Biography of Clare Grundman and Analysis of Selected Works* (master's thesis, Bowling Green State University, 1988).

18. *Let Me Entertain You: A Ruth Lyons Memoir*, a seventy-minute overview in cassette format, was narrated by Jane Pauley (WVXU FM–X-Star Radio Network, 1997).

19. For a sense of Martin's relationship to his hometown, see Jeff Robinson, "The Dean of Steubenville," *Ohio* (Jan. 2002): 62–67.

20. Zamecnik contributed to scores for at least four other silent films, as well as several in the new era of sound. Nineteen of his film cues can be heard on *Cinema. Silent Film Music by J. S. Zamecnik*, a CD self-published in 1999 by the Mont Alto Motion Picture Orchestra, based in Louisville, Colo. My knowledge of Zamecnik is based to a large extent on the scholarship of its director and pianist, Rodney Sauer.

21. See several articles in *Billboard*'s one-hundredth-anniversary issue of November 1, 1994, particularly Ken Schlager, "On the Boards 1894–1920" (19–34), Irv Lichtman, "It All Starts with a Song" (79–88), and Fred Bronson, "Charts: Billboard's Greatest Hits" (112 and 256).

APPENDIX B: A SAMPLING OF SHEET MUSIC PUBLISHED
IN OHIO, 1857–1943

1. This, plus Albert's *First Rate Schottisch*, was found in a bound, two-volume anthology of songs that belonged to Eliza Joanna Zimmer (1840–1918) of Miamisburg and her sisters, now at the Ohio Historical Society. A semilegible comment suggests that the women began their collection about 1855.

2. Although the first commercially successful oil well was drilled in Venango County, Pennsylvania, in 1859, it was only after the cessation of hostilities that the boom in "black gold" exploded. These and many other oil-fever songs suggest the public's newfound awareness of the potential impact of easily accessible petroleum.

3. This was found in a bound, nine-volume set of period music bearing the name of Josephine Klippart, which came to the Ohio Historical Society from the library of her father, John Hancock Klippart (1823–78), a widely published agriculturist. Volume 4 consists in large part of an extended series of *Golden Leaves* by Charles Kinkel, dances for the piano published in Cleveland by S. Brainard and Sons in 1867. Some sample titles: *Fairy Queen Mazurka, Faust Quickstep, Early Dawn Schottisch, Reindeer Quickstep, First Love Mazurka, Sea*

Bird Polka, Strike the Harp Waltz, and *Enchanter's Galop.* Volume 5 contains items taken from periodicals such as *Peter's Musical Monthly* and *Whitney's Musical Guest* of 1868 and 1869. Volume 8 contains Nos. 1–72 of *Hitchcock's Half Dime Series: Music for the Millions,* issued by Benj. W. Hitchcock in New York and Cincinnati, probably in 1869.

4. And adorned with an engraving of "Ohio's Great Brewery" with an invitation to visit the firm's exhibit in the Power Hall of the Exposition and also to sample "National Export, 'The Queen of Beers,'" brewed for the event. "Do Not Fail to Try It!"

5. Smith and Nixon (who advertised their piano wares on the back cover) offered the $150 prize awarded to this work as "the best Concert Waltz for Orchestra."

6. This has to do with the Cleveland, Cincinnati, Chicago, and St. Louis Railroad, created in 1889 through the amalgamation of several smaller lines. Strongly influenced by the New York Central system, the CCC & St.L was finally leased to that larger carrier in 1930.

7. The work is dedicated to J. G. Schmidlapp and the structure portrayed (visually as well) was his Union Trust Building.

8. The piece is dedicated to the Freibergs, Cincinnati distillers, as a tribute to their Gannymede "76" Pure Rye, of which they boldly claimed, "There are others, but none so good." The cover is adorned with a handsome engraving of the mythological Ganymede being whisked away to become cupbearer to the gods, carrying a bottle of you-know-what in his hand.

9. The number of songs about Ohio is legion. One list includes 138 items, including twenty-one simply with the title "Ohio" (for instance, Oley Speaks's "Ohio," published by G. Schirmer in 1938). Many were bundled together in *Songs of Ohio,* a booklet issued by the Lima City Loan and Savings Company in 1953, the result of a "nation-wide contest."

10. Newman was described as of the Newman-Stern Company, "Ohio's Greatest Sporting Goods Store–Pioneers in Radio."

11. *The Goodrich Rubber Company Hour* was broadcast each Wednesday evening on WEAF "and twenty associated stations"; the Silvertown Cord Tire Ensemble is pictured on the front cover.

12. This was one of several pieces penned by faculty members of the Awanda operation. For example, "Once in a Lifetime of Years" (1928) was written by Drewes, Berger, and George Luyster, three of the seven faculty pictured on its cover. The hype is quite incredible. Awanda students were told that once they placed themselves at a piano during a party, they immediately became "the center of attraction, the director of festivities, the one upon whom the Good Time depends, the one upon whom praise and favors are lavished and the one who will really have the best time of all. An AWANDA education is the stepping stone to social, moral and financial betterment." The AWANDA method was guaranteed. After all, "The imaginary obstacles and fears your imagination has conjured up disappear before our instruction like mist before the sunshine. We call your attention to our 5,500 graduates, 1,000 students awaiting graduation, and the fact that we are the largest Studio in the world teaching Popular Music on the Piano—exclusively." Lots of Cincinnatians must have been studying popular music at that time, since the Original Leffingwell Studio, the "First School of Syncopation," established in 1910, also issued at least one song in 1928.

13. This bit of boosterism even includes a pep message from the city manager and an extensive list of "Interesting Facts about Cincinnati," including such information as, "Every 24 hours 113 passenger trains arrive in Cincinnati and a like number depart"; "Cincinnati street cars

operate over 286 miles of track. The service carries more than 125 million passengers a year"; and "Cincinnati's total wealth is estimated at $1,843,481,500. This is about $4,500 per person."

14. Touted as having been "Featured on the 'AIR' with Marvelous Success by Elaine and Sis[,] 'The Original Hillbilly Girls' of Cleveland" (who are pictured) and having been recorded eleven times, with more releases to follow.

15. The Jahco Melodie Boys and many Jahco employees at the their assigned wartime jobs are pictured on the back cover.

Bibliography

Books

Adams, Deanna R. *Rock 'n' Roll and the Cleveland Connection*. Kent: Kent State Univ. Press, 2002.

Aiken, Charles, Alfred Squire, J. P. Powell, and Victor Williams. *The Young Singer's Manual*. Cincinnati: Van Antwerp, Bragg, 1866.

Akers, William Joseph. *Cleveland Schools in the Nineteenth Century*. Cleveland: W. M. Bayne, 1901.

Alexander, J. Heywood. *It Must Be Heard: A Survey of the Musical Life of Cleveland, 1836–1918*. Cleveland: Western Reserve Historical Society, 1981.

Atwater, Caleb. *An Essay on Education*. Cincinnati: Kendall and Henry, 1841[?].

———. *A History of the State of Ohio, Natural and Civil*. Cincinnati: Glezen and Shepard, 1838.

Auld, Alexander. *The Farmers' and Mechanics' Minstrel of Sacred Music*. Deersville: published for the author, 1866.

———. *The Key of the West or, The Ohio Collection of Sacred Music*. Columbus: J. H. Riley, 1856.

———. *The Ohio Harmonist*. Revised. Pittsburgh, Pa.: W. S. Haven, 1850.

———. *The Ohio Harmonist*. 3d. ed. Columbus: J. H. Riley, 1852.

Barker, Joseph. *Recollections of the First Settlement of Ohio*. Ed. George Jordan Blazier. Marietta: Marietta College, 1958.

Bierley, Paul E. *Hallelujah Trombone! The Story of Henry Fillmore*. Columbus: Integrity, 1982; 2d ed., New York: Carl Fisher, 2003.

———. *The Music of Henry Fillmore and Will Huff*. Columbus: Integrity, 1982.

Bloch, Ernst. *Ernest Bloch: Romaine Lettres 1911–1933*. Ed. José-Flore Tappy. Lausanne, Switz.: Editions Payot Lausanne, 1984.

Boice, Martha, Dale Covington, and Richard Spence. *Maps of the Shaker West: A Journey of Discovery*. Dayton: Knot Garden, 1997.

Brandt, Harry A. *Meet Henry Kurtz*. Elgin, Ill.: Brethren, 1941.

Brasher, John Lawrence, ed. *Warren's Minstrel*. Athens: Ohio Univ. Press, 1984.

Cincinnati Musical Directory, 1886–87. Cincinnati: Cincinnati Wesleyan College for Young Women, 1886.

Cincinnati Symphony Orchestra: A Tribute to Max Rudolf and Highlights of its History. Cincinnati: Cincinnati Symphony Orchestra Association, 1967.

Cist, Charles. *Cincinnati in 1841: Its Early Annals and Future Prospects.* Cincinnati: published for the author, 1841.

———. *Sketches and Statistics of Cincinnati in 1851.* Cincinnati: Wm. H. Moore, 1851.

———. *The Cincinnati Miscellany: or Antiquities of the West, and Pioneer History, and General and Local Statistics Compiled from the Western General Advertiser, from April 1st, 1845 to April 1st, 1846.* 2 vols. Cincinnati: Robinson and Jones, 1846.

———. *Sketches and Statistics of Cincinnati in 1859.* Cincinnati: published for the author, 1859.

Cohen, Gustave M. *The Sacred Harp of Judah: A Choice Collection of Music for the Use of Synagogues, Schools, and Home.* Part 1. Sabbath Living. Cleveland: S. Brainard, 1864.

———. *The Orpheus, or Musical Recreations, for the Family Circle and Public Worship.* Cleveland: S. Brainard, 1878.

Copland, Aaron, and Vivian Perlis. *Copland Since 1943.* New York: St. Martin's, 1989.

Creswell, Nicholas. *The Journal of Nicholas Creswell 1774–1777.* New York: Dial, 1928.

Cuming, F. *Sketches of a Tour to the Western Country, through the States of Ohio and Kentucky.* Pittsburgh, Pa.: Cramer, Spear, and Eichbaum, 1810.

Cummins, Kenneth. *Dutchtown: Your Days in History: A Complete History of New Washington and Cranberry Township.* New Washington: New Washington Centennial Committee, 1974.

Current Biography 1940. New York: H. W. Wilson, 1940.

Dolge, Alfred. *Pianos and Their Makers: A Comprehensive History of the Development of the Piano from the Monochord to the Concert Grand Player Piano.* Vol. 1. Covina, Calif.: Covina Publishing, 1911. Repr., New York: Dover, 1972.

———. *Pianos and Their Makers: Development of the Piano Industry in American Since the Centennial Exhibition at Philadelphia, 1876.* Vol. 2. Covina, Calif.: Covina Publishing, 1913.

Drake, B[enjamin], and E[dward] D[eering] Mansfield. *Cincinnati in 1826.* Cincinnati: Morgan, Lodge, and Fisher, 1827.

Eddy, Mary O. *Ballads and Songs from Ohio.* New York: J. J. Augustin, 1939. Repr., Hatboro, Pa.: Folklore Associates, 1964.

Eldridge, Mabel, et al., *The History of Franklin in the Great Miami Valley.* Ed. Harriet E. Foley. Franklin: Franklin Area Historical Society, 1982.

England, J. Merton, ed. *Buckeye Schoolmaster: A Chronicle of Midwestern Rural Life, 1853–1865.* Bowling Green: Bowling Green State Univ. Popular Press, 1996.

Everhart, J. F. *History of Muskingum County, Ohio, with Illustrations and Biographical Sketches of Prominent Men and Pioneers.* [Columbus]: J. F. Everhart, 1882.

Fast, J. J. *The Cantica Sacra: A Collection of Church Music, Embracing, Besides Some New Pieces, a Choice Selection of German and English Chorals, Set Pieces, Chants, etc.* Hudson: Hudson Book, 1854.

Fellers, Frederick P., and Betty Meyers, comp. *Discographies of Commercial Recordings of the Cleveland Orchestra (1924–1977) and the Cincinnati Symphony Orchestra (1917–1977).* Westport, Conn.: Greenwood, 1978.

Ferguson, John Allen. *Walter Holtkamp: American Organ Builder.* Kent: Kent State Univ. Press, 1979.

Field, Al. G. *Watch Yourself Go By.* Columbus, 1912.

Fillmore, Augustus Dameron. *The Universal Musician: A New Collection of Secular and Sacred Music Designed for Schools, Musical Associations, and Social Music Parties.* 12th ed. Cincinnati: Applegate, 1859.

Fleming, John E. *The Underground Railroad: Resources and Sites to Visit.* Columbus: Ohio Historical Society, 1995.

Flint, Timothy. *The Columbian Harmonist: In Two Parts. To Which Is Prefixed a Dissertation upon the True Taste in Church Music.* Cincinnati: Coleman and Phillips, 1816.

————. *Recollections of the Last Ten Years Passed in Occasional Residences and Journeyings in the Valley of the Mississippi.* Boston: Cummings, Hilliard, and Co., 1826. Repr., New York: Johnson Reprint, 1968.

Folson, James K. *Timothy Flint.* New York: Twayne, 1965.

Foote, Henry Wilder. *Three Centuries of American Hymnody.* Cambridge, Mass.: Harvard Univ. Press, 1940.

Forman, Samuel S. *Narrative of a Journey Down the Ohio and Mississippi in 1789–90.* Cincinnati: Robert Clarke, 1888. Repr., New York: Arno, 1971.

Frank, Leonie C. *Musical Life in Early Cincinnati and the Origin of the May Festival.* Cincinnati: Ruter, 1932.

Freedland, Michael. *Music Man: The Story of Frank Simon.* Portland, Ore.: Vallentine Mitchell, 1994.

Freese, Andrew. *Early History of the Cleveland Public Schools.* Cleveland: Robison, Savage, and Co., 1876.

Gierk, Jack. *A Photo Album of Ohio's Canal Era.* Kent: Kent State Univ. Press, 1988.

Gist, Christopher. *Christopher Gist's Journals.* Pittsburgh, Pa.: J. R. Weldin, 1893.

Goodspeed, Thomas Wakefield. *William Rainey Harper: First President of the University of Chicago.* Chicago: Univ. of Chicago Press, 1928.

Goss, Charles Frederic. *Cincinnati: The Queen City, 1788–1912.* Chicago: S. J. Clarke, 1912.

Greve, Charles Theodore. *Centennial History of Cincinnati and Representative Citizens.* Vol. 1. Chicago: Biographical, 1904.

Grossman, F. Karl. *A History of Music in Cleveland.* Cleveland: Case Western Reserve University, 1972.

Gould, Nathaniel D. *History of Church Music in America.* Boston, Mass.: Gould and Lincoln, 1853.

Hagedorn, Ann. *Beyond the River: The Untold Story of the Heroes of the Underground Railroad.* New York: Simon and Schuster, 2002.

Hall, J. H. *Biography of Gospel Song and Hymn Writers.* New York: Fleming H. Revel, 1914.

Hall, James. *Letters from the West; Containing Sketches of Scenery, Manners, and Customs; and Anecdotes Connected with the First Settlements of the Western Sections of the United States.* London: Henry Colburn, 1828.

Hall, Roger L. *The Story of "Simple Gifts."* Holland, Mich.: World of Shaker, 1992.

Harrison, Thomas. *The Juvenile Numeral Singer.* Cincinnati: published for the author, 1852.

————. *Music Simplified: or A New System of Music, Founded on Natural Principles; Designed Either for Separate Use, or as an Introduction to the Old System, and Intended Chiefly for Educational and Religious Purposes: To Which is Added a Collection of Christian Melodies.* Springfield: printed at the office of "The Republic," 1839.

Hartzell, Lawrence W. *Ohio Moravian Music.* Winston-Salem, N.C.: Moravian Music Foundation Press, 1988.

Hazen, Margaret Hindle, and Robert M. Hazen. *The Music Men: An Illustrated History of Brass Bands in American, 1800–1920.* Washington, D.C.: Smithsonian Institution Press, 1987.

Heintze, James R., ed. *American Musical Life in Context and Practice to 1865.* New York: Garland, 1994.

Hildreth, S[amuel] P[rescott]. *Biographical and Historical Memoirs of the Early Pioneer Settlers of Ohio.* Cincinnati: H. W. Derby, 1852.

Historical Sketches of Public Schools in Cities, Villages and Townships of the State of Ohio. Columbus: Ohio Teachers' Association Centennial Committee, 1876.

Hitchcock, H. Wiley, and Sadie Stanley. *The New Grove Dictionary of American Music.* Vol. 2. London: Macmillan, 1986.

Hooper, Osman Castle. *History of the City of Columbus, Ohio.* Columbus: Memorial, 1921.

Horton, John J. *The Jonathan Hale Farm: A Chronicle of the Cuyahoga Valley.* Cleveland: Western Reserve Historical Society, 1990.

Howard, Tasker. *Our American Music.* New York: Thomas Y. Crowell, 1930.

Howe, G. L., and W. S. B. Mathews, eds. *A Hundred Years of Music in America.* Chicago: G. L. Howe, 1889.

Howe, Henry, ed. *Historical Collections of Ohio.* Cincinnati: Derby, Bradley, 1847. Ohio Centennial ed. 3 vols. in 2. Norwalk: Laning, 1896.

Howells, William Cooper. *Recollections of Life in Ohio, from 1813 to 1840.* Cincinnati: Robert Clarke, 1895.

Hughes, Adella Prentiss. *Music Is My Life.* Cleveland: World, 1947.

Jackson, George Pullen. *White Spirituals in the Southern Uplands.* Chapel Hill: Univ. of North Carolina Press, 1933.

Jackson, John A. *Big Beat Heat: Alan Freed and the Early Years of Rock and Roll.* New York: Schirmer, 1991.

Joyce, Patrick Weston. *Old Irish Folk Music and Songs: A Collection of 842 Irish Airs and Songs Hitherto Unpublished.* London: Longmans, Green, and Co., 1909. Repr., New York: Cooper Square, 1965.

Junkermann, G. F., and J. L. Zelltz. *The Cincinnati Music Reader.* Part 1. Revised. Cincinnati: John Church, 1893.

Kaufman, Stanley A., ed. *Moravians in Ohio.* Walnut Creek: German Culture Museum, 1987.

Keck, George R., and Sherrill Martin, eds. *Feel the Spirit: Studies in Nineteenth Century Afro-American Music.* Westport, Conn.: Greenwood, 1988.

Knepper, George W. *Ohio and Its People.* Kent: Kent State Univ. Press, 1989.

Krehbiel, Henry Edward. *Review of the New York Musical Scene, 1887–88.* New York: Novello, Ewer, and Co., 1888.

Lane, Leasure Porter. *Tone, Silence and Time: A Comprehensive and Logical Treatment of the True Meaning of Characters That Represent Music.* Zanesville: published for the author, 1907.

Launius, Roger D. *The Kirtland Temple: A Historical Narrative.* Independence, Mo.: Herald House, 1986.

Lax, Roger, and Frederick Smith. *The Great Song Thesaurus.* 2d ed. New York: Oxford Univ. Press, 1989.

Lee, Alfred E. *History of the City of Columbus: Capital of Ohio.* New York: Munsell, 1892.

Leonard, J. W. *The Centennial Review of Cincinnati: One Hundred Years.* Cincinnati: J. M. Elstner, 1888.

Lewis, Thomas W. *Zanesville and Muskingum County, Ohio.* Chicago: S. J. Clarke, 1927.

Listen for the Jazz: Key Notes in Columbus History. 2d ed. Columbus: Columbus Arts Foundation of Olde Town, 1992.

Lomax, John A. *Adventures of a Ballad Hunter.* New York: MacMillan, 1947.

Loucks, Richard. *Arthur Shepherd: American Composer.* Provo, Utah: Brigham Young Univ. Press, 1980.

MacLean, J. P. *Shakers of Ohio: Fugitive Papers Concerning the Shakers of Ohio, With Unpublished Manuscripts.* Columbus: F. J. Heer, 1907.

Marsh, Robert C. *The Cleveland Orchestra.* Cleveland: World, 1967.

———. *Dialogues and Discoveries: James Levine: His Life and His Music.* New York: Scribner, 1998.

Marshall, George Sidney. *The History of Music in Columbus, Ohio: February 14, 1812–July 1, 1953.* Columbus: F. J. Heer, 1953.

Martineau, Harriet. *Retrospect of Foreign Travel.* London: Saunders and Otley, 1838.

Mason, Lowell, and Timothy B. Mason. *The Sacred Harp, or Eclectic Harmony.* New ed. Cincinnati: Truman and Smith, 1840.

Mason, Luther Whiting, D. H. Baldwin, Elisha Locke, and Charles Aiken. *The Young Singer: A Collection of Juvenile Music, Compiled (at the Request of the Board of Trustees) for the Cincinnati Public Schools, by Messrs. Mason, Baldwin, Locke and Aiken, Teachers of Music in Those Schools.* Part 1. Cincinnati: Sargent, Wilson, and Hinkle, 1860.

Mason, Timothy B. *The Sacred Harp, or Beauties of Church Music.* Vol. 2. New ed. Boston: Kidder and Wright, 1845.

May, John. *Journal and Letters of Col. John May, of Boston Relative to Two Journeys to the Ohio Country in 1788 and '89.* Cincinnati: Robert Clarke, 1873.

Melish, John. *Travels through the United States of America, in the Years 1806 and 1807, and 1809, 1810, and 1811.* Philadelphia, Pa.: printed for the author, 1815. London: George Cowie, 1818. Repr., New York: Johnson Reprint, 1970.

Men of Northwestern Ohio: A Collection of Portraits and Biographies. Bowling Green: C. S. van Tassel, 1898.

Merz, Karl. *Musical Hints for the Million.* Cleveland: S. Brainard's Sons, 1875.

Michel, N. E. *Piano Atlas.* Rivera, Calif., 1953.

Miller, Zane. *Cincinnati's Music Hall.* Virginia Beach, Va.: Jordan, 1978.

Millet, William E. *Stephen Foster: Youth's Golden Gleam: A Sketch of His Life and Background in Cincinnati, 1846–1850.* Princeton, N.J.: Princeton Univ. Press, 1936.

Mixter, James Murchie Eaton. *Music Was My Business: My Life and Times with Baldwin.* Cincinnati: published for the author, 1996.

Moore, Jerrold Northrop. *Edward Elgar: A Creative Life.* Oxford, U.K.: Oxford Univ. Press, 1984.

Morgan, Russell V. The Fine Arts Guide of Ohio: Season 1929–1930. Cleveland: Fine Arts Service of Ohio, 1929.

Morhart, Hilda Dischinger. *The Zoar Story.* 3d ed. Strasburg: Gordon, 1981.

Mosbrook, Joe. *Cleveland Jazz History.* Cleveland Heights: Northeast Ohio Jazz Society, 1993.

Muenschner, Joseph. *The Church Choir. A Collection of Sacred Music: Comprising a Great Variety of Psalm and Hymn Tunes, Anthems, and Chants.* Columbus: Isaac N. Whiting, 1839.

The Musical Personnel of Cincinnati and Vicinity for 1896. Cincinnati: Universal, 1896.

Mussulman, Joseph A. *Dear People... Robert Shaw: A Biography.* Bloomington: Indiana Univ. Press, 1979.

Nathan, Hans. *Dan Emmett and the Rise of Early Negro Minstrelsy.* Norman: Univ. of Oklahoma Press, 1962.

Nicholas, Luis. *Thor Johnson: American Conductor.* Fish Creek, Wis.: Music Festival Committee of the Peninsula Arts Association, 1982.

Nordhoff, Charles. *The Communistic Societies of the United States from Personal Visit and Observation.* New York: Harper and Brothers, 1874. Repr., New York: Dover, 1966.

Olmstead, Earl P. *Blackcoats among the Delaware: David Ziesberger on the Ohio Frontier.* Kent: Kent State Univ. Press, 1991.

———. *David Zeisberger: A Life Among the Indians.* Kent: Kent State Univ. Press, 1997.

Osburn, Mary Hubbell. *Ohio Composers and Musical Authors.* Columbus: F. J. Heer, 1942.

Patterson, Daniel W. *The Shaker Spiritual.* Princeton, N.J.: Princeton Univ. Press, 1979.

Pierce, Bob. *Pierce Piano Atlas.* Long Beach, Calif.: Bob Pierce, 1965.

Randall, E. O. *The Separatist Society of Zoar: An Experiment in Communism from Its Commencement to Its Conclusion.* Columbus: Ohio State Archaeological and History Society, 1900. Indexed and Repr., [S.I.]: Arthur W. McGraw, 1990.

Revett, Marion S. *A Minstrel Town.* New York: Pageant, 1955.

Rice, Edward Le Roy. *Monarchs of Minstrelsy, from "Daddy" Rice to Date.* New York: Kenny, 1911.

Ritter, Frédéric Louis. *Music in America.* New York: Scribner, 1883. Rev., 1895.

Rodzinski, Halina. *Our Two Lives.* New York: Scribner, 1976.

Roe, George Mortimer. *Cincinnati: The Queen City of the West.* Cincinnati: Cincinnati Times-Star, 1895.

Roell, Craig H. *The Piano in America, 1890–1940.* Chapel Hill: Univ. of North Carolina Press, 1989.

Rosen, Carole. *The Goossens: A Musical Century.* Boston, Mass.: Northeastern Univ. Press, 1993.

Rosenberg, Donald. *The Cleveland Orchestra Story: "Second to None."* Cleveland: Gray, 2000.

Roy, Klaus G. *Not Responsible for Lost Articles: Thoughts and Second Thoughts from Severance Hall, 1958–1988.* Cleveland: Musical Arts Association, 1993.

Sacks, Howard L., and Judith Rose. *Way Up North in Dixie: A Black Family's Claim to the Confederate Anthem.* Washington, D.C.: Smithsonian Institution Press, 1993.

Safford, William H. *The Life of Harman Blennerhasset.* Cincinnati: Ely, Allen, and Locker, 1850.

Salt, Elizabeth Anne. *Buckeye Heritage: Ohio's History in Song.* Columbus: Enthea, 1992.

Schabas, Ezra. *Theodore Thomas: America's Conductor and Builder of Orchestras, 1835–1905.* Urbana: Univ. of Illinois Press, 1989.

Schneider, Norris F. *Y Bridge City: The Story of Zanesville and Muskingum County, Ohio.* Cleveland: World, 1950.

Scribner, Harvey, ed. *Memoirs of Lucas County and the City of Toledo.* Vol. 1. Madison, Wis.: Western Historical Association, 1910.

Seidensticker, Oswald. *Geschichte des Männerchors in Philadelphia, 1835–1885.* Philadelphia, Pa.: Verlag des Männerchors, 1885.

Sheblessy, Sylvia Kleve. *100 Years of the Cincinnati May Festival.* Cincinnati, Ohio, 1973.

Shoemaker, Dacia Custer. *Choose You This Day: The Legacy of the Hanbys.* Westerville: Westerville Historical Society, 1983.

Simpson, Joshua McCarty. *The Emancipation Car, Being an Original Composition of Anti-Slavery Ballads Composed Exclusively for the Underground Railroad.* Zanesville: Edwin C. Church, 1854, 1874.

Smith, Emma. *A Collection of Sacred Hymns, for the Church of the Latter Day Saints.* Kirtland: F. G. Williams, 1835. Repr., n.p.: Herald Heritage, 1973.

Smith, James. *An Account of the Remarkable Occurrences in the Life and Travels of Col. James Smith, during his Captivity with the Indians in the Years 1755, '56, '57, '58, and '59.* Cincinnati: Robert Clarke, 1870.

Smith, Ophia D. *The Life and Times of Giles Richards (1820–1860).* Columbus: State Archaeological and Historical Society, 1936.

Speary, Nellie Best. *Music and Life in Marietta, Ohio.* Marietta: MacDonald, 1939.

Studer, Jacob H. *Columbus, Ohio: Its History, Resources and Progress.* Columbus: J. H. Studer, 1873.

Sutor, J. Hope. *Past and Present of the City of Zanesville and Muskingum County, Ohio; Together with Biographical Sketches of Many of Its Leading and Prominent Citizens and Illustrious Dead.* Chicago: S. J. Clarke, 1905.

Symmes, Thomas. *The Reasonableness of Regular Singing, or Singing by Note.* Boston, Mass.: B. Green, 1720.

Talevski, Nick. *The Unofficial Encyclopedia of the Rock and Roll Hall of Fame.* Westport, Conn.: Greenwood, 1998.

Thierstein, Eldred A. *Cincinnati Opera: From the Zoo to Music Hall.* Hillsdale, Mich.: Deerstone, 1995.

Thomas, Rose Fay. *Memoirs of Theodore Thomas.* New York: Moffat, Yeard, and Co., 1911.

Thomas, Theodore. *Theodore Thomas: A Musical Autobiography.* Vol. 1. Ed. George P. Upton. Chicago: A. C. McClurg, 1905.

Thwaites, Reuben Gold. *Early Western Travels, 1748–1846.* Vol. 4. Cleveland: Arthur H. Clark, 1904.

Tolzmann, Don Heinrich, ed. *The First Mayor of Cincinnati: George A. Katzenberger's Biography of Major David Ziegler.* Lanham, Md.: University Press of America, 1990.

Tracey, Steven C. *Going to Cincinnati: A History of the Blues in the Queen City.* Urbana: Univ. of Illinois Press, 1993.

Trollope, Frances. *Domestic Manners of the Americans.* 5th ed. London: George Routledge and Sons, 1839.

Tunison, F[rank] E. *Presto! From the Singing School to the May Musical Festival.* Cincinnati: Criterion, 1888.

Turk, John R. *The Musical Danas of Warren, Ohio: The History of the Dana School of Music.* Youngstown: Dana Press of Youngstown State University, 1999.

Van Grundy, Paul, ed. *Stories of the Fountain City, 1840–1900.* Bryan: Bryan Area Foundation, 1975.

Vincent, Rickey. *Funk: The Music, the People, and the Rhythm of The One.* New York: St. Martin's Griffin, 1996.

Vitz, Robert C. *Cincinnati Symphony Orchestra: Centennial Portraits.* Cincinnati: Cincinnati Symphony Orchestra, 1994.

———. *The Queen and the Arts: Cultural Life in Nineteenth-Century Cincinnati.* Kent: Kent State Univ. Press, 1989.

Vonada, Damaine, ed. *The Ohio Almanac.* Wilmington: Orange Frazer, 1992.

Warch, Willard. *Our First 100 Years: A Brief History of the Oberlin College Conservatory of Music.* Oberlin: Oberlin College, 1967.

Ward, Andrew. *Dark Midnight When I Rise: The Story of the Jubilee Singers Who Introduced the World to the Music of Black America.* New York: Farrar, Straus, and Giroux, 2000.

Waters, Wilson. *The History of Saint Luke's Church, Marietta, Ohio.* Marietta: for the author by J. Mueller and Son, 1884.

Wetzel, Richard D. "Catholic Church Music in the Midwest before the Civil War: The Firm of W. C. Peters and Sons." In *American Musical Life in Context and Practice to 1865,* ed. James R. Heintze, 203–30. New York: Garland, 1994.

————. *Frontier Musicians on the Connoquenessing, Wabash, and Ohio: A History of the Music and Musicians of George Rapp's Harmony Society (1805–1906).* Athens: Ohio Univ. Press, 1976.

————. *"Oh! Sing No More That Gentle Song": The Musical Life and Times of William Cumming Peters (1805–66).* Warren, Mich.: Harmonie Park, 2000.

Witchey, Holly Rarick, and John Vacha. *Fine Arts in Cleveland: An Illustrated History.* Bloomington: Indiana Univ. Press, 1994.

Wittke, Carl. *The First Fifty Years: The Cleveland Museum of Art 1916–1966.* Cleveland: Cleveland Museum of Art, 1966.

Woods, Terry K, comp. *The Ohio and Erie Canal: A Glossary of Terms.* Kent: Kent State Univ. Press, 1995.

Yankovic, Frankie. *The Polka King: The Life of Frankie Yankovic as Told to Robert Dolgan.* Cleveland: Dillon-Liederbach, 1977.

Zverina, Silvia. *And They Shall Have Music: The History of the Cleveland Music School Settlement.* Cleveland: Cobham and Hatherton, 1988.

Theses and Dissertations

Breitmayer, Douglas Reece. "Seventy-Five Years of Sacred Music in Cleveland, Ohio, 1800–1875." Master's thesis, Union Theological Seminary, 1951.

Campbell, David Eugene. "The Purveyor as Patron: The Contribution of American Piano Manufacturers and Merchants to Musical Culture in the United States 1851–1914." Ph.D. diss., City University of New York, 1984.

Christensen, Donald E. "Music of the Shakers from Union Village, Ohio: A Repertory Study and Tune Index of the Manuscripts Originating in the 1840s." Ann Arbor, Mich.: UMI, 1988.

————. "A Transcription to Modern Notation of a Shaker Hymnal by Issac Youngs Based on His Theory Book." Master's thesis, Indiana University of Pennsylvania, 1976.

Gary, Charles L. "A History of Music Education in the Cincinnati Public Schools." Ph.D. diss., University of Cincinnati, 1951.

Grant, Francis Hawthore. "Foundations of Music Education in the Cleveland Public Schools." Ph.D. diss., Western Reserve University, 1963.

Gross, Jeanne Bilger. "Benjamin Russell Hanby, Ohio Composer-Educator, 1833–1876: His Contributions to Early Music Education." Ph.D. diss., Ohio State University, 1987.

Hart, Kenneth Wayne. "Cincinnati Organ Builders of the Nineteenth Century." Ph.D. diss., University of Cincinnati, 1972.

Kapfer, Miriam B. "Music Instruction and Supervision in the Public Schools of Columb[us], Ohio, from 1845 to 1900." Ph.D. diss., Ohio State University, 1964.

Kares, Hans Martin Heinrich. "Das Deutsche Element im amerikanischen Orgelbau" ("Th[e] German Element in American Organbuilding"). Ph.D. diss., Philipps-Universität a[t] Marburg-Lahn, 1990.

Klassen, Hope M. "Maestros and Management: The Cleveland Orchestra, 1918–1994." Master's thesis, University of Akron, 1995.

Lewis, John, Jr. "An Historical Study of the Origin and Development of the Cincinnati Conservatory of Music." Ph.D. diss., University of Cincinnati, 1943.

Martin, Michael D. "The Band School of Dana's Musical Institute, Warren, Ohio, 1869–1941." Ann Arbor, Mich.. University of Michigan Microfilms, 1996.

Massman, Richard Lee. "Lillian Baldwin and the Cleveland Plan for Education Concerts." Ph.D. diss., University of Michigan, 1972.

McVicker, Ronald R. "A Biography of Clare Grundman and Analysis of Selected Works." Master's thesis, Bowling Green State University, 1988.

Mennel, Christina Chenevert. "Change in Early Cincinnati's Musical Identity: Shape-Note Tunebooks from Timothy Flint's *Columbian Harmonist* (1816) to Timothy and Lowell Mason's *Sacred Harp* (1834)." Ph.D. diss., Ohio State University, 1997.

Miller, Terry E. "Alexander Auld and American Shape-Note Music." Master's thesis, Indiana University, 1971.

Mitchell, Hamer. "The Eisteddfod in Ohio." Master's thesis, Ohio State University, 1943.

Nixon, Edgar Burkhardt. "The Society of Separatists at Zoar." Ph.D. diss., Ohio State University, 1933.

Orlando, Vincent A. "An Historical Study of the Origin and Development of the College of Music of Cincinnati." Ph.D. diss., University of Cincinnati, 1946.

Pisoni, Michael J. "Operatic War in New York City, 1883–84: Colonel James H. Mapelson at the Academy of Music vs. Henry E. Abbey at the Metropolitan Opera House." Ph.D. diss., Indiana University, 1975.

Pohly, Linda Louise. "Welsh Choral Music in America in the Nineteenth Century." Ph.D. diss., Ohio State University, 1989.

Pool, Jeannie Gayle. "The Life and Music of Zenobia Powell Perry: An American Composer." Ph.D. diss., Claremont Graduate University, 2001.

Scholten, James William. "The Chapins: A Study of Men and Sacred Music West of the Alleghenies, 1795–1842." Ph.D. diss., University of Michigan, 1972.

Schroeder, Vernon D. "Cincinnati's Musical Growth, 1870–1875." Master's thesis, University of Cincinnati, 1971.

Script Ohio: 110 Years of the Ohio State Marching Band. [Columbus]: Ohio State University, Kappa Kappa Psi, 1989.

Skrym, Richard Dean. "Oberlin Conservatory: A Century of Musical Growth and Influence." Ph.D. diss., University of Southern California, 1962.

Snyder, Suzanne Gail. "The Männerchor Tradition in the United States: A Historical Analysis of its Contribution to American Musical Culture." Ph.D. diss., University of Iowa, 1991.

Soriano, Constantine F. "Cincinnati Music Readers." Master's thesis, College-Conservatory of Music of Cincinnati, 1957.

Sprunger, Orlo Omer. "The North American Saengers Union." Master's thesis, Ohio State University, 1951.

Thomas, Louis R. "A History of the Cincinnati Symphony Orchestra to 1931." Ph.D. diss., University of Cincinnati, 1972.

Wagner, Mary Cleveland. "Early Orchestras in Cleveland (1900–1915)." Master's thesis, Kent State University, 1998.

Wolz, Larry Robert. "Opera in Cincinnati: The Years before the Zoo, 1801–1920." Ph.D. diss., University of Cincinnati 1983.

Wyrick, Charles B. "Concert and Criticism in Cincinnati, 1840–1850." Master's thesis, University of Cincinnati, 1965.

PAMPHLETS, ARTICLES, AND SHEET MUSIC

Adams, Dennis P. "Journal, Sept. 1845–Nov. 1846, of a Trip from Marietta, O., to Boston, Mass., on a Sailing Vessel built at Harmar, O., and return Overland." Typescript, 1937. Ohio Historical Society: VFM 3.

Aiken, Walter H. "Music in the Cincinnati Schools." *Musician* 11, no. 5 (May 1906): 52–53.

———. "Music in the Cincinnati Schools." *Journal of the Proceedings of the Annual Meeting of the Music Supervisor's National Conference* (April 7–11, 1924): 46–55.

Allen, Jim. "The Norwich Area Cornet Bands." Typescript, n.d. Ohio Historical Society: 977.191/A537a4.

Alexander, J. Heywood. "Brainard's (Western) Musical World." *Notes: The Quarterly Journal of the Music Library Association* 36, no. 3 (March 1980): 601–14.

Atwater, Caleb. *An Essay on Education.* Pamphlet. Cincinnati: Kendall and Henry, 1841.

Barber, Elinore. "The Baldwin-Wallace College Bach Festival, 1965 1982." In *A History of the Baldwin Wallace Bach Festival.* Booklet. Berea: Riemenschneider Bach Institute, 1982.

———. "Dr. Albert Riemenschneider: A Centenary Tribute." *Diapason* 69, no. 10 (Sept. 1978): 1, 8–9.

Bastastini, Robert J. "From Correspondence Course to Worship III: The Story of G. I. A." *Pastoral Music* 10, no. 4 (Apr.–May 1986): 46–48.

Becker, Carl. M. "Brighten the Corner Where You Are: Homer Rodeheaver." *Timeline* 17, no. 3 (May–June 2000): 38–53.

Boehm, Richard Theodore. "Tod B. Galloway: Buckeye Jongleur, Composer of 'The Whiffenpoof Song.'" *Ohio History* 83 (1974): 256–82.

Boehne, Rich. "Baldwin Ashes at Stake." *Cincinnati Post,* March, 26, 1987.

Boothe, Raymond L. "Unique Singing Tradition in the Jackson City Schools Celebrates 69th Anniversary." *Triad* 59 (Apr. 1992): 52–53.

Brown, Vernon. "Carl Barckhoff and the Barckhoff Church Organ Company." *Tracker* 22, no. 4 (Summer 1978): 1–7. Repr., *Tracker* 39, no. 4 (Summer 1995): 1, 7–11.

"Bryan City Band: History and Highlights." *Bryan Times,* June 5, 2001.

Cincinnati's Music Hall: A Brief History of the Grand Old Lady of Elm Street, in Timeline Form." Pamphlet. Comp. Ashley L. Ford. Cincinnati: Society for the Preservation of Music Hall, 1998. Public Library of Cincinnati and Hamilton County.

"Cincinnati Sings—A Choral History—1788 to 1988." In *Saengerfest 1988: A Choral Celebration of the Greater Cincinnati Bicentennial, Sunday, May 1, 1988.* Pamphlet. Florence, Ky.: Willis, 1988. Public Library of Cincinnati and Hamilton County.

Cincinnati Symphony Orchestra Concerts: Fritz Reiner, Music Director: 1922–1931. Booklet. Chicago: Fritz Reiner Society, 1989.

The City of Cincinnati and Its Resources. Pamphlet. Cincinnati: *Cincinnati Times-Star,* 1891.

"Cleveland's Orchestra." *Fortune,* November 1931.

Coleberd, Robert E., Jr. "Philipp Wirsching[,] the Consummate Builder." *American Organist* 51, no. 10 (Oct. 1968): 13–15, 24–29.

———. "Stevens of Marietta: A Forgotten Builder in a Bygone Era," *Diapason* 93, no. 6 (June 2002): 18–21.

Condon, Randall J. "A Supervisor as Seen by a Superintendent." *Journal of Proceedings of the Fifteenth Annual Meeting of the Music Supervisors National Conference* (1922): 37.

Connin, John. "The Beginning of the Bryan Band." In *Stories of the Fountain City 1840–1900,* ed. Paul Van Gundy, 21–23. Bryan: Bryan Area Foundation, 1975.

Craig, Lois Zimmer. "Moravian Lovefeast." *Wonderful World of Ohio* (Dec. 1967): 17–19.

Descriptive Catalogue of Upright and Cabinet Pianos. Norwalk: A. B. Chase, 1901[?]. Ohio Historical Society: PA Box 489/21.

Dickinson, Edward. "The Conservatory of Music." *Oberlin Alumni Magazine* 19, no. 8 (May 1923): 3–15.

Diehl, William, Jr. "A Cool New Image for a Staid Old Firm." *Cincinnati* (Jan. 1968): 44–47, 63–65.

Dobbert, G. A. "The 'Zinzinnati' In Cincinnati." *Bulletin of the Cincinnati Historical Society* 22, no. 4 (Oct. 1964): 209–20.

Dooley, Dennis. "The Orchestra Nobody Knows." *Cleveland* (Jan. 1978): 58–64, 137–47.

Durnbaugh, Donald F. "Henry Kurtz: Man of the Book." *Ohio History* 76, no. 3 (Summer 1967): 114–31.

"Eclectic Academy of Music in Cincinnati." *American Annals of Education and Instruction for the Year 1834* (1834): 289.

Elward, Thomas J. "Thomas Harrison's Patented Numeral Notation System." *Journal of Research in Music Education* 28, no. 4 (Winter 1980): 218–24.

Fanfare: Portraits of the Cleveland Orchestra. Booklets in 3 vols. Ed. Susan Sackman. Cleveland: Junior Committee of the Cleveland Orchestra, 1974, 1984. Ed. Marilyn Eppich, 1995. Cleveland Public Library.

Ferguson, John. "A Conversation with Walter Holtkamp Jr." *American Organist* 35, no. 2 (Feb. 2001): 52–55.

Field, Al. G. "Lish Murn's Pledge." *Ohio* 1, no. 3 (Sept. 1906): 241–43.

Fillmore, Henry. "Frank Simon." *Musical Messenger* 13, no. 7 (July 1917): 2–3.

Foreman, B. J. *CCM 125.* Booklet. Cincinnati: University of Cincinnati, 1992. College-Conservatory of Music in Cincinnati.

Galbreath, C[harles] B. "Benjamin Russell Hanby: Author of 'Darling Nelly Gray.'" *Ohio Illustrated Magazine* 1, no. 2 (1906): 182–88.

———. "Daniel Decatur Emmett, Author of 'Dixie.'" *Ohio State Archaeological and Historical Quarterly* 13 (Oct. 1904): 504–50.

———. "Will Lamartine Thompson." *Ohio Archaeological and Historical Quarterly* 14, no. 3 (1905): 291–312.

Gelfand, Janelle. "De Blasis Led with Business Head, Artistic Soul." *Cincinnati Enquirer*, June 30, 1996.

Goehring, Susan. *Schoenbrunn: A Meeting of Cultures*. Pamphlet. Columbus: Ohio Historical Society, 1997.

Grant, Francis Hawthorne. "The Emergence of Cultural Patterns in a Great American City: Cleveland." *Fine Arts* 19, no. 893 (July 19, 1971): 2, 4–5, 13; no. 894 (July 26, 1971): 3–4, 6–7, 11, 13; no. 895 (Aug. 2, 1971): 3–5, 16–17; no. 900 (Sept. 6, 1971): 4, 7, 11–13; no. 901 (Sept. 13, 1971): 6–7, 10–13; no. 909 (Nov. 8, 1971): 4–8.

Grayson, Frank W. "Singing Cincinnati." *Cincinnati Times-Star*, January 6–March 5, 1937. *A Half Century of Golden Music: Golden Jubilee Year: The Story of the Cincinnati Symphony Orchestra*. Pamphlet. Cincinnati: Cincinnati Symphony Orchestra Association, 1945[?]. Public Library of Cincinnati and Hamilton County.

Hamm, Charles. "Patent Notes in Cincinnati." *Historical and Philosophical Society of Ohio Bulletin* 16 (1958): 293–310.

Hanby, B[enjamin] R. "Little Tillie's Grave." Sheet music. Cincinnati: John Church Jr., 1860.

———. "Terrible Tough!" Sheet music. Cincinnati: John Church Jr., 1864.

———. "Willie's Temptation: A Song for Children." Sheet music. Cincinnati: J. Church Jr, 1868.

Hartzell, Lawrence W. "Musical Moravian Missionaries: Part II: Johann Jakob Schmick." *Moravian Music Journal* 30, no. 3 (Fall 1985): 36–37.

Heller, George N. "N. Coe Stewart (1838–1921): Cleveland Composer, Author, Compiler, Music Educator, and Administrator." Unpublished paper delivered to members of the College Music Society meeting in Cleveland, November 1997.

A History of the Baldwin-Wallace Bach Festival. Booklet. Berea: Riemenschneider Bach Institute, 1982.

Hobbs, Lenora. "Sizing Up the Queen City: Frances Trollope and Harriet Martineau." *Timeline* 21, no. 3 (May–June 2004): 14–27.

Holliday, Joseph E. "Cincinnati Opera Festivals During the Gilded Age." *Bulletin of The Cincinnati Historical Society* 24, no. 2 (Apr. 1966): 131–49.

———. "The Cincinnati Philharmonic and Hopkins Hall Orchestra 1856–1868." *Bulletin of the Cincinnati Historical Society* 26, no. 2 (Apr. 1968): 158–73.

———. "The Musical Legacy of Theodore Thomas." *Bulletin of the Cincinnati Historical Society* 27, no. 3 (Fall 1969): 191–205.

———. "Notes on Samuel N. Pike and his Opera Houses." *Bulletin of the Cincinnati Historical Society* 25, no. 3 (July 1967): 165–83.

———. "Three World Premières of Grand Opera." *Bulletin of the Cincinnati Historical Society* 36, no. 2 (Summer 1978): 117–23.

Hoover, Earl R. "Our Bard—Benjamin R. Hanby: The Stephen Foster of Ohio." *Report* 5 (1965): 1–2. Ohio Genealogical Society.

Horstman, Denise, and Judith Arnold. *The Cleveland Orchestra Discography*. Pamphlet. Cleveland: Cleveland Orchestra, 1985. Cleveland Public Library.

Huber, Donald L. "The Prophet Joseph in Ohio." *Timeline* 16, no. 6 (Nov.–Dec. 1999): 2–17.

Huntington, Peletiah W. "Old-Time Music of Columbus." *The "Old Northwest" Genealogical Quarterly* 8 (Apr. 1905): 136–40.

Jones, William Harvey. "Welsh Settlements in Ohio." *Ohio Archaeological and Historical Society Quarterly* 16 (Apr. 1907): 194–227.

The Journal of Colonel Ichabod Nye. Vol. 2. Typescript, 1937. Dawes Memorial Library. Marietta College, Marietta, Ohio.

Jozwiak, Kathleen L. *Cleveland-Style Polka Directory*. Willoughby: St. Monica, 1998.

Kapfer, Miriam B. "Early Public School Music in Columbus, Ohio, 1845–54." *Journal of Research in Music Education* 15 (Fall 1967): 191–200.

Keiger, Dale. "What You Didn't Learn About Baldwin . . . Until It Was Too Late." *Cincinnati* (Dec. 1983): 74–79.

Knittle, Rhea Mansfield. *Early Ohio Taverns*. Booklet. Ashland: privately printed, 1937. Repr., *Ohio Frontier Series*. Vol. 1. Ashland: privately printed, 1976.

Kushner, David. "Ernst Bloch in Cleveland (1920–1925)." Unpublished paper presented to members of the College Music Society in Cleveland, November 1997.

The Lane Conservatory of Music: 1899–1900. Pamphlet. Zanesville: *Times Recorder*, 1899[?]. Ohio Historical Society: PA Box 281/1.

Lane, Leasure Porter. "Loved Though It Be." Sheet music. Zanesville: printed for the author, 1910.

Lasky, Joe. "The Art Tatum." *Ohio* 18, no. 9 (Feb. 1996): 29–31, 72–74.

Louderback, Jeff. "The Heritage of Hopalong." *Ohio* 22, no. 2 (May 1999): 46–47.

Malitz, Nancy. "A Hardy Survivor Rides the Wave of the Future." *New York Times*, March 19, 1995.

Mason, Timothy, and Charles Beecher, "Report on Vocal Music, as a Branch of Common School Education." *Western Academician and Journal of Education and Science* 1, no. 11 (1837–38): 631–50.

McCormick, Alexander S. "The History of the Military Bands of Akron." Typescript, 1940s[?]. Akron-Summit County Library.

Milford, Gene F. "George T. 'Red' Bird; Innovations and Developments of Marching Band Techniques at Massillon, Ohio (1938–1946)." *Contributions to Music Education, 1999* 26, no. 1 (1999): 86–95.

———. "The Ohio March Connection." *Triad* 64 (Dec. 1995–Jan. 1996): 41–44.

Miller, Charles G. "The Background of Calvin E. Stowe's 'Report on Elementary Instruction in Europe' (1837)." *Ohio State Archaeological and Historical Quarterly* 49 (Jan.-Mar. 1940): 185–90.

Miller, Terry E. "Alexander Auld: Early Ohio Musician." *Bulletin of the Cincinnati Historical Society*, 33 (1975): 244–60.

Myers, Carol Bishop. "The Musical Expression of Anti-Slavery Sentiment in Ohio." *Sonneck Society Bulletin* 18, no. 1 (Spring 1992): 8–11.

Nye, Captain Pearl R. *Scenes and Songs of the Ohio-Erie Canal*. Booklet. Ed. Cloea Thomas. Columbus: Ohio Historical Society, 1952. Repr., 1971.

O'Connell, Tom. "Something to Sing About." *Cleveland Plain Dealer*, February 24, 1957.

Official Souvenir of the Twenty-Seventh Saengerfest of the North American Saengerbund, Held at Cleveland, Ohio, July 11, 12, 13, and 14, 1893. Comp. Calvin P. Wilcox. Booklet. Cleveland: Williams, 1893. Western Reserve Historical Society.

Ogden, Rebecca R. "Glory Light Shines for Me: The Black Tradition of Shape Note Singing in Ohio." Unpublished paper, 1991.

Osborne, William. "The Echoes of His Songs Go from Lip to Lip the World 'Round: William Howard Doane: Industrialist, Composer, and Philanthropist." *Queen City Heritage* 56, no. 2 (Summer 1998): 2–28.

Ostrander, Stephen. "Tracing Zane." *Ohio* (Apr. 1996): 34–42, 90–91.

Pantsios, Anastasia. "Polka Is King." *Cleveland Free Times,* May 15, 1996.

Peskin, Allan. *The Tempting Freedom: The Early Years of Cleveland Judaism and Anshe Chesed Congregation.* Pamphlet. Cleveland: n.p., 1973. Western Reserve Historical Society.

Pitkin, Mrs. Fred S. "Music in Tallmadge." *A History of Tallmadge, Ohio.* Booklet. Tallmadge: Tallmadge Historical Society, 1957. Western Reserve Historical Society.

Pool, Jeannie Gayle. "Zenobia Powell Perry: An American Composer," *Journal of the International Alliance for Women in Music* 9, no. 1 (2003): 13–16.

Porter, Susan L. "Music in 19th-Century Lima." Unpublished paper. University of Colorado.

Preston, Diana. "Why Fear Death? Charles Frohman aboard the *Lusitania,*" *Timeline* 19, no. 6 (Nov.–Dec. 2002): 36–53.

Rarick, Ron. "The Baroque Organ at Elgin: A Saga." *Diapason* 86, no. 9 (Sept. 1998): 14–16.

Ratterman, H[einrich] A. *Early Music in Cincinnati. An Essay Read before the Literary Club, November 9, 1879.* Pamphlet. Cincinnati: s.n., [1879]. Ohio Historical Society: 780.77178/R189.

Reeb, Mary. "Adella Prentiss Hughes and the Founding, Fostering, and Financing of the Cleveland Orchestra." *Gamut* 15 (Spring–Summer 1985): 62–68.

Riddell, Cecilia, ed. *Handy Play Party Book.* Booklet. Burnsville, N.C.: World Around Songs, 1981.

Riemenschneider, Selma Marting. "A History of the Baldwin-Wallace College Bach Festival (1933–1964)." In *A History of the Baldwin-Wallace Bach Festival.* Booklet. Berea: Riemenschneider Bach Institute, 1982.

Riepenhoff, Jill. "The Band Plays On." *Columbus Dispatch,* August 21, 1994.

Rippley, La Vern J. "German Theater in Columbus, Ohio," *German-American Studies* 1, no. 2 (1970): 78–101.

Robinson, Jeff. "The Dean of Steubenville." *Ohio* (Jan. 2002): 62–67.

Rosenberg, Don[ald]. "Bringing Bach and His Buddies to Berea." *Akron Beacon Journal, The Sunday Magazine,* March 18, 1979, 4–7, 22–23.

Rosenberg, Donald. "Putting Music in the Picture." *Cleveland Plain Dealer,* June 16, 1996.

Royse, Noble K[ibby]. *Charles Aiken: An Address Delivered In Music Hall, Cincinnati, November 15, 1884, at the Unveiling of the Aiken Memorial.* Pamphlet. Cincinnati: Robert Clarke, 1885. State Library of Ohio: MT3.U6/R69X.

Sanders, Paul D. "Caleb Atwater's Contribution to Music Education in Ohio." *Contributions to Music Education* 24, no. 2 (Dec.1997): 7–15.

————. "Early Public School Music Education in Zanesville, Ohio." *Bulletin of Historical Research in Music Education* 19 (May 1998): 187–96.

————. "Early Public School Music in the State of Ohio." *Triad* 63, no. 5 (Apr. 1996): 37–39.

Sanders, Rory Meshenberg. "A Conservatory of Excellence." In *Notes,* newsletter of the Cleveland Institute of Music.

Savage, Lloyd C. "A Bicentennial Celebration from the Music Archives!" *First Capitol Chronicle* 1, no. 1 (Dec. 1990): 3–9.

Schneider, Norris F. "Zanesville Heard First Important Musicians from 1850 to 1860." *Zanesville News,* March 14, 1943.

————. "Zanesville's Music." *Zanesville Times Signal,* January 9, 16, and 23, 1955.

Schreiber, William I. "Karl Merz: German-American Musician." *The American-German Review* (Feb. 1941): 4–7, 33; (June 1941): 24–27.

Smith, Ophia D. "Joseph Tasso, the Arkansaw Traveler." *Ohio Archaeological and Historical Quarterly* 56 (Jan. 1947): 16–43.

Smodic, Frank, Jr. *The Legendary Frankie Yankovic "Through the Years": The Life and Times of America's Polka King.* Pamphlet. Scottsdale, Pa.: Frank Smodic Jr., 1991. Cleveland-Style Polka Hall of Fame.

Stark, James M. "The Phillipp Wirsching at First Unitarian Church, Pittsburgh." *Tracker* 47, no. 1 (Jan. 2003): 25–29.

Stevens, Harry R. "Adventure in Refinement: Early Concert Life in Cincinnati. 1810–1826." *Bulletin of the Historical and Philosophical Society of Ohio* 5, no. 3 (Sept. 1947): 8–22.

———. "The Haydn Society of Cincinnati, 1819–1824." *Ohio State Archaeological and Historical Quarterly* 52, no. 3 (Apr.–June 1943): 95–119.

Stowe, C[alvin] E. "Report on the Course of Instruction in the Common Schools of Prussia and Wirtemberg." *The Western Academician and Journal of Education and Science* 1. Repr., pamphlet. Cincinnati: James R. Allbach, 1837–38.

Sutton, Walter. "Cincinnati As a General Publishing Center: The Middle Years, 1830–1860." *Bulletin of the Historical and Philosophical Society of Ohio* 16 (1958): 311–23.

Swain, Richard H. "Captain Pearl R. Nye's Ohio Canal Songs." *Gamut* (Fall 1983): 20–34.

"Syndicated Syncopation." *C[leveland] A[thletic] C[lub] Journal* (July 1943): 8–10.

Thompson, Morley P. *D. H. Baldwin: The Multibank Music Company.* Pamphlet. New York: Newcomen Society in North America, 1974 [c 1973].

"Thompson [Will L.] & Co. Confidential Price List." East Liverpool: Thompson and Company, 188[?]. Ohio Historical Society: PA Box 514/17.

Thuman, J. H[erman]. *The College of Music of Cincinnati: An Address Delivered before the Optimists Club at the Queen City Club, Cincinnati, Ohio, Saturday, November 13, 1920.* Pamphlet. Cincinnati: s.n., 1920. Cincinnati Historical Society: 780.7.

Titus, Parvin. "Famous Cincinnati Music Hall Organ Has Interesting History." *Tracker* 9, no. 3 (Spring 1965): 9–13.

Tolzmann, Don Heinrich. "Musenklänge aus Cincinnati." *Bulletin of the Cincinnati Historical Society* 35, no. 2 (Summer 1977): 115–29.

Vacha, John E. "Biggest Bash: Cleveland's Great Lakes Exposition." *Timeline* 13, no. 2 (Mar.–Apr. 1996): 2–23.

———. "The Selling of Szell: The Cleveland Orchestra Meets Its Maestro." *Timeline* 15, no. 6 (Nov.–Dec. 1998): 2–13.

Van Pelt, Derek. "Polka[,] the Dance That Refuses to Die." *Cleveland* 4 (Apr. 1975): 82–90.

Wetzel, Richard D. "The Search of William Cumming Peters." *American Music* 1, no. 4 (Winter 1983): 27–41.

Whitney's Musical Guest 4, no. 1 (Nov. 1870). Ohio Historical Society: PA Box 550/17.

Wohlgemuth, E. Jay. *Within Three Chords: The Place of Cincinnati in the Life of Stephen Collins Foster: [A] Paper Read before the Literary Club of Cincinnati.* Pamphlet. Indianapolis: Rough Notes, 1928.

Wolf, Edward C. "The Convivial Side of Scottish Psalm Tunes," *American Music* 14, no. 2 (Summer 1996): 141–60.

Wulsin, Lucien. *Dwight Hamilton Baldwin (1821–1899) and the Baldwin Piano.* Pamphlet. New York: Newcomen Society in North America, 1953.

Wurlitzer World of Music, 1856–1956: 100 Years of Musical Achievement. Booklet. Cincinnati: Rudolph Wurlitzer, 1956. Ohio Historical Society: PA Box 498/16.

Zoar: An Ohio Experiment in Communalism. Pamphlet. Columbus: Ohio State Archaeological and Historical Society, 1952. Repr., Ohio Historical Society, 1996. Ohio Historical Society: 977.1661/Oh3z.

AUDIO AND VIDEO RECORDINGS

Buckley, Bruce. *Ohio Valley Ballads,* 1955. Folkways FA 2025.

Gibson, Bob. *Folksongs of Ohio,* 1963. Granada Hills, Calif.: Stinson SLP 76.

Let Me Entertain You: A Ruth Lyons Memoir, 1997. Audiocassette. WVXU FM–X-Star Radio Network.

Masters of Music and Gifted Young People Play Great Music of the Past and Present, 1962. Fiftieth anniversary recording. Cleveland: Cleveland Music School Settlement. Self-produced.

Mester, Jorge, dir. *Fanfares,* 1981. London Philharmonic Orchestra. North Hollywood, Calif.: Varese Sarabande VCDM 1000–240.

Ohio State Ballads: History through Folksongs, 1958. New York: Folkways FH 5217.

Salute to the Armco Band, 1993. Videocassette. Middletown: Globe Productions.

Seems Like Romance to Me: Traditional Fiddle Tunes from Ohio, 1985. Gambier: Gambier Folklore Society GFS 901.

Songs of the Ohio Country, 1975[?]. Mark Records MC 1039.

TBDBITL: The Ohio State University Marching Band. Videocassette. WOSU-TV.

Traditional Music from Central Ohio, 1979. Columbus: Ohio Arts Council TALP–001.

Where Home Is: Life in Nineteenth-Century Cincinnati, 1995 [1977]. Compact disc. New York. New World Records 80251–2.

Zamecnik, J. S. *Cinema: Silent Film Music.* 1999. Compact disc. Louisville, Colo.: Mont Alto Motion Picture Orchestra.

NEWSPAPERS

Cincinnati Commercial Gazette, October 2, 1843–June 15, 1896.

Cincinnati Daily Gazette, June 25, 1827–January 3, 1883.

Cincinnati Enquirer, April 10, 1841–present.

Cincinnati Independent Press and Freedom's Advocate, July 4, 1822–November 13, 1823.

Cincinnati Journal, 1829–1839.

Cincinnati Post, January 3, 1881–present.

Cincinnati Times-Star, April 25, 1840–July 19, 1958.

Cleveland Daily Herald and Gazette, May 30, 1835–March 15, 1885.

Cleveland Daily True Democrat, January 12, 1847–October 14, 1853.

Cleveland Plain Dealer, April 7, 1845–present.

Cleveland Press, November 2, 1878–1982.

Columbus Ohio State Journal, August 11, 1847–November 7, 1959.

Columbus Westbote, October 2, 1843–August 1918.

Daily Cincinnati Atlas, 1843–1854.

Daily Cincinnati Republican, 1831–1842.

Liberty Hall and Cincinnati Gazette, April 7, 1815–October 29, 1857.

Lima Gazette, 1854–1891.

New Concord Enterprise, July 22, 1880–June 23, 1966.

Ohio City Argus, 1836–1838.

Toledo Blade, April 17, 1848–present.

Tuscarawas Advocate, 1835–1911.

[Warren] Western Reserve Chronicle, October 4, 1816–July 1921.

Western Spy; Western Spy and Cincinnati General Advertiser; Western Spy and Literary Cadet,
    September 1, 1810–December 28, 1822.

Youngstown Vindicator, September 23, 1889–present.

Zanesville News, October 22, 1939–January 23, 1954.

Zanesville Times Signal, March 21, 1882–November 30, 1959.

Zanesville Weekly Courier, 1845–1915.

Index

Cavini String Quartet, 198
Cecilia Society (Cincinnati), 38, 208
Centerville, 361
Central Musical Association (Cleveland), 124
Central Ohio Sängerbund, 354
Central Ohio Singers, 347–48
Cerone, David, 198
Chadwick, George Whitefield, 216
Chalifoux, Alice, 197
Chamber Orchestra (Lancaster), 279
Champlain, Polly, 321
Chantry Music Press, 518–20
Chapin, Amzi, 71–72
Chapman, Tracy, 478–79
Charters, George, 21
Chase, Philander, 13
Chávez, Carlos, 248
Chester Park (Cincinnati), 268
Chevalier des Grieux, 273
Chicago Grand Opera Company, 269
Chicago Symphony Orchestra, 167, 232–35, 292
Chillicothe, 72, 392–93; German singing societies
   in, 346, 354–55; on Ohio-Erie Canal, 402–3
"Chillicothe" (Nye), 402
Choir, the, 473
Chookasian, Lili, 274
Choralist's Companion, The 105, 110
Christian Psalmist, The (Fillmore and Leonard), 82–
   83, 323
Christians' Duty, The 308
Christiansen, Olaf C., 168–69
Christy, George N., 411
Christy Minstrels, 127, 409–10
Church, John, Jr., 422–25, 514
Church Choir, The (Muenscher), 308–9
Church Harp, The (Hanby), 421
Churchill, Charles H., 158–59
Church's Musical Visitor, 514–15
Cincinnati, 18, 130, 345, 399, 410; American Classical
   Music Hall of Fame in, 203; Baldwin Piano and
   Organ Company in, 483–92; ballet at the zoo,
   269–70, 272; bands in, 19, 459; Cleveland compared to, 51, 227; early music schools in, 18–21,
   28, 34, 36–38; early promotion of public school
   music in, 34, 38, 100–102, 106, 108; German
   singing societies in, 38, 210, 344, 346–47, 351–53,
   355; German-born residents in, 343–44; instrument manufacture in, 21, 29, 492–94, 501–4,
   507–8; minstrelsy in, 39, 410, 412–13; music in,
   pre–Civil War, 18–40; music publishers in, 21–
   22, 36, 510–16, 520–23; opera in, 255, 257–61,
   268–75; pre–Civil War, 18–40; public school music in, 91–115, 234; record companies in, 525–26;

Sängerfests in, 79, 281–82, 344–45, 347, 357–58;
   singing schools in, 19, 34–35, 68; singing societies in, 210, 283, 288; Welsh music in, 363, 368–
   69; Wurlitzer company in, 495–97. *See also*
   specific organizations, locations, and events
Cincinnati Academy of Music, 37
Cincinnati Band, 25
Cincinnati Civic Ballet, 192
Cincinnati Conservatory of Music, 173–82, 193,
   269; College of Music and, 183, 187–91; expan-
   sion, 176–77; facilities, 174–75, 177–78; faculty,
   174, 176, 179, 181, 184, 532. *See also* College-Con-
   servatory of Music of the University
Cincinnati Conservatory of Music Society, 174
Cincinnati Deutsche Liedertafel, 344
Cincinnati Deutscher Gesangverein, 344
Cincinnati Eisteddfod Association, 365
Cincinnati Euphonical Society, 21
Cincinnati Gardens, 273
Cincinnati Grand Orchestra, 212–13, 283, 354
Cincinnati Hotel: ballroom, 24, 26
Cincinnati Institute of Fine Arts, 180, 182, 191
Cincinnati Mothersingers, 181
Cincinnati Music Hall Association, 285–86
Cincinnati Music Readers, The, 108
Cincinnati Music School, 534
Cincinnati Opera Association, 276
Cincinnati Opera Ensemble, 276
Cincinnati Orchestra Association Company, 213–14
Cincinnati Orchestra Company, 213
Cincinnati Orpheus, 262
Cincinnati Philharmonic Orchestra, 208
Cincinnati Pops Orchestra, 225
Cincinnati Sacred Music Society, 37
Cincinnati Sängverein, 358
Cincinnati Summer Opera, 275
Cincinnati Summer Opera Association, 273, 276
Cincinnati Summer Opera Orchestra, 272
Cincinnati Symphony Orchestra, 112, 167, 192, 205,
   207–26, 270, 460; in Cleveland, 231, 233; Con-
   servatory of Music and, 176, 181; directors,
   214–19, 223–25, 295; under Goossens, 220–22,
   221, 295–96; guest conductors, 292; under
   Kunwald, 292–93, 292–94; opera and, 269, 276;
   radio broadcasts, 219; recordings, 217–18, 222–
   24, 226; under Stokowski, 216–17; tours, 218–
   20, 224–25, 297; under Van der Stucken, 214–
   15, 291–92; venues, 162, 485
Cincinnati Symphony Orchestra Association Company, 217, 226
Cincinnati Symphony Orchestra Chambers Players
   series, 225–26
Cincinnati Theatre: orchestra of, 28

Cincinnati Wesleyan College, 175
Cincinnati Zoo Opera ensemble, 270
Cincinnatus Minstrels, 418
Cist, Charles, 492–93, 503–4
Clapp, Willard, 197
Clark, J. H., 122–23
Clarke, Herbert L., 460–61
Claussen, Julia, 359
Cleaveland, Moses, 41, 359
Cleva, Fausto, 271–74
Cleveland, 201, 369, 412, 437; German singing societies in, 47, 231–32, 343, 346–47, 351; growth, 41–42, 51, 227; instrument manufacture in, 46, 505–6, 508; invention of Muzak in, 525; music pre–Civil War, 41–51; music publishers in, 124, 516–18; music schools in, 118–20, 122, 227; Ohio-Erie Canal to, 399, 402; opera in, 49, 255; orchestra in, 227–31; polka of, 437–41; public school music in, 46, 116–28, 234; public schools of, and Cleveland Orchestra, 237, 249, 252; record companies in, 526; rock in, 468, 474; Sängerfests in, 345, 358–59; singing societies in, 227, 239; synagogues in, 47, 311–12. *See also* specific organizations, locations, and events
Cleveland Academy, 118
Cleveland Amateur Philharmonic Society, 228
Cleveland Brass Band, 46
Cleveland Browns: music for, 445–46
Cleveland Chamber Symphony, 534
Cleveland Choral Union, 47
Cleveland City Band, 46
Cleveland City Guard, 46
Cleveland Composers' Guild, 527
Cleveland Foundation, 139, 141
Cleveland Gesangverein, 346
Cleveland Grand Orchestra, 228
Cleveland Grays Band, 46, 447
Cleveland Harmonic Society, 43–44
Cleveland Institute of Music, 138, 195–98, 529–30, 535
Cleveland Juvenile Music Society, 120
Cleveland Mendelssohn Society, 47
Cleveland Municipal Symphony Orchestra, 228, 230
Cleveland Museum of Art, 201–3
Cleveland Music School Settlement, 134–41, 478
Cleveland Musical Association, 536–37
Cleveland Musical Society, 42–43, 47
Cleveland Musical Union, 47
Cleveland Oratorio Society, 228
Cleveland Orchestra, 135, 137, 205, 228–29, 239; children's concerts, 126, 249, 252; and choral works, 249–50; Cleveland Institute of Music and, 195, 197–98; and Festival Orchestra, 359–

60; guest conductors, 238, 243, 245–46, 248, 250–51; and opera, 252; personnel, 140, 245–47, 251–52, 432, 536; recordings, 237, 244, 246, 250, 252–53; under Rodzinski, 241–45; under Sokoloff, 233–39; summer festival of, 250–51; under Szell, 247–51; tours, 235–37, 250, 252–53; venues, 239–41, 250, *251*
Cleveland Orchestra Chorus, 249–50
Cleveland Orchestra Youth Chorus, 252
Cleveland Orchestra Youth Orchestra, 252
Cleveland Philharmonic Orchestra, 228
Cleveland Philharmonic Society, 47
Cleveland Plan, 237, 249
"Cleveland Polka, The" (Lausche), 441
Cleveland Quartet, 198
Cleveland Sacred Music Society, 43, 46
Cleveland School of Music, 195, 227–28
Cleveland State Hospital, 141
Cleveland String Quartet, 235–36
Cleveland Symphony Orchestra, 228, 230–31, 234–37, 235
Cleveland Trio, 197
Cleveland Vocal Society, 228
"Clever Skipper, The" (Nye), 403
Clifton Heights Gesangverein, 352–53
Clinton, Bill, 473
Clinton, George, 478
Clokey, James W[addell], 528
Cohen, Gustave M., 47, 311–14
Colburn, William F., 36, 100–101
Collection of Revival Hymns and Plantation Melodies, A (Taylor), 392
Collection of Sacred Hymns, for the Church of the Latter Day Saints, A (Smith), 315–16
Collection of Welsh and English Hymns, A 365
College of Music of Cincinnati, 173–74, 182–91, 212; opera department of, 266–68; personnel of, 216, 289, 528–29, 531; radio department of, 189–90; and University of Cincinnati, 180, 187–91. *See also* College-Conservatory of Music of the University
College of Wooster, 255–56, 534
College-Conservatory of Music of the University of Cincinnati, 173, 191–94, 224, 462
Colliere, L. Corradi, 30, 212
Collins, Bootsy, 475, 477, 478
Collins, Phelps "Catfish," 475
Colonel Mack's Ball Room (Cincinnati), 25–27
Columbian Harmonist, The (Flint), 21, 34, 68, 84–86
Columbian Orchestra, The, 30
Columbus, 255, 343, 406, 416, 509; German singing societies in, 346–47, 350, 354; John Kerr in, 67–68; music education in, 68, 126–33; public school